Hail Hail!

Matt Corr

HARRY HOOD

TWICE AS GOOD

The official biography by Matt Corr

Forewords by
Tommy Callaghan, Kenny Dalglish,
Davie Hay & Willie Wallace

THE CELTIC STAR

Harry Hood - Twice As Good

The official biography by Matt Corr

Published by The Celtic Star
in cooperation with Matt Corr Media.

First Published in the UK in 2021 by The Celtic Star.

ISBN 978-1-8380207-3-6

A catalogue for this book is available from the British Library and the Irish Library in Dublin.

Cover & page design and typesetting by Stephen Cameron.

Back cover collage by Mark Lewis.

Publisher - David Faulds: email editor@thecelticstar.co.uk

Printed by Replika Press

Contents

Dedication

For Billy Lindsay, my dear friend and brother-in-law and Robert McGuire, my beloved 'wee cousin' and the heartbeat of Team McGuire. Both of whom lost their long battles with illness during the writing of this book.

For all those who have lost their lives to this dreadful disease of cancer, including, of course, the wonderful and much-loved Harry Hood, my own dad, Matt Corr and his 'big brother' Dan, who passed on his love of Celtic to my dad, and was a neighbour of the Hood family in Gartons Road. Both Corr brothers spent their final hours in Marie Curie's Glasgow Huntershill hospice.

For all the fabulous Marie Curie staff who make the most difficult burden just that bit lighter, with their dedication and devotion to everything they do.

And my long-suffering wife, Lesley, who put her own life on hold for a year to allow me to research and write this book. Above and beyond.

Acknowledgements

Marie Curie Scotland • Brunswick Community & Youth Centre • Robin Bacon • Tommy Callaghan • Denis Connaghan • Malcolm Cook • Robert Corr • Bernie Curran • Ian & Betty Dalgleish • Kenny Dalglish • Siobhan Edwards • Tom Forrest • Martin Gorman • Stuart Graham • Jimmy Hamilton • Gordon Hammond • Robert Harvey • Davie Hay • George Herd • Jack & Lil Hood • Kathleen Hood • Nicky Hood • Graham Macfarlane • Rob Mason • Mike Maher • Alan Maxwell • Jim McCalliog • Iain McCartney • John McHugh • Malcolm McNeill • Stephen Mill • Stephen Mullen • David Potter • Jim Pryde • Davie Reilly • Stuart Ross • Dick Staite • Rod Stewart • Gordon Sydney • John Scott • John Taylor • John Wagner • Willie Wallace • Lisa Wishart

The Celtic View • The Celtic Wiki • The Evening Times • The Glasgow Herald

Special thanks to the Hood family, for their time, patience, input, support and provision of photographs. To Tommy Callaghan, Kenny Dalglish, Davie Hay and Willie Wallace for kindly writing the forewords. To Stephen Cameron, David Faulds and Mark Lewis for editorial and design input and Martin Gorman, Rob Mason, Alan Maxwell, David Potter and Gordon Sydney for proof reading.

Visit - https://theceltiestar.com

Shop - https://celticstarbooks.com

Forewords by

Tommy Callaghan, Kenny Dalglish, Davie Hay and Willie Wallace

Tommy Callaghan

I was delighted to be asked by Harry's family to write a short foreword for this book, which celebrates his life, and it was my great pleasure to accept. Harry and I go back a long way, 50 years in fact, having roomed together many times as Celtic teammates and friends. It made perfect sense to pair us 'new guys' together back in the late sixties, with most of the players already having established friendships over many years. Cesar would room with John Clark, for instance, whilst Jinky and Bobby Lennox were pretty much inseparable. Tommy Gemmell and Bertie Auld, Stevie Chalmers and Ronnie Simpson, Bobby Murdoch and John Fallon, Willie Wallace and Jim Craig. Always together at Seamill and on European trips. It was 'one of those Jock Stein things,' I guess. He sized up who would most likely get on together and inevitably it worked. Harry and I just seemed to 'click' from the outset, and we became great friends.

Our careers at Celtic ran very much in parallel, looking back, as Harry moved to Parkhead from Clyde in March 1969, just four months after I had signed from Dunfermline Athletic. We both managed to hit the 300-appearance mark over the next seven years, 150 of those together, playing at the top-level of European football, before leaving the club again within a few months of each other in 1976. And I've often heard it said that we were 'typical Jock Stein signings,' that is players who had excelled in Scottish football with other teams before adding that experience and quality to the group of youngsters developed by the club through the ranks. Other men in that category who immediately spring to mind are Joe McBride, Willie Wallace and Dixie Deans. It was a hugely successful formula for Jock and Celtic for many years, albeit I used to joke that I couldn't be a typical Jock signing, and that I was unique, as I don't believe he signed anyone else twice! The Boss had brought me to Dunfermline back in 1962.

Those were very special times to be at Celtic. We were fortunate enough to experience some wonderful occasions together on the pitch, winning cup finals at Hampden and being part of the historic march to nine-in-a-row, whilst facing the best that European football had to offer. And of course, there were disappointments along the way, Milan and the European Cup final of 1970 undoubtedly the one which still hurts most. Even after all these years. Such is football.

Harry was a wonderful footballer. He had it all. A real thinking man's player, with an excellent football brain. Creative, with a lovely touch and a good striker's instinct. A great fit for Celtic.

And he was a good lad to be around off the field. Great company and he loved his golf. Harry was one of a number of players who thought about going into the pub business, and he had his head screwed on. A very good mind for business. I remember he talked about buying his first pub, just on the outskirts of Uddingston from memory, which the family then worked in. His brother George and wife Kathy very much involved. They would be very successful and build that business up, with Angels and others to follow. A very intelligent and shrewd man.

Harry was also behind the American adventure my family and I had as things were drawing to a close for me at Celtic. He was playing out in Texas with San Antonio Thunder and made the approach to Jock Stein which saw us team up again for six weeks under the captaincy of Bobby Moore, my great idol growing up. The stories from that episode in our careers would justify a book in itself! Great times.

I do hope you enjoy revisiting some of these memorable matches and recalling the characters who made Celtic such a powerful force in football during this period, and of finding out a bit more about Harry's life before and after his career at Parkhead. It's a wonderful story and I'm delighted it is now being shared and passed down through generations of Celtic supporters who were perhaps too young to see Harry in action wearing those famous green and white Hoops first-hand.

I am honoured and privileged to have counted Harry Hood not just as a Celtic teammate but as my dear friend.

This is for you, Harry.

Tommy Callaghan

Kenny Dalglish

It was really nice to be asked by the family to say a few words about Harry and our time together at Celtic. Chatting about those days brought back so many memories.

My career at Celtic pre-dated Harry's by a couple of years. I was provisionally signed in May 1967, just before Lisbon, at the same time as Danny McGrain, who was a year older. Freddie Pethard and I were playing for Glasgow United in a friendly against a team from Celtic's groundstaff at Barrowfield. We beat them that day and Big Jock was there with Sean Fallon. Jock told our manager that he liked the number 4, but that he had heard he was going to Rangers. "Well, he hasn't heard that," was the reply. So, shortly afterwards, Sean came round to ours and I signed. A group of us all came through together. Danny and myself, Lou Macari, Vic Davidson, Paul Wilson and Pat McCluskey. We all trained together on the pitch with the first team and then we got farmed out to the juniors to develop and toughen up a bit. That's how it was back then. I played at Cumbernauld United, whilst Danny, Pat and Paul were at Maryhill,

Lou was at Largs Thistle from memory and Vic at Ashfield.

I signed full professional forms for Celtic the following summer and made my debut from the bench in the League Cup against Hamilton Accies at Douglas Park that September. I think we were about 14 goals up in the tie before Jock brought me off the bench. He obviously wasn't taking any chances!

Harry was still at Clyde at that time but by the time I got my first start, in October 1969 – a 7-1 home win over Raith Rovers – he was at the club. I played at right-half that afternoon, then again in a couple of League Cup semi-final matches against Ayr United at Hampden. That would be the first time we teamed up together. Harry was real quality on the pitch. He was a player. You will recall that big Jock didn't sign too many, but when he did... His main asset, for me, was his technical ability. And Harry didn't mind heading up the park and having a skelp at goal. He knew where the goal was.

Like all the senior players at the club, Harry was very accommodating to the younger guys like myself. Always welcoming and encouraging. Not arrogant in any way. He used to take us golfing at one of the courses up behind the King's Park Hotel – Cathkin Braes or Kirkhill perhaps – where he was a member. The senior pros couldn't beat us right enough. It must have got a wee bit embarrassing for them! Kidding aside, it was a fantastic dressing-room. The patter was always good with so many different characters in there. Guys like Jim Brogan. Everyone contributed. You've got to be strong and be able to have a chuckle. Success happens on and off the pitch.

It would be the summer of 1971 before Harry and I consistently lined up together. Jock would know when to bring you in and take you out of the side. You have to remember that the quality of player at the club at that time was frightening. I remember the Frank Beattie testimonial at Kilmarnock, then a friendly in Limerick before we played in the Drybrough Cup. We beat Dumbarton at Parkhead then St Johnstone at Firhill but lost the final to Aberdeen at Pittodrie. Then there were the three victories at Ibrox in a month. Matt mentioned me scoring something like 20 goals in that period but that sounds more like some of Harry's golf scores! In fact, I reckon he still owes me some golf balls!

My very best regards to Kathy and the family.

I hope they enjoy seeing Harry's story playing out in this book.

Kenny Dalglish

Davie Hay

My earliest recollections of Harry are probably when he moved from Clyde to Sunderland and him being there at the same time as Jim Baxter. I was a few years younger than him, so we didn't play against each other at schoolboy level. The first time I came up against him was a Scottish Cup replay against Clyde at Celtic Park in February 1969. Ronnie had suffered that bad shoulder injury in the first game at

Shawfield and we had a few other defenders struggling, so I came in beside Billy for the replay. It was one of my earliest appearances for Celtic. Harry was up front for Clyde and you could tell he was a top player. There was talk of him coming in and he signed for Celtic shortly afterwards. We knew we would be signing a good player and there was also a Celtic connection, as he was a supporter. In my only other first-team match that season, we both played together. That was a Friday night Glasgow Cup match against Rangers at Parkhead, with a big crowd in. We lost but Harry scored one of the goals.

We really made our breakthroughs together the following season and in October of that year, we both won our first medals, against St Johnstone at Hampden in the League Cup final. I had been playing at right-back, then Jim Craig and Tommy Gemmell paired up again. Jock named the team in the dressing room beforehand and I was in…at left-back! Tommy had been sent off playing for Scotland in midweek and he was left out. Neither of us had any inkling that Jock was thinking about making that change. We found out at Hampden. Bertie scored early on to win the cup and I ended up at a small party back in Harry's house in Simshill that night. I always remember that. He and Kathy made me most welcome.

Those were special times. We trained with the Lions every day and they were so supportive, which is to their eternal credit, as that was to their own sacrifice if you think of it. Over time, the Quality Street Gang - as we were often referred to as - would be fighting for and taking their places in the team. The Lions changed in the home dressing-room and the younger players in the away lockers. I was one of the first to be 'moved through.' There were some characters in there. You learned early doors to keep your mouth shut. Just sit there, like the three wise monkeys! They were a phenomenal squad.

Harry was a silky forward who scored a lot of goals for Celtic. Most memorable for me probably was his hat-trick against Rangers at Hampden in 1973, That was special. And another memory involving Rangers at Hampden was the cup final a couple of years earlier. Harry scored from the spot and he had this beauty of a black eye. I'm not sure if that was from the penalty incident or not but later on, the bold Harry appears wearing these sunglasses in all the photos. Like a film star. I think he loved it.

There were so many highs back then. Just playing for Celtic. So many cup finals and I always enjoyed beating Rangers. We would be desperate not to lose those games, as they meant so much. You had to make sure you gave your all. If I was really pushed to choose one personal memory, I'd pick out the night against Leeds United at Hampden. Leeds were favourites in many people's eyes, but I knew we were going to win. That incredible crowd and Jimmy's performance. When you play for Celtic, you either rise to the demands or you falter. The supporters took you to another level on nights like that.

No doubt about the biggest disappointment, which was the European Cup final in Milan immediately afterwards. So many memories of that night. Unlike Lisbon, both clubs had a similar support inside the San Siro, but it felt like there were more Dutch, and I think that was down to two things. The first was that they seemed to have the middle section of the stadium. That's my recollection anyway. And the second was the noise created by those klaxons. I often say that the Dutch 'out- klaxoned' the Celtic support. We went 2 v 3 in midfield, which I think was a big factor. We didn't match them up in there. It's been said many times, but I genuinely believe that we would have won the replay on the Friday if we had held out for just a few more minutes.

Harry was always good company. Like most of us, he liked a wee moan now and again. But I always thought of him as a good husband and father. I spoke to him occasionally over the years after our time at Celtic. I remember once when I was manager at Motherwell, around 1981/82, I was taking training at the red blaes pitch at Calder and Harry came over for a chat and asked if it would be ok if he watched us. I think he was coaching at Albion Rovers at the time, or possibly Queen of the South. I remember he was very friendly with one of the directors at Motherwell, Malcolm McNeill. They were great friends for many years and Malcolm read a lovely eulogy for Harry. They were holidaying together in the south of France when they bumped into Rod Stewart. Harry would have enjoyed that.

We would bump into Harry a few times ourselves over the years, sometimes in his pubs at functions, like the Castle Rooms in Uddingston, or other events. One such occasion was the time we met at the Neil Diamond concert at Hampden, back in the summer of 2011. Harry was there with Kathy and Catherine and I were in the same section. And we met Dom Sullivan there also. Small world. I may not have the timing spot on, but I seem to remember that Harry had a wee cancer scare previously, but he was looking well.

The last time we spoke, things were not looking so great. I had given him a call just to see how he was doing. You're always a wee bit wary calling out of the blue in those circumstances but he was chirpy enough and he wasn't down about it. He said he appreciated the call. I was glad we had that chat.

Please give my regards to Kathy and the family and my very best wishes for the success of the book.

Davie Hay

Willie Wallace

For all the games we played together at Celtic, it might seem strange that my first thought of Harry when Matt asked me about him was of a magic week we spent together in Las Vegas as guests of the North American Celtic Supporters. I had flown up from Australia and found I was rooming with Harry. We had always got on well together and I found him a really nice guy. That was a great week.

I remember Harry as a young lad at Clyde when I played with Hearts. I always thought of him as a young player with good ability. A very skilful player who could change a game, just like a couple of other old teammates of mine, Jim Baxter at Raith Rovers and later Scotland, and of course, Jimmy Johnstone at Celtic. Clyde were a good side at that time. They were doing alright.

Big Jock perhaps surprised us all a bit when he went for Harry, although he was one of the opposition players he would identify as a threat before the match. Jock would say something like, "Make sure you give him a good rattle and let him know he's in a game." I remember we matched up directly in a Scottish Cup semi-final at Hampden just before Lisbon. Bobby Murdoch was out, and I was playing further back in the middle of the park, wearing the number four shorts. My job was to make sure Harry didn't give us too much trouble. Stay close to him and cut out the service. Harry was their main player, although Sam Hastings wasn't a bad winger, and I remember Stan Anderson, who later went to Rangers as a coach. That game finished in a goalless draw and we won the replay on the Wednesday, again at Hampden, to go through to the final against Aberdeen.

Clyde's manager by then was Davie White. We had faced up a few times as players and Celtic usually had the upper hand. I remember Davie was a bit upset after one game. We were due to play Rangers shortly afterwards and he said to me coming off the pitch, "Wait until the big team gets you!"

Harry joined Celtic part way through the run to nine-in-a-row. He joined a club with the most fantastic characters in that dressing-room. Ronnie Simpson, for example. What a lovely, funny man he was with the most incredible story. And the young boys who came through around that time. George Connelly. Davie Hay. Danny McGrain. Kenny Dalglish. Great players. And we did all get on as well as it looked from the outside. It wasn't staged for the media. We were all great friends. Wonderful times.

Harry would go on to score a few important goals for Celtic. We played together quite a bit at Celtic then he was there for a few seasons after I left for Crystal Palace in 1971. I saw him a few times afterwards, over the years, when the players would get together for reunions and suchlike and Harry and I were included. I think the last time we spoke was at a funeral in the Jock Stein Lounge at Celtic Park. It may have been Tommy Gemmell's. Ironically, when I heard the sad news of Harry's passing, I had not long returned to Australia after Billy McNeill's funeral, and whilst I was travelling over to Glasgow for that, Stevie Chalmers passed away. I had heard that Stevie wasn't keeping too well but I didn't expect that. I flew back to Australia immediately after Stevie's service and I was on my way once again to the Celtic Convention in Las Vegas, of which I had such great memories of my time there in Harry's company, when I heard about Harry. As I said at that time, not only was he a great player but he was also a genuine person who will be fondly remembered by the Celtic family.

I look forward to reading Harry's story and wish you all the very best for the success of the book.

Willie Wallace

Prologue: New Year matches in Glasgow

Football has an incredible habit of intertwining with life, sometimes over a number of decades, to produce fascinating quirks of fate which never cease to amaze and amuse.

The Celtic supporters who made their way happily home in their Brake Clubs from Govan in the early evening of Tuesday, 1 January 1895 would be blissfully unaware that they had just witnessed a piece of history. Earlier that afternoon, their team which included early heroes such as James Kelly, Willie Maley, Dan McArthur and Johnny Madden had recovered from the loss of an early penalty to beat Glasgow rivals Rangers 3-2 at the original Ibrox Park. The match had been billed as a 'holiday fixture,' the second such game between the clubs to kick off the new year following the success of the inaugural Ne'erday derby played at Celtic Park 12 months earlier, which Rangers had won by the same scoreline. *The Glasgow Herald* reporter who commented that the fixture had "all the appearance of becoming an annual institution" must have been blessed with 20/20 foresight. By 1899, as Rangers prepared to move to a new home on an adjacent site near Copland Road, built in an attempt to compete with Celtic Park for the lucrative International matches and Scottish Cup finals of the day, the meeting of the city rivals on the opening day of the calendar year had become a traditional part of the League programme which would stretch with few exceptions into the third millennium. Thus, the 18,000 spectators present at Ibrox that day in 1895 had witnessed Celtic's first-ever victory in a series of matches which would last for more than a century.

There would be a second deja-vu experience for the Celtic supporters just 24 hours later, Wednesday, 2 January 1895, as Everton visited Glasgow's east end for a friendly match, as they had done on the same date the previous year. The Merseyside club had won the English First Division title in 1890/91 and would finish second in the spring of this year. They boasted a number of Scots in their squad, most notably defender Bob Kelso, who had lined up beside James Kelly at 'world champions' Renton, and Tom McInnes, the inside-forward from Springburn who had played for local outfit Cowlairs in the tussles with 'The Irishmen' Celtic in their inaugural season of 1888/89. 'Oor Tam' had then created his own personal niche in English football history – not once but twice! Having joined Notts County from Cowlairs in December 1889, thus becoming one of the first Scottish professional players to move to England, McInnes was selected to represent the Football League in the inaugural Inter League fixture, which just happened to be against his old pals in the Scottish League. The match was played at Pike's Lane, Bolton, in April 1892, and Tam duly opened the scoring just before the interval to become the first man ever to do so for the Football League select team. Following spells with Rangers and 3rd Lanarkshire Rifle Volunteers (later renamed Third Lanark), McInnes joined Everton in 1894. In October of that year, just three months before the second Parkhead clash, 'Oor Tam' was in the record books again, when he scored the first-ever goal in a Merseyside derby, McInnes doing so within 10 minutes when he headed home from a corner- kick at Goodison Park. You can take the boy out of Springburn...

The Everton side who had defeated a weakened Celtic selection 4-1 in January 1894 had also featured another legendary figure. John 'Jack' Bell had won the first two Scottish League Championship titles with hometown club Dumbarton, before moving to Everton's new Goodison Park base in 1893. Jack would then sign for Celtic five years later for £300, a significant sum of money for those days, joining a team which had become the first to go through a Scottish League season undefeated, doing so in new manager Willie Maley's first campaign in charge. In April 1899, despite being a virtual passenger after suffering an injury, Bell would set up the clinching goal for Johnny Hodge as Celtic beat Rangers 2-0 at Second Hampden (latterly known as Cathkin Park) to win the Scottish Cup for the second time. On Monday, 1 January 1900, Jack Bell had the honour of scoring the first Celtic goal of the new century, doing so in the 15th minute of the 3-2 victory over Rangers at Parkhead. And three months later, he was once again on target as Celtic retained their Scottish Cup with a 4-3 victory over Queen's Park at the new Ibrox, a game which marked the last appearance in Scottish football's showpiece for the famous Hampden amateur club who had dominated the early years of the competition.

Just as Celtic had reversed the 3-2 defeat from Rangers in January 1894, winning by the same scoreline 12 months later, so they would avenge the loss to Everton 24 hours later by inflicting their own 4-1 victory on the Merseyside outfit on Wednesday, 2 January 1895. One member of the Glasgow Irish Roman Catholic community who would definitely not have been present at Celtic Park that afternoon was Peter Doran Hood, a 28-year-old steam crane worker from Clyde Place, on the south bank of the river. He had his own New Year match to attend that day.

At the turn of the 20th century, the Ne'erday holiday was a very popular time for young couples to marry in Scotland, being one of the few periods that time-off from work could be guaranteed. Earlier that day, Peter Hood had married his sweetheart Maggie - Margaret Ferguson - at St John's RC Church in Portugal Street in the city's Gorbals district, the service conducted by Father Patrick Ryan. Maggie, some three years younger than her new husband, lived literally around the corner from the Hoods with her parents Henry and Catherine Ferguson at 63 King Street – later renamed as Kingston Street - in Tradeston. On the marriage certificate, Peter's late father, William Hood, is listed as having been a labourer, and is survived by his wife, also Margaret, whilst Peter's new father-in-law, Henry Ferguson, is described as a gasworks stoker.

Six years later, at the time of the 1901 Census process, Peter and Maggie Hood have moved across to the north side of the River Clyde and are living in a two-roomed tenement flat at 9 Dover Street in Anderston, just west of the city centre. It would have been a busy home, to say the least, as the couple now have three children,

Maggie junior at four years old, Peter junior who is 12 months younger, and two-year-old Kate. In addition, Maggie's father Henry Ferguson, now 62 years of age and widowed, is sharing their home with his two other grown-up children, 24-year-old factory worker Sarah and 18-year-old labourer Henry junior.

A decade on, and the list of Hood home occupants has undergone some significant changes. The 1911 Census makes no mention of any of the three Fergusons – Peter's in-laws - nor Maggie Hood junior, his oldest daughter, who by now would have been in her mid-teens. Peter junior and Kate have been joined by another three sisters, Sarah and Lizzie, nine and eight years old respectively, and toddler Mary, who is two. And there is now another brother on the scene, Henry, at that time six years of age.

Henry Ferguson Hood, the second son and sixth child from the marriage of Peter Hood and Maggie Ferguson, and presumably named directly after Maggie's father, was born at 11.40pm on Thursday, 25 August 1904 in the family home at 9 Dover Street. His baby sister, Mary Ann Ferguson Hood, is also a Thursday's child, arriving four years later, at 11am on 23 July 1908.

So, let's recap. What do we have thus far?

In a football context, we have wonderful Celtic sides breaking records under a legendary manager, with heroic forwards scoring goals which would still be spoken about decades later.

We have Celtic beating Rangers in a Scottish Cup final at Hampden, then retaining the trophy the following season.

We have a much sought-after young footballer from the Springburn area heading south to a top club.

And a New Year match of a different type has ultimately given us a Henry Hood, who would later come to be known as Harry, born into a large, loving family in Glasgow in the early years of the 20th century.

There has just got to be a story in there somewhere.

Chapter 1

The Highland Connection

Friday, 8 February 1889 saw huge excitement in the Irish community in Glasgow, as supporters of the new club, Celtic, prepared to meet the 3rd Lanarkshire Rifle Volunteers (3rd LRV) in their first-ever Scottish Cup final the following day, less than nine months after they had played their inaugural match. This would be a replay of the infamous 'Snow Final' from the previous Saturday and would end in disappointment for the 'Bould Bhoys' at the second Hampden, as the 'Thirds' won 2-1 to win the most prestigious silverware of the day for the first time. By 1903, 3rd LRV had been renamed Third Lanark and the club had made the short journey from their original Cathkin Park base to take up residence at that same Hampden arena, replacing previous owners Queen's Park, who had recently moved to the third and current national stadium site in Mount Florida. Third Lanark would change the name of their new ground to New Cathkin Park and this would remain their home until their sad liquidation in the summer of 1967, ironically just as Celtic, the team they had defeated back in February 1889, were achieving the ultimate accolade of being crowned European Champions in Lisbon. Such were the very different fates of the two early Scottish Cup final protagonists in the eight decades which followed.

Some 200 miles to the north of Glasgow, the rural hamlet of Rosskeen in Ross county - just along the coast from Dingwall on the shores of the Cromarty Firth - was experiencing its own excitement for a rather different type of match on Friday, 8 February 1889. The Morrison home farm of Nonikiln was the venue for the wedding of Ann, daughter of William and Elizabeth Morrison, to Walter John Scott, a 24-year-old journeyman shoemaker from Buckie, a Banffshire town on the Moray Firth coast. The service was conducted by the Reverend John Ross from the Free Church of Scotland. Ann is listed on the marriage certificate as being 23 years of age and a domestic servant. Her new husband Walter was clearly following in the footsteps of his father George, described at that time as a master shoemaker.

Newlyweds Walter and Ann Scott initially set up home back in Buckie and their first three children are born there, daughter Elizabeth followed by sons George and William Reynold, who will be referred to simply as Reynold in future. The family then appear to return to Ann's home village, as a fourth child, Margaret, also known by her middle name of Lottie, is born at Bridgend, Rosskeen in November 1896. The next phase of Walter and Ann's married life takes them south to the Highland capital of Inverness, the Scott family extended to seven by the arrival of a third son, Walter John junior, in May 1899.

By the time of the 1901 Census, the family are residing at 3 Stephen's Street, near the city's Eastgate. A third daughter duly arrives in October of the next year, the baby named Ann Morrison Scott after her mother, followed by a fourth son, Alexander, born on 8 November 1904. That would appear to be that in terms of the Scott family composition, before there is a perhaps unexpected twist in the tale. Six months after the couple celebrated their 20th wedding anniversary, there would be one final addition to the nest. At 3pm on Tuesday, 3 August 1909, on her brother George's 18th birthday, Mary Morrison Scott entered the world at 3 Glebe Terrace, Glebe Street, Inverness, on the east bank of the River Ness, a fourth daughter and eighth child for Walter and Ann Scott, now both in their mid-forties.

All 10 members of the Scott clan are still going strong as the Census of April 1911 finds them living in a five-roomed house at 45 Rose Street, Inverness. By now, the three eldest Scott offspring are all in employment. Elizabeth, at 21, is a nurse at the rather unfortunately named lunatic asylum, whilst George, two years younger, is a clerk at the electricity works. Reynold is now 17 years old and is an apprentice house carpenter with a building firm. Four of the younger children are at school in Inverness, whilst toddler Mary has not yet reached her second birthday.

The next few years, however, will involve a major relocation which will have life-changing implications for the family. By 1915, with the world now at war, the Scott's have moved to Glasgow. Reynold is a journeyman joiner to trade but is also listed on his marriage certificate as a Gunner in the 3rd Lowland Brigade of the Royal Field Artillery. He married domestic servant Jessie Margaret Spiers from the city's Kingston district in the registry office at 102 Parson Street, Townhead on 8 October 1915. Reynold's normal residence is given as 70 Garngadhill, so presumably that is the Scott family home at that time. However, in the 1915/16 Valuation Roll, shoemaker Walter John Scott is the named householder for a tenement flat at 45 Glenfield Street, in the shadow of Glasgow's Royal Infirmary (in fact, on the site of the extension at Alexandra Parade). It is not clear what prompted the decision to move south, and as we lose track of a couple of the children at this point, it is possible that some remained in the Highlands, perhaps to marry and rear families of their own. On balance, however, I think it more likely that the entire Scott family made the journey down to Glasgow to commence a new life together.

At the onset of the next decade, with Europe easing into a cautious truce following the carnage of the first world war, the new Scott family base in Glasgow would be the scene of some celebrations. Oldest daughter Elizabeth would be the next to wed, doing so at home in Glenfield Street on 5 April 1920, when she married James Armstrong. Elizabeth is almost 31 (albeit she is listed as being 29 on the marriage certificate) and her new husband, a stationer from Mansfield in Nottinghamshire, is 32.

Within 10 months, those bells would be chiming again, this time in St Mary's RC

Church in Duntocher, where local cotton mill worker Nellie Small, known as Helen, married Walter Scott junior on 4 February 1921. The groom is described as an acetylene welder and is listed as being 23, the same age as his new bride, although he is not yet 22. Their grandson, John Scott, provides some background on the couple.

"I believe my grandad Walter may have been a conscript in the army and met my granny Nellie whilst doing training at Auchentoshan. That's why he was around Duntocher. I don't remember my grandad, but my sister Ann does a little. He was a shoemaker, as opposed to a cobbler. They had five children, Walter, Michael – my father, Henry, Morris and Sheila, who is still going strong as she approaches 90."

"In terms of his siblings, Ann thinks Lottie was married to a police inspector called Thompson and that Reynold had a cobbler's shop in Glasgow. That follows a theme, as my great grandad had a cobbler's hut in Hamilton Street, Inverness, apparently, around the time that Mary – Harry's mum – was born."

A third Scott wedding in four years then takes place on 17 August 1923 at Robertson Memorial Church, which was in Taylor Street, Townhead, adjacent to the Rottenrow hospitals. On that day, Walter and Ann's youngest son, Alexander Scott, married Jane Bennie Watson of nearby Barony Street. Both bride and groom are 18 years of age, with Alexander's 'wee sister' Mary being one of the witnesses to the ceremony. Her own time for the starring role on such an occasion would come soon.

Having left her hometown of Inverness as a child, Mary Morrison Scott would have attended school in Scotland's largest city, most likely in either the Dennistoun or Townhead district in the northern part of Glasgow. Upon completion of her secondary education, the teenager would eventually take up employment as a confectionery saleswoman, during the course of which she would be introduced to Henry Hood, known as Harry, a young grocery salesman from Anderston, in the city's west end.

That meeting would change the course of their young lives forever.

Romance would blossom between Harry, the teenage Glaswegian, and Mary, his Highland sweetheart, culminating in their marriage on Friday, 24 October 1924 at St Patrick's RC Church in Anderston. The beautiful old red sandstone building, at the junction of William Street and North Street, just south of Charing Cross, now stares across at the concrete ramps of the Kingston Bridge and the towering Hilton skyscraper hotel beyond, as a nod to a bygone century. However, back in the autumn of 1924, it was the hub of the Roman Catholic community of busy Anderston. Having only been opened for worship in 1898, the church was not much older than most of the excited newlyweds who pledged their marriage vows there. As Father McLaughlin blessed the pair as one, Harry and Mary, the new Mr and Mrs Hood, could happily contemplate the beginning of the rest of their lives.

Chapter 2

Hatches, matches and the saddest of dispatches

As an 11-year-old boy growing up in Anderston, Henry Hood had the misfortune to experience family tragedy at first hand. In the early afternoon of Monday, 8 November 1915, his older brother Peter would pass away in the nearby Western Infirmary, having suffered a fractured skull. Young Peter Doran Hood was an apprentice boilermaker. He was just 18 years old and still living at home with his parents, who had by this time moved to the next close at 3 Dover Street. So, there would undoubtedly be emotional scenes in the Hood household when Henry's wife Mary gave birth to a baby boy a decade later, a first grandchild for Peter and Maggie Hood. Poignantly, the new addition to the Hood family would be called Peter Anthony, 'Peter' in honour of both his paternal grandfather and his late uncle.

The following year, as they continued to adapt to their new roles of parents and grandparents, fate would deal another bitter blow to the Hoods. Henry's 24-year-old sister Sarah lost her fight for life in the early hours of Monday, 15 March 1926, at the family home at 3 Dover Street, with the cause of death given as anaemia and miliary tuberculosis. Dress finisher Sarah had been ill for several months.

The grieving Hoods would then move across the River Clyde to a new home at 363 Calder Street in Govanhill, in the shadow of Hampden Park. Having witnessed a birth and a death in the family over the past two years, there would once again be love in the air as Henry's older sister Kate - Catherine McSherry Hood - married engine fitter Bernard Burns on Friday, 7 September 1928, in their new home parish of Holy Cross RC Church in Crosshill. Kate was one month short of her 30th birthday on her wedding day, whilst Bernard was 32 and had been living at 16 Minerva Street in Finnieston, just around the corner from the old Hood family home at Dover Street.

The Hoods had not had the monopoly on tears in the second half of the Roaring Twenties. Just a few months before her sister-in-law Kate's marriage, young Mary Hood would lose her own brother. In the early hours of Monday, 23 April 1928, Alexander Scott would succumb to pulmonary tuberculosis at his parents' home at 45 Glenfield Street, just off Alexandra Parade, as Townhead morphs into Dennistoun. Carpenter Alexander was just 23 years old and lived with wife Jane at number 6 Glenfield Street. Less than five years earlier, Mary had been an excited witness at the wedding of her older brother. Now she would have to watch as he was laid to rest, as life continued to shell the newlyweds from all sides, long after that horrific war had ended. And fate had not quite finished with them yet.

There would be further tragedy for the Scotts, the knife twisted further by it taking place on the first anniversary of Alexander's death, Tuesday, 23 April 1929. Still mourning the loss of his youngest son, Mary's father Walter, the Highland shoemaker, would now be bidding farewell to Ann, his wife of 40 years, and the mother of his eight children. The 63-year-old lady from Ross-shire suffered heart failure in the early hours at 39 Gretna Street, Dalmarnock, the home of her son Reynold and his wife Jessie, a few minutes' walk from Celtic Park. It is not clear if the couple had moved in there permanently from Glenfield Street, in the aftermath of Alexander's passing, or temporarily to allow Ann to be cared for there by her family. She had been fighting womb cancer for nine months prior to her death. In any case, Walter's name does not appear in the Valuation Roll for Glenfield Street the following year. The next record of Mary's father places him with another son, George, in Stranraer, so it is reasonable to assume that he moved to the south-west of Scotland following the death of his beloved wife.

Thankfully, the 1930s would be kinder, with Henry and Mary Hood now raising a family in Springburn, an area at the northern tip of the city of Glasgow, which had thrived with the growth of the railway engineering industry at the latter end of the previous century. We pick up their trail in 1935 at a flat at 401 Keppochhill Road, at the junction with Pinkston Road, looking across to Cowlairs Park. By this time, their 9-year-old son Peter Anthony has been joined by sisters Irene Ann and Patricia, born in 1930 and 1933 respectively, with baby brother George Scott Hood arriving the next year, on Thursday, 24 October 1935. The six-strong Hood family will then move a mile or so east to a 'four in a block' house at 44 Avonspark Street, where Springburn meets Balornock. A third son for Henry and Mary - John O'Dornan Hood, later to be known as Jack or Jackie - is born there on Saturday, 8 January 1938.

Despite the carnage inflicted on Europe and beyond between 1914 and 1918, lessons had clearly not been learned or wounds healed. Just over two decades later, the world would be blighted by another global conflict, following the invasion of Poland by German forces in September 1939. Air raid shelters and gas masks would now be the new normal for the working-class families of Springburn, including milkman Harry Hood, his wife Mary, and their five children. Five would become six for 18 brief months before tragedy dealt the family another hammer blow. The spring of 1940 had brought the arrival of a third daughter for Harry and Mary, named Margaret Ferguson Hood after Harry's mother. Tragically, the little girl would contract bronchopneumonia, and baby Maggie's short life would end in Stobhill Hospital at 10.35pm on the evening of Tuesday, 7 October 1941. Another little angel sleeps in heaven.

The previous winter had seen the marriage of Harry's younger sister, Mary Ann, known as May, to a journalist, Henry Joseph O'Gara, described on the marriage certificate as 'now engaged in war service,' being a 2nd Lieutenant of the Royal Scots Fusiliers.

The ceremony took place on Saturday, 21 December 1940, once again at Holy Cross RC Church, Crosshill, where the now 74-year-old Peter Hood had given daughter Kate away 12 years earlier. At the time of her wedding, confectionery saleswoman May was 32 and living with her parents and older sister Betty at the family home at 363 Calder Street, a few minutes' drive away from the church, whilst new husband Henry was five years younger.

Henry O'Gara was born on Friday, 14 November 1913 at 273 Saracen Street, Possilpark, Glasgow to chartered accountant Michael O'Gara and his wife Mary, both of whom are deceased by the time of their son's wedding. The outbreak of war would see Henry leave his civilian profession as a journalist to join the Royal Scots Fusiliers, duly promoted to the rank of 2nd Lieutenant on 18 August 1940, just four months before his marriage.

By January 1943, Henry O'Gara had joined the RAF Volunteer Reserve, as a War Substantive Flying Officer, and in the autumn of that year, he was stationed at RAF Millom, just north of Barrow-in-Furness on the West Cumberland (now Cumbrian) coast.

Thursday, 14 October 1943 was a day of celebration in the nearby town of Whitehaven. A fundraising initiative under the RAF's 'Wings for Victory' campaign had seen the local population raise a six-figure sum for the purchase of Lancaster and Spitfire aircraft to support the war effort, and a Battle of Britain veteran – Flight Lieutenant David Moore Crook DFC - was on hand to present the town's mayor with a plaque to recognise that effort in the afternoon. The ceremony over, a few hours later David Crook was being escorted to the scene of a tragedy by a local newspaper editor, John Roger Williams.

Flying Officer Harry O'Gara and four colleagues had been heading home from a routine navigational exercise over the Irish Sea and were minutes from home above the Cumbrian coastline when the Avro Anson R9780 training aircraft in which they were travelling developed a defect in one of its wingspans, causing the pilot to lose control. The five-man crew would attempt to bail out using their parachutes, however, tragically, the time and space available would prevent the devices from opening safely.

Around 4pm, the children of Whitehaven emerged at the end of their school day to the alarming noise and sight of an aircraft falling from the sky above the range of hills known locally as The Brows. Within minutes, David Crook and John Williams would be amongst the rescue party surveying the wreckage on the hillside. There would be no survivors.

Harry O'Gara, beloved husband of May Hood, died on active service on the afternoon of 14 October 1943, on or above the hills at Kells Brows, near Whitehaven in West Cumbria. The couple had been married for less than three years. Harry was around eight weeks short of completing his training and just one month shy of his 30th birthday. His four companions in eternity would be those with whom he spent his last hours.

- Sergeant Thomas Inman, aged 20, from Yorkshire.
- Sergeant Rene Harold Murphy, also 20, from Ontario, Canada.
- Sergeant Vincent James Dunnigan, 26, from Buffalo, New York State, United States of America.
- Sergeant Cyril Johnson, aged 33, from Cheshire.

In another cruel twist of fate, on Monday, 18 December 1944, just 14 months after the crash at Kells Brows, the Spitfire piloted by David Moore Crook crashed into the North Sea off the coast at Aberdeen. He had celebrated his 30th birthday the previous month.

Six young men. Cut off in their prime.

Yet more victims to the absolute futility of the man-made madness which is war.

Harry O'Gara, Rene Murphy and Vincent Dunnigan are all buried in the RAF section of the cemetery at Blacon, on the northern outskirts of Chester, just yards from the Welsh border. Their two English colleagues, Tommy and Cyril, lie in rest in their own home counties of Yorkshire and Cheshire respectively. The body of David Crooks was never recovered. He was declared missing in action.

Sad would be the heart of May Hood O'Gara, as word came through on the loss of the love of her life.

However, the story of Henry Joseph O'Gara does not end there.

His death would create a legacy for another male member of the Hood family named Harry, Henry O'Gara's nephew, who would be born in his home city of Glasgow, almost exactly one year later.

Chapter 3

The impressive sporting family Hood gains a new addition

As the first anniversary of the death of her beloved husband approached, a new Harry was introduced to the world of May Hood O'Gara. On Tuesday, 3 October 1944, her sister-in-law Mary Hood delivered a baby boy in Stobhill Hospital, just three years after she had said a heart-breaking goodbye to her own infant daughter Margaret in that same Springburn institution. May's new nephew Henry Anthony would be a fourth son for the Hoods and would complete the family unit when he arrived at their new home at 60 Menzies Road, Balornock, in a modern housing estate built just a short walk from Stobhill. Like his father and late uncle before him, he would be christened Henry but would be known as Harry.

That family unit would be rather unique, with four of the six surviving Hood children going on to enjoy careers in professional sport. Those genes had more than likely been passed down from Harry senior, described as quite a footballer in his day. Now aged 40, he had spent many years as a popular milkman with the Cowlairs Co-operative Society – the Co-op – then Scottish Farmers, and old friends recalled him travelling down Lamont Road, or along Burnbrae Street, in his electric float. Harry senior would later run a dairy and general grocery in Queenshill Street in Springburn. Those familiar with the area would know that street as the home of Santi's famous New Yorker fish and chip restaurant and takeaway, the mecca for many a Friday night treat in those days.

Mum Mary worked in Brownlee & Company's City Sawmills, a well-known landmark at the junction of Keppochhill and Craighall Roads, just a few hundred yards from their first flat as a married couple.

Harry and Mary's eldest son, Peter, now 19 years old, was a keen amateur boxer. Peter would soon have the opportunity to continue that whilst serving in the Royal Navy, which he entered in February 1946 as an engine room artificer. The story goes that famous boxing promoter Jack Solomons tried to convince him to turn professional, but Peter turned him down, suggesting that he would be happy to take the management role if Solomon took the punches! Peter would become the first of the six Hood children to take the plunge, marrying Margaret Winter, known as Meg, in Bridgeton in 1949.

The lives of Harry and Mary's remaining two daughters - Irene and Patricia, known as Pat – would follow remarkably similar paths. Both girls would become professional ice skaters, the two beautiful, elegant Hood ladies appearing in venues across Britain and continental Europe throughout the 1950's, performing with the major stars of the day, such as singer Frankie Vaughan. They would also both wed US servicemen before raising their families on the other side of the Atlantic. Irene's childhood friend Delia would marry the well-known Glasgow criminal defence solicitor, Joe Beltrami, in 1959.

The Hoods' second son, George, was just about to turn nine years old when Harry was born. George had suffered with polio as a child, thus perhaps putting paid to any hopes of a career in sport for him. However, younger brother John – known as Jack or Jackie and now approaching his seventh birthday - would already be showing the early promise which would take him to one of the biggest football clubs on these islands. It was quite a talented and impressive family cast for Harry to join.

The earliest recollections of the young Harry Hood and his family are provided by his first school friend, Bernie Curran.

"When I first met Harry, the family lived in a four-in-a-block house in Menzies Road, adjacent to a lane which led to the shops in Balornock Road. Just opposite Springburn Park. I lived in Drumbottie Road, just across from there. I remember the Hood house vividly because they had a chicken coup in the back garden. They later moved to a top floor flat in Barmulloch Road. Harry and I were primary school pals at St Bede's, which was a wooden structure at the top of the hill on the right as you came up Red Road from Petershill, just before the Broomfield Road roundabout."

"His sisters were professional ice skaters and lived in the USA, and Harry had at least one brother, but they were all much older, and as a result he was pretty much spoiled, as I remember. When we went fishing in Springburn Park and Harry would catch a perch - much bigger than the usual minnows - he was allowed to keep them... in the family bath!"

"Harry's mum was a lovely lady, very elegant, and his dad was a real character, a milkman who drove a bright red float. Lunchtime at St Bede's consisted of four or five of us jumping on to Harry senior's electric milk float, chapping doors and asking, "Need any milk, missus?" We did it for the sheer joy of getting a free hurl. One particularly hot day, there was a bottle of Irn Bru at Harry senior's feet. I grabbed the bottle, only to be told, "Don't touch that!" When I enquired, I was told it was poison. Suffice to say there were no public toilets on Harry's dad's milk round!"

"One day, Harry and I were going to my house and on the way along Drumbottie Road, we passed an area which contained many plots, some with greenhouses. They could not be seen from the road, but we knew they were there. We threw a couple of stones over and to our horror, we heard an enormous crash. A man ran out and grabbed us and gave us a good skelp. He then marched us to my house and told my mother what we had done. She thanked him and then proceeded to belt Harry and I

harder than the man had done. Lesson learned!"

"Harry's dad was his biggest fan and motivator. When we played Boys Guild football for Immaculate Heart of Mary, he was an ever-present at the games. Our strip was all green with a white diamond, similar to the Airdrie kit. He would run the line in those matches but was inclined to be a bit biased. His dad never, as I recall, gave as much as a throw-in to the opposing team and he always did it with a straight face."

Aunt May would play a key role in the early development of young Harry beyond his spell at St Bede's. Like her older sister, Betty, who had never married, she had set up her own business, in her case selling confectionery, whilst they also owned a hairdressing salon. In the language of the day used in Springburn, the sisters would be described as "financially comfortable." Hood family history suggests that May took a special interest in Harry, the namesake of her late husband. Through her 'adoption,' he would then attend the private St Aloysius College - a prestigious fee-paying seat of learning in Garnethill, north of the city centre, rather than any of the local schools in Springburn or, indeed, the adjacent St Martha's Primary in Menzies Road, which would not be completed until 1953. Bernie picks up the story again.

"I remember that time vividly. Harry told me in the playground at St Bede's. He was a bit quiet about it. I remember thinking at the time that this was obviously a family decision. Harry's dad – as dad's do – always wanted the best for him. Harry was very much younger than his older siblings and, in my opinion, he was treated as the special one. That is not meant as derogatory. Harry's mum and dad were wonderful people."

There would one huge problem with all of this for Harry, standing out amongst the other kids with his bright green school blazer. In 1954, after more than half a century as valued members of the Glasgow Schools Football Association, the trustees of St Aloysius College made a strategic change in its sporting direction which would have major implications for the 10-year-old Harry Hood and his football-mad classmates. From that point onwards, the preferred sport at its Garnethill campus would be rugby rather than football, and although described as "a useful hooker," a career chasing the egg-shape ball was not really for Harry. He was emerging as a real talent as a footballer, starring with the local street teams, such as Menzies Star. That would be his forte, and within a few years, the change of direction at St Aloysius would present a challenge to his hopes of forging a career in the game.

All that was yet to come to pass. In the meantime, the relentless circle of life would give young Harry his first experience of death in the family, as he lost two of his three surviving grandparents, either side of his ninth birthday. On Friday, 6 February 1953, Harry's grandmother Margaret Ferguson Hood died in the family home at 363 Calder Street, Govanhill. She was 83 years old and had suffered a coronary thrombosis. Having spent the best part of six decades married to Maggie, husband Peter would not have to wait too long to be reunited with the love of his life. On the evening of Sunday, 21 March 1954, 88-year-old Peter Doran Hood would take his leave of this world through a combination of cardio-vascular degeneration and senility, once again at home in Calder Street.

Harry's maternal grandmother, Ann Morrison Scott, had passed away 25 years earlier, back in April 1929, thus widower Walter, the now-retired Highland master shoemaker, would find himself the sole surviving grandparent of the six Hood siblings in March 1954, at the grand old age of 89. By that time, Mary Hood's elderly dad had left Glasgow, having spent some time living with daughter Mary and the Hood family at Menzies Road, and was staying with his son George in Stranraer, in the south-west corner of Scotland. George, by now 62 years old, had retired from his role as the Chief Constable of Wigtownshire, having earlier played professional football with Grimsby Town - as a goalkeeper, I believe - as they joined the English League set-up. George would later become a noted police athlete.

Jack Hood recalled an unusual habit of his grandfather.

"Granda lived with us for a while in Menzies Road. He used to drink a glass of water with a rusty nail in it and tell us that was how he got his iron intake!"

By the autumn of 1956, the current members of the sporting family Hood are making progress in two very different areas. Back in Balornock, young Harry was continuing to develop as a footballer of some note who would potentially carry that family tradition into another generation. Jim Pryde, now a sprightly 85-year-old, remembers the weekly kickabouts enjoyed by the locals at Springburn Park.

"We would play up there every Sunday afternoon, without fail. I would bring my ball, one of those big size fives, all patched up, and there would be guys of all ages playing. Sometimes we arranged to play another team from the area. Jackie Hood would be there. He was a six-footer. Powerful guy. His brother George would also play, from memory, and I recall that Harry would show up wearing long trousers, with his football socks pulled all the way up to his knees over his trousers. I hadn't seen anyone do that before. Harry had a certain finesse. He was a player. We knew even then that he was going places."

Jack recalled memories of his younger brother, the aspiring footballer, when we met recently.

"Harry was always football crazy. When I was 18, he was 11, but we practised a lot together on specific skills, such as how to get up a bit early to beat a defender to a high ball. Lots of heading practice and how to swerve the ball from free-kicks. That kind of thing. Harry was a sensible lad. He always thought things through and was never in any bother."

Apprentice plasterer Jackie Hood had enjoyed a successful 1955/56 season with amateur football side Metro Vicks (his dad would work as a security guard for the same company in Springburn before his retirement) before stepping up to the junior grade with Shettleston. *The Evening Times* of Saturday, 1 September 1956 mentions the increasing senior interest in him, with Blackpool and Queen's Park the latest clubs to be linked, Jackie having apparently already rejected offers from Nottingham Forest and Everton. The previous evening, the still-amateur 18-year-old had played for a Glasgow East End Junior select beaten 1-0 by their Lanarkshire rivals. The only goal was scored by a young outside-right from Douglas Water Thistle called Ian St John, who was on Motherwell's books at that time. Following over a century of appearances with the Ancell Babes at Fir Park, St John would end up a hero to the red half of Liverpool, Bill Shankly paying a club record fee of £37,500 to bring him south in May 1961. He would also become Scotland's first-choice centre-forward in perhaps our finest generation of talent ever. Sadly, Ian passed away during the writing of this book, on 1 March 2021, aged 82.

With Celtic now added to the list of potential suitors, the Jackie Hood transfer saga finally ended by the end of that month. Everton had played a friendly against Aberdeen at Pittodrie on Monday, 24 September 1956, losing 3-2, and their Scottish first-team coach, Ian Buchan, had invited Jackie to travel back to Liverpool with the squad to have a look around. Whilst in Aberdeen, the Everton party had been based in the Caledonian Hotel in the city's Union Terrace, and the following offer was made in writing by the club's Admin Officer on hotel notepaper on the day of the game.

"On behalf of the Everton Football Club, I hereby promise to pay John Hood the maximum wages applicable to his age at the time of signing. I further promise that he will be allowed to continue with his apprenticeship (plasterer) and that the forms duly signed will only be lodged when his club, Shettleston Juniors, have lost interest in the Scottish Junior Cup."

The VIP treatment clearly worked, the talented teenager agreeing to join Everton two days later for what would be the highest transfer fee ever received by a Scottish Junior club of £1,500, as Celtic boss Jimmy McGrory awaited his return for a chat which would never happen. Great things were predicted for the talented youngster, with Shettleston's vice-president Bob Brown boldly predicting that Jackie Hood would one day play for the full Scotland team. As an aside, Jackie's junior transfer record set in 1956 would incredibly remain in place for the best part of a decade, before Watford manager Ken Furphy paid £2,500 to bring Renfrew Juniors right-half Sandy Pate to Vicarage Road in February 1965.

As was the custom at that time, it was agreed that Jackie would move to Everton once Shettleston's involvement in the Scottish Junior Cup was over (Incidentally, the current holders of the national trophy at that time were Petershill, a well-known Springburn team). That cup involvement duly ended the following weekend, Shettleston suffering a 5-1 first-round defeat at the hands of Ayrshire outfit Whitletts Victoria, at the wonderfully named Voluntary Park, thus triggering the transfer. Jackie Hood would officially become an Everton player on Friday, 5 October 1956, just two days after his younger brother Harry turned 12 years old.

Jack remembers that period well.

"I scored my favourite-ever goal whilst at Shettleston. It was set up for me by Johnny 'Non-stop' Kelly, who played with Celtic for a spell afterwards. His cross came into me at shoulder height and I managed to catch it with one foot and score with the other. There was a lot of talk about me going to Queen's Park, who were signing up a lot of amateur players at that time. And I had guested for Blackpool in a practice game, playing the first half with their reserves then the second half with their first team. What about this for a forward line...Stanley Matthews, Ernie Taylor, Jack Hood, Allan Brown and Bill Perry? And I scored a goal! Ernie Taylor was the greatest player I ever played with. Constantly supporting you and available to take the ball. He signed for Manchester United in the aftermath of Munich, which was the greatest thing they ever done."

"Everton then asked me to join them for a match at Pittodrie, and we stayed in the Gleneagles Hotel. I liked the set-up and agreed to sign for them. My dad was most disappointed that I didn't join Celtic."

Jackie's photo in that aforementioned *Evening Times* article is published beside that of older sister, Irene, at that time starring as a professional ice skater in the resort of Garmisch-Partenkirchen in the shadow of the Bavarian Alps in southern Germany. Her decade-long skating career had commenced in 1950 and would see her introduced to British royalty, having made her name at London's Empress Hall, where she appeared in Dick Whittington, indeed she is featured on the programme cover of the Pocahontas-inspired Wildfire with Frankie Vaughan. The Empress arena in Earls Court held 7,000 spectators and was home to London's renowned 'Ice Spectaculars' - a series of extravagant musical performances on ice - before closing its doors for the last time in 1958. Irene's final European tour took her to the US Army recreational base in Garmisch-Partenkirchen to perform in the Ice Reviews held in the Casa Carioca nightclub before an audience of American servicemen and their families on vacation. It was there that Irene would meet her future husband, Colonel Robert Coleman Bacon.

Texas-born Bobby Bacon was third-generation US military, following in his father's footsteps when he graduated from Westpoint Military Academy in 1956, his roommate and friend being none other than Norman Schwarzkopf, the infamous 'Stormin' Norman' who led American troops during the Gulf War. Bobby himself would progress through the ranks and was a captain when selected as a special advisor to the South Vietnamese army in 1964. It was then he was photographed leading his men through the Mekong Delta, an iconic image which made the front cover of the multi-million selling *Life* magazine.

After his second tour of South-East Asia, now a decorated war hero, Bobby moved into a protocol role with the military and planned the funerals of assassinated US Senator Robert Kennedy in June 1968 and former US President Dwight Eisenhower in March of the following year. He received a personal letter of thanks from Kennedy's widow and an invitation to the White House, where he and his wife, Irene Hood

Bacon, were introduced to President Lyndon Johnson. Irene and Bob had married at the Bacon family home in Brownsville, Texas, near the Mexican border, on Tuesday, 6 June 1961. The couple would have three sons, two of whom - Robin and Bill - became American football coaches for rival high school teams, the event (when their sides clashed) affectionately labelled the "Bacon Bowl!"

Irene's sister Pat married Robert Duane 'Robie' Robinson in Springburn in 1954, before moving to Missoula, Montana and building a life in the American mid-west with their children Dominique – known as Dede, Mary Ann and Robert junior - known as Bob, including a spell, would you believe, in Glasgow, Montana! Robie won an Academy Award in 1970 for Best Visual Effects for *Marooned*, a science fiction movie released just after the Apollo 11 moon landing the year before and starring Gregory Peck and Gene Hackman. He later enjoyed more success as a writer, most notably with the wonderfully named cult TV movie *Flatbed Annie and Sweetie Pie: Lady Truckers*, which starred Annie Potts, Kim Darby and Harry Dean Stanton. Pat later married Arthur Wagner from Havre, Montana, a caboose conductor with Northern Pacific Railway, their son John born in 1969. Arthur and Pat Wagner divorced around 1971, Pat then devoting her life to bringing up her four children in Missoula.

From amateur boxing to professional ice skating, from schoolboy rugby to senior football, and from Hollywood Oscars to White House Presidential audiences, there is little doubt that the sporting family Hood from Glasgow's north-east were an exceptionally talented bunch with more than a hint of glamour and a sense of adventure.

And that tradition would now be continued by its youngest member.

Chapter 4

Life-changing decisions as Harry goes to Holyrood ...via Barmulloch

The year 1956, would also be a significant one for Irene, Pat and Jackie's younger brother, Harry. The Hood family had moved from Menzies Road to a top-floor tenement flat at 10 Barmulloch Road in another part of Balornock and then to a new semi-detached home at 50 Gartons Road, in nearby Barmulloch. Number 50 was a corner plot leading into a small circular conclave, where another five housing blocks were located. Closest to the Hoods, beyond a large corner garden area, was number 48 Gartons Road, the home of the Dalgleish family. They had moved there three years earlier, in 1953, and had a son named Ian, who being aged 11, was one year younger than Harry. The two lads hit it off immediately and would become lifelong friends, pretty much inseparable over the years to follow.

Whilst researching for this book, I had the pleasure of speaking with Ian several times. Inevitably, the conversation would end in laughter, as he regaled me with tales of escapades with his old friend.

"We had some great times, Harry and I. We were always together. We used to go on fishing trips, take the bikes out to Lennoxtown, where the burn runs into the Campsies. We'd have an all-nighter in a wee tent. Not a care in the world. Harry loved his fishing. I didn't like handling the fish, but Harry didn't care. One time we woke up feeling hungry during the night, but when we dug out our sandwiches, they were completely covered in maggots. I go back to sleep, raging, but the bold Harry just flicks them off his pieces with his finger and ate them. Can you believe that? He ate the f'n pieces! Every time I see a maggot now, I think of Harry! He was something else."

"He also loved the golf. Between our two blocks, there was a big garden, which stretched around the corner of Gartons Road, effectively serving both houses. One morning, I walk outside and Harry's already out there with the golf clubs. We cut the grass to make the garden into a pitch and putt course, with five holes. We played for hours around the big tree in the garden, until it got dark. Magic."

"We would play up at Littlehill golf course in the summer, joining the course at that

lane that comes up at The Cairn. Walk up to the Auchinairn Road end, near the burn. Around the 14th hole. We would get the lost balls and play the last four or five holes and we didn't have to pay. Then I would get fed up playing with Harry, because he was really good at it, and I would usually end up carrying the bags."

"Harry enjoyed sport in general and football in particular. His favourite player was Pele. Harry was different class as a footballer. I went to school at the Albert, in Springburn, and Harry and I joined their former pupils' club training sessions. You'll remember the script. Two captains were appointed and took turns at choosing players to form the teams. Everyone wanted to be picked for Harry's team. Basically, if you were not chosen in Harry's team that night then you lost. Harry was always the best at everything. He always wanted to win. That was just his nature. All his life he was the same."

There was one sport, though, which the two friends could enjoy on a more equal footing, if you pardon the pun. Ian picks up the story once more.

"I used to go to Springburn Harriers, who met in the old hall on Auchinairn Road, near where the new Huntershill complex is today. Harry joined up as well. He wanted to be involved and it was level terms for once. Harry had a distinctive running style, which I would describe as a 'slow moving swagger.' His arms would be sort of half-bent. It was a gait which stayed with him throughout his football career. When Harry was running out of the tunnel on to the park, or chasing the ball on the pitch, you could see it. It was exactly the same."

Ian also confirmed that, as a boy, Harry did not really find television or indoor hobbies of any interest, other than playing cards, although perhaps you could briefly have added darts to that list…

"The Hood family house at Gartons Road was a gable end, and they had a dartboard over a coal bunker. I remember one day Harry was playing with his older brother George, who was taking so long to remove his darts after his shot that Harry took his next turn a bit too quickly. Bang! The dart ending up sticking out of poor George's head! Fortunately, there was no harm done. George was nine years older than Harry, having been born in 1935. He was a gentle giant. I never knew him to get upset about anything. George idolised Harry. He was always so proud and pleased when Harry did well."

As Harry's darts/javelin career came to a premature end, he would no doubt be keeping up to date with the progress of his other brother, Jackie, some 200 miles south in Merseyside. Jackie's first season at Goodison would be spent in the reserves, as the first team struggled in the lower half of the English First Division. The Toffees eventually finished 15th for the second successive campaign under their young Scottish coach, Ian Buchan, despite an incredible 5-2 victory over the defending champions, Manchester United, at Old Trafford, followed by a 4-0 win over Arsenal at Goodison seven days later, all within the first month of Jackie's arrival in Liverpool.

The Busby Babes would take their revenge by knocking the Blues out of the FA Cup at Old Trafford in February 1957, en route to the final, United only narrowly missing out on winning the first English League and Cup double of the 20th century as they lost to Aston Villa at Wembley. Tragically, within 12 months of that victory over Everton, most of that fabulous young squad, the Flowers of Manchester, would perish on the runway at Munich Airport.

There would be some silverware for Everton come the spring of 1957, though. The Liverpool Senior Cup is perhaps the equivalent of the Glasgow Cup, with the two giants, Everton and Liverpool, often fielding weakened sides against the first-choice teams from across Merseyside. Their main opposition that season came in the shape of Southport and Tranmere Rovers, who had just finished in two of the bottom three places in the old Third Division (North), at that time the lowest rung in the English League ladder. They would both surprise the big two, Southport eliminating Phil Taylor's Second Division Liverpool, who had only missed out on promotion by a single point, whilst Rovers took Everton to a replay, following a 1-1 draw at Prenton Park. Jackie was drafted into the team for the replay with Tranmere, played at Goodison Park on Tuesday, 7 May 1957, one of only three home players without first-team experience. He would vindicate that decision by setting up the winning goal on the hour.

Five days later, Jackie retained his place as Everton met Southport in the final on a sodden pitch at neutral Anfield. The Blues would fall behind within four minutes, thanks to a header from legendary inside-forward Stan Mortensen. Just four years earlier, Mortensen had scored a hat-trick for Blackpool as they beat Bolton Wanderers to win the FA Cup final at Wembley, albeit he may not have been too happy that this match is always referred to as the "Stanley Matthews Final!" Jackie led the line well, creating several chances whilst denied himself by goalkeeper Richardson on more than one occasion. Southport would threaten another shock win before eventually succumbing to the odd goal in three.

Although he was identified as one of the "four for the future" from that cup-winning side, that would be as good as it got for Jackie at Goodison. As the new 1957/58 season opens, he is listed as being one of the players now serving in HM Forces, as his National Service commenced. He picks up the story.

"Things were going well at Everton and then I was called up for National Service and sent to a base in Wiltshire, where football was frowned upon a bit. It was all rugby and cricket. I asked to be transferred up to Longtown, north of Carlisle, where a few of the other players were based, but I was refused. When I came out of the army things had changed. The spark had gone and a trainer at Goodison took a dislike to me for some reason. I was doing extra sessions with Eddie O'Hara and Alex Parker, a couple of the other Scottish boys who had come down from Falkirk, and he basically told me "I decide when training starts and ends. It just wasn't the same place when I came back."

Returning to the club on completion of his service in 1959, Jackie would be aware that things had changed at Everton. Having taken Blackburn Rovers to promotion in 1958, former Manchester United and Ireland captain Johnny Carey had replaced coach Ian Buchan in charge of first-team affairs, after six straight defeats in the opening matches of the 1958-59 League campaign – including a 6-1 mauling by Arsenal at Goodison – had threatened the perennial 15/16th placing which had almost become a tradition at the once-mighty institution. Carey continued in his Irish national team manager role in tandem with club duties. His growing colony of Scots was led by the inspirational Bobby Collins, finally joining Everton in 1958, a decade after he had agreed to do so as a teenage midfielder with Pollok Juniors. A contractual dispute had seen the Govanhill boy sign for Celtic, where he would be part of every success Jimmy McGrory's side achieved in his 20-year tenure as Parkhead manager. That would include two Scottish Cups, with one completing a League and Cup Double under Jock Stein's captaincy in 1954. The Coronation Cup had memorably been won against the odds the previous year, and the first two League Cups in the club's history would follow from 1956. The second of those would be the 7-1 'Hampden in the Sun' match of October 1957. Bobby Collins was undoubtedly a Celtic great.

Whilst Bobby would now be revered on Merseyside, Jackie would be on his way out. An article appears in the Glasgow *Evening Times* of 2 October 1959, under the heading *"The runaway is suspended."* It seems that Jackie had travelled back to Glasgow the previous weekend and had duly received a letter from Everton advising that he had been suspended for 14 days, presumably for going AWOL. On calling manager Johnny Carey, the outcome was that Everton would consider offers from any Scottish club for his transfer, and, if no such offers were forthcoming, he would return to Goodison on completion of the suspension. At that point Jackie is 21 and, as mentioned, has just completed his national service. Presumably, nothing materialised at that time from Scotland, and on 1 December 1959, Jackie Hood signed for Tranmere Rovers, against whom he had got his only real break at Goodison, in that replayed Senior Cup semi-final. Jackie would take his leave of Everton just as Bill Shankly, Huddersfield Town's exciting Scottish manager, was being handed the reins at Anfield, and being tasked with reviving the ailing club who played across Stanley Park. What an incredible decision that would prove to be.

As a sad footnote to Jackie's spell at Everton, Ian Buchan, the coach who brought him south – he was never described as the manager, for whatever reason – would tragically be killed in a car crash in his native Scotland six years later. Ian was just 45 years old at that time.

As Jackie's ferry crossed the Mersey to Birkenhead and Prenton Park, his younger brother Harry would keep the tenuous Scouse musical theme alive by making plans to go to Holyrood. The decision by St Aloysius College to adopt rugby as the main sport was by this time proving problematic to his dreams of playing senior, and more immediately to his hopes of representing Scotland at schoolboy level. There would be no shortage of opportunities to play football, Harry turning out for the Boys Guild team at Immaculate Heart of Mary in Balornock, his local parish – where manager Willie Birt quickly identified that *"he would go places in fitba'"* - and for informal teams drawn from schoolmates. But something was missing. Harry would then make two decisions which would impact his career - albeit in terms of his schoolboy international ambitions, perhaps not in the way he hoped – and ultimately his life. Focusing on the football first, I'll let Harry himself pick up the story, as quoted in Stratton Smith's *International Football Book No.12* from 1970.

"One of my biggest disappointments in football is that I never got a school's international honour. I went to St Aloysius College, where rugby was the official game. I had to toe the line and play it too. I was a hooker and enjoyed it, but I still missed my football, so much so, indeed, that eventually some of us got together a football team to play friendlies against other schools."

"I did get a chance to play football more seriously when I signed for St Roch's, at the age of 14 years and 9 months. Still keen to get a school's international cap, I finally changed to Holyrood school. Selected for the Holyrood school team, I went on to play in an East v West school's international trial. I scored two goals and seemed well on the way to that cap, but the authorities took a dim view when it was discovered that I had played for St Roch's, and I was passed over."

Harry's new status as a signed amateur player at St Roch's in the summer of 1959 would not present any opportunities to play in the Central League, the top-flight in Scottish Junior football, at that time. He would actually spend the following season on the south side of the river, with Queen's Park's Under-18 side, known as the Victoria XI. Hampden in the spring of 1960 was the centre of the footballing universe, having just played host to that incredible European Cup final between Real Madrid and Eintracht Frankfurt, where Ferenc Puskas and Alfredo Di Stefano had shared seven goals between them as the Spanish masters thrilled 120,000 Scottish supporters to retain their continental crown for a fifth successive year. Into such illustrious, magical footsteps strolled the young, confident and talented Harry Hood of Balornock.

As an aside, Real Madrid would win a sixth European Cup in 1966, prompting UEFA to award them the original trophy on a permanent basis. That would lead to a new design entirely for the trophy to be awarded from 1967 onwards, with Billy McNeill of Celtic having the honour of being the first captain to lift what is now the iconic European Cup, awarded to winners of the Champions League since 1993.

One of Harry's teammates for that 1960/61 campaign at Queen's Park was right-back Jimmy Hamilton. Now in his late seventies, Jimmy can still recall the events of six decades ago with a wonderful clarity and enthusiasm more typical of a teenager.

"I remember that season at Hampden with Harry really well. I had come over from Drumchapel Amateurs after winning the Scottish Under 16 Cup and Harry had been playing for his school team, Holyrood. At that time, Queen's Park ran four sides. The

first team played in the Scottish League, in the old Second Division, under a man called Willie Gibson. Another former Drumchapel Amateurs player - Alex Ferguson - had just turned professional with St Johnstone, who had been promoted to the First Division and Jim Cruickshank and Davie Holt had signed for Hearts, who were Scottish champions. There was a stack of players coming through at that time. The Strollers played in the Combined Reserve League, which featured third-string sides from Celtic and Rangers plus a number of reserve teams from other clubs. Then there was a Hampden XI, who played in the Scottish Amateur League, and our team, the Victoria XI, who were all aged 16 or 17 and so competed in the Under 18 League. Our side was packed with names you would recognise, guys like Doug Houston and Alex Ingram, and of course Harry, who all went on to professional careers. We had Bobby Clark in goal, I played at full-back and Harry was up front with a guy called Andy Roxburgh. You might remember him! Our manager revelled in the name of William S Burgess. He worked for a whisky company, from memory."

"In those days, the four Queen's Park teams all trained together, on Mondays and Thursdays. There were no floodlights at Hampden back then, so we would often use the facilities at Brig O'Lea, Neilston Juniors ground, for training or matches on the dark nights. I remember seeing a young Dixie Deans up there. Daylight matches would be played on one of the Lesser Hampden pitches, either the old ash park outside the main stand or the one folk are more familiar with, behind the west end of the stadium."

"My recollection is that Harry was very self-confident. He knew he was a good player. He played every week but perhaps didn't see himself making the progression through the teams quickly enough. Sometimes that was more to do with whether your face fitted or not. It could be a bit of a closed shop. Anyway, Harry left after one season to play with Brunswick Boys Club up in Carntyne. He played against us the following season at Under 18 level, then he went to St Roch's. His elder brother was there. He was some player. Inside-left. All left peg. I also recall that Bobby Waddell and Malcolm Cook were in that side. Malcolm had played with me at Drumchapel and went to Motherwell after St Roch's. He moved into coaching and ended up Director of Youth Football under Kenny Dalglish at Anfield. I stuck around at Hampden for another few years and eventually played a couple of times for the first team. Willie Gibson was later replaced as Queen's Park's first team coach by Eddie Turnbull, who took Bobby Clark with him to Pittodrie as his first signing when he, in turn, got the Aberdeen job a few years later."

If the Hood family move to Gartons Road, Barmulloch in 1956 had inadvertently led to a lifelong friendship with Ian Dalgleish, then Harry's decision to change school from St Aloysius College to Holyrood Secondary four years later would prove to be the real 'sliding doors' moment of his life.

On Thursday, 8 August 1940, four months before May Hood married Harry O'Gara at Holy Cross RC Church in Glasgow's Crosshill district, another wedding took place in the nearby church of St Francis in Cumberland Street, deep in the heart of the Gorbals community. On that day, engineer's labourer Anthony McGinley married domestic servant Mary Boyle, the service conducted by Father Frederick Furlong. Tony was the son of farmer Edward McGinley and his wife Rose McGarvey McGinley, whilst Mary's parents were James Boyle, a railway platelayer to trade, and Mary Gallagher Boyle.

Both Mary Boyle and Tony McGinley had been born in Ireland - Tony in June 1909 and Mary in September 1912 - before moving to Scotland with their respective parents. The couple then met in Paisley before moving to Glasgow. By August 1940, only one of the newlyweds' four parents – Tony's dad Edward McGinley - was still alive, and their marriage certificate would suggest that both Mary and Tony were living with him at the McGinley family home at 336 Crown Street, Gorbals at that time.

The marriage of Tony and Mary McGinley would duly be blessed by three daughters, in their home just along from Edward at 295 Crown Street, with a certain Patrick Timothy Crerand and his family living in the adjacent close. First-born to the young McGinley's was baby Mary Rose, presumably named after both of her grandmothers and entering the world on Thursday, 2 April 1942. She would be followed two years later by Kathleen, born in Stobhill Hospital, Balornock on Monday, 29 May 1944. As an aside, a little over four months later, a newborn Harry Hood would also get his first sense of this world there. Such is fate. More than a decade would then pass before Tony and Mary's third child was introduced, baby Anne completing the McGinley family on Wednesday, 9 February 1955.

As their family grew, the young couple would prosper through sheer hard work, becoming successful publicans and opening their first licensed premises, Tony's Bar in Bridgeton. In 1956, Tony, Mary and their three young daughters relocated from the Gorbals to a new home at 8 Orcades Drive, Simshill.

In the summer of 1960, the 16-year-old Kathleen McGinley commenced her fifth year of studies at Holyrood Secondary School on Dixon Road. Unawares to Kathleen, her life was about to change with the arrival of a new student, a young lad from the north of the city called Harry Hood. She recalls it clearly.

"Harry transferred to Holyrood from St Aloysius in fifth year, whilst I had attended Holyrood for all of my secondary education. We were in the same class and Harry was always late coming to school, as he travelled from Balornock to the south side of Glasgow via two buses. He always had a training bag with him, plus a joke to explain why he was late to the class, which brought great hilarity to the teacher and pupils, but I was not at all amused, being a studious young girl. We were both 16/17. But I quickly changed my mind at the Christmas school dance of 1960, and I accepted his offer to walk me home."

A decade on from the spring of 1961, Bobby Clark, Eddie Turnbull, Aberdeen and Hampden would all feature prominently in the Harry Hood story, by which time the beautiful Miss Kathleen McGinley was Mrs Kathleen Hood, mother of the couple's three children.

But that's for another day.

Chapter 5

Braunschweig, the Black Watch and the Candy Roch

In December 1943, two months after Harry O'Gara and four colleagues had tragically lost their lives at Kells Brow, a new prisoner-of-war camp for Allied officers was established by the German army in the town of Braunschweig, just east of Hanover, on the main route between there and Berlin. It would be named Offizierslager 79 – Officer's Camp 79 in English – and known by its abbreviation of Oflag 79.

By January 1945, with the Allied bombing of Germany having severely impacted communications and the deliveries of Red Cross parcels into the camp, a combination of hunger, freezing cold weather and boredom had damaged the morale of the occupants of Oflag 79. As always in times of adversity, some folk will step up to the plate. One of the officers, Percy Flood, contemplated that these conditions of hardship being endured by the prisoners in Braunschweig were not dissimilar to those experienced by many young men back in the UK in times of peace. He floated a concept where the prisoners of Oflag 79 would work together to establish a Boys Club to provide opportunities for developing the potential of those who would not otherwise have access to such amenities. The club would be located in one of the major UK cities, most likely London, and would serve as an enduring memorial to the comradeship shared by the men of Oflag 79 and to their friends and colleagues who would not survive the war.

On St Valentine's Day 1945, the vision became a reality when several hundred men from the camp voted overwhelmingly to set up the club. By the time the camp was liberated by the US Army in April 1945, a sum equivalent in today's terms to £175,000 had been raised or promised by the men of Oflag 79, and three years later, the construction of premises in Fulham in the west end of London had been completed, including a gymnasium which resembled an old airport hangar. The club was named after the camp in Braunschweig where the idea had originated, using the English translation of Brunswick.

A second branch of Brunswick Boys Club was opened the same year, in the Toxteth area of Liverpool, and in 1951 a third club was opened in Balornock, in north-eastern Glasgow, again with that distinctive curved gymnasium building, looking like an enlarged version of the Anderson wartime air raid shelter. The new club proved hugely popular, with football just one of the wide range of sports on offer for the youth of Balornock and Barmulloch. One young lad who spent many hours playing in or for the Brunswick was Thomas Stephen Chalmers from nearby Lamont Road. Known as Stevie, he would be picked up by junior side Kirkintilloch Rob Roy as a 17-year-old in 1953. Shortly afterwards, Jackie Hood from Menzies Road would also take the first steps with the Brunswick on a path that would lead him through the junior football ranks with Shettleston to sign for Everton in October 1956. The careers of the two Brunswick Boys would then follow very different paths over the coming years.

By the summer of 1961, Stevie Chalmers was an automatic choice and approaching the 50-goal mark for his beloved Celtic, having suffered the agony of a Scottish Cup final replay defeat a few months earlier at the hands of Dunfermline Athletic and their charismatic young manager, Jock Stein, the former Parkhead captain and reserve team coach. Stevie had returned for a second spell at Brunswick after a two-year stint in the RAF on National Service followed by a brush with death in the autumn of 1956 had severely curtailed his football ambitions. Now back at Rob Roy, Stevie was struck down by the often-deadly illness tuberculosis meningitis, before defying his doctors and the accepted medical science to make a full recovery. Within 12 months he was back with the Brunswick Club and working non-stop to get his football dream back on track. Stevie would then step up to the junior game for a second spell, this time with crack local outfit Ashfield, where one of his teammates was his future brother-in-law, Willie Brackenridge. Chalmers was capped at junior international level against Ireland at Firhill before signing for Celtic in February 1959. Jimmy McGrory handed the 24-year-old Garngad-born forward his debut against Airdrieonians at Parkhead the following month, and by the end of his first full season as a professional footballer - 1959/60 - Stevie Chalmers was scoring regularly for Celtic.

As mentioned previously, Jackie Hood had returned from completing his own National Service in 1959 to find his first-team opportunities at Everton somewhat limited. In December of that year, he joined the ex-Blues colony at Tranmere Rovers, led by two Irish internationalists, former Goodison skipper Peter Farrell – now player/manager at Prenton Park – and Tommy Eglington. Jackie scored three goals in five games for Rovers, including a double in his final match away to Mansfield Town which saved the club from relegation from English League Division Three. In July 1960, he asked to be placed on the transfer list in the hope of securing a move home to Scotland, the Birkenhead club placing a notional £250 price on his signature. The 22-year-old striker would quickly have his wish granted, Jackie heading back north to join Second Division East Fife on Monday, 15 August 1960.

Jackie Hood made his Scottish senior football debut in a League Cup sectional match five days later, a 2-2 draw with Stranraer at Stair Park. The man he replaced in the number 10 jersey for East Fife that afternoon was Ian Stewart. More on Ian to follow. Jackie would retain his place for the two remaining League Cup ties, opening his scoring account with East Fife's third in the 4-3 victory over Forfar Athletic in Methil in the final group match on Saturday, 3 September 1960, sadly another goal from each team still required to give us that immortal scoreline of 'East Fife five, Forfar four.' Hood then scored his first Scottish League goal seven days later, a 25-yard rocket to give the hosts the lead in the Fife derby with Cowdenbeath at Bayview. The Blue Brazil had won the League Cup section which included both local rivals the previous month and they would prove too strong again, bouncing back to win 4-1 to go top of the Second Division, whilst leaving East Fife pointless after three matches.

Jackie would be on target again as a 4-2 victory over Albion Rovers at Bayview on Wednesday, 14 September 1960 produced a very welcome first win of the campaign, and he scored his fourth goal of the season to give the Fifers an interval lead against Berwick Rangers at the same venue ten days later, the eventual 4-0 win lifting them off the foot of the table. Now partnering Ian Stewart up front, both men would be on the scoresheet against Queen's Park in a 2-2 draw in Methil on Wednesday, 28 September, the second successive midweek League clash with the Hampden amateurs where their direct opponent was a 16-year-old centre-half, Alan Gray. More on Alan also to follow in due course.

The opening day of October saw East Fife come up short against a rampant Hamilton Academical side at Douglas Park, highly rated Accies winger Jim McLean netting a double in a 5-2 triumph for the hosts. The following Saturday, 8 October 1960, it was the Fifers number seven - Norrie Tran – who was the star of the show, the former Hibernian forward scoring a hat-trick in East Fife's 3-1 win over Falkirk at Bayview, to leapfrog Jackie Hood and Ian Stewart as the club's top goalscorer with seven.

Jackie made his 14th consecutive appearance in the East Fife forward-line at Cappielow, seven days later in a 1-1 draw. He had scored four goals in 11 Second Division appearances at Methil, whilst adding another one from his three League Cup matches, for a more-than-decent return of a strike every three games. He then disappears completely from the first-team picture. Jackie clears that one up.

"I had thought my last game was against Queen's Park at Hampden, but I remember coming in after the match and literally hanging my boots up on the peg and saying, "That's it." I had always wanted to play at the top level rather than in the lower Leagues. I was 'scunnered' with football and wanted to make a life for myself, so I picked up a job in insurance and they wanted me to work on a Saturday."

The biggest match of Jackie's season though happened back on Merseyside the following month, as he married Lilian Roden from – appropriately enough - the Everton district of Liverpool, in Prescot on Monday, 21 November 1960. The couple had first met 'at the dancing,' introduced by friends when Jackie was on the Goodison Park books, but the new Mrs Lilian Hood – known in family circles as Lil – would now follow her footballer husband to Scotland. Jackie was released by East Fife at the end of that season, having not made a first-team appearance since the previous October.

His application to be reinstated to the junior ranks with St Roch's - nicknamed The Candy Rock - was duly approved at a formal Scottish Junior FA meeting held in August 1961.

As Jackie Hood was experiencing the full range of emotions offered by senior football north and south of the border, his younger brother Harry was progressing well much closer to home. Having left Queen's Park to join the Brunswick Boys Club, the 16-year-old inside-forward had formed an effective right-flank partnership with John McHugh. Harry's senior by one year, John was a Springburn boy, educated at the local St Aloysius schools before moving up to St Mungo's Academy. The McHughs had moved from Springburn Road up to Lamont Road, and would now be neighbours of both the Chalmers and Hood families. The teenagers had actually been opponents in their Boys Guild days, as John recalls.

"Harry played with the Immaculate Heart of Mary, whilst I turned out for St Catherine's Laboure - the church on Lamont Road just around the corner from the Brunswick Centre. That would be back in 1957 or 1958. Incidentally, the manager of St Catherine's at that time was a certain Jimmy Chalmers, who was Stevie's brother! Harry and I played for one season together for the Brunswick, in the Scottish Under 18 Amateur League. Home games took place at Hogarth Park, over in Carntyne. It was non-stop football back then. We played for our school teams on the Saturday morning, then for the Brunswick in the afternoon. Harry was a great player. Very skilful. And as a person, he was very likeable. I would describe him as mischievous, but not in any bad way. He was just great fun. Those were good times."

That successful Brunswick pairing would temporarily be broken up in the spring of 1961, as John McHugh signed for junior outfit Dennistoun Waverley. He would spend just a few short months at that level, playing on Waverley's infamous black ash surface at Haghill Park – just a stone's throw from the Brunswick's Hogarth Park - before joining Clyde, John turning out for the reserves in a 2-0 win over Queen's Park Strollers at Shawfield on Saturday, 9 September 1961. His teammates that afternoon included Graham Macfarlane and Jim McLean. McHugh would not know then that within 12 months, his Boys Guild opponent then Brunswick teammate Harry Hood would be joining them at Shawfield.

In the interim, Harry would cram an enormous amount of football into his schedule. His outings with Queen's Park and Brunswick had been supplemented by appearances for his school team at Holyrood and top amateur outfit Campsie Black Watch, who played out in Lennoxtown, at the foot of the Campsie Fells. And the 1961/62 season would now see his introduction to the junior game with St Roch's, where his brother Jackie now plied his trade, as did a third forward with the Hood surname – 17-year-old Gerald - who was unrelated. Gerry had also been playing with Campsie Black Watch before making his debut for St Roch's against Cambuslang Rangers at a packed Provanmill Park in the fourth round of the Scottish Junior Cup on Tuesday, 3 January 1961, the full-house crowd of 6,500 that afternoon including the full Celtic team and their manager - ex-Candy Man Jimmy McGrory – just 24 hours after they had lost the Ne'erday Derby by 2-1 at Ibrox.

The St Roch's team that day also featured John McStay – nephew of former Celtic captains Willie and Jimmy and later to become the father of 1980's Celts Willie and Paul – at right-back, and left-winger Frank Brogan, who scored twice in a 4-3 defeat. Two months earlier, on Saturday, 9 November 1960, Frank had played against Glencairn at that same venue, unaware that Celtic assistant manager and chief scout Sean Fallon was in the crowd. Sligo's Iron Man would then make the Celtic-mad Brogan's dreams come true by signing him after the match. He would be joined two years later at Parkhead by younger brother Jim, both siblings following that path from the Candy to the Celtic. Frank's 13 League goals in three seasons at Parkhead would include the 5,000th in the club's history, as he joined an incredible list of Celts – including his new manager Jimmy McGrory – who had notched the previous landmark goals. Frank would later enjoy an excellent career at Ipswich Town but sadly was another wonderful Celt who passed away during the writing of this book, aged 78, on Thursday, 29 April 2021.

In addition to playing with the Brunswick, the Black Watch and the Candy Rock, Harry was also training twice-weekly with the youths at Parkhead, another potentially huge opportunity for the Celtic-daft teenager, whilst the three youngest Hood brothers could all be found together on a local set of playing fields - the red-ash pitches on Broomfield Road, Balornock - on Sunday afternoons. It was there where a lovely family tradition began. Harry's boyhood pal, Ian Dalgleish, takes up the story again.

"Harry played at Campsie Black Watch for a couple of years, between the ages of 15 and 17. He was also training at Celtic Park two evenings a week at that time - on Tuesdays and Thursdays. And we would be going to the dancing at Kirkintilloch Town Hall at the weekend, catching the old Bluebird bus from Springburn Road, opposite Woolworth's at the Balgray swing park. So, the week was pretty much all mapped out."

"I also have it in my mind that Harry played briefly for St Roch's, perhaps just four to six games, before joining Clyde. And he and Jackie would play together for a local outfit - Balornock Real - on the pitches up at Broomfield. Sunday League standard, although those two could really play. Harry was skilful and Jackie powerful. I would go along to watch with their brother, George. That's where I first remember George using the "Viva!" cry, which would become his trademark. He would shout that after a goal, and Harry would turn and acknowledge his brother, right arm in the air. That continued throughout Harry's career, albeit at a full Celtic Park it would be less pronounced because of the noise around us."

Jack Hood also remembered those Sundays with Balornock Real and Harry's reaction to scoring.

"There would be three or four professionals playing up there on the pitches. John McHugh was one and a lad called McGuigan, from memory, and Harry and I.

Harry's goal celebrations were always fairly muted, even as a senior. I sometimes thought he could have been a bit more exuberant but there were never any hysterics. That was just Harry. He was the ultimate, consummate professional."

Ian's mention of Harry's occasional St Roch's outings would appear to be spot on. Gordon Hammond is the honorary president of the famous junior outfit, who have provided so many players to Celtic over the years, none greater than the man after whom their home ground on the Royston Road is now named, James McGrory. Gordon watched his first Candy game back in 1953 and was the 'hamper boy' between 1959 and 1964, when the Hood trio of forwards were playing for the club. His passion for and knowledge of St Roch's is on a different level. When I told him that I was looking for information on Harry and Jackie's spell with the Saints, he was immediately able to tell me that the brothers had managed five goals between them in season 1961/62 – Jackie with three of those – before producing a meticulous handwritten record of every St Roch's result from that and several other seasons.

The St Roch's squad who began that campaign had several links to Celtic. In addition to John McStay, inside-forward Tommy McGunnigle's father of the same name had spent the ill-fated 1931/32 season – during which Celtic's young international goalkeeper John Thomson had tragically been killed at Ibrox - as understudy to winger Bertie Thomson, albeit his solitary first-team appearance had been as a replacement for Charlie Napier – on international duty for Scotland at Wembley – in a 1-1 League draw with Airdrieonians at Celtic Park on Saturday, 9 April 1932. At left-back for the Hoops that day was Willie/Peter McGonagle, Tommy's cousin, despite the different spelling of their surnames. After leaving Celtic, Tommy would enjoy spells in Ireland with Glentoran and Cork and back in Scotland with Dumbarton and Brechin City, before ending his career at Polkemmet Juniors. Tommy junior would catch the eye of the Queen's Park scouts and would move to Hampden at the end of the season.

Two other young forwards had taken the 'McGrory route' of joining the 'Big Candy' from St Roch's Boys Guild before being provisionally signed by Celtic. Sadly, neither of the boys - Dick Lowrie and Junior McLaughlin - would follow the great man into the first-team scene at Parkhead, although Lowrie would enjoy a senior career with Stenhousemuir before tasting Scottish Junior Cup glory twice with the dominant Cambuslang Rangers side of the early 1970's.

Central defender Jim Hannah was actually Jimmy McGrory's nephew. Hannah's performances during the first half of the campaign would see him leave St Roch's to sign for First Division Airdrieonians in December 1961, the young pivot immediately promoted to the first team where he would remain for the rest of the season. Hannah would spend five years at Broomfield before joining St Mirren in 1966.

And the name John Taylor will be familiar to Celtic supporters of the current generation, as his son John Paul is their Liaison Officer at Parkhead, having spent many years as the Ticket Office manager.

The final Parkhead link was inside-right Davie Robertson, who was training with the club's part-timers. He was one of three players joining St Roch's that summer from top Glasgow youth outfit Drumchapel Amateurs, the others being Matt Brennan and Malcolm Cook. Now a highly respected football coach and author, Malcolm picks up the story.

"I had just turned 18 and was working in the shipyards, which was a tough and very cold environment. I had been training with Rangers, which involved running multiple laps around the track until every part of you ached. All the big names were there, Ian McColl, Bobby Brown, John Prentice, Scot Symon and a real tough customer called Willie Telfer, who came from St Mirren. I used to see him head medicine balls. Something else. But it wasn't for me. I had quite a few offers, including my local junior team, Benburb. I lived in Govan, but I chose to go to St Roch's for one reason, and that was their manager, Willie Smith. He was a brilliant little guy. So enthusiastic and so good to me. He came to see my dad and I at home and we just took to him. He said to me, "You're good enough to make it as a pro. Come to us. You'll love it." And I did. They were a brilliant bunch of players. He sold me on his model, which was to take guys with talent and polish them up a bit. Get them through that final stage of grooming required to become a professional player. I ended up down at Arsenal on trial, spending time down there with my parents. That was fantastic. I played for their reserves against the first team and I loved it, but it was too far to move away from home for me at that time. I ended up at Motherwell, which with hindsight was not a great move. They had a plethora of top-class midfield players already."

"Harry and I got on really well. He was a great lad and we used to talk about our dreams. Unlike me, he had what I describe as an economy of effort on the pitch. He reminded me of Willie Fernie in some ways although he didn't have to dribble his way past several players. He could play a ball off early and he could ride tackles and not get caught. The junior game could be rough, and Harry had a slight build. He was not excessively quick, but he was very mobile. We could tell he was going to be a player."

Having trawled through the newspaper archives for every single day of that 1961/62 season, I can find only two records of Harry playing for St Roch's. The first of those is on Saturday, 26 August 1961, the 16-year-old Harry giving the Candy a 1-0 half-time lead against Vale of Clyde at a waterlogged Provanmill Park when *"he hit the roof of the net."* St Roch's eventually won the Central League match 3-0, with the following line-up.

Boyle; Newman & Phil Lynch; Tommy Collins, Jim Hannah & Dougie Kerr; Jimmy McQuillan, Tommy McGunnigle, George Fellowes, Harry Hood & Keily.

Three weeks later, Saturday, 16 September 1961, Harry is again included in the St Roch's team which fights back from two goals down to secure a draw with Strathclyde in a Central League fixture played at Springfield Park, in the shadow of Celtic Park. On the same day, two supporters were killed and more than 50 injured in an accident on Ibrox's notorious Stairway 13. With horrific similarities to the disaster which would claim 66 lives at the same part of the stadium a decade later, the incident took place after Rangers had scored a late equaliser against Celtic, in this case Jim Baxter to make it 2-2. Over in the east end of the city, the following St Roch's team had shared four goals with the Strathies.

Boyle; Phil Lynch & Jim McInally; Malcolm Cook, Jim Hannah & Newman; Bremner, R Watson, George Fellowes, Harry Hood & John Taylor.

Neither of the above matches featured the other Hood forwards, and I can find no record of the trio ever appearing together for the Candy in the media, although Jack confirmed that they did so once.

"I went to St Roch's that season as Harry was there and I wanted to look after him. We played one game together, but I can't recall the opposition. I do remember they had a hard man who hammered Harry early on. I sorted that out!"

There are several mentions of Jack struggling to recover from injury throughout the season – indeed, he featured in one match in goals for St Roch's in August whilst in that situation – and his playing career would appear to end at this stage at the age of 24. By the end of the decade, though, he would be back at Provanmill Park, this time as the president of St Roch's, having spent some time coaching at Ayrshire junior outfit Dalry Thistle from August 1967.

Gerry Hood ended a highly successful 1961/62 campaign with 19 goals, having featured most weeks at inside-forward as St Roch's won three of the four cup finals in which they featured. His strike partner John Taylor managed 35 goals that campaign, both men then joining Albion Rovers before the calendar year was out. The Candy had lost out to Pollok in the final of the Glasgow Junior Cup, played at Celtic Park on Saturday, 12 May 1962, whilst they would beat St Anthony's to clinch both the Glasgow North Eastern Cup and the Kirkwood Shield.

However, the highlight of the season was a 2-1 win over local rivals Petershill in the replayed final of the Central League Cup at Shawfield, on Wednesday, 6 June 1962. This would be some measure of revenge for their controversial exit from the Scottish Junior Cup at the hands of 'The Peasy,' seven months earlier. St Roch's had actually won the original Junior Cup first-round tie 1-0, thanks to a bizarre, early own goal from Petershill defender Tony Weldon, at a packed Provanmill Park on Saturday, 4 November 1961. The Springburn club would then successfully lodge a protest, stating that Candy full-back Phil Lynch had been ineligible for the match, and the great sense of injustice around the Garngad was heightened when Petershill scored a late winner to knock them out at the same venue two weeks later, after John McStay had given St Roch's the lead from the penalty spot.

My take on all of this is that the young Harry Hood was possibly utilised as cover for injuries to Jackie and Gerry in the early weeks of the season, before focusing on making appearances for Brunswick Boys Club and his school team, Holyrood

Secondary, beyond September 1961.

As a footnote to that junior season, I found it interesting to note the development of the next batch of Lisbon Lions who were going through their apprenticeships at that level before being called up to Parkhead. First to catch my eye was the incomparable Jinky, referred to at that time as Jim Johnstone, *"Blantyre Celtic's Tom Thumb outside-right, who is 5' 2" tall and a real box of tricks."* On Saturday, 27 January 1962, Jinky and three other future Lions played in the fourth round of the Scottish Junior Cup for their respective sides. Jimmy featured for Blantyre Celtic in their 5-2 defeat at home to Glencairn, as did Tommy Gemmell for Coltness United in a 2-2 home draw with Camelon, whilst Bobby Lennox opened the scoring for Ayrshire amateurs Ardeer Recreation in a 2-1 defeat to Newburgh in Fife.

The following Saturday, Jinky played for Blantyre Celtic – managed by Ned Cushley, father of Celtic's John, who had moved from Craighead Park to Parkhead in July 1960 – in their 5-0 defeat to St Roch's in the Central League clash at Provanmill Park. And the shape of things to come was demonstrated in the replayed Scottish Junior Cup-tie between Coltness United and Camelon, as Tommy Gemmell scored "with an amazing shot from the halfway line." Undisputed team of that season was Kirkintilloch Rob Roy, who won the coveted double of Scottish Junior Cup and Central League, their star man being wing-half Martin Ferguson – brother of Alex – who joined Partick Thistle at the end of the campaign. The Rabs had knocked St Roch's out of the other major competition – the West of Scotland Cup – in early September, after the Candy had lost defender Brian Savage to injury in the first minute.

Back with Harry at Holyrood, he would almost certainly have been involved in the Under 18 trials for the Glasgow Schools team, which took place at Nether Pollok on Saturday, 4 November 1961. Jim McCalliog represented Holyrood in the Under 15 trials at the same venue, whilst 11-year-old Danny McGrain of Camus Place played for Glasgow West's under 12s against West Lothian in Blackburn. Harry would progress to the final trials for Glasgow at the senior age level, played at Lesser Hampden on Monday, 13 November before being selected with Holyrood teammate Tommy Doherty and former Queen's Park colleague Alex Ingram in the following line-up to face the Rest of Scotland at Cathkin at the end of that month.

Melville (St Augustine's); Milliken (Hyndland) & Doherty (Holyrood); Wyper (Whitehill), McCarron (Lourdes) & McLellan (Eastwood);

Ingram (Eastwood), Samson (Whitehill), McNulty (Lourdes), Hood (Holyrood) & Kilpatrick (John Neilston Institution).

Reserves: Wishart (Shawlands, Rankin (St Mungo's), Mackay (Shawlands), Neilson (Rutherglen) & Miller (Queen's Park).

That major step towards Harry's dream of schoolboy international honours was cruelly crushed when the selectors realised that he had signed amateur forms and played for St Roch's earlier that season. On Thursday, 23 Nov 1961, it was announced that an *"enforced change"* would see Hood of Holyrood replaced by Neilson of Rutherglen Academy for the clash with Rest of Scotland at Cathkin the following Monday. It would be small consolation, if any, to Harry that Glasgow duly lost 4-0 that evening.

Harry would pick himself up, dust himself down and focus on doing well for Holyrood and Brunswick for the rest of the campaign, albeit that contract with St Roch's would have another sting in its tail later that season. Holyrood commenced their League programme in devastating style, an unbeaten run taking them to the top of Division 1D of the Glasgow Schools League, where they would enjoy a season-long tussle with Lourdes for the title. The goalkeeper was a youngster from Pollokshields by the name of Denis Connaghan, who, of course, would feature again in the Harry Hood story. Sixty years down the line, former Celtic keeper Denis still has fond memories of those times at Holyrood.

"We had a great side back then. The manager was a chap called John Murphy, who was actually the stadium matchday announcer at Celtic Park. Unusually, he had looked after us each year, whereas normally you got a new coach as you moved through the age levels. My family had moved from Coburg Street in the Gorbals to Pollokshields in 1957, so I had been at Holyrood from the outset, but I remember Harry and John McCafferty only moved across from St Aloysius in fifth year. A lot of boys did that at the time, as St Aloysius was a rugby-playing school. You could tell right away that Harry was a player. He stood out like a sore thumb. We got on like a house on fire from the start and I became and remained close friends with Harry and Kathie. We both loved our football. He was very modest. Never boasted. Harry did his talking on the park."

"I remember some of the other boys well. Tommy Doherty at full-back was from Priesthill. He later married Kathie's best pal, Angela Canning. Defender Andy McManus and winger Harry Murphy both went on trial with Bolton Wanderers, and big Conrad La Pointe was a fabulous athlete. He was six foot plus and a 400m runner. He spoke with a broad Glaswegian accent, and I'm not certain but I think his family origins may have been French Canadian."

"At outside-right was John Gartland, who revelled in the nickname "Judy" for obvious reasons. He was greased lightning and could run 100 yards in 10 seconds. His parents owned Gartland's Rolls, a bakery in Rutherglen. It was a family business which was later taken over by one of the bigger companies, Morton's I believe. John went on a supporters' charter to Milan for the European Cup final in 1970. One of the stewardesses on the flight was Rae Stein, Jock's daughter, and they later married."

"There was only one problem for Harry. He had signed an amateur form for St Roch's, which prevented him playing in the Scottish Secondary Shield – the schoolboy equivalent of the Scottish Cup."

It is unclear whether that ban covered all rounds of the major competition or just the final. Holyrood progressed steadily with the key tie being a last-16 clash with Lanark

Grammar, Willie Waddell's old school. The Glasgow boys would eventually win 4-1 at the fourth attempt to reach the quarter-final. There they would face Our Lady's High from Motherwell, whose colours had been worn with such distinction by both Billy McNeill and Bobby Murdoch. Indeed, Bobby would have been part of their 1960 winning team, as was the aforementioned John Cushley.

Holyrood would again triumph by 4-1, on Saturday, 24 February 1962, to set up a semi-final clash with St Gerard's from Govan, where yet more future Lisbon Lions had developed their craft, Jim Craig winning Scotland schoolboy caps there the previous season whilst a 16-year-old Joe McBride would possibly have played in their cup-winning side of 1954. For the third successive Saturday, Holyrood would record a 4-1 win in the Scottish Secondary Shield, Harry's boys now awaiting the winner of great rivals Lourdes and Falkirk High in the final. As an aside, as Holyrood were beating St Gerard's at their Dixon Road home, just a few miles away at Parkhead another of the immortal Lions was making his debut in the Hoops. With Ardeer Recreation's Scottish Junior Cup dreams over, Bobby Lennox had been called up by Celtic, and on Saturday, 3 March 1962, the Saltcoats Bhoy played his part as a late Billy McNeill header secured a 2-1 win over Dundee, handing the title initiative to Rangers with just eight games remaining. Three years earlier, McGrory's Hoops had beaten Hearts on the final day of the League season to literally hand the flag to Rangers. Bob Kelly may have divided opinion, however, there was certainly never any question around Celtic's sporting integrity when he was at the helm.

The last day of March 1962 saw a virtual League decider for the Holyrood team, as they travelled to Cardonald to face Lourdes with the following line-up.

Denis Connaghan; Rigby & Tommy Doherty; P McLean, Andy McManus & Conrad La Pointe;

John Gartland, Harry Murphy, John McCafferty, Harry Hood & Gray.

The visitors had led the Division from the outset but would now see Lourdes overtake them following a 4-3 defeat. Holyrood were 3-0 down before John McCafferty pulled a goal back, and it was 4-1 before their two Harry's – Hood and Murphy – set up a cliffhanger of a finish. Harry Hood's direct opponent, Frank McCarron, had been selected with him for the Glasgow Schools side back in November, and the powerful Scotland Schoolboys' skipper would sign for Celtic on Monday, 28 May 1962. Lourdes would go on to clinch the Glasgow League title after the four Division 1 leaders played-off that same month.

As an aside, whilst Holyrood were going down at Cardonald, just a few miles away at Ibrox there were disgraceful scenes as Celtic lost their Scottish Cup semi-final to a Willie Fernie-inspired St Mirren. Bob Kelly allegedly conceded the tie before the pitch was cleared and the game restarted. Celtic lost 3-1.

April began with the postponement of the Scottish Secondary Shield final at Hampden due to concerns over the pitch cutting up ahead of the Scotland v England clash and the Scottish Cup final, where St Mirren would face Rangers after their Ibrox victory over Celtic. Monday, 9 April 1962 saw Lourdes once again come out on top with a 2-1 victory over Holyrood in the Cameronian Cup final at Cathkin. Five days later, there was finally some joy for Holyrood against their nemesis, as Harry's boys beat Lourdes 5-1 in the first round of the Maley Trophy at Dixon Road. John Gartland opened the scoring within three minutes, before Harry *"cleverly netted"* the second and John McCafferty added a third. Gartland and McCafferty would each complete their doubles before a large crowd at the school in the shadow of Hampden. Meanwhile, inside the national stadium, a Scotland side including Billy McNeill and Paddy Crerand were beating England at home for the first time in 25 years, before more than 132,000 supporters. The Holyrood team who triumphed on Saturday, 14 April 1962 was as follows.

Denis Connaghan; Tommy Doherty & Gray; P McLean, Andy McManus & Conrad La Pointe;

John Gartland, T Jones, John McCafferty, Harry Hood & Harry Murphy.

Whether Harry had been forced to sit out the earlier rounds of the Scottish Secondary Shield remains unknown, however, there is no doubt that he missed out on the final. His replacement on the day would be none other than Jim McCalliog, who would later famously make his senior Scotland debut in the 3-2 victory over World Champions England at Wembley in April 1967, the 20-year-old Sheffield Wednesday forward scoring the winning goal on the day 36-year-old Celtic keeper Ronnie Simpson became the oldest Scotland debutant ever. Jim remembers the lead-up to that schools' final very well.

"I was playing with Holyrood's under 15's at the time. Denis Cuddihy, who I believe is the uncle of Paul who works at Celtic, was our teacher, whilst John Murphy was the Head of PE and took charge of the seniors. It was Denis who gave me the heads-up that John wanted me to take Harry's place in the final, as Harry was ineligible. I wasn't that comfortable about it, to be honest. It was an honour to be asked but I was worried that it wouldn't go down well with the team. It felt to me that there were others who had played their part in getting the team to the final, and that one of those reserves should step in. I remember thinking that, apart from anything else, I didn't want a clip around the ear from one of the older guys. I asked Denis for time to think about it."

"The decision was then taken out of my hands. John Murphy was adamant that I would play. He told the Under 18 squad that there were to be no repercussions for me. From memory, he said that the decision was his baby – not mine. And that was that. It was the only game I ever played for that team."

On Tuesday, 15 May 1962, the Holyrood team lined up at Hampden for the Scottish Secondary Shield final against Falkirk High, as follows.

Denis Connaghan; J McQuillan & Tommy Doherty; P McLean, Andy McManus &

Conrad La Pointe; John Gartland, T Jones, John McCafferty, Jim McCalliog & Harry Murphy.

The match would turn out to be a one-sided affair, with John McCafferty putting Holyrood in front as early as the second minute, the powerful striker completing his hat-trick before half-time. He would grab his fourth late on, with John Gartland and Harry Murphy also on target as the blue-clad Holyrood boys won 6-0 to lift the prestigious shield for the first time in the school's history. The cup final win would cap a pretty memorable few days in the life of the 15-year-old Jim McCalliog.

"That was a huge week for me personally. On the Saturday, I had played for the Scottish Schoolboys team who beat England 4-3 at Ibrox to lift the Victory Shield. Jim O'Rourke and Peter Lorimer, God rest him, were in that side. I walked from Ibrox to our home in the Gorbals and later that evening there was a knock on the door, and there's a man standing outside who asked to speak with my mum. Turns out he was a Manchester United scout and they wanted me to go down to Old Trafford for a trial. But I had already promised Don Revie at Leeds I would go there, and I wanted to honour my word."

"Strangely, although myself and the rest of the Under 15's liked to watch the older team whenever we could, I don't recall seeing Harry play at that time. I do remember him, and I would get to know him well. Harry was a clever guy, with a mischievous sense of humour. I do recall having a crush on his girlfriend Kathleen at school though! Usually, it was the teachers that was supposed to happen with!"

Whilst Harry had missed out on that success, his star was still very much in the ascendancy. The Juniors football correspondent for many years in *The Evening Times* was a chap called George Manson, who worked tirelessly to promote the game at that level. In his newspaper column of Saturday, 26 May 1962, he suggests that English interest in the young Hood had stepped up.

"Harry Hood, the clever 17-year-old forward who has been playing for one of the minor Queen's Park sides, has been invited south for talks with Bolton Wanderers and Barnsley."

England would have to wait, as by the end of June, Harry's immediate future was committed to Clyde.

His teenage friend Ian Dalgleish recalls.

"Whatever happened with that or whatever offer was made, it didn't come to pass. Harry had a lot of respect for his dad and would have taken any advice from him on board. Harry senior knew the Dunn family, who ran Clyde at that time, and they then came up with an offer for Harry to go senior with Clyde plus take up a job as a rep with their company - Dunn's Lemonade - which would effectively make him a full-time footballer at just 17. So, Harry ended up at Shawfield."

As a footnote to this part of Harry's life, my own first recollection of seeing his name mentioned was in the 1965 edition of Hugh Taylor's *Scottish Football Book* annual, which my brother owned, and still does, in fact. It was within an article on how to start a football club – in this case Bo'ness Thistle – and a photo of the young, smiling Harry was captioned with a description of how he had started his early career with the Brunswick Boys Club. The Brunswick, as mentioned earlier, was a well-known youth outfit based in Balornock, a mile or so from my home in Springburn, hence the reason it jumped out.

It would later transpire that the Hood family at that time lived at Gartons Road, in nearby Barmulloch, where they were neighbours with Dan Corr - my dad's brother. My Celtic-mad uncle.

It's a small world.

Chapter 6

The Bully Wee Clyde battle for survival

The Clyde which 17-year-old Brunswick Boy Harry Hood joined on Saturday, 23 June 1962 – just six days after a Brazilian side minus their brilliant injured star Pele, Harry's all-time favourite player, had beaten Czechoslovakia 3-1 in Santiago to retain their World Cup - was certainly an interesting club with an intriguing recent history. The decade or so which preceded Harry's arrival had witnessed no fewer than three relegations from the top division, with the Shawfield side returning immediately the following season as champions on each occasion, whilst, remarkably, Clyde had won the Scottish Cup twice in amongst all of that, in 1955 then again in 1958.

The first of those cup wins had been the swansong of their legendary manager Paddy Travers, who had also brought the Scottish Cup to Rutherglen for the first-time ever in 1939, following a 4-0 victory over Motherwell. He was regarded as a bit of a cup specialist, having taken Aberdeen to their inaugural Scottish Cup final in 1937, where the gold-and-black clad Dons were beaten 2-1 by Willie Maley's Celtic before a European club record attendance of 147,365, which stands to this day.

Paddy had actually played under Maley at Parkhead in season 1911/12, with both Clyde and Aberdeen – his two previous clubs - featuring prominently in his brief career there. He made the first of his 24 appearances in the Hoops against the Shawfield outfit in a 3-2 home League win on Saturday, 2 September 1911, and his double in the 2-0 Scottish Cup victory over the Dons at Celtic Park six months later were the last of his six goals scored. The quality and strength of competition in that Celtic side is illustrated by considering Paddy's inside-forward partners for the vast majority of those games, Jimmy McMenemy or Patsy Gallacher lining up with him, either side of the mighty Jimmy Quinn, three of the all-time great Celts. When both McMenemy and Gallacher were declared fit to play for the Scottish Cup semi-final against Hearts which followed that win over Aberdeen, sadly Paddy would lose his place in the team which then went on to defeat - you've guessed it - Clyde in the Ibrox final. In search of regular first-team football, Travers would return to Pittodrie for a second spell that summer.

As Willie Maley approached his Golden Jubilee of service in the late 1930s, Paddy

Travers was one of the men heavily tipped to succeed him at Celtic Park. However, his next destination would be a mile or so south, to pick up the managerial reins at Shawfield. Having won the Scottish Cup at the end of his first season there, Paddy returned to Hampden with Clyde a decade later, in 1949, this time losing the final to Rangers. Travers was 73 years old when the club nicknamed the Bully Wee were relegated in the spring of 1956, just 12 months after they had beaten Jimmy McGrory's Celtic 1-0 in a replay to claim the prestigious trophy for a second time at Hampden. That would be Paddy's cue to retire.

Travers would be succeeded by former Dumbarton forward Johnny Haddow, who would continue the club's yo-yo record by winning the Second Division title then the Scottish Cup in his first two seasons before suffering relegation at the end of 1960/61. They would then win the Second Division title the following season, Harry Hood thus joining the newly promoted Shawfield outfit ahead of their first campaign back in the big time. This would also be the final season for their red first-choice kit before a return to the white jersey and black shorts combination, which supporters of my vintage will recall.

Harry would perhaps get to wear that red jersey for the first time at the pre-season public trial match, held at Shawfield on the evening of Tuesday, 7 August 1962. He would start the season five days later in the reserves, appearing at inside-left in the line-up for a friendly against Stirling Albion at Shawfield, which Clyde won 3-1. A few miles across the river, that afternoon of Saturday, 11 August 1962 was momentous for another two youngsters with Celtic in their blood. Bobby Murdoch was still six days short of his 18th birthday when manager Jimmy McGrory handed him the number 10 shorts for the opening match of the campaign, a League Cup section tie against Hearts at Celtic Park, the teenager marking his Hoops debut with Celtic's opening goal in seven minutes. Leading the Hoops out that day for the first time was Billy McNeill, having replaced Dunky MacKay as club captain during the summer.

Cesar's direct opponent was a certain Willie Wallace, a key piece of the Lisbon jigsaw which had yet to be placed. And it was also a memorable day - for the wrong reason - for another man who was an established inside-forward for Celtic, John Divers. He had been one of five Celts in the Glasgow Select who had faced Manchester United at Hampden in midweek, as the authorities revamped the jaded Glasgow Charity Cup from a knockout competition to a one-off showpiece season opener. Divers had then rolled up to Celtic Park on the Saturday oblivious to the fact that his boots were still at home, rather than in the Parkhead boot room! He was promptly dropped, with Charlie Gallagher handed his inside-right slot. Gallagher would celebrate his good fortune by scoring Celtic's second goal of the afternoon, three minutes after the restart, with John Hughes sealing a 3-1 win just before the hour.

Back at Clyde, Harry Hood would make his competitive debut against Hibernian's reserves at Easter Road on Wednesday, 22 August 1962. The hosts featured their own teenage prodigies, 15-year-old Jim O'Rourke and Peter Cormack, the latter a relative veteran at 16 years and one month. Both had played for Scotland's schoolboys with Jim McCalliog in that 4-3 Victory Shield triumph over England at Ibrox a few months earlier. Harry's Clyde would take the honours that evening, though, to open their Reserve League campaign with a fine 2-1 win.

Harry would retain his place for the 2-1 friendly victory over Queen of the South reserves in Dumfries on the last Saturday in August, before lining up against Partick Thistle's second-string at Shawfield on Saturday, 8 September 1962, where his direct opponent was future Clyde colleague Dick Staite. Hood would continue his positive start, as the hosts won 3-1. The following week saw Harry turn out twice for the reserves within 24 hours. On Thursday, 13 September 1962, he was part of the Clyde team which defeated Stranraer 3-0 at Shawfield to progress to the next round of the Scottish Second XI Cup. The Friday night would be a different kettle of fish entirely, future Lisbon Lions Bobby Murdoch, John Hughes and Jimmy Johnstone all on target as Celts beat Clyde 4-0 in Harry's first senior appearance at Parkhead, Rutherglen Bhoy Murdoch enhancing his growing reputation with a double. The previous Monday, the old ground had been packed to the rafters as 72,000 spectators watched Celtic produce a valiant second-half performance before succumbing 3-1 to former European masters Real Madrid. As in 1960 at Hampden, the young Harry Hood was once again following in the footsteps of the giants.

Eight days later, it was Scottish champions Dundee who sent a strong reserve side to Rutherglen, with Harry's former Queen's Park teammate, Doug Houston and future Shawfield boss Craig Brown in the visiting line-up. But Clyde, with Harry Haddock at right-back, enjoyed an emphatic 5-2 win on the day.

Having missed out on the 3-0 defeat by Dunfermline Athletic at the end of September, Saturday, 6 October 1962 marks the first mention I have found of a Harry Hood senior goal in the mainstream media. He belatedly celebrated his 18th birthday of three days earlier by opening the scoring for Clyde reserves in the seventh minute of the 4-0 victory over Airdrieonians at Shawfield, knocking the ball home after a shot had come back off the crossbar. Harry repeated the feat seven days later, with a rocket from outside the box to put the Bully Wee second-string ahead after 12 minutes against Queen of the South at Palmerston. The Doonhamers would eventually prevail to win 3-1, but the Shawfield reserves would be sitting in a highly respectable fifth position in the table after edging a seven-goal home thriller with Raith Rovers the following Saturday, before finishing the month with a thumping 5-0 victory over Third Lanark in front of their recently opened new main stand at Cathkin. That particular structure would prove highly significant in the history of Thirds, as we shall discover later.

November then opened with an excellent 4-1 win over Kilmarnock at Rugby Park, which saw Harry and the Shawfield Colts rise to second position in the Reserve League, ahead of Rangers and just one point behind Celtic's Kelly Kids at the summit. Harry's initial spell in the Clyde reserve team would then end with a 4-2 defeat by Hearts at

Shawfield on Saturday, 10 November 1962. Celtic would eventually claim the Reserve League title for the fourth time in five seasons, continuing the great work started by coach Jock Stein before he had left in 1960 to take up the managerial reins at Dunfermline Athletic.

Whilst the second string were excelling against the big boys, the same could not be said for the first team. Clyde could certainly consider themselves unfortunate to exit the League Cup at the section stage, losing out to St Johnstone by a whisker under the old 'goal average' system, despite a 5-1 victory over the Perth men at Shawfield. However, a dreadful run of just one win in 12 League games, which included five-goal defeats at the hands of both Partick Thistle and Kilmarnock, saw manager Johnny Haddow under pressure as he took his side to face Rangers at Ibrox on Saturday, 24 November 1962.

Haddow would go for bust, dropping both Harry Haddock, his veteran defender and former captain - who would not feature in the first team again after 13 years of wonderful service - and wing-half Alex Blain, allowing the Clyde boss to introduce two debutants. Making first senior appearances for a baptism of fire against Scot Symon's men were Donald McDonald - plucked from Anniesland Waverley by Renfrew Juniors in December 1961 whilst under scrutiny by Rangers - in place of Haddock at right-back, and Harry Hood at inside-right. The Clyde forward line that afternoon in Govan included future Dundee United manager Jim McLean and former Celt John Colrain, whilst Harry's old friend and Brunswick colleague John McHugh dropped back to left-half to partner a man who would feature prominently for both Clyde and Rangers over the next few seasons – Davie White. White had been captaining the side prior to the match at Ibrox, before giving it up, presumably in light of his expressed desire to leave Shawfield, following his recent transfer request. Danny Malloy, a close-season signing from Doncaster Rovers, where he had been player/manager, would assume the skipper's role for the visitors in the interim.

The full line-ups for Harry's senior debut were as follows.

RANGERS:

Billy Ritchie; Bobby Shearer & Eric Caldow; Harold Davis, Doug Baillie & Jim Baxter; Willie Henderson, Ian McMillan, Jimmy Millar, Ralph Brand & Davie Wilson.

CLYDE:

Tommy McCulloch; Donald McDonald & John Finnigan; Davie White, Danny Malloy & John McHugh; Jim McLean, Harry Hood, Dick Grant, John Colrain & Billy Muir.

Harry's appearance in the Clyde first team at Ibrox would appear to have caught the sports reporters of the day unawares, the teenager described in *The Evening Times* as a "*St Aloysius College schoolboy,*" despite the fact that he had moved from Garnethill to Holyrood Secondary some two years earlier. In the hosts line-up, Ronnie McKinnon and John Greig paid the price for the 3-2 midweek defeat at Celtic Park in the semi-final of the Glasgow Cup, the duo making way for Harold Davis and Ian McMillan.

Harry would immediately be involved in the action, taking a long through ball from Davie White in his stride to test Ibrox keeper Billy Ritchie with a shot from outside the box. Within 15 minutes Ritchie was beaten, as Billy Muir took advantage of an error from Doug Baillie to give Clyde the lead. Rangers drew level through a Ralph Brand header just before half-time, with the final action of the half seeing Jim Baxter volley a ball into the enclosure beneath the main stand, the hosts leaving the field to howls of derision from the 26,000 spectators. They would be forgiven as Rangers improved after the break, an early Brand shot followed by a late strike from Jimmy Millar producing a 3-1 home win, although a late Tommy McCulloch save from Willie Henderson's penalty prevented him from notching a fourth. Despite the defeat, Peter Hendry's review for Monday's *Evening Times* believed Clyde's performance to have been their best of the season, with both debutants described as having *"first-rate displays."*

Bizarrely, Harry's senior debut would turn out to be Johnny Haddow's last match in charge of Clyde. Despite having managed them to a Scottish Cup victory over Hibernian in 1958, two Second Division titles in 1957 and 1962, the Glasgow Cup in 1959 and the Glasgow Charity Cup in both 1958 and 1961, a quite unprecedented run of success at Shawfield, Haddow resigned, with some suggestion that the pressure he was under had forced a choice between his job or his health. Also leaving the club was long-serving trainer Dawson Walker, a man often involved in quiz questions due to his spell as Scotland manager in 1958 whilst Matt Busby was recovering from the serious injuries sustained at Munich Airport in February of that year. In our chats about Harry's time at Shawfield, John McHugh mentioned that at a time when most clubs had former players carrying out the role of trainer, in Dawson Walker, Clyde could boast the only full-time qualified physiotherapist in the League. He would carry out the same role for Scotland, hence his inadvertent interim role during Matt's convalescence. With both men gone by the Monday, Clyde chairman Willie Dunn would take charge of first team matters whilst a replacement for Haddow was sought, his first task being to grant a new transfer request from Davie White, whilst goalkeeper Tommy McCulloch had also announced his intention to leave Shawfield. What is that infamous saying about *"it never rains but it pours?"*

The 1-3 Ibrox result was replicated in Harry's home debut the following week, Saturday, 1 December 1962, against Aberdeen, albeit the young inside-forward would open his scoring account in League football within 10 minutes. The Dons, minus their injured young talent Charlie Cooke – another product of Renfrew Juniors - had dominated the opening spell before Billy Muir's cross from the left was headed home by Hood, *"as brilliant a goal as has been scored at Shawfield in months,"* according to Gair Henderson in that day's *Evening Times*. Despite Harry – *"just about the most dangerous inside-forward on the field"* – testing Aberdeen's legendary goalkeeper

John 'Tubby' Ogston twice with great efforts in the second half, the points would head back to the Granite City as Clyde dropped into the second relegation slot, with only winless Raith Rovers below them. On the same day, Scotland striker Alan Gilzean scored seven goals for champions Dundee in their 10-2 win over Queen of the South at Dens Park, six of those notched by Gilly before half-time.

The final comment on the Aberdeen match would go to *Evening Times* sports reporter Gair Henderson.

"This boy Hood, I think, will figure largely in the plans of the new manager. He is big...he is well skilled in the game...and most of all, he can shoot."

Seven days later, Harry was on target again, scoring the first of Clyde's three goals at Brockville from close-range with 17 minutes remaining. Sadly, for the Bully Wee faithful, Falkirk were already 6-0 ahead at that point and would eventually manage seven of their own that afternoon – six of those scored by future Celt Hugh Maxwell - as the Shawfield club's latest stay in the top division began to look increasingly precarious even before the halfway point in the current campaign had been reached.

Johnny Haddow would finally be succeeded as Clyde boss by former Rangers and Falkirk wing-half John Prentice the following Saturday, 15 December 1962, with Bruce Hay coming in as trainer to replace Dawson Walker. Prentice had recently resigned as Arbroath's manager, following some issues with housing arrangements in the town. He had skippered Falkirk to Scottish Cup glory in 1957, just 12 months before Haddow won the trophy with Clyde. His appointment would bring a brief respite, Harry scoring for the third successive League match that afternoon, Clyde's second in a 2-0 victory over St Mirren at Shawfield, before a 6-2 defeat by Motherwell at Fir Park seven days later piled the misery back on ahead of the festive break. Joe McBride scored twice for the hosts that afternoon.

Harry made it four goals from five League games with the opener in a 2-1 win over fellow basement-dwellers Hibernian at Easter Road on Saturday, 29 December 1962. However, he would not be in the team for the New Year's Day derby clash with high-flying Partick Thistle at Shawfield, which the Jags fought back to win by the odd goal in three, or the 3-2 victory over defending champions Dundee at the same venue four days later, his inside-left spot on both occasions taken by John Colrain.

The winter of 1962/63 was extremely harsh, with the Scottish football calendar decimated until March. Clyde's next fixture would prove to be their second round Scottish Cup-tie at the end of January, a precarious trip to face the one team struggling below them in Division One, Raith Rovers. The eminent Celtic historian David Potter is a local man. He recalls that only the proximity of Stark's Park to the sea saved this game, with the pitch in good trim, and that it was watched by former Raith star Jim Baxter, a future colleague of Harry at Sunderland. The hosts would eventually edge a five-goal thriller, as Harry's first experience of the prestigious cup competition ended in disappointment, his clever shot beating Kirkcaldy keeper Jim

Thorburn all ends up but coming back off the junction of crossbar and post with the scoresheet still blank.

The remainder of Clyde's season would now all be about survival in the top-flight, the month of February being a complete wipe-out with no matches played whatsoever by the Shawfield outfit. Harry would then miss out on the 2-1 defeat to Third Lanark at Cathkin Park which opened March, before returning with a spectacular headed goal in the 3-2 last-minute defeat to Kilmarnock at Rugby Park, seven days later. As an aside, Celtic would lose 6-0 at the same venue before the end of that month, rather underwhelming debuts for teenagers Jimmy Johnstone, Dick Madden and John Cushley.

Harry would face his own six-goal thrashing in March, as a rampant Hearts inflicted that same scoreline on his shell-shocked Clyde team at Shawfield on Saturday, 16 March 1963, doubles from Willie Wallace and Alan Gordon making it an unhappy first start for new full-back Harry Glasgow, signed that morning from Falkirk. Clyde would then hit their best form of the season, with four wins in their next six League games, home victories over Airdrieonians and bottom-dogs Raith Rovers topped up by the full points secured from trips to Aberdeen and Paisley. Despite the concern that a home defeat by Falkirk over the Easter Weekend could come back to haunt them, that excellent run had given the Bully Wee more than a fighting chance of survival. The 2-2 draw with Dunfermline Athletic at East End Park which followed on Wednesday, 24 April 1963, despite the early dismissal of restored captain Davie White, meant that Clyde remained four points clear of second-bottom Hibernian with four fixtures remaining, albeit the Leith side did have a game in hand and what appeared an easier run-in, on paper anyway.

Those final four matches would produce just one solitary point for Clyde, with the pivotal afternoon in the season being Saturday, 27 April 1963. A double from John Colrain had the Bully Wee 2-0 ahead against Motherwell at Shawfield by the interval, with Hibernian on their way to a 3-0 defeat at home to Falkirk. Crucially, Motherwell would also score three times in the second half in Rutherglen to claim victory, hence a wonderful opportunity to move six points clear with three matches to play was lost.

A second survival lifeline was then passed up seven days later. Harry had been on the periphery since the 4-1 defeat at Tannadice in March, however, he replaced John Colrain for the visit to Palmerston Park and was immediately to the fore, setting up Sammy Reid to beat George Farm in the Queen of the South goal within eight minutes. The Doonhamers quickly equalised through their much-wanted inside-forward, Neil Martin, before the visitors regained their lead through Jackie Ferguson. At half-time, Clyde led 2-1, whilst Hibernian were 2-0 down to Hearts at Tynecastle, a combination of results which would see the Bully Wee safe and the Dumfries side left to sort out the final relegation slot with Hibs over the closing weeks of the season. All that would change completely over the next 45 minutes, though, Hibernian recovering brilliantly to draw 3-3 in Gorgie, whilst Willie McLean, brother of Clyde's

Jim, secured a vital point for Queen of the South, as their match also ended in a tie, 2-2 in that case. Future Clyde player and manager Stan Anderson also featured at left-half for the hosts that afternoon.

As an aside, some 60 miles north of Dumfries that same day, Celtic were also involved in a draw. An equaliser from first-season professional Bobby Murdoch just before half-time at Hampden saw their Scottish Cup final with Rangers end 1-1 in front of more than 130,000 spectators. This was the first meeting between the Glasgow clubs in that showpiece game since 1928 and their first clash at the National Stadium since the 7-1 'Hampden in the Sun' League Cup final rout of October 1957. Rangers would win the replay by 3-0, 11 days later, following some bizarre team selection changes by Celtic.

The weekend relegation dogfight had claimed a managerial victim who had faced Celtic in another of those iconic 1950s Hampden occasions. Hugh Shaw had managed the great Hibernian side of the Famous Five era to three Scottish League titles before his men faced Jimmy McGrory's Celtic in the Coronation Cup final of 1953. He would lose out that day, then again to Johnny Haddow's Clyde in the Scottish Cup final at the same venue five years later. In November 1961, Shaw left Easter Road to take over the reins at Starks Park, prompting the Hibernian board's attempt to woo Jock Stein away from Scottish Cup-holders Dunfermline Athletic as his replacement. That courtship would be unsuccessful, for the time being anyway, as the Fifers held on to their prized asset. On Friday, 3 May 1963, after just 18 months in the role, and with his Raith Rovers side doomed to relegation from the top-flight, Hugh Shaw resigned as the Kirkcaldy club's manager.

Celtic would be next up for John Prentice's Clyde, 48 hours after the Scottish Cup final. A quirk of the rearranged fixture calendar meant that Clyde's final two games would now be against the cup finalists, with the added twist that their final match, a home clash with Rangers, would not be played until Wednesday, 22 May 1963, by which time rivals Hibernian would have completed their programme.

Harry would again be missing for the short trip to Parkhead, on Monday, 6 May 1963, John McHugh and Sammy Reid occupying the inside-forward roles for Clyde. When you're struggling, bad luck seems to follow as a consequence, and so it was that night as a speculative shot from Celtic defender John McNamee struck Shawfield counterpart Jim Fraser on the hand after half an hour. Referee Hamilton awarded a penalty which was duly converted by Dunky MacKay to give the sparse 8,000 crowd something to cheer about at last. With 10 minutes remaining, John Hughes sealed the points with a fine solo effort. Rangers would succeed Dundee as Scottish champions the same night with a 2-0 win over Airdrieonians at Broomfield, McGrory's Celtic settling for fourth spot behind Kilmarnock and Partick Thistle. It would be difficult to imagine that exactly seven years later, several members of that Celtic side would be chasing a second European Cup-winners medal in Milan's giant San Siro stadium.

Clyde's immediate fate now lay squarely in the hands of Hibernian, a club now under the management of a former Bully Wee player, Walter Galbraith. Four points behind with three games remaining, there was no margin for error for Hibernian, with the Shawfield side retaining one distinct advantage. They would know exactly what was required ahead of their final match of the season at home to Rangers.

Having won just two games since early November, remarkably Galbraith's men would turn it on at the most critical part of the season. First up for his Hibernian side was a home match with St Mirren, with goalkeepers Ronnie Simpson and Dick Beattie representing the past and future of Celtic stoppers. With half an hour to play, Ronnie's immediate future looked like being in the Second Division, as Saints held on to their early lead. Then another Easter Road life was used up, as goals from John Baxter and Gerry Baker brought a vital 2-1 win, leaving Hibernian just two points behind Clyde in the battle for survival.

The Edinburgh side would then edge ahead of Clyde on goal average, following their 4-0 victory over Queen of the South at Palmerston, four nights later, Wednesday, 15 May 1963. They would now just have to match the Shawfield club's result in the final fixture, Hibernian facing relegated Raith Rovers whilst Clyde entertained Double-winning Rangers the following midweek. Whilst football can be scarily unpredictable at times, few would dispute that the scales had now firmly swung back in favour of Hibernian surviving.

So, it would prove. Hibernian duly repeated their 4-0 Dumfries performance against Raith Rovers in Kirkcaldy at the weekend, leaving Clyde requiring the football equivalent of snookers - a massive 9-0 victory against Rangers four days later. Harry would return at Shawfield on Wednesday, 22 May 1963 for a final taste of top-flight football for the time being as Clyde took an early lead through Dan Currie, before Alex Willoughby, a Springburn teenager whom Harry would almost certainly have known from his days in schools, youth and amateur football, opened his Ibrox account with a double in just his second start. Ralph Brand added a late third for Rangers as Clyde ended the season with another defeat, the Bully Wee finishing two points behind Hibernian to join Raith Rovers in the Second Division for 1963/64.

Five years after the Hibernian supporters had watched their last chance of Scottish Cup glory for their greatest team disappear at the hands of Clyde, stretching their drought in that competition into a 57th year, there would be some measure of revenge as they survived in the top-flight at Clyde's expense. They would not be aware that another 57 long years would pass before that particular Scottish Cup hoodoo would end in May 2016. Hibernian's Class of 1963 would be joined by Second Division title-winners St Johnstone, managed by former Queen's Park and Rangers goalkeeper and future Scotland boss, Bobby Brown, and East Stirlingshire, now under the control of the Steedman brothers. The Falkirk-based Shire had pipped favourites Morton to win promotion for the first time in 30 years – when co-incidentally they had come up with St Johnstone – and only the second time in their history, despite selling star full-back Eddie McCreadie to Chelsea the previous spring. The Steedmans would later, and controversially, merge the club with Clydebank for one season before eventually taking an independent Bankies and their all-seated Kilbowie into the Premier League more than a decade later.

Whilst relegation with Clyde in 1962/63 would, inevitably, be a huge disappointment to Harry Hood, the teenage forward had managed to score five goals in his 16 appearances in his debut campaign, a more than respectable strike rate of one in three in the top-flight, particularly given the context of six months spent struggling for survival with Clyde against mainly full-time opponents.

It would now be time for Harry and his teammates to regroup ahead of his first full season at first-team level, as Clyde endeavoured to gain immediate promotion back to the top-flight for the fourth time in just over a decade.

Chapter 7

Goals galore as Harry and the Clydesiders cruise the Second Division

Harry and Clyde would fare much better in that following season, which commenced with the annual trial match between the first team and reserves at Shawfield on Tuesday, 6 August 1963. Harry showed up well as the *"leader of the Red side, scoring a fine goal,"* whilst new inside-forward Jimmy Copeland, signed that summer from Montrose, grabbed a brace. Five days later, both Harry and Jimmy would start - as would wing-half Eddie Mulheron, a close-season signing from junior outfit Benburb - as the Bully Wee opened their League Cup campaign with a 2-0 victory over Stranraer at Stair Park, Jim McLean and Sammy Reid the men on target.

McLean's brother, Willie, had scored a damaging equaliser against Clyde for Queen of the South in the crucial relegation tussle at Palmerston back in May. Willie had now joined his sibling at Shawfield and took his place on the left-wing for the visit of Ayr United, opening the scoring early on in what would be a man-of-the-match performance from him. Clyde led 3-1 with just half an hour to play, before an inexplicable collapse saw the not-quite-so Honest Men steal the points late on in a seven-goal thriller.

Next up for the Bully Wee was a rampant Morton side, who had opened the section with two wins. Having missed out on promotion to the top-flight by a single point, as East Stirlingshire followed St Johnstone into the First Division, the Greenock side had started the new season on fire with maximum points and two clean sheets. Harry would breach that record when he opened the scoring within 10 minutes, albeit *The Evening Times* credited Jimmy Copeland with the final touch, before the hosts thrilled the majority of the 12,000 Cappielow crowd by scoring three of their own to secure the points.

Four days later, Harry made his first appearance in the Second Division, as Clyde opened their League campaign with a visit to Douglas Park, Hamilton. He would mark the occasion by scoring his first double in senior football, John McHugh completing the Brunswick Old Boys act by grabbing Clyde's third as they edged a five-goal thriller. On the scoresheet for the Accies that afternoon was left-winger Sam

Hastings, who would join Clyde the next summer and become a Shawfield stalwart for many years.

League Cup business resumed on Saturday, 24 August 1963, with Harry again to the fore as Clyde beat Stranraer 4-1 at Shawfield. Within 25 seconds of kick-off, he had set up Willie McLean for the opener before heading home a cross from his brother Jim to double the lead. Harry then completed his second brace in four days, converting Davie White's pass to end the scoring, 10 minutes into the second half.

That would become a remarkable three successive doubles in one week for the impressive Hood, as Clyde took revenge by beating Ayr United 4-2 at Somerset Park on Wednesday, 28 August 1963, albeit Morton's 2-1 victory at Stranraer the same evening saw them clinch the section. The top two then met at Shawfield in the final match three days later, with only pride at stake. Harry had a vicious shot cleared off the line by a defender as the hosts looked for a morale-boosting win, before Morton turned on the style, the Greenock men eventually maintaining their 100% record with an emphatic 4-0 win.

Clyde's misfortune in being paired with Morton would be reinforced as the Cappielow side eliminated First Division outfits Motherwell and Hibernian to go all the way to the Hampden final in October. They would thus become the first second-tier team to do so since Kilmarnock lost to Dundee in 1952, some 11 years earlier. My uncle, Willie Jack, had been in the Killie line-up that day, having scored a last-minute winner against Rangers at the same venue in the semi-final, the part of his anatomy used to score varying depending on your preference for hilarity or accuracy! Willie was originally from the Garngad, and it would be another striker from the Roystonhill area who would finally end the Morton League Cup dream, Jim Forrest scoring four of Rangers five goals on the day as they won 5-0. The other goal was scored by Springburn boy Alex Willoughby, whose mother was a cousin of Forrest's mum. Both men will feature in a later chapter of Harry's story, albeit wearing different colours at that time.

Harry's first senior hat-trick arrived four days after the defeat by Morton, in a 5-0 victory over Forfar Athletic at Station Park on Wednesday, 4 September 1963, Clyde's second League match of the 1963/64 campaign being a thoroughly depressing experience for young Forfar supporter David Potter, which he recalls well! Harry's five goals in his first two Second Division games saw the Bully Wee level with Morton at the top, the Clydeside duo setting a pace which others would then struggle to match.

The third club on maximum points after two games was Queen's Park, Harry's former team, and they would provide the opposition for Clyde in their next match, played at Shawfield on Saturday, 7 September 1963. This was one of three derbies played in Glasgow that afternoon, with Celtic travelling to Ibrox and Partick Thistle to Cathkin. The home teams would take the honours in all three fixtures, with Harry notching another first as his penalty kick conversion three minutes before the break proved to be the only goal of the game, after he had been fouled in the box. No doubt the 'patter' would have been flowing after the game, as the Spiders featured two of Harry's old under-18 colleagues from his Hampden days. Bobby Clark was the keeper who failed to stop his well-placed spot kick – which must have presented an interesting dilemma of conscience for his father Tom, Clyde's treasurer, sitting with his fellow directors in the Shawfield stand - whilst the Queen's attack was led by Alex 'Dixie' Ingram, who would later make his name with Ayr United. Partnering Ingram in attack was Malcolm MacKay, who had played with Tommy Gemmell at Coltness United. With six goals in just three League outings, Harry's name was now beginning to be noticed, a point reinforced by his photograph appearing in the Sports Edition of The *Evening Times* later that afternoon.

A regular quirk of the Scottish fixture calendar in the early 1960s was the scheduling of home and away matches against the same opponent really close together early on in the programme, albeit I have never quite understood the reason for this. In any case, Forfar Athletic would provide the opposition for Clyde on matchday four, Wednesday, 11 September 1963, just as they had seven days earlier. The Loons had lost their opening three games, and that figure would rise to four by the end of their clash at Shawfield. Harry grabbed another brace, to make it eight goals scored in his first four Second Division matches, whilst pacey winger Graham Macfarlane went one better with a hat-trick, as Clyde won 5-2 to move to the top of the table. On the same night, title rivals Morton were holding Motherwell to a goalless draw in the quarter-final of the League Cup, in front of more than 25,000 spectators at Fir Park, around half of those apparently having travelled from Greenock.

Clyde's blistering start to their League campaign would come to a halt at Annfield, three days later, as the Bully Wee fought out a 1-1 draw with Stirling Albion, whilst Morton edged a nine-goal thriller with Stenhousemuir at nearby Ochilview, to close to within one point of the leaders. There had been an audacious attempt to take Harry from Shawfield to Firhill, 24 hours earlier, Partick Thistle boss Willie Thornton following up his midweek visit to watch the teenager in scoring action against Forfar by making a written offer to sign him, ahead of their home match with Rangers and the trip to Belfast to face Glentoran in the Inter-Cities Fairs Cup. However, Clyde manager John Prentice was adamant that Harry was going nowhere, despite suggestions of an £8,000 bid on the table from First Division Jags.

"Hood will not be moving to Partick Thistle. He is not for sale. We are trying to build at Shawfield. Selling players won't help us."

If Harry had been unsettled by the transfer talk then that did not last long, the striker hitting Clyde's second goal in the 2-2 draw with Stenhousemuir at Shawfield in midweek. The Bully Wee were now two points clear of Morton at the summit, having played two games more, as a mere 20,000 crowd watched the Greenock side knock Motherwell out of the League Cup at Cappielow the same night. Three days later, on Saturday, 21 September 1963, he volleyed home Clyde's opener from a Sammy Reid cross on the half-hour at Shawfield against Arbroath, Davie White adding a second after the break as the hosts won 2-0. Harry's scoring tally now stood at an impressive 10 goals in seven League games.

The next match - with Stenhousemuir - was brought forward 24 hours to the Tuesday evening, to avoid a clash with the Rangers v Real Madrid European Cup-tie at Ibrox, Clyde visiting Ochilview just six days after the sides had drawn 2-2 at Shawfield. The League leaders would be more clinical on this occasion, Harry netting the third goal in a 3-1 victory. That win set things up perfectly for the Second Division's match of the season thus far, as Clyde and Morton faced off at Shawfield on Saturday, 28 September 1963, both clubs hoping to preserve their unbeaten record. That prospect brought more than 10,000 noisy supporters rolling into Rutherglen, together with Kilmarnock manager Willie Waddell, coming along apparently to run the rule over Harry Hood. The teenager's stock continued to rise, Harry now the top goalscorer in the country ahead of kick-off, with 16 goals in League and League Cup games.

The cup-tie atmosphere seemed to inspire the hosts, Harry twice sending Graham Macfarlane in on goal for great opportunities before missing the post by inches with his own header. As often happens, though, that failure to turn superiority into goals would come back to haunt Clyde, as Allan McGraw, resplendent in Morton's new white-and-blue pin-stripe kit – a real 1960's classic – gave the visitors the lead with an unerring finish after 20 minutes. A Jim McLean header brought Clyde level within five minutes, and the match looked to heading for a fair 1-1 draw before McGraw struck again with just 90 seconds remaining, the Greenock striker diving full-length to bullet the ball past Tommy McCulloch with his head, piercing a dagger through Clyde hearts and preserving Morton's perfect record.

Having turned 19 years old on Thursday, 3 October 1963, Harry grabbed Clyde's second goal at Glebe Park 48 hours later, in a disappointing 2-2 draw with a Brechin City side who had shipped eight to Morton in midweek. The Greenock side then added another six goals against East Fife at Cappielow to move one point clear of Clyde at the top of the table, whilst still retaining their two games in hand of the second-placed Shawfield outfit.

For once Harry would not be on the scoresheet the following Saturday, as Allan Gray became the latest Clyde player to grab a hat-trick, in the 4-1 win over Alloa Athletic at Recreation Park. That was a story in itself, which Clyde FC Historian, Gordon 'Syd' Sydney had previously picked up.

"Allan made his debut for Clyde in August 1961 and played a number of games at centre-half before settling down at full-back, so he was a defender. However, for that game against Alloa, he was drafted in as a replacement centre-forward. After 54 games without a goal, it took Allan only 40 minutes to bag a double and give us the interval lead. In the 64th minute, Jim Copeland got our third, then Allan got his hat trick with 20 minutes remaining! He retained his place at centre-forward in the

next game, against Albion Rovers, without any joy whatsoever, then normal service resumed, with Allan moving back to full-back and not scoring any goals!"

Scottish Amateur International defender Gray had joined Clyde in 1961, having spent the previous two years with Queen's Park, so he would have been a clubmate of both Harry and Jimmy Hamilton in their Hampden season together. Indeed, Allan would also have known Jimmy from his spell at crack Glasgow youth outfit, Drumchapel Amateurs.

Normal service had also resumed for Harry, as he netted a double in the 3-2 victory over Albion Rovers at Shawfield on Saturday, 19 October 1963. Hood was first to threaten, albeit that was Gerry – Harry's former St Roch's teammate – who had joined Rovers from the junior club the previous year. Harry would claim the Hood bragging rights that weekend by opening the scoring with a low drive after 20 minutes then netting a late winner, after the Coatbridge side had fought back bravely from two goals down to level the match.

Saturday, 26 October 1963 was League Cup final day, Morton suffering their first defeat of the season and doing so in some style, going down 5-0 to Rangers before 106,000 spectators at Hampden. Clyde took full advantage, regaining the top slot in the Second Division table by winning 3-2 at Central Park, Cowdenbeath, the Bully Wee showing some real character by coming back from the loss of two goals in the opening 15 minutes to secure the points. Harry started the Clyde fightback, converting a penalty kick after 25 minutes for his 20th strike of the season, with John McHugh making it a good day for the Brunswick Boys by netting a double either side of the break. Back in Glasgow, consistently inconsistent Celtic were also making the headlines by beating Airdrieonians 9-0 at Parkhead, to move up to sixth spot in the First Division. Both John Hughes and John Divers managed hat-tricks, whilst goalkeeper Frank Haffey watched his spot kick saved by opposite number Roddie McKenzie to prevent Jimmy McGrory's men reaching double figures. This was Celtic's biggest League win since McGrory himself had scored eight goals against Dunfermline Athletic in a 9-0 home win on Saturday, 14 January 1928.

November opened with victories for both of the table-topping Clydeside teams in the second tier, the Bully Wee beating shock League Cup semi-finalists Berwick Rangers 3-1 at Shawfield, whilst Morton were involved in a 10-goal thriller with Forfar Athletic at Station Park, the visitors with six of those to maintain their 100% League record, an impressive 11 straight wins. That would stretch to 12 within 48 hours, following an 8-0 mauling of Hamilton Academical at Cappielow, which took Morton back to the top of the table, Allan McGraw netting another hat-trick to take his season's tally to 29, nine ahead of Harry, his closest challenger. On the same day, four of Third Lanark's five directors resigned, amidst claims that the club faced debts which could lead to the liquidation of the famous old club.

Harry added another two to his total on Saturday, 9 November 1963, in Clyde's 2-1 win over Raith Rovers at Starks Park, only denied a hat-trick by a linesman's flag after ex-Celt Neil Mochan had briefly given the Kirkcaldy side parity. That prompted a £13,000 offer for Harry's services from Ipswich Town. The Portman Road outfit were enduring a difficult campaign, with one win in their opening 17 League games leaving them adrift at the foot of the English First Division, less than 18 months after winning the title under Alf Ramsey in their first season in the English top-flight. Now under Jackie Milburn, the Newcastle United legend and uncle of the Charlton brothers, the Suffolk side would fail in their bid for Harry's signature and, ultimately, in their attempt to avoid relegation at the end of that season.

Harry's second senior hat-trick was only delayed until the following Saturday. The hitman was in lethal form in a 6-0 rout of Ayr United at Shawfield on Saturday, 16 November 1963, his third a rebound after visiting keeper John Gallagher saved his spot kick. That treble took him on to 25 for the campaign.

With an odd number of teams in the Second Division – there were 19 at that time – the following weekend would see Clyde as the team with a free League Saturday. Their friendly with English Non-League side South Shields at Simonside Hall on the south bank of the Tyne would be played in the immediate aftermath of the assassination of US President John Fitzgerald Kennedy in Dallas, as the world recoiled from the news. For the record, Harry scored the winner as the Shawfield club won 3-2.

That victory on Tyneside would precede a shock home defeat by East Fife on the last day of November. Jim McLean headed Clyde in front, after Harry's fierce shot had come crashing back off the crossbar. However, the Methil outfit rallied to win 3-1, allowing Morton to move five points clear after a 3-0 victory at Alloa, a 16th consecutive League win for the rampant Greenock side. There was now a posse of clubs fighting for that second promotion place, Montrose's 8-2 win at Forfar bringing them to within two points of Clyde, with two games in hand, with Arbroath and Queen's Park now also in the mix. That made the meeting of Montrose and Clyde at Links Park on Saturday, 7 December 1963 extra special. The Angus club boasted two of the finest young attacking prospects in the country, Joe Gilroy and Gordon Wallace, and it would be Gilroy who equalised after Graham Macfarlane had given the visitors an early lead. The match was settled before the interval, Harry following up to net the rebound after Montrose keeper Les Cameron had blocked his first attempt from the penalty spot.

The next two games would see Harry fail to get on the scoresheet, albeit in the second of those, a 1-0 victory over Dumbarton at Boghead on Saturday, 21 December 1963, he did everything but score, hitting the bar then the post before being involved in a collision with Doug Robertson, which saw the Sons keeper stretchered off, all within the opening 15 minutes. At that match was Harry's cousin, Michael Scott – one of Walter junior's sons – and his own eight-year-old son John, who recalls it well.

"Seeing Harry after the game was like meeting a film star. He looked so cool in a long

white raincoat, and my dad and him were having a joke. It had been quite a rough game. After mass the next morning, I remember my dad telling his brother, my Uncle Henry, that I had never shut up about Harry as we walked the six miles home to Duntocher, having missed the bus!"

Seven days earlier, Stranraer had left Rutherglen with a point following a 1-1 draw, with Jim McLean scoring for Clyde in both matches. Harry would end the calendar year on a high, though, his fifth-minute strike proving to be the winner as the Bully Wee beat Hamilton Academical 1-0 at Shawfield on Saturday, 28 December 1963. That left Clyde clear in second place, six points behind leaders Morton and their perfect record of 40 points from their opening 20 games, but currently seven ahead of Montrose and Arbroath, albeit the former had played two games less.

The New Year's Day fixture saw Harry first-footing at his old Hampden stomping ground by scoring Clyde's second in a 4-2 victory over Queen's Park, beating his old teammate Bobby Clark in the Spiders goal after half an hour. Graham Macfarlane netted his second hat-trick of the campaign to get 1964 off to a winning start. That was followed by two successive goalless draws over the next three days, Stirling Albion defending heroically at Shawfield before Clyde maintained their advantage over third-placed Arbroath at Gayfield on Saturday, 4 January 1964.

Clyde would then have a free weekend, the squad heading down to Inverclyde for a training camp as the farcical situation of 'byes' for a number of teams in the first round of the Scottish Cup continued, despite pressure from clubs and customers alike to amend the format. There would be controversy of a different kind closer to home, though, as news then emerged of plans to amalgamate the Bully Wee with East Kilbride Juniors and relocate from Shawfield to the Lanarkshire New Town, with a stadium already under construction. Clyde chairman Willie Dunn explained the rationale behind the proposal.

"The club is in with a very good chance of winning promotion this year, but our attendances are averaging no more than 3,000 at home games. No club, even a Second Division club, can live on that income, and we think that, by moving house, we can give East Kilbride a football team worthy of a new town, and definitely improve our own future. [The stadium] is a beautiful bowl, well sited, and the turf on the playing pitch has already been laid. We would need to erect a stand worthy of a First or Second Division club, but that is not an insuperable barrier. The ground should certainly be able to hold more than 50,000 fans."

Within 24 hours of that story breaking, Clyde were hitting the headlines again, this time on the pitch. Having made his debut at Ibrox in a 3-1 League defeat in November 1962, Harry found himself lining up once again in Govan against Rangers on Wednesday, 15 January 1964, this time in the semi-final of the Glasgow Cup. The visitors were written off, one newspaper talking of a miracle being required to prevent the first Glasgow Cup final between Celtic and Rangers since 1956 taking place.

In fairness, it was a stretch. Whilst Rangers had been humiliated in Europe by Real Madrid, losing 6-0 in the Estadio Santiago Bernabeu after a late Ferenc Puskas goal had won the first leg at Ibrox, they were on course for a domestic Treble, tucked in behind Kilmarnock at the top of the First Division with the League Cup already secured after their 5-0 victory over Morton. Ibrox boss Scot Symon now declared his intent by naming the same eleven men who had won 5-1 at Ochilview on the Saturday, to knock Stenhousemuir out of the Scottish Cup. On the other hand, Second Division Clyde boasted a small squad made up entirely of part-time players. A win for the underdogs would therefore be a huge ask, as the following teams took the field.

RANGERS:

Billy Ritchie; Davie Provan & Eric Caldow; Harold Davis, Ronnie McKinnon & Jim Baxter; Willie Henderson, John Greig, Jimmy Millar, Ralph Brand & Craig Watson.

CLYDE:

Tommy McCulloch; Eddie Mulheron & Alex Blain; Jim Murray, Jim Fraser & Davie White; Jim McLean, Sammy Reid, Graham Macfarlane, John McHugh & Harry Hood.

Clyde would enjoy the better of the first half, that superiority rewarded when Harry *"spooned the ball past Ritchie"* for the opening goal five minutes before the interval, as the majority of the 10,000 crowd expressed their dissatisfaction in the traditional manner. The second turning point of the night would arrive just after the hour, Ibrox winger Craig Watson's shot handled on the line by Shawfield skipper Davie White with keeper Tommy McCulloch beaten, with some suggestion that the ball had actually crossed the line. Any sense of injustice being harboured by the home support would be exacerbated by McCulloch's wonderful save from Davie Provan's spot kick. That would be it for the hosts, as Clyde defied the odds to secure a cup final date with Celtic or Third Lanark, a first for the young Harry. No doubt that left arm of his was raised in triumph, as he acknowledged the presence of his dad, his brothers and his best pal in the Ibrox crowd. A "Viva" overload for the Hood family that night, I'd bet.

Author and historian David Potter recalls a joke of the day which he heard from and attributes to his father, which went along the following lines.

"I hear Scot Symon phoned Jimmy McGrory asking for Divers."

"Why?"

"To get Harry Hood out of the Clyde!"

Harry's efforts at Ibrox had seen him struggle with a bout of cramp towards the end of the 90 minutes, with newspaper reports suggesting he was an injury doubt for the weekend. Thankfully, he would be judged fit enough to start the League match that Saturday, a top of the table clash with Morton at a packed Cappielow. The Greenock outfit had already inflicted three defeats on Clyde that season, and they would again succeed where Rangers had failed with a 3-0 victory. The final goal was scored by Allan McGraw, a 44th of the campaign for Britain's top marksman. That would also be the 100th League goal of the season for Morton, whose record now stretched to an incredible 23 wins from 23 games since the opening day of what would now inevitably be a title-winning campaign. As an aside, McGraw had also scored the goal which took Morton to the century mark the previous season, their last of a campaign which saw them narrowly miss out on promotion on the final day.

Saturday, 25 January 1964 was Scottish Cup second-round day, Clyde drawn at home to Forfar Athletic whilst the much-anticipated tie of the round would see an-ticket crowd of 22,000 cramming into Cappielow to see Morton host Celtic, with many observers predicting a home win. That game would take on extra significance for Harry and his Shawfield teammates, following Celtic's 3-0 victory over Third Lanark at Cathkin in the replayed Glasgow Cup semi-final on the Monday evening. The teenager's superb strike at Ibrox the previous midweek now meant that his first cup final in senior football would be against his beloved Celtic at Parkhead. That would be pretty special, being the first time that Harry would face his boyhood club at that level.

That final would have to wait until March. Meantime, there was the small matter of Forfar Athletic. The two League meetings earlier in the season had seen Clyde score 10 goals for the loss of only two, however, the Loons would do much better in the Scottish Cup. They would come back twice from a goal behind at Shawfield, a late own goal from Jim Fraser ending the scoring at 2-2, before knocking Clyde out by the odd goal in five at Station Park on the afternoon of Wednesday, 29 January 1964, thus denying the Bully Wee a trip to Dens Park in the next round. The visitors were 0-3 down at the interval, Davie White's late double not enough to save them from a disappointing cup exit in Angus. That would, however, provide a nerve-wracking finish for the group of local schoolboys who had cycled in an impressive flotilla at full speed from Forfar Academy to reach the ground shortly after half-time at 4.00pm, with a certain David Potter in the vanguard. At least one future Forfar Athletic chairman disobeyed his headmaster, took the afternoon off to watch the match then got belted for his pains the following morning!

In the match of the day on the Saturday, Allan McGraw had given Morton hope by netting his 45th of the season to give the hosts a first-half lead, albeit he was hurt in the process. Celtic would prove once again to be the greatest cup-fighters in the country, John Hughes equalising with a wonderful solo goal 10 minutes from the break, Celts then missing the opportunity to take a lead down the tunnel when Bobby Murdoch sent his penalty kick past the post with the last kick of the half, after Hughes had been tripped in the box. The tie turned seven minutes after the restart, as Charlie Gallagher, only playing due to an injury to John Divers, curled the ball into the net directly from a corner kick. Gallagher was a master of the art of taking those kicks, and in the years to come would produce two of the most iconic winning goals in Celtic's history for Billy McNeill, against Dunfermline Athletic and Vojvodina. Jimmy Johnstone blasted home a third goal five minutes later, prompting the remarkable sight of Celtic goalkeeper John Fallon being warned on the pitch by the local constabulary for the heinous crime of raising his arms to the crowd behind the goal in celebration. Morton's day of misery was then complete as Allan McGraw was carried off in the closing minutes of the match, the Greenock talisman having suffered injuries to his ankle, arm and thigh in three separate incidents over the 90 minutes.

Morton's incredible winning sequence in the League was finally ended the following week, on the opening day of February 1964. East Fife had been the only side other than Morton to beat Clyde in the championship race, winning 3-1 at Shawfield at the end of November, and they would now defeat the League leaders at Bayview by the same scoreline. The Shawfield club closed the gap to six points by scoring five without reply at home to Brechin City, Harry netting a double in the final 15 minutes to round off a good day, taking his personal tally in the three main domestic competitions to 30 in the process. He would have a less productive afternoon the following Saturday, blazing an early second-half penalty over the crossbar as Clyde suffered a shock 1-0 defeat at home to Alloa Athletic.

The Bully Wee would then have a three-week wait before resuming action, the next round of the Scottish Cup then a weather-enforced cancellation of their home match with Cowdenbeath meaning it would be the last day of February before a trip across the border to face Berwick Rangers at Shielfield Park got them back on track. Following Harry's spot kick miss against Alloa, Davie White would find himself on penalty duty after Hood was crudely brought down in the box, the skipper making no mistake with Clyde's second in a 3-1 win. This Leap Year Saturday would be a momentous day for Morton, their 6-1 win over Forfar Athletic at Cappielow, coupled with third-placed Arbroath's home defeat by Ayr United, guaranteeing their promotion to the First Division for the first time since 1951.

Harry was on fire seven days later, Saturday, 7 March 1964, setting up Jimmy Morrison for the opener then adding a second as Clyde entertained Raith Rovers, in a meeting of the two sides relegated from the top-flight the previous spring. Sammy Reid scored a third on the stroke of half-time and with that 3-0 lead still intact with 15 minutes remaining, it appeared to the 1,100 spectators that the points were secured. But football can be the cruellest of games sometimes, the Kirkcaldy club fighting back with three late goals to stun their hosts by stealing an unlikely draw at Shawfield, thus allowing both East Fife and Arbroath to close the gap below Clyde to just four points, with Montrose still in the hunt.

The Bully Wee were back in winning form the following Saturday, with a 2-0 victory over Ayr United at Somerset, whilst back in Glasgow, Morton were crowned Second Division champions. Having failed to win the League Cup at Hampden the previous October, the Greenock side would clinch the title there with a 3-0 win over Queen's Park, which was more difficult than the scoreline would suggest, Allan McGraw on target with his 51st goal of an incredible campaign.

With Clyde requiring just eight points from their final six League games to join Morton in the top-flight for season 1964/65, Saturday, 21 March 1964 was a pivotal day in the campaign. The Bully Wee fought back from a goal down to beat Cowdenbeath 2-1 at Shawfield, Harry heading home the equaliser after half-an-hour, whilst their three nearest challengers all slipped up. That would see Clyde in fine fettle ahead of their next match, the midweek Glasgow Cup final with Celtic at Parkhead, certainly more so than the hosts, who had been on the end of a 4-0 hiding from title-chasing Kilmarnock at Rugby Park.

The choice of venue had actually been suggested by Clyde, perhaps a decision based on the likelihood of a higher attendance there than the other, neutral options, given chairman Willie Dunn's previous comments around the lack of income at the club. It would be the most important game to date in the fledgling senior career of Harry Hood, the 33-goal teenager featured and identified by Gair Henderson of *The Evening Times* as a possible transfer target for Celtic in the pre-match build-up.

"Celtic fans, disgruntled and disappointed at that 4-0 Kilmarnock defeat, should not stay by the fireside tomorrow night when Clyde visit Celtic Park for the final of the Glasgow Cup. The supporters should turn out for three good reasons.

1) They will be on more than an even-money chance of seeing the team win their first silverware this season (there is still a very good chance of another and bigger trophy to come – the European Cup-Winners' Cup).

2) They will definitely see a Clyde team playing all out to win from the first whistle and…

3) They MAY see a possible new Celtic star.

The man who may swap his white Clyde jersey for the famous green-and-white very soon is Harry Hood, mainstay of the Shawfield attack all season. Hood is good, so good that Jimmy McGrory watched him on Saturday, and at 19 is one of the brightest prospects to arrive on the Scottish football season for years. Young Harry has the height and build PLUS the football needed to make a star inside-forward, but tomorrow night he may be playing at centre-forward again for Graham Macfarlane is still on his honeymoon and will miss the final."

Harry would indeed be leading the Clyde attack in his first cup final in senior football, the teams lining up as follows at Celtic Park on Wednesday, 25 March 1964.

CELTIC:

John Fallon; Ian Young & Tommy Gemmell; John Clark, Billy McNeill & Jim Kennedy; Jimmy Johnstone, Bobby Murdoch, Steve Chalmers, John Divers & John Hughes.

CLYDE:

Tommy McCulloch; Eddie Mulheron & Alec Blain; Harry Glasgow, Jim Fraser & Davie White; Jim McLean, Sammy Reid, Harry Hood, Jimmy Morrison & Jimmy Copeland.

Hoops fans of a certain vintage may feel a song coming on when they read through that home team.

Celts would win the Glasgow Cup for the second time in three seasons, thanks to two goals in a five-minute spell early in the second half from former Brunswick Bhoy Stevie Chalmers and the underrated but prolific John Divers, before 13,500 spectators. That would be a first trophy success for new captain, Billy McNeill, and a timely boost ahead of the imminent European Cup Winners' Cup semi-final against MTK Budapest. Harry had played up front in direct opposition to the man known as Cesar that night, Gair Henderson following up his earlier article with this review of his performance.

"The game was a stern, maybe alarming test, for centre-forward Harry Hood. There he was, playing out of position against the club which may shortly be handing him his wage packet, and he was also being asked to shine against one of the best pivots in Europe. Hood had the idea that industry might bring success, and for 15 minutes he tried to put on a Denis Law show – roaming, chasing and even defending. But McNeill stood there and waited, unworried. As long as the centre-forward kept away from the middle of the field there was no hint of danger, and when Harry did come in, Billy showed him that 19-year-olds still have a deal to learn. Nevertheless, I thought Harry showed quite a lot of promise, and he will doubtless be a vastly different player in one of the inside-forward positions. I doubt if Celtic will now write him off on the evidence of one game, playing in just about the most difficult circumstances."

Celtic most certainly did not write him off, and there would be more on that story to follow.

In the meantime, there was still promotion to be secured for Harry and Clyde, and they took another huge step to making that dream a reality by securing a 1-1 draw with third-placed East Fife at Bayview three days later, on Saturday 28 March 1964. Harry scored the vital equaliser, 10 minutes before the break, robbing full-back Bobby Stirrat before squeezing the ball home. Another Hood goal prompted more transfer speculation, this time Sunderland, neck-and-neck with Don Revie's Leeds United in the race for the English Second Division title, the latest club credited with an interest in *The Evening Times*.

"Celtic have so far made no move for Clyde's inside-forward, Harry Hood, but that does not mean to say they have given up interest in the player. Hood, the hardest football worker inside Shawfield, did not have an outstanding match against Billy McNeill in the Glasgow Cup final, but Celtic will not condemn him on this showing, for very few centre-forwards get much change out of their centre-half. There may be developments inside the next two or three days, for I hear that Sunderland still think very highly of Hood, despite the fact that Johnny Crossan and another [former] Clyde player, George Herd, are still playing more than just well at Roker Park."

As an aside, one notable transfer which did go ahead that weekend was the signing of highly-rated Danish international goalkeeper Erik Sorensen by Morton's enterprising manager Hal Stewart. That would set the tone for the so-called 'Scandinavian invasion of Scottish football' which would follow. The other major news was that Dunfermline Athletic manager Jock Stein would now be taking over at Easter Road, replacing Walter Galbraith following his resignation as Hibernian boss. Stein had earlier announced his intention to quit his post at East End Park at the end of that season, having enjoyed a very successful four years in Fife. Meantime in Glasgow's east end, Celtic announced plans to build a stand on the site of the existing Jungle at Parkhead, as they launched their new Development Fund.

The point earned by Harry's strike at Methil meant that only Montrose – currently in fifth place but with a game in hand - could overtake Clyde in the race to the top-flight, and a quirk of the fixtures had the two clubs meeting next, at Shawfield on Saturday, 4 April 1964. Fittingly, Harry was the man who secured promotion, his second-half double giving the Bully Wee a 2-0 victory. Just after the hour, he headed a Jim McLean corner home to give the hosts the lead, and the champagne corks were popping in Rutherglen when the high-scoring teenager added a second with nine minutes remaining, his 36th goal in all competitions that season.

Bill Hutchison was full of praise for Harry's performance in Monday's edition of *The Evening Times*.

"The Bully Wee eventually got the point they needed, achieved their objective and are due congratulations. For this happy result and much of their success throughout the season they must thank Harry Hood, the man of the match as far as Clyde were concerned. In addition to scoring both goals, he was well ahead of his mates in poise, positional sense and distribution."

There was no such happy result three days later, Clyde three goals down within 20 minutes of the kick-off in the clash with Stranraer at Stair Park, before a Jim McLean penalty ended the scoring at 3-1. The campaign then closed with two midweek fixtures. Dumbarton were dispatched 4-2 at Shawfield on Thursday, 23 April 1964, Harry grabbing Clyde's second goal of the evening, and he was on target again six nights later, netting the club's first in a 2-2 draw with Albion Rovers at Cliftonhill. That would take his personal tally to 38 goals, having played in all 47 of Clyde's games that season. A fabulous return.

As Clyde looked forward to their return to the top-flight, it was unclear who they would face there as some incredible manoeuvring behind the scenes saw a vote taken at a meeting of Scottish League clubs at Ibrox on Tuesday, 28 April 1964 which would see Airdrieonians and Third Lanark join already relegated Queen of the South and East Stirlingshire in the Second Division, that quartet occupying the bottom four slots in the table. Morton and Clyde's hard-earned promotions would stand, and they would take their place in a new 16-club elite division for season 1964/65.

That same number would then be secured in the second tier by removing five clubs from the Scottish League structure altogether, presumably on the basis of attendance figures or geography, given that the five teams involved – Stranraer, Albion Rovers, Stenhousemuir, Berwick Rangers and Brechin City - had finished between eighth and 15th in the Second Division, thus only the last-named had been one of the five lowest-ranked sides that season. The controversial proposal was being driven by Rangers.

Other than the 'condemned five', Celtic had been one of only two of the remaining Scottish League clubs not represented at the meeting – East Stirlingshire were the other - with the Parkhead directors in Budapest for the return match with MTK the following day. However, when told of the outcome, Celtic chairman Bob Kelly commented that the plans *"had left a bad taste in his mouth."* Sadly, he would soon have another of those to worry about, after a horrific 4-0 second-leg defeat in the giant Nepstadion shattered Celtic dreams of a first-ever European final appearance.

The proposal to reduce the composition of the Scottish League by five teams was then the subject of an interim interdict which prevented it from even being discussed at the League's AGM at the end of May. Thus, the status quo would prevail for season 1964/65, for the time being at least.

Chapter 8

Back in the big time...and the headlines

Following the broken collarbone sustained by Graham Macfarlane in pre-season training, the new season brought three new strike partners for Harry as Clyde prepared for life back in the top-flight. Joe Gilroy signed from Montrose, having previously been a predecessor of Harry's at Queen's Park, whilst Sam Hastings joined from Hamilton Academical and Alex Bryce from Third Lanark. Bryce would be the only one of that trio to feature in the opening game of the campaign, a League Cup section tie at Hampden against that same Queen's Park on Saturday, 8 August 1964. For once, Harry was unable to get one over on his old friends, Bobby Clark and Alex Ingram, as the match ended goalless, the closest either side coming to breaking the deadlock being when Sammy Reid hit the bar from Harry's cross in the second half. Other notable events on that opening day of the Scottish season included the first-ever match played by the new East Stirlingshire Clydebank – a 2-2 draw with Stenhousemuir at Kilbowie Park – and a meeting of those two wonderful Celts from the 1950's, Jock Stein and Bobby Evans, now both in charge of their new clubs, Hibernian and Third Lanark respectively. Jock would hold the bragging nights on that Saturday evening following a 3-0 victory for the hosts at Easter Road.

Celtic followed up their own disappointing goalless draw with Partick Thistle with perhaps the most audacious transfer bid in the club's history, as they made an offer to sign legendary Argentinian striker Alfredo Di Stefano, recently released from Real Madrid, manager Jimmy McGrory poised to fly to Spain *"at a moment's notice"* if he received any encouragement to the original offer cabled on the Saturday evening. He duly did so anyway on the Tuesday, accompanied by reserve centre-half John Cushley, a fluent Spanish speaker, despite no replies whatsoever being forthcoming from Di Stefano's camp. The following day, the great man did advise Celtic that he had already committed his future to Espanyol. Closer to home, chairman Bob Kelly also confirmed that Celtic would not be bidding for Motherwell's unsettled striker Joe McBride, as per Celtic's policy, as Joe was not currently officially transfer-listed.

Another transfer tug-of-war had seen Hamilton Academical winger Sam Hastings reject an offer from the Steedman brothers at ES Clydebank to sign for John Prentice at Clyde. He would mark his debut on Wednesday, 12 August 1964 by scoring Clyde's equaliser in the 1-1 draw with Arbroath at Shawfield, which kept the Bully Wee tucked in behind section leaders Queen's Park after two games.

Harry would then open his own account for season 1964/65, hitting a double either side of the interval against Albion Rovers at Cliftonhill, as Clyde followed up their opening two draws with a 5-0 win on Saturday, 15 August 1964, which saw them go top of the group. The beaten keeper was Dick Madden, who had signed for Rovers just the previous week after his release by Celtic, where his only first-team appearance had been the infamous 6-0 defeat by Kilmarnock at Rugby Park in March 1963. His fellow debutants that evening had been Jimmy Johnstone and the aforementioned John Cushley.

Clyde's return to First Division football would see Jock Stein bring his Hibernian side to Shawfield on Wednesday, 19 August 1964. Stein had galvanised the club since moving from Dunfermline in the spring, taking them to the final of the Summer Cup, where their matches with Aberdeen had been deferred to early August following an outbreak of typhoid in the Granite City. With the sides level after home and away legs, a play-off would be required in September to settle the destination of the trophy.

Stein had made Celtic's John McNamee – a defender he had worked with whilst reserve team coach at Parkhead – his first signing for Hibernian, and he joined the young midfielder Pat Stanton and an exciting array of attacking talent at Easter Road. Those included Peter Cormack, Willie Hamilton, Jim Scott and Neil Martin, the latter having faced Harry and Clyde whilst with Queen of the South. Martin would again be a key man at Shawfield that night, scoring a double in Hibernian's 3-1 win, whilst Harry would face frustration as his goalbound header was cleared off the line. Jim McLean scored for Clyde.

The League Cup action resumed three days later, with the return game with Queen's Park at Shawfield. Clyde dominated from the outset, Harry's cross headed past his own keeper in spectacular style by Spiders' centre-half Billy Neil to open the scoring after 20 minutes, before Jim McLean made it 2-0. Harry then added a third just before the break, after Bobby Clark had spilled Joe Gilroy's effort. Sam Hastings then put Clyde 4-0 up early in the second half before Niall Hopper grabbed a consolation strike for the visitors.

The pivotal match in the section took place on Wednesday, 26 August 1964, as leaders Clyde travelled to face second-placed Arbroath at Gayfield. Harry set Joe Gilroy up to break the deadlock early in the second half, Sam Hastings' goal shortly afterwards enough to secure the points and allow the Bully Wee to join Celtic, Dundee United and Rangers in qualifying with a match to spare, despite a late Ian Brown goal for the hosts.

Clyde would then turn on the style in the final 'dead rubber' with Albion Rovers at Shawfield, Harry feeding Sam Hastings for an early tap-in before scoring himself from the edge of the box on the stroke of half-time. Joe Gilroy would make it 3-1 to Clyde with 15 minutes remaining before both Hastings and Hood beat Dick Madden to complete their doubles in the final stages to end the scoring at 5-1.

Over in East Ayrshire, there was nothing dead about the rubber at Rugby Park, as Willie Waddell's Kilmarnock appeared to vent their frustration at section winners Celtic, both Bobby Murdoch and Billy McNeill stretchered off with bad injuries in the second half of a violent encounter. Clyde's satisfaction at a League Cup job well done may then have been tempered as they were drawn against their old nemesis Morton in the quarter-final, the Greenock club having won all four of their clashes in the previous campaign.

Hibernian manager Jock Stein was in the headlines in midweek, as he added the brand-new Summer Cup to the 1961 Scottish Cup won by his Dunfermline Athletic side to his growingly impressive CV after a play-off win over Aberdeen at Pittodrie, whilst agreeing to sell his transfer-listed goalkeeper Ronnie Simpson to Celtic. The 33-year-old Simpson had announced his likely retirement the previous week, but would now be back-up to John Fallon at Parkhead, allowing the Celtic board to accept the transfer request from Frank Haffey. How significant that transfer would later prove for all parties involved!

Back at Clyde, Harry had opened the season with an impressive five goals in six League Cup matches and he would notch his first League counter of the campaign at Firhill on Saturday, 5 September 1964, in an excellent 3-0 victory over Partick Thistle. Harry created the first goal for Sam Hastings in the fourth minute, leaving two defenders for dead, capping an outstanding first half-hour when he made it 2-0 with an unstoppable shot high past George Niven. Jim McLean completed an excellent Derby Day for Clyde by heading a third with 15 minutes remaining, but the headlines belonged to Harry, this article from Jimmy Dunbar in Monday's edition of *The Evening Times* was titled *"Hood in the Mood."*

"Some time ago, Partick Thistle made an unsuccessful transfer bid for Clyde centre-forward Harry Hood. Accordingly, it must have been with mixed feelings that manager Willie Thornton viewed Thistle's 3-0 home defeat by the newly promoted Bully Wee. Hustling, bustling Harry was the main difference between the sides. He gave Thistle centre-half John Harvey his most uncomfortable afternoon for months and led the attack with both skill and purpose."

Next up for Harry and Clyde was the visit of Morton in midweek for the first leg of their League Cup quarter-final tie, the winners facing the prospect of a semi-final with Celtic if the Parkhead men could overcome Second Division East Fife. There was a "Strip-gate" sideshow before the match, with Clyde planning to wear their brand-new red-and-white striped kit – described, as it would turn out ironically, as "Sunderland-style" – whilst Hal Stewart feared that would clash with Morton's pin-striped jersey. Clyde would win that battle but would lose the war, as a Morton side clad in 'Real Madrid' all-white strips inflicted a 3-0 defeat on their hosts to take a huge step towards the last four of the competition.

The big time was well and truly back at Shawfield three days later, Saturday, 12 September 1964, as 21,177 spectators crammed into the Rutherglen stadium for the visit of Jimmy McGrory's Celtic. Even by the Parkhead club's standards the previous seven days had summed up the great inconsistencies of that period, the Bhoys securing a first League victory over Rangers in four years, despite the absence of the injured Billy McNeill and Bobby Murdoch, before slumping to a shock 2-0 defeat to East Fife at Bayview in midweek. McNeill's leg was still in plaster after breaking his ankle at Kilmarnock two weeks earlier, John Cushley continuing to deputise in central defence, whilst there was a surprise return for Murdoch in his hometown. Clyde striker Graham Macfarlane also made his comeback, following the broken collarbone sustained in pre-season. He replaced Jim McLean as the teams lined up as follows:

CLYDE:

Tommy McCulloch; Harry Glasgow & Eddie Mulheron; John McHugh, Jim Fraser & Davie White; Alex Bryce, Joe Gilroy, Graham Macfarlane, Harry Hood & Sam Hastings.

CELTIC:

John Fallon; Ian Young & Tommy Gemmell; John Clark, John Cushley & Jim Kennedy; Jimmy Johnstone, Bobby Murdoch, Steve Chalmers, Charlie Gallagher & Bobby Lennox.

Clyde started the match on the front foot, with Harry very much to the fore, and it was no surprise when Macfarlane opened the scoring within 15 minutes with a tremendous solo effort. Other than a Stevie Chalmers header which struck the inside of the post before rolling to safety, it was the hosts who emerged with most of the credit from the afternoon. Only a late Chalmers equaliser saved Celtic blushes and prevented Clyde from taking both points, with Gair Henderson commenting specifically on Harry's performance in his review of the game for the Sports Edition of that day's *Evening Times* and then again in his weekend summary on the following Monday.

"Harry Hood immediately produced half-a-dozen conjuring tricks with the ball inside the Celtic 18-yard line, as Cushley and Clark looked on in wonder. Hood had two shots blocked in Clyde's big offensive, and after just 10 minutes, the Celtic fans were calling on their team to wake up. Harry Hood was the man who did most to put the Celtic machine out of gear. In the first 20 minutes, he showed such great ball control and dash that he had to be marked by three men thereafter, and that took a big burden off players like Fraser, White and Glasgow."

The following midweek saw Clyde almost salvage what had looked a hopeless cause by beating Morton 2-0 at Cappielow, to lose out on a semi-final place by the odd goal in five. Harry put Clyde in front in the early stages with Sam Hastings reducing the deficit to just a single goal on the stroke of half-time. Try as they might, that third goal would not arrive and so the opportunity of an Ibrox clash with Celtic in the last four – Hood's fellow former Brunswick boy Stevie Chalmers scored five goals in the Hoops 6-0 destruction of East Fife at Parkhead - would elude the Shawfield outfit. On a positive note, yet again, Harry had emerged as the outstanding player of the night, as Morton's unbeaten record was shattered. Jimmy Dunbar of *The Evening Times* pulled this piece together the following day, whilst the same newspaper carried a photograph of the teenager - described as a *"bottle stock controller with a Glasgow firm"* - at his work.

"[Clyde] *had the finest attacker on view in Harry Hood. As often as not, Harry was a one-man forward line, but it is a tribute to his ability that he caused the home defence as much trouble as not one, not two but THREE ordinary attackers. For my money, Hood is the youngster with the greatest potential in Scotland. His reflexes are needle-sharp, and he knows where the goal lies. He had his BACK to the Morton goal when he hooked the ball over his head to beat an astonished* [Erik] *Sorensen for Clyde's first goal in 11 minutes."*

High-flying Clyde would then come crashing back to earth three days later, Saturday, 19 September 1964, following a 7-2 mauling by Dunfermline Athletic at East End Park. Alex Ferguson was the tormentor-in-chief with a hat-trick. That defeat would be quickly followed by the sad news that former Shawfield trainer Dawson Walker had passed away the next day in Ruchill Hospital at the age of 56 after a short illness. Walker had resigned together with Clyde manager Johnny Haddow in November 1962, on the weekend of Harry's senior debut at Ibrox, and had been planning to get back into the game with ES Clydebank before being hospitalised with a chest complaint.

The Bully Wee would get back on track the following Saturday, with a 1-0 win over Third Lanark at Shawfield. Once again, Harry was the man who mattered, his header in the 11th minute from a Sam Hastings corner proving to be the only goal of the game. That would take him on to eight for the season, only the crossbar preventing another first-half header from making that nine. Cathkin player-manager Bobby Evans, the former Celtic legend, was Harry's direct opponent on the day.

Harry celebrated his 20th birthday on Saturday, 3 October 1964 with another starring role in Clyde's excellent 2-1 victory over Dundee at Dens Park. The hosts featured his former Queen's Park colleague Doug Houston at wing-half, and they took an early lead through Kenny Cameron. Harry then set up Joe Gilroy for the equaliser on the stroke of half-time, before scoring the winner himself with six minutes remaining. Clyde would end the match with 10 men after John McHugh was ordered off.

That late winner would seem to pay testament to an astute observation made by Clyde manager John Prentice, as an *Evening Times* article published the following Saturday revealed.

"When Harry Hood played inside-left for Clyde against Celtic in the 1-1 draw he was a brilliant player for half an hour and then faded quietly from the Shawfield scene.

When he played against Dundee at Dens Park last week, he was brilliant, not just for half an hour but for an hour and a half. Clyde are now convinced that they have 'tamed' Harry and that from now on they will be an even better team than they are today, and that is by no means bad. Trouble up until last week was that Harry, a whirlwind starter in every game, put so much concentration and effort into his work early on that he was forced to take a breather in the spell just before half-time and after the restart."

"Manager John Prentice realised this commendable failing immediately after the Celtic match and since then he has spent a large portion of his training time in a bid to force Hood to pace himself. From Shawfield, I am told that in all of the practice matches of the past two weeks, Harry has been nagged into holding himself back just a shade in the first half-hour. The plan was a hundred per cent success at Dens Park with the result that Hood was a deadly dangerous player from the first minute to the last, and not just from the first minute to the 30th. Today, Hood was told a split-second before he went out against Airdrie – "Remember. Pace yourself."

Harry would certainly be involved throughout the match against Airdrieonians at Shawfield, played on Saturday, 10 October 1964, setting up Clyde's second goal for Sam Hastings as they built up a 3-0 interval lead before eventually winning by the odd goal in seven, Jim McLean and a Joe Gilroy double the other scorers securing the two points which lifted the Bully Wee into a lofty fifth place in the table. Yet another clash with Hal Stewart's Morton followed seven days later, Clyde denied the victory they probably deserved when Danish keeper Erik Sorensen superbly saved Jim McLean's late penalty at Cappielow, neither side managing a goal on the day before another 10,000 crowd.

Clyde's players would again follow the new routine of training on the morning of a match, introduced by John Prentice and Bruce Hay in an attempt to offset the disadvantages of being a part-time team in a predominantly full-time Division. Hay also revealed that Harry had been carrying out training exercises in a hot bath in an effort to remove muscle tensions being experienced by the player. It seemed to be working, as the Bully Wee made it nine points from five games with a 4-1 win over St Johnstone at Shawfield on Saturday, 24 October 1964. Once again, it would be Harry who opened the scoring, forcing the ball home from close-range after 25 minutes, in front of a posse of English scouts. Sam Hastings continued his excellent start to his Clyde career with a double either side of the break, taking the winger to an impressive 12 for the season. Jim McLean, like Hastings signed as a winger from Hamilton Academical but now thriving in an inside-forward role, rounded off the scoring late on.

The great run came to an end at Ibrox on the last day of October, although there had been no sign of what was to come as Clyde enjoyed the best chances in a goalless first-half, Harry coming close on several occasions. A Jimmy Millar header broke the deadlock eight minutes into the second half, with the goals coming thick and fast thereafter, sadly all at the one end. Clyde were 6-0 down before Jim McLean grabbed a crumb of comfort with a last-minute penalty conversion, after Sam Hastings had been fouled in the box by John Greig.

If Harry was down in the dumps after such a disappointing result, then the events of the next few days would quickly help him to forget that. Having watched him train with their youngsters some three years earlier, then see him develop into a top-class professional talent with Clyde, Celtic would finally make their move for Harry. Raymond Jacobs writing in *The Glasgow Herald* described Harry as the outstanding player on the field at Ibrox – a match watched by Sean Fallon - and revealed that Celtic had *"started inquiries"* regarding his joining up at Parkhead, with discussions having taken place between officials of both clubs after the match, albeit manager Jimmy McGrory did not expect any developments until midweek. A smiling Harry was photographed outside Celtic Park on the back page of *The Evening Times* on Monday, 2 November 1964, with the accompanying article by Peter Hendry suggesting that the move might depend on the views of another Harry Hood.

"Celtic's search for a goalscoring inside-forward could end with the signing of Harry Hood of Clyde, but it all depends on a talk between Harry and his father later today. The clubs had agreed on a fee – about £20,000 – before Hood went to Celtic Park today with manager John Prentice and chairman Willie Dunn. Hood spoke for half-an-hour with manager Jimmy McGrory and then told me – "I'll have to see my dad before I make any decision and he is on night-shift." Then Hood went back to work – he is employed in Mr Willie Dunn's business in Glasgow – to make a phone call home. However, it could be six o'clock tonight before he can see his father and decide whether or not to join Celtic. The answer seems certain to be YES. Hood, who joined Clyde from Brunswick Youth Club in 1962 and made his debut against Rangers at Ibrox in November of that year, has always wanted to become a full-time player. Now that he has the chance, it is most unlikely he will turn it down."

The reporter called it wrong, as turning it down is exactly what Harry did, in a telephone call to Jimmy McGrory on that Monday evening. With Harry combining his job at Dunn's with part-time football at Clyde, then clearly the terms for him to move into full-time football with Celtic would have to be right. The 20-year-old Hood himself was forthright in his comment to the press the following day.

"Unless Celtic come up with a vastly increased offer, I cannot consider moving from Shawfield to Celtic Park."

According to the press and Jimmy McGrory, Celtic did come back with an improved offer for Harry the following day. However, by the Wednesday the deal looked dead in the water, as reported by Gair Henderson in *The Evening Times*.

"Harry Hood, the Clyde centre-forward and the man who two days ago looked all set to bring punch to the Parkhead forward line, will not now be signing for Celtic. All transfer negotiations have ended and today manager Jimmy McGrory completed the

Hood serial story with these four terse words – "THE DEAL IS OFF."

"Obviously, the terms Celtic offered did not meet with Hood's assessment of his value, for McGrory said – "We are no longer interested in the player. We made him an offer on Monday, and a revised and better offer yesterday, but he would not sign. We could not go on talking indefinitely and as far as we are concerned, the matter is finished."

"Earlier today – before the official Celtic announcement – I spoke to Hood and he admitted that he did not know exactly the position. "As far as I am concerned, I have no plans for making a third visit to Celtic Park," he told me, "but you never know what can happen."

"I understand that Hood, who is a stock clerk in the bottling factory of Joseph Dunn Ltd, gave the Celtic offer careful thought, and apparently decided that his wages at the factory and his weekly pay from Clyde were not worth swapping for a full-time player's job with Celtic."

Harry would later ruefully reflect on that decision, once again quoted in Stratton Smith's *International Football Book No.12* from 1970.

"I'll never know why I turned down the chance to go to Celtic several years ago. Maybe it was sprung on me so quickly that I was in a daze when I was asked to sign. Celtic and Clyde had reached agreement about a transfer fee. I was called in to complete the deal but because of a few snags I didn't sign. Celtic got impatient and I lost the chance to join them."

Apart from Harry's dad, there was another special person in his life whose views he sought about a potential transfer to Celtic at that time. That was his girlfriend, Kathleen McGinley, and she has vivid recollections of those events from November 1964, as well as an insight into their life post-Holyrood.

"We had both left Holyrood Secondary in the summer of 1962. I went to Strathclyde University to study Commerce & Business and Harry pursued his football career by signing for Clyde, whilst working part-time with Dunn & Moore – a soft drinks company – as a rep. That was a job he excelled at, as he was a great 'people person' and raconteur. Many of Glasgow's old publicans still remember him calling into the pubs to get orders. I seem to recall that happening even after he joined Celtic in 1969."

"We enjoyed going to the cinema and playing 10-pin bowling. Harry taught me to swim and he tried to encourage me to play golf but unfortunately, though I tried many times, I was not at all interested. Ironically, we later owned our own golf club at Dalziel! Staying in to listen to music was in keeping with both Harry's strict training regime and my university studies."

"Harry was extremely good fun to be with and had a superb, cheeky sense of humour. My poor mum was on the receiving end of that once when he introduced

her to reporters as his Gran! That was when they were chasing Harry at the time Celtic were trying to sign him. He was also very kind-hearted and showed me immense sympathy when my dad died suddenly in June 1964. He definitely had a strong supportive nature. He was also a very proud person with high moral standings."

That last sentence appears to be key in why Harry did not end up at Celtic Park in November 1964. Jimmy McGrory is one of my all-time Parkhead heroes. I met him once as a youngster at the signing of his autobiography – one of my most prized possessions – and he was every inch the gentleman he was made out to be. That being the case, perhaps the approach adopted in the transfer dealings reflected more on the culture of the time. Kathleen continues.

"Harry went into the manager's office at the agreed time and Jimmy McGrory's opening was "What's your name, son?" He didn't even know who Harry was. He then outlined Celtic's offer and asked if Harry was interested. Harry came back with "I'm getting x at Clyde and y with Dunn & Moore, so z would be required to make it worth my while going full-time." Jimmy's response was, "Son, if you're interested, then you'll sign." Harry left and we drove over to Shawfield. We're sitting in the car park and he asks me, "What will I do?" I told him it was his career. He felt he had been disrespected and as I said, he was a proud man with principles, and he was also financially astute. It just didn't feel right. There was a "Why should I?" moment and in the end he didn't sign."

Celtic could certainly have done with Harry three days later, a revamped forward line of John Hughes, Jimmy Johnstone, Stevie Chalmers, John Divers and Bobby Lennox failing to spark as Jimmy McGrory's men lost three goals in the opening half-hour to St Johnstone at Muirton Park, the game ending 3-0. Back in the outskirts of Glasgow, Harry was lining up for Clyde against Dundee United at Shawfield, the youngster showing no signs of being affected by the events of the week as he was closely involved in the play throughout the match, unlucky not to score when his header hit the top of the crossbar in the second half. Jim McLean was the man who grabbed the headlines in the fog, scoring twice against the team he would lead to the last four of the European Cup two decades later to secure the points which allowed Clyde to leapfrog both Morton and Motherwell into sixth spot in the table, now behind Celtic and Dunfermline Athletic only on goal average. The 2-0 victory over Jerry Kerr's men on Saturday, 7 November 1964 would prove to be the last match of Harry's first spell at Clyde, the teams having lined up as follows.

CLYDE:

Tommy McCulloch; Harry Glasgow & Eddie Mulheron; John McHugh, Jim Fraser & Davie White; Alex Bryce, Joe Gilroy, Harry Hood, Jim McLean & Sam Hastings.

DUNDEE UNITED:

Donald Mackay; Tommy Millar & Jimmy Briggs; Tommy Neilson, Doug Smith & Stewart Fraser; Johnny Graham, Frank Munro, Bert Howieson, Denis Gillespie & Lewis Thom.

Despite an article in that day's *Evening Times* featuring a caricature of Harry with the message that he would be staying at Clyde, within 48 hours Harry Hood would indeed be on the move from Shawfield.

But that would involve crossing the English border rather than the River Clyde.

Chapter 9

Harry joins a Scots colony at Sunderland

The 1963/64 campaign had ended very differently for two of the English clubs linked with an interest in signing talented young Clyde forward, Harry Hood. Two years after becoming champions under Alf Ramsay, Ipswich Town found themselves relegated to the Second Division under the stewardship of Geordie hero Jackie Milburn. Milburn's rebuild plans for the new campaign would include the signing of Celtic winger Frank Brogan in June 1964. The scorer of Celtic's 5,000th League goal against Partick Thistle in April 1962, both Frank and younger brother Jim had signed up at Parkhead from St Roch's Juniors, the Brogan siblings having played at Provanmill Park either side of the Hood brothers' brief involvement there in autumn 1961. As I mentioned earlier, Frank sadly passed away during the writing of this chapter, on Thursday, 29 April 2021, Jim having predeceased his brother in September 2018.

Ipswich and Bolton Wanderers would be replaced in the First Division for season 1964/65 by Leeds United and Sunderland. Don Revie's Leeds had won the Second Division title by two points from the Wearside outfit, with Sunderland perhaps missing out on top spot due to some incredible displays in the FA Cup in the spring of 1964. On Saturday, 15 February 1964, they eliminated reigning English champions Everton with a 3-1 win at Roker Park in front of 63,000 spectators. That set up a quarter-final tie on the last day of the month against Manchester United at Old Trafford. The Second Division visitors were 3-1 up with four minutes remaining before another 62,000 supporters when goals from Bobby Charlton and George Best secured a replay for the FA Cup-holders. That took place at Roker Park four days later, Wednesday, 4 March 1964, with Sunderland this time seconds from glory as they led 2-1 in the last minute of extra-time before that man Charlton again broke Wearside hearts with a last-gasp equaliser. The epic tie was finally decided at Leeds Road, Huddersfield on Monday, 9 March 1964, in front of another massive attendance of 55,000. Nick Sharkey gave Sunderland the lead early in the second half before United flexed their muscles with five goals in a devastating 18-minute spell, which included a Denis Law hat-trick, to end Roker dreams of an FA Cup/promotion double.

Still, the return to the top-flight would trigger wild celebrations on Wearside after their team had agonisingly missed out in each of the previous two seasons following final-day heartbreaks. Those celebrations would be tempered by the shock resignation of popular, 'morally-compassed' manager, Alan Brown, who accepted an offer to take over the reins at Sheffield Wednesday at the end of July after seven years in charge of Sunderland.

Whilst Revie would openly express his interest in the Roker Park vacancy, in the absence of a new manager the Sunderland team would be chosen by a selection committee as they rejoined the English top-flight in August 1964. The opening 15 League matches were quite remarkable in the sense that an almost perfect trend developed, with home draws followed by away defeats, the only exception to that sequence being a 1-0 win over Blackburn Rovers at Roker Park on Saturday, 19 September 1964.

The winning goal that day was scored by the aforementioned Nick Sharkey, one of several Scots on Sunderland's books at that time, continuing a link with the country which went all the way back to the club's formation by Ayrshireman James Allan in 1879. The 21-year-old Sharkey had moved to Wearside directly from schools' football with that well-known nursery St Patrick's, Dumbarton in 1959, making his first-team debut the following year. Sharkeyabecome one of a select group of three Sunderland players to score five goals in a League match – the only one to do so post-war - when he managed the feat in a 7-1 rout of Norwich City at Roker Park in March 1963, including a 10-minute hat-trick just before the interval. Alan Brown's men had then only required a point from their final match at home to Chelsea two months later to secure promotion from the Second Division, but a 1-0 defeat allowed Tommy Docherty's men to steal the prize from their grasp. Twelve months earlier, Leyton Orient had also leapfrogged Sunderland on the final day to clinch the second promotion spot by 0.01 of a goal at their expense. Thankfully it had been third-time lucky for the Rokerites in 1963/64.

Keeping goal for Sunderland against Blackburn had been Kilwinning-born Sandy McLaughlan, signed from Kilmarnock that summer and debuting in the 2-2 draw with West Bromwich Albion at Roker Park on Wednesday, 2 September 1964, a game which marked the return of striker Brian Clough after a two-year injury absence. Clough would remain in the side for that weekend's visit of Leeds United – scoring Sunderland's opener in a 3-3 draw – and the home game with Aston Villa the following midweek, where the sides shared four goals, before being replaced by Sharkey for the trip to Highbury three days later. Sadly, the prolific Clough would never play again, eventually turning to management and incredible success at Derby County and Nottingham Forest, where his strict management style was widely acknowledged as being closely based on that of Sunderland's Alan Brown.

In addition to Nick Sharkey, there would be other Scottish candidates vying for the role of long-term successor to the legendary Clough. John O'Hare was another teenager plucked from the Dumbarton area, handed his Sunderland debut at Stamford Bridge on Saturday, 29 August 1964 whilst still one month shy of his 18th birthday. Young John obviously made an impression on Brian Clough during their spell together at Roker Park, as he would later sign him for Derby County, Leeds United and Nottingham Forest. The Sunderland goal that afternoon in a 3-1 defeat was scored by George Herd, yet another Scot. Herd had moved to Wearside from Clyde for £42,500 in May 1961, having been part of their Scottish Cup-winning team at Hampden under Johnny Haddow three years earlier. Capped five times by Scotland whilst at Shawfield - netting once in a 3-3 draw with Hungary in Budapest in June 1960 - he was now 28 years old and as such considered very much a senior player at Roker Park.

As an aside, George made his Scotland debut against England before 128,000 spectators at Hampden on Saturday, 19 April 1958, in a side captained by the aforementioned Chelsea manager Tommy Docherty, then playing with Preston North End. Also making their international bows that afternoon were both Jimmy Murray of Hearts, who would later join Clyde, and England's Bobby Charlton, who made a scoring debut in a 4-0 victory for the visitors, whilst Shawfield trainer Dawson Walker took charge of Scotland for the first time as manager Matt Busby recovered from injuries sustained in the Munich air tragedy. Playing in navy blue for the final time were Clyde captain Harry Haddock and future Scotland and Sunderland boss Ian McColl. Seven days later, Haddock, Herd and Walker would all be celebrating at the same venue after Johnny Coyle's goal saw Clyde beat Hibernian in the Scottish Cup final. Jimmy Murray would also enjoy his summer, winning the League title with Hearts in record-breaking style before becoming the first Scottish player to score in a World Cup finals tournament, when he equalised against Yugoslavia in Vasteras in eastern Sweden on Sunday, 8 June 1958.

Two days younger than George Herd was another member of the Scots colony at Roker Park, George Mulhall. The Falkirk-born left-winger had made over a century of appearances for Aberdeen and his international debut for Scotland before signing for Sunderland in September 1962. He would receive a further two caps within his first year on Wearside. Curiously, all three of his Scotland matches were against Ireland - the Six Counties - where his opponents included Sunderland colleagues Martin Harvey and Johnny Crossan, as well as his future Roker teammate John Parke.

Herd, Mulhall, Sharkey, Harvey and Crossan were all in the Sunderland team which opened the 1964/65 season with a 3-3 draw with Leicester City at Roker Park on Saturday, 22 August 1964, as was left-half Jimmy McNab, another Scotsman who had moved to Wearside from schoolboy football, in his case from Stirlingshire in the summer of 1957, and 15-year-old debutant goalkeeper Derek Forster. George Mulhall grabbed a double and George Herd a third as the team often called the Black Cats opened their top-flight campaign with a point against a Foxes side which included Gordon Banks, Frank McLintock and former Hibernian striker David Gibson.

The final member of the Scots colony at Roker Park, for now, had a rather different background. John Watters was born in Fife on 5 September 1919 and played for St Aloysius College and St Roch's before joining Celtic on a provisional contract in 1935. That arrangement would be formalised in January 1937 with the young inside-forward making his senior debut in November of the following year as a replacement for appendicitis victim Malky MacDonald in a 2-0 League win over Arbroath at Gayfield. The 17-year-old Watters – known as Jackie or Johnny - would be in good company that afternoon, as he lined up with the 10 remaining members of Celtic's wonderful Empire Exhibition Cup-winning team.

Johnny would open his scoring account for the Hoops seven days later, netting a double as a last-gasp Frank Murphy strike gave Celtic a 5-4 victory against Hibernian at Parkhead. He maintained his place in the team through December, repeating his brace against the other Edinburgh club, Hearts, on Hogmanay. This time it was the visitors who scored right at the death to deny Celtic both points, after Johnny's late second had looked like the winner. Two days later, Monday, 2 January 1939, he lined up for Celtic at Ibrox in front of 118,730, still the largest attendance ever to watch a League match on these islands. Watters would then make his final appearance of the season in his native Fife against Burntisland Shipyard in the first round of the Scottish Cup on Saturday, 21 January 1939, Johnny scoring Celtic's seventh goal in the 8-3 win over the Kirkton Park amateurs.

His place would then be taken by John Divers, and Johnny would not reappear in the Celtic first team until Saturday, 7 October 1939, in a 1-0 defeat to Queen's Park in the replayed Glasgow Cup semi-final at Hampden. The 1939/40 Scottish League season had been suspended in early September after five games, due to the outbreak of war, ironically an injury to Divers now allowing Johnny to play in Celtic's first-ever wartime Regional League match, a 4-3 home defeat by Hamilton Academical.

Watters would then slip back into first-team exile before re-appearing the following March for his final run in the side. By this time, the legendary Celtic manager Willie Maley had retired – voluntarily or otherwise – and former skipper Jimmy McStay was now in charge of team affairs. Johnny featured in eight of the remaining Regional League games between March and May 1940, his last game being a 2-1 defeat by St Mirren at Love Street, which saw Celtic finish the season 13th in a 16-team League!

In the summer of 1940, as he approached his 21st birthday, Johnny Watters joined the war effort, serving in the Royal Navy as a medic until his demob in 1947. Formally released by new Celtic manager Jimmy McGrory in April of that year, he moved to Airdrieonians in September, his first season there ending in the disappointment of relegation. The Broomfield club finished four points below Johnny's former team Celtic, for whom a Jock Weir hat-trick at Dens Park on Saturday, 17 April 1948 finally removed the horrific possibility of a humiliating, first-ever demotion from the top-flight.

After two seasons in the second tier, Airdrieonians would be promoted back to Division A in April 1950, and they would remain there until the end of the 1953/54 campaign. The final part of Johnny's career involved another link with the Empire Exhibition Cup of 1938. Sunderland had faced Celtic in the first game of that competition, and in 1955, now a 36-year-old qualified physiotherapist, Johnny joined the Roker Park backroom team, beginning a love affair that would last the best part of 30 years.

Johnny Watters and Harry Hood would meet up soon enough, and no doubt would compare notes on their spells at St Aloysius and St Roch's. Meantime, on Saturday, 7 November 1964, as Harry was lining up for the final time for Clyde against Dundee United at Shawfield, Johnny and a Sunderland side still without a first-team manager travelled to White Hart Lane to face Tottenham Hotspur. The eighth away match of the season would end just as the previous seven had, in defeat, this time thanks to three second-half goals from Jimmy Greaves, Cliff Jones and Jimmy Robertson.

Welsh internationalist Jones, normally a winger, was wearing the number 10 jersey, previously worn with such distinction for Spurs by Scottish international inside-forward John White, who had tragically been killed in a lightning strike on a Middlesex golf course just four months earlier, aged 27. Their third goalscorer against Sunderland, Glasgow-born Jimmy Robertson, was also a winger, a contemporary of Harry's in both schools and amateur football before joining Cowdenbeath in 1961. He would spend one season in Fife then two in Paisley with St Mirren before joining Spurs that summer, receiving his international debut in a 3-2 defeat by Wales at Cardiff five weeks before the clash with Sunderland. Robertson was one of three Scots who received his first cap from manager Ian McColl that afternoon, Saturday, 3 October 1964, Harry's 20th birthday, Liverpool's Ron Yeats and Celtic's Jimmy Johnstone being the others, although he would be the only one of that trio not to play for his country again. Robertson's Spurs clubmate Cliff Jones was on the right wing for the Welsh as two goals in the final three minutes from the man with the best Welsh name ever – Birmingham City's Ken Leek – allowed the hosts to snatch a 3-2 victory from the jaws of defeat at Ninian Park. Stevie Chalmers and Leicester's David Gibson had given Scotland a 2-1 lead within the opening half hour in front of 37,000 spectators.

Back at White Hart Lane, Sunderland's continuing woes on the road were highlighted by the last-gasp penalty miss by Irishman Johnny Crossan, who sent his international colleague Pat Jennings the wrong way from the spot only to see the ball hit the post and bounce to safety. That defeat saw Sunderland remain in 20th spot in the First Division with eight points from 15 games, ahead of Aston Villa in the relegation zone only on goal average, with Wolverhampton Wanderers propping up the table.

As an aside, Crossan's route to Sunderland is a strange story in itself. The Roker Park club had offered Irish League outfit Derry City - his hometown team - £6,000 for Johnny's signature back in 1957. As an amateur, strictly neither player nor club could accept financial compensation, albeit this was common practice in Ireland at that time. Derry City offered to split the £6,000 fee with Johnny on the basis that he would sign a professional contract to enable that to happen, however, Crossan felt that City should receive only £1,000 rather than £3,000, and the ensuing stalemate ensured that no deal could take place. On expiry of his amateur contract at the end of the 1957/58 campaign, free agent Johnny moved to Coleraine, where a £7,000 fee was agreed with Bristol City for his transfer in October 1958. Unhappy at how this was playing out, Derry City then reported themselves to the Irish FA for offering the illegal payment, aware that this would bring Crossan's part in the situation to the fore. The ploy worked. Derry received a token fine whilst Johnny was banned indefinitely from playing football anywhere.

It would be August 1959 before an appeal restricted that ban to clubs within the British Isles, Crossan duly signing for Dutch champions Sparta Rotterdam. He would score a critical goal for his new side in the European Cup first-round play-off against IFK Gothenburg in Bremen that November, which saw Sparta paired with Rangers in the quarter-final. Both teams would win their away legs by 3-2 before the Ibrox club won the Highbury play-off by the same scoreline. Johnny would take his revenge two years later. Now playing with Belgian champions Standard Liege and facing Rangers again at the same stage of the competition, Crossan scored twice in a 4-1 first-leg victory in Liege which would prove enough to take the Belgians through to a semi-final with five-times winners Real Madrid in April 1962.

The story had a happy albeit a curious, suspiciously convenient ending. The following month, whilst in South America for the Chile World Cup finals, England selector and Sunderland chairman Syd Collings had an informal chat with Irish FA President Harry Cavan. By October 1962, the Irish association had lifted the ban and Sunderland manager Alan Brown had paid £27,500 to bring Johnny Crossan to Wearside, the Derry man making his debut in a 6-2 victory over Grimsby Town at Roker Park in November, just three weeks before Harry Hood made his own senior breakthrough for Clyde at Ibrox.

Two years later, Sunderland's poor start to the 1964/65 season now prompted action at boardroom level. Overtures were made to Rangers to sign former Scotland captain Eric Caldow, and when that approach was rejected by the Ibrox board, the Rokerites turned to Jock Stein's Hibernian to agree a £36,000 fee for Irish international left-back John Parke. Sunderland then headed due west to improve their attacking options by paying £26,000 to Clyde for their talented teenage forward Harry Hood.

A contract was duly signed on Monday, 9 November 1964, between Sunderland FC secretary Edward Marshall, on behalf of the club, and Henry Anthony Hood of 50 Gartons Road, Glasgow N1. Harry agreed *"to play in an efficient manner and to the best of his ability for the club for the period of two years from that day until 30 June*

1966." Harry would receive a £2,000 signing-on fee and his basic weekly wage would be £40, and there were financial incentives for finishing in the top six of the First Division and progression in the FA and League Cups, all based on appearances. Harry would also qualify for *"talent money"* at the rate of £20 per League point gained where he played and *"normal match bonuses according to rules."* The contract was witnessed by Chief Scout, Charles Ferguson and offered the club an option of extending for a further two years from 30 June 1966.

Just 24 hours after putting pen to paper, Harry watched his new side in action for the first time, the League Cup providing a welcome diversion from the First Division struggle as the fourth-round draw sent Sunderland to Coventry on Tuesday, 10 November 1964. Having already beaten two top-flight sides in West Ham United and Blackpool – with their combined trio of future World Cup-winners Martin Peters, Geoff Hurst and Alan Ball – Sunderland were favourites to dispose of Jimmy Hill's Coventry City, newly promoted to the Second Division. The tie would not go to script, however, the Sky Blues 4-0 up at Highfield Road before a second-half John O'Hare double put some semblance of respectability on the scoreline. The following evening, back in North London, a Scottish international select beat Tottenham Hotspur 6-2 at White Hart Lane in a testimonial match for John White, the opening goal for the hosts scored by Hearts Tommy White, brother of the late Spurs and Scotland star.

The silver lining in the Sunderland cloud would be the introduction of Harry Hood at centre-forward for the visit of Burnley the following Saturday, 14 November 1964, the new signing one of four Scots in their forward line as Johnny Crossan found himself the man left out after the midweek cup defeat in the West Midlands. The teams lined up as follows in front of 36,000 supporters at Roker Park.

SUNDERLAND:

Jim Montgomery; Colin Nelson & Len Ashurst; Dave Elliott, Dickie Rooks & Jimmy McNab; Brian Usher, George Herd, Harry Hood, John O'Hare & George Mulhall.

BURNLEY:

Adam Blacklaw; Fred Smith & Mick Buxton; Brian O'Neil, John Talbut & Brian Miller; Willie Morgan, Andy Lochhead, Ray Pointer, Arthur Bellamy & John Price.

Scots were very much to the fore as Andy Lochhead gave the visitors an early lead before George Herd and George Mulhall beat international goalkeeper Adam Blacklaw to give Sunderland a 2-1 lead at the interval. A Dickie Rooks penalty stretched that lead before boyhood Rokerite Arthur Bellamy ended the scoring at 3-2. It was a winning start to his life as a full-time footballer which left an indelible impression on the young Harry.

"I was absolutely stunned when I ran out at Roker Park for my debut. Remember,

in my career I would ultimately play in front of huge raucous crowds in Glasgow, but I've never forgotten what the noise and atmosphere was like inside Roker Park."

There was no raucous crowd in the east end of Glasgow that same afternoon. Having failed to lure Harry to Parkhead, Celtic switched their attention to Falkirk, signing inside-forward Hugh Maxwell for £15,000 on Friday, 13 November 1964. The move was pretty much ignored in the media, thus leading to some puzzled looks amongst the home supporters in the 15,000 crowd who rolled up the next day to find a tall redhead wearing the number 10 shorts as Celts lost 2-0 to Dundee. The transfer date would prove to be a suitable omen for the new Bhoy. He had scored six goals for Falkirk against Clyde at Brockville in one of Harry's early appearances for the club, however, he would manage only two in eight matches for Celtic before joining St Johnstone at the end of that season. Strangely, life after Harry for Clyde would continue with another trip to Brockville, Dave Souter plucked recently from his former club Arbroath by Shawfield manager John Prentice and handed the number nine jersey for his debut. There would be no repeat of the 7-3 mauling of two years earlier, as the match ended goalless.

Harry's first away appearance in English football came seven days later, Saturday, 21 November 1964, at Bramall Lane against Sheffield United. The Sunderland selection committee made six changes to the team which had beaten Burnley the previous week, with debuts for two Irishmen, John Parke, their recent signing from Hibernian, and winger Billy Campbell, a £7,000 acquisition from Belfast's Distillery. There was also a return for three other Irish stars, Martin Harvey, club captain Charlie Hurley – future Distillery midfielder Martin O'Neill's boyhood idol – and Johnny Crossan, as Sunderland lined up as follows.

SUNDERLAND:

Jim Montgomery; Cec Irwin & John Parke; Martin Harvey, Charlie Hurley & Jimmy McNab; Billy Campbell, George Herd, Harry Hood, Johnny Crossan & George Mulhall.

The hosts fielded future Leeds United and England striker Mick Jones, albeit he was not on target as they ran out comfortable 3-0 winners on the day, to inflict a ninth successive defeat on the road for the Wearsiders. Sunderland were a goal down within the first minute, then played for most of the second half with 10 men, after Hurley was forced from the field with a recurrence of his thigh problem.

Two days later, Monday, 23 November 1964, the Sunderland board appointed former England captain George Hardwick as caretaker manager until the end of the season. 'Gentleman George' had spent 13 seasons at Middlesbrough and was considered a legend by the Ayresome Park faithful due to his performances at the heart of the Boro defence, his statue adorning the concourse of their present Riverside home. He is also one of the few men to skipper a Great Britain side, doing so in a 6-1 win over a Rest of Europe select at Hampden in May 1947 to mark the home nations return to

FIFA. His first Sunderland team selection saw the return of striker Nick Sharkey for that Saturday's visit of Everton, one of four Scots in the forward line, alongside Harry Hood, George Herd and George Mulhall.

Everton had been on a steep upward curve since the days when Harry's brother Jackie had been on the books, largely due to the replacement of Johnny Carey as manager by Harry Catterick in 1961. The Goodison men won the English title in 1962/63 and would remain a top-class side for several seasons thereafter. On the day of George Hardwick's appointment at Sunderland earlier that week, they had completed a 6-1 dissection of Willie Waddell's Kilmarnock in the Inter-Cities Fairs Cup, but they would be no match for Sunderland at Roker Park on Saturday, 28 November 1964. Harry scored his first goal for the club with two minutes remaining, their final blow in a 4-0 victory before 41,581 ecstatic Wearsiders, after his fellow Scots Herd, Mulhall and Sharkey had taken the game beyond Everton.

The Scottish influence was again very much to the fore as December opened - appropriately enough - with a visit to St Andrews, to face fellow-strugglers Birmingham City. Sunderland would eventually lose out to the Blues in a seven-goal thriller, despite a double from Nick Sharkey and a late strike from Jimmy McNab, but the away duck was finally broken, at the 11th attempt, on Saturday, 12 December 1964, when Sharkey beat Gordon Banks with just five minutes remaining to secure a 1-0 win over eighth-placed Leicester City at Filbert Street.

The ante was raised significantly the following Saturday, as Tommy Docherty brought his high-flying Chelsea side to Roker Park. The Stamford Bridge outfit sat second in the table, sandwiched between leaders Manchester United and Don Revie's Leeds United, with only two points separating first from third in a nip-and-tuck contest which would prevail until the final minutes of the season. Former Holyrood boy Jim McCalliog had left Elland Road to join Docherty in West London the previous year, however, he would not feature as the following sides lined up in front of another 41,000 Roker crowd.

SUNDERLAND:

Sandy McLaughlan; John Parke & Len Ashurst; Martin Harvey, Dickie Rooks & Jimmy McNab; Brian Usher, Harry Hood, Nick Sharkey, George Herd & George Mulhall.

CHELSEA:

Peter Bonetti; Marvin Hinton & Eddie McCreadie; John Hollins, John Mortimore & Ron Harris; Bert Murray, George Graham, Barry Bridges, Terry Venables & Tommy Knox.

Sunderland would revert to their traditional black shorts that afternoon, having worn white from the opening games of the season. Whatever the reason for that, it would bring the Black Cats good luck as they hammered Chelsea 3-0 to record a third consecutive home win, thus putting some daylight between themselves and the bottom duo of Aston Villa and Wolverhampton Wanderers. Nick Sharkey was again on target, opening the scoring after 20 minutes. Martin Harvey then doubled Sunderland's lead on the half-hour, before George Herd sealed the two vital points with 10 minutes remaining.

Boxing Day 1964 then threw up a real Christmas cracker as Bill Shankly brought defending champions Liverpool to Wearside, with 50,000 spectators cramming into the ground. George Hardwick's only change from the victory over Chelsea was to bring back Jim Montgomery in place of former Kilmarnock keeper Sandy McLaughlan. Scotland striker Ian St John would miss out for the visitors, to be replaced by the aptly-named target man Alf Arrowsmith, as the teams lined up as follows.

SUNDERLAND:

Jim Montgomery; John Parke & Len Ashurst; Martin Harvey, Dickie Rooks & Jimmy McNab; Brian Usher, Harry Hood, Nick Sharkey, George Herd & George Mulhall.

LIVERPOOL:

Tommy Lawrence; Chris Lawler & Gerry Byrne; Gordon Milne, Ron Yeats & Billy Stevenson; Ian Callaghan, Roger Hunt, Alf Arrowsmith, Tommy Smith & Peter Thompson.

Shankly's wing-half pairing of Gordon Milne and Billy Stevenson – the latter signed from Rangers two years earlier after losing his place to Jim Baxter – would give the visitors a 2-0 interval lead, before a storming fightback saw Nick Sharkey and George Mulhall draw Sunderland level with 20 minutes to play. There would be another twist on the tale late on, though, as Stevenson scored his second of the afternoon in the 82nd minute to hand Sunderland their first home defeat of the season. News of Aston Villa's 1-0 victory over Midland rivals Wolves at Molyneux then filtered through, further darkening the festive mood on Wearside.

The second leg of the holiday double-header with Shankly's men took place at Anfield two days later, Monday, 28 December 1964. Harry dropped out of the team, as did Jim Montgomery and Brian Usher, the recast Sunderland side recording a creditable goalless draw in front of 44,000 spectators.

The tough run of League fixtures for Sunderland continued into the new year. Saturday, 2 January 1965 saw them travel to Yorkshire to take on Leeds United, Don Revie's men chasing a first-ever top-flight title. Even at that stage, the side which would later dominate English football was taking shape, albeit it is interesting to see Terry Cooper playing at outside-left. Harry Hood and Brian Usher returned to the forward line at the expense of Cec Irwin and Johnny Crossan, as the following 22 men took the field in front of 44,000 supporters at Elland Road.

LEEDS UNITED:

Gary Sprake; Paul Reaney & Paul Madeley; Billy Bremner, Jack Charlton & Norman Hunter; Johnny Giles, Jim Storrie, Rod Johnson, Bobby Collins & Terry Cooper.

SUNDERLAND:

Sandy McLaughlan; John Parke & Len Ashurst; Martin Harvey, Dickie Rooks & Jimmy McNab; Brian Usher, Harry Hood, Nick Sharkey, George Herd & George Mulhall.

McLaughlan's goal would remain intact until the 70th minute, at which point Jack Charlton gave the hosts the lead. Then with seven minutes remaining, Norman Hunter was the unlikely goalscorer who appeared to have sealed the win, only for Harry to notch his second Sunderland strike two minutes later. Revie's men would duly see the game out to overtake Manchester United at the top of the table.

Despite his goal at Elland Road, Harry would miss out on a place in the team which commenced Sunderland's FA Cup campaign with a 3-0 win over Luton Town at Kennilworth Road seven days later. The Third Division hosts included future Luton manager David Pleat and a young Bruce Rioch, Scotland's captain at the Argentina World Cup of 1978, and they were just 12 minutes away from a money-spinning replay at Roker Park before a Nick Sharkey double either side of George Mulhall's counter gave Sunderland a 3-0 win and late but safe passage into the fourth round. Harry remained on the sidelines for the visit of Arsenal to Wearside the following Saturday, goals from former Hibernian striker Joe Baker and John Radford giving the Gunners a 2-0 win, which combined with Villa's win over Blackpool, saw Sunderland drop into the relegation positions for the first time that season.

The next weekend saw Sunderland's trip to Blackburn one of several fixtures which fell victim to the winter weather, but on Saturday, 30 January 1965, Harry was restored to the line-up and vindicated that selection by netting on his FA Cup debut for Sunderland at Roker Park. The young Scot briefly brought the hosts back into the fourth-round tie with Nottingham Forest, before a late Charlie Hurley own goal sealed a 3-1 victory for Johnny Carey's men. League business resumed on the first Saturday in February with the visit of Blackpool, a late Nick Sharkey goal clinching two precious points on the day Mike Hellawell made his Sunderland debut. The right-winger had played on the opposite flank to Bertie Auld in the Birmingham City side which lost the Inter-Cities Fairs Cup final to Roma back in 1961.

Tuesday, 8 February 1965 witnessed a very productive trip back to Scotland for Harry, as he scored his first hat-trick for his new club. The occasion was the opening of the new floodlights at Kilbowie Park, as the Steedman brothers controversial merger of East Stirlingshire Clydebank drew 10,000 spectators to see the English side win 5-1. Nick Sharkey's double bookended Harry's second-half treble, whilst the Steedman's nephew, Andy Roxburgh, grabbed a late consolation goal for the hosts. Roxburgh, of course, had been a teammate of Harry's at Queen's Park. Hibernian manager Jock Stein and his captain John McNamee were amongst those looking on, the Leith men having been held to a 1-1 draw by ES Clydebank in their Scottish Cup-tie at Easter Road three days earlier. By this time, Jock was essentially working his notice, having agreed to take over as manager of Celtic. The current incumbent of that post – Jimmy McGrory – was also taking in a match that night. McGrory was at Brig O'Lea in Neilston, watching young St Mirin's Boy Guild left-half David Hay in action for a Secondary Juveniles select.

The following Saturday saw Sunderland up against their former manager Alan Brown for the visit to Hillsborough, two late goals giving Sheffield Wednesday a 2-0 win which, together with Villa's 1-0 victory in another Midlands derby away to Birmingham City, sent the Black Cats tumbling back down into the second relegation slot and in danger of an immediate return to English football's second tier.

The fightback would start seven days later, though, on Saturday, 20 February 1965, Harry opening the scoring 10 minutes before the interval in a 3-2 win over Ron Greenwood's FA Cup-holders West Ham United at Roker Park. His direct opponent that day was England captain Bobby Moore, whilst another of the Hammers' World Cup-winning trio of the following year – Martin Peters – was listed at left-back and the third, Geoff Hurst, brought the visitors level at 2-2, after Nick Sharkey then Johnny Byrne had scored in a see-saw match. Sharkey would have the last word with the winning goal in the last-minute, and with relegation rivals Aston Villa and Wolverhampton Wanderers clashing in the last 16 of that season's FA Cup the same afternoon, Sunderland moved back up into 20th slot in the First Division. The teams had lined up at Roker Park as follows.

SUNDERLAND:

Sandy McLaughlan; John Parke & Len Ashurst; Martin Harvey, Charlie Hurley & Jimmy McNab; Brian Usher, George Herd, Harry Hood, Nick Sharkey & George Mulhall.

WEST HAM UNITED:

Jim Standen; John Bond & Martin Peters; Eddie Bovington, Ken Brown & Bobby Moore; Alan Sealey, Ronnie Boyce, Johnny Byrne, Geoff Hurst & John Sissons.

The big names kept on coming. Undoubtedly, the highlight of Harry's stay on Wearside took place on Wednesday, 24 February 1965, as he scored the only goal of the game against Matt Busby's Double-chasing, star-studded Manchester United side - Best, Law, Charlton, Crerand et al - in front of more than 51,000 jubilant home fans. His fierce shot was struck from an impossible angle, 20 yards out, the ball dipping and swinging viciously to beat United's Irish keeper Pat Dunne after just eight minutes. The high-profile visitors would then lay siege to Sunderland's goal but without success, as the hosts leap-frogged Birmingham City to sit 19th in the table.

That evening had marked the debuts in English football for another two young Scotsmen, Alan Black and John Fitzpatrick. Black had left his local club Dumbarton to sign for Sunderland and replaced Len Ashurst at left-back, whilst Aberdonian Fitzpatrick came into the United side for Nobby Stiles. Wing-half Stiles was on the verge of a full international call-up for England and was representing the Under 23 side against Scotland the same evening in a goalless draw at Pittodrie. The combative Stiles and Blackpool's Alan Ball were involved in a number of tasty challenges with Billy Bremner of Leeds United, as promising Celtic full-back Ian Young made his only appearance at that level in John Fitzpatrick's home city. Back in the cauldron of Roker Park, the teams had lined up as follows.

SUNDERLAND:

Sandy McLaughlan; John Parke & Alan Black; Martin Harvey, Charlie Hurley & Jimmy McNab; Mike Hellawell, George Herd, Harry Hood, Nick Sharkey & George Mulhall.

MANCHESTER UNITED:

Pat Dunne; Shay Brennan & Tony Dunne; Pat Crerand, Bill Foulkes & John Fitzpatrick; John Connelly, Bobby Charlton, David Herd, Denis Law & George Best.

The euphoria would be slightly deflated three days later, as an unchanged Sunderland went down by the only goal of the game at Craven Cottage to a Fulham side which included Bobby Robson, Johnny Haynes, Rodney Marsh and yet another of England's World Cup-winners, full-back George Cohen. A home fixture with Nottingham Forest opened March, Harry on the scoresheet again as a measure of revenge was taken against their FA-Cup conquerors. He grabbed Sunderland's third goal in a 4-0 win, after a Nick Sharkey double had provided some breathing space by the interval. Mike Hellawell scored his first goal for the Rokerites late on to send most of the 35,000 supporters heading home on a high.

Up in Scotland, Jock Stein's last act as Hibernian manager was to knock holders Rangers out of the Scottish Cup in the quarter-final at Easter Road, leaving the Leith men still with high hopes of a Double. Stein's former side Dunfermline Athletic were in the same position, whilst the other two clubs who could realistically have achieved the feat, Hearts and Kilmarnock, both bowed out of the cup the same day, the latter 3-2 at Parkhead to the Celtic side which Jock would take charge of 48 hours later.

March would continue to be a positive month for Sunderland, as they repeated their 3-2 victory over West Ham United of a few weeks earlier, this time at the Boleyn Ground, to record a second away win in the Division the following Saturday. The Hammers were one goal up through Brian Dear when they lost centre-half Eddie Bovington to injury, in those pre-substitution times. Martin Harvey and George Herd would give the full-strength Wearsiders the lead before the break, with Herd scoring what proved to be the winner on the hour mark after Dear had completed his own brace one minute earlier.

An impressive London double was secured seven days later, Saturday, 20 March 1965, as Bill Nicholson brought his expensively assembled Tottenham Hotspur side to Roker Park, including former Dundee stars Bill Brown and Alan Gilzean. Ex-Clyde striker George Herd continued his recent scoring form with the opener on the half-hour, before England's prince of poachers, Jimmy Greaves, levelled things early in the second half. With just four minutes remaining, Nick Sharkey notched the all-important winner. Six victories in their last eight League games was anything but relegation form, Sunderland now sitting in 16th position in the table, having bypassed Leicester City, West Bromwich Albion and Fulham, to remain well-clear of basement-dwellers Birmingham City, Aston Villa and Wolverhampton Wanderers. The teams at Roker Park that afternoon lined up as follows.

SUNDERLAND:

Sandy McLaughlan; John Parke & Len Ashurst; Martin Harvey, Charlie Hurley & Jimmy McNab; Mike Hellawell, George Herd, Harry Hood, Nick Sharkey & George Mulhall.

TOTTENHAM HOTSPUR:

Bill Brown; Cyril Knowles & Ron Henry; Alan Mullery, Laurie Brown & Eddie Clayton; Jimmy Robertson, Jimmy Greaves, Alan Gilzean, Cliff Jones & Terry Dyson.

The good run seemed set to continue three nights later, as Sunderland led 2-0 after 15 minutes of the rescheduled clash with Blackburn Rovers at Ewood Park, thanks to early strikes from Len Ashurst and Nick Sharkey. The hosts would then fight back to score three of their own to clinch an unlikely two points in front of just 10,000 spectators. The Wearsiders returned to East Lancashire to face Burnley that weekend, the point secured from a goalless draw capping off what had been a productive month.

Harry opened April with Sunderland's first goal in a 3-1 win over Sheffield United at Roker Park, a Dickie Rooks penalty and late strike from George Mulhall making the game safe, before a last-minute consolation effort from Mick Jones ended the scoring. On the same day, Dunfermline Athletic beat Hibernian at Tynecastle to reach the Scottish Cup final, whilst two goals from Motherwell's Joe McBride at Hampden meant they and Celtic would replay for the right to meet the Pars in the final.

The following Saturday saw Harry play his first match at Goodison Park, where elder brother Jackie had plied his trade with Everton several years earlier. Nick Sharkey's first-half opener would earn the visitors a creditable 1-1 draw, on an afternoon where most of the attention was focused on the England v Scotland clash at Wembley. That match also ended all-square, Scotland coming back from two goals down to earn a draw, albeit the hosts played most of the second half with only nine fit men.

The Good Friday home fixture with second-bottom Wolverhampton Wanderers appeared to be going to plan when Mike Hellawell's second-minute strike saw Sunderland lead at the break. However, the Black Country men would fight back to claim two desperately needed points in their battle for survival and dampen the hopes of the 43,000 Rokerites. There were 10,000 fewer of them inside the stadium 24 hours later, Saturday, 17 April 1965, for the visit of fellow strugglers Birmingham City, who propped up the table. Those who did attend were rewarded with another Harry Hood goal, as Sunderland edged a three-goal thriller with the Blues, George Mulhall sealing the win with 15 minutes remaining.

Harry had a new strike partner for the midweek trip to Molyneux as Gary Moore, a local lad capped by England as a schoolboy international, made his Sunderland debut. It would be a night to forget for both youngsters as Wolves – who had appointed former Scotland manager Andy Beattie in a caretaker capacity to succeed legendary, long-serving boss Stan Cullis in November 1964, with the Black Country club rooted to the bottom of the table – continued their late but ultimately unsuccessful push to remain in the English top-flight with a 3-0 victory, thanks to a Bobby Woodruff hat-trick. Despite their back-to-back successes over Sunderland, Wolves would take the dreaded drop with Birmingham City.

Whilst Gary Moore retained his place, Harry would be missing from the much-changed Sunderland team which lost 3-1 to Stoke City at the Victoria Ground four days later, another local debutant Mel Slack netting a second-half consolation after the visitors had trailed by three goals at the break. Some 200 miles to the north, Celtic's seven-year-plus trophy drought was coming to an end at Hampden under Jock Stein, thanks to a Bertie Auld double and Cesar's dramatic late winner in the Scottish Cup final against his old club, Dunfermline Athletic. Stein's successor at East End Park, Willie Cunningham, had dropped a bombshell before the kick-off by dropping top scorer, Alex Ferguson. Strange to think that had those contract talks ended in a different way some five months earlier, Harry may have been part of that historic Hoops line-up. His day would come, as would that of Tommy Callaghan, who had lined up with elder brother Willie for the Pars. Willie Waddell's Kilmarnock were also in a celebratory mood, after a thrilling 2-0 victory at Tynecastle over hosts Hearts - the League leaders at 3pm that afternoon - had given the Ayrshire club their first-ever Scottish title by a mathematical fraction on goal average. Curiously, the English champions would be decided on the same basis, as Manchester United edged out Leeds United to claim a first title since the tragic Busby Babes' last hurrah in 1956/57.

The last match of the 1964/65 English Football League season saw a restored Harry grab Sunderland's final goal of the campaign, his strike just after the hour sealing a 3-0 win over Sheffield Wednesday at Roker Park on Wednesday, 28 April 1965, after Len Ashurst and George Mulhall had established a two-goal lead. It had been a productive start for the new man on Wearside, his eight goals from 24 League appearances giving him a decent return of 1:3, in addition to a goal in his only FA Cup-tie to date. Only Nick Sharkey and George Mulhall would beat Harry's total – with both men enjoying the benefit of a full season - as Sunderland finished a respectable 15th in their first season back in the 22-club Division.

It had been a new experience for Harry's brother George and his closest friend, Ian Dalgleish, who had followed him throughout his career at Clyde and now continued that by travelling south of the border to support him. Ian recalls that season well.

"George and I travelled to watch Harry play football every week. Home and away. I always thought of it as an outlet for George, if that makes sense. Next best thing to playing. And he was the only one I knew with a car, so he did all the driving, taking us both down to Roker. Harry had moved down to Sunderland in late 1964, and they had put him in a club house. About two weeks after he signed for them, he turns up at my door in this big red-and-white Vauxhall Velux, a club car. We didn't even know he had taken a driving lesson. Turns out that Sunderland had put him through a crash course."

Chapter 10

Weary on Wearside

The chain of events which would shape the next stage of Harry's career on Wearside was triggered on the Clyde coast on the evening of Wednesday, 12 May 1965. A series of meetings between the SFA office-bearers earlier that afternoon ended with a statement announcing the resignation of Scotland national team manager Ian McColl with immediate effect, with the former Rangers skipper quickly countering that by claiming he had been sacked. McColl had received the news whilst working with the players at their training camp at Inverclyde, Largs. Jock Stein had been the Hibernian manager just two months earlier, and now found himself carrying the hopes of not just the massive Celtic support, but those of every Scottish football fan, albeit he was clear that the international appointment would cover just two games, the World Cup qualifiers in Poland and Finland falling later that month.

Nine days later, Friday, 21 May 1965, Ian McColl was announced as the successor to George Hardwick as the manager of Sunderland, with reports immediately linking him with a move to sign Jim Baxter, the Scottish international having so far refused to sign a new contract with Rangers. That deal did go through the following Tuesday, chairman Syd Collings travelling through to Edinburgh to make Baxter the latest member of the Scots colony at Roker Park, in a deal believed to have cost around £72,000.

As Harry watched the drama unfold from the sidelines, he would have another match on his mind, the biggest and happiest of his life, as he married his childhood sweetheart, Kathleen McGinley. The new Mrs Hood picks up the story.

"Harry asked me to marry him when he was asked to sign for Sunderland – on the telephone!! We were married in Christ the King RC Church in King's Park, on Tuesday, 8 June 1965, during the close-season, and the reception was in the King's Park Hotel. Harry actually crashed his car two days before the wedding, and so we set off on our honeymoon with the priest, a Father Seamus O'Kane, who had befriended Harry in Sunderland and had come to Glasgow to perform the marriage ceremony. He was lending us his car to drive to Newquay, where we had our honeymoon."

Whilst he would be in a good place in his personal life, Harry's second season as a Sunderland player would be a huge disappointment, effectively over almost before it had begun, thanks to a combination of injury and the aforementioned new manager, Ian McColl. The football fates would decree that the first test for McColl and his new signing Jim Baxter would be the visit of Harry's boyhood team, Celtic - under Jock Stein, ironically the man who had replaced McColl as Scotland boss - to Wearside on Saturday, 7 August 1965, a game attended by my dad and my elder brother, Robert. We still have the tiny match programme, with the two teams displayed in the centrefold. Despite George Herd being listed as Sunderland's number eight, the former Clyde and Scotland star had injured his ankle in training and would miss out, with Hood and Baxter occupying the inside-forward positions.

The following teams lined up at Roker Park that afternoon before 37,000 spectators.

SUNDERLAND:

Sandy McLaughlan; John Parke & Len Ashurst; Martin Harvey, Charlie Hurley & Jimmy McNab; Mike Hellawell, Harry Hood, Nick Sharkey, Jim Baxter & George Mulhall.

CELTIC:

John Fallon; Ian Young & Tommy Gemmell; Bobby Murdoch, Billy McNeill & John Clark; Jimmy Johnstone, Charlie Gallagher, Joe McBride, Bobby Lennox & John Hughes. Substitute: Bertie Auld

Celtic fielded Joe McBride, their £22,000 close-season signing from Motherwell, but there was no sign of the two trialists who had arrived from Brazil, inside-forwards Marco Di Sousa and Ayrton Inacio. The duo had remained behind to train at Celtic Park following the long journey from South America.

Around 10,000 Hoops fans had made the shorter trip to Wearside and they would thoroughly enjoy their afternoon as a rampant Celtic side – clad in a new all-green kit to begin a first full season under Stein - roared to a 5-0 victory. Bobby Lennox opened the scoring in 15 minutes, before Bobby Murdoch doubled the lead with a wonderful 20-yard shot eight minutes from the break. Stein's men then blew the Roker men away with a devastating start to the second half, new Bhoy Joe McBride making it 3-0 before John Hughes unleashed a ferocious long-distance drive which flashed past Sandy McLaughlan in the home goal, both goals coming before two minutes had elapsed. With the visiting support taunting Baxter with that "Easy! Easy!" chant which they had been on the receiving end of so many times in the early 1960's, the onslaught continued with the only surprise being the solitary addition to the scoresheet five minutes from time. The injured Joe McBride had been replaced by Bertie Auld, forcing Hughes to adopt the central striking position which had been his domain since joining the first team five years earlier until the arrival of Stein. Big Yogi would duly get his double with another superb solo effort before Lennox was only denied a sixth by the width of the post. It had been an exhilarating display of attacking power by Celtic as the momentum and optimism generated by Jock Stein's appointment a few months earlier was cranked up yet another level.

This was a real 'rite of passage' afternoon for my brother, Robert Corr. Over half a century later, he still recalls the events vividly.

"There are many memorable dates in my Celtic calendar over the years. Many 'firsts' that fill my memory, whether they are first trophies, first game, first visit to each away venue and so on. However, one date is forever etched there and that is my first trip abroad to watch my beloved team. It wasn't glamorous - it wasn't the San Siro, the Camp Nou or the Bernabeu or anything like that. My first trip 'abroad' was all the way to Sunderland for a pre-season friendly in August 1965: I was just 10 years old and I thought I was a world traveller."

"I made the trip south that Saturday morning with my Dad, Matt Corr, on board the Springburn CSC bus, but I had been waiting for this moment ever since he had first told me we were going. I remember when we arrived, we parked up on the beach promenade alongside many other Celtic buses - it looked like Janefield Street had come to the seaside."

"When we went into the ground, I found myself behind the goal and, as always, perched up on a stanchion with my dad behind me to keep me safe. The terracing was packed with Celtic fans and, while we waited for the kick-off, our Celtic songs rang out across Roker Park. One of the first things I noticed was the front of the main stand, which (apart from being painted in red and not blue) looked exactly like the photographs I had seen from Ibrox. The Ibrox connection was even more real that afternoon as ex-Ranger Jim Baxter would be making his debut. What we didn't know however, was that Sunderland's other inside-forward - a certain Harry Hood - would go on to become a Celtic legend."

"The game passed by very quickly, mainly because we were unstoppable and completely outplayed our hosts, winning comfortably by five goals to nil. Baxter was anonymous and Celtic were sensational. The reports of the game all refer to the fact that it could easily have been so many more. Goals from Lennox, Murdoch, McBride and Hughes (2) meant that our journey back to Glasgow was accompanied by more singing and much discussion. Just how good could this new Celtic team be? I'm sure none of us at Roker Park that day even dared dream that in less than two years, our beloved Celtic would be crowned Champions of Europe."

David Potter's recollections of that day include some rather less-savoury memories.

"There was some awful hooliganism, not so much inside Roker Park as in the surrounding areas, with some Newcastle fans unashamedly joining in on the Celtic side. At the game itself, someone threw an orange at Jim Baxter!"

It had obviously not been Baxter's day. Sunderland club historian Rob Mason was kind enough to share an extract from a recent interview he conducted with John Hughes, who scored twice for Celtic that afternoon and later, briefly, joined his younger brother Billy on the books at Roker Park.

Rob: *"You played at Sunderland for Celtic in a 5-0 win in 1966 and scored twice. Can you remember that at all?"*

John: *"I remember someone came into the dressing-room beforehand to say that Jim Baxter had told the Sunderland boys that we would give them a hard game. He was right."*

Whilst the Hoops attackers were thriving, sadly that 90 minutes against his favourite team would be it for Harry in terms of first-team action for several months, following a double hernia injury sustained during weight training shortly afterwards. Whilst he and Roker Park physio Johnny Watters would be spending most of their days together, manager Ian McColl would go back into the Scottish market to sign Neil Martin from Hibernian for £45,000 in October 1965, a serious rival for his position perhaps not the 21st birthday gift Harry would have chosen.

The previous month, there had been personal sadness for Harry when his last remaining grandparent, maternal grandfather Walter John Scott, passed away in Stranraer. Born to George and Charlotte Scott in the Scottish Highland town of Buckie on Thursday, 5 January 1865 – three months before the assassination of US President Abraham Lincoln - the retired master shoemaker was nearing his 101st birthday when he succumbed to a combination of left ventricular failure and coronary atherosclerosis on Wednesday, 1 September 1965. Walter had survived his wife Ann by 36 years and at least three of their eight children, Alexander who died back in April 1928, Walter junior in July 1959 and Reynold just a few months earlier in June 1965. Walter's death was recorded by another son, George, at that time 74 years young himself. There can't be too many men of that age who notify the authorities of the death of their centenarian father.

Having played against Celtic in the opening fixture of the season back in August, curiously Harry's only other appearance in the Sunderland first team in that entire campaign would come in a friendly with Dukla Prague on Tuesday, 7 December 1965. The touring Czechs were en route to a domestic title win which would eventually see them meet Stein's Lisbon Lions in the semi-final of the European Cup the following season. Dukla Prague – 1962 Ballon D'Or winner Josef Masopust et al - would comfortably win that December Roker Park encounter by 3-0, before just 7,000 spectators.

The teams had lined up as follows.

SUNDERLAND:

Sandy McLaughlan; John Parke & Len Ashurst; Martin Harvey, Charlie Hurley & Dave Elliott; Mike Hellawell, Harry Hood, Gary Moore, Jim Baxter & George Mulhall. Substitute: Nick Sharkey

DUKLA PRAGUE:

Ivo Viktor; Milan Dvorak & Ladislav Novak; Ivan Novak, Svatopluck Pluskal & Jan Gelata; Jan Brumovsky, Frantisek Knebort, Josef Masopust, Josef Moravek

& Stanislav Strunc. Substitutes: Miroslav Cmarada, Jiri Cadek, Josef Nedorost & Miroslav Rodr.

Neil Martin and George Herd would return to claim the inside-forward positions for that weekend's visit of champions Manchester United, whilst Harry - the man who had scored the winning goal against the Old Trafford superstars at Roker Park less than 10 months earlier - would go back to cooling his heels on the sidelines. A decent start in the League for McColl's men had them sitting in the top six of the First Division in mid-September. Form dipped badly as 1965 rolled into 1966, culminating in three successive home defeats from Burnley, Manchester United and West Bromwich Albion where 12 goals were conceded and just three scored, albeit that was followed by a 2-0 win over promoted local rivals Newcastle United in front of 55,000 at Roker Park, with George Herd and John O'Hare on target, then an impressive 1-1 draw in the return with Matt Busby's men in Manchester.

Harry's former Holyrood cup final replacement, Jim McCalliog – now a Celtic Park regular - would score for his new side Sheffield Wednesday in a 2-0 win at Roker Park at the end of January, before a dreadful run of five consecutive defeats, which culminated in a 2-0 loss to Newcastle United at St James' Park in early March, saw the Black Cats flirting with relegation in the lead-up to the crucial Easter programme. Sunderland's home form would then come to the rescue, with only three points dropped in seven games, which included victories over Tottenham Hotspur, Chelsea and FA Cup-winners Everton, plus a draw with new champions Liverpool. Even with that final home flourish, they finished the 1965/66 campaign just three points ahead of relegated Northampton Town in 19th place.

If it had been a disappointing season for the club, then it was a complete non-event for Harry Hood. His wife Kathleen remembers that period well, with mixed emotions.

"Our first home together was a club house at 10 Harewood Gardens in Barnes Park, and Lisa - our first child - was born in the nearby Sunderland Royal Hospital's maternity unit. The club had quite a few houses in the area. Jim Baxter was a neighbour and the captain at that time - Charlie Hurley - was next door. We had happy memories and made really good friends with many north-easterners. Lovely people. But Harry had a disappointing career with Sunderland. The manager who signed him was sacked and replaced by Ian McCall, who did not appreciate Harry's talent. Harry was a slightly-built player, but McColl insisted he took up weight training to increase his bulk and Harry ended up with a double hernia and was out of the game for a full season."

One positive aspect of Harry's lack of football action that campaign was the surprise appearance of the Hoods at the wedding of his childhood friend Ian Dalgleish and new bride Betty at Colston Wellpark Church on the Glasgow/Bishopbriggs boundary on Saturday, 23 April 1966. Ian had met Elizabeth Steel at her sister's wedding reception some three years earlier, and the couples had become close friends. With the first-team squad down south to face Arsenal then Northampton town in a 48-hour double-header, no requirement for Harry to play for any of the club's other sides that weekend and passing up the opportunity to see Celtic play Rangers in the Scottish Cup final at Hampden, Harry and Kathleen turned up unannounced to surprise their friends at the church. They then invited the new Mr and Mrs Dalgleish to return with them and spend their honeymoon in Sunderland!

Despite the club taking up its option to extend Harry's contract by a further two years from July 1966, his third and final season on Wearside would see him make just eight competitive starts, with one further appearance from the bench. Just as they had done the previous summer, Sunderland opened the 1966/67 campaign with a home friendly against Scottish opposition, in this case Kilmarnock, now under the leadership of former Celt Malky MacDonald, Willie Waddell having moved into sports journalism after leading his team to the title. Harry came off the bench at the interval to replace George Herd, as the sides shared six second-half goals at Roker Park on Saturday, 6 August 1966. He then started in the goalless draw with the same side at Rugby Park four nights later, listed beside Neil Martin for the first time. The second half in east Ayrshire saw the introduction of 17-year-old winger Billy Hughes in a Sunderland shirt. The younger brother of Celtic's John, he would go on to enjoy a wonderful decade on Wearside, a key man in Sunderland's epic run to Wembley in the spring of 1973, which saw the FA Cup return to Roker Park after their shock 1-0 victory over holders and odds-on favourites Leeds United.

Sunderland's pre-season preparations were then completed with a trip to face Hull City at Boothferry Park on Saturday, 13 August 1966. Harry scored the only goal of the game in the 17th minute, the Second Division hosts missing a wonderful opportunity to equalise when Ken Houghton struck the underside of the crossbar with his penalty kick just seconds later.

Those appearances saw Harry chosen in the side which began the First Division campaign with a 3-1 defeat by Arsenal at Roker Park on Saturday, 20 August 1966. The Gunners had sprung a surprise by promoting physio Bertie Mee to replace England legend Billy Wright as their new manager. Mee would bring Dave Sexton and Don Howe on board as he took the first steps on his illustrious Arsenal career by winning on Wearside, thanks to a double from Alan Skirton and a third from George Armstrong. Jim Baxter had levelled Skirton's opener as the following teams faced off before 38,000 spectators.

SUNDERLAND:

Jim Montgomery; John Parke & Len Ashurst; Martin Harvey, Charlie Hurley & Jimmy McNab; Mike Hellawell, Harry Hood, Neil Martin, Jim Baxter & Allan Gauden. Substitute: George Herd

ARSENAL:

Jim Furnell; David Court & Peter Storey; Frank McLintock, Ian Ure & Terry Neill; Alan Skirton, Tommy Baldwin, John Radford, Jon Sammels & George Armstrong. Substitute: Jimmy McGill

Four nights later, Harry retained his place and George Herd featured, rather unusually, at right-half as Sunderland put their first points on the board with a 2-0 victory over newly promoted Southampton - beginning their first-ever top-flight campaign - thanks to goals from wingers Allan Gauden and the restored George Mulhall either side of the interval.

I took the opportunity to ask George Herd about that positional switch when we spoke to discuss Harry's time on Wearside and his recollections of that period and some of the characters involved. Now in his mid-80s, George married a local girl and still stays on Wearside.

"Yes, I played in midfield that night. I was happy enough to play anywhere, to be honest, except centre-forward. The way the game was played back then you didn't see as much of the ball playing through the middle as on the wing or inside-forward. I remember Harry coming in. He was a young lad, and I was getting on a bit! We had a raft of Scots in the team back then, and that was largely down to a man called Charlie Ferguson, who was Sunderland's Scottish scout. Half the team was Scottish."

"Alan Brown was the manager who brought me down to Wearside from Clyde in 1961. Sunderland had come in for me before, but Clyde wouldn't sell, and then they needed the money, so off I went. Alan was a lovely man and, for me, the best coach ever. His interest was in developing kids. We used to do this thing at training called 'shadow play', with Alan repeating his mantra, "See the ball, see the man." Simple stuff but really effective. He made sure you carried out the basics until they had become second nature. He was also a disciplinarian. I was a smoker. He tried to get me to stop but I told him I enjoyed a smoke. I never did it in front of him, though. Alan tried to take me with him to Sheffield Wednesday, but I was happy at Sunderland so stayed there. A media friend of mine asked him later which player he missed most from his Roker Park days, and he told him "George Herd." I was made up with that."

"The managers who followed him were very different. George Hardwick had been a great player with Middlesbrough and England but I'm not sure he was really cut out to be a manager. He had a different style. He made me captain of Sunderland when Charlie Hurley was out, which I really appreciated. Ian McColl? I had played against him when he was at Rangers and with him once for Scotland. I did some coaching under him for a while, but we didn't really hit it off. We saw things differently. I remember driving down to Halifax with him one night to watch a lad called Bruce Stuckey, a winger from Torquay. When we compared notes later, we had very different views. I ended up coaching the youths and left him to it. My career at Sunderland ended under him so it's not a time I remember with great fondness. He also seemed to take a dislike to certain players for whatever reason."

"Getting back to Harry, as I say, I was quite a bit older, so we didn't really socialise away from football, as such. He was a good player. Trained hard. Everything you would want as a pro. But more than that, Harry was a quality man. I remember

him and his wife and their wee girl. I think they moved into Martin Harvey's house in Barnes Park."

Saturday, 27 August 1966 saw the Black Cats travel to face the other promoted side, last season's Second Division champions Manchester City. Joe Mercer's team featured an old Sunderland favourite, Johnny Crossan, the 27-year-old Derry man bought from Wearside in January 1965 for £40,000 to help City's promising but inexperienced youngsters regain the club's place amongst the elite, an objective duly achieved under their new captain. The sides lined up at Maine Road as follows.

MANCHESTER CITY:

Harry Dowd; Tony Book & Bobby Kennedy; Glyn Pardoe, George Heslop & Alan Oakes; Mike Summerbee, Colin Bell, Jimmy Murray, Johnny Crossan & Neil Young. Substitute: Dave Connor

SUNDERLAND:

Jim Montgomery; Cec Irwin & Len Ashurst; John Parke, Charlie Hurley & Jimmy McNab; George Herd, Harry Hood, Neil Martin, Jim Baxter & Allan Gauden Substitute: Martin Harvey

Like Bertie Mee, Joe Mercer was developing a young side which would soon be competing for and winning trophies against the English elite, indeed City would be champions the following season under new skipper Tony Book. The only goal of this match was scored by Alan Oakes after an hour's play. The second successive midweek match with Southampton which followed saw another defeat for Ian McColl's men, despite George Mulhall's opener at The Dell early in the second half. Terry Paine's spot kick just after the hour brought the hosts level, before late strikes from John Sydenham and Ron Davies sent the Black Cats on the long drive north to Wearside empty-handed.

The opening Saturday in September saw Harry open his League account for the 1966/67 season in the fifth match, a 4-0 win over Blackpool at Roker Park. The Seasiders had sold their World Cup-winning midfielder Alan Ball to Everton the previous month for a record transfer fee of £112,000, however they did feature another future England captain, Emlyn Hughes, at left-back. Harry's strike partner Neil Martin gave Sunderland an early two-goal lead before Harry made it 3-0 on the hour. Martin then completed his hat-trick with 10 minutes remaining to round off a resounding 4-0 win for Sunderland. Harry's goal at Roker Park that afternoon of Saturday, 3 September 1966, would prove to be his 10th and final strike for the club.

He would feature in both matches of the away double-header which followed, a 2-1 midweek loss to Leeds United at Elland Road then a 1-1 draw with Chelsea at Stamford Bridge, where the changing times were illustrated by the replacement of Sunderland's legendary Irish captain Charlie Hurley by debutant Colin Todd – another future England star – late in the second half.

Harry would play in his first English League Cup-tie, a 1-1 draw against Sheffield United in the second round at Roker Park on Wednesday, 14 September 1966, but would then be replaced by John O'Hare for the League visit of Leicester City three days later. Sunderland lost Jim Baxter to injury after just 10 minutes then lost the match by the odd goal in five, after goals from Scottish duo Neil Martin and O'Hare had seen them fight back from two goals down. That result, a fifth defeat in eight League games, saw the Black Cats drop to 18th place in the table.

The mood on Wearside would not be helped by a League Cup exit in Sheffield three nights later. Harry was named as a substitute for the first and only time in his Sunderland career for the replayed second-round tie with Sheffield United at Bramall Lane, on Tuesday, 20 September 1966. He would replace wing-half Jimmy McNab with three minutes remaining and the game still goalless, and two minutes into extra-time, Blades winger Alan Woodward scored what would prove to be the winning goal. That brief appearance from the bench would prove to be Harry Hood's last action as a Sunderland player.

Negotiations would soon commence quietly behind the scenes with a view to bringing Harry back to Clyde and end his two-year stay on Wearside. The Shawfield club had once again been victims of their own success in the interim, as they continued to hold their own in the top-flight. As opposed to losing their star players such as George Herd and Harry to wealthier suitors, in March 1966 they would see manager John Prentice headhunted to succeed Jock Stein as manager of Scotland. Clyde responded to this latest compliment/setback by promoting club captain and coach Davie White to the manager's office. White had played at right-half as Harry made his senior debut for Clyde at Ibrox some four years earlier. On Wednesday, 5 October 1966, two days after Harry's 22nd birthday, a transfer fee of £11,000 – around half that which had taken him south in November 1964 - was agreed between his current and former clubs. Harry then made the journey by car to Shawfield on the Friday afternoon for talks with Clyde officials which would make him a Bully Wee player for the second time.

In a strange quirk of timing, as Harry prepared for his second Clyde debut the following morning, Scottish football supporters were rocked by the news that national team manager John Prentice - his old boss - had been sacked. David Potter recalls the day clearly.

"Celtic beat Hibs 5-3 that afternoon at Easter Road in a brilliant game, and I remember being terrified that Jock Stein would take the Scotland job on a permanent basis."

Relations between Prentice and the SFA had been tense following his decision to speak with Canadian outfit Vancouver about the manager's role there. His tenure in the international hotseat had been brief and largely unsuccessful, his four games in charge in the spring of 1966 bringing three home defeats – to England, Netherlands and Portugal – followed by a draw with World Cup-holders Brazil at Hampden. In the final match, former Brunswick Boy Stevie Chalmers had opened the scoring in the first minute and was later rewarded with the great Pele's jersey at full-time, whilst another, John McHugh, was an unused reserve. Harry's old colleague from youth football was one of two Clyde players brought into the international fold by their old club manager John Prentice for the three friendly games, former Third Lanark midfielder Alex Bryce being the other, albeit he would sign for Dundee before the clashes with Portugal and Brazil took place.

Back at Shawfield, whilst clearly placing the responsibility for his lack of appearances at Sunderland beyond the first season there firmly at the door of the new manager, Ian McColl, another Prentice old boy Harry Hood would remain philosophical about his time at Roker Park.

"I wasn't seeing eye to eye with Ian McColl and I felt he never gave the likes of myself or John O'Hare the run we deserved. Although I felt I was playing well enough to be a regular member of the first team at Roker Park, the manager obviously didn't, so I returned to Clyde. I do feel, however, that my spell in England has stood me in good stead. My experience has been widened, but not only that. Despite some other opinions, I didn't consider I was a failure down south and believed I was a better player when Clyde bought me back for £11,000."

He was correct.

For Harry Hood, the best was definitely still to come.

Chapter 11

A season of seasons for Clyde and a Scotland call-up for Harry

New Clyde manager Davie White began his first full season in charge of the club he had served with such distinction as a player for over a decade with a tough League Cup challenge, the Shawfield side drawn in a section which included Jock Stein's champions Celtic, Hearts and St Mirren. The group would pretty much go with the form displayed in the previous League campaign, Clyde's tally of four points from six games coming from 1-0 wins in the two clashes with a Paisley outfit who had narrowly avoided the drop to the Second Division a few months earlier. The opening fixture with Saints at Shawfield, played on Saturday, 13 August 1966, saw a little bit of Scottish football history created when teenage midfielder Archie Gemmill became the first 'tactical substitute' to be utilised following the recent rule change, which allowed injured players to be replaced. Gemmill would carve his name into Scottish football folklore for a very different reason 12 years later, with THAT goal in Argentina. Speaking of great Scots, Willie Wallace was the main man in the matches with Hearts, the future Lisbon Lion scoring four goals in the first half at Tynecastle as the Gorgie men edged out the Bully Wee by the odd goal in seven, then adding the third in their 3-1 win at Shawfield two weeks later.

The two meetings with Celtic would also end in defeat. Joe McBride helped himself to a hat-trick in the 6-0 rout of Clyde at Celtic Park on Wednesday, 17 August 1966, with a Bobby Lennox double and a late strike from Stevie Chalmers completing the scoring. McBride then added a double in the 3-1 victory at Shawfield which sealed Celtic's qualification a fortnight later. The former Motherwell striker had started the season on fire and would continue to run riot until Christmas in what would ultimately be his most bittersweet of campaigns.

Joe would make it six goals in three matches against Clyde by scoring Celtic's second as the champions opened the defence of their League title with a 3-0 win at Shawfield on Saturday, 10 September 1966. The hosts had taken the field in their 'Sunderland' striped change kit with the players all wearing squad numbers rather than the traditional 1-11, albeit they would emerge after the break having reverted to protocol. Consolation from three defeats would come in the share of gate receipts from the near 80,000 customers who had paid to watch the east end trilogy. That welcome windfall prompted Clyde chairman Willie Dunn to declare after the match that "at least two new players would be signed shortly." So, I guess that Celtic supporters, indirectly at least, had an involvement in the return of Harry Hood to Shawfield.

That was still a few weeks away. In the interim, Clyde would put their first League points on the board seven days later, Joe Gilroy's header after just 30 seconds at Firhill enough to beat Partick Thistle. A 3-1 home defeat to Kilmarnock followed as an attack of gastric flu claimed several Shawfield first team stars, including Eddie Mulheron, Davie Souter and John McHugh. All three would recover for the trip to Pittodrie which opened October, a late Ian Stewart penalty rescuing a point for Clyde in a 1-1 draw. After four matches, only Celtic and Hibernian could claim the maximum eight points, with Airdrieonians tucked in one point behind the leaders, who were scheduled to meet at Easter Road the following Saturday. By that time, Harry Hood would be back at his first senior club, wearing the white, black and red of Clyde.

Harry's second Clyde debut took place at Shawfield on Saturday, 8 October 1966, the new old boy ditching superstition by taking the field sporting the number 13 shirt vacated by Sammy Reid in a 3-1 win over Motherwell in front of 4,000 spectators. More on Sammy to follow. Despite an impressive showing - Harry setting up the second Clyde goal for Davie Souter when visiting keeper Peter McCloy could only parry his fierce drive - he would not manage to get on the scoresheet on that occasion against a Motherwell side which included his future friend and teammate John 'Dixie' Deans up front.

The teams had lined up as follows:

CLYDE:

John Wright; Harry Glasgow & Eddie Mulheron; John McHugh, Jim Fraser & Stan Anderson; Davie Souter, Ian Stewart, Joe Gilroy, Harry Hood & Sam Hastings. Substitute: Dick Staite

MOTHERWELL:

Peter McCloy; Matt Thomson & Bobby McCallum; Willie McCallum, John Martis & George Murray; Willie Hunter, Bobby Campbell, John Deans, Benny Cairney & Gus Moffat. Substitute: Andy Weir

Harry would also draw a blank in the midweek defeat at Firhill in the semi-final of the Glasgow Cup, Clyde thus missing out on the opportunity to face Celtic in the final, but he was back on the goal trail the following weekend as the Bully Wee lost 4-3 to Dundee United at Tannadice. The hosts, with excitement growing ahead of their double-header with Inter-Cities Fairs Cup-holders Barcelona, had actually led 4-0 by the half-hour mark, after a burst of three goals in as many minutes, before Harry kick-started the comeback with a close-range finish. As an aside, Dundee United's fourth goal that day was scored by Ian Mitchell, who had been part of the Falkirk High School team which lost to Holyrood in the Scottish Secondary Shield final at

Hampden back in 1962, making his United debut later that year whilst still just 16 years of age. He would taste glory this season by scoring the Hogmanay winner at Tannadice which cost Jock Stein's Celtic their unbeaten record, a few weeks after his strike against Barcelona which helped knock the Catalans out of European football. Ian would make over 300 appearances on Tayside but would sadly pass away in April 1996, one month before his 50th birthday.

Both Harry Hood and goalkeeper John Wright were flu victims as the next League match saw Clyde score four times without reply in the first half against Falkirk at Shawfield, on Saturday, 22 October 1966. There would be no repeat feast after the interval as the Bully Wee's excellent 4-0 win saw them join a cluster of clubs on seven points from seven games in mid-table. Next up was a second visit of the season to Tynecastle, Harry combining well with Ian Stewart whose goal just before the interval was enough to secure the two points. Home striker Willie Wallace, who had scored a quadruple in the previous clash between the clubs in Gorgie, had a rather less profitable afternoon this time around, the Kirkintilloch-born forward dismissed near the end for a challenge on Clyde keeper Tommy McCulloch. Meantime, 40 miles to the west, Jock Stein's Celtic retained the League Cup with a Bobby Lennox goal at Hampden, the Hoops defeating Rangers in the third successive meeting of the clubs in that particular fixture. Within 10 days the Saltcoats Bhoy would add another hat-trick to that he had scored at Ibrox in August as Celtic recorded a third 4-0 victory in that season's Glasgow Cup to beat Partick Thistle in the final at Parkhead. Two of the five trophies up for grabs in 1966/67 now resided in the club's trophy room. This could be a season to remember for Jock Stein's exciting team.

November opened with a baby boom at Shawfield, the Rutherglen air scented by cigar smoke as Dick Staite, Graham Macfarlane then Davie Souter all celebrated fatherhood in the traditional fashion. There was also a managerial decision which would have later consequences for the club, as Aberdeen boss Eddie Turnbull rejected the offer of the number two job at Ibrox under Scot Symon. On the field, Guy Fawkes' Day proved a damp squid as the Bully Wee suffered a 4-0 defeat at the hands of Dunfermline Athletic at East End Park. The afternoon also produced a dreadful ending for the younger of the Callaghan brothers on display for the Pars, 20-year-old wing-half Tommy stretchered off with a suspected broken leg 20 minutes from time following a collision with Graham Macfarlane. Alex Ferguson then netted the fourth and final goal for the hosts.

Clyde bounced back in sensational style seven days later, Saturday, 12 November 1966, with a 5-1 win over previously high-flying Hibernian at Shawfield. There was a return to Rutherglen for previous nemesis Alan McGraw, the former Morton hitman now wearing the green and white of the Hibs, his deflection from Jim O'Rourke's shot giving the visitors an early lead after Harry had twice gone close to opening the scoring. Joe Gilroy would quickly bring the Bully Wee level before Harry's flashing header from Graham Macfarlane's corner saw the hosts lead 2-1 at the break. The second half was the stuff of dreams for the Shawfield faithful, as their forwards tore Hibernian apart. Sam Hastings had struck the bar before Macfarlane's diving header extended the lead on 50 minutes, and the same man made it 4-1 midway through the half after Harry's shot had come back off a post. Hood then set up Ian Stewart to complete the route to send the home supporters in the 2,600-strong crowd home in a great mood. Harry's outstanding performance was picked up by the media, triggering calls for his selection in the Scotland Under 23's squad for the upcoming match with Wales at Wrexham.

Clyde continued in the winning groove by beating Airdrieonians thanks to a late Ian Stewart goal at Shawfield the following Saturday. The Diamonds had also been in high-scoring form the previous weekend, with a 7-0 victory over Stirling Albion but it was the Bully Wee who secured the two points which lifted them into fifth spot in the table. Leaders Celtic maintained their three-point advantage at the top after an incredible game at East End Park, Dunfermline. Three times, Jock Stein's men came back from two goals down to win 5-4, thanks to a last-minute penalty conversion from Joe McBride. The former Motherwell man had been one of six Celts involved in Scotland's 2-1 win over Ireland at Hampden in midweek, and his double in Fife had taken his tally for the season to 30 in all competitions with half the campaign still to play. Currently in the form of his life, the man born in Govan on the same day that Celtic won the Empire Exhibition Cup at nearby Ibrox in June 1938 now looked odds-on to beat both Jimmy McGrory's club record of 50 League goals in a season and the Scottish landmark of 52, set by Motherwell's Willie MacFadyen in 1932.

Harry was on target again as Clyde recorded a third consecutive League victory with a 3-1 win at Love Street against struggling St Mirren. The Paisley club had suffered rejection in midweek as former Shawfield boss John Prentice turned down the chance to become Saints manager due to "potential travel fatigue" and they would suffer again on the pitch as Graham Macfarlane gave the visitors an interval lead. Harry's moment of glory on the hour mark would come at the expense of his school team goalkeeper Denis Connaghan, a long range shot from one old Holyrood old boy beating another to make it 2-0. Connaghan would then feel harshly done by as he saved a late penalty from Sam Hastings only to see the kick retaken after encroachment. Harry Glasgow's second attempt only just escaped the keeper's grasp to end the scoring and maintain Clyde's position in the top five. Elsewhere, future colleagues of Harry's were in the news. John 'Dixie' Deans scored a four-minute hat-trick either side of the interval in Motherwell's 6-2 demolition of Dunfermline Athletic at Fir Park, whilst the Pars wing-half Tommy Callaghan was making excellent progress from his recently sustained broken leg.

December 1966 opened with the announcement of a 'round the world' tour for Scotland's footballers to take place at the season's end the following spring, with Israel, Iran, Malaysia, Hong Kong, New Zealand, Australia and Canada listed as the exotic destinations. The news was greeted with disdain in the media, with criticism of the level of opposition involved and benefit to be gained, whilst SFA Secretary Willie Allan was at pains to paint a different picture.

"We will be taking some of our bright young players who are expected to be of great value to Scotland in coming internationals. With them, we will have a nucleus of our established stars and at least one of the ideas will be to introduce new men to the international scene."

Whilst that news would no doubt provoke some excitement for one of those young prospects, Harry Hood, there was domestic disappointment for the player as Clyde's excellent winning sequence came to a halt at home to bottom-of-the-table Ayr United on the opening Saturday of the month. The hosts actually had Eddie Mulheron to thank for salvaging a point in the goalless draw, the defender twice kicking the ball off the line in the second half with Tommy McCulloch beaten. That result saw Dundee leapfrog Clyde into fifth place in the League table.

The two clubs would meet the following Saturday, 10 December 1966, at Dens Park, Clyde edging a seven-goal thriller to reclaim their spot after an incredible afternoon. The host squad included former Shawfield stars Jim McLean and Alex Bryce but there was no old pals act in evidence as Clyde raced to a 3-0 lead by the interval, Joe Gilroy and Sam Hastings with early counters before Harry rounded Dundee centre-half Jim Easton and fired past keeper John Arrol seconds before the break. Harry grabbed his own second goal with a low shot from a tight angle with 20 minutes remaining, after Dundee had fought back to 2-3, Clyde returning home with the points despite the hosts grabbing a third in the closing stages. Elsewhere, having watched Celtic's midweek victory over Nantes from the stand, Joe McBride again missed out with a knee injury in the eventful 4-2 win over his former club Motherwell at Celtic Park. Scotland's top scorer was replaced by midweek signing Willie Wallace from Hearts, the £30,000 player on the verge of emigrating to Canada before opting for Glasgow, dashing Gilroy's hopes of a widely-touted dream move to Parkhead. But it was two other strikers who grabbed the headlines, Stevie Chalmers with a hat-trick whilst John 'Dixie' Deans was sent off following a foul on future friend and teammate, Jimmy Johnstone.

Midweek would see the Clyde players swap their football strips for tuxedos, as the club held its annual dance in one of the function suites at Shawfield. That would provide an opportunity for trainer Bruce Hay to say his farewells, ahead of his move to, ironically enough, Dens Park. Hay would replace Bobby Seith there, the Dundee trainer having agreed to a switch to Ibrox.

There was a touch of deja-vu the following Saturday as Clyde once again headed to Tayside and built up a 3-0 lead, this time Bobby Brown's St Johnstone the victims as goals from Sam Hastings, Harry Hood and Ian Stewart effectively sealed the points within 17 minutes at Muirton Park. As at Dens Park the previous weekend, the hosts then pulled two goals back, before Ian Stewart relieved the late pressure with a last-minute strike. With 11 points gained from six League games, Clyde now replaced

Kilmarnock in fourth spot in the First Division table, with only Celtic, Rangers and Aberdeen above them. This progress prompted manager Davie White to review his previously set 'one point per game' target, as the Shawfield club started to dream about the possibility of European football the following autumn.

The snow which arrived in Glasgow ahead of a white Christmas put paid to the clash between Clyde and Rangers on Saturday, 24 December 1966. That meant the Bully Wee players had to wait until the home match with Stirling Albion on Hogmanay for their next taste of action. It would not quite be the end to the excellent first half of the campaign envisaged by anyone at Shawfield, as the struggling Binos inflicted a shock 1-0 defeat on the hosts to bring the long unbeaten run to an end. Dundee's point at Ibrox enabled them to replace Clyde in fourth spot in the table, albeit the Tayside outfit had played a game more. However, the biggest shock of the day involved their neighbours, Dundee United, who came from 2-1 down at Tannadice to become the first team to beat Jock Stein's Celtic in any competition that season, thanks to Ian Mitchell's late winner. Another prize scalp for Jerry Kerr's men to add to their home and away victories over Barcelona. Although it was not known at that time, there would be a greater concern for those whose heart lay at Parkhead. An injury sustained at training 24 hours earlier had ruled Joe McBride out of the Tannadice game. Sadly, Scotland's top goalscorer would not feature again in that incredible campaign.

The big freeze continued to decimate the holiday football fixtures with Clyde suffering more than most. Having lost their lucrative Christmas Eve clash with Rangers, they then saw the New Year's Day match at Celtic Park and the home derby with Partick Thistle two days later fall victim to the weather, before plans to reschedule their Parkhead visit for the evening of Wednesday, 4 January 1967 were also dashed. The sting in that particular winter's tale was that most of the clubs around Clyde did manage to play and accumulate points, Davie White's team finding themselves dropping to eighth position, having been fourth two weeks earlier.

Clyde took the first steps to rectifying that situation with an excellent 3-1 win over current fourth-placed side Kilmarnock, at Rugby Park on Saturday, 7 January 1967. Two Joe Gilroy headers either side of a Tommy McLean penalty kick gave the visitors an interval lead, with a late third from Graham Macfarlane completing a memorable afternoon for the travelling support. That win saw Clyde leapfrog both Dundee clubs to tuck in behind Kilmarnock and Hibernian in fourth spot, both of those clubs having played three games more.

Whilst the calendar year 1967 would be a momentous one for both of the old east end rivals, Celtic and Clyde, it would sadly spell the end of the road for another historic Glasgow club, Third Lanark. As Clyde were winning in Ayrshire and Celtic were taking five goals off Dundee in Glasgow to move four points clear of Aberdeen at the top of the table, Thirds were losing 1-0 to Brechin City at Glebe Park in the second preliminary round of the Scottish Cup, the only goal, perhaps ironically, scored in the 13th minute. That would prove to be their farewell tie in the competition in which, as 3rd LRV, they had beaten Celtic in the new east end club's first-ever final back in February 1889. Now sitting mid table in the Second Division, Thirds' failure to meet the guarantees of visiting clubs and pay supplier invoices, together with a series of resignations at board and managerial level and grave dissatisfaction amongst the players regarding the conditions at Cathkin Park was triggering suggestions that the club would struggle to complete the season.

The signs for the survival of the Hi Hi were growing increasingly desperate as Celts hosted the Bully Wee on Wednesday, 11 January 1967, the match deferred from Ne'erday due to the frozen conditions. Despite pre-match speculation that Joe McBride would return, the heavy conditions ensured that he would take no part in proceedings. And it was a ninth successive unchanged line-up for Clyde as the following teams took to the field before 38,000 spectators.

CELTIC:

Ronnie Simpson; Jim Craig & Tommy Gemmell; Bobby Murdoch, Billy McNeill & John Clark; Jimmy Johnstone, Willie Wallace, Stevie Chalmers, Charlie Gallagher & Bobby Lennox. Substitute: Bertie Auld

CLYDE:

Tommy McCulloch; Harry Glasgow & Eddie Mulheron; John McHugh, Dick Staite & Stan Anderson; Graham Macfarlane, Harry Hood, Joe Gilroy, Ian Stewart & Sam Hastings. Substitute: Davie Souter

The Hoops continued life minus their injured 33-goal striker by thrashing the Shawfield outfit 5-1, a second successive Parkhead win by that margin to open 1967. Stevie Chalmers netted Celtic's opener within 12 minutes, with the visitors' leading marksman, Joe Gilroy restoring parity just after the half-hour mark. Charlie Gallagher had been the star man in the weekend victory over Dundee and he put the hosts ahead again early in the second period. Chalmers then made it 3-1 with 20 minutes remaining with the goal of the game arriving immediately afterwards, Tommy Gemmell marking his 99th consecutive appearance for Celtic by blasting a ridiculous volley past Tommy McCulloch from fully 30 yards. Within seconds, Bobby Lennox rounded off the four-minute scoring burst and a wonderful attacking display from Jock Stein's men by heading home Celtic's fifth goal. It was only a second defeat in 10 matches for the visitors and brought to a halt Clyde's run of four successive away League victories.

Having faced the League leaders in midweek, next up for Clyde was a home match with Eddie Turnbull's second-placed Aberdeen, the Dons travelling to Shawfield on Saturday, 14 January 1967. The game would end goalless, despite the dominance enjoyed by the hosts against a blanket defence. Harry was denied a goal on several occasions by the brilliance of his old Queen's Park teammate Bobby Clark, the son of a serving Clyde director and currently training at Shawfield – as indeed was Dundee's John Arrol – and now staking his claim to be Scotland's first choice between the posts. As an aside, 50 miles to the north, Jock Stein fielded the 11 men who would later become revered as the Lisbon Lions for the first time together, the historic afternoon marked by a 4-0 victory over St Johnstone at Muirton Park, Perth.

Seven days later, the Bully Wee travelled to Fir Park to face a Motherwell side buoyed by the return from suspension of striker John 'Dixie' Deans. A game of many missed chances looked to be heading for stalemate before Clyde inside-left Ian Stewart blasted the ball past Peter McCloy with 15 minutes remaining. The Steelmen would then fight back to salvage a point thanks to a superb late solo effort from their young winger, Gus Moffat.

The first round of the Scottish Cup took place on Saturday, 28 January 1967 and saw Clyde head 'doon the watter' to face old foes Morton at Cappielow. The Greenock club had held the Indian sign over the Bully Wee during Harry's first spell at Shawfield and were once again running away with the Second Division title, just as they had done in 1963/64, largely due to their 58-goal strike partnership Joe Mason and Joe Harper. Charismatic manager/director Hal Stewart was up to his usual brinkmanship, sending Morton out in light blue 'Rangers' kits in a bid to intimidate his visitors. The sides lined up as follows, in front of 14,000 spectators.

MORTON:

Erik Sorensen; John Boyd & Jim Kennedy; Borge Thorup, Hugh Strachan & Billy Gray; Joe Harper, Benny Arentoft, Joe Mason, Gerry Sweeney & Morris Stevenson Substitute: Jack Bolton

CLYDE:

Tommy McCulloch; Harry Glasgow & Eddie Mulheron; Stan Anderson, Dick Staite & John McHugh; Graham Macfarlane, Harry Hood, Joe Gilroy, Ian Stewart & Sam Hastings. Substitute: Davie Souter

Hal Stewart's attempts to unsettle Clyde would backfire spectacularly as the visitors raced out of the traps to take the lead within 25 seconds, Harry finding Graham Macfarlane on the right for the winger to hammer the ball past Erik Sorensen from the tightest of angles. The tone for much of this tie was set early on, a bad challenge by debutant Gerry Sweeney after 15 minutes ending Shawfield skipper Harry Glasgow's afternoon and quickly followed by a series of dangerous tackles from players on both sides, former Celt Jim Kennedy and Clyde pivot Dick Staite both cautioned. With Davie Souter on at full-back, Clyde's opening to the second half was almost as dramatic as the first, Macfarlane's shot beating Sorensen all ends up but crashing back off the underside of the crossbar, Harry missing a glorious chance from the rebound to secure the Bully Wee's place in the next round. As the Shawfield men continued to press, referee Robert Holley Davidson was next to find himself in the spotlight, the controversial Airdrie official surely the only man in the stadium who felt John Boyd's lunge on Sam Hastings did not merit a penalty kick. Morton then threw everything into a late bid to rescue the game, Clyde surviving some scary moments to progress after the most pulsating of Scottish Cup-ties.

A player who had kicked off the 1966/67 season in Clyde colours was involved in the major shock of the afternoon, and indeed possibly in the history of the competition. Inside-forward Sammy Reid would see his rare first-team opportunities at Shawfield restricted further by the arrival of Harry Hood from Sunderland in October 1966. He would then join Second Division Berwick Rangers and would now find his name entering the record books as the scorer of the Borderers' goal which knocked the cup-holders Rangers out on English soil at Shielfield Park.

League action resumed the following Saturday as Clyde hosted Dundee United at Shawfield. Davie Souter retained his place for the injured and suspended Harry Glasgow, the first change to a Bully Wee starting line-up since early November, with former schoolboy internationalist Henry Quinn – released by Celtic the previous summer after spells at Burnley and St Mirren – taking a seat on the bench. Jerry Kerr's men boasted recent victories over Barcelona and Celtic, but they found themselves trailing in Rutherglen within five minutes, thanks to a Graham Macfarlane header. The goalscoring winger would move to full-back 10 minutes later, after Eddie Mulheron tragically broke his leg in a collision with United's Danish centre-forward Finn Dossing, Quinn coming on for his Clyde debut at outside-right. Despite the circumstances, the hosts showed great courage and resolution and deservedly went 2-0 up five minutes from the break, Harry following up to score after a Sam Hastings effort had come back off the post. The second half would produce no further scoring as Clyde edged ahead of Kilmarnock into fifth place on goal average, with Hibernian and Aberdeen now clearly in their sights.

There was a setback for the Bully Wee in midweek, as a Rangers side still reeling from the events at Berwick 10 days later exploited a Clyde defence featuring makeshift full-backs Dave Souter and John McHugh to run out 5-1 winners at Shawfield, in the match held over from Christmas Eve. With Ibrox forwards George McLean and Jim Forrest scapegoated for the shock Scottish Cup exit, it would be the latter's cousin Alex Willoughby who would profit from their misfortune with his second hat-trick in the space of four days. The only positive moment on the night for the home fans within the near 20,000 crowd was a second half headed goal by Ian Stewart, which brought the score back to 3-1.

Davie White shuffled his pack for the weekend trip to face Falkirk at Brockville, with Graham Macfarlane pushed back into the right-back position he had adopted in the Scottish Cup-tie at Cappielow two weeks earlier, to partner Davie Souter. That allowed a starting debut for Henry Quinn on the right flank, with Jim Fraser continuing in central defence and knee injury victim Dick Staite dropping out of the team. The visitors struck first in 20 minutes, Joe Gilroy tapping home after John McHugh's vicious free-kick had beaten former Dunfermline Athletic cup-winning hero Eddie Connachan only to strike the crossbar. Bairns defender John Lambie had conceded that free-kick and his afternoon went from bad to worse when he fouled

Sam Hastings in the box just before the interval, the future Partick Thistle boss then watching Ian Stewart dispatch the kick past Connachan for 2-0. As with the previous Saturday, that would prove to be the final score, despite Harry being presented with two wonderful opportunities to increase that lead. On a negative note, Clyde's injury woes continued with Joe Gilroy the latest casualty, the club's top scorer suffering ankle ligament damage at Brockville.

The second round of the Scottish Cup on Saturday, 18 February 1967 saw another of the giant-killers head to Shawfield. Second Division East Fife had knocked out top-flight opponents Motherwell at Fir Park in their previous tie and headed to Rutherglen optimistic of a repeat. Harry's elder brother Jackie had spent the 1960/61 season at Bayview, and another one of those quirks thrown up so often by football now saw his strike partner of the time – Ian Stewart – line up alongside the younger Hood sibling against the Fifers. Clyde welcomed back captain Harry Glasgow from injury, allowing Graham Macfarlane to resume in the attacking role in which he had been excelling all season, whilst 'want away' inside-forward Kenny Knox replaced Joe Gilroy up front.

Having crashed a wonderful long-range effort off the crossbar in the 20th minute, Harry duly opened his Scottish Cup account for the season with a double in the 4-1 win over the Methil outfit. The first of those arrived eight minutes before the break, Harry beating debutant Fife keeper John O'Hara after Macfarlane had done brilliantly down the right wing. Hood then turned goal maker, setting up Sam Hastings for a far post header six minutes after the restart. There was a show of defiance from the visitors, as winger Andy Waddell reduced the deficit on the hour, however, 10 minutes later, Harry completed his brace and Ian Stewart ended the scoring at 4-1 when he converted a penalty against his old club with 20 minutes remaining. It was a performance which did not go unnoticed by *Evening Times* reporter, Jimmy Dunbar.

"Shawfield boss David White certainly knew what he was doing when he persuaded Harry Hood to rejoin the club after a spell with Sunderland. Hood scored two of Clyde's four goals, was the mastermind behind another, and was obviously Mr Entertainment to the small but enthusiastic band of Shawfield supporters who cheered the home team's every move."

Sam Hastings' ankle injury sustained against East Fife and a recurrence of Harry Glasgow's problem were the latest woes to stretch David White's limited first-team resources ahead of the League clash with Hearts at Shawfield on Saturday, 25 February 1967. With only 11 fit players, the Clyde manager's response was to sign former Celtic wing-half Mike Jackson, who had been on trial with Partick Thistle after spells at Third Lanark and St Johnstone. Jackson was on the bench for the visit of the Gorgie men, with Henry Quinn restored on the right wing, Graham Macfarlane reverting to right-back, Kenny Knox wide left and central defender Dick Staite introduced as an emergency striker against the club he had supported as a boy in Edinburgh. Of course, the stand-in centre-forward would duly open the scoring with a header, eight minutes before the break. White's next master stroke was to swap the roles of Staite and Knox for the final 20 minutes, and it was the latter who made it 2-0 shortly afterwards. The patched-up hosts would then see out the game to secure another two points, despite a late consolation goal from Hearts' wing-half George Miller. With Hibernian beating Aberdeen 1-0 at Easter Road, the part-time Shawfield outfit were now just two points behind that illustrious duo with a game in hand and 10 to play, European football still very much a possibility.

Skipper Harry Glasgow's return to action eased David White's selection issues slightly for the following week's home clash with Dunfermline Athletic. That allowed Graham Macfarlane to move forward, with Henry Quinn replacing Mike Jackson on the bench. The only goal of a tight contest came 20 minutes in, Kenny Knox beating former Celtic keeper Bent Martin in the Pars goal as Clyde continued their fine run with another two points. A few miles across the river, the on-off return from injury of Scotland's top goalscorer, Celtic's Joe McBride, a player who would later feature for both of those clubs, took another twist as it was announced that he would be going into hospital in midweek ahead of surgery on a torn cartilage.

McBride duly checked into Killearn Hospital on Thursday, 9 March 1967, a few hours after his Celtic teammates had dramatically pulled back the 1-0 deficit from the previous week's European Cup quarter-final first leg in Novi Sad against Yugoslav champions Vojvodina at Celtic Park. That had also been a red-letter day for Harry, as new Scotland boss Bobby Brown – the St Johnstone manager a shock appointment by the SFA two weeks earlier – named him in a 17-strong international squad to tour the Middle & Far East, Australasia and Canada across the months of May and June.

The full Scotland pool named by Brown for the 11-match series – with one place still up for grabs – was as follows:

GOALKEEPERS: ***Jim Cruickshank (Hearts) & Bobby Ferguson (Kilmarnock).***

FULL-BACKS: ***Willie Bell (Leeds United), Willie Callaghan (Dunfermline Athletic) & Tommy Gemmell (Celtic).***

HALF-BACKS: ***Billy Bremner & Eddie Gray (both Leeds United), John Greig & Ronnie McKinnon (both Rangers) & Jim Townsend (St Johnstone).***

FORWARDS: ***Alex Ferguson (Dunfermline Athletic), Willie Henderson (Rangers), Harry Hood (Clyde), Peter Lorimer (Leeds United), Jim McCalliog (Sheffield Wednesday), Tommy McLean (Kilmarnock) & Willie Wallace (Celtic).***

Arsenal wing-half Frank McLintock would subsequently be announced as the 18th player by the end of the month, whilst Jim Townsend moved from St Johnstone to Hearts for £20,000 in April.

Back on the domestic front, Joe Gilroy returned to lead the Clyde attack for the home Scottish Cup quarter-final clash with Second Division Hamilton Academical, conquerors of St Mirren at Love Street in the previous round. A near 10,000 crowd watched Clyde launch an all-out attack on the visiting goal, Ian Stewart's drive striking the bar before Harry saw his effort ruled out for offside just before the break. The second period was much of the same, the hosts frustrated as the match ended goalless. The replay took on additional significance, Monday's draw pairing the winner with European Cup semi-finalists Celtic at Hampden in the last four.

That prompted an interview with Harry, under the heading *"Harry's got three scores to settle,"* a copy kindly sent to me by Clyde FC historian, Gordon Sydney.

"It just had to be Celtic!" That was Clyde's Harry Hood's reaction to Monday's Scottish Cup draw. "I used to dream about playing FOR them, but I always seem to be playing AGAINST them," says Harry."

"Harry's hopes were ALMOST fulfilled three times. When he was a pupil at Holyrood School he was invited to train at Celtic Park, However, before his 17th birthday came along and Celtic could sign him, he joined Queen's Park. To keep himself fit in the close season, Harry at that time played for Brunswick Boys Club. He was a prolific scorer for them. Sean Fallon heard about it, went to see him one Saturday, only to find that Harry had quietly signed for Clyde the previous evening. The final "miss" was a couple of seasons ago when Celtic tried to buy him from Clyde. The terms were not quite to Harry's liking and, in the end, he went to Sunderland."

"Harry now feels that a Scottish Cup medal would cap what has, for him, been a wonderful year. Twelve months ago, he was recovering from a hernia operation, feeling down in the dumps and completely out of favour at Sunderland. He returned to Clyde. Now they're going strong in the League campaign, in the semi-final of the Scottish Cup and Harry is earmarked for a round-the-world trip with Scotland in May."

Saturday, 18 March 1967 involved a trip to Broomfield to face another Scottish success story of the 1966/67 season, Airdrieonians. Former Clyde wing-half Archie Wright had managed the Diamonds since replacing Willie Steel in 1963, the club suffering relegation at the end of the 1964/65 season as they took the drop to the second tier together with Third Lanark. Whilst the Cathkin side would never recover from that demotion, Airdrieonians would secure instant promotion behind Ayr United to rejoin the top-flight for the current campaign. The Somerset men were toiling badly at the foot of the League, certainties for relegation with just six points from 27 games. In contrast, Wright had worked miracles to lift the Broomfield men up to mid table, keeping company with Hearts, Dunfermline Athletic and Dundee United.

The clash of two of Scotland's outstanding young managers produced five goals, all scored in the first half. Unchanged Clyde came out of the blocks quickest, Kenny Knox with an effort which struck Irish goalkeeper Roddie McKenzie's upright before Ian Stewart opened the scoring in 10 minutes. Harry then took the score to 3-0 with a double strike inside 5 minutes, his second a 25-yard drive which screamed past McKenzie into the roof of the net. Debutant home striker Willie McLelland had only stepped up from the junior ranks with Largs Thistle the previous week, but he marked his first senior outing with a brace before the interval. The Diamonds would then be robbed of a point when a late Dave Marshall effort came back off the crossbar with Tommy McCulloch beaten, Clyde returning from Lanarkshire with a 3-2 win.

Harry would repeat his two-goal feat in the replayed Scottish Cup quarter-final tie against Hamilton Academical, played at 4.45pm on Wednesday, 22 March 1967, as the Bully Wee won 5-1 at Douglas Park in front of 9,232 spectators, the Celtic management team and most of the squad. With Sam Hastings still deemed unfit to turn out against his former club, David White's only change was to bring back Dick Staite at centre-half, with Jim Fraser moving to the bench. Clyde had the tie sewn up by the interval, by which time they were 4-0 up. Kenny Knox got the party started in the 12th minute, Harry notched his double with two "splendidly taken" goals in a six-minute spell midway through the half and Graham Macfarlane added a fourth just before the break. The Accies night of misery would continue as Ian Gilmour missed a penalty shortly after the restart then saw Joe Gilroy make it 5-0 before the hour. A last-minute consolation goal from Alan Thomson – a schoolboy football opponent of Harry's back in the day who had spent some time at Rangers – would be the only moment of relief for the home supporters, as their Scottish Cup dreams ended. That win set up a last four clash between Clyde and Celtic at Hampden on the opening day in April.

In the meantime, there was League business to attend to. With Celtic and Rangers slugging it out for the title, the prize up for grabs for Clyde was third spot, the Shawfield men battling with Aberdeen, Hibernian and Kilmarnock for that honour. The next visitors to Rutherglen on Saturday, 25 March 1967 were a feisty St Mirren side struggling near the foot of the table but buoyed by a 3-0 win over Hearts the previous week. The hosts, still on a high after their midweek Cup success, once again started well and took the lead through Ian Stewart in the sixth minute, following good build-up play by Harry Hood and Kenny Knox. Harry was in dazzling form, setting up Stan Anderson for a strike on goal before being denied by his old Holyrood pal Denis Connaghan from point-blank range. As often happens, all the first-half pressure was negated by a sucker punch just before the break, Paisley striker Peter Kane's effort deflected past Tommy McCulloch by Davie Souter to send the teams in level. Both sides went all out for a winner in the second period, the only goal scored with 15 minutes remaining as Ian Stewart completed his double with a flashing header past Connaghan. With Aberdeen and Hibernian both losing that day, Clyde now moved past the Dons to sit level on points with the third-placed Leith outfit, behind them only on goal average and having one game in hand.

A huge week for the Bully Wee commenced with a visit to Easter Road on Tuesday, 28 March 1967. The progress made by Clyde so far that campaign was reflected not just in their lofty League position, but also by the presence of no fewer than four of their forwards in the list of goalscorers in Scotland who had reached double figures. Ian Stewart's brace against St Mirren saw him overtake Joe Gilroy to sit on 15 goals, with Harry now one behind Joe on 13. Winger Graham Macfarlane had also scored an impressive 10, despite his recent spells filling in at right-back. Stewart would improve his tally with a spectacular solo effort for Clyde's opener at Easter Road, their 50th League goal of the campaign, midway through the second half. Former Morton nemesis Alan McGraw then once again hurt the Shawfield side by heading the equaliser within five minutes, as the match ended 1-1. There was also pain of a different sort for both Stan Anderson and Joe Gilroy, their muscle injuries causing some concern ahead of the Scottish Cup semi-final clash with Celtic at Hampden five days later.

Both players would recover to be in their normal positions as almost 57,000 spectators – the biggest attendance before which Harry had played to date - braved a blustery afternoon to watch the following sides battle the elements and each other before settling for a 0-0 draw.

CELTIC:

Ronnie Simpson; Jim Craig & Tommy Gemmell; Willie Wallace, Billy McNeill & John Clark; Jimmy Johnstone, Bertie Auld, Stevie Chalmers, Bobby Lennox & John Hughes. Substitute: Charlie Gallagher

CLYDE:

Tommy McCulloch; Harry Glasgow & Davie Souter; Stan Anderson, Dick Staite & John McHugh; Graham Macfarlane, Harry Hood, Joe Gilroy, Ian Stewart & Kenny Knox. Substitute: Jim Fraser

The infamous swirling wind at Hampden would sadly ruin the match as a contest. Celts twice came close in the first half when first John McHugh cleared a Billy McNeill header from under his own crossbar then Clyde's Scottish Cup-winning goalkeeper of 1958, Tommy McCulloch, kept his hopes of a second medal alive by blocking a Tommy Gemmell piledriver. The two big incidents of the afternoon occurred in the closing quarter, Ronnie Simpson pulling off a fabulous one-handed save from Joe Gilroy before Celts were denied a penalty by Fife referee J R P Gordon, when Jimmy Johnstone's goalbound shot was stopped on the line by Dave Souter's elbow with just four minutes remaining. The disappointment felt by both clubs after the goalless stalemate would be somewhat alleviated as the League results filtered through from the other games. Rangers' 1-0 defeat at home to Dunfermline Athletic tilted the title advantage significantly towards Parkhead, whilst struggling Stirling Albion's win by the same scoreline at home to Hibernian boosted Clyde's hopes of a third-placed finish.

An ankle injury suffered by Harry as early as the 10th minute at Hampden required three stitches and caused him to miss the replay, played before 55,000 spectators at the same venue four days later. Winger Sam Hastings returned after his own spell on the sidelines to replace Hood in a reshuffled attack, whilst Celtic also made one change, weekend substitute Charlie Gallagher replacing John Hughes. As it transpired, Clyde had also missed their chance of glory, goals from Bobby Lennox and

Bertie Auld settling the tie within the opening 20 minutes, Celts duly progressing to a final meeting with Aberdeen later that month.

A key component of the Clyde defence which defied the European Champions-elect for much of the two encounters at Hampden was Dick Staite. His ability and willingness to perform at a high standard in any number of positions for the Shawfield side pretty much summed up for me the attitude and desire which enabled Davie White's men to punch above their weight over a number of seasons. Dick very kindly provided a unique insight into the events leading up to and during those semi-final ties.

"The week preceding the match was pretty hectic. We had a critical away match at Easter Road on the Tuesday night against a strong Hibs side vying with ourselves - along with Aberdeen and Kilmarnock - for third in the League and a European place. A draw, overseen by a watchful Jock Stein in the stand, kept us in contention and reasonably positive for the semi-final. The build-up from then to the Saturday was inescapable: more than usual press coverage; pictures taken in training; speculation as to team selection due to injury in both camps; the near certainty, according to the pundits, of outcome."

"On the Saturday morning, we followed our usual routine: the usual light training session at Shawfield which allowed the whole squad to come together. This was necessary as several of the players lived firth of Glasgow and did not join us in midweek training. By then it was clear that Stan [Anderson] and Joe [Gilroy], both of whom had been injured along with Sam [Hastings], would be fit to play, but Sam would not make it."

"Following hotel lunch on the south side of the city, we made our way to Hampden where, as the team bus approached the streets near the ground, crowds were already milling. The sense of anticipation was palpable. A walk on the pitch, checking the surface (dry and firm on largely a fine Spring day, with some wind), soaking in the atmosphere, then repairing to the dressing room giving some thought to the great players of the past that had shared that space."

"Then, at 2.15, the news came through of the Celtic eleven, and with it a real boost. Bobby Murdoch would not be fit to play. This led to the unusual selection of Willie Wallace in a deeper role and this was another boost, as he too had been, in our opinion, key to the fluency and interchange of the Celtic attack. Bobby, as I'm sure you'll know, was the quarter back releasing fast flowing and darting Celtic attacks which, when they were fully on song, were almost mesmeric to play against."

"We were used to playing in front of large crowds at Parkhead, where 35,000-40,000 would not be unexpected, so the 57,000 attendance at Hampden was not, in itself, a huge increase. However, the largest mass of fans had congregated to the centre of the ground. These terraces were then topped by a full North Stand. So, as we emerged from the tunnel, the effect of this clamorous vertical wall of people was staggering."

"Harry had been badly bruised in that first match of the semi-final and missed the replay. The Celtic defenders certainly understood his worth and the danger he

presented. Interestingly, Jock Stein, by all accounts, refused to accept Clyde's 'injury smokescreen' prior to the replay but in Harry's case, as evidenced by the bruising to his leg, reports of the injury were entirely true. He had taken a bit of a hammering on the Saturday and did not make it. This was a big loss."

"As for the replay, although the loss of Harry was crucial, softened albeit by the return of Sam, our players had also been back at their places of work from the Monday. Some might have been doing shifts on the day of the match. That we did not reach the heights of the first leg might be understandable. Turned out that we were not alone: first Dukla, then Inter were about to find out the calibre of the opposition."

Harry would also sit out the next two games, joined on the injury list by Ian Stewart as Jim McLean and Alex Bryce enjoyed a 3-1 win on their return to Shawfield in the colours of Dundee, Dick Staite adding inside-right to the list of positions covered by him for Clyde in recent weeks. The home clash with St Johnstone - three nights later, Tuesday, 11 April 1967 - was highly significant, as the points gained from a 2-0 win allowed Clyde to jump ahead of Hibernian and Aberdeen into third spot in the First Division, with just four matches remaining. Stewart was back for this one but yet again Davie White had to ring the changes, the most significant being John Wright replacing Tommy McCulloch between the sticks. The versatile Staite moved back to his central defensive role and he marked that return with Clyde's second goal, 10 minutes after the break, whilst Mike Jackson made his Bully Wee debut in Harry's inside-right position and Graham Macfarlane reverted to full-back in the absence of Davie Souter. Joe Gilroy – watched by Blackpool's scouts - had headed the opener for the revamped hosts on the 20-minute mark.

Harry recovered sufficiently from injury to play in the final four fixtures of the campaign. John Wright continued in goal but otherwise Clyde's line-up was back on more familiar lines as they beat relegated Ayr United 1-0 at Somerset Park on Wednesday, 19 April 1967. Hood was involved in the only goal of the game, five minutes into the second half, his right-wing cross nodded down by Sam Hastings for Ian Stewart to edge further ahead of Joe Gilroy once again in the club scoring stakes, the former East Fife striker collecting his 17th goal of the season.

Three days later, Clyde faced a daunting trip to Ibrox to face a Rangers side on a high after a midweek victory in Bulgaria which had given them one foot in the final of the European Cup-Winners' Cup in Nuremberg. Three points behind Celtic in the title race with three games to play, the crowd of less than 20,000 suggested the home support held out little hope of their favourites wrestling the League flag from Parkhead as the teams lined up as follows.

RANGERS:

Norrie Martin; Kai Johansen & Davie Provan; Sandy Jardine, Ron McKinnon & John Greig; Willie Henderson, Alex Willoughby, Alex Smith, Dave Smith & Davie Wilson Substitute: Colin Jackson

CLYDE:

John Wright; Harry Glasgow & Davie Souter; Stan Anderson, Dick Staite & John McHugh; Graham Macfarlane, Harry Hood, Joe Gilroy, Ian Stewart & Sam Hastings Substitute: Jim Fraser

Harry was first to threaten with a shot which only just cleared Norrie Martin's crossbar early on, before John Greig's last-ditch challenge prevented the striker from adding to his Ibrox tally as the visitors showed no sign whatsoever of any inferiority complex. Just after the half-hour, it looked like that promising start would receive the reward it deserved, Harry combining well with Graham Macfarlane to set Joe Gilroy up to shoot past Martin before Clyde celebrations were muted by the sight of the linesman's raised flag. That knife was turned on the stroke of half-time, Davy Wilson, midweek goalscoring hero against Slavia Sofia, beating Wright with a low shot to give the hosts a slightly flattering interval lead. The Clyde keeper then proceeded to keep his team in the match with a string of saves as Rangers ramped up the pressure after the break, and it was against the run of play when Ian Stewart found himself in splendid isolation at the edge of the box with 17 minutes remaining, the striker coolly placing a shot into the corner to give the Bully Wee another priceless point in the battle for a European slot.

Clyde's penultimate match was the rescheduled fixture with Partick Thistle at Shawfield, one of the weather casualties from the festive period. It finally took place on Wednesday, 26 April 1967, with the Bully Wee securing qualification for the Inter-Cities Fairs Cup with an emphatic 4-1 victory. Mike Jackson was handed a rare start on the right wing in place of Graham Macfarlane and he duly opened his Clyde scoring account within 30 seconds of kick-off, the former Celt adding a second on the half-hour as the hosts took control. Top marksmen Ian Stewart and Joe Gilroy upped Clyde's tally to four in the second half before an injured Harry made way for Henry Quinn with 10 minutes remaining. A consolation strike from Tommy Rae in the 87th minute then brought an end to the scoring, Clyde requiring just one point from their final game now to guarantee a third-place finish in the top division. Despite his two-goal haul against Partick Thistle, this match would mark the end of the brief Shawfield career of Mike Jackson. Both he and used substitute Henry Quinn were handed free transfers by Clyde two days later, as the club reverted to a pool of just 15 first-team players.

Clyde ensured that the drama continued right to the end of the season, finding themselves two goals down to Stirling Albion at Annfield on Saturday, 29 April 1967, to a Les Thomson penalty and a strike from future St Johnstone and Dundee United winger, Henry Hall. Davie White's final half-time talk of the campaign would pay off handsomely, the Bully Wee scoring five without reply in the second period to secure third place in the First Division, equalling the club's highest League finish of all time, last achieved 55 years earlier in season 1911/12 and only once before that, in 1908/09. Harry ended the domestic season on a high with another double, giving him an excellent return of 14 goals from 33 appearances since his move from Wearside the previous October. Graham Macfarlane, Stan Anderson and Joe Gilroy were also on target. The Bully Wee would finish the campaign with an impressive tally of 46 points from 34 games, four ahead of Hibernian who had completed their campaign the same afternoon with a 2-0 defeat at home to Airdrieonians. Aberdeen were a further point behind but with one League game remaining, the Dons having played and lost the Scottish Cup final to Jock Stein's Celtic thanks to a Willie Wallace brace at Hampden.

The evening before the cup final and Clyde's great fightback in Stirling, two of the powerhouse clubs from the early years of Scottish football were concluding their Second Division programme, almost disregarded by the mainstream press. However, Dumbarton's 5-1 win over Third Lanark at Boghead on Friday, 28 April 1967 would later enter the record books as the last match ever played by the Hi Hi. The club had been struggling with debt for several years and perhaps ironically, the petition to wind Third Lanark up was brought by the building company who had constructed the new main stand at Cathkin back in 1963, as the club attempted to bring in additional revenue. After several continuations, the Court of Session in Edinburgh appointed a liquidator and issued the winding order on Wednesday, June 7, 1967. Later that evening, Celtic, the club Thirds had defeated at what would become Cathkin Park some 80 years earlier to win its first Scottish Cup, would reinforce their new position as European champions by beating their 1966 predecessors Real Madrid 1-0 in the Estadio Bernabeu in a benefit match for Argentinian legend Alfredo Di Stefano. How differently the Football Gods had treated the two early protagonists in the modern era.

As Thirds were consigned to history their old rivals Clyde were looking back on a wonderful campaign and ahead to a bright future. It had been a truly remarkable effort from the part-time Shawfield outfit, Davie White juggling with the smallest player pool in the top division and his players overcoming horrendous injury difficulties in recent months to outperform clubs with substantial additional resources and now deservedly looking forward to making their formal debut in European football.

Sadly, there would be a cruel twist to that story.

More than 50 years down the line, Dick Staite recalls the events of that monumental season for Clyde with remarkable clarity and insight, as perhaps befits the Midlothian head teacher knighted in the New Year's honours list of 2005 for his outstanding contribution to education.

"From November 1966, a month after Harry signed from Sunderland, the Press was waking up to what Clyde had to offer. References are made to the speed and sharpness of passing; to fluidity and what is now referred to as 'transition;' to robust defence and positional awareness. Match after match reports tell the story. "The Bully Wee have perfected such a smooth soccer system that when one man replaces another the style remains unchanged......there are few more attractive sides

to watch at the moment;" "They have a team of rare talent;" "Few teams play more precise outfield football." And from the semi-final against Celtic: "They marshalled their defensive ranks so magnificently that Scotland's most deadly attack was made to look sadly incompetent."

"Manager John Prentice had developed the '66/67 Clyde team over successive seasons. What leadership manuals now call strategic planning by identifying players to fit a system. As I recall, at least 12 of the squad had been signed by John, several from the lower Leagues, gelling with players who had been there for some time. When Davie [White] took over, two critical signings were made; and with Stan [Anderson] and Harry now added to the squad, the balance of the side was truly in place."

"Due to their positional role, a great deal of that transition and crispness came from them. Harry - with quicksilver feet and speed of thought - and Stan, with his 'big-picture' football brain; but there were others, hugely gifted individuals, gelling as a collective. The team was a combination of football brain: quick thinking, seeing the space, the change of direction, the bigger patterns. But the 'brains' are not always the most industrious, so we had the heart and lungs, the guys that gave us the 'out,' the breather, the chasing and harrying and carrying. And we had the muscle, the defending that you would expect of the necessarily 'industrial' 1960s football. With Harry's return, and with much already there, everything clicked into place. He was the right player at the right moment for the right collective."

"In that system - and what the Press were picking up on - the fast moving from defence to attack, (transition); the sharp, smart inter-passing (fluidity), Harry had a key role. He played in front of the middle pairing of Stan and Ian [Stewart] with a free role just behind Joe [Gilroy] at centre. And with our wingers, Graham [Macfarlane] and Sam [Hastings] operating like modern wing-backs - full of running, tricky in attack, unselfish in covering back with huge reserves of stamina - Harry fitted right into that system as key to transition in bringing others into play."

"Add to that the extremely gifted individual skills that he brought. Almost instantaneously in a crowded box, for example, he would receive a pass, create space, deceive his immediate marker and engineer room for a shot. He had exceptional balance, plus the mid-twenties' awareness and speed of thought to anticipate and exploit a space; and muscle memory to exploit the opening. With very little backlift, he was able to generate fierce power in shooting, coupled with accuracy and direction. When Tom McCulloch would be asked to name the hardest shot in football, Harry's power in training drills was his number one choice."

Chapter 12

Around the world in 30 days ...but Europe is out of bounds for Clyde

The success enjoyed by Scottish clubs – and indeed Leeds United - in Europe during that unique 1966/67 season did have a negative impact on the international scene, a clash of dates between the final stages of continental competition and the upcoming world tour robbing Scotland of the services of no fewer than 10 of the 18 players previously selected. An emergency meeting of the SFA was held on Saturday, 29 April 1967, the day of the Scottish Cup final, to decide if the tour was still viable in these circumstances. Perhaps predictably, the governing body chose to go ahead with the month-long trip, attempting to deflect further media and supporter criticism by rebranding the squad as a touring select rather than a full international side. It feels correct and appropriate in these circumstances to emphasise that Harry Hood had been chosen on merit in that initial 18-man squad, which very much represented the cream of Scottish talent, with Denis Law the most notable established international player excluded, the Manchester United icon required for a club tour of Australasia at the same time. Another Wembley hero, Jim Baxter, would also be away with Harry's old Sunderland mates in Canada.

Three days before that Hampden Scottish Cup final, Celtic had secured the 0-0 draw in Prague against Czech champions and army club Dukla, which set up a first-ever European Cup final for a side from the British Isles. Jock Stein's men would now meet either twice-world champions Internazionale of Milan or Bulgarians CSKA Sofia, who were scheduled to meet in a play-off to decide who would progress to Lisbon for that day of days on Thursday, 25 May 1967. Thus, Tommy Gemmell and Willie Wallace would be wearing the green-and-white of Celtic rather than the navy blue of Scotland that evening.

The coming midweek would also surely see Rangers book their place in the final of the competition for national cup-winners, having established a 1-0 lead in the away leg of their semi-final against another Bulgarian outfit, Slavia Sofia. Scotland would duly lose the services of John Greig, Ronnie McKinnon and Willie Henderson. The Ibrox club had recently agreed a 'swap-plus-cash' deal with Dundee, which saw

Berwick scapegoat George McLean head for Tayside with Dens inside-forward Andy Penman making the opposite journey. Penman would be ineligible for the expected Nuremberg final against Standard Liege or Bayern Munich, so the new Ranger would now find himself instantly promoted to the international scene.

The Inter-Cities Fairs Cup schedule was somewhat behind that of the other two tournaments, the last-four tie between Leeds United and Kilmarnock due to take place in tandem with the aforementioned finals. That clash of dates would cost Scotland the Killie duo of Bobby Ferguson and Tommy McLean, plus Don Revie's Anglo quartet of Willie Bell, Billy Bremner, Eddie Gray and Peter Lorimer.

Some of the replacements announced by Scotland manager Bobby Brown on Monday, 1 May 1967 were familiar names, with others much less so. From Arsenal came former Dundee defender Ian Ure and teenage wing-half John Woodward, the latter originally from Glasgow's Possilpark. Burnley provided goalkeeper Harry Thomson and winger Willie Morgan. Left-back Hugh Tinney had enjoyed five years at Partick Thistle before moving south to Bury, whilst Joe Harper had scored a barrowload of goals with strike partner Joe Mason as Morton romped to the Second Division title and had recently signed for Huddersfield Town. Both would now find themselves unexpectedly representing Scotland.

Three players from West Bromwich Albion joined the group, defenders Doug Fraser and Eddie Colquhoun, plus inside-forward Bobby Hope, who had edged Harry out of the Scotland Under 23 team in the season just ended. The final name listed was former East Stirlingshire full-back Eddie McCreadie, now starring under Tommy Docherty at FA Cup-finalists Chelsea. Due to the European date clashes, McCreadie and Jim McCalliog would now be the only members of the Scotland team which beat world champions England at Wembley the previous month to make the trip.

The revamped squad list was as follows.

GOALKEEPERS: ***Jim Cruickshank (Hearts) & Harry Thomson (Burnley).***

FULL-BACKS: ***Willie Callaghan (Dunfermline Athletic), Hugh Tinney (Bury) & Eddie McCreadie (Chelsea).***

HALF-BACKS: ***Alan Anderson & Jim Townsend (Hearts), Eddie Colquhoun & Doug Fraser (West Bromwich Albion), Frank McLintock, Ian Ure & John Woodward (Arsenal).***

FORWARDS: ***Alex Ferguson (Dunfermline Athletic), Joe Harper (Huddersfield Town), Bobby Hope (West Bromwich Albion), Harry Hood (Clyde), Jim McCalliog (Sheffield Wednesday), Willie Morgan (Burnley) & Andy Penman (Rangers).***

McCalliog, McCreadie and McLintock were also named in a 16-man Scotland squad to face the USSR in a Hampden friendly the following midweek, Celtic manager Jock Stein perplexed and angry that no fewer than nine of his players had been selected and would thus miss out on part of the team's preparation for the European Cup final in Lisbon, later that month. A knee injury suffered by Frank McLintock in the 2-0 defeat to the Soviets then ruled him out of the forthcoming tour, whilst Chelsea's progression to meet Tottenham Hotspur in the FA Cup final at Wembley on Saturday, 20 May 1967 had seen full-back Eddie McCreadie hurt and subsequently prevented from joining up with the party.

The trans-global trip commenced in the Ramat-Gan Nation Stadium in Tel Aviv on Tuesday, 16 May 1967, as Scotland faced Israel in front of 27,000 spectators. With only two-full-backs travelling, that lack of cover was exposed as Hugh Tinney suffered a reaction to his smallpox jab, forcing Bobby Brown to field Eddie Colquhoun at left-back. Harry was listed as 12th man as the Scots lined up as follows.

Harry Thomson; Willie Callaghan & Eddie Colquhoun; Alan Anderson, Ian Ure & Doug Fraser; Andy Penman, Bobby Hope, Jim McCalliog, Alex Ferguson & Willie Morgan. Substitute: Harry Hood.

Harry would come off the bench after just half-an-hour to get his first taste of international football, replacing another debutant Andy Penman who had suffered an ankle injury. At that stage, the visitors led 1-0, Burnley winger Willie Morgan opening his Scotland account in the 20th minute with a wonderful goal. Israeli striker Giora Speigel then beat another Turf Moor star, Scots goalkeeper Harry Thomson, to equalise five minutes before the break. Morgan would also be involved in the game's decisive goal, scored by Alex Ferguson six minutes from time, the scramble which ensued from his corner ended by the head of the Dunfermline Athletic hitman to give the Touring XI a winning start, albeit some newspaper reports cited both Eddie Colquhoun and Harry as the scorer. On a more negative note, a facial injury to captain Ian Ure meant that he would take no further part in the tour, the Arsenal central defender returning home after playing just 90 minutes of football.

The second game of the tour was due to take place against a Chinese XI in Hong Kong six days later, however, rioting in the colony caused the introduction of a 'dusk to dawn' curfew, which in turn forced the cancellation of the match. The next fixture did take place at the Hong Kong Stadium on Thursday, 25 May 1967, a few hours before Celtic took on Internazionale in Lisbon, Hugh Tinney restored at full-back allowing Eddie Colquhoun to revert to his normal central defensive berth to replace Ian Ure whilst Harry Hood started instead of Andy Penman. Like his boyhood club, Harry would also enjoy the taste of victory that day, scoring his first international goal in Scotland's 4-1 win over Hong Kong before just 7,000 spectators. The Scots had fallen behind early on, Ken Wills taking advantage after Alan Anderson had been short with a passback. Alex Ferguson was on target again, this time with a double strike either side of the half-hour. The Dunfermline Athletic marksman took a Jim McCalliog pass to equalise before Harry's cross allowed him to head Scotland into the lead. Harry's own moment of glory would arrive on the hour, the young Clyde hitman making it 3-1 with a lovely solo effort. With 10 minutes remaining, it would be another Pars player who would complete the scoring, full-back Willie Callaghan –

the elder brother of Tommy – firing home from a tight angle for the tourists.

The party then moved on to Australia for a series of three matches against the hosts, SFA secretary Willie Allan confirming the status of these fixtures as full internationals due to a FIFA ruling where the home side is fielding its strongest team. The Scotland squad was boosted by the arrival of Kilmarnock duo Jackie McGrory and Tommy McLean, following the Ayrshire club's two-leg defeat by Leeds United in the semi-final of the Inter-Cities Fairs Cup.

The first test against Australia took place at the Sydney Showground on Sunday, 28 May 1967 in front of 35,000 spectators, the hosts managed by a certain Jozef Venglos. Colquhoun again deputised for Tinney at left-back whilst new Hearts wing-half Jim Townsend, who had replaced the Bury defender against Hong Kong, was awarded his first international start by his old St Johnstone manager, Bobby Brown. Harry was again listed wide left in an unchanged forward line. On a surface totally unsuitable for football – it was normally used for livestock shows - the only goal of the game was scored after half-an-hour by Alex Ferguson, the third consecutive tour match in which he had netted, this one a simple tap-in after the ball had rebounded his way in front of goal. Scotland boss Brown was scathing afterwards in both his assessment of the way Australia had approached the match and repeated criticism of his own team.

"I can't recall any match of this standard where the tackling was so brutal. It was downright dangerous to be caught in possession. I think the critics have been unfair to the Scottish players. We are being treated as a full international team, which we are not. Due to circumstances well-known, including the success of teams like Celtic, Rangers, Kilmarnock and Leeds United in cup competitions, I brought a young and inexperienced squad of players to Australia. These players met something they had never experienced before when they played at the Showground on Sunday. The big crowd, the international atmosphere and the way the Australian team fought. All this was new to some members of the Scottish team. I am sure we shall put on a better exhibition in the remaining two matches in Adelaide and Melbourne and I look to Australia to play better too."

The injury fallout plus the opportunity to introduce fresh players to a depleted squad saw Brown revamp his side for the second match against the Australians, played at Adelaide's Norwood Oval before a full-house 20,000 crowd on Wednesday, 31 May 1967. Harry was actually named in the team beforehand, but it would be Tommy McLean and Willie Morgan occupying the wing positions as the players took the field, the former's Kilmarnock teammate Jackie McGrory replacing broken toe victim Eddie Colquhoun in defence, in front of Hearts goalkeeper Jim Cruickshank. Tynecastle new boy Jim Townsend scored his first goal for his country with a long-range strike in the 25th minute, Cruickshank at fault as the hosts levelled through Ray Beartz before the break. Scotland would eventually edge the match by 2-1 when Willie Morgan headed home a cross from Doug Fraser with 20 minutes remaining.

The Scots duly completed a hat-trick of wins over Australia in six days with a 2-0 victory in Melbourne's Olympic Park on Saturday, 3 June 1967, Alex Ferguson the hero with a second-half double to take his personal tally to six goals in five games. His reward was a rest for the next match, Scotland up against a New Zealand Under 23 select in Wellington two days later. Harry returned to the starting line-up as did both Hugh Tinney and Andy Penman, and there were places for youngsters John Woodward and Joe Harper. The Huddersfield Town striker would remember his first international start, as he notched a hat-trick of his own in a 7-2 romp at the Lower Hutt Recreation Ground. Tommy McLean's penalty had brought the Scots level early on and Jim McCalliog's double and a late Gary Lake own goal saw the visitors tally rise to seven, with Earl Thomas grabbing a consolation second for the New Zealanders.

Alex Ferguson returned to net his own first-half treble as Scotland completed the Australasian leg of their world tour with a 4-0 win over an Auckland Select on Thursday, 8 June 1967. Andy Penman added a fourth with 15 minutes remaining to open his own international scoring account.

The final two matches on the tour took place on Canadian soil, the first of those at Vancouver's Empire Stadium on Saturday, 10 June 1967 as Scotland beat a local All-Stars select 4-1 having only arrived from New Zealand 12 hours before the kick-off. Former Holyrood old boy Jim McCalliog scored a first-half double before becoming the latest Scot to suffer an injury, the Sheffield Wednesday striker replaced by Joe Harper. Alex Ferguson and Tommy McLean would add goals either side of the interval before All-Star left-half Hazeldene gave the home support something to cheer in the closing moments.

The tourists then brought the curtain down with another 7-2 win, this time over Canada at Alexander Park, Winnipeg, on Tuesday, 13 June 1967. Having missed the previous two games, Harry was deemed fit enough to start the match, coming in at inside-left as Joe Harper scored five to make it eight goals in two games for the former Morton hitman. Bobby Hope and Willie Morgan completed the scoring as Bobby Brown's men made it nine wins out of nine on the gruelling tour. Harry would eventually be replaced by Jim McCalliog, now being viewed as a hot property back home and the subject of a rumoured six-figure bid from Manchester United. Alex Ferguson had also caught the eye, netting 10 goals in his seven appearances, which would see the Dunfermline Athletic inside-forward move to Ibrox on the last day of July in a club record £60,000 transfer, whilst Burnley winger Willie Morgan received most plaudits as the 'find of the tour' and would end up at Old Trafford the following year. Of the 19 players who travelled, seven would not receive full caps for Scotland beyond the tour games, Harry and Alex Ferguson being the most high-profile of those. To this day, I would struggle to name many better uncapped Scottish players than Harry Hood, however, there were no failures in the eyes of Scotland manager Bobby Brown.

"Throughout the tour, each and every player has been a credit to Scotland, both on and off the field."

Back on the domestic front, Rangers' 1-0 defeat by Bayern Munich in the final of the European Cup-Winners' Cup in Nuremberg on the last day in May now posed a threat to Clyde's dream of continental football. Comments relating to the rule whereby only one club from each city could compete in the Inter-Cities Fairs Cup began to appear in the media in mid-June, with the SFA apparently writing to UEFA to request Clyde's inclusion on the basis of sporting merit. As League runners-up, the Ibrox club would have a legitimate first claim on Glasgow's solitary spot, whilst Aberdeen and Hibernian - the teams finishing immediately below Clyde in the table - would also qualify for Europe on their own merits, the Dons taking Scotland's Cup-Winners' Cup slot as runner's-up to champions Celtic.

Whilst they awaited their European fate, there would be frustration and disappointment for Clyde in their attempts to build on their success. Joe Gilroy became one of the first Scottish players to be tempted to join the rebel National Professional Soccer League of America, the former Queen's Park and Montrose striker reported to have accepted an offer to sign for Chicago Spurs, meaning the Shawfield club would receive no transfer fee whatsoever. As manager Davie White awaited the opportunity to speak with Gilroy on his return from the USA, and to convince a number of other players - including Harry - that their futures lay at Shawfield, the Clyde boss was then offered and accepted the post of assistant manager of Rangers, with Archie Wright of Airdrieonians named immediately as his successor. Gilroy would eventually reject the offer to cross the Atlantic and an opportunity to join Kilmarnock by signing back on at Shawfield, on the condition that any subsequent approaches which would allow him to move into full-time football would be considered by the club.

Clyde's worst fears were duly confirmed on Friday, 4 August 1967, when UEFA confirmed that the 'one city, one club' rule would be applied for the new season's Inter-Cities Fairs Cup, sixth-placed Dundee getting the nod to replace them as Scotland's third representative in the first-round draw. To rub salt into the Shawfield wounds, the Dens Park men would then go all the way to the last four of the competition, before following both Hibernian and Rangers as the third Scottish club to be defeated by eventual winners Leeds United.

Those wounds would take some time to heal. Last word on those two events in the summer of 1967, Scotland's round-the-world trip and Clyde's treatment at the hands of UEFA, goes to Harry Hood, who was in a unique position to assess both. Typical of the man, he did not miss the target when he looked back at those situations in 1968.

"A place in Europe. That's the dream for every club in Scotland, the incentive which livens up the fight for the top League places. I know how much it helped Clyde two seasons ago. Remember that season of 1966/67? It was the year Celtic became the first-ever British team to win the European Cup, the year Rangers made the final of the European Cup-Winners' Cup. Everyone wanted a taste of that European honey. Clyde were no different, although many people were stunned to see a part-time team right up beside the giants, Celtic and Rangers."

"Eventually, we went on to take third place behind champions Celtic and runner's-up Rangers, and everyone at Shawfield looked forward to a place in the Fairs Cities Cup. We knew that as a part-time team, one of our problems would be getting time off from our ordinary work for the European trips, so as we crept up the table and the chances of that Fairs Cup spot moved closer to reality, many of the players worked on days off, to make sure they would have a backlog of extra days when we went to the continent. Alas for all our hopes, they were cruelly – and I feel unfairly – smashed when the Fairs Cup committee ruled that there could only be one team from one city in the competition. So, Rangers got the place for Glasgow and Clyde were out in the continental cold."

"We had to sit back and watch teams who finished beneath us march happily into Europe. There were defeated Scottish Cup-finalists Aberdeen, who got a place in the Cup-Winners' Cup. There were Hibs, two places below us, who got a Fairs Cup place. So did Dundee, who were three spots below us, and got the passport to Europe that we earned. Dundee certainly did not let Scotland down. They were the only one of the five sides who reached a semi-final place in Europe, and all credit to them. But can you blame the players at Shawfield for thinking a little bitterly to themselves at times… "it could have been us."

"I think this 'one city, one team' [rule] in the Fairs Cup was responsible for some of our League defeats later on last season. The incentive had gone. We knew that Celtic, as League Cup holders, were already in the Fairs Cup. We knew that if they won the championship and made the European Cup again then [likely] runner's-up Rangers would again get the Fairs Cup place. Frankly, I feel the approach of the Scottish football authorities to the problem was not good enough. I wonder if the position would have been accepted so timidly if the League had finished the other way, with Clyde ahead of Rangers, or Celtic. I can hardly believe that pressure would not have been brought to bear to make sure the 'Old Firm' also got a place."

"It was the same approach which typified Scotland's round the world tour last season. Afterwards, we were told that there had been discoveries who would be helpful in the World Cup campaign. To me, the two most successful players in that team were Doug Fraser and Bobby Hope of West Brom, but when the home internationals came around the next season, they never got a mention."

Chapter 13

A dream fulfilled as Harry scores against England at Hampden

As Dundee looked forward to visiting Amsterdam, Clyde kicked off the 1967/68 campaign in the rather less-exotic surroundings of Roots Hall, Southend on Saturday, 5 August 1967, normal service quickly resumed as Harry set up Ian Stewart for the opener in 15 minutes before crashing an effort off the upright. Stewart would grab a second in the second half with Sam Hastings also on target in a 3-1 win. The second and final pre-season friendly took place much closer to home 48 hours later, Morton's top scorer from the previous campaign Joe Mason continuing where he had left off in the spring with the only goal as the newly promoted Greenock outfit secured a morale-boosting victory at Cappielow.

The competitive season kicked off with another tough-looking League Cup sectional draw for Clyde, the Shawfield men paired with Hibernian, Dundee and Motherwell. The Bully Wee had to twice come from behind to secure a 2-2 draw at Fir Park in the opening match on Saturday, 12 August 1967, Harry with the second equaliser 10 minutes from time. There may have been a whiff of revenge in the air as Bobby Ancell brought his Dundee side to Rutherglen four nights later, the Dens men controversially awarded the Fairs Cup slot earned on the field by Clyde the previous season, that decision still the subject of heated correspondence between Shawfield chairman Willie Dunn and SFA secretary Willie Allan. Former Clyde favourite Jim McLean bit the hand which once fed him with the opening goal for the visitors, with Irish winger Sammy Wilson doubling that lead early in the second half. The points would head to Tayside despite a Stan Anderson strike reducing the deficit to 2-1 before the finish.

The third sectional match would also end in defeat, this time by 3-1 to Hibernian at Easter Road on Saturday, 19 August 1967, Scotland boss Bobby Brown amongst the 10,000 spectators and hopefully as impressed by Harry's performance as Shearer Borthwick of *The Evening Times*, who named him as star man. Sam Hastings had kept Clyde in the match with a tremendous shot just before the interval. Harry would open his account for the season seven days later, in the return match with Motherwell at Shawfield, coolly slipping the ball past Peter McCloy in the 13th minute to give Clyde the lead. Graham Macfarlane added a second 10 minutes after the restart, the hosts notching a first win of the campaign despite a last-minute consolation effort from the Steelmen's Benny Cairney.

Midweek brought a 1-0 defeat at Dens Park, Dundee qualifying as Group 3 winners thanks to Sammy Wilson's solitary strike on the half-hour, and a hugely disappointing League Cup programme for Clyde ended with a fourth loss in six games, as Hibernian won 2-0 at Shawfield on Saturday, 2 September 1967, Colin Stein and Peter Cormack with the goals either side of half-time. Archie Wright's men would play at Hampden 48 hours later, albeit against Second Division Queen's Park in the semi-final of the Glasgow Cup, the top-flight Shawfield side still trailing to an early John McLaughlan goal with just six minutes remaining before late strikes from Stan Anderson and Sam Hastings squeezed them through to a final meeting with either Celtic or Rangers.

Clyde would open their League campaign at the home of the European champions, Celtic, on Saturday, 9 September 1967, the majority of the 37,000 spectators enjoying the sight of a second consecutive championship flag being raised above the Jungle by the wife of chairman Bob Kelly beforehand. With Jimmy Johnstone struggling with flu and Jim Craig injured in the midweek victory over current world champions Penarol, Jock Stein handed League debuts to close-season signings Chris Shevlane and Pat McMahon. The two had taken very different paths to Paradise, full-back Shevlane freed by Hearts after his ankle injury was deemed career-ending then picked up by Celtic after a second specialist opinion suggested that was far from the case, with the Tynecastle club refusing to change their stance. Croy Bhoy McMahon had been the star of Kilsyth Rangers' Scottish Junior Cup-winning team in May, and the skilful inside-forward had seemed destined to join Tommy Docherty at Chelsea before Jock Stein swooped for his signature. He had already made two starts in the Hoops, against Partick Thistle in the Glasgow Cup and Aberdeen in the League Cup, scoring three times across those games.

Clyde would be minus last season's top goalscorer Ian Stewart, injured against Queen's Park, versatile Dick Staite taking his place with winger Russell Steele, their recent recruit from Ibrox, on the bench.

The teams lined up as follows.

CELTIC:

Ronnie Simpson; Chris Shevlane & Tommy Gemmell; Bobby Murdoch, Billy McNeill & John Clark; Stevie Chalmers, Pat McMahon, Willie Wallace, Bertie Auld & Bobby Lennox. Substitute: John Hughes

CLYDE:

John Wright; Harry Glasgow & Davie Souter; Stan Anderson, Jim Fraser & John McHugh; Graham Macfarlane, Harry Hood, Joe Gilroy, Dick Staite & Sam Hastings. Substitute: Russell Steele

The game would be won by half-time, by which time Pat McMahon had added a fourth goal to his fledgling Celtic tally, Lisbon Lions Bobby Lennox and Bertie Auld had made it 3-0 and Shawfield wing-half John McHugh had limped off the field with a leg knock. Harry had gone close to netting for Clyde on two occasions in that first period but there would be no further scoring with the only incident of note being the return from injury of John Hughes from the Celtic bench, replacing Stevie Chalmers, who left the field much quicker than his old Brunswick colleague. This created some comment, given that substitutes at this stage were still only allowed where a player was deemed unfit to continue.

It was another Glasgow derby clash up next for Clyde, with the visit of Partick Thistle to Shawfield on Saturday, 16 September 1967. Dick Staite replaced the injured John McHugh at left-half whilst Ian Stewart returned to his normal role up front. Harry had already gone close with one effort then saw a goal ruled out for offside before Stewart opened the scoring from the spot in the 15th minute, Hood beating George Niven again on the half-hour to make it 2-0 at the break. Both of the prolific duo would claim their doubles after the break, as would home striker Tommy Rae, as Clyde ran out 4-2 winners. As an aside, the two managers on duty that afternoon had been on opposing sides in the Scottish Cup final of April 1949, Archie Wright for Clyde and current Jags boss Willie Thornton for Rangers, as was present Scotland supremo Bobby Brown and Harry's old Sunderland manager, Ian McColl.

That victory was followed by two excellent points at Pittodrie, seven days later, despite Stan Anderson joining John McHugh on the injured list. Graham Macfarlane moved back to right-half with Kenny Knox coming in at outside-right. Aberdeen took an early lead against their under-strength visitors, Willie Watt giving John Wright no chance with a fierce strike, but Harry restored parity before the half-hour, beating his old Queen's Park teammate Bobby Clark from close range after good work from Harry Glasgow. A late winner from Joe Gilroy then made it a long but happy journey back to Rutherglen.

The run came to an end with a 2-0 defeat by Falkirk at Shawfield on Saturday, 30 September 1967. The scoreline was actually something of a travesty, unchanged Clyde on top throughout before being hit with a late double sucker-punch, Bairns striker Johnny Graham scoring via the crossbar then seeing his shot deflected past John Wright by substitute Russell Steele to secure an unlikely away win.

John McHugh returned to the line-up for the visit to Tynecastle which opened October, the wing-half marking the occasion with a fabulous strike from outside the box which gave Clyde the lead just before the interval. The game erupted in the closing 20 minutes, as first Hearts skipper George Miller scored a double within 60 seconds - the first from the spot - before late goals from Ian Stewart and Joe Gilroy snatched victory from the jaws of defeat, the visitors eventually edging a genuine five-goal thriller.

Next up for Clyde was a visit from League leaders Rangers, and the return of their former manager Davie White - now assisting Scot Symon in the Ibrox hotseat - before 24,509 spectators on Saturday, 14 October 1967. The hosts were unchanged, whilst Symon handed first starts of the current campaign to goalkeeper Norrie Martin and 'want-away' striker Alex Willoughby, with the full line-ups as follows.

CLYDE:

John Wright; Harry Glasgow & Davie Souter; John McHugh, Jim Fraser & Dick Staite; Graham Macfarlane, Harry Hood, Joe Gilroy, Ian Stewart & Sam Hastings. Substitute: Stan Anderson

RANGERS:

Norrie Martin; Kai Johansen & Willie Mathieson; John Greig, Ronnie McKinnon & Dave Smith; Orjan Persson, Andy Penman, Alex Ferguson, Alex Willoughby & Willie Johnston. Substitute: Roger Hynd

Harry was denied three times in the opening half-hour before John Greig fired home from close-range for 1-0. As with Tynecastle the previous week, the match would then spring to life in the final quarter, new Rangers signings Orjan Persson and Alex Ferguson heading goals either side of an Ian Stewart counter, as the match ended 3-1 to the visitors. Despite Clyde's defeat, sports reporter Peter Hendry described Harry's performance as "*superb*" in his column in *The Evening Times*, 48 hours later.

An injury sustained by captain Harry Glasgow against Rangers saw him miss out on the trip to Airdrie seven days later, Dick Staite yet again showing his versatility by moving back to partner Dave Souter, with Stan Anderson returning at wing-half. The hosts were wearing an unusual royal blue kit as they welcomed their old boss back to Broomfield and took the lead midway through the first half through striker Dave Marshall. Things then looked ominous for Clyde when Souter was dismissed after giving away a penalty seven minutes from the break, but John Wright saved George Fyfe's kick to keep the 10 men in the match, a sixth consecutive spot kick failure for the Diamonds. The second half was a different matter entirely, Harry going close himself before setting up Joe Gilroy for the equaliser within the first five minutes. With three minutes remaining, Harry turned goal-taker, beating keeper Roddy McKenzie from close-range to secure the points, his sixth goal of the season. The home side's misery was complete when winger John Phillips was sent off in the dying seconds for a challenge on Staite.

There would have been a certain amount of trepidation in the Shawfield air on Saturday, 28 October 1967, as Clyde entertained Kilmarnock, the Ayrshire side having won on their previous eight visits. The Bully Wee were also dealing with the loss of star striker Joe Gilroy, signed by Fulham 24 hours earlier in a £20,000 deal, the former Montrose man thus finally achieving his dream of full-time football. No prizes for guessing that Gilroy's replacement up front was…Dick Staite but the hosts would yet again overcome the loss of a key player, goals from Harry and Sam Hastings enough for Clyde to win 2-1 and secure the two points which lifted them above Killie,

Falkirk and Morton into sixth spot in the table.

Leading that table as we entered November 1967 were Scot Symon's Rangers, although on the first day of the month that would read Davie White's Rangers, after the long-term Ibrox boss was sacked, despite the official line that he had resigned. With European champions Celtic in Argentina preparing to fight for the World Club Championship, the timing of such a move would suggest that those who made the key decisions in Govan had begun to fear, feel then resent the chill in Jock Stein's shadow.

Back at White's old club, his successor Archie Wright moved into the transfer market to spend some of the Joe Gilroy fee on Dunfermline Athletic's Pat Delaney, son of the great Jimmy. Formerly an Ancell Babe at Motherwell, Delaney was equally comfortable playing in central defence or attack. He would not feature against his old teammates that weekend, the only goal of the East End Park encounter coming from the penalty spot with 20 minutes remaining, Pars winger Hugh Robertson the scorer.

Pat Delaney would make his Clyde debut seven days later, Saturday, 11 November 1967, the new man up front as struggling Stirling Albion visited Shawfield. Dick Staite duly added left-back to his list of recent positions but still managed to break the deadlock on the hour, after Harry's effort had been blocked. The points were sealed three minutes later by Ian Stewart, Clyde now moving past Willie Ormond's St Johnstone into an impressive fourth place. Celtic's chief scout Sean Fallon had been an interested observer at the match, raising speculation once again that Shawfield top scorer Harry Hood was the target for the Parkhead club. Reports had also linked Harry with moves to both Birmingham City and Aberdeen, but Clyde manager Archie Wright dismissed all of this out of hand, 48 hours later.

"In spite of reports that we are on the point of selling Harry Hood, I can truthfully say that we have not had an offer from any club for his transfer. I can also say that the only club officials I spoke to at Shawfield on Saturday were Stirling Albion men. I read that Sean Fallon was at the game. but we never met."

Harry was in his normal place for the latest clash of old rivals Clyde and Morton, played at Cappielow on Saturday, 18 November 1967, the in-demand forward going close early on before the hosts took command of the game. A Joe Mason double either side of the interval was followed by a third from Danish striker Bjarne Jensen. Harry did set up Dick Staite for yet another goal just after the hour, but the 3-1 win allowed the Greenock side to leapfrog Clyde in the Division standings on goal average.

That position would be reversed the following weekend, following Clyde's 1-0 victory over Dundee at Shawfield and Morton's 0-3 home defeat to Dunfermline Athletic. Harry turned in another man-of-the-match performance and it was from his cross that Sam Hastings headed the winner 10 minutes from the break. Ron Trevorrow was lavish in his praise of Harry's partnership with Stan Anderson in his Monday review of the match for *The Evening Times*.

"Most significant aspect of Clyde's thoroughly deserved 1-0 win over Dundee at

Shawfield on Saturday was the vast difference in understanding between the respective half-backs and inside-forwards. Clyde had obviously done their homework. The link-up work of right-half Stan Anderson and inside-right Harry Hood was well-nigh perfect, and a constant source of worry to an unusually panicky Dundee defence. Anderson and Hood were the Clyde aces. They read the game brilliantly and practically every Clyde attack – and there were plenty – emanated from their splendid inter-passing, which the Dundee defenders were never able to counter. It was from one such move that Clyde, who should have won this game by three clear goals, got the one that mattered in the 36th minute. Anderson, just inside the Dundee half on the right, stroked a perfect pass to Hood, whose equally perfectly judged cross into the goalmouth was neatly headed past a statuesque John Arrol by Sam Hastings."

Harry's form prompted calls yet again for his inclusion in the Scotland set-up. The eligibility deadline for the Under 23 squad for that season had been September 1967, Harry meeting the selection criteria by one month with the next list of names due to be announced by Bobby Brown in the coming days, ahead of the December 13 meeting with Wales at Pittodrie. Sadly, he would once again be overlooked.

December at Shawfield opened with a transfer request from Dick Staite, who had dropped to the bench for the win over Dundee. He would be restored to the attack for the visit to Muirton Park, Perth, with Pat Delaney moving to full-back to replace flu victim Harry Glasgow. Staite would do his chances of a move no harm with both goals in Clyde's 2-0 win, the man of many positions twice finding himself picked out alone in the box to beat St Johnstone keeper Jim Donaldson with clinical finishes. The next match scheduled was against Hibernian at Easter Road, the first icy blasts of winter weather seeing that fixture cancelled on the morning of Saturday, 9 December 1967. Preparations for the following weekend's home clash with Dundee United were then thrown into disarray with the shock resignation of Clyde manager Archie Wright for health reasons, 24 hours before the kick-off. The 43-year-old had only been in the Shawfield post for five months and would no longer be involved in senior football.

Football being the crazy game that it is, the match which followed was the highlight of Clyde's season to date, a 5-0 win over Jerry Kerr's men who had taken a point at Celtic Park two weeks earlier. Harry was in the midst of the action from the outset, the only surprise being that his opening goal did not arrive until just before the break, Dick Staite laying on the chance with a cushioned header. And the second half opened in the same fashion, Harry going close twice before his low shot deceived Donald Mackay in the visitors' goal for 2-0 in the 55th minute. Clyde piled on the agony in the closing quarter, with three goals in a four-minute spell. Ian Stewart converted a penalty before Sam Hastings and Dick Staite gave the managerless hosts their biggest win of the campaign in front of just 2,000 spectators. That would set the players up nicely for their annual dance at Shawfield the following Tuesday night.

That feelgood factor took a dent seven days later, as a Motherwell side struggling at the foot of the table built up a three-goal lead by the interval, thanks to strikes from Jimmy Wilson, Alex McCall and John 'Dixie' Deans. Clyde fought back well in the second half, Harry taking advantage of a defensive slip to beat Peter McCloy three minutes after the restart for his 10th goal of the season. But the hosts would have to wait until five minutes from time before Dick Staite added a second, as Motherwell edged a five-goal thriller to secure a first away victory of the campaign.

The calendar year 1967 ended with a 1-1 draw with Raith Rovers at Starks Park, the Fifers battling with Motherwell and Stirling Albion at the foot of the table and reeling from the loss of midfield star Ian Porterfield to Ian McColl's Sunderland the day before for £45,000. The visitors started on the front foot, Harry beating 16-year-old debutant goalkeeper Robert Aitken with a low shot in the eighth minute to give Clyde the lead. He then beat the youngster for a second time just before the break, looking on as his drive hit the inside of the post before being cleared. In the interim, Rovers equalised, top scorer Gordon Wallace setting up Jim Murphy to beat John Wright with a volley from a tight angle.

The new year opened with a visit from Celtic, Jock Stein choosing to rest several key men ahead of the following day's crunch League clash with leaders Rangers at Parkhead. Still without a manager, Clyde were along the usual lines, as the following teams ran out at Shawfield on Monday, 1 January 1968.

CLYDE:

John Wright; Harry Glasgow & Davie Souter; Stan Anderson, Jim Fraser & John McHugh; Graham Macfarlane, Harry Hood, Dick Staite, Ian Stewart & Sam Hastings. Substitute: Pat Delaney

CELTIC:

Ronnie Simpson; Davie Cattenach & Tommy Gemmell; Bobby Murdoch, Billy McNeill & Jim Brogan; Bobby Lennox, Stevie Chalmers, Joe McBride, Bertie Auld & John Hughes. Substitute: Charlie Gallagher

Clyde made it a perfect start to the new year with a wonderful opening goal within six minutes from Stan Anderson, his fierce dipping shot beating Ronnie Simpson all ends up. With Celtic's fragile grip on the Scottish title looking increasingly precarious, Jock Stein's Bhoys then showed the spirit of champions with a devastating three goal burst before the break, Stevie Chalmers with a double either side of a strike from the returning Joe McBride. The Bully Wee opened the second period once again on the front foot. Graham Macfarlane bringing it back to 3-2 just minutes after the restart. Chalmers would then be denied a hat-trick near the end due to a controversial offside call as the Hoops secured a precious two points. Despite the defeat, Harry had been very much to the fore, if Raymond Jacobs of *The Glasgow Herald* is to be believed.

"The power of Murdoch and Brogan at wing-half and the hard running of Chalmers and McBride, who scored Celtic's goals between them, were unmatchable over the

whole game by Clyde, for whom Anderson, Hood and Macfarlane took the eye in much briefer glimpses. Clyde forestalled any thoughts of a rout two minutes after the interval, when Macfarlane took Anderson's pass and shot home from an angle. Indeed, they played their best football in the next 15 minutes, during which Hood hit a post and Simpson made timely saves from Hood and Stewart."

Veteran goalkeeper Ronnie Simpson sustained a rib injury at Shawfield which would rule him out of the vital meeting with Rangers 24 hours later, the two Glasgow rivals now neck-and-neck for the title. John Fallon would take Ronnie's place between the sticks and would sadly be blamed for the two goals which gave Rangers an undeserved draw and left the advantage for the flag race very much with the Ibrox club. Across the city at a snow-covered Firhill, an unchanged Clyde side went down 2-0 to Partick Thistle, in front of watching Scotland boss, Bobby Brown. The Jags goals came in the second half from strikers Tommy Rae and Frank Coulston. The Shawfield team's disappointing festive programme had produced just one point from a possible eight, thus allowing both Dunfermline Athletic and Kilmarnock to push Clyde down into seventh place in the Division.

Spirits were immediately lifted as the Clyde board announced their latest managerial appointment, former player Archie Robertson. Currently dividing his time between a fuel technology role with the National Coal Board in Edinburgh and managerial duties at Second Division Cowdenbeath, Robertson had the perfect Shawfield pedigree, with over 300 appearances. It was his last-minute Hampden goal directly from a corner kick which had prevented Jimmy McGrory's Celtic from retaining their Scottish Cup in April 1955, Tommy Ring striking to win the trophy in the midweek replay. Both men would then play in the Clyde team which beat Hibernian to claim the old trophy three years later as well as international colleagues with Scotland during a golden era at Shawfield in the later part of that decade.

There was also a personal lift for Harry on Friday, 5 January 1968, Scotland manager Bobby Brown picking the Clyde star in the 14-man squad to represent Glasgow against Arsenal in the annual Glasgow Charity Cup match to be played at Hampden the following midweek. The full squad was as follows.

GOALKEEPERS: ***Ronnie Simpson (Celtic) & John Wright (Clyde).***

FULL-BACKS: ***Tommy Gemmell (Celtic) & Kai Johansen (Rangers).***

HALF-BACKS: ***Tommy Gibb (Partick Thistle) & John Greig, Ronnie McKinnon & Dave Smith (all Rangers).***

FORWARDS: ***Harry Hood (Clyde), John Hughes & Bobby Lennox (both Celtic), Willie Johnston & Andy Penman (both Rangers) & Tommy Rae (Partick Thistle).***

The weather claimed the planned fixture between Clyde and Aberdeen at Shawfield, whilst injury claimed John Greig and Bobby Lennox, the Rangers skipper replaced by Celtic's Bobby Murdoch and Lennox by teammate Willie Wallace, as the media reported that Harry would be the only player not from either of the two biggest Glasgow clubs in the following line-up.

Ronnie Simpson; Kai Johansen & Tommy Gemmell; Bobby Murdoch, Ronnie McKinnon & Dave Smith; Andy Penman, Harry Hood, Willie Wallace, Willie Johnston & John Hughes.

Despite assurances that the game would be played at Celtic Park or Ibrox if Hampden was unplayable, the organising committee announced on the Tuesday evening that the fixture had been postponed. It was actually never played, with the drawn match between Glasgow and Leeds United at Hampden in August 1966 remaining the final competition for the old Glasgow Merchants Charity Cup to this day.

Whilst most of the weekend football calendar was wiped out, Clyde's match with Falkirk at Brockville on Saturday, 13 January 1968 was given the all-clear. Kenny Knox came in for the injured Sam Hastings and marked his rare first-team start with the only goal of the game, played in treacherous conditions. Harry's corner kick found him in the right place with just five minutes remaining, a nod of his head giving the visitors a very welcome two points in Archie Robertson's first game in charge.

Harry would be on fire seven days later with a hat-trick for Clyde in a 6-3 win over Hearts at Shawfield. Graham Macfarlane got the party started in the third minute, when his corner kick deceived Jim Cruickshank to find the net. Shades of Hampden 1955 for Archie Robertson no doubt. It was also a corner which led to Clyde's second goal, 20 minutes later, Harry meeting Sam Hastings' curling cross to head home. After Bobby Kemp had pulled one back for Hearts, Harry turned goalmaker to tee up Kenny Knox and restore the two-goal cushion. Two minutes from the break, the roles were reversed, Cruickshank parrying Knox's header only as far as Hood, whose left-foot drive made it 4-1. The Gorgie men refused to lie down, Jimmy Irvine slamming home seconds before the half-time whistle ended a tremendous 45 minutes with Clyde 4-2 ahead. The scoreline remained thus until the closing 15 minutes, Kemp bringing the Tynecastle outfit right back into the match with a header. The final twist was saved for the closing 120 seconds. First Ian Stewart's excellent strike made it 5-3 before Harry got the hat-trick he richly deserved with virtually the last kick of the ball, the two points lifting Clyde above Hearts into fifth place in the table, with Dunfermline Athletic and Hibernian very much in their sights.

It was a performance which encouraged reporter Ron Trevorrow to wax lyrical about Harry's talents.

"In Harry Hood, Clyde manager Archie Robertson has inherited one of the best 'uncapped' players in Scotland. This game was a personal triumph for the inside-right. He scored three goals, made two others and generally tore the Hearts defence apart at the seams."

And those thoughts were echoed later in the week by his *Evening Times* colleague,

Gair Henderson.

"The return of Harry Hood has probably made all the difference to the football flow of the Clyde this season. He has been a bit of a genius in making the goals that have wrecked teams of the class of Hearts, Dundee United, Kilmarnock and Aberdeen."

The final Saturday of the month was Scottish Cup first-round day, Clyde welcoming the giant-killers of 12 months earlier, Berwick Rangers, to Shawfield. There would be no repeat fairytale for Borderers goalkeeper/manager Jock Wallace, beaten twice in the opening 20 minutes by Ian Stewart before putting the shutters up for the next 70. The shock of the round would take place a few miles away, as George Farm's excellent Dunfermline Athletic side, featuring the ghosts of Parkhead Past and Future – Bent Martin and Tommy Callaghan – eliminated cup-holders Celtic by the same 2-0 margin.

Clyde's reward for progression against Berwick Rangers was a second-round awayday to Partick Thistle or Kilmarnock, whilst Harry's own excellent form saw him again selected by Scotland manager Bobby Brown, this time for the Under 23 squad which would face England at Hampden in early February. The full list of 16 players announced was as follows.

GOALKEEPERS: ***Bobby Clark (Aberdeen) & Bobby Ferguson (West Ham United).***

FULL-BACKS: ***Francis Burns (Manchester United), Eddie Colquhoun (West Bromwich Albion) & Jim Whyte (Aberdeen).***

HALF-BACKS: ***Tommy Gibb (Partick Thistle), Bobby Moncur (Newcastle United), Steve Murray (Dundee) & Pat Stanton (Hibernian).***

FORWARDS: ***Peter Cormack & Colin Stein (both Hibernian), Harry Hood (Clyde), Willie Johnston (Rangers), Jim McCalliog (Sheffield Wednesday), Willie Morgan (Burnley) & Jimmy Robertson (Tottenham Hotspur).***

Archie Robertson left his NCB job to assume the manager's role full-time at Shawfield at the beginning of February. His first task was to watch Partick Thistle surprise Kilmarnock in the Rugby Park replay to qualify for a Scottish Cup-tie against his Clyde charges and his second was to take those same charges to Ibrox for a clash with League leaders Rangers at Ibrox on the opening Saturday of the month. The Bully Wee returned from Govan pointless, thanks to a solitary strike from John Greig on the half-hour.

Wednesday, 7 February 1968 was a red-letter day in the career of Harry Hood as he made his first Under 23 appearance for Scotland…against Alf Ramsay's powerful England youngsters at Hampden. The near-15,000 crowd included the full Celtic first-team squad and backroom staff, and they watched the following 22 players take the field.

SCOTLAND:

Bobby Ferguson (West Ham United); Eddie Colquhoun (West Bromwich Albion) & Francis Burns (Manchester United); Pat Stanton (Hibernian), Bobby Moncur (Newcastle United) & Steve Murray (Dundee); Willie Morgan (Burnley), Harry Hood (Clyde), Colin Stein, Peter Cormack (both Hibernian) & Jimmy Robertson (Tottenham Hotspur).

Substitutes: Bobby Clark (Aberdeen), Tommy Gibb (Partick Thistle) & Jim Whyte (Aberdeen).

ENGLAND:

Peter Springett (Sheffield Wednesday); Tommy Wright (Everton) & Emlyn Hughes (Liverpool); Tommy Smith (Liverpool), Alan Stephenson (Crystal Palace) & John Hollins (Chelsea); Colin Bell (Manchester City), Rodney Marsh (Queen's Park Rangers), Brian Kidd (Manchester United), Martin Chivers (Tottenham Hotspur) & Peter Osgood (Chelsea).

Substitutes: Roger Jones (Bournemouth), Howard Kendall (Everton) & Peter Knowles (Wolverhampton Wanderers).

The match would prove to be a personal disappointment for Scotland keeper Bobby Ferguson, the former Killie man widely criticised for both English goals in their 2-1 win. His fumble of Rodney Marsh's cross fell nicely at the feet of Martin Chivers in the 15th minute, the man recently signed by Spurs from Southampton for a British record £125,000 transfer fee needing no second invitation to score. Things looked bleak for the Scots when they lost Chivers' new club teammate Jimmy Robertson shortly afterwards to injury, Partick Thistle's Tommy Gibb replacing the winger. The best spell for the home crowd came immediately after the restart. Harry had watched his goalbound shot kicked off the line by Tommy Wright in the first half, but his moment of glory arrived seconds after the break, a fine curling shot which beat England keeper Peter Springett all ends up to crash off the far post into those famous huge nets. The winning goal would come somewhat against the run of play midway through the second half, Brian Kidd's corner flicked on by Chivers for the unmarked Rodney Marsh to knock home. Manchester United youngster Kidd would win the hearts of the nation a few months later when he scored against Benfica at Wembley in the European Cup Final on his 19th birthday. However, his gestures to the spectators in the main stand after that goal would leave a sour taste in the mouth.

Gair Henderson of *The Evening Times* was scathing in his review of England's approach, whilst very complimentary of the effort and talent on display from the young Scottish players.

"In the second half, when the Scots had levelled the score at 1-1 and were proceeding to get on top and to give their opponents a lesson in skilful football, England clearly decided that if they could not win by fair means they would win by foul. And foul

they did, from that point to the final whistle. All Scottish attacks were stopped by bone-crushing tackles and trainer Walter McRae was on the field almost as often as he was in the dugout. Scotland's goal, scored by Harry Hood just after the interval, was easily the best of the night – a spectacular 16-yard shot that cracked against the inside of a post with Springett helpless. Had Ferguson been in his true form in the Scottish goal, that Hood drive would have ended the scoring and the Scots would have won. There were plenty of young men with a big future wearing Scotland's jerseys. Willie Morgan showed more ball control in five minutes than the entire England team did in 90, and the slightly built Burns will shortly be a threat to [our] international full-backs. I also liked the coolness of Moncur, the enterprise of Hood and the skill of Cormack."

The fallout would continue into the next day, with angry Scotland manager Bobby Brown describing some of the English tackling as *"nauseating."* And another boss with the surname Brown was also in the headlines the same day, Sheffield Wednesday's manager Alan released from his own Hillsborough agreement and expected to return to Sunderland to replace Ian McColl, sacked from Roker Park after his side's recent FA Cup exit to Norwich City. Brown had left Wearside for South Yorkshire in July 1964, a few months before Harry's arrival at the club.

It was back to domestic business at the weekend, Archie Robertson returning to Cowdenbeath to sign Jimmy Burns. The new midfielder started on the bench for Clyde against Airdrieonians at Broomfield 24 hours later but was called into action within 15 minutes, after Stan Anderson suffered a knee injury. Harry went close with one effort in the first half, but a disappointing match would end goalless. The dropped point faded into insignificance with the news that the talented Anderson would require a cartilage operation, just one week after teammate Russell Steele had undergone the same surgery.

The Scottish Cup second-round tie with Partick Thistle was twice postponed due to snow on the Firhill pitch but finally went ahead on Friday, 23 February 1968, the evening before the full international between Scotland and England at Hampden. More than 14,000 spectators rolled up to Maryhill to see which of the two Glasgow rivals would travel to face Dunfermline Athletic in the next round. Thistle scored first through Frank Coulson, just five minutes in, with Ian Stewart restoring parity after an hour where Clyde had made and missed the better chances. Within two minutes, the hosts were ahead again through winger Brian Gallagher. Harry *"pulled Clyde together with his sheer skill and class,"* but despite that it would be his Scotland Under 23 colleague Tommy Rae who was heavily involved in the next and ultimately decisive goal, 10 minutes later, his shot at the end of a solo run beating John Wright before coming back off the post, leaving John Flanagan a tap-in for 3-1. The never-say-die Dick Staite reduced the leeway in the closing stages, however, Thistle held out to progress to that quarter-final date with Celtic's conquerors in Fife.

Clyde would suffer further disappointment the following midweek, when they came up against a Kilmarnock side on top form at Rugby Park. Scotland prospect Tommy McLean was the inspiration behind the Ayrshire side's 5-1 victory, the tiny winger setting up Gerry Queen for goals at the start of each half before scoring a tremendous third himself with 20 minutes remaining. Graham Macfarlane had briefly pulled the visitors back into the game but further strikes from Kenny Cameron and John Gilmour completed the rout, the heaviest defeat of the season to date for the Shawfield club.

Archie Robertson's men would bounce back in spectacular style three days later, Saturday, 2 March 1968, despite missing the suspended Dick Staite. Veteran keeper Tommy McCulloch was restored between the posts and left-back Eddie Mulheron made a welcome return to the bench after 14 months out with a broken leg but it was two new boys who would make the headlines on the day, Pat Delaney and Jimmy Burns both scoring doubles as Clyde edged a seven-goal thriller with high-flying Dunfermline Athletic at Shawfield. The hosts led 3-1 at the break and were cruising three goals clear by the hour before late counters from Hugh Robertson and John Lunn put a somewhat misleading complexion on the final scoreline. Harry had been paid the ultimate compliment, Dunfermline's Alex Totten handed a man-marking role on the Clyde talisman, and whilst this perhaps curtailed his direct involvement in proceedings, it did free up space for Burns to turn in a man-of-the-match performance from right midfield, whilst Delaney had a field day up front against his former colleagues.

That win meant Clyde headed to Annfield for the match against bottom-of-the-table Stirling Albion the following Saturday full of confidence. The hosts had the better of the goalless first half before the roof caved in on the Shawfield men within two minutes of the restart, a double from Beanos striker Joe Hughes setting Albion up for a very welcome two points. Those would be confirmed just after the hour when winger George Peebles finished off a counter-attack and the match with a third goal, the home side thus recording just their second League win of the campaign after 25 attempts.

Next up for Archie Robertson's men was a visit from Scottish Cup semi-finalists Morton, on Saturday, 16 March 1968. Clyde welcomed back Dick Staite and Ian Stewart, with Pat Delaney and Kenny Knox dropping out. The opening goal after 25 minutes was a personal disaster for Greenock defender Billy Gray, who nodded a Graham Macfarlane corner past his own keeper Bobby Russell for 1-0. The match was then turned on its head before the interval, as Willie Allan struck twice for Morton to leave the Bully Wee facing a second consecutive defeat. That prospect looked more certain as we entered the final minute before Harry popped up with a last-gasp equaliser to rescue an unlikely point.

Clyde's disappointing spell continued with a 3-0 defeat to Dundee at Dens Park seven days later. The hosts carried the majority of the attacking threat throughout, but the game remained goalless with 20 minutes remaining before George McLean struck an eight-minute hat-trick to leave Clyde with just that one win against Dunfermline Athletic from their last eight matches and eighth in the League table.

They would get back on the rails in midweek, Stan Anderson making a remarkably early return from knee surgery and pivotal in the 1-0 victory over Aberdeen at Shawfield. The game's only goal arrived seven minutes into the second half, John McHugh picking out Kenny Knox superbly for the winger to beat Dons keeper Bobby Clark at the far post. Jock Stein had recently made Aberdeen an offer for their much-fancied inside-forward Jimmy Smith, however, *The Glasgow Herald* reporter on duty in Rutherglen had no doubt who the star player was on this particular Wednesday evening.

"Only an occasional glimpse of imaginative football was had at Shawfield Stadium last night and most of that came from one talented player – Harry Hood, Clyde's centre-forward. Hood's intelligence created all sorts of problems for Aberdeen's defence, particularly in the first half, and had Stewart and Anderson been more alert goals must surely have come."

The Scottish Cup semi-finals produced a 10-day gap in the fixture list for Clyde, Hibernian the next visitors to Shawfield on Saturday, 6 April 1968. Archie Robertson brought back keeper John Wright and winger Graham Macfarlane with Tommy McCulloch and Aberdeen matchwinner Kenny Knox missing out. Things were looking bright at the interval as the hosts enjoyed a 2-0 lead, courtesy of an early Stan Anderson strike and Ian Stewart's bundled effort just before the break. The Leith fightback started on the hour, Colin Stein following up to score from close-range after Wright failed to hold a shot, and it was complete five minutes later when Jim O'Rourke capitalised on another goalkeeping error to finish the scoring at 2-2.

Clyde would lose Graham Macfarlane and Ian Stewart to injury and flu respectively for the midweek visit of St Johnstone to Shawfield. Willie Ormond's men were battling with Motherwell to avoid the dreaded drop to Division Two with already-doomed Stirling Albion, and they took a huge step towards safety with a 1-0 victory. The only goal came with 10 minutes remaining, Alex MacDonald netting after a goalmouth scramble. The match is notable for Harry receiving a booking for dissent, as did his skipper Stan Anderson. The Bully Wee would then travel to Tayside three days later, Saturday, 13 April 1968, to face Dundee United at Tannadice. The hosts would dominate a first half in which they scored twice, through Ian Scott and former Rangers and Scotland winger Davie Wilson. Sam Hastings did get on the end of a Stan Anderson free-kick to reduce the deficit with 15 minutes to play, however, Jerry Kerr's side would hold on for a 2-1 win as Clyde's recent poor run of form continued.

That being the case, the last team the Shawfield players would want to meet was Jock Stein's high-scoring Celtic, fighting desperately to retain their title with an avalanche of goals which now topped the century in League games alone. But that was the challenge as Clyde ran into a rampant Hoops side in the final of the Glasgow

Cup, on Wednesday, 17 April 1968. There had been controversy in the semi-final when Rangers refused to play Celtic at Ibrox on the date put forward by the Glasgow Football Association at a time when they faced a Scottish Cup quarter-final tie with Hearts, an Inter-Cities Fairs Cup match at the same stage with Leeds United and a League run-in which saw them hold a slender advantage over Celtic. They had duly been expelled from the competition then lost both cup ties, thus only the League Championship remained a possibility for Ibrox. As it happened, Rangers would face Morton at Cappielow in their game in hand, whilst Celtic and Clyde contested the Glasgow Cup final.

The following teams lined up at Hampden as follows, before 25,000 spectators.

CLYDE:

Tommy McCulloch; Harry Glasgow & Davie Souter; Stan Anderson, Jim Fraser & John McHugh; Harry Hood, Dick Staite, Pat Delaney, Ian Stewart & Sam Hastings. Substitute: Jimmy Burns

CELTIC:

Ronnie Simpson; Jim Craig & Tommy Gemmell; Bobby Murdoch, Billy McNeill & Jim Brogan; Jimmy Johnstone, Bobby Lennox, Willie Wallace, Charlie Gallagher & John Hughes. Substitute: John Clark

Following the high of playing for his country at Hampden in February, Harry would suffer the heaviest defeat of his professional career at the same venue two months later. The Hoops had held the Glasgow Cup since the 2-0 victory over Clyde at Celtic Park four years earlier, when a teenage Harry had scored the winner in the Ibrox semi-final then saw his hopes of a first cup-winner's medal dashed against his favourite team. They showed no inclination to give the trophy up anytime soon, scoring seven goals in a breathtaking 24-minute spell in the first half, Jimmy Johnstone, Bobby Lennox with a 10-minute hat-trick, John Hughes with a brace and Tommy Gemmell doing the damage. Fortunately, for Harry and Clyde, Celts eased off in the second half, only a Bobby Murdoch strike early on adding to the Bully Wee misery. The stunning 8-0 victory equalled a record scoreline for this final which had stood since Queen's Park's demolition of Partick Thistle back in 1889, the year after Celtic was founded. A perfect evening for Jock Stein's men was complete as news filtered through of Rangers draw at Cappielow, a result which finally tilted the scales in favour of the Hoops with just two League games remaining.

Clyde had three matches still to play, the first of those three days later away to a Motherwell side whose hopes of remaining in the top Division were hanging by a thread, the Steelmen two points behind St Johnstone having played one game more. Archie Robertson's plan to field Eddie Mulheron failed to come to pass, young Jim McGregor making his senior debut at left-back following his recent call-up from Yoker Athletic and Davie Souter pushed up to outside-right in the continued absence of Graham Macfarlane. Souter would be replaced by Ian Stewart after a goalless first half, and it would be the substitute's goal with 20 minutes left on the clock which would call time on Motherwell's 14-year tenure in the top-flight, their 1-0 defeat combined with St Johnstone's 4-0 victory over Partick Thistle at Firhill enough to send them down with Stirling Albion.

The penultimate League fixture presented a more difficult challenge, third-placed Hibernian at Easter road, on Wednesday, 24 April 1968. A Joe Davis penalty was followed by a second from Jim O'Rourke as the host took control of proceedings early on. Clyde did pull one back just before the break, Sam Hastings netting after Hibs keeper Willie Wilson had misjudged Harry's cross, but the second period failed to produce another goal as the points stayed in Leith.

Archie Robertson's men then brought the curtain down on the 1967/68 season with a dazzling display of attacking football against Raith Rovers at Shawfield on Tuesday, 30 April 1968. The Fifers included their newly crowned Scottish Football Writers Player of the Year Gordon Wallace up front, but the stars on the night would be wearing the colours of Clyde. Harry produced an outstanding performance at inside-right, despite failing to improve on his 15-goal tally for the season, whilst 'play anywhere' Dick Staite recorded a hat-trick in the hosts' 5-0 victory. That lifted Clyde above Dundee into a highly respectable eighth position in the first Division table, with a perfectly symmetrical record of 34 points from 34 games, 15 wins and 15 losses, and 55 goals both scored and conceded.

Whilst not quite matching the dizzy heights of the previous campaign, the part-time Shawfield outfit had continued to punch above its weight against clubs with much more substantial resources, with Harry again earning rave reviews for his displays and attracting the attention of potential suitors.

Chapter 14

Harry's Shawfield legacy: Goals, memories...and floodlights!

There was a lovely Hood family cameo to kick off the new campaign, as Clyde travelled to face junior outfit Cumbernauld United at Ravenswood on Saturday, 27 July 1968, as part of their pre-season preparations. Harry's brother Jack picks up the story.

"We lived in Garrowhill at the time. Harry called to tell me that Clyde were playing Cumbernauld, so I went along with him. When we arrived at the ground, their manager asked me if I had my boots with me, which of course I hadn't. Anyway, long story short, they sorted me out with a pair, and I ended up playing for Cumbernauld against Harry and Clyde. John McHugh and I were good pals. We had played at Brunswick together. At one point, I beat him, then I looked behind me and there's big John coming after me. Clyde won 7-3 but after the match, their manager Archie Robertson asked me to consider coming back."

The as yet unsigned Harry Hood commenced what would be his final season with Clyde by scoring in a 4-1 win over Aberdeen in the opening League Cup sectional tie at Shawfield, on Saturday, 10 August 1968. The Dons included their new signings Jim Forrest and Tommy Rae, signed from Preston North End and Partick Thistle respectively, and they took an early lead through Davie Robb. They would then be blown away by the response from the home side, featuring leg-break victim Eddie Mulheron for the first time in 18 months, the long-serving full-back made skipper for the day following a request from regular captain Harry Glasgow on behalf of the players, a lovely touch. Stan Anderson crashed two tremendous strikes past Bobby Clark in the space of six minutes, just before the interval, and Clyde went 3-1 up when Harry fastened on to Dick Staite's cushioned header to volley home within seconds of the restart. Staite was again involved in the final goal of the game, on the hour, this time setting up Jimmy Burns to round off a perfect afternoon's work with a low shot into the far corner.

Clyde were handed the by-now annual difficult League Cup group, Scottish Cup-winners Dunfermline Athletic and Jerry Kerr's dangerous Dundee United the other clubs involved. The midweek trip to Tannadice saw all three of Saturday's main men – Stan Anderson, Harry Hood and Dick Staite - on the scoresheet, as the Bully Wee edged a five-goal thriller to maintain their 100% start to the campaign. That run was halted at East End Park on Saturday, 17 August 1968. With Jim Fraser injured, Pat Delaney came in at centre-half against his old club and it was his error which allowed Barry Mitchell in to give the Pars the lead after 20 minutes. Anderson equalised just before the break, the wing-half taking a short free-kick before blasting the ball past Bent Martin for his fourth goal in three games. The winner arrived 10 minutes after the restart, and it went the way of the home side, Tommy Callaghan's flighted cross headed home by Bert Paton. At the halfway stage, Clyde, Aberdeen and Dunfermline Athletic all shared top spot with four points, Dundee United effectively out of the running after three defeats. The report in Monday's *Evening Times* summed up the key factors involved in the disappointing result.

"Most disillusioned football boss in Scotland must have been Clyde's Archie Robertson, who saw his hopes of a hat-trick of cup wins crumble at East End Park. Dunfermline cashed in on two defensive blunders to take the points and leave their section wide open. At the start, it didn't look as if Dunfermline were in that frame of mind, for Harry Hood and right-winger Graham Macfarlane were slicing through the defence almost with contempt. But gradually, and with a lot more menace in front of goal, Dunfermline came into the game. After Mitchell gave them their opening goal, they took charge. Clyde, in contrast, were jaded up front, Staite limping with a heavily bandaged knee, and Hood being carefully marked by left-half Callaghan and Thomson. Clyde, however, scored the best goal of the game, a raging 30-yarder from Stan Anderson. Clyde relied too much on Anderson in defence and Hood up front and, in the end, they could not complain at their 2-1 defeat."

The Bully Wee bounced back to take control of the group seven days later, first-half goals from Graham Macfarlane and Dick Staite producing an excellent 2-0 victory over Aberdeen at Pittodrie. The first of two home games that week which would decide their fate took place against Dundee United on Wednesday, 28 August 1968. Archie Robertson received some bad news 24 hours before kick-off, as Harry was forced to call off, the Clyde star confined to bed with a stomach complaint. There would be a few more of those around Shawfield the following morning after the shock 4-0 defeat to Dundee United, which left all four clubs capable of qualifying for the last-eight ahead of the final round of fixtures that weekend.

Harry declared himself fit enough to play against Dunfermline Athletic at Shawfield a few hours before the kick-off at Shawfield, on the last day of the month, and what a call that would turn out to be. Hood was unstoppable, hitting a hat-trick as the Bully Wee finished two points clear of Aberdeen and Dundee United and six ahead of the Pars. His first arrived midway through the first half, a 25-yard shot which flew past debutant keeper Stewart Kennedy. Three minutes after the restart, Harry was even further out when his swerving effort beat the young Pars stopper all ends up for the second time. The unfortunate Kennedy was 'celebrating' his 19th birthday, and his big day was further ruined when Hood duly completed his treble and the scoring from the spot in the 56th minute.

Daily Express reporter James Sanderson ran with the story in his Monday column.

"Clyde manager Archie Robertson spoke out last night about the gamble to play "invalid" Harry Hood that sent the Shawfield club smashing through to the last eight in the League Cup. And it was a gamble that could put three-goal Hood into Scotland's World Cup pool, to be announced on Wednesday. For sitting in a director's box seat, Scottish team boss Bobby Brown saw the 23-year-old come straight from four days in a sick bed, after a week without solid food, and sent Dunfermline crashing 3-0. This display, allied to Hood's goal-getting talents in previous games, has made a deep impression on Brown. Watch for Hood's name in that pool. For me, it's a certainty."

"And Robertson, the man who took the calculated risk of bringing this "invalid" back, earned high praise for his faith and a public "thank you" from his players. As they crowded into the dressing-room, jubilant and grinning, I was told: "The boss said we could do it. Just to forget the four-goal thumping we took from Dundee United in midweek."

"Robertson, talking of his calculated risk, said: "Of course it was a risk. Harry was pretty ill, as we all knew. But the important thing, an object lesson to a lot of players, is that he wanted to play. Not for himself, but for what it could mean for the team, to get out of his sick bed, determined and courageous."

"After he had taken the back slaps, Hood could only say: "Thanks. Now I just want to get back to bed and eat properly for the first time in seven days."

"Hood's "one-two-three" was a shattering experience for Dunfermline goalkeeper Stewart Kennedy, celebrating...what a misnomer that is...his 19th birthday! It was a nightmare for him, but it is unfair to blame him for all three goals. He can take a share of the blame on his young shoulders for the first, but not the next two. After all, how many top-class goalkeepers save a penalty? And Hood's was a model of everything a spot kick should be."

Before that clash, Clyde found themselves facing the champions Celtic in the opening League game of the season for the second successive year, this time at Shawfield on Saturday, 7 September 1968. Jock Stein would be missing three players injured in Dublin in midweek whilst representing the Scottish League, Willie O'Neill, Bobby Murdoch and Willie Wallace. Back into the side came Tommy Gemmell and John Clark, whilst there was a first start of the campaign for Joe McBride. Clyde would be missing Stan Anderson – the influential midfielder hurt in training - and long-term casualty Sam Hastings, but welcomed back Ian Stewart, as the sides lined up as follows.

CLYDE:

Tommy McCulloch; Harry Glasgow & Eddie Mulheron; Jimmy Burns, Jim Fraser & John McHugh; Graham Macfarlane, Harry Hood, Dick Staite, Ian Stewart & Jim McGregor. Substitute: Pat Delaney.

CELTIC:

Ronnie Simpson; Jim Craig & Tommy Gemmell; Jim Brogan, Billy McNeill & John Clark; Jimmy Johnstone, Bobby Lennox, Joe McBride, George Connelly & John Hughes. Substitute: Stevie Chalmers.

The old Rutherglen stadium was crammed with 22,000 fans, most expecting to watch Celts continue the high-scoring form which had seen them blow away Rangers, Morton and Partick Thistle in their own League Cup section. They would see three goals from Jock Stein's men, two of them late on from Bobby Lennox and a Tommy Gemmell spot kick, to put a rather flattering look on the scoreline at 3-0, after Jim Brogan had scored perhaps the finest goal of his Celtic career midway through the first half.

Clyde won both legs of the League Cup quarter-final against Ally McLeod's Ayr United side, who would be promoted from the Second Division at the end of the season. Ian Stewart's 25-yard rocket midway through the first half – his first goal of the season - was the only score in the first leg, played at Somerset Park on Wednesday, 11 Sep 1968. The hosts featured keeper Dave Stewart, who had played with Pat McMahon in Kilsyth Rangers' Scottish Junior Cup-winning team the previous season and would play in the 1975 European Cup final for Leeds United, plus Alex Ingram, a teammate of Harry's at Queen's Park. Both Harry and Ian Stewart would be on target with late strikes in Clyde's 2-0 win in the return leg at Shawfield, two weeks later, Wednesday, 25 September 1968. On the same night, two youngsters called David Hay and Kenny Dalglish were given their Celtic debuts by Jock Stein at Douglas Park, as the Hoops followed up their 10-0 first-leg humiliation of Hamilton Academical – Stevie Chalmers and Bobby Lennox each scoring five goals – with a 4-2 victory. Davie started whilst Kenny came on at half-time for Charlie Gallagher, and that would prove to be the final Celtic game for the Gorbals Bhoy, another wonderful player and gentleman who sadly passed away during the writing of this chapter, on Sunday, 11 July 2021. The two east end clubs would now meet at Hampden for the third time in 18 months, on Wednesday, 9 October 1968, with a place in the League Cup final at stake.

Between those last-eight ties with Ayr United, Clyde had played two League games with very different outcomes. The Glasgow derby at Firhill on Saturday, 14 September 1968 was a one-sided affair, Partick Thistle scoring twice in each half without reply, to record a resounding 4-0 victory. The Jags would be under new management by the following weekend, Willie Thornton moving to become assistant to Davie White at Ibrox, with Scot Symon - the man White had replaced - taking over the reins at Firhill. Clyde finally put some League points on the board against Raith Rovers at Shawfield, albeit only just. Harry opened the scoring with a tremendous header after 20 minutes, with Dick Staite doubling that lead 10 minutes from the break. When Sam Hastings made it 3-0 just after the restart, the points looked secure, but the Fifers replied with two goals of their own through Dave Millar and George Falconer to set up a nervous last 25 minutes. The hosts would eventually hold on for a 3-2 victory, and Peter Hendry of *The Evening Times* was fulsome in his praise of Harry as he looked ahead to the second leg of the League Cup tie with Ayr United.

"As I see it, Clyde hold all the aces. In addition to their 1-0 lead they have ground advantage, confidence after the win over Raith Rovers and Harry Hood is their forward line. On his day – and that is fairly often – Hood has no superior in inside-forward play. It is also polish with punch when Harry is in the mood. His goal against Raith keeps him out in front as Clyde's leading scorer with six of the best."

The next League match involved a tricky visit to Muirton Park, Perth to face St Johnstone, on Saturday, 28 September 1968. The best chance of the goalless game arrived just before the interval, Harry twice denied by Saints keeper Derek Robertson as the sides settled for a point apiece. The week which followed provided a cause for double celebration in the Hood household. On Wednesday, 2 October 1968, on the eve of Harry's 24th birthday, Kathleen delivered baby Siobhan Pauline Hood, a second daughter for the couple to join toddler Lisa. As Harry enjoyed spending some time with his newly extended family, he also had to settle for a continuation of his stay at Shawfield in the immediate future, his latest request to leave the club for full-time football rejected on the basis of the size of the Clyde squad, as manager Archie Robertson explained to the media after speaking with the player.

"With only a small staff of players, we can't consider selling any players. That is why we turned down transfer requests from Pat Delaney and John Wright earlier. If [that] changes in the future, we would then be in a position to reconsider."

If Harry was disappointed by that decision, then it appeared to make no difference to his performance the following day, as he and Clyde faced their old manager John Prentice, the former Shawfield boss having moved from Falkirk to Dundee in midweek. Hood had already brought out an excellent save from home keeper Ally Donaldson before he set Jimmy Burns up for the opening goal 10 minutes from half-time. Within two minutes a Harry Glasgow header had doubled that lead although John Duncan immediately pulled one back for the Dark Blues. The second half was only 10 minutes old when Harry's free-kick deflected off the Dundee wall to allow Burns to score his second of the afternoon, with home winger Alex Bryce netting against his old teammates just after the hour to make it 3-2. There would be no further scoring as Clyde made it five points from the last six available in the League.

A foot injury suffered by his star striker Harry Hood at Dens Park made for a very anxious few days for Clyde manager Archie Robertson ahead of the Scottish League Cup semi-final with holders Celtic in midweek. Harry attended Shawfield daily from the following Monday to undergo heat lamp treatment under the watchful eye of Clyde physio Tom Craig, the effort paying off as he was declared fit ahead of the Hampden kick-off on Wednesday, 9 October 1968. Robertson was in upbeat mood beforehand.

"We expect to give Celtic a real game tonight but obviously our chances will be greatly improved if Hood can play. His presence will be a great morale boost to the team. The players feel that if they can get the breaks [then] they can cause a big surprise and Hood is a great goalscorer."

With Jimmy Johnstone beginning a club suspension following an altercation with Jock Stein during the victory over Dundee United at the weekend, Bobby Lennox made a rare appearance on the right wing for Celtic as the teams lined up at Hampden as follows.

CELTIC:

Ronnie Simpson; Jim Craig & Tommy Gemmell; Bobby Murdoch, Billy McNeill & Jim Brogan; Bobby Lennox, Willie Wallace, Stevie Chalmers, Joe McBride & John Hughes. Substitute: George Connelly.

CLYDE:

John Wright; Harry Glasgow & Eddie Mulheron; Stan Anderson, Jim Fraser & John McHugh; Graham Macfarlane, Harry Hood, Dick Staite, Jimmy Burns & Jim McGregor. Substitute: Ian Stewart.

Archie Robertson was correct to be optimistic, as his Clyde team defended for their lives whilst causing several problems for Ronnie Simpson at the other end of the field. Harry Hood was described as a *"constant threat,"* but it would be Celtic who would progress to a final meeting with Hibernian, thanks to a late George Connelly strike. The big Fifer scored with a fierce shot off the crossbar just three minutes after replacing the injured Joe McBride, to send most of the 35,000 spectators home happy.

Celtic's future Hampden opponents would provide the next challenge for Clyde as Hibernian rolled up to Shawfield three days later, the visitors enjoying the better of the opening half-hour before Graham Macfarlane's break down the right saw the winger set up Harry for a neat finish, his eighth goal of the season coming very much against the run of play. Justice was served on the hour when another much sought after young Scottish target - Peter Cormack - took aim from fully 30 yards to beat John Wright in the home goal, the match duly ending with honours even at 1-1.

A trip to the Granite City on Saturday, 19 October 1968 gave Clyde the opportunity to record a third victory of the season over League Cup group opponents, Aberdeen. This they duly achieved, thanks to an own goal from Dons wing-half Martin Buchan after 20 minutes. The Bully Wee had a second slice of good luck in the closing moments, a shot from Aberdeen's Danish right-half Jens Petersen beating John Wright to come crashing down off the crossbar onto the line, before being scrambled clear.

The two points earned at Pittodrie had enabled Clyde to move into the top half of the table, and that push continued seven days later with a 2-0 win over Falkirk at Shawfield. Dick Staite had recovered from his ongoing thigh problem to take his place again at centre-forward, with Graham Macfarlane reverting to the right wing, whilst

Tommy McCulloch replaced John Wright between the sticks. Willie Cunningham had replaced John Prentice in the Brockville dugout but his first match in charge of the Bairns would end in defeat, despite an excellent display from young keeper Stewart Rennie. Harry did manage to beat him midway through the first half, then crossed for the returning Staite to double the lead seven minutes from the break, the Bully Wee extending their good form to move up to sixth place in the division, behind Rangers only on goal average and just two points behind league leaders Celtic.

November opened with a visit to Tannadice, Dundee United enjoying the majority of possession but Clyde defending resolutely until conceding with just six minutes remaining. There was a certain irony in that the scorer Andy Rolland had been a target for the club whilst the full-back was at Cowdenbeath. Seven days later, the roles were reversed at Shawfield. This time Airdrieonians withstanding a barrage of Clyde attacks before Sam Hastings snatched the only goal of the game in the 88th minute. The see-saw month continued with a second 2-1 defeat away to Dunfermline Athletic in three months. The Pars were two goals ahead within 25 minutes through Barrie Mitchell and Willie Renton before Jimmy Burns clawed one back for the below-par Bully Wee seconds from the break with a long-range strike.

Clyde faced a major challenge the following Saturday, 23 November 1968, with the visit of former manager Davie White and his expensively assembled Rangers team to Shawfield. They included Colin Stein, involved in Scotland's first-ever internal six-figure transfer when he moved from Easter Road to Ibrox on the last day of October for £100,000, and Alex MacDonald, the midfielder making his debut having signed from St Johnstone for half that amount in midweek. The full line-ups were as follows.

CLYDE:

John Wright; Harry Glasgow & Eddie Mulheron; Stan Anderson, Jim Fraser & John McHugh; Graham Macfarlane, Harry Hood, Dick Staite, Jimmy Burns & Sam Hastings. Substitute: Ian Stewart.

RANGERS:

Norrie Martin; Kai Johansen & Willie Mathieson; John Greig, Ronnie McKinnon & Dave Smith; Alex Willoughby, Alex MacDonald, Colin Stein, Willie Johnston & Orjan Persson. Substitute: Roger Hynd.

The visitors would enjoy the majority of the chances in the first half in front of 21,000 spectators, and they took the lead eight minutes after the restart when Colin Stein continued his high-scoring start to his Ibrox career by forcing the ball home from close-range. Jimmy Burns squandered a glorious chance to equalise immediately with a fresh air swipe in front of goal and Harry escaped the personal attention of Rangers captain John Greig to force a decent save out of Norrie Martin but as the clock ticked down, it looked like the points were heading to Govan. Cue Clyde hero Harry Glasgow, Shawfield belonging to him that evening after he charged through the Rangers defence to head home a Sam Hastings free-kick with just three minutes remaining. As an aside, a few miles to the north, Tommy Callaghan made his Celtic debut at Firhill on the same day, having signed for £35,000 from Dunfermline Athletic 24 hours earlier, the wing-half celebrating the event by scoring an excellent first goal in the Hoops in the 4-0 win. Jock Stein had brought the player to East End Park as a youngster from Fife junior outfit Lochore Welfare six years earlier. Thus Tommy has a unique claim to fame, as the only man ever to be signed twice by the legendary Celtic boss.

There was another late rescue act at Shawfield seven days later, as a Kilmarnock side including the McLean brothers Jim and Tommy came to Rutherglen and took the lead within 90 seconds through Eddie Morrison, the striker nodding home a corner-kick from the younger McLean sibling. That goal would still separate the teams as we headed into the closing 10 minutes before Clyde came storming back to win the match. Stan Anderson brought the hosts level, but the final word would go to Harry, his 85th minute header beating his old Sunderland goalkeeper Sandy McLaughlan to clinch the points and move him into double figures for the season.

Clyde travelled through to Edinburgh on the first Saturday of December for a meeting with Hearts at Tynecastle. Dick Staite's latest battle with injury saw Davie Souter drafted into the centre-forward role but, as always, the Bully Wee adapted, Stan Anderson giving them the lead midway through the first half with another special goal, a 30-yard drive which beat Jim Cruickshank all ends up. Within five minutes Jimmy Burns converted a Graham Macfarlane cross to make it 2-0, with the prolific Alan Gordon halving the deficit just before the break. The crucial next goal would go the way of the visitors, Harry netting his 11th of the season five minutes after the restart, after a mistake in the Hearts defence. Gordon would collect his double with 20 minutes to go but Clyde would follow up their win over Kilmarnock with another impressive victory over one of sides alongside them in the League table.

The Evening Times' Shearer Borthwick was glowing in his praise of the Shawfield outfit 48 hours later.

"The teamwork, the understanding, the one-for-all spirit were the main ingredients of Clyde's success, and the polish was provided by two brilliant wingers, Macfarlane and Hastings, plus some highly intelligent play by Hood. The goals were mainly spectacular affairs. Stan Anderson's long-range effort was a beauty and the goals from Burns and Hood followed some really brilliant approach play."

Morton arrived at an icy Shawfield on Saturday, 14 December 1968 and left with a hard-earned point, both sides contriving to miss a number of decent chances as the match ended goalless. Nevertheless, there had been enough to entertain and impress *The Evening Times* match reporter Ron Trevorrow.

"Despite Morton's more effective all-round teamwork in the later stages, Clyde had in Harry Hood and John McHugh the outstanding men on the field. Hood, as so often in the past, was the man who made Clyde's attack tick. Some of his close dribbling on the bumpy surface was delightful. Unfortunately, the other forwards never mastered

the conditions enough to take advantage of the inside-right's good work. One delicate touch of Hood magic in the first half is worth mentioning. Eight yards out and with his back to the Morton goal, he tamed a Graham Macfarlane pass ever so delicately and swivelled to hit the ball straight at a thankful Andy Crawford. And in John McHugh, Clyde had the best defender on view. The left-half seldom put a foot wrong and was always on hand to clear with intelligent use of the ball with head or foot."

The cold weather continued to threaten Scotland's League programme, Clyde's visit to Paisley one match which did survive on the Saturday before Christmas. Regular Saints keeper Denis Connaghan was declared unfit to face his old Holyrood teammate Harry Hood, Jim Thorburn between the home posts. The stand-in stopper would enjoy a clean sheet, the only goal of the game coming from Buddies striker Peter Kane, five minutes into the second half, as St Mirren duly edged above Clyde in the table. That would be the last action of 1968 for Archie Robertson's men, an early pitch inspection by match referee Tom 'Tiny' Wharton on the morning of Saturday, 28 December declaring Shawfield unplayable for that afternoon's visit of Arbroath.

Instead, the next game would involve the short trip across the river to 'first foot' at Celtic Park, on Wednesday, 1 January 1969. Clyde would face a Hoops side on the back of three successive draws, two of them goalless, a quite unique set of results for the reigning champions in those days. The 31,000 spectators who braved the cold weather watched the following teams take the field.

CELTIC:

John Fallon; Jim Craig & Tommy Gemmell; Bobby Murdoch, Billy McNeill & Jim Brogan; Jimmy Johnstone, Bobby Lennox, Willie Wallace, Tommy Callaghan & John Hughes. Substitute: Bertie Auld.

CLYDE:

John Wright; Harry Glasgow & Eddie Mulheron; Stan Anderson, Jim Fraser & John McHugh; Graham Macfarlane, Harry Hood, Dick Staite, Jimmy Burns & Sam Hastings. Substitute: Davie Souter.

Celtic would open the new year with a devastating display of firepower, new signing Tommy Callaghan helping himself to a double – the first a fabulous shot from fully 30 yards which crashed in off the post - whilst a ferocious Tommy Gemmell penalty kick and two second-half strikes from Willie Wallace and Bobby Lennox made it a comfortable 5-0 victory for the hosts.

The English scouts and managers were out in force at Shawfield 24 hours later, as Clyde welcomed Partick Thistle for another Glasgow derby. Tommy McCulloch was back between the home posts, and he was a hero within six minutes as he dived to save Jimmy Bone's spot-kick, John McHugh penalised for bringing down Thistle's highly rated winger Arthur Duncan. It would be Duncan who would grab the only goal of the first half, this time McCulloch helpless as the shot beat him low at the

Meet the family, as Pat Hood marries Bob Robinson in 1954. Back left is Peter and wife Meg, Jack and Irene. Harry is on the extreme right with his parents and brother George.

Proud Harry with George, Irene and Jack. This wouldn't be the last time he would wear a Stetson!

Harry & Mary Hood - Harry's parents. Photo taken around 1965.

Harry (second right) in that distinctive diamond kit of Immaculate Heart of Mary Boys Guild in Balornock.

Harry with niece Irene and nephew John Hood.

A young Harry at his front door in Balornock

ST ROCH'S F.C.
1920

The Brunswick and the Candy Roch

Jack Hood is back left in this Everton squad photo for 1959/60. Ex-Celt Bobby Collins is in the front row.

Harry with sister-in-law Lil Hood, sister Irene and brother George in 1959

The Celtic squad of 1906/07

Irene and Pat, the beautiful, elegant and talented Hood sisters who starred in Ice Reviews across Europe.

Harry and Kathleen pursued by media as speculation mounts that he will sign for Celtic on 2 November 1964

Harry and Kathleen marry at Christ the King Church in King's Park, Glasgow on 8 June 1965

Clyde FC players and wives looking elegant at the club's annual dance at Shawfield on 13 December 1966

Harry signs an autograph for a young Australian football fan on the Scotland tour in May 1967

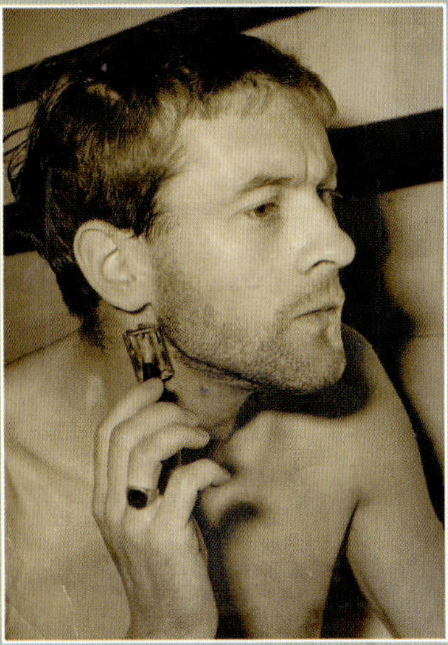

Harry gets out of his sick bed to play for Clyde at Dunfermline in August 1968

Harry and Kathleen share a toast after he signs for Celtic in March 1969

Harry leaves Celtic Park for Hampden for his first cup final in October 1969

Fashion icon Harry

Harry admiring the natty headgear worn by Celtic captain Billy McNeill en route to Basel

The Hood family takes shape.

A tender moment for mum and dad.

1977

ily
cord
SFRONT

Anne is the latest Stein star

CELTIC boss, Jock Stein, had to share the limelight yesterday—for once.

His son, George, 23, stole the scene from him when he married 22-year-old Anne McGi ey, from Burnside, Ruth glen.

For er Celtic star, Harry Hood married to Anne's sister, gave the bride away at a service in St Columbkille's Church, Rutherglen.

And later he also got in the act by giving Anne a real smacker of a kiss.

After the reception at a Glasgow hotel, George and Anne set off for their honeymoon in the north of Scotland.

George, who works with Strathclyde Regional Council, joked: "Anne's not as keen on football as I am—but I'm sure she'll learn."

If he takes after his father, she certainly will . . .

BUT THERE'S BAD NEWS

JOHANNES MAY BE MOVING ON

JOHANNES EDVALDSSON, Celtic's Icelandic international, wants to leave Celtic Park.

The 26-year-old defender or midfield player yesterday handed a written transfer request to assistant manager Davie McParland.

Edvaldsson said last night: "I ... feel it's time to mo..."

Harry gives sister-in-law Anne away at her wedding to George Stein in 1977 as a proud Jock Stein looks on.

A young Nicky Hood intimidating Scotland manager Jock Stein!

When Harry met Miss World… American beauty Marjorie Wallace won the title in 1973.

Left: Harry on horseback with Jack, Siobhan and Lisa. Right: "I played that shot too good!"

Harry looks back at THAT hat-trick with son Nicky and another fabulous Celtic striker, Chris Sutton

Left: Harry and Malcolm McNeill. "Might need a ruling on that bunker shot, Harry!"
Right: Harry and Kathleen enjoy dinner with close friends Billy and Liz McNeill

Harry and daughter Lisa with Stuart Ross

Left: When Harry ******* Hood met Rod Stewart.
Right: "You should have worn your flatties, Penny." "I'm wearing them, Harry."

Blondes have more fun

Five decades in the making…the award-winning Lisini Pub Co

The warmest of welcomes awaits you at

The Sherwood Manor Hotel

Personally supervised by Mr HARRY HOOD

Enjoy a quiet meal in our Restaurant

Business Lunch available from 11.30 a.m.-3 p.m. from 10/-

Watch your favourite TV Show in colour, in either our Public Lounge Bar, or our Cocktail Bar.

We can accommodate overnight guests, and of course enjoy a

SEVEN-DAY LICENCE

The Hotel is situated at

315 NEW EDINBURGH ROAD, FALLSIDE

UDDINGSTON **Telephone Bellshill 2275**

(½-mile from Bellshill Cross)

Mr Stephen O'Connor and his Staff will be pleased to serve you.

When Harry met Moussa…

Harry with his brothers Jack and George

Harry and Kathleen with his sister Irene 'Tai Tai' Bacon, surrounded by her grandchildren.

Harry and George with sister Irene and one of her three sons, Robin Bacon.

Harry with his favourite teams.

post to send the visitors in 1-0 up at the break. A cat-and-mouse second period then exploded into life in the closing 15 minutes. First, Jimmy Burns was in the right place to equalise following good work from substitute Dick Staite, but the cheers had hardly died down when Frank Coulson headed home from Duncan's cross to give the Jags a first away win of the season and consign Clyde to a third successive defeat. Those three losses would see the Bully Wee slump into the bottom half of the table in 10th place.

There was an immediate opportunity to start putting that right within 48 hours, the Shawfield men travelling to face struggling Raith Rovers at Stark's Park on Saturday, 4 January 1969. The Kirkcaldy side had lost all six previous League matches but they looked set for a very welcome two points in their relegation battle when substitute Bobby Stein – Colin's brother - headed them in front on the hour, against a Clyde team minus injury victims Stan Anderson, Sam Hastings and Harry Glasgow. Raith were denied no fewer than four times by the woodwork but held that lead until just three minutes from time, when John McHugh salvaged an unlikely point for the visitors following a goalmouth melee.

Archie Robertson's ongoing injury woes increased as Harry Hood had to undergo a sinus operation in Glasgow's Ear, Nose and Throat Hospital in midweek. The Clyde boss moved to plug the latest gap by bringing in young Jimmy Quinn from Celtic - grandson of the legendary Hoops striker of the same name - on a loan basis. He would make his debut in the home game with St Johnstone on Saturday, 11 January 1969, both Stan Anderson and Sam Hastings returning to action on what would prove to be a miserable afternoon for the Bully Wee faithful. Goals from Henry Hall and Fred Aitken just before the break put Willie Ormond's men in a commanding position, former Stirling Albion winger Hall completing his double in the 88th minute with his 17th goal of the season to end the scoring at 3-0.

Harry had a short convalescent break in the Sunderland area before resuming training on Thursday evening. Against all the odds, he was included in the team which faced Dundee at Shawfield on the Saturday, partnering Jimmy Quinn. The Dens side included three players who had worn Clyde's colours in the past, Jim McLean, Joe Gilroy and Alex Bryce. Hood, Quinn and McLean all struck the woodwork in the first half of a match which ultimately ended in a goalless stalemate.

Saturday, 25 January 1969 was Scottish Cup first round day, with Clyde drawn away to Second Division leaders Motherwell. Scotland manager Bobby Brown was one of more than 10,000 spectators who made their way to Fir Park to see the following teams take the field.

MOTHERWELL:

Peter McCloy; Davie Whiteford & Joe Wark; Tom Donnelly, Willie McCallum & Bobby Campbell; Jimmy Wilson, Jackie McInally, John 'Dixie' Deans, Tom Forsyth & John Murray. Substitute: Jim Muir.

CLYDE:

John Wright; Harry Glasgow & Eddie Mulheron; Stan Anderson, Jim Fraser & John McHugh; Graham Macfarlane, Harry Hood, Jimmy Quinn, Jimmy Burns & Sam Hastings. Substitute: Dick Staite.

This would be a remarkable cup-tie, the restored Eddie Mulheron involved in an early exchange with Jackie McInally which saw the former Kilmarnock man – the father of Alan who would play for Celtic two decades later – stretchered off. Harry then forced three excellent saves from Peter McCloy, the Motherwell keeper thought to be the main focus of Bobby Brown's attention. As McInally hobbled back on to the pitch, the next action saw Joe Wark drag Harry down in the box for a stick-on penalty kick. Clyde's joy was short-lived though, as Sam Hastings' effort beat McCloy but rolled to safety off the inside of his post. With 'Jumbo' Muir replacing the unfortunate McInally immediately afterwards, the visitors seized the initiative on the half-hour. Jimmy Quinn's pursuit of a long ball looked a hopeless cause, until the Celtic loanee deceived McCloy with a low shot which beat the keeper at his near post, his first goal for Clyde. The final attack of the half then saw a Dixie Deans strike ruled out for offside.

The second period got off to an explosive start with Jimmy Quinn dismissed after an incident involving former Aberdeen winger Jimmy Wilson. Motherwell pressed home their advantage and equalised on the hour thanks to a wonderful strike from Deans from outside the box. Things looked hopeless as Eddie Mulheron was sent off minutes later for dissent but somehow the nine men held out to take the tie to a midweek replay at 1-1. There would be added incentive for both clubs before that rematch as Monday's second-round draw saw their names come out of the hat first to be immediately paired with the winner of the Partick Thistle v Celtic tie, the Jags having equalised through Jimmy Bone in the dying seconds at Firhill to force their own Wednesday night replay at Celtic Park after a six-goal thriller.

The first part of that second-round puzzle was solved on Tuesday, 28 January 1969, as the Shawfield men won the home replay 2-1, before another healthy crowd of 8,000. The disciplinary system of the day meant that both Jimmy Quinn and Eddie Mulheron were free to play, as was Dixie Deans, who had just been handed a 14-day suspension for an earlier offence. With both Jackie McInally and John Murray unfit, Motherwell introduced two teenagers to their forward line, Ramsay Bryson and Keith McRae. If you are thinking that the latter's name is familiar you would be correct. McRae would later play for Motherwell, Manchester City and indeed the Scottish League between the sticks!

Young Bryson would make a dream start by scoring the opening goal within three minutes, his only strike for the club. The visitors would enjoy the best of the first half before being hit by a sucker punch seven minutes from the break. Peter McCloy had been at fault for Clyde's goal on the Saturday and had not been included in the Scotland squad announced two days later, Tommy Lawrence of Liverpool getting the nod. He would now suffer a third disappointment as he fumbled a header from Graham Macfarlane straight to Jimmy Burns who gleefully tapped home for the equaliser. The hosts improved greatly after the break, but it was one minute into stoppage time before the third and clinching goal arrived. Harry connected perfectly from Macfarlane's corner to send a shot rocketing goalwards, the ball striking a posse of defenders on the line to spin up into the air where Stan Anderson won the race to head home. That would set up a money-spinning sell-out clash with Treble-chasing Celtic for the following month, as the Hoops destroyed Partick Thistle 8-1 in their replayed tie the next night – with no fewer than SEVEN different goalscorers, Tommy Gemmell actually managing to net for both teams!

It was back to League business on the first day of February, with a trip to face League Cup-finalists Hibernian at Easter Road. With Eddie Mulheron and Jimmy Quinn now both joining the injury list, Archie Robertson took the opportunity to bring Davie Souter and Dick Staite back into his starting line-up. Hibs had responded to the loss of star striker Colin Stein to Rangers by spending some of that transfer fee across the city at Celtic Park to secure Joe McBride, the hitman starting on fire with a glut of goals at Easter Road and he would again be in the midst of the action against Clyde. It would also prove to be an eventful afternoon in Leith for Hibernian's prodigious young talent Peter Cormack. He opened the scoring in the sixth minute, firing home after a typical cushioned header from McBride had set him up. Joe then doubled that lead after 15 minutes, beating John Wright via the post, before Sam Hastings gave the visitors a lifeline from a Graham Macfarlane corner-kick, midway through the half. As at Motherwell the previous Saturday, the 47th minute would prove to be the end of the match for one of the players. This time it was Peter Cormack taking the early bath, the youngster retaliating after being fouled by Jim Fraser to leave his team a man short. He would be a relieved man as the game ended without further scoring, Clyde's winless run in the League now stretching to eight games.

As an aside, it was also a momentous day for Davie Souter. He had travelled by train from his Aberdeen home to the match which marked his return to the first team. He alighted at Dundee to check on the progress of his heavily pregnant wife, to find out that she had just delivered a baby daughter. On his arrival in Edinburgh, he made a further phone call to be told that he was now the father of twin girls. His humorous response was that he was thankful he hadn't been travelling much further!

Things would not get any easier in the short term, for Davie or Clyde presumably. Next up for the Bully Wee was a visit by a Celtic side which had followed up the eight goals scored against Partick Thistle with a nap hand in the defeat of Hearts three days later. The Scottish Cup second-round tie was due to go ahead at Shawfield on Saturday, 8 February 1969, however, as the icy blasts brought much of central Scotland to a standstill in the latter part of that week, the big match became an early casualty, much to the frustration of the 25,000 ticket holders. This meant that for the second successive round, both sides would know their potential opponents should they progress, Monday's quarter-final draw producing a home tie with either East Stirlingshire or St Johnstone.

The second-round tie did take place four days later with a 4.30 kick-off, due to police insistence that the initially agreed maximum crowd limit was unsafe for a match played under floodlights. It also went ahead much against the wishes of Celtic manager Jock Stein, who declared himself unhappy with the condition of the pitch, as match referee Bill Mullen declared it playable at 8am on the day of the game. With both Eddie Mulheron and Jimmy Quinn back for the hosts, the following sides took the field.

CLYDE:

John Wright; Harry Glasgow & Eddie Mulheron; Stan Anderson, Dick Staite & John McHugh; Graham Macfarlane, Harry Hood, Jimmy Quinn, Jimmy Burns & Sam Hastings. Substitute: Ian Stewart.

CELTIC:

Ronnie Simpson; Jim Craig & Tommy Gemmell; Bobby Murdoch, Billy McNeill & Jim Brogan; Jimmy Johnstone, Bobby Lennox, Willie Wallace, Tommy Callaghan & Stevie Chalmers. Substitute: Bertie Auld.

It would prove to be a significant occasion for two wonderful Celts, albeit for vastly different reasons. Those crammed into the Rutherglen arena would see Celtic goalkeeper Ronnie Simpson dislocate his shoulder early on following a clash with – would you believe it – Hoops loanee Jimmy Quinn, the veteran stopper preventing a certain goal but landing heavily on the frozen surface. Tommy Gemmell would replace the man affectionately known as 'Faither' in goals, at first temporarily, whilst the 38-year-old goalkeeper received treatment. Heroically, Simpson insisted on returning with the joint forced back into place, only to leave the field for a second and final time after just 17 minutes. With Bertie Auld off the bench and Tommy Gemmell once again wearing the gloves, Celtic's Scottish Cup hopes were quite literally on thin ice. In those circumstances, it is remarkable that they would still enjoy the better chances as the match petered out to a goalless draw. Sadly, that afternoon would be the start of Ronnie Simpson's injury problems which would ultimately cause his retirement from football after a 25-year career in May 1970. One can only imagine the thoughts of Jock Stein, who had not wanted the game to go ahead in the first place. Such a cruel and crazy game is football sometimes.

The Ronnie Simpson/Tommy Gemmell situation raised the question across Scottish football as to which outfield player would take over in the event of such an emergency. Clyde boss Archie Robertson said that Dick Staite would be his nomination, and in his absence, it would be a certain Harry Hood.

Three days later, Clyde's fixture with Falkirk at Brockville would be one of only three

First Division matches to survive the weather. Harry would be in his normal role threatening goals rather than defending them, his 17th minute header from Graham Macfarlane's cross giving the Bully Wee the lead on another difficult surface. He was then denied a double immediately afterwards as Stuart Rennie produced a wonderful save from his fiercely dipping free-kick. Eight minutes from the break, the Shawfield side did go 2-0 up, thanks to a dreadful blunder from Falkirk right-back John Lambie, the future Partick Thistle icon contriving to pass the ball beyond Rennie into an empty net. The Bairns did get back into the match on the hour, Johnny Graham following up his own shot to score, but within five minutes the visitors' two-goal advantage was restored. Some magic from Harry left two defenders in his wake before Jimmy Burns took his pass to beat Rennie for 3-1. Hood was denied yet again by the home keeper after another wonderful piece of skill, before a late fightback salvaged a vital point for Falkirk. Graham's low drive beat John Wright with 20 minutes remaining and as the game entered its closing stages, Bairns skipper George Miller equalised to deny Clyde a much-needed away win.

The big freeze continued to play havoc with the February fixture calendar, Clyde's home games with both Aberdeen and Dundee United the latest to be cancelled. That did allow Archie Robertson to take his players down to Inverclyde ahead of the replayed Scottish Cup clash with Celtic, which finally got the go ahead on Monday, 24 February 1969. The Hoops were buoyant, after an excellent 0-0 draw in the snow-covered San Siro the previous midweek raised Parkhead hopes of a second European Cup triumph in three seasons. A higher-than-normal crowd of 38,000 turned out on an icy evening to see the teams fight it out for a home quarter-final slot against East Stirlingshire or St Johnstone, who met in their own replay in Perth the same evening. With Jim Craig, John Clark and Jim Brogan all joining Ronnie Simpson on the injured list, there was a Celtic Park debut for Davie Hay in a much-changed line-up from the first tie at Shawfield, whilst Jimmy Johnstone played despite suffering from an ear infection. Clyde were unchanged, as Jock Stein and Archie Robertson named the following players.

CELTIC:

John Fallon; Tommy Gemmell & Willie O'Neill; Bobby Murdoch, Billy McNeill & Davie Hay; Jimmy Johnstone, Bobby Lennox, Willie Wallace, Stevie Chalmers & John Hughes. Substitute: Tommy Callaghan.

CLYDE:

John Wright; Harry Glasgow & Eddie Mulheron; Stan Anderson, Dick Staite & John McHugh; Graham Macfarlane, Harry Hood, Jimmy Quinn, Jimmy Burns & Sam Hastings. Substitute: Ian Stewart.

Stevie Chalmers gave Celts the lead midway through the first half, heading home after John Wright had parried a Bobby Lennox shot. Despite incessant attacking, Clyde always looked a threat on the break, Harry missing a golden opportunity to level the tie when he fired wide of the target. Stein's men would have to wait until the closing 15 minutes of the tie before further strikes from John Hughes and Bobby Murdoch sealed the 3-0 victory and a last-eight clash with St Johnstone, Tommy Gemmell seeing his last-gasp penalty kick well blocked by Wright to prevent a fourth on the night. That save was all the more remarkable considering that the Clyde keeper had been injured in the lead-up to Celtic's second goal, his elbow subsequently being encased in protective plaster.

As Celts and St Johnstone played off their last eight cup-tie at Parkhead on the opening day of March, the hosts winning by the odd goal in five, Harry was scoring twice in a 4-0 friendly win over Clydebank at Kilbowie Park. Jimmy Quinn and Ian Stewart were also on target with all the goals coming after the interval. The beaten Bankies keeper that afternoon was none other than Dick Madden, who had made his one and only Celtic appearance with fellow debutants Jimmy Johnstone and John Cushley at Rugby Park, Kilmarnock, in a horrific 6-0 defeat back in March 1963.

The Bully Wee's search for a League win extended into double figures as a late goal from former Sunderland striker Willie McPheat consigned them to a 1-0 defeat in the rescheduled fixture with Airdrieonians, played at Broomfield four days later. As an aside, McPheat's career on Wearside had ended in August 1962, when he broke his leg in a challenge with fellow Scot Bobby Collins of Leeds United. The latest loss saw Clyde sink to a season's low 14th in the First Division table. The fightback would start that weekend, with the visit of third-placed Dunfermline Athletic to Shawfield on Saturday, 8 March 1969. With Jimmy Quinn commencing his suspension following his ordering off at Motherwell in January – strangely, Eddie Mulheron was available despite being dismissed in the same match – Stan Anderson was moved into the centre-forward role. Anderson was enjoying an excellent season at wing-half and that would continue in his new attacking role, the former Ranger opening the scoring in the third minute following a mistake from Pars keeper Willie Duff, a member of the Hearts team which beat Celtic in the Scottish Cup final of 1956. The veteran stopper was then beaten twice in a five-minute burst just before the interval, Anderson bundling the ball home for his second before Harry made it 3-0 with a tremendous rising shot, his 13th goal of the campaign and his last for the club. There would be no further scoring after the break, Clyde finally enjoying two League points for the first time since the victory at Tynecastle in early December to move past Dundee in the standings.

It was the Dark Blues' Tannadice Street neighbours who were the next visitors to Shawfield, three nights later. Stan Anderson continued up front in an unchanged team and instigated the move which led to Sam Hastings giving the hosts an early lead. Scotland's top scorer Kenny Cameron brought Dundee United level on the half-hour with his 29th goal of the season. The end-to-end match swung back in favour of Clyde just before the break, Anderson again involved by chasing a 'lost cause' ball to the byeline, Davie Souter converting his cross to send the Bully Wee down the tunnel 2-1 in front. The pivotal moment of the night arrived midway through the second period, Hastings denied his second by the width of the crossbar just before Cameron's deceptive shot dipped over Clyde keeper Tommy McCulloch to complete his own brace and take him to the 30 mark, as the sides settled for a 2-2 draw.

There was a touch of symmetry about the match with Rangers at Ibrox on Saturday, 15 March 1969. Back in November 1962, Harry had made his debut for Clyde in the same venue as an 18-year-old hopeful. This day would now mark his final game for the club.

Despite pre-match optimism, John Wright and Graham Macfarlane had still not recovered sufficiently from their injuries sustained against Celtic, Archie Robertson duly naming an unchanged line-up again.

RANGERS:

Norrie Martin; Kai Johansen & Willie Mathieson; John Greig, Ronnie McKinnon & Dave Smith; Willie Henderson, Andy Penman, Colin Stein, Alex Ferguson & Willie Johnston. Substitute: Alex MacDonald.

CLYDE:

Tommy McCulloch; Harry Glasgow & Eddie Mulheron; Jimmy Burns, Jim Fraser & John McHugh; Davie Souter, Harry Hood, Stan Anderson, Ian Stewart & Sam Hastings. Substitute: Dick Staite.

It would be an afternoon to forget for the Clyde faithful amongst the 35,000 crowd, Dave Smith putting the hosts ahead within three minutes. By the half-hour mark it was 3-0, Colin Stein's header then a deflected Andy Penman shot finding their way past Tommy McCulloch, the former Hibernian striker claiming a double before the interval as the roof threatened to cave in on Clyde completely. The start to the second half was equally horrific for the visitors, Alex Ferguson and Stein both on target before three minutes had elapsed to take the score to 6-0. With Dick Staite on for Jim Fraser, Clyde's day went from worse to ridiculous when Ian Stewart was stretchered off, leaving the Bully Wee to play the remaining 16 minutes with 10 men. The match still had two surprises in store, the first being that there was no further scoring and the second when hat-trick hero Stein contrived to get himself sent off for the third time that season in the final minute, the £100,000 man retaliating after an incident with Eddie Mulheron, who was also dismissed. Stein's latest act of folly – his team 6-0 up against 10 men with seconds to play – would have consequences. The severe winter weather had given him a huge break by reducing his 28-day suspension to effectively a one-match ban. He would not be so lucky this time, the Ibrox centre-forward's next sentence causing him to miss the Scottish Cup final.

As one Glasgow-based striker contemplated his actions, there would finally be a dream move for another. On Sunday, 16 March 1969, after 96 goals in 197 matches for Clyde, Henry Anthony Hood became Harry Hood of the Celtic. *The Glasgow*

Herald carried the story the following morning, with news of Harry's successor at Shawfield included in the article.

"Harry Hood, Clyde's Scottish Under 23 international inside-forward, was last night transferred to Celtic for an undisclosed fee. The player recently expressed a wish to leave Clyde and, in the past, has made no secret of the fact that he would like to play for Celtic."

"It is the second time that Hood has left Clyde. He was transferred to Sunderland in 1964, but after two seasons with the English club he returned to Shawfield. Hood played in the Scottish Under 23 team who were beaten 2-1 by England at Hampden last season and was in the Scottish party who toured the Far East in the summer of 1967."

"Clyde later signed Billy Hulston, East Stirling's leading scorer, for what was described as a substantial fee. Archie Robertson, Clyde's manager, completed the deal after having travelled through to Stirling."

As well as the signing of Hulston, the £30,000 transfer fee received from Celtic was utilised in a quite unique and, with due respect to Billy, much longer-lasting way. Current Clyde FC chairman John Taylor has been a passionate follower of the Bully Wee for 60 years, his first match being a 6-0 destruction of Jock Stein's Dunfermline Athletic at Shawfield in April 1961, just a few weeks before Charlie Dickson and his pin-striped Fifers won the Scottish Cup and his beloved Clyde took the drop to the Second Division. The hosts even enjoyed the luxury of a missed penalty by the legendary Harry Haddock!

John took that wonderful photo of a teenage Harry in his early days at Shawfield which is featured in this book, as far as I can ascertain the first image of his senior football career. He would be too young to remember the occasion back in 1953 when Clyde inaugurated their new floodlight system against Matt Busby's Manchester United, the first club in Glasgow to take such a step forward. The original system would soon be upgraded, thanks to Celtic's cheque. John picks up the story.

"My main memories of Harry are from when he came back from Sunderland. He was the silkiest, classiest player. The most talented man I ever saw play for Clyde. Not a lot of people know this but his transfer to Celtic paid for the new floodlighting system to be installed at Shawfield. We always referred to them as the 'Harry Hood floodlights.' I guess we must be unique in that sense."

Life would never be quite the same, albeit not just for Harry.

Alan Maxwell is also a lifelong Clyde supporter. There is no doubt about his favourite Bully Wee player of all-time or of his sense of loss and disappointment as a teenager when Harry Hood joined Celtic.

"I was eight years of age when Harry signed for Clyde in 1962. By that time, I had been going to Clyde games with my dad for about three years. Harry became an instant hit with the fans and was certainly an idol in our house from the very start.

I particularly remember getting ready for school one morning when my dad was as high as a kite. He'd been at Ibrox the night before to see Clyde win in the Glasgow Cup. Harry scored the only goal and I'm sure Tommy McCulloch saved a penalty."

"I have a lot of memories of season 1963/64. That was a Second Division campaign. Morton ran away with the League, with Clyde as runners up. I think Harry really made his name that season. I was probably a bit too young to remember game specifics around that time, but I do vividly recall meeting the great man behind the main stand at Love Street. He was probably only about 19 but I am sure my dad asked him why he wasn't playing, and Harry told us that he had failed a fitness test. I recall it being a sad day in the Maxwell household when he departed for Roker Park. Again, I was too young to say I followed his career with Sunderland. It would be easy now with social media but not in those days. I will say though, Harry never left the memory of the Clyde faithful, including our own household."

"By the time Harry returned to Shawfield, in the autumn of 1966, I was in my first year at secondary school. There had been rumours of his return, but it was the end of the week before his signing was confirmed. I remember the Saturday morning of his first game back. I was playing for the school team at Scotstoun Showgrounds and I couldn't wait to get that match out the way to get to the Clyde game in the afternoon. This was immediately after England had won the World Cup (allegedly!). Clyde had famously started that campaign with each player having his own individual squad number, rather than the traditional 1-11 numbering. I'm sure Harry was given number 13 for the remainder of the season."

"1966/67 was a fantastic season to be a Clyde supporter. The standard of football was brilliant, needless to say greatly influenced by Harry. Just look at any match report and you'll see the references to "the flowing Clyde" or our opponents being "Hoodwinked." That was game after game. I particularly remember the first Scottish Cup semi-final tie with Celtic, which ended goalless. Harry had a great influence, as he always did. Very late in the game, The Evening Times reported that "It might have been Clyde who contested the April 29th final, but for a superb, one-handed save from Ronnie Simpson from Joe Gilroy in the 67th minute." Remember, this was the Celtic team who just a few weeks later were to lift the European Cup. Now, if only the great Harry Hood had been playing for Inter! Sadly, Harry would miss the cup replay. I remember finding that out on the night of the replay and I was heartbroken. The replay was a non-event with 'Hoodless Clyde' presenting no challenge on the night."

"Harry continued as a talisman at Shawfield for another two years and I probably saw the vast majority of his Clyde appearances. The League Cup section of 1968/69 was memorable. Clyde shared a section with Aberdeen, Dundee United and Dunfermline, and won it. Can you imagine that now? This was a hugely Hood-inspired Clyde side. They still managed to retain most of the 66/67 personnel. A 3-0 home win against the Pars always lingers in the memory banks. This was a 'Harry supershow' and he scored all three goals. In goal for Dunfermline and not blameless was a very young

Stewart Kennedy. I'd need to check but I think that may have been his senior debut. Clyde lost out 1-0 in the semi-final, once again to Celtic, thanks to a brilliant George Connelly strike. The Evening Times gave a glowing report of the Clyde performance and I recall that Ronnie Simpson produced a number of memorable saves, not least a great dive to thwart a Hood header. This was just a few months before Celtic sealed his signature."

"Harry moved on in March 1969. I was delivering morning papers in Jordanhill by that time. I always got to the shop early to scan the 'fitba pages' and, very sadly, 50-odd years on, I still do that. I was shocked to see that Harry had gone. He had been linked with Celtic for years but there had been nothing to prepare me for that sudden news. It was a like death in the family to me."

"I have met him a few times, most recently at Clyde award nights. He always loved the Bully Wee. In 2003, I met him at the baggage carousel at Glasgow Airport. We had been on the same flight back from Malaga. He asked me if I had been at a memorable 6-0 defeat for Clyde at Ibrox in the late 60's, when Eddie Mulheron got sent off for chasing Colin Stein around the park and repeatedly kicking out at him. Of course, I was there, and I remembered the incident. Harry told me the Clyde players were unhappy at Stein that day due to his gamesmanship. Happily, Colin was also sent off, albeit I was never quite sure why! I have just discovered that this was the same weekend Harry signed for Celtic, so the 6-0 defeat at Ibrox would be his last game for Clyde."

"I have a signed photo of the great man in action. It's a fantastic picture of Harry which shows perfectly his combination of balance, poise and concentration. A 1960's Messi....just a wee bit better! "Feed the Hood," as was the chant some 50 years ago. Harry is easily the single best player to play for Clyde since the early sixties. Graceful, sharp, fantastic football brain and skilful. He had the lot. He was brilliant at making other good players play above themselves."

Harry's departure from Shawfield would also be felt in the dressing-room. One constant across both of his spells there was Graham Macfarlane, whom I had the pleasure of chatting to about those days. Graham had taken the first steps in his football career with Strathclyde Juniors, before being called up for National Service aged 19 in 1958. I had seen him referred to as the 'Brigton Dynamo' and assumed that he was either an east end man or the name had arisen from his time with the Strathies, who were based in the shadow of Celtic Park, but Graham set the record straight.

"It was actually the 'Bridgeton Bomber' and would you believe it related to my job working in a bank! I'm a Cambuslang boy but I took a job in the Bridgeton branch of the bank and for whatever reason that name stuck. When I joined the army, I was placed into the Pay Corps in Germany. All of the corps based there had their own football teams and we played matches all over the country. When my two years' service was over, I had options to go to a few senior clubs and I chose my local team, Clyde."

By the time the teenage Harry was lining up for St Roch's against Strathclyde Juniors in September 1961, Macfarlane was already making appearances in the Clyde first team, playing beside Shawfield legends such as Tommy McCulloch and Harry Haddock. And when Harry moved to Shawfield the following summer, Graham would be the centre-forward as the youngster made his senior debut in Clyde's reserve side. With the exception of Harry's two-year stint on Wearside, the pair would line up together on innumerable occasions for the Bully Wee until the end of the decade, Graham showing his versatility by playing through the centre, on the right-wing and even as an attacking right-back, much to the chagrin of Stan Anderson, who believed that defenders were only there to defend and would often make comment accordingly! Graham retains many fond memories of Harry.

"When Harry arrived at Shawfield he blended in really well. He had a strong belief in his ability to score goals and to improve with experience. We had some great times there, particularly during his second spell. We had a marvellous mix of personalities and a huge belief in our talent and capabilities. So much so, in fact, that we would often hang our jackets on 'our peg' even before the team was announced. Our exclusion from the Inter-Cities Fairs Cup in 1967 was a real blow, but we did receive an invite to tour Rhodesia two years later, which was memorable. We won all of our games over there. Of course, Harry had left just before that, which was a real shame, as he would have enjoyed Rhodesia. Sam Hastings and I wound Harry and Joe Gilroy up when news of their transfers came through. We said they would have to start working now at their new clubs, as they wouldn't have Sam or I to do all their fetching and carrying for them, to let them score their goals! Both men loved to score goals. I had no doubt that Harry's dream was always a move to Parkhead, and I always looked for the Celtic results to see if his scoring touch was still active. We met at Broadwood several years ago, when the Clyde players of that era were invited to meet and remember the 'good old days.' They certainly were that."

Final word on 'Harry of the Clyde' goes to Dick Staite. As a young Partick Thistle centre-half, he had first come up against the 17-year-old Harry in a reserve fixture at Shawfield back in September 1962, a match in which the slightly more experienced Graham MacFarlane also featured. Dick would then be an established first-team player with the Bully Wee when Harry swapped Wearside for Clydeside four years later, his versatility allowing him to appreciate Hood's talents from a number of different positional perspectives over the next 30 months or so.

"My recollections of Harry really begin on his return to Shawfield, as I was still at Thistle, during his first spell with Clyde. Those who had played with him in that first period though were pretty clear that Harry was the real deal; that he would make a difference. On his return, aged 22, primed in the perfect mid-twenties for professional football, and after a few games settling-in, he lived up to the billing."

"In any dressing room, there will be characters who are extrovert and larger than life. Others prefer to identify as part of their own group within The Group; others

are happy to be more solitary, at ease in their own space while sharing in the vibe of the dressing room at that remove. Harry, as I recall, was not fixed in any of these categories. He mixed easily, naturally and confidently as part of the wider group, a squad that blended really well. The mood of a dressing room, of course, varies with the success or otherwise of the team. Results matter. And in Harry's time with the Bully Wee, we had a pretty successful time, finishing 3rd in 1967, 8th in '68 – both times in a League of 18 clubs - and he left part way through the following season. His status off the field was secured by his ability on the pitch. As for socialising outwith football, our squad had players from further afield, some of whom only linked up on the morning of a match, but some of the Glasgow-based boys - Harry included – would meet from time to time as a group with spouses, usually on a Saturday evening."

"Harry signed for Celtic in March 1969, but we were aware of their reported interest in him much earlier than that: even before the Scottish Cup semi-final in April 1967. The subsequent delay of nearly two years before his transfer was certainly a surprise to me. There was never any question around Shawfield that Harry was worthy of the switch."

Chapter 15

The new Bhoy makes an immediate impact for the Treble-chasing Celts

Having finally signed for his Bhoyhood club, more than four years after rejecting Celtic's initial approach, Harry would find his dream debut delayed still further. He was in the 14-man squad listed for the League game at Dens Park on Tuesday, 18 March 1969, two days after joining Celtic, however, unseasonal weather in the city of Jute, Jam and Jim Spence put paid to that. And he was ineligible for the Scottish Cup semi-final against Morton the following Saturday - my first visit to the national stadium, an eighth birthday gift from my dad – having played against the Hoops for Clyde in an earlier round. Like myself, Harry would have to watch from the stand as Jock Stein's men – clad in that all-white 'St Etienne' kit - recovered from the loss of a second-minute Willie Allan goal to clinch a place in the final with a 4-1 win over a Greenock outfit managed by former Celtic wing-half, Eric Smith. Four Lisbon Lions were on target, Willie Wallace and Billy McNeill turning the deficit around before half-time with Stevie Chalmers and Jimmy Johnstone scoring after the break to set up a Scottish Cup final meeting with Rangers.

It was a bittersweet time for Celtic, the Bhoys still very much on for a second domestic Treble in three seasons, having lost out agonisingly by a single goal to AC Milan in the quarter-final of the European Cup, *"the Final before the Final"* as the Italian media had described it. Many took the view that the Celtic squad of 1969 was even better than their famous predecessors of two years earlier. There was no doubt that having done the hard work securing a goalless draw in the San Siro, Celtic's failure to beat the Rossoneri in Glasgow a few days before Harry signed for the club had been a huge opportunity scorned. There would soon be others, with the city of Milan again involved.

Harry would finally get to wear those Hoops on Monday, 24 March 1969, albeit he remained on the bench as fellow League Cup-finalists Hibernian left Celtic Park with a well-earned point from the 1-1 draw. With Tommy Gemmell injured, Willie O'Neill returned for the hosts, as did Bobby Lennox for Stevie Chalmers, whilst both Joe McBride and Chris Shevlane faced their former club, the Govan-born striker captaining Hibernian on the night as the teams lined up as follows.

CELTIC:

John Fallon; Jim Craig & Willie O'Neill; Bobby Murdoch, Billy McNeill & Jim Brogan; Jimmy Johnstone, Bobby Lennox, Willie Wallace, Bertie Auld & John Hughes. Substitute; Harry Hood.

HIBERNIAN:

Thomson Allan; Joe Davis & Chris Shevlane; John Blackley, John Madsen & Pat Stanton; Peter Marinello, Allan McGraw, Joe McBride, Peter Cormack & Eric Stevenson. Substitute; Colin Grant.

Willie Wallace headed Celts in front within 15 minutes, however, the visitors would withstand the Celtic barrage which followed before gaining the upper hand in the second half. It was no surprise when McBride came back to bite the hand which once fed him by equalising on 72 minutes. It was the Hoops turn to be under pressure then as the Leith men looked for a winner. Disappointment at the 'dropped point' in a tight title race soon turned to joy for the bulk of the 30,000 spectators as news came through that closest rivals Rangers had been beaten 3-2 by Airdrieonians at Bromfield, Celts thus pulling three points clear at the top with seven matches to play in the quest for four-in-a-row.

There was also good news for Harry, as Jock Stein dropped the widest of hints to the media that his long wait to play for Celtic's first team was about to end.

"Hood has been running himself in with the reserve team, but obviously he must come into the top 11 very soon. It could well be against St Mirren."

Five days later, Saturday, 29 March 1969, Harry would indeed make his debut as a Celtic player, as the Bhoys travelled to Paisley to face St Mirren. He would replace Bertie Auld in a rejigged forward line, whilst Tommy Gemmell returned in place of Willie O'Neill and Tommy Callaghan was on the bench. Another former Celt, Ian Young, lined up for a Saints team wearing an all-scarlet outfit. The teams on this red-letter day for the Hood family were as follows.

ST MIRREN:

Jim Thorburn; Cammy Murray & Tony Connell; Billy Fulton, Ian Young & Eric Murray; Bobby Adamson, George Urquhart, Peter Kane, Bobby Pinkerton & Hugh Gilshan. Substitute; Jim Blair.

CELTIC:

John Fallon; Jim Craig & Tommy Gemmell; Bobby Murdoch, Billy McNeill & Jim Brogan; Jimmy Johnstone, Harry Hood, Willie Wallace, Bobby Lennox & John Hughes. Substitute; Tommy Callaghan.

It was Gemmell's full-back partner Jim Craig who opened the scoring with a lob which went in off the far post just before the break, the outstanding John Hughes then doubling that lead 10 minutes into the second half with a powerful finish. With 20 minutes remaining, Harry marked his Celtic debut with a goal, the stuff of dreams. The new Bhoy lashed the ball past Saints keeper Jim Thorburn with former Third Lanark defender Tony Connell helpless to stop it on the line, after shots from Bobby Lennox and Bobby Murdoch had been blocked, to complete the scoring at 3-0 with his 14th strike of the season.

It had been a highly effective start to his career as a Celt, as picked up by Gair Henderson in his *Evening Times* match report on the Monday.

"Naturally, the Celtic fans had two interests in this game. They wanted to see the goals scored and the points collected but they came too to see how their newcomer, Harry Hood from Clyde, would fit into the scheme of things, particularly with a view to Europe next season. Hood played this one with great intelligence. With Clyde, he was something of an individualist, a man who could win games on his own, but with Celtic, in his debut, he made no attempt to steal the scene from any of the other established players. Quietly and efficiently he [went about] his work, and the indications are that when he settles down and increases his pace a little, he will be a great asset."

Harry got his first live experience of the fairytale club on his second appearance, the following night, as an unchanged Celtic side took on St Johnstone at Muirton Park, five days before the delayed League Cup final with Hibernian. Willie Ormond's men had been in tremendous form, with nine wins in their previous 10 games. At half-time, Stein's defending champions looked down and out against a side who continually caused Celtic problems at that time, two goals down following strikes from Henry Hall and John Connolly and the in-form John Hughes stretchered off following one bad challenge too many. Still trailing with just 20 minutes remaining, they would show the spirit for which they were renowned, first Willie Wallace then Tommy Gemmell finding the net to set up a frantic finish. With just seconds left on the clock, it would be the new hero, Harry Hood, who would follow up a Wallace header to force home a dramatic winner, as Celts stretched their lead at the top of the table to five points.

Hood would again be ineligible as Celtic won the first leg of the Treble at Hampden by claiming the League Cup, hammering a Hibernian side who had recently held their own at Parkhead by 6-2. Indeed, it could and should have been worse, the Hoops six goals clear with 15 minutes to play before two late goals gave the Leith supporters something to cheer about on the day. The Celtic Wiki refers to the Bhoys effectively winning two trophies on the same day, as a 2-1 win for Dundee United over Rangers at Tannadice all but secured four-titles-in-a-row for Jock Stein's men. Celtic thus became the first club to win the League Cup on four successive occasions, a feat they duly repeated in the next millennium.

Whilst Harry would watch the Hampden triumph from the sidelines, there was no doubt that Jock Stein saw him as an integral part of his plans moving forward, the Celtic boss quoted within an *Evening Times* article on the day of the game.

"When Harry Hood left Shawfield and Clyde to move a mile along the road to Parkhead, everybody expected the inside-forward with the shining bright future to be put through a crash course to raise himself to the Celtic standard of stamina. But without even doing one extra stint of hard graft on the track, Harry already starting to pay back his transfer fee, and you can take it from me that you can add on a few thousand pounds to the quoted deal of £30,000 already."

"In two appearances in Celtic's top team Hood has scored two goals, the one that destroyed all hopes of a St Mirren recovery at Love Street and the one that will almost surely win the League Championship flag for Celtic this season. Need I say that the all-important goal was that last-gasp touch in the St Johnstone game at Perth on Tuesday night? Mr Stein is highly delighted with his new boy, but he has no intention of forcing Hood to produce even more spectacular results this season."

"Said Jock: "Harry could not play in the League Cup final today and is not eligible for the Scottish Cup final. I have no intention of rushing him to the front. I want to let him settle in with his new teammates and in his new surroundings. I feel certain that when he starts up on our commando training course at the end of July he will be as fit as any man on the Celtic staff. Next season will really show Hood's value. It will then be up to the player to prove that Celtic were right when they brought him to Parkhead."

Harry would be restored to the Celtic side for the midweek clash with struggling Falkirk at Parkhead, Stevie Chalmers the player making way. The new Bhoy marked his "*splendid*" home debut with the goal of the night, his third in three starts, putting Celts 2-0 up after half an hour, having been set up by Willie Wallace, who had earlier opened the scoring from the penalty spot. Wispy would conclude the scoring at 5-2 in the final moments, following a Bobby Lennox double, the Buzz Bomb adding to his Hampden hat-trick to give him five goals in four days.

With six of the Celtic side away on international duty for Scotland ahead of the World Cup qualifying clash with West Germany at Hampden, it was a shadow Hoops line-up which faced Rangers in the semi-final of the Glasgow Cup on Friday, 11 April 1969 at Parkhead, with the Ibrox side missing two of their own. Around 40,000 supporters rolled up to Glasgow's East End to see the following teams fight for the right to face Partick Thistle in the final and receive a confidence boost ahead of the Scottish Cup showpiece at Hampden later that month.

CELTIC:

John Fallon; Jim Craig & Willie O'Neill; Jim Brogan, Davie Hay & John Clark; Willie Wallace, George Connelly, Stevie Chalmers, Harry Hood & Tommy Callaghan. Substitute; Pat McMahon.

RANGERS:

Norrie Martin; Kai Johansen & Willie Mathieson; Sandy Jardine, Colin Jackson & Dave Smith; Willie Henderson, Andy Penman, Alex Ferguson, Willie Johnston & Orjan Persson. Substitute; Alex Miller.

Harry continued his goal-a-game start by opening the scoring in the 13th minute of his first appearance in the major Glasgow derby fixture. Sadly, his Friday strike would prove to be unlucky for Celts. His former Scotland colleague Alex Ferguson equalised within three minutes before a Willie Johnston hat-trick won the match for the Ibrox club by the odd goal in seven, despite a brave second-half fightback from the makeshift Celts which saw goals from Tommy Callaghan and Stevie Chalmers bring them level at 3-3 before Johnston's clincher in the dying seconds.

League flag business was resumed on Saturday, 19 April 1969, Celtic sharing four goals at home with Airdrieonians. Tommy Gemmell only just beat the Diamonds' Irish keeper Roddy McKenzie from the spot to open the scoring three minutes from the interval, the visitors turning the game around in a 10-minute spell in the second half, with goals from Willie McPheat and Dave Marshall. Celtic had been beaten by only three Scottish teams in the past three seasons, but that record was under threat until Bobby Lennox levelled on 79 minutes. A Billy McNeill 'winning goal' from Harry's cross was then controversially disallowed in the last minute on the strength of the Jungle-side linesman's raised flag, the Hoops skipper furiously remonstrating with referee Currie all the way down the tunnel as the boos rang out across Parkhead. This was the first match in which Harry played for Celtic and did not score, the defending champions now five points clear of second-placed Rangers with three matches to play, the champagne remaining on ice meantime.

That 2-2 scoreline would be repeated two nights later, at Rugby Park, Kilmarnock, as Harry came up against another two of his former teammates. Goalkeeper Sandy McLaughlan had spent three years at Roker Park before replicating Hood's career path by returning to his former club - in his case to Killie - in 1967. Jim McLean had played with Harry for two seasons at Shawfield before moving to Dundee in 1965 and was now lining up beside his younger brother Tommy at Rugby Park. Celts were two goals down within half an hour to strikes from Eddie Morrison and Gerry Queen on an evening where victory would secure the title. However, just as at Muirton Park at the beginning of the month, the champions would storm back. Just after the hour, Kilmarnock captain Frank Beattie made a hash of a cross from Scotland's Player of the Year Bobby Murdoch to head past his own keeper, halving the deficit. McLaughlan would then finally concede a second goal in stoppage time, as Tommy Gemmell's 18-yard shot pretty much secured the title, the last-gasp point sending Hoops six clear, Rangers with three games remaining now requiring a miracle. Still, as Kilmarnock themselves would know from their own final-day triumph at Tynecastle four years earlier, 'it ain't over until it's over.' Any mathematical uncertainty was duly removed 24 hours later, as Davie White's side suffered another defeat in Dundee, this time by 3-2 at Dens Park. After more than six years in senior football, and now playing for his third different club, Harry had finally won his first major honour.

Celtic would pile on the misery for the Ibrox club the following Saturday, a quite sensational Hoops performance blowing Rangers away to win the Scottish Cup by 4-0, in front of 133,000 spectators. Billy McNeill effectively ended Alex Ferguson's Ibrox career by losing his marker from a corner-kick to head Celts in front after just two minutes. The cup and Treble were then secured in a crazy 60-second spell just before the interval. First the explosive Bobby Lennox left the Rangers defence trailing in his wake to beat Norrie Martin with a low shot. Then, as the King's Park end celebrated, it was 3-0, George Connelly showing ridiculous confidence and composure to dispossess John Greig, waltz around the Ibrox keeper and tap the ball home as if it were a training match. Many thousands had fled from the Mount Florida terracing long before Stevie Chalmers cheekily beat Martin for Celtic's fourth on one of THE great days in the Jock Stein tenure.

Cup-tied Harry Hood, for that night at least, could enjoy the Treble-winning party as a non-playing observer. He would not have to wait too much longer to taste that Hampden feeling for himself.

Two League games remained before the boots could be put away for the summer. Harry returned for the first of those, a home game with Morton just 48 hours after the Scottish Cup triumph. With the 30,000 crowd in party mood and the three domestic trophies on parade in the centre of the pitch, the Greenock side had clearly not read the script. Danish winger Per Bartram completed perhaps the quickest hat-trick ever scored by a visiting player at Celtic Park, only six minutes elapsing between his fourth-minute opener and his own personal treble. Willie Wallace managed to pull one back at 0-2 but three minutes into the second period, Joe Harper put Morton out of sight at 4-1. Despite suffering his first defeat as a Celtic player, Harry would at least have the last word, successfully converting a Davie Cattenach delivery just after the hour to end the scoring with his 18th goal of the season.

That tally would be 19 two nights later as Jock Stein's men completed their Treble-winning campaign with a 2-1 win over Dundee at Dens Park. There would be more familiar faces on Tayside to greet Harry on arrival, his old boss John Prentice fielding former Clyde stars Joe Gilroy and Alex Bryce, but it would be the newest Celt who would take the honours, with the winner, after teenager Lou Macari's first goal for the club on his League debut had been cancelled out by a Bobby Murdoch own goal. The match at Dens would be the 94th and final Celtic appearance for defender Willie O'Neill, after a decade of great service for the team he loved. He would join English Second Division outfit Carlisle United in May but would be reunited with his old teammates before the summer was out. Watch this space!

As new signing Harry and the young Macari looked forward to developing their own reputations at Parkhead, amongst the glittering array of attacking talent available to Jock Stein, the ever-changing football fortunes were once again illustrated by news of the release of Pat McMahon. The Kilsyth Bhoy had started the 1967/68 season as Celtic's inside-right, the new kid on the block scoring the opening goal of the Hoops League campaign in a 3-0 win over Clyde on Saturday, 9 September 1967, whilst Harry wore the number eight for the Bully Wee. Pat would now follow a very different career path, although he would be an opponent for Harry many years later in the most unlikely of settings.

But that's a story for another day.

Harry, Harry and Lou Macari.

Now that's quite catchy.

Chapter 16

The toss of a coin separates the Lions and the Eagles of Lisbon

Harry would start his first full season as a Celt by featuring in three very different friendly matches. First of those was against St Etienne, on Wednesday, 30 July 1969, the French champions memorably defeated by the Bhoys in the previous European Cup campaign. Celtic's return to the Stade Geoffroy-Guichard ended with honours even following a 1-1 draw, Bobby Lennox with the first goal of the new season. If Les Verts reflected the ghost of Celtic's European past, then the visitors to Celtic Park six days later would represent the future, Don Revie's newly crowned English champions Leeds United attracting 65,000 spectators to watch the clubs battle out another 1-1 tie, Harry setting up Lennox for Celtic's equaliser. The hosts wore an unusual combination of Hoops with their dark green away socks to prevent a colour clash with their visitors. Later in the campaign, that same problem would produce one of the iconic Celtic images of the era under the lights at Elland Road.

Sandwiched between those matches in St Etienne and Glasgow was a meeting with an old friend just over the English border, as Jock Stein took his side down the A74 to face Willie O'Neill's Carlisle United. The huge Celtic support inside Brunton Park headed home disappointed after former Airdrieonians striker Tommy Murray beat Ronnie Simpson from the edge of the box for the only goal of the game.

There was a brief glimpse of his new-found celebrity status for Harry, as he found himself one of the invited guests at the opening of East Kilbride Thistle's new Showfield Park home in early August. Five years earlier, that had been the proposed relocation for Harry's Clyde, the initiative aimed at boosting attendances ironically failing to secure the required support, as the Bully Wee remained at Shawfield.

Harry would be on fire as the competitive action got underway, scoring five goals in the six League Cup sectional fixtures as the Bhoys continued their love affair with the trophy they had won for the previous four seasons. With Rangers and Raith Rovers the other sides in the group, the opening match saw Airdrieonians visit Celtic Park on Saturday, 9 August 1969, having enjoyed two League draws against the champions the previous season. They would not enjoy this afternoon, Celts 4-0 up by the interval thanks to a double from John Hughes and strikes Willie Wallace and George Connelly, the latter deputising for the out-of-favour Jimmy Johnstone. After Dave Marshall had clawed one back for the Diamonds, Harry – "who although playing as a striker, was the guy who constantly kept the Parkhead frontline humming on the sweetest note" - added a fifth goal for Celtic with 12 minutes remaining, following great work from man-of-the-match Hughes. Tommy Gemmell's 82nd minute header from another Yogi assist made the final score 6-1.

Raith Rovers also faced a first-half blitz when they visited Parkhead seven days later, Celts 3-0 ahead within 17 minutes through Willie Wallace, Harry and Billy McNeill, the latter after Hood's shot had struck a post. Having scored one and made one, Harry then made way for Stevie Chalmers on the hour mark, just before Wallace made it a double against his old club. John Hughes made it a nap hand with 10 minutes remaining. Peter Hendry in his Monday *Evening Times* column explained the rationale behind Harry's substitution.

"Celtic boss Jock Stein picked up the ace of trumps when he persuaded Clyde to part with Harry Hood last season. Hood was in brilliant form in the 5-0 win over Raith Rovers and played easily his best game since joining Celtic. Stein put his mark of approval on Hood's display by taking him off the field in the 61st minute, evidently a move calculated to ensure Hood's fitness for Wednesday's game against Rangers at Celtic Park."

The only blemish in Celtic's progress through the section stage had been a defeat at Ibrox, three days earlier, on Wednesday, 13 August 1969, a match where Harry had come up against familiar faces. Jim Baxter had recently returned to Govan from Sunderland via Nottingham Forest, a free transfer signing by Rangers manager Davie White, Hood's old Clyde teammate and the man who brought him back to Shawfield from Roker Park in 1966. There would be no old pals act, as the following teams lined up.

RANGERS:

Gerhard Neef; Kai Johansen & Davie Provan; John Greig, Ron McKinnon & Jim Baxter; Willie Johnston, Bobby Watson, Colin Stein, Sandy Jardine & Orjan Persson. Substitute; Dave Smith.

CELTIC:

John Fallon; Davie Hay & Tommy Gemmell; Bobby Murdoch, Billy McNeill & John Clark; George Connelly, Harry Hood, Willie Wallace, Bobby Lennox & John Hughes. Substitute; Bertie Auld.

Harry opened the scoring within eight minutes with a superb solo goal, taking John Clark's pass to beat German keeper Neef, a lead which Celts held until the interval. However, two goals in two minutes early in the second half from Orjan Persson and Willie Johnston would secure the points for Rangers in front of 72,000 spectators. With Jimmy Johnstone making his long-awaited return to the first team in place of

George Connelly, and Jim Craig replacing another youngster, Davie Hay, at right-back, a second-half Tommy Gemmell header redressed the balance at Celtic Park the following midweek. Following their 1-0 defeat, Rangers then appealed to the SFA regarding referee Jim Callaghan's failure to send John Hughes off for a challenge on Willie Johnston, a move which would incredibly bring about an unprecedented eight-week suspension for the official.

There would be some justice, happily, Rangers requiring a late equaliser to scrape a point from their next fixture, at home to Raith Rovers, as Celts scored another three without reply to beat Airdrieonians at Broomfield, Willie Wallace, Bobby Lennox and Billy McNeill on target. Jock Stein's men would not relinquish that advantage, Harry being one of several injured Celts to recover ahead of the midweek trip to Stark's Park. With three of his less fortunate colleagues – Bobby Lennox, Bobby Lennox and John Hughes – deployed as scouts at Easter Road to watch potential quarter-final opponents Hibernian and Aberdeen, and Jimmy Johnstone on the bench, Harry would help himself to a double as the much-changed Celts built up an unassailable 4-0 lead before the hour, his first an unbelievable strike from a wide position. With the job done, Stein again withdrew his new talisman to allow the Kirkcaldy crowd half an hour of Jinky magic. Raith would manage to pull two goals back as Celtic not surprisingly took a collective foot off the gas, before Stevie Chalmers finished the scoring at 5-2 with his second of the evening after Rovers keeper Bobby Reid saved a Tommy Gemmell spot kick. Rangers would thus lose out yet again to the Bhoys in the League Cup, the fifth successive season they had done so.

The Celtic manager confirmed his logic to the media afterwards.

"Harry is playing very well, even although he has not been with us for that long. We definitely made a good buy when we brought him to Parkhead, but we are not going to kill him. It takes a bit of time for a player to get used to the speed at which we try to play the game. Two games a week are hard enough for any player in my panel and they have to be used carefully. We recognise the Hood potential, and I am deliberately breaking him in slowly, pacing him so that he will not lose form because he has been overplayed. The player knows this, and he not only accepts but agrees with the policy."

The first League game of the campaign was one I remember very well, Willie Ormond's St Johnstone – Britain's top goalscorers and boasting a 100% League Cup record - the visitors to a beautiful, sunny Parkhead on Saturday, 30 August 1969, as the Championship flag was raised once again above the Jungle. The thing that sticks out for me, though, was the huge crowd inside the old ground, officially recorded as 60,000. That level of attendance was remarkably rare in those days, outwith the visits of Rangers and top English or continental opposition. With Bertie Auld joining the Celtic casualty list, the team chosen by Jock Stein to begin the assault on a fifth successive Scottish League title was as follows.

John Fallon; Jim Craig & Tommy Gemmell; Jim Brogan, Billy McNeill & John Clark; Jimmy Johnstone, George Connelly, Willie Wallace, Harry Hood & Stevie Chalmers. Substitute; Lou Macari.

Defending champions Celtic trailed with half an hour remaining, Saints scoring twice through Bill McCarry and Fred Aitken either side of a Stevie Chalmers strike. The last word would go to Harry, his fine header from Chalmers left-wing cross buried past keeper Jim Donaldson for 2-2. That would be a fitting end to a day on which work commenced on erecting the 'Harry Hood floodlights' at Shawfield.

Gair Henderson was full of praise for Harry in his Monday match report for *The Evening Times*.

"Most pleasing thing for the Celtic fans is the form of Harry Hood. He is now becoming a star who no longer needs to lean on colleagues, and his finishing is deadly accurate as he showed when he scored the second equalising goal."

Celtic's tricky start to their title defence continued with a midweek visit to Rugby Park, early goals from Willie Wallace and Bobby Lennox sending the Hoops in 2-1 ahead at the break, Ross Mathie pulling one back for Kilmarnock. Harry set Wallace up for his double on the hour but Eddie Morrison kept the hosts in the match at 3-2, setting up a nervous finish. It would be Lennox who would remove all doubts with Celtic's fourth from Harry's headed assist in the closing stages to move the Hoops into a posse of clubs on three points, tucked in behind League leaders Motherwell and Morton.

Willie Wallace would not enjoy the next match so much, the striker sent off with Dunfermline Athletic defender Willie Renton after just 13 minutes as Celts went down 2-1 at East End Park on Saturday, 6 September 1969. Pat Gardner, the Pars Scottish Cup final hero from 1968, was the man who done the damage with a double either side of that incident. Tommy Gemmell pulled one back 10 minutes into the second half with a ferocious shot from fully 30 yards, but the hosts held on to inflict a season's first defeat on the champions.

The big games kept on coming. Next up was a trip to Pittodrie four nights later to face Aberdeen in the first leg of the League Cup quarter-final. The Dons had emerged unbeaten from a tough section ahead of Hibernian, Saturday's conquerors Dunfermline Athletic and Clyde, and with Celts again missing a number of key men – notably star wingers Jimmy Johnstone and John Hughes – there was a real possibility of an upset. Both sides went all out for goals, the excellent form of keepers Ernie McGarr and John Fallon the main reason for the goalless scoreline, both men now being touted for international recognition. Worryingly, Jock Stein's attacking injury worries increased as Harry limped off after an hour to be replaced by Jim Brogan.

Saturday, 13 September 1969 is another afternoon which remains clear in my memory more than half a century later. Bob Shankly had recently resigned as manager of Hibernian citing his disillusionment with the game, trainer Tom McNiven in charge of the team which arrived to face the champions. And with Jimmy Johnstone and

Harry in the starting line-up things looked ominous for the visitors when the little winger headed past England Under 23 keeper Gordon Marshall to give Celts an interval lead. The mood of the home fans was further cheered when news came through of Ayr United's two-goal advantage over Rangers at Somerset Park. Whilst Ally McLeod's man would hold out for both points, things would go downhill for the Hoops at Celtic Park in the second half. Johnny Hamilton brought Hibernian level within three minutes, triggering a bombardment on the visitors' goal, the match still level as Harry made way for Tommy Callaghan with 10 minutes remaining. He would have barely taken his seat in the dugout as Pat Stanton blasted the winner past John Fallon to leave Celtic in the bottom half of the table, with three points from four games. My routine at that time was to go home from the game then re-enact it in our backcourt in Springburn afterwards. Usually, I would be Jinky, or Willie Wallace or local hero Stevie Chalmers, scoring great goals. Tonight, Matthew, I would be Pat Stanton.

Midweek brought another new adventure for Harry, Swiss champions Basel the opposition for his first European match. It was also a first opportunity for a couple of highly-rated youngsters to sample that continental experience, Danny McGrain and Kenny Dalglish included in the 18-man party which flew to Switzerland from Prestwick 48 hours after the defeat by Hibernian. Bobby Murdoch was the latest casualty, Scotland's current Player of the Year failing to recover from a bout of flu, whilst John Hughes returned and there would be a European debut for Davie Hay. Harry started on the bench at the St Jakob Stadion as Jock Stein named the following team.

John Fallon; Davie Hay & Tommy Gemmell; Jim Brogan, Billy McNeill & John Clark; Jimmy Johnstone, Bobby Lennox, Stevie Chalmers, Willie Wallace & John Hughes. Substitutes; Ronnie Simpson, Jim Craig & Harry Hood.

The form of goalkeeper John Fallon had been one of the high spots in Celtic's uncharacteristically poor start to the season and he was again the key man as the Hoops reached the interval still level before 38,000 spectators. Harry replaced Stevie Chalmers for the second half and that change coincided with a much better performance, the only negative being Celtic's failure to convert that superiority into a first-leg lead to take back to Glasgow, as the match ended goalless in Switzerland.

Harry's continental debut was followed by a starting slot at Ibrox three days later, a pivotal afternoon in his career and indeed in Celtic's season. He replaced Stevie Chalmers as the Bhoys sought to end a winless run of League games in Govan which stretched back to September 1957, a few weeks before Hampden in the Sun, goals from Bobby Collins, Billy McPhail and Sammy Wilson edging a five-goal thriller, Celtic's only such success in that competition there since the war. Jock Stein's selection for the match was restricted still further as John Hughes' comeback had started and ended in Basel, Yogi joining Bobby Murdoch, Bertie Auld, George Connelly and Tommy Callaghan on the sidelines.

The following teams ran out at a rainy Ibrox in front of 75,000 spectators.

RANGERS:

Gerhard Neef; Kai Johansen & Davie Provan; John Greig, Ron McKinnon & Jim Baxter; Willie Henderson, Sandy Jardine, Colin Stein, Dave Smith & Willie Johnston. Substitute; Bobby Watson.

CELTIC:

John Fallon; Jim Craig & Tommy Gemmell; John Clark, Billy McNeill & Jim Brogan; Jimmy Johnstone, Harry Hood, Willie Wallace, Davie Hay & Bobby Lennox. Substitute; Stevie Chalmers.

Harry would prove to be the matchwinner on a day of incessant rain, the new Bhoy scoring for the third time against Rangers since joining Celtic six months earlier. His goal early in the second half was enough to secure two valuable points for Celtic and end the 12-year League drought at Ibrox. Chasing a Billy McNeill through ball, he sold Ronnie McKinnon a beautiful dummy before clinically striking the ball inside Gerry Neef's near post in front of an ecstatic Broomloan Road end, as John Greig came lunging in to block. The drama did not end there. With the fallout from Jim Callaghan's ridiculous eight-week punishment for failing to send John Hughes off against Rangers at Parkhead the previous month dominating the pre-match build-up, there was no way that Jim Craig's 67th minute kick out at Willie Johnston – the player involved with Yogi in the August incident – would go unpunished by referee Tom 'Tiny' Wharton. The burly official duly sent Craig down the tunnel, leaving Celts to play the last quarter of the match one man down. To their credit, the Bhoys saw the game out comfortably to win the day.

The hectic schedule continued in midweek as Aberdeen headed to Celtic Park for the second leg of the League Cup quarter-final, the sides level after the Pittodrie stalemate a fortnight earlier. A crowd of 47,000 watched under the lights as Jock Stein tried something a little bit different, Jimmy Johnstone utilised as a deep-lying centre forward. An excellent display by the Hoops somehow saw them head down the tunnel a goal down, former Rangers striker Jim Forrest adding another to his tally against Celtic on the half-hour. Two moment of magic from Jinky early in the second period settled the tie, first setting up his friend Bobby Lennox then Willie Wallace to beat Ernie McGarr in the Dons goal.

The last eight clubs in the competition included some unfamiliar names. Ayr United had completed a comfortable victory over Dumbarton and would now face Celtic in the semi-final. Morton and Motherwell had been surprise League leaders in the opening month or so of the season and their tie had been the most dramatic, the Steelmen recovering from a 3-0 defeat at Cappielow to inflict the same result on the Greenock men at Fir Park. They would now play-off at Ibrox to meet St Johnstone, Willie Ormond's men on fire and very much the dark horses for the trophy after an 11-goal demolition of Falkirk over two legs.

The month ended with Harry lining up against his old Clyde teammates for the first time, as Celts warmed up for the return leg with Basel with an unconvincing 2-1 victory on Saturday, 27 September 1969. There was an unfamiliar look about the Bully Wee forward line, which included recent signings Miller Hay from Queen's Park and Jackie McBride from Cumnock Juniors, as the following teams ran out in front of 35,000 spectators at Celtic Park.

CELTIC:

John Fallon; Davie Hay & Tommy Gemmell; Jim Brogan, Billy McNeill & John Clark; Jimmy Johnstone, Harry Hood, Willie Wallace, Bobby Lennox & John Hughes. Substitute: Jim Craig.

CLYDE:

John Wright; Harry Glasgow & Davie Souter; Stan Anderson, John McHugh & Jimmy Burns; Graham Macfarlane, Miller Hay, Jackie McBride, Billy Hulston & Sam Hastings. Substitute: Dick Staite.

Harry was denied several times by his old keeper John Wright as the hosts struggled to break through. Celtic's eventual matchwinner was Bobby Lennox, with goals either side of the break, the first set up by Harry in the 40th minute. It was all-square 10 minutes after the break, Miller Hay squeezing the ball home through a ruck of players, Tommy Gemmell then suffering the indignity of a second successive missed penalty, the big defender blasting wide after Harry and his old Brunswick teammate John McHugh clashed in the box. Lennox capitalised on a Wright error to seal the points just after the hour, Harry immediately withdrawn by Jock Stein with midweek in mind, Jim Craig his replacement.

On his first home European appearance for Celtic, the second leg against Basel, played on the first evening in October, Harry scored his first goal in continental competition inside the first minute, following up to net before many of the 50,000 crowd had taken their places after great work from Jimmy Johnstone. With an hour played and Celts 1-0 to the good, an away goal from a potential exit, there was anxiety in the stadium until that European expert Tommy Gemmell blasted a shot from fully 25 yards past Swiss international keeper Marcel Kunz and into the roof of the net to finish the tie.

Elsewhere in the European Cup, the ties went with form, both Leeds United and Feyenoord racking up 16 goals against outclassed opposition from Norway and Iceland whilst Benfica and Fiorentina also progressed over Scandinavian sides with much narrower margins. Main headline of the night was St Etienne's thrilling comeback over Bayern Munich, the French champions overcoming a 2-0 first leg deficit to win 3-2 on aggregate, thanks to a late winner from Malian striker Salif Keita. Friday's second round draw paired Celtic with Benfica, a return to Lisbon for Jock Stein and his remaining Lions and an exciting 25th birthday gift for Harry, whilst cup-holders AC Milan would face the high-scoring but little-known Dutch champions Feyenoord Rotterdam.

Whilst I was still "too wee" to attend the midweek European match with Basel, I was lucky enough to witness the home debut of a future Celtic superstar three days later. In the absence of Bobby Murdoch and his deputy Jim Brogan, 18-year-old Kenny Dalglish ran out against Raith Rovers for his first Celtic start, wearing the number four on his green jersey, whilst at the other end of the age spectrum Ronnie Simpson made his first appearance since the shoulder injury sustained at Shawfield back in February, just one week short of his 39th birthday. My abiding memory of that game is how the Press managed to mis-spell Kenny's surname, adding an 'e' for whatever reason. Harry would have to settle for a place on the bench, eventually coming on for two-goal Jimmy Johnstone with 17 minutes remaining and the Bhoys already 6-1 ahead. Bobby Lennox also netted a double whilst Willie Wallace, Tommy Callaghan and finally John Hughes were all on target as Celts won 7-1 to climb to sixth spot in the table.

Harry would start in place of Jinky in the midweek League Cup semi-final with Ayr United at Hampden, the winger suffering from an ear infection. The honours on the night would go to his old Queen's Park teammate, Alex 'Dixie' Ingram, wingers Quinton Young and Bobby Rough and the other Honest Men, as Ally McLeod's underdogs gave the favourites the fright of their lives. Rough twice gave Ayr United the lead, his second in extra-time threatening to eliminate the cup-holders before Bertie Auld, who had replaced Harry, earned Celtic a replay at 3-3. John Hughes and Tommy Gemmell - from the penalty spot - were the other Hoops scorers, with Dave McCulloch also on target for the Somerset Park outfit.

A clean sheet as captain for the day in Celtic's 2-0 win over Airdrieonians at Broomfield on Saturday, 11 October 1969 was a nice way for Ronnie Simpson to enter his 40th year, goals either side of the interval from fellow Lions Stevie Chalmers and Willie Wallace lifting a Hoops team showing six changes from midweek up to fourth in the table. Leaders Hibernian followed up their victory over Celtic in Glasgow the previous month with a 3-1 win over Rangers at Ibrox, young winger Peter Marinello adding to his growing reputation with a double.

Harry had drawn a blank against Airdrieonians, but he was back amongst the goals again in the League Cup semi-final replay against Ayr United at Hampden, 48 hours later. Alex Ingram had beaten Billy McNeill to nod the Honest Men into an early lead and cause a few Celtic hearts to flutter before Harry headed the equaliser from Tommy Gemmell's cross midway through the first half. Stevie Chalmers snatched the winner 10 minutes after the break from Kenny Dalglish's excellent through ball, the youngster continuing to impress. Whilst Celts would hold on to reach a sixth successive League Cup final, it would be at a cost, Ronnie Simpson stretchered off late on after dislocating the same shoulder as before saving a netbound Ingram effort. The legendary Celtic keeper would not play senior football again, a sad end to an incredible near 25-year career which had begun as a 14-year-old schoolboy in the same stadium all the way back in 1945. There will never be another 'Faither,' that's for sure.

Presumably to make up for not taking me to Hampden on the Monday night, dad took me to Parkhead on the Wednesday, as former Third Lanark and Wolverhampton

Wanderers goalkeeper Evan Williams made his Celtic debut, 24 hours after signing for his boyhood club. I had always thought that Williams had been brought to Celtic as a consequence of the injury to Ronnie Simpson, however, he was watching in the stand at Hampden as the great Celt suffered that career-ending blow. Sometimes, timing is everything in football, as a man unable to command a place at Molyneux and currently on loan at Midland rivals Aston Villa would succeed Simpson as the second Celtic goalkeeper to appear in a European Cup final. All that was yet to pass. The opposition for Evan's first appearance as a Celt was Clyde, in a Glasgow Cup semi-final, Harry one of several first-team players missing as Jock Stein watched youngsters Vic Davidson and Lou Macari grab the goals and most of the honours in a 4-1 win. Dick Staite became the first player to beat the new Celtic keeper when he headed Clyde into the lead midway through the first half, but with Bertie Auld, Stevie Chalmers and Bobby Murdoch supporting the youngsters – the latter around one stone lighter following a two-week spell at an English health farm – that would be it for the Bully Wee. Auld equalised within a minute before a Davidson double and a superb long-range shot from Macari had Celtic coasting within three minutes of the restart. Only John Wright's excellent save from Davidson's late penalty prevented the prolific teenager - born Victor Salvatore Feria Davidson in the shadow of Celtic Park - from completing his hat-trick, as Jock Stein's men progressed to a second cup final in three days.

Saturday, 25 October 1969 was the date of Harry's first cup final as a Celtic player. The opposition at Hampden for the 1969/70 Scottish League Cup final was Willie Ormond's St Johnstone, a first-ever major showpiece for the Perth outfit. They had won all six games in a tough section which included Kilmarnock, Dundee and Partick Thistle, before hammering Second Division Falkirk 11-3 on aggregate in the quarter-final. Their last-four opponents at Hampden had been Motherwell, League leaders at that time, Saints comfortably disposing of them by 2-0 to progress to the final.

St Johnstone boasted their own HH at inside-right, Scotland's top scorer Henry Hall, with 18 goals to his name already, plus talented youngster John Connolly and two former Parkhead youth prospects, Kenny Aird and captain Benny Rooney, the latter the son of Celtic physiotherapist Bob. Already without Bobby Lennox - a scorer in all three of the previous League Cup finals - and the suspended Willie Wallace, Jock Stein made two surprising omissions from his team, as he sought a fifth successive triumph in the competition. Despite scoring for Scotland on World Cup duty in midweek, Jimmy Johnstone moved to the bench, whilst Tommy Gemmell was dropped completely following his comical but ultimately costly episode of 'one-man-hunt' with West Germany's Helmut Haller in Hamburg. Davie Hay was drafted in at full-back for his first major final. An unhappy Gemmell would subsequently submit a transfer request and this would effectively mark the beginning of the end of his wonderful career at Celtic Park.

Jock Stein and Willie Ormond went with the following team selections, in front of 73,000 spectators.

CELTIC:

John Fallon; Jim Craig & Davie Hay; Bobby Murdoch, Billy McNeill & Jim Brogan; Tommy Callaghan, Harry Hood, John Hughes, Stevie Chalmers & Bertie Auld. Substitute; Jimmy Johnstone.

ST JOHNSTONE:

Jim Donaldson; John Lambie & Willie Coburn; Alex Gordon, Benny Rooney & Ian McPhee; Kenny Aird, Henry Hall, Bill McCarry, John Connolly & Fred Aitken Substitute; Gordon Whitelaw.

The final was settled by a goal after just two minutes, Harry nodding a John Hughes cross against the crossbar with Bertie Auld the first to react to knock the ball home, just as he had at the other end of Hampden in that era-defining 1965 Scottish Cup final, a second consecutive League Cup final goal for the much-loved Celt. It should have been 2-0, a John Hughes goal controversially disallowed in the second half for a foul on Jim Donaldson which was obvious only to referee John Paterson of Bothwell. The keeper then inexplicably passed the resulting free-kick straight to Harry, before manhandling him to the ground in his attempts to retrieve the ball and being booked for his troubles. In fairness, only the excellence of John Fallon prevented St Johnstone from registering on the scoresheet, the original 'Holy Goalie' in outstanding form for the second successive Hampden cup final. But the main negative on the day was the injury suffered by Stevie Chalmers in the opening minutes of the second half. He was stretchered off, to be replaced by Jimmy Johnstone, the problem later diagnosed as a hairline fracture of the ankle, which would eventually put Stevie out of action for a calendar year, the second Lisbon Lion to be struck down with a serious injury that month.

As Billy McNeill, the captain of that immortal team, raised the League Cup aloft for the fifth successive season, Harry waited patiently on the rostrum behind goalkeeper John Fallon and matchwinner Bertie Auld for his first taste of cup-winning glory, doing so as a Celtic player at that. A fairytale moment for anyone with Hoops in their heart.

There would be many more to follow.

Four days after the cup final high of Hampden, Harry would experience the other side of football, forced off the Pittodrie pitch with an ankle injury as Celtic came from behind to edge a five-goal thriller with Aberdeen, his substitute Jim Brogan netting the winner in the closing minutes. Lou Macari would be in Harry's place as Celts opened November with a hard fought 4-2 victory over League Cup semi-finalists Ayr United at Somerset Park, Bobby Murdoch continuing his explosive return to first-team action to win the match with a sensational late double, after Jimmy Johnstone and Alex Ingram had traded their own brace of goals apiece.

Harry would also miss the shock 2-0 home defeat by Hearts the following Saturday but had recovered to take his place in the Celtic team for the biggest game of his life, the European Cup second-round tie with Benfica at Parkhead on Wednesday, 12 November 1969. Almost 75,000 supporters crammed into the east end cauldron to see the two heavyweights battle it out for the right to progress to the quarter-final, in the days before seeding protocols rendered such fixtures impossible. The Lisbon Eagles had been vying with the Milan duo of Inter and AC for the right to succeed Real Madrid as the new continental masters, all three clubs having managed two successes in the decade to date. Benfica had also reached the finals of 1963, 1965 and 1968, whilst Celts had broken the Latin monopoly in the heat of their home city in May 1967 and were now considered amongst the greatest sides on the planet. This was a clash of serious European royalty. Football Hollywood.

The following line-ups were selected by Jock Stein and his Benfica counterpart, Otto Gloria.

CELTIC:

John Fallon; Jim Craig & Tommy Gemmell; Bobby Murdoch, Billy McNeill & John Clark; Jimmy Johnstone, Harry Hood, Willie Wallace, Bertie Auld & John Hughes Substitutes; Evan Williams, Tommy Callaghan, George Connelly, Jim Brogan & Davie Hay.

BENFICA:

Jose Henrique; Malta Da Silva, Humberto Coelho, Zeca Miglietti & Humberto Fernandes; Jaime Graca & Mario Coluna; Antonio Simoes, Jose Torres, Eusebio Ferreira & Diamantino Costa. Substitutes; Jose Augusto & Artur Jorge.

The opening blockbuster came from the right boot of Tommy Gemmell, restored to the side from the naughty step and blasting a shot home from a free-kick within two minutes which if anything was even better than his strike in Lisbon. Willie Wallace – also back after the 28-day suspension imposed for his sending-off at Dunfermline in September - doubled Celtic's lead just before the break, rifling home from an impossible angle. It should have been 3-0 at half-time, Italian referee Concetto Lo Bello disallowing John Hughes' headed finish for reasons known only to himself. That would prove a very important call. The great Eusebio failed to reappear for the second half and with 20 minutes remaining, Jock Stein's men did get the third goal their play deserved on the night, Harry drifting in to nod Bobby Murdoch's cross past Jose Henrique to give Celts one foot in the last eight.

Three days later, I made my first visit to Fir Park to watch an unchanged Celtic take on a home team which included Peter McCloy, Tom Forsyth and John 'Dixie' Deans in their ranks. Harry would take advantage of hesitation between the future Ibrox defenders to give the Hoops an early lead, his 10th goal of the season, his future teammate Deans equalising for Motherwell just before the interval. With 15 minutes to play, man-of-the-match Bertie Auld sent over a cross from the left which John Hughes reached first to glance the ball past McCloy and win the game for Celtic.

As an aside, it may not be widely known that prior to joining Motherwell, attacking inside-forward Tommy Forsyth had been attracting the attention of Jock Stein whilst playing with junior outfit Stonehouse Violet.

Jock Stein led his men back to Lisbon for the first time since that unforgettable evening two years earlier, the players staying in the same Estoril hotel and training on the Estadio Nacional ahead of the return leg. Seven of the men who had started that match would again be in the team, the injured Ronnie Simpson, John Clark, Stevie Chalmers and Bobby Lennox missing out, as did Harry, who started on the bench as Stein went with the more defensively-minded Tommy Callaghan.

It would be a very different Lisbon, a monsoon prevailing for most of the night and a storm brewing on the pitch, as goals from Eusebio and 1968 final scorer Jaime Graca had reduced Celtic's aggregate lead to one before the interval. With no further score and the clock ticking past the 90-minute mark, the Dutch referee awarded Benfica a final corner-kick. You could write the script as the ball was knocked all the way to the far post before being headed back across the Celtic goalmouth, John Fallon stranded as Diamantino Costa levelled the tie in the most dramatic circumstances.

With a full pitch invasion in progress, the teams had to leave the Estadio da Luz field before extra-time could commence. When it did, with Harry and George Connelly on for Callaghan and Bertie Auld, perhaps the only surprise was that the shellshocked Celts did not concede a fourth goal to blow a 3-0 lead, as their predecessors had done five years earlier against MTK in Budapest, thus avoiding a most unwanted record. Instead, by now in the early hours of Thursday morning, legendary captains Billy McNeill and the great Mario Coluna of Benfica would squeeze into the referee's dressing-room where Cesar would correctly guess 'Heads' twice to send the Hoops into the quarter-final via the most unsatisfactory of methods. I seem to remember only finding out the result of the match the following day, such were the problems with communications that night. As a footnote to this outcome, Celtic chairman Bob Kelly would successfully lobby UEFA to have this scenario abolished. We would soon see the introduction of a penalty shootout as a means of deciding drawn ties, Celtic, ironically, one of the earliest clubs to lose out by this new method which they had fought to introduce. Perhaps, Bob should have just kept quiet!

On the same night, there were dramatic events taking place in the runners-up part of Glasgow as Rangers manager Davie White, Harry's old colleague and boss, was sacked following back-to-back 3-1 defeats in the Cup Winners' Cup at the hands of Poland's Gornik Zabrze. The Poles were no mugs. Led by the great Lubanski, they would go on to eliminate Roma on a coin toss in the semi-final before losing the Vienna final to Manchester City, still the only European trophy won to this day by the Middle East-backed English club.

Three days after Lisbon, Saturday, 29 November 1969, a Celtic side showing three changes ended the month by going to an icy Cappielow for a tricky League fixture with Morton, who had drawn 2-2 with Rangers the previous week. In came Davie Hay, Lou Macari and Harry Hood, whilst Celtic legend Bobby Collins featured for the hosts, following his recent transfer from Bury. Macari opened the scoring after eight minutes from Harry's corner, with Hood himself adding a second 10 minutes from time. Sadly, when a third Celtic goal went in just before the final whistle, it wasn't Kevin Barry on target, or we would no doubt have heard the very popular chant of the day. Somehow, "Oh Harry, Harry, Lou Macari…and Willie Wallace" just isn't as catchy.

The decade would end with Stein's defending champions sending out the most powerful of messages, with eight straight League wins. The victories at Motherwell and Greenock were followed by home successes over St Mirren and Dundee, the Monday night meeting with the Paisley side seeing Evan Williams make his League debut but perhaps overshadowed by his counterpart at the other end, Denis Connaghan, who was outstanding, limiting Celtic to a Lou Macari double either side of the break. John Fallon was back between the sticks five days later as a rather generous penalty award allowed Tommy Gemmell to score the only goal of the game against Dundee, six minutes into the second half, Celts closing ominously to within one point of League leaders Hibernian.

Wednesday, 10 December 1969 saw the European Cup quarter-final draw in Zurich pair Celtic with Italian champions Fiorentina, whilst new favourites Leeds United would face Standard Liege, conquerors of Real Madrid. The lop-sided match-ups left the four lowest-ranked clubs effectively in their own half of the draw, meaning that two of those would progress to the semi-final. In fairness, they had earned that slice of luck. Legia Warsaw had eliminated French champions St Etienne, whilst East Germans Vorwarts had defeated Red Star Belgrade on away goals. The outstanding performance had come from Feyenoord, recovering from a 1-0 defeat in the San Siro to beat cup-holders AC Milan 2-0 in Rotterdam, thanks to the two Wims, Jansen and Van Hanegem. Turkish champions Galatasaray had gone to the wire like Celtic, qualifying at the expense of Czechs Spartak Trnava on the toss of a coin.

Three days later, Celtic's League challenge continued with a 4-1 win over League Cup finalists St Johnstone at Muirton Park. This would be a much more comfortable afternoon than that at Hampden, a Willie Wallace double and a Tommy Gemmell special having the Bhoys on Easy Street before Harry made it 4-0 six minutes after the break with his 12th goal of the season. Kenny Aird completed the scoring on the hour. Domestically, Jock Stein's men were now going through the gears, however, the best was saved for the following midweek.

On Wednesday, 17 December 1969, Jerry Kerr brought his newly-Tangerined Dundee United side to Parkhead, watched by 26,000 and the current League leaders, Hibernian, in the stand. In all my years of following Celtic, I have rarely seen a performance of such power, and I never saw Jimmy Johnstone play better. The wee man was simply incredible, perhaps at his peak that night as he destroyed and toyed with the visitors.

Bertie Auld had given Celts a second-minute lead before Harry doubled that on the 15-minute mark. By half-time it was 4-1, John Hughes obliging after Ian Mitchell and Tommy Gemmell had traded penalty conversions, and within seven minutes of the restart it was 6-1, Willie Wallace with a quickfire double. Most of Celtic's attacking prowess stemmed from the genius of Johnstone, who would do everything but get on the scoresheet, at one stage hitting the post with a shot that gets further out each time I tell this story. Alan Gordon and Bobby Murdoch would manage to get on target before the Hoops declared at a magnificent 7-2. I was eight years old at the time and recall standing towards the back of the Celtic End, watching this magic unfold as if it were yesterday. As Simple Minds frontman Jim Kerr would later sing, I saw Jimmy Johnstone set the night on fire. Fifty years on, it remains one of my all-time favourite memories of watching our beloved club.

The greatest decade in Celtic's fabulous, unbroken history would then end with another two home wins. The 3-1 victory over Kilmarnock five days before Christmas was soured by the broken leg suffered by visiting captain Frank Beattie after an early collision with man-of-the-moment Jimmy Johnstone. Despite the setback, Eddie Morrison gave Killie the lead before a Tommy Gemmell penalty and a John Hughes double secured the points for Celtic.

Stein's men then saw the 1960's out in some style, seven days later, with an 8-1 mauling of bottom dogs Partick Thistle, the second time they had inflicted that scoreline on the Jags in nine months. The only surprise this time was that Harry was not amongst the goalscorers, the former Sunderland and Clyde man involved in most of Celtic's attacks before being replaced by long-term injury victim Bobby Lennox at 5-1, as his strike partners John Hughes and Willie Wallace hoovered up the goals. Yogi hit a hat-trick in the type of conditions he traditionally revelled in whilst Wispy grabbed a brace, the second from the penalty spot marking his 100th goal for Celtic. Bertie Auld also scored twice with captain Billy McNeill completing the rout.

Two months earlier, Jock Stein had set his men the challenge of being top of the League table by Christmas, and despite the shakiest of campaign starts, his new combination of youth and experience had delivered, whilst progressing in Europe at the expense of one of THE great sides and putting the first domestic silverware of the season in the Parkhead trophy room.

As 1970 beckoned, this had all the makings of another wonderful season for the fairytale club.

Chapter 17

Celts beat the cream of European football before a dream dies in Milan

I marked the first changing of a decade in my lifetime with a trip to Shawfield in my dad's car to see Celtic take on Clyde, the supporters' bus not running on Thursday, 1 January 1970. It was weird to see a date on the programme which was not from the 1960's. Funny the things which stick in your mind. Harry returned to his first senior ground and Celtic returned with the two points after a hard-fought 2-0 win, the former Clyde striker instrumental in setting up the first goal of the '70s for John Hughes before young Lou Macari sealed victory right at the death with an excellent solo effort. Harry may well have enjoyed a goal on his own stomping ground, but for a most unusual opponent. The Celtic Wiki describes him being "dispossessed by a black mongrel, which jumped a five-foot fence to take to the field," such athleticism and defending surely entitling him to the Dog of the Match award later.

Two days later, new Rangers manager Willie Waddell brought his team to Parkhead and left with a creditable point after a goalless draw, the major talking point the ruling out of a Billy McNeill goal just before the break, referee John Paterson of Bothwell deciding that keeper Gerry Neef had been impeded. Neef was only playing after a deal to bring Aberdeen keeper Bobby Clark to Ibrox fell through when Bobby Watson refused to move to Pittodrie.

The following Saturday's match at Firhill was a victim of the snow which covered Scotland, but Cesar would score an identical goal from Bertie Auld's free-kick a fortnight later at Easter Road, which was allowed to stand, before Harry set up John Hughes for a late winner with a sublime flick at the edge of the box. Yogi beat future Celtic keeper Gordon Marshall at his near post in the 86th minute to clinch a 2-1 win after Hibernian debutant Arthur Duncan had brought the hosts level early in the second half in the vital League clash. Duncan had moved to Easter Road from Partick Thistle the previous week to replace Peter Marinello, after Hibernian's teenage winger had joined Arsenal for £100,000.

Next followed a memorable double-header with Dunfermline Athletic at Parkhead, again games I can recall so clearly for whatever reason. Saturday, 24 January 1970 saw the Pars face Celtic in a rematch of the Scottish Cup third-round tie which they had won 2-0 two years earlier, en route to winning the trophy. More than 50,000 fans packed into the ground to see if Jock Stein could avoid a repeat of his only loss in the competition as Celtic boss to date, outwith a final itself, a record he would incredibly retain until his final season, a decade later. However, with 10 minutes remaining, a Dunfermline win looked the likelier outcome, the Fifers ahead on the hour when winger Jim Gillespie took advantage of a poor Jim Brogan pass-back to beat Evan Williams. The fact that a similar mistake by Davie Cattenach in the 1968 tie had cost the Bhoys a goal that day would not be lost on anyone who attended. As the game entered its final stages, once again it was John Hughes to the rescue, Yogi turning brilliantly to beat John Arrol for 1-1. Due to the size of the crowd, I had been sent down to the front barrier with the other young kids, and as was the practice of the day, over we went onto the grass behind the goal to celebrate, in my case praying desperately that my dad wouldn't spot me amongst the throng. He would not have approved of that. I really pushed my luck 10 minutes later, with a repeat performance, following Harry's last-gasp header which won the match for Celtic, in his first Scottish Cup tie wearing the Hoops. Pars manager George Farm would have his replay tickets for company on the bus journey home to Fife, as the holders progressed to the second round.

Harry, Jimmy Johnstone and Bertie Auld would all drop out of the squad as Celts defeated Dunfermline 3-1 the following Saturday, Jock Stein ringing the changes with the introduction of youngsters Lou Macari, Davie Hay and the evergreen Bobby Lennox to the forward line. This would be a welcome first start in almost four months for the Lisbon Lion, who celebrated his return with Celtic's final goal, after Willie Wallace and Macari had netted either side of the interval.

Harry returned for the visit of Dundee United in the second round of the Scottish Cup on Saturday, 7 February 1970, Jerry Kerr's men possibly feeling a sense of trepidation following their 7-2 mauling at the same ground in December. Any sense of relief felt when they heard that Jimmy Johnstone would not be playing would be misplaced, as the damage that afternoon came from Celtic's other star winger. A John Hughes first-half brace helped secure a safe passage into the quarter-final for the Bhoys after a 4-0 win, with Lou Macari and Willie Wallace on target after the break. United's side featured Walter Smith at inside-right, like Tom Forsyth another player watched by Jock Stein whilst plying his trade in the Junior game – in his case with Ashfield – who would later be associated with Rangers.

The prize for that victory was a home tie with Rangers in the last eight, the first time I could recall the sides meeting before the final. That draw was made on the Monday, whilst 24 hours earlier, 40,000 tickets were snapped up for the visit of Fiorentina in March, as the Celtic support looked forward to another very special night under the lights. These were truly great times to follow Jock Stein's men, although not so kind to the man who had lost out to the Hoops on the toss of a Dutch Guilder back in November, Benfica manager Otto Gloria, who was sacked by the Lisbon club. The list of successors contacted by Benfica included England manager Alf Ramsey and Harry's old Clyde boss, Davie White.

That excitement was dampened somewhat by the wintry weather, which saw the matches at Dens Park then at home to Morton postponed. The latter cancellation saw Jock Stein head for Firhill to take a look at next opponents Partick Thistle against Airdrieonians, which was also the occasion of my first visit to the Maryhill stadium, as dad managed to get his Saturday match fix squeezed in. He was back at Firhill 48 hours later - minus his *"it's a school night"* son - to see a battle of the classic Hoops, Harry putting the green-and-white variety into an early lead with an excellent strike, his 15th of the season, before Jimmy Johnstone, Lou Macari and a Tommy Gemmell double from the penalty spot set Celts up nicely for the big Scottish Cup-tie five days later with a 5-1 win over the struggling Jags.

Saturday, 21 February 1970 saw the much-anticipated clash of Glasgow's big two at Celtic Park in the quarter-final of the Scottish Cup. Jock Stein decided to go with Davie Hay in a more advanced role, Harry the man to drop to the bench as the following teams lined up.

CELTIC:

Evan Williams; Jim Craig & Tommy Gemmell; Bobby Murdoch, Billy McNeill & Jim Brogan; Jimmy Johnstone, Bobby Lennox, Willie Wallace, Davie Hay & John Hughes. Substitute; Harry Hood.

RANGERS:

Gerhard Neef; Kai Johansen & Willie Mathieson; John Greig, Ron McKinnon & Dave Smith; Alfie Conn, Andy Penman, Colin Stein, Alex MacDonald & Willie Johnston. Substitute; Willie Henderson.

A full house of 75,000 which included Fiorentina manager Bruno Pesaola saw an incredible start to the match, Bobby Lennox the latest Celt to have a goal disallowed, the ball clearly crossing the line before being knocked out by Willie Mathieson, then Jim Craig inadvertently giving the visitors the lead within 60 seconds, his misplaced header beating Evan Williams. The class act which is Willie Johnston then decided to have a bit of fun at Craig's expense, running over to give him a celebratory pat on the head, an act copied by his strike partner, Colin Stein. The Karma Police would soon sort that nonsense out.

Lennox would get his name on the scoresheet just before the interval, beating Gerry Neef from a tight angle, and on the hour mark, Harry replaced the limping John Hughes as Celts tried to seal the tie. The second controversial moment in the match occurred immediately after his introduction, Rangers midfielder Alex MacDonald sliding into the prone Williams as he gathered the ball and being promptly sent off by referee Tom 'Tiny' Wharton, as Jim Brogan sought to take matters into his own hands. With the match seemingly destined for an Ibrox replay, Stein's tactical deployment of Davie Hay would reap dividends. There were only five minutes left on the clock when the youngster strode through the midfield mud to unleash the most glorious shot past the German keeper into the roof of the net, as Parkhead erupted, not a bad way to score your first goal for Celtic. Jimmy Johnstone then made certain of a semi-final place for the holders by netting a third in the final minute, the little winger lifted into the air in triumph by Harry in front of the Jungle, in another iconic Celtic moment, as Willie Waddell's unbeaten record as Rangers manager bit the Parkhead dust.

Monday's semi-final draw then paired Celtic with John Prentice's Dundee, the first of what would be a regular series of meetings between the two clubs at that stage of the competition throughout the decade. Aberdeen would face Kilmarnock at Muirton Park, Perth in the other tie, with the Ayrshire side deemed the slight favourites to go through. Two nights later, Harry was back in the starting line-up for the visit to Stark's Park, goals from Lisbon Lions Billy McNeill and Tommy Gemmell giving Celts a comfortable 2-0 victory on the night over Raith Rovers, Harry making way for the return of Bertie Auld once the points were secured, the Fiorentina match presumably on Jock Stein's mind.

Before the Italians arrived in Glasgow, there was a visit of Airdrieonians on the last day of February to be addressed. The clubs had shared four goals in the last Parkhead meeting, a scoreline repeated as we headed into the closing 10 minutes of this one, the two-goal lead established by another two Lions, Jimmy Johnstone and Bobby Lennox cancelled by strikes from Davie Marshall and Ian Cowan. Harry had come off the bench to replace cup hero Davie Hay before Johnstone made it 3-2, Willie Wallace quickly adding a fourth to give the Hoops another two points in the quest for the title.

March commenced with the visit of Italian champions Fiorentina to Celtic Park in the quarter-final of the European Cup, 12 months after AC Milan had denied the Hoops the chance of a potential second quadruple, and thus the chance to match the achievements of the immortals of Lisbon two years earlier. Jock Stein had expressed a desire to avoid English champions Leeds United *"until later,"* the UEFA draw duly obliging. However, he was given the most serious of tests as Celts were paired with the latest Florentine Masters, La Viola having a renaissance of their own by lifting Lo Scudetto in 1969 for only the second time in the club's history. Their previous success had been back in 1956, one solitary Serie A defeat seeing them finish well clear of the Milan giants. Fiorentina's goalkeeper then had been a certain Giuliano Sarti, the young stopper and his teammates going all the way to the following season's European Cup final, before losing out to holders Real Madrid in front of 120,000 spectators at their own Estadio Santiago Bernabeu.

La Viola would enjoy continental success within three years, an extra-time defeat in the final of the Coppa Italia to double-winning Juventus in the San Siro in September

1960 seeing them qualify for the first-ever competition for national cup-winners, the tournament at that time not recognised by UEFA and featuring only 10 teams. Fiorentina would comfortably beat Swiss outfit Lucerne and Yugoslavs Dinamo Zagreb to progress to a two-legged final with Rangers. Two goals from the ironically named Luigi Milan effectively settled the destination of the trophy at Ibrox, the same Milan and legendary Swedish star Kurt Hamrin repeating the dose in Florence as the local favourites became the first Italian side to win a European honour. As an aside, a few months later, Bertie Auld and his Birmingham City team failed to prevent Roma becoming the second Italian success, when they lost over two legs in the Inter-Cities Fairs Cup final. It's not always appreciated that "10.30" played in three European finals.

In 1963, Giuliano Sarti moved to Inter Milan, where he would win back-to-back European Cups in 1964 and 1965, adding two World Club Championships for good measure, before even his unbelievable performance in the heat of Lisbon in May 1967 could not stop Jock Stein's fantastic Celtic side from taking the Big Cup home to Glasgow. Fiorentina's latest title-winning team featured two men effective at the other end of the pitch, Luciano Chiarugi and Amarildo. Italian striker Chiarugi delighted in the nickname 'Crazy Horse,' thanks to his style of play, whilst Brazilian Amarildo's name would be familiar to those who recalled the World Cup of Chile in 1962, where his three goals included a double against Spain and Brazil's equaliser in their final victory over Czechoslovakia. Whilst Amarildo started the first leg, top-scorer Chiarugi did not even travel to Glasgow, amidst suggestions that Bruno Pesaola would adopt an ultra-defensive approach to the tie. A record midweek crowd of 77,240 packed into Celtic Park for the mouth-watering tie, on Wednesday, 4 March 1970, with the teams lining up as follows.

CELTIC:

Evan Williams; Davie Hay & Tommy Gemmell; Bobby Murdoch, Billy McNeill & Jim Brogan; Jimmy Johnstone, Bobby Lennox, Willie Wallace, Bertie Auld & John Hughes. Substitutes; John Fallon, Jim Craig, Harry Hood, Tommy Callaghan & Lou Macari.

FIORENTINA:

Franco Superchi; Bernardo Rogora & Giuseppe Longoni; Francesco Carpenetti, Ugo Ferrante & Giuseppe Brizi; Salvatore Eposito, Claudio Merlo, Mario Maraschi, Giancarlo De Sisti & Amarildo. Substitutes; Claudio Bandoni, Pierluigi Cencetti, Giorgio Mariani, Francesco Rizzo & Giovan Pirovana.

Bertie Auld was the surprise inclusion for Celtic, having not started a game since mid-January due to injury. Once again, Jock Stein would come up trumps, the veteran midfielder running the show, scoring the opening goal – remarkably his only strike for Celtic in Europe – with a low left-foot shot from the edge of the box on the half-hour, then playing in the cross from which poor Francesco Carpenetti launched the ball into his own net five minutes into the second period. The Italians resorted to some uncompromising challenges to avoid further damage, John Hughes taking a level of punishment which forced him from the field and allowed Stein to introduce Harry. He would be wearing the number 13 shorts, however, that would prove unlucky for Fiorentina. Seconds from the final whistle, Auld centred again from the left, his cross taking out goalkeeper Franco Superchi but seemingly drifting out for a goal-kick beyond the far post. Then there is a tremendous leap from Harry, outjumping his marker to head the ball perfectly back across the goal, Superchi left stranded as Willie Wallace finds himself on the line and presented with the easiest goal of his illustrious career. Justice is done at 3-0, although no-one will know at that point that this is Harry's final on-field contribution on the Road to Milan.

Seconds later, it is all over, and a jubilant Hoops team are taking a bow in front of an ecstatic Jungle. There will still be an Italian Job to be done in a fortnight, however, they have taken a huge step towards a second European Cup.

The dream is on.

The quest for a second consecutive domestic Treble continued at Tannadice three days later, although I had to make do with a much shorter trip, the few hundred yards from my home to Petershill Park. The occasion was a Scottish Junior Cup fifth-round second replay between St Roch's and Larkhall Thistle, with Candy winger Dominic Sullivan the main topic of interest, having been signed by Clyde. He would of course later join Celtic, whilst the substitute for St Roch's that afternoon had already played with both clubs, Henry Quinn. On the other flank for the men in green was Denis McQuade, who will feature later on in this story. I have clear memories of that match, one being the trouble inside the ground – anyone familiar with the background of the two clubs will understand perhaps why such animosity was prevalent in all three of these cup-ties – another being Dom's equaliser just in front of us and the third that the Candy won 2-1, favourites Larkhall Thistle suffering defeat for the first time in six months as Jimmy McGrory's first club marched into the last eight of Junior football's showpiece. The great man had played in the team which brought the trophy back to the Garngad – to their original Millburn Park home - in 1921, their first and to date only success in this competition.

Some 90 miles north, the man who would later bring Dom Sullivan to Celtic was securing another two vital points in the title race, Billy McNeill with headers either side of the interval the only goalscorer in Celtic's 2-0 win over Dundee United. Harry and Tommy Callaghan had come back into the starting line-up in place of Bertie Auld and John Hughes on Tayside, but it was all-change again three nights later for the visit of Morton, Harry and Bobby Murdoch the players to drop out for the 4-0 win, Auld and Lou Macari marking their returns with second-half goals. Before Bobby Lennox completed the scoring.

Both Macari and Lennox would again be on target the following Saturday as Celtic beat Dundee 2-1 at Hampden to reach a fifth Scottish Cup final in six years. Harry successfully came through a Reserve League match with Dundee United on the Thursday evening, but he was missing from the list of 12 players named for duty by Jock Stein, testament to the incredible array of attacking talent at the Celtic manager's disposal. The final would now be a repeat of the 1967 showpiece between Celtic and Aberdeen, the Dons edging a trouble-strewn semi-final with Kilmarnock at a packed Muirton Park thanks to a solitary first-half goal from Derek 'Cup-tie' McKay.

The Bhoys had actually closed in significantly on both of the remaining components of the Treble that afternoon, Rangers failing to reduce Celtic's seven-point advantage at the top of the table, despite playing their two games in hand that week. Their 2-1 defeat to Dunfermline Athletic at East End Park in Peter McCloy's debut had followed another loss by the same score in Fife in midweek, relegation-threatened Raith Rovers the unlikely victors as Willie Waddell's early promise began to disintegrate just as the season reached its climax.

His nemesis across the city continued to work his magic as Celtic progressed to the last four of the European Cup in midweek, restricting Fiorentina to just the one goal from returning striker Luciano Chiarugi and very few chances, Stein bringing George Connelly into the team for the first time that season, the big Fifer repaying his faith with an outstanding performance on the night. Following the victory over Inter Milan in Lisbon three years earlier, Celtic's latest successful Italian Job saw them become the first side from these islands to win a two-legged tie against Italian opposition, a nice way for Harry to celebrate his first anniversary as a Celt, albeit he would no doubt be disappointed to have remained on the bench in Florence's Stadio Comunale.

Celtic's opposition in the semi-final would come from Poland, the Netherlands or England. Legia Warsaw had followed up a 1-1 draw in Istanbul with a 2-0 win over Galatasaray, whilst Feyenoord again recovered from a single-goal deficit to beat Vorwarts Berlin by the same score in Rotterdam. A late Johnny Giles penalty secured a second 1-0 victory for Leeds United over Standard Liege, as Don Revie's men reached the penultimate stage of the European having yet to concede a goal. Jock Stein had openly discussed his preference to avoid the English champions at each stage, however, Friday's draw paired the two together, with the first match scheduled for Elland Road. Celtic had already announced that should they reach the semi-final, the home leg would be played at Hampden, due to work scheduled to commence imminently at the east end of Celtic Park. That would now ensure a record European club attendance on Wednesday, 15 April 1970.

Before that wonderful prospect, domestic business would take precedence. Harry was back in the team named to face Ayr United at Celtic Park, one of three changes from midweek as second-half strikes from Bobby Lennox and Willie Wallace, the latter with a double to keep him out in front as the club's top goalscorer, saw off the Honest Men by 3-0. That same afternoon, Rangers suffered a third successive League defeat for the first time in over 40 years, this time to a Jocky Scott goal at Dens Park, to leave

Celtic nine points ahead with just five matches remaining. A fifth consecutive title for Jock Stein's men was now within touching distance.

The opportunity to clinch that flag came four nights later, Aberdeen the visitors in a dress rehearsal for the Scottish Cup final, which looking back should have fired up a warning to all-conquering Celtic. Stein continued his squad rotation policy by bringing back the three players rested at the weekend, Jimmy Johnstone, Bobby Murdoch and Bertie Auld, with Harry, Lou Macari and Tommy Callaghan the men to miss out. This was a miserable night in all senses, as the rain poured down, one I remember very well as we picked up my older brother on his return from a school trip to Belgium. That was the only good news as Celts squandered the chance to win the title before the soaked home support. Second-half goals from George Murray and self-confessed Castlemilk Bhoy Arthur Graham in his debut gave the Dons a huge morale boost ahead of the Hampden meeting of the clubs the following month. A last-gasp Tommy Gemmell free-kick was not enough to stop Celts suffering a third home League defeat of the season, as the champagne remained on ice.

Having failed to beat Aberdeen at home in midweek, the point required for the title was secured by a Celtic side minus a number of first-team players at Tynecastle on Saturday, 28 March 1970. How my dad managed to secure a day pass on what was my sister's seventh birthday is another matter entirely, however, the charm offensive obviously worked, he and I travelling through that morning for what would be my first visit to Edinburgh and the first time I would see us win a trophy. A wonderful Celtic 'rite of passage' day. It would have been absolutely perfect had Jim Cruickshank not saved Tommy Gemmell's penalty early in the second half denying Celts the win, Harry then replacing Jimmy Quinn as the Hoops effort ended in a 0-0 draw. Still, it was five-in-a-row for Stein's men and Harry maintained his own record of having won all five competitions Celtic had entered since he joined in March 1969.

The first day of April saw Celts in Yorkshire for a much-awaited 'Battle of Britain' at Elland Road in the first leg of the European Cup semi-final. Jock Stein's stated preference had been Feyenoord, however, instead he got Leeds United, *"the final before the final,"* just as with AC Milan the previous season. The teams lined up as follows in front of 45,505 spectators at Elland Road.

LEEDS UNITED:

Gary Sprake; Paul Reaney & Terry Cooper; Billy Bremner, Jack Charlton & Paul Madeley; Peter Lorimer, Allan Clarke, Mick Jones, Johnny Giles & Eddie Gray Substitutes; David Harvey, Mick Bates, Terry Yorath, Terry Hibbert & Rod Belfitt.

CELTIC:

Evan Williams; Davie Hay & Tommy Gemmell; Bobby Murdoch, Billy McNeill & Jim Brogan; Jimmy Johnstone, George Connelly, Willie Wallace, Bobby Lennox & Bertie Auld. Substitutes; John Fallon, Jim Craig, Harry Hood, Tommy Callaghan & John Hughes.

The Celtic manager once again played a master stroke, young George Connelly wearing the number eight shorts to match his bright red/orange socks, with Harry on the bench. Connelly scored the only goal of the game within the first minute and Celtic would not look back. It was the first goal Leeds had conceded in the competition and the first the Hoops had managed on the road, albeit both of those records should have read 'two,' Connelly repeating the feat in the opening minute of the second half and becoming the latest Celt to have a goal mysteriously disallowed. Still the win was a win and a huge one at that. My recollection of that game is listening to the radio commentary whilst attending the cub scout night in the church hall of St Aloysius in Springburn, spending hours the following day after school watching for my dad to return home from Leeds with the customary pennant and programme.

Harry found himself on reserve team duty 48 hours later, scoring twice in a 3-2 win over Motherwell's second-string at Fir Park, in a match which marked the welcome return of Stevie Chalmers to action following the broken ankle he sustained in the League Cup final. Bobby Lennox would help himself to a hat-trick the following day, as the five-time Scottish champions beat the Steelmen's first-choice selection 6-1 at Celtic Park. A Willie Wallace penalty plus strikes from Jimmy Johnstone and Bobby Murdoch had Celts six goals clear before John 'Dixie' Deans pulled one back for Motherwell late on, the Bhoys finishing their home programme in some style to delight most of the 30,000 crowd.

There was sadness across the city as Partick Thistle's goalless draw at home to St Mirren consigned Scot Symon's team to relegation from the top-flight, where they had competed since 1902. That would mark a parting of the ways for assistant manager Adam McLean, who had been three years old at that point! He had joined his boyhood club a decade earlier after a legendary career as a winger at Celtic. The Jags would now be replaced in the new season by Cowdenbeath, who had last featured in the First Division in September 1939. The Fife club would claim a unique but unwanted record that season. Having won Division Two at a canter in the spring of that year, they would be bottom of the table after five games, their only two points coming from an opening day victory over Third Lanark at Central Park. Cowdenbeath's penultimate match had been a 2-1 defeat to Willie Maley's Celtic at the same venue, which was followed by a 4-0 loss to St Mirren at Love Street on Saturday, 2 September 1939. The declaration of war the following day saw senior football suspended until 1946/47, with the Central Park side remaining in Scottish football's second tier until clinching promotion in April 1970. Ironically, their heaviest defeat in that brief return to the First Division in the autumn of 1939 had been a 7-1 thrashing at Brockville, and Falkirk would now be favourites to take the step back up beside them.

Harry returned to the first-team line-up for the trip to Dens Park on Monday, 6 April 1970, one of five changes as Jock Stein continued to spin the plates with his squad ahead of the hectic run-in. It was another of the incoming players - Bertie Auld - who gave Celts the lead within two minutes, Bobby Lennox securing the points just before the break after Gordon Wallace had levelled for the hosts. The Bhoys duly moved 10 points clear of second-placed Rangers, with just one League fixture remaining.

The inclusion of Harry in the reserve side which faced Raith Rovers at Celtic Park the following Friday, the eve of the Scottish Cup final confirmed that he would be missing from the showpiece for the second successive occasion. He would add to a Kenny Dalglish strike and a Vic Davidson double as the second-string Hoops won 4-1 on the night. The first team would not fare so well in Mount Florida the following afternoon. I found a perch on a railing in the North Enclosure to peer through the 108,000 crowd to see the lethal combination of referee Bobby Davidson and teenage winger Derek McKay win the Scottish Cup for Aberdeen, my first Hampden final and a game I still find it difficult to write about 50 years down the line. Suffice to say it was Bobby Lennox's name which came out of the hat that day to have a vital Celtic goal disallowed, the Airdrie official then denying a blatant penalty for a foul on the same player having earlier awarded Aberdeen a spot kick when the ball was driven against Bobby Murdoch at close range, which Joe Harper duly converted. McKay had scored winning goals in both the quarter and semi-finals and would now add a Hampden double to create his own piece of Aberdeen folklore. Davidson would also enjoy his Saturday night after his very own three-card trick and sadly there would be no quintuple for Celtic.

Harry would take his place on the bench at the same venue four nights later, as the largest crowd in the history of European competition, 136,505, crammed into the vast arena to watch Celts complete a home and away double over the pride of English football. Each side made one change to the starting line-up from the first leg at Elland Road, Norman Hunter replacing broken leg victim Paul Reaney for Leeds United whilst John Hughes was at centre-forward for Celtic in place of the injured Willie Wallace. Yet again, Jock Stein got it right, Yogi and Bobby Murdoch scoring early in the second half to send Celts into the final, after a long-range rocket from Hoops-daft Leeds skipper Billy Bremner had flown past Evan Williams into the top corner to level the tie. As the players took their lap of honour before the record-breaking crowd it was hard to imagine any other outcome than a second European Cup for this incredible team. Their opponents in the Milan final would be Dutch champions Feyenooord, who had followed up a goalless draw in Poland with a comfortable 2-0 victory over Legia Warsaw in Rotterdam.

Before that meeting in the San Siro there was one final piece of domestic business to attend to. Three days after the elation of Hampden, Celtic's League campaign ended with a 3-2 victory over St Mirren in my first visit to Love Street. Jock Stein brought back Harry, Jim Craig and Tommy Callaghan and handed a debut to Vic Davidson, with Davie Cattenach offered the possibility of some rare first-team action from the bench. Harry would grab his 16th competitive goal of the season, equalising an early Jim Blair strike from a Tommy Gemmell corner five minutes before the interval, young Davidson grabbing his first goal for Celtic two minutes later. Callaghan would head home a third for Celtic from Harry's corner kick immediately after the restart, Blair adding his second just before the final whistle to end the scoring at 3-2 as the curtain came down on another Scottish season. Celts would finish 12 points clear of Rangers at the top of the table, Bobby Collins scoring Morton's late second in their 2-0 win at Ibrox.

Celtic would then have an 18-day gap to plug before the European Cup final with Feyenoord in Milan on Wednesday, 6 May 1970, a critical factor which I think is often overlooked. Harry featured and scored in the first of two warm-up games arranged in the countdown to the final, a 7-0 victory in Fraserburgh, but was missing in the 8-0 rout of Stenhousemuir at Celtic Park on the Friday before the big match. He would be amongst the squad which flew out from Prestwick Airport to Milan, Jock Stein taking his entire playing staff with the exception of Charlie Gallagher - handed a free transfer on the opening day in May - and Ronnie Simpson, who was standing as a councillor in an Edinburgh election. The legend known as "Faither" would then announce his retirement the day after the match.

Harry would no doubt be extremely disappointed at not being named amongst the 11 players chosen to win a second European crown for Celtic against the Dutch underdogs, although I can imagine that he would still have retained his sense of humour even as the butt of Bertie Auld's sharp wit. Malcolm Munro of *The Evening Times* told the story.

"Best crack of the tour came from my Maryhill 'china,' Bertie Auld. He was talking to me in the hotel foyer with a brand-new pair of boots hanging by the laces around his neck.

"Harry Hood came up and said, "They look great. Do we all get a pair?"

"No," said the Fox. "Only the players!"

Ernst Happel and Jock Stein finally settled on the following line-ups at a noisy, wet Stadio San Siro.

FEYENOORD:

Eddy Pieters Graafland; Piet Romeijn & Rinus Israel; Theo Laseroms, Theo van Duivenbode & Franz Hasil; Wim Jansen, Henk Wery, Ove Kindvall, Willem van Hanegem & Coen Moulijn. Substitutes; Eddy Treijtel, Cor Veldhoen, Gus Haak, Piet Vrauwdeunt & Joop van Daele.

CELTIC:

Evan Williams; Davie Hay & Tommy Gemmell; Bobby Murdoch, Billy McNeill & Jim Brogan; Jimmy Johnstone, Bobby Lennox, Willie Wallace, Bertie Auld & John Hughes. Substitutes; John Fallon, Jim Craig, George Connelly, Tommy Callaghan & Harry Hood.

The disappointment and pain felt by those players excluded would be mirrored within a couple of hours by all of those with Celtic in their hearts across the world, after the dream died on a night best summed up by the newspaper headline which paraphrased Jock Stein's own pre-match comment, *"It's Lisbon in reverse."*

Despite an opener from Tommy Gemmell, his second European Cup final strike, the Dutch and not the Scots would be the masters on the night. Feyenoord captain Rinus Israel's looping header brought the Rotterdam side level within two minutes of Gemmell's opener, the only surprise being that the goal which won the cup did not arrive until three minutes before the end of extra-time, Swedish striker Ove Kindvall toe-ending the ball over Evan Williams after Billy McNeill had handled in the box.

Three minutes from another opportunity to deliver the dream. Surely we could not play so badly again.

The biggest *"if only"* in our history, for me.

The players too would feel that gut-wrenching sense of what might have been, even five decades later. Tommy Callaghan sat with Harry on the bench at the San Siro as events unfolded. The anguish in his voice was still evident as I broached the subject in the spring of 2021.

"Well, there's no doubt about the biggest disappointment of my career. That was Milan in 1970. We underestimated Feyenoord, who were an excellent team. Lots have been said and written about that match over the years, but it was their turn. They were a great team."

Whilst admiring Harry's medal collection at his home a few months later, his wife Kathy mentioned to me that there was one missing, the one from Milan, from the biggest game in European club football.

"Well, to use a good Glasgow word he was "scunnered" about being on the bench and not picked to play. He thought he was not worthy of receiving the medal, so he just walked away at the final whistle. He was bitterly disappointed about the result, of course, and quite frankly at the time I didn't quite pick up on it. It was 1970, and Harry's parents were both ill, and I assume Harry's thoughts were very much on that situation. On top of that, I was expecting our son, Nicky, and we were in the midst of purchasing the Sherwood Manor. So, as disappointing as the result was, we both obviously had other things to contend with. He never gave the medal another thought until later years, by which time it was too late."

Chapter 18

A full gauntlet of emotions for Harry

There would be little time for wound-licking for the Celtic players following the heartache of Milan, a squad minus the injured trio of Jimmy Johnstone, John Hughes and Jim Brogan flying to Canada to commence the post-season tour. Harry was part of a three-man forward line with Lou Macari and Bobby Lennox, as Jock Stein used the opening match with Manchester United at Toronto's Varsity Stadium on Saturday, 9 May 1970 to experiment with a 4-3-3 formation. Only Jock will know how successful that was, but the result was certainly in favour of Wilf McGuinness' side, who won 2-0 thanks to an early Billy McNeill own goal and a late strike from John Aston.

Harry was on target against a Bari side newly relegated from Serie A as the tour party moved to New York for a match on Randall's Island four nights later. His strike 10 minutes into the second half ended the scoring at 1-1 after the defensively minded Italians had scored from the penalty spot following a rare counterattack, Harry immediately making way for Vic Davidson. The two sides met again the following Sunday back in Toronto, in a game which was destined never to complete. Postponed from the Saturday due to torrential rain, it finally went ahead at the Canadian National Exhibition Centre 24 hours later. With the score tied at 2-2 after 72 minutes, Macari and Davidson on target, the local referee sent three Bari players off in the space of 10 minutes, before awarding a penalty to Celtic for a trip on Jim Craig. That kick would never be taken. As Bertie Auld waited patiently with the ball for things to calm down, resisting a plea from Bari officials to deliberately miss in the interests of peace, the remaining eight Italians walked from the field, the match subsequently abandoned by the referee.

The tour continued to be problematic, the hectic travel schedule as the players flew back and forth along the eastern seaboard not helping the mood of a squad still deflated from the events in Milan. Both Tommy Gemmell and Jimmy Johnstone were heavily linked with moves away from the club, the winger apparently only two years into a Jim McLean-esque 12-year contract, whilst the big full-back and Bertie Auld were sent home by Sean Fallon following an alleged incident in Toronto, manager Jock Stein already back in Scotland by this time for reasons varying between club business and hospital appointments. It seemed so far removed from the tour of 1966 which launched that incredible season.

On the field, there was at least a victory to enjoy, albeit the opposition was a select team from Boston, Vic Davidson hitting a first hat-trick for the senior squad in a 7-1 romp on Wednesday, 20 May 1970. The final match against top-class opposition took place back at Randall's Island in New York City, 48 hours later, Bundesliga outfit Eintracht Frankfurt claiming the honours with a 3-1 win after Bobby Lennox had brought Celtic level on the stroke of half-time. The Celtic party then flew to Bermuda for a week of relaxation - albeit they did manage two comfortable wins over local sides – before finally calling time on the rollercoaster of emotions which was the 1969/70 campaign.

The Celtic squad would be back in Scotland to witness the incredible football extravaganza that was the Mexico World Cup of June 1970, an experience which lit up my own nine-year-old world, despite a period spent in Glasgow's Oakbank hospital for an emergency appendectomy. Pele, Harry's favourite player, was at the absolute peak of his powers, he and his fabulous attacking Brazilian teammates providing moments which still capture my imagination, five decades later. Pele's lob from the halfway line which drifted inches past the Czechoslovakian post. His mid-air chest control and volleyed finish in the same game. His unbelievable dummy on the Uruguayan keeper. His salmon-like leap to open the scoring and that wonderful Carlos Alberto goal to seal the 4-1 final victory over Italy in the Azteca. This was football for the Gods.

Of course, any mention of Pele brings Harry's sense of humour immediately to the fore. Of the many anecdotes I heard from speaking to his family and friends, two of my favourites related to the great man. There was Harry's explanation for calling his dog 'Pele.'

"It was only fair, given that he had called his dog Harry Hood!"

Or the time the subject came up in one of his bars – Cheers in Bellshill, perhaps – when Harry advised one of the customers that Pele was staying overnight with him. Coaxed by the punters, Harry agreed to bring him to the pub the following morning. Cue the expressions on the faces on the long line of star-struck football fans as Harry opened his car boot the next morning to allow the non-Brazilian Pele to come bounding out to meet his adoring audience!

There was the thrilling prospect of Harry playing against the two-legged Pele as Jock Stein's plans for the new season included a friendly with the Brazilian's club team, Santos, at Hampden Park in October 1970. The Parkhead boss expressed his confidence that such a game could go ahead, perhaps as part of a tour, and was awaiting confirmation that the South American superstars would travel to Scotland. One fixture which would go ahead in Glasgow before that was the first round of the 1970/71 European Cup, Finnish champions KPV Kokkola the first stage of the recovery process for Celtic players and fans.

Following the disappointing end to the campaign, for Harry personally in terms of first-team starts and for the club as a whole with the devastating loss of those two cup finals, both he and Celtic would bounce back in spectacular fashion the following season. Harry was on target in a 6-0 victory over Limerick, as Celts opened their pre-season schedule with a short trip to south-west Ireland followed by a glamour friendly against Manchester City at Hampden, on Tuesday, 4 August 1970. For me, this was the Lancashire side's finest era, winning the English First Division title in the spring of 1968, their FA Cup final at Wembley the following year then the European Cup-Winners' Cup in Vienna, three months before facing Jock Stein's Bhoys in front of 63,000 spectators at Hampden in what would have been an early forerunner of the European Super Cup. If only. Harry was part of a four-man forward line which did everything but score that night, as Joe Mercer's side returned to Manchester with a fortunate goalless draw. It would be 40 years before City could follow up that level of success in a very different world under Roberto Mancini, Manuel Pellegrini then Pep Guardiola.

The competitive business commenced at Tynecastle, scene of that title-clinching match back in March, four days later, as the League Cup sections got underway. Harry was closely involved in both of Celtic's goals in their 2-1 win, setting up John Hughes to open the scoring 10 minutes before the break then his quick thinking catching the Hearts defence unawares after substitute Kevin Hegarty had grabbed an equaliser. As the home side claimed a throw-in, Harry took it quickly to set Bobby Lennox free, the Saltcoats Express laying on the winner for Jimmy Johnstone, as Celtic's quest for a sixth successive League Cup triumph – the Parkhead club having won it only twice previously - got off to a great start.

Harry was one of six players then rested by Jock Stein 48 hours later, as an effectively second-string Hoops side beat Rangers 3-1 to reclaim the Glasgow Cup, the final held over from the previous season. Celtic's monopoly of the old trophy thus stretched to six wins in the last seven competitions. He was back to face his old Clyde mates as the Bully Wee came to Celtic Park on the Wednesday night for the second League Cup fixture. Harry was "a standout" against his former club, pulling the strings as a Bobby Lennox hat-trick and a Jimmy Johnstone strike had Celts 4-0 up before well the hour. In fairness, the honours for the closing half-hour went to the visitors, who scored three times through Jimmy Burns, Sam Hastings and Dick Staite for the loss of a second from Jinky, as the crazy evening ended in a 5-3 win for the cup-holders. Only Eusebio's Benfica had managed to score three goals against Celtic in one match the previous season, and even at that they had required 120 minutes in Lisbon to do so.

Saturday, 15 August 1970 brought the third team in the section - Jerry Kerr's Dundee United - to Celtic Park. Harry was again on top form, crashing a shot off the crossbar from 20 yards in the opening minute then crossing for Tommy Callaghan to volley Celts into the lead 10 minutes later. The Hoops were only seconds away from a third successive win - Bobby Lennox having restored their lead following an Alex Reid equaliser on the hour - before striker Alan Gordon secured a share of the points for United.

The return fixture with Clyde took place at Shawfield on Wednesday, 19 August 1970, and it was another eventful evening. Celtic were reduced to 10-men five minutes before the break, when Willie Wallace was dismissed following a clash with Sam Hastings. The same player then pulled Harry down in the box in the opening minutes of the second half, Tommy Gemmell showing Tommy McCulloch no mercy from the spot. And the full-back, who had recently settled his differences with Celtic, struck once again from 12 yards in the final 15 minutes to seal the points, this time after Eddie Mulheron had punched a Tommy Callaghan header off the line.

Next up for Jock Stein's men was a visit from Hearts, the Edinburgh side looking to repeat their Celtic Park victory of the previous November. Those hopes would take nose-dive after the returning John Hughes took Harry's pass to blast Celts into the lead within 30 seconds, triggering the chants for The Bear and Harry, Harry to ring out from sections of the 40,000 spectators. The party was temporarily halted as Kevin Hegarty scored his second consecutive goal against the Hoops on 15 minutes, and it was not until midway through the second period when Yogi waltzed around Jim Cruickshank to restore Celtic's lead. With 10 minutes remaining, a second 2-2 home draw in a week looked the likely outcome as Hegarty netted yet again. Cue the Quality Street Gang to win the match for the Bhoys. George Connelly had been in outstanding form, now tipped as the next, big international prospect, although just where was unclear, as he appeared capable of playing pretty much anywhere on the park without any detriment to his performance. With five minutes to go he turned striker to blast Celtic into a 3-2 lead from outside the box, before substitute Lou Macari – on for Bobby Lennox – completed the scoring on 87 minutes with a cute header, the Hoops duly qualifying with one game to spare.

Despite his lack of goals, Harry's impressive start to the season had not gone unnoticed, Scotland boss Bobby Brown choosing "Celtic's class inside man" 48 hours later in a 14-man squad to represent the Scottish League against their Irish counterparts at Celtic Park in early September. George Connelly and Davie Hay would also receive their first call-ups, with Tommy Gemmell and Jimmy Johnstone taking the Celtic representation to five. On the same day, the players learned their League Cup fate, Dundee, beaten finalists three years earlier, would provide the quarter-final opposition for the holders.

It was up to Tayside on Wednesday, 26 August 1970, as Celts completed their group fixtures with a visit to Tannadice, Jock Stein taking the opportunity to blood another of his rising stars, full-back Danny McGrain. Having started all six section matches, Harry made way for the final 25 minutes to allow McGrain a Hoops debut, with Dundee United leading through a first-half Davie Wilson goal. Davie Hay equalised with eight minutes remaining but that looked in vain as Alan Gordon repeated his Celtic Park feat by scoring in the final minute. Then with Celts unbeaten record hanging by a thread, up popped Lou Macari straight from the restart to make it 2-2.

The League Cup sections looked like marking the end of the road for Harry's old club, Clyde, as news broke on the Friday morning of Hamilton Academical's resignation from the Scottish League, ahead of a planned merger with Clyde. The report confirmed that the Harry Hood Floodlights would now be erected at the home of the new club, Douglas Park, rather than Shawfield, with names such as Strathclyde Academical in the mix, albeit it appeared to me that Clyde would simply absorb the Hamilton outfit, with Accies players and management released. In any case, like the planned move to East Kilbride a few years earlier, this latest Clyde proposal would fall through. Hamilton Academical quickly withdrew its resignation, a new board of directors came in and after just one weekend of two 18-club Divisions, things reverted to the status quo in terms of the existence of both clubs involved.

With Jim Craig still recovering from cracked ribs and Davie Hay now established in midfield, the new Danny Bhoy was handed his first senior start as Celtic began the defence of their League title with a 2-0 victory over Morton at Parkhead. The afternoon began with the now traditional unfurling of the League Championship flag, five of those now flying proudly over the Jungle. Once the football was underway, normal service was resumed on the pitch also. Harry was involved in both Celtic goals, setting up Bobby Lennox for clinical finishes past Morton keeper Erik Sorensen – the Man in Black back in Greenock following his release from Ibrox - either side of the break. The big negative on the day was the sight of Tommy Gemmell being stretchered off after sustaining an ankle injury in the second half, which would rule him out of the Inter-League match in midweek. An 18-year-old Joe Jordan also made an appearance from the bench for the visitors, shortly before his £15k transfer to Leeds United.

Harry's continued good form saw Bobby Brown select him for the following side, 48 hours later.

SCOTTISH LEAGUE:

Jim Cruickshank (Hearts); Davie Hay (Celtic) & Billy Dickson (Kilmarnock);

Pat Stanton (Hibernian - captain), Ron McKinnon (Rangers) & Jim Henry (Dundee United);

Jimmy Johnstone, George Connelly & Harry Hood (all Celtic), Johnny Graham & Arthur Duncan (both Hibernian).

Substitutes; Bobby Clark (Aberdeen), Peter Oliver (Hearts) & Tommy McLean (Kilmarnock).

The League of Ireland side was largely drawn from national champions Waterford and runner's-up Shamrock Rovers, whilst right-half Joe O'Mahoney had played well for Limerick against Celtic in the pre-season friendly at the end of July. His teammate Al Finucane had been on Jock Stein's radar and had made his full international debut beside Charlie Gallagher against Turkey in Ankara in February 1967. He enjoys mythical status in Ireland, having played more league games there than any other player in a staggering 28-year career. He also holds the distinction of being the oldest player to play in European competition, appearing against Bordeaux in September 1986 not far short of his 44th birthday. I guess he is Ireland's equivalent of Alec McNair, Celtic's Icicle. The best-known player in the Irish squad was Shay Brennan. Manchester-born, he made his debut for Matt Busby's United in the infamous FA Cup-tie against Sheffield Wednesday in February 1958, which marked the first game after the Munich tragedy, the match programme unable to list the players who would be involved. Brennan replaced David Pegg, one of the victims, scoring twice in a 4-0 victory on an emotional night. A decade later he would be a European Cup-winner, after United succeeded Celtic as continental champions by beating Benfica 4-1 at Wembley. Shay was in England's initial 40-man squad for the World Cup in Chile in 1962, however, three years later he became the first player not born in Ireland to represent the country. In 1967, Charlie Gallagher would be the first man born in Scotland to achieve that accolade.

The following players would proudly wear the green at Celtic Park on Wednesday, 2 September 1970.

LEAGUE OF IRELAND:

Peter Thomas; Peter Bryan & Shay Brennan (all Waterford);

Joe O'Mahoney, Al Finucane (both Limerick) & Paddy Dunning (Shelbourne):

Jimmy McGeogh (Waterford), Mick Lawlor (Shamrock Rovers), Alfie Hale (Waterford), John Minnock (Athlone Town) & Johnny Matthews (Waterford).

Substitutes; Michael Smyth, Mick Kearin & Damien Richardson (all Shamrock Rovers).

In Tommy Gemmell's absence, Harry found himself one of four Hoops men playing on home soil that evening. David Hay and George Connelly were also making their debuts at this level whilst there was a fifth appearance for Jimmy Johnstone, which ended with an injury ruling him out of Celtic's weekend fixture. The match was viewed as the first step on the road to West Germany for the next World Cup finals, four years hence, but it would probably be a disappointing affair for under-pressure manager Bobby Brown and the 8,000 underwhelmed spectators. Brown was duly slaughtered in the media for his negative tactics, as Connelly scored the only goal of the game just after the hour to give the Scots a narrow victory rather than the cricket score suggested beforehand. Both Paddy Dunning and Mick Lawlor would play for Dundalk against Celtic in the European Cup at the end of the decade.

Five days later, Clyde faced Celtic for the third time that season, the second round of League fixtures pairing the clubs at the reprieved Shawfield. This would be the afternoon of the Quality Street Gang, Lou Macari opening and closing the scoring in a 5-0 win, whilst Davie Hay and substitute Vic Davidson – on for Bobby Murdoch - were also on target. Celtic's other goal came early in the second half when John McHugh could only deflect a Billy McNeill header past Tommy McCulloch. Harry had also beaten his old keeper a few minutes earlier, his strike knocked off as the referee felt his last touch had been a punch rather than a header. There was an outbreak of shadow boxing late on which saw Billy Beattie harshly sent off and Macari cautioned, as Celtic's 100% opening to the new League season continued.

The midweek trip to Dundee for the first leg of the League Cup quarter-final at Dens Park would prove to be the proverbial game of two halves. Jimmy Johnstone – restored to the starting line-up following his injury against the League of Ireland seven nights earlier - put Celts in a commanding position with a double midway through the first half, his second following a powerful shot from Harry which Dundee keeper Ally Donaldson failed to hold. The hosts came out after the interval and did exactly the same thing to Celtic, strikes from Alex Kinninmonth and Jocky Scott either side of the hour mark leaving the sides level at 2-2 ahead of the return leg at Celtic Park a fortnight later.

League business resumed with the visit of Rangers on Saturday, 12 September 1970. Celts made an incredible start to the match, John Hughes earning a penalty in the second minute – which Jim Brogan blasted over the crossbar – before beating Peter McCloy with a deft header four minutes later. Celts added a second killer goal early in the second half, and a work of art it was, Jimmy Johnstone's cute dummy from Yogi's cross allowing Bobby Murdoch to explode a shot behind McCloy before running to the Jungle, arm aloft, for one of Celtic Park's enduring images. The 2-0 victory saw Jock Stein's men move on to six points after three games, ominously already three ahead of Willie Waddell's Rangers.

Harry's excellent start to the new season had produced everything except goals. The feelgood factor extended to his family life, the Hood home now complete as the couple's son Nicholas Henry was born the following day, their third child in five years.

On the same day, a new set of fixtures appeared in the schedule for the first time, as Motherwell, Morton and Airdrieonians met English opposition in the first batch of British Cup ties. I have no recollection of that term being used, having always understood it to be known as the Texaco Cup. Hearts, Dundee and Dunfermline Athletic would also take part, the first two of those falling victim to the same 'one club from each city' rule which had prevented Clyde playing in the Inter-Cities Fairs Cup in 1967/68. With Hibernian and Dundee United finishing above their city rivals, seventh-placed Kilmarnock would be the beneficiaries, albeit Hearts would perhaps take some comfort from going all the way to the British/Texaco Cup final, before losing to Wolverhampton Wanderers over two legs.

Two nights later, Wednesday, 16 September 1970, was a landmark occasion for both new dad Harry and I, together with the late and much-missed Paul Wilson. Finnish champions KPV Kokkola were the opposition for my first-ever European Cup match, the Celtic striker marking the occasion with his first hat-trick for the club in the opening 35 minutes, to break his scoring duck for the season in some style. With a 6-0 lead at the interval - John Hughes, Billy McNeill and Jimmy Johnstone had also been on target - Jock Stein withdrew Harry and Davie Hay and introduced youngsters Vic Davidson and Paul Wilson to the fray, a senior debut for the latter. Paul would net twice either side of a Davidson goal as the yellow-clad Celts won 9-0 to set a European scoring record for the club which stands to this day.

Celtic's unbeaten start to the season finally came to an end at Easter Road three days later, the man who did the damage being Joe McBride, the former Parkhead hitman following up his midweek hat-trick against Malmo with a second-half double in Hibernian's 2-0 win, his first a thing of beauty as he volleyed the ball spectacularly past Evan Williams. The Hoops first defeat allowed Airdrieonians to assume an unlikely position at the top of the First Division table, one point ahead of a cluster of clubs which included the defending champions.

The week to follow involved a Parkhead double-header with Dundee. Having opened his European account against Kokkola, Harry finally got off the mark domestically, and in some style, on Wednesday, 23 September 1970, his bullet header three minutes from the break giving Celts a three-goal cushion in the second leg of their quarter-final tie, before 41,000 spectators. The goal is beautifully described by Malcolm Munro of *The Evening Times*.

"The third goal, scored by Harry Hood, was a masterpiece. I saw it coming all the way. Danny McGrain ran forward with the ball, tailed by the wee man, Jimmy Johnstone. As the back went forward, you could hear Johnstone yelling for a pass. McGrain side-flicked the ball to Johnstone, who made ground, then gave the ball back to the right-back. Danny immediately controlled the ball and clipped a wonderful cross to the far post, where Harry Hood rose like a bird and met the ball squarely with his forehead to score. It is goals like this which demoralise the opposition. There was no question of a foul or offside, or of any infringement. It was a goal, and a bonny one at that. A goal that was inevitable on the run of play."

Lou Macari had opened the scoring early on and - just as he had done at Shawfield at the beginning of the month – and he would also round off a great night's work with Celtic's fifth goal in the closing stages. John Hughes was also on target in the first half, before being replaced by Paul Wilson, who duly scored for the second successive midweek. Gordon Wallace managed a solitary reply for the visitors as a 5-1 win on the night saw Jock Stein's men through to the last-four draw on a 7-3 aggregate.

The somewhat lop-sided format adopted by the League Cup at that time – where all the First Division sides were grouped together, meaning most would not survive the section stage – produced the usual surprise semi-finalists, newly-promoted

Cowdenbeath and Second Division Dumbarton joining Celtic and Rangers in 'the hat' two days later. There were few gasps of astonishment, I suspect, when the Glasgow giants were kept apart, Charlie Gallagher and his Sons of the Rock drawn to face the Hoops at Hampden, just a few months after leaving his beloved Celtic Park. His old boss was out of the country at that point, Jock Stein and club secretary Desmond White in Paris to pick up the prestigious award from France Football and adidas as Europe's Team of the Year for 1969/70, having been runner's up in each of the previous two seasons. The beautiful 'Winged Victory of Samothrace' statuette is a much-loved display item in the Celtic Park boardroom to this day.

The third and final part of the Celtic v Dundee September trilogy was played out at Parkhead 24 hours later, John Hughes midweek injury allowing Paul Wilson a first start in the Hoops. It was Celtic's other winger who made the difference on the day, Jimmy Johnstone with a second-half double either side of a Lou Macari strike as the Bhoys won 3-0, with Dens wing-half Ron Selway dismissed late on following an incident with Macari. The League table would now take on a look which would become familiar for much of the remainder of the season, Celtic ahead of Aberdeen only on goal difference and St Johnstone the third team on the eight-point mark after five games.

There was a lovely Hood family occasion on the holiday Monday afternoon, as Harry kicked off a charity match at Provanmill Park between a Celtic Old Crock side and the Northern Police. Elder brother Jackie was now the president at St Roch's Juniors, the host club where both Hood siblings had played almost a decade earlier. Jackie would finally get to wear the Hoops, having signed for Everton in 1956 as Celtic manager Jimmy McGrory waited for his opportunity to make the teenager an offer.

September ended with a visit to Finland for the dead-rubber with KPV Kokkola, albeit it would be an afternoon of huge significance for Stevie Chalmers, who returned to the starting line-up for the first time since breaking his ankle against St Johnstone in the League Cup final 11 months earlier. The man who scored the goal which put the star above the crest three years earlier went close to opening the scoring with a trademark header, before fellow Lisbon hero Willie Wallace took the aggregate score to double figures midway through the first half. Tommy Callaghan doubled the lead before the break, Wispy grabbed his second and a third Lion – Bobby Lennox - completed the scoring after Vic Davidson, one of the Quality Street Gang had put his name on the scoresheet. Harry was one of a virtual first team rested for this match, testimony to the incredible depth of talent now available to Jock Stein.

Celtic's overall 14-0 victory was not the highest winning margin of the first round. That honour went to Borussia Monchengladbach, who managed another two in their romp over Cypriots EPA Larnaca. The undoubted shock was the elimination of holders and reigning world champions Feyenoord, who failed to win either leg of their tie with Uzina Textila Arad of Romania, duly exiting on away goals, an outcome described by coach Ernst Happel as *"equivalent to the eighth wonder of the world."*

Like Jock Stein's Celtic in 1967, they would relinquish their grip on the famous trophy at the first time of asking. There would be still be Dutch representation in the European Cup, in the form of Feyenoord's bitter rivals Ajax of Amsterdam - the current national titleholders - who were the beaten finalists in 1969.

The opening Saturday in October saw Celts make the trip to East End Park to take on bottom-of-the-table Dunfermline Athletic. The struggling Fifers had sacked their 1968 Scottish Cup-winning manager George Farm 48 hours earlier, although strangely he was sitting in the stand. The weekend wouldn't bring an uplift in his fortunes, nor for those of Pars captain Dave McNicoll, who broke his leg in a collision with Jimmy Johnstone just before the interval. With Harry off the bench at half-time in place of Vic Davidson, Celts stepped up a gear. Willie Wallace beat former Hoops defender John Cushley to set up Lou Macari for Celtic's opener midway through the half, before sealing the points from the spot with six minutes remaining, after John Lunn had handled a Harry cross. Aberdeen's surprise 2-0 defeat at Cappielow left Celtic and St Johnstone out on their own now as joint League leaders, with the sides due to meet the following Saturday.

Tuesday's European Cup draw in the Netherlands paired Celtic with Irish opposition competitively for the first time, as Waterford and the Hoops were the first two names produced. The Blues had won an All-Ireland first-round tie with Glentoran, and immediately announced that their home leg would be played at Dublin's Lansdowne Road, where they had hosted Manchester United in front of 49,000 spectators in the same competition two years earlier. A number of their players would be familiar to Harry and the other three Celts who had faced the League of Ireland at Parkhead the previous month.

The following night Celts met Second Division Dumbarton at Hampden in the semi-final of the League Cup. There would be no goals on a night when recently freed Charlie Gallagher was the man-of-the-match, the Hoops playing for around 40 minutes with 10 men after an injury to Bobby Murdoch, during which time Sons keeper Laurie Williams saved a Willie Wallace penalty. This was the last time Celtic wore the all-white kit most often associated with the memorable St Etienne victory two years earlier.

The afternoon of Saturday, 10 October 1970 saw a top-of-table battle between an injury-ravaged Celtic and St Johnstone at Parkhead, an ill-tempered game decided by a controversial goal. Tommy Callaghan was stretchered off after half an hour with a bad injury, Jimmy Quinn coming off the bench to play at left-back with Davie Hay moving into midfield. The only goal of the game arrived 10 minutes later, Willie Wallace shooting home before a group of Saints players rounded on Edinburgh referee Eddie Thomson, claiming that a penalty should have been awarded instead! After a consultation with his linesman, Thomson confirmed the goal, Celts now out in front, one point clear of the chasing pack.

The League Cup semi-final replay with Dumbarton, 48 hours later, involved another controversial winner. A severe nosebleed which had kept him up all of Sunday night meant Harry would not start a match in the competition for the first time that season. Despite a perfect start - a Bobby Lennox double within 15 minutes - Celts would again struggle against the second-tier Sons. Charlie Gallagher scored from the spot just after the hour to start the fightback from 0-2 and it would take extra-time before Jock Stein's men edged a seven-goal thriller, thanks to goals from Willie Wallace and Lou Macari, with Dumbarton defenders claiming that the ball had swerved back into play before Macari headed home.

League business resumed five days later with a tricky visit to Broomfield to face an Airdrieonians side tucked in just two points behind the leaders and boasting their double-Drew strike force of Busby and Jarvie. That gap would be four later that afternoon, as Harry celebrated his return with an outstanding performance, which included his first two League goals of the season, not the nicest reunion for his direct opponent that afternoon, former Clyde teammate Pat Delaney, the son of Celtic legend Jimmy. Harry's 15th-minute header from a Bobby Lennox cross equalised the opening goal from Diamonds winger Billy Wilson, another member of that Kilsyth Rangers Scottish Junior Cup-winning side of 1967. As an aside, Drew Jarvie would also have played at Hampden that day but for injury. Within 10 minutes Harry turned goalmaker, returning the compliment to Lennox, allowing the Lisbon Lion to volley past Roddy McKenzie. With 20 minutes remaining, Harry scored the goal of the game, a 20-yard drive which left Airdrie's Irish international keeper helpless. Aberdeen's 2-0 win at Ibrox allowed them to stay in touch with Celtic at the top of the table, both the Dons and St Johnstone remaining two points behind.

There was a lovely family postscript to that match at Broomfield. A scene featuring Harry was featured in the popular *'Place the ball'* competition in *The Evening Times* and the main prize of £1,000 was duly won by a 43-year-old Duntocher joiner, Henry Scott, who just happened to be Harry's first cousin! The son of Walter Scott junior – Harry's maternal uncle - was delighted, his wife Betty expecting their first child in February 1971.

"It's quite incredible that I should win the big prize this particular week. Harry must have brought the luck. Harry was making his own luck that Saturday at Broomfield. I remember he scored two goals."

Harry was now enjoying the best form of his career, prompting suggestions of a full international call-up. Jim Blair waxed lyrical over his weekend performance in his Monday column for *The Evening Times*.

"Clap hands, here comes Harry! That could well be Celtic's slogan this week - seven days that soak up a European Cup-tie in Ireland and a League Cup final date at Hampden against Rangers – after their fine 3-1 win on Saturday over Airdrie. No doubt about it, this was a 24-carat performance from Harry Hood, a player of

unquestionable ability. Whilst Scotland team manager Bobby Brown was at Ibrox watching Rangers slump to defeat against Aberdeen – he was checking on Bobby Clark, John Greig and Colin Stein – Hood had the Celtic fans singing his praises at Broomfield with an exhibition of almost flawless football."

"He scored two goals. His first came from a header after Airdrie had taken the lead and his second wrapped up the game 20 minutes from time. It was a beauty. He picked up the ball in the outside-left position, veered inside and from about 25 yards out, looked up and cracked in an unsavable shot that even moved his normally modest self to raise both hands above his head in salute, when he saw it crash into the net behind McKenzie."

"It wasn't just his goals that made him the top man. Far from it. His distribution was a treat to watch, and I honestly don't remember him wasting a ball all afternoon. It was Hood who set up Celtic's second goal. He chested down a good Murdoch pass in the inside-right position and crossed to the far post. Wallace jumped and missed, right-back Jonquin decided to let it go – which is suicidal against Celtic – and in stepped Lennox to slam it home."

"Scotland's game with Denmark is only a couple of weeks away, and if Hood continues to turn in this sort of football, he may well swap his green-and-white jersey for the dark blue of his country."

Harry's first overseas commitment that season would be a brief affair, 36 minutes to be exact, by which time Celtic were already 4-0 ahead of Waterford in front of 50,000 spectators at Lansdowne Road. With the tie effectively over, and Harry limping slightly after taking a knock, Jock Stein took the opportunity to give substitute Stevie Chalmers some more game time and Harry some respite in the dugout. He would no doubt have a bird's-eye view of the terracing trouble which flared up behind one of the goals, causing the Danish referee to delay the start of the second half. Harry had set things rolling directly from the kick-off, his touch to Bobby Lennox seeing the lightning-fast winger leave Irish defenders trailing in his wake before crossing for Willie Wallace to score the earliest-ever goal in European competition, just 10 seconds in. Lou Macari, Bobby Murdoch and Wallace then all added doubles – the latter thus completing his hat-trick - as Celts racked up a 7-0 victory, a club record away win in European competition which, like the 9-0 landslide over KPV Kokkola, remains intact to this day.

As Celtic prepared for their seventh consecutive League Cup final that Saturday, Clyde manager Archie Robertson made an audacious bid to bring Bertie Auld to Shawfield, the Celtic midfielder currently serving a suspension and yet to make a first-team appearance since being sent home from Toronto.

Harry would be back in the side which faced Rangers at Hampden on Saturday, 24 October 1970, his second national cup final appearance as a Celt, following the victory over St Johnstone in the League Cup at the same stadium 12 months earlier.

Jock Stein went for youth over experience as the following teams lined up in front of 106,263 spectators, the last six-figure crowd to attend a League Cup game.

CELTIC:

Evan Williams; Jim Craig & Jimmy Quinn; Bobby Murdoch, Billy McNeill & Davie Hay; Jimmy Johnstone, George Connelly, Willie Wallace, Harry Hood & Lou Macari. Substitute; Bobby Lennox.

RANGERS:

Peter McCloy; Sandy Jardine & Alex Miller; Alfie Conn, Ron McKinnon & Colin Jackson; Willie Henderson, Alex MacDonald, Derek Johnstone, Colin Stein, & Willie Johnston. Substitute; Graham Fyfe.

Sadly, Celtic's third major cup final of the calendar year 1970 would end the same way as the previous two, in defeat, thanks to a first-half header from 16-year-old Ibrox striker Derek Johnstone, ending the grip on this particular trophy which Stein's men had enjoyed for five years. Harry's disappointing afternoon ended after 65 minutes, with the evergreen Bobby Lennox introduced from the bench to add to his wonderful record in these clashes. It was not to be, Willie Wallace uncharacteristically missing Celtic's best chance late on. Instead, it would be a first success for Willie Waddell as Rangers manager and a first for anyone at Ibrox since their extra-time victory in the Scottish Cup final over Celtic four years earlier. The arrival of Jock Stein had triggered a steep decline in the fortunes of the Govan outfit, with only those two cup successes secured since his arrival at Parkhead in March 1965.

My own recollection of that afternoon was slightly different. Still deemed too young to attend such fixtures, I had negotiated the boundary wall at Petershill Park to take in the Central League clash with Lesmahagow. The huge roar of the crowd when the half-time score from Hampden was announced over the tannoy system confirmed that I was very much in the minority inside the ground that day.

Harry was on target again four nights later, scoring the late winner as Celts immediately bounced back from that Hampden defeat. Jock Stein's men showed the courage of champions, recovering from two goals down against Hearts at Parkhead with just 25 minutes remaining to win 3-2. Donald Ford's brace for the Gorgie side was matched by Willie Wallace against his old team, Bobby Murdoch - Celtic's outstanding player on the evening - setting up Harry to smash the ball home with 13 minutes to play. But he saved his best for the last day of the month. On a pitch covered in muddy puddles which would have had Peppa Pig declaring a huff, Harry ran riot at Fir Park, scoring a hat-trick – his second in six weeks - as Celts hammered Motherwell 5-0 to end October two points clear of Aberdeen at the top of the table. Harry's first goal was a powerful left-foot shot which left Keith MacRae helpless after 20 minutes, the second arriving just before the interval as he headed home a Bobby Lennox cross. George Connelly added a third before Harry completed his treble from the spot on the hour, after MacRae had dragged Jimmy Johnstone down in the box. The winger then completed the rout in the closing stages, a few minutes after Harry had left the mudbath for a well-earned rest, Lou Macari coming on. Monday's *Evening Times* match report led with the memorable headline *"HMS Hood sinks the 'Well."*

"Ridiculous!" we sages up in the Press seats decided. "You can't ask players to splash about in this." Then Harry Hood got the first goal. He killed a pass, veered to the left and without too much fuss steered the ball home. The ball went in against the tide, as it were. Hood's whole attitude appeared to be – "Now you've seen how it's done, let's do it again." And Celtic did it. From a team that had been slipping and slithering they began to walk upon the water and take the ball with them too. Wee Jimmy Johnstone was jinking...Bobby Murdoch sailing over puddles with all the majesty of a Spanish galleon under full sail...and there was HMS Hood blasting at the opposition whenever half a chance came up. 'Appy 'Arry showed how it could be done twice more before being taken off after his hat-trick and replaced by Macari, who, immediately, had the impertinence to attempt to score."

There was another monsoon as November commenced with the return leg of the European Cup second-round tie against Waterford at Celtic Park. The match would play out very differently from that in Dublin, Celts finding themselves 2-0 down at the break before the introduction of Harry for Bobby Lennox provided the platform for a second successive Parkhead recovery from that position to win 3-2. Having scored 21 goals without reply in their opening three goals in the competition, there was some talk in the media of Celtic beating Real Madrid's European Cup record of 31 in a season, established in their incredible 1959/60 campaign. The Irish clearly had not read that particular script, taking the lead on 20 minutes, Alfie Hale's header deflected past Evan Williams by Billy McNeill. Things went from bad to worse on the half-hour, as Johnny Matthew – another who had played for the League of Ireland at Celtic Park in September - volleyed past Williams for 2-0. Jock Stein shuffled his attacking pack at the interval, bringing on Harry to play through the middle with John Hughes. That switch paid immediate dividends, as Yogi – making a welcome return from a lengthy injury lay-off, as was Tommy Gemmell – pulled a goal back seconds after the restart, following good work from Jimmy Johnstone. The little winger then added another two goals to his European collection to give Celts a narrow win on the night and a 10-2 aggregate victory. Two of the big guns exited the competition at this stage. With Real Madrid missing from the European Cup for the first time ever, neighbours Atletico eliminated Italian champions Cagliari, Luigi Riva et al, to progress, whilst Everton became the first side to win in a penalty shootout, Borussia Monchengladbach the unfortunate victims after two 1-1 draws. With Celtic and Ajax, this pair would make up the quartet of favourites in the eyes of many observers.

Back on the domestic front, three days later promoted Cowdenbeath made their first League visit to Celtic Park since a 7-0 defeat in September 1933, an afternoon when both Jimmy McGrory and Charlie Napier scored hat-tricks. Two of 'Happy Feet' Napier's goals had come from the penalty spot, the first award conceded by his elder brother George. The other was given away by Napier's full-back partner Charlie Gronbach, who now returned to Glasgow's east end as Cowdenbeath chairman. Small world. Harry's first task that afternoon was to gently remove a small dog from the field, the Blue Brazil perhaps bringing their own Pele with them! Half an hour later Harry set George Connelly up for the opening goal, the big Fifer doubling the lead on the stroke of half-time following a glorious dummy from Jimmy Johnstone. Willie Wallace scored Celtic's third with 15 minutes remaining and there was a brief blip just before the end, as Harry saw his penalty kick saved by visiting keeper Allan Wyllie.

Harry had yet again been overlooked for the full Scotland set-up, despite his impressive start to the season, Coventry City's Willie Carr the latest inside-forward introduced by Bobby Brown for the match with Denmark at Hampden in midweek. On this occasion, though, perhaps he would consider himself fortunate to miss out, spared the appalling abuse meted out to the two Celts in the team – Davie Hay and Jimmy Johnstone – booed every time they touched the ball by a large section of the crowd behind one goal, for the crime of playing for Celtic. The crowd then started up a chant for Sandy Jardine, and shamefully Brown obliged, removing the young Celtic full-back from the fray. *The Evening Times* headline the following morning was *"Night of shame - for fans,"* which pretty much summed it up.

The excitement felt by Harry as he took his first steps into a business career by opening the Sherwood Manor hotel on Uddingston's New Edinburgh Road would be followed by personal heartbreak, the new owner tragically losing both of his beloved parents within a three-week spell as November rolled into December. Whether his father's illness was a factor in Harry dropping to the bench for the home match with Kilmarnock on Saturday, 14 November 1970 is unclear, but he came on to replace opening goalscorer Bobby Murdoch, with Celtic already 3-0 up, Willie Wallace and Jimmy Johnstone the others on target. There would be no further scoring, largely due to the efforts of Kilmarnock's impressive young keeper, Alistair Hunter. At 1pm the following day, 66-year-old retired security officer Henry Ferguson Hood passed away peacefully in Glasgow's Stobhill Hospital, just a mile or so from the current family home at 120 Burnbrae Street in Balornock. He had been suffering from prostate cancer. His son Henry Anthony Hood would register the death on the Monday, 16 November, as his Celtic teammates headed to London to play West Ham United in Bobby Moore's testimonial that evening.

As Harry and his family attended his dad's funeral on the morning of Wednesday, 18 November 1970, the quarter-final draw for the European Cup in Paris paired Celtic with highly-fancied Ajax. Jock Stein expressed his delight at the tie but in terms of Celtic's hopes of progression it could scarcely have been more difficult, as events would later prove. That would also finally put paid to plans to match up Celtic and Santos in Jamaica in February 1971 - an opportunity for Harry to face his hero Pele - the likelihood now being that the Bhoys would seek a game with Feyenoord in that window, ahead of the clash with their Dutch rivals the following month. UEFA also announced that the European Cup final would be played at Wembley, a huge incentive for Celtic and a mouth-watering prospect for the supporters.

Harry would miss out on the goalless draw with Falkirk at Brockville three days later but would then bravely turn out against St Mirren at Parkhead on Saturday, 28 November 1970, setting up Tommy Gemmell's early opener before being replaced by George Connelly for the final 18 minutes in Celtic's 3-0 win, which kept them one point ahead of Aberdeen at the summit. Vic Davidson – wearing number seven in the absence of Jimmy Johnstone, who had said beforehand that he was *"not keen to play"* – completed the victory with a second half double.

As Celts prepared to travel to Tannadice for the vital League match with Dundee United, Harry would then suffer the tragic loss of his mother. Just two weeks after saying goodbye to the love of her life, Mary Morrison Scott Hood suffered cardiac failure and passed away at 9.45am on Saturday, 5 December 1970, aged 61, in the same Stobhill Hospital which had featured so prominently in her life. The teenage confectionery salesman from Anderston and his Highland sweetheart had shared the highs and lows of life together for more than four decades. They would now be reunited after the briefest of partings, and their love story could carry on forever.

It was a time which is still vivid in the memory of Harry's nephew, John Scott, more than 50 years later, as he shared his recollections of the Hoods, the Scotts and football from his childhood.

"My parents Michael and Margaret Scott were married at St Mary's in Duntocher on 23 September 1950. We were always under the impression that Harry's dad was a bit of an entrepreneur, as there is a family story that he provided a case of whiskey at the reception, at a time, apparently, when whiskey was rationed or difficult to come by."

"I knew about the football connection early on. Harry's cousins all liked football but Duntocher Hibs were on the go and there were other junior or amateur teams around, so they tended to watch them, although Walter and Henry in particular would go to the big games, like the cup final. There were at least three supporters' buses leaving from Duntocher, and I was a regular from 11 years old. My mother's uncle used to take me, and I couldn't have had a better introduction, as my first regular season was 1966/67. I remember the Scottish Cup semi-final versus Clyde that year. I think Willie Wallace wore number four for Celtic and he and Harry had a bit of a niggle throughout the game. We used to be in a bit of a huff with Wispy, as we thought he'd gone to Celtic when Harry should have. Word around our campfire was that Willie stole Harry's place. All untrue of course."

"I think all four of Harry's cousins were decent players, but Morris and Henry were very good, indeed Henry had trials down south. Henry was a great laugh and he and my dad were very close. Morris went to Jersey in 1961 and has never come back. I've spoken to him on the phone once or twice and I know he follows the Celtic from afar. My dad liked the juniors, and in my life, I was only ever at four senior games

with him. The first one was a Motherwell v Dumbarton Scottish Cup-tie in the early 1960's. My dad worked in Dumbarton and a supporters' bus picked us up at the Boulevard in Duntocher. That would be classed as a 'wee day out' and was the first time I had seen 'cairy oots.' It was all good fun even though the Sons lost. The next game was that Dumbarton v Clyde game in 1963 when Harry was playing, and after that I saw him score a hat-trick for Sunderland at Clydebank, in the match to inaugurate the floodlights. My uncles Henry and Walter and my cousin Ian were all at that one with me. Ian got his name as it's Gaelic for John, which was what my grandad (Walter John) was called. Sadly, Ian died at just 14."

"The only time I saw Celtic with my dad was the 3-2 victory over Hearts just after the Derek Johnstone cup final. I always thought it was odd my dad saying out of the blue that he and Uncle Henry were going with me. I may be putting two and two together and making five, but I think Harry's dad passed away shortly afterwards, and I think his mother died just before Christmas. Anyway, my dad and Henry were at both funerals. I asked if they had seen Harry at the first one and they said they had been talking to him, and that Harry had said we should go to a game. The night of the Hearts match we arrived at Celtic Park and Henry disappeared for five minutes. We then went to the game and it was only the second and last time I ever sat in the main stand. We were right in the middle. I'm wondering if Henry had picked up comps from Harry, as they were certainly in touch around then. Harry scored the winner that night. When I came home from games, my dad would always ask firstly if Harry had been playing, rather than the score."

"Being a gawky teenager back then, I never had the courage to say hello when I saw Harry outside the ground before games, but before that brilliant 2-2 match with St Johnstone at the start of the season in 1969, I said hello to his mother and brother George, after he'd left. His mother gave me a shiny 50p piece, which was greatly appreciated."

"The overriding aspect of all this, which I'd like to convey, is that despite not always being in touch with Harry, all of us Scott's were, and always will be, so proud of his tremendous achievements."

Later that day, Harry's Celtic teammates would recover from the loss of an early Billy McNeill own goal to beat Dundee United 2-1, Vic Davidson equalising on the hour before Stuart Markland evened things up in the own goal stakes with 15 minutes remaining. Some 70 miles north, Aberdeen sent out a clear message with a 7-0 demolition of Cowdenbeath at Pittodrie. There was just one point and two goals between the Bhoys and the Dons ahead of the clash of the teams in Glasgow seven days later, and a further seven points between Aberdeen and the nearest clubs. The title was already a two-horse race.

Harry would endure another sad week following his mum's funeral on the Tuesday before returning to matters football. Jock Stein named him on the bench for the top-of-the-table clash with the Dons at Celtic Park on Saturday, 12 December 1970, a match which drew an enormous crowd of over 63,000 to the east end, meaning the 10-year-old Yours Truly would have to make do with radio commentary and brief highlights on the Saturday night. The teams lined up as follows for a 2.50pm kick-off, threats of national power cuts forcing both that decision and the halving of the half-time break to five minutes to ensure the game would finish in daylight.

CELTIC:

John Fallon; Jim Craig & Tommy Gemmell; Bobby Murdoch, Billy McNeill & Jim Brogan; Jimmy Johnstone, George Connelly, Lou Macari, Davie Hay & John Hughes. Substitute; Harry Hood.

ABERDEEN:

Bobby Clark; Henning Boel & Jim Hermiston; Steve Murray, Tommy McMillan & Martin Buchan; Ian Taylor, Davie Robb, Jim Forrest, Joe Harper, & Arthur Graham. Substitute; Alex Willoughby.

The Dons were in superb form leading up to this match, their nine straight League wins including six consecutive clean sheets for keeper Bobby Clark and his defence. At the other end of the pitch, they boasted Scotland's top scorer, Joe Harper, with 19 goals. Harper had played with Harry on Scotland's tour of the Far East, Australasia and Canada in the summer of 1967, having moved from his local team Morton to Huddersfield Town at that time. He duly returned to Greenock before being picked up by Eddie Turnbull for Aberdeen in 1969. That would prove to be an astute piece of business.

More than 50 years later, having not been at the game, I still see the winning goal clearly in memory's view. Jim Hermiston's long throw from the Jungle at what I would deem the far end – the east terracing – is flicked on by Davie Robb for Harper to nod past John Fallon. Simple and clean as a whistle, eight minutes into the second half. Still trailing as we passed the hour mark, and with the crowd chanting for "Harry, Harry," Jock Stein did indeed introduce him for George Connelly, in a last throw of the dice. Whilst Harry would then notably improve Celtic's performance in those final 25 minutes, he would be unable to conjure up a goal, his 30-yard drive beating Clark but squeezing agonisingly past the post. Turnbull's men saw the match out to leapfrog Celtic and move one point clear at the top, both teams now sharing an identical record of 37 goals scored and just seven conceded. Game on.

Celtic would finish 1970 with two victories, as Jock Stein denied rumours that he was trying to sign striker John 'Dixie' Deans from Motherwell. Seven days after the defeat by Aberdeen, Harry scored what would prove to be the winner early in the second half of the 2-1 win over Ally MacLeod's Ayr United at Somerset, the striker following up after a Bobby Lennox drive had come back off the crossbar to beat David Stewart for his 11th goal of the season. John Hughes had memorably opened the scoring directly from a corner midway through the first half, home debutant Jim Flynn pulling one back for the hosts just 30 seconds after Harry's goal.

Monday's Scottish Cup third-round draw handed Celts a home tie with Second Division Queen of the South, with Jock Stein taking the opportunity to watch European Cup opponents Ajax play out a 1-1 draw with Feyenoord in Rotterdam before a 67,000 crowd the previous day. And news of a third cup competition to be introduced the following season for Scottish clubs emerged, sponsored by brewers Drybrough. This would involve the four top-scoring teams in each Division competing on a straight knock-out basis ahead of the League Cup sectional stage.

And 24 hours after what must have been the saddest of Christmas Days for the Hood family, Harry was in action for Celtic at Cappielow, as Stevie Chalmers marked his first domestic appearance of the campaign on his 34th birthday with a wonderful opening goal in a 3-0 win over a Morton side clad in Aberdeen red strips - Hal Stewart up to his old mischief again. Fellow Lions Bobby Lennox and Willie Wallace then secured the points before the interval, whilst two significant others – Billy McNeill and Jimmy Johnstone – were missing from the line-up without explanation. The Class of 1970 ended the year still tucked in one point behind Aberdeen at the top of the table, with 16 games remaining which would decide the destiny of the Scottish League title.

It had been a roller-coaster of a year for Harry, professional highs and major lows mixed in with the full range of personal emotions, the joyous birth of his son then the anguish of losing both parents.

He would no doubt be hoping that 1971 would be kinder.

Chapter 19

It's high-scoring Harry at the Double

Reeling from the recent loss of his parents, the second day of 1971 would see Harry play in a match which still sends a shiver through me 50 years later. The traditional Ne-erday fixture between Celtic and Rangers drew over 80,000 supporters to Ibrox on a foggy afternoon which those present will never forget. As Jock Stein sought to maintain his challenge to League-leaders Aberdeen – now three points clear at the summit following their 3-0 victory over Dundee at Pittodrie 24 hours earlier, Celtic's match with Clyde frozen off - he again left his captain Billy McNeill out in favour of George Connelly, Tommy Gemmell wearing the armband. Willie Waddell's response to the 3-1 defeat to Falkirk at Brockville on New Year's Day – a sixth League defeat of the season for Rangers - was to hand German keeper Gerry Neef his first start of the campaign, as the following sides ran out at Ibrox on this fateful afternoon.

RANGERS:

Gerry Neef; Sandy Jardine & Willie Mathieson; John Greig, Ron McKinnon & Colin Jackson; Willie Henderson, Alfie Conn, Derek Johnstone, Colin Stein & Dave Smith. Substitute; Alex MacDonald.

CELTIC:

Evan Williams; Jim Craig & Tommy Gemmell; Jim Brogan, George Connelly & Davie Hay; Jimmy Johnstone, Harry Hood, Willie Wallace, Tommy Callaghan & Bobby Lennox. Substitute; Lou Macari.

In conditions which did football a huge disservice, the only goal action took place in the closing minute of the match. First Jimmy Johnstone followed up on a shot from his pal Bobby Lennox which beat Rangers goalkeeper Gerry Neef all ends up but crashed off the crossbar, the little winger then grabbing one of so many headed goals he would enjoy in these fixtures. He would not have time to savour this one though, as a long, desperate free-kick from Dave Smith was propelled into the packed Celtic penalty area for Colin Stein to scramble past the tracksuit-bottomed Evan Williams. Celtic's 50-year wait to savour the taste of victory at Ibrox in the Ne-erday fixture would thus continue, whilst former Rangers striker Jim Forrest scored a late winner at Muirton Park which sent Aberdeen four points clear at the top of the table. Sadly, the weekend match details would prove later to be irrelevant.

My dad had decided, for his own reasons, that he was not going back to Ibrox, and as I was still considered in the 'too wee' category for such games, we were paying his brother a visit at his home in Barmulloch, as we did at New Year. Both men had teenage sons at the game, albeit not together, so when word came through of *"trouble at Ibrox,"* there was genuine concern for their safety. Eventually, my cousin would arrive home, saying he had heard there had been "bother" at the other end, like most folk, I guess, assuming violence rather than the tragedy which later unfolded. I can recall watching the scenes on black-and-white television later that night - not sure if it was Scotsport or the news - then in the newspapers, bodies laid out on the Ibrox pitch and the expressions of Jock Stein, Neil Mochan, Bob Rooney and other club officials as they tended to the injured, with the thick fog and lack of colour only adding to the surreal scenario. Irrespective of who was to blame and why, or what colour their scarves were, on Saturday, 2 January 1971, 66 supporters went to a football match and didn't return to their families, almost half of those teenagers or younger. May they rest in peace.

I made my way with 28,000 others to Celtic Park seven days later, as some degree of normality was reintroduced by the playing of the next League fixture, Hibernian the visitors with their new manager, Dave Ewing in charge, following the sacking of Willie MacFarlane. An eerie silence descended over the ground as the players stood, heads bowed, for a minute's silence before the kick-off, impeccably observed as if that required to be said. Jock Stein brought back his Lions, Bobby Murdoch and Billy McNeill, with youngsters George Connelly and Davie Hay making way, the latter moving to the bench. Harry would be the main man as Celts won the match 2-1, setting up Tommy Callaghan to head past Roy Baines 10 minutes before the break then nodding home what would prove to be the winner himself, shortly after the restart. Pat Stanton tapped home a last-minute consolation goal for the visitors to produce a result which did not in any way reflect the domination of Celtic from start to finish.

As an aside, all three goals on the day were scored by what I would describe as identikit Jock Stein signings for Celtic, proven experienced players in the Scottish game with creative or attacking flair and commanding a cheque in the region of £30/£40k. That would start with Joe McBride of Motherwell in the summer of 1965, his first major capture, then continue with Willie Wallace from Hearts the next year, Tommy Callaghan from Dunfermline Athletic in 1968 and Harry himself the following March. He would go back to the well, literally, for Dixie Deans, before former Dundee and Aberdeen midfielder Steve Murray arrived at Parkhead. Ronnie Glavin from Partick Thistle would require the Celtic board to dig a lot deeper in 1974, as would Johnny Doyle from Ayr United two years later, however, they would then acquire the veteran Stanton from Hibernian that summer for the cost of Jackie McNamara senior's contract, and he would repay that with a Double in his only season. Whilst his ability to secure a goalkeeper of the correct standard for Celtic – only Ally Hunter from Kilmarnock in 1973 really fitting that particular bill, and only for a short time at that – was and is open to debate, there was no doubt that Jock got most of those outfield signings bang on the money.

Stanton and Hibernian would then do Celtic a huge favour the following Saturday, 16 January 1971, defeating Aberdeen 2-1 at Easter Road to end both the Dons 15-match unbeaten run and European record 'clean sheet' tally of 1,157 minutes. On the other side of the Forth, the Hoops were going goal crazy, beating Dundee 8-1 at Dens Park with Harry opening and closing the scoring and denied a hat-trick first by the post and then by Doug Houston's last touch on his cross for 4-0. Willie Wallace and an unstoppable Jimmy Johnstone also added doubles, with Tommy Callaghan completing the rout on the day Bertie Auld made his first top-team appearance since the European Cup final in Milan the previous May. It was a pivotal day in the title race, Jock Stein's men now two points behind Aberdeen but with that home game with Clyde in hand. As it happens, that would turn out to be a rather special occasion for Bertie and indeed a few other Celts, but that story is for later.

Despite his excellent form and 14 goals so far that season, there would be no place for Harry in the squad announced by Scotland boss Bobby Brown on the Monday for the European Nations Cup-tie with Belgium in February. Joe Harper, Jim Forrest, Tony Green of Blackpool and Kilmarnock's Tommy McLean were the latest to get the nod, Harry's omission not lost on Jim Blair of *The Evening Times*.

"I am amazed that not one Celtic half-back or forward has been chosen. Certainly, Harry Hood would have been in my pool the way he has been playing in recent weeks."

Harry would grab another brace five days later, scoring either side of the interval, as Celtic's bid to regain the Scottish Cup commenced with a home tie against Second Division Queen of the South, the first time I had watched the Dumfries side in action. They would head south with a healthy cheque and no disgrace, having been on the end of a 5-1 defeat, Willie Wallace, Tommy Callaghan and Billy McNeill the other scorers for Celtic. The fourth-round draw made in Glasgow 48 hours later saw Celtic paired with Dunfermline Athletic yet again at home, for the third time in four years. By a strange quirk of fate, the teams met on League business that weekend, a Willie Wallace header early in the second half giving Celtic the points and a psychological advantage ahead of a cup meeting a fortnight later, although that was offset by the loss of Bobby Murdoch with a dislocated shoulder.

The pressure of a tight title race was beginning to tell, as February opened with defeats for both title contenders. Aberdeen lost 1-0 to second-bottom Dunfermline Athletic at East End Park, whilst St Johnstone edged a five-goal thriller with Celtic at Muirton Park, Harry equalising an early opening goal from teenage Perth striker Jim Pearson before the hosts moved into a 3-1 lead through Henry Hall and Ian McPhee. Willie Wallace provided hopes of a Hoops comeback with an 81st minute strike, however, that would prove to be too little too late as the Dons maintained their two-point advantage at the summit, Stein's men still with a vital game in hand. Aberdeen would have more immediate matters to address, as a significant section of the main stand at Pittodrie was completely destroyed in a fire in the early hours of Saturday morning. Indeed, it took firemen wearing breathing apparatus to retrieve the precious and priceless Scottish Cup from the Dons boardroom with only minutes to spare.

Tuesday, 9 February 1971 provided an opportunity for Celtic to take a measure of revenge for THAT night in Milan when world club champions Feyenoord rolled up to Hampden before 51,000 spectators. There were many similarities on the night, Tommy Gemmell again opening the scoring – this time from the penalty spot – only for the Dutch to quickly equalise through the ominously-named Posthumus. Thankfully, there was no sickening Ove Kindvall blow late on and indeed Celtic could count themselves unfortunate not to win the match as the final whistle blew on a 1-1 draw. Jock Stein had once again taken the opportunity to experiment, Harry and Bobby Lennox either side of Jimmy Johnstone in an attacking 4-3-3 formation, supported by man-of-the-match Tommy Callaghan, Bertie Auld and Davie Hay.

Tom's elder brother Willie was with the Pars team who travelled through to Glasgow the following Saturday on a high after their win over Aberdeen the previous week, albeit a late fitness test ruled him out of another match-up with his sibling. His side would leave Celtic Park with a replay though, after Joe McBride once again scored against his boyhood club, his equaliser early in the second half cancelling out Willie Wallace's header just before the break as the sides fought out a 1-1 draw in the fourth round of the Scottish Cup. Monday's quarter-final pairings gave the winners a home tie against either Clyde or Raith Rovers, whilst cup-holders Aberdeen would go to Ibrox if they could overcome Dundee United at Pittodrie in their own replay.

As Scotland prepared to move into a new Decimal Age, Harry would be the matchwinner in the replay, at East End Park four nights later in front of 23,000 spectators, scoring the only goal of the game on 20 minutes, following a Bobby Lennox cross. He would no doubt be disappointed to hear that the last-eight opposition would be Raith Rovers, rather than his old Clyde colleagues, the Second Division Fifers upsetting the form book with a 2-0 win at Shawfield the same night.

It was back to League business on Saturday, 17 February 1971, Airdrieonians the visitors to Celtic Park on another pivotal day in the title race. Aberdeen would drop a point in a goalless draw at home to Rangers, whilst the Hoops closed the gap to one point with an emphatic 4-1 victory over the Diamonds. Harry made it 3-0 with 20 minutes remaining with a fine strike from outside the box after a Willie Wallace double had put Celts in the driving seat, Airdrie keeper Tom Gourlay having saved a first-half Tommy Gemmell penalty. Drew Jarvie and home substitute Lou Macari completed the scoring late on.

Both of the top two would slip up the following Saturday, the Dons held again at

Pittodrie, this time 1-1 by struggling St Mirren, whilst Celts could only manage the same result at Tynecastle, despite Harry's headed opener on the half hour. His 20th goal of the season was disputed by Hearts, who claimed that their defenders had stopped after a whistle was blown, presumably by someone in the crowd. Scotland youth international Eric Carruthers then struck back three minutes later for the hosts.

The old '6/-' entry sign on the boundary wall as you approached from Janefield Street was replaced by '30p,' as decimal prices were displayed at Celtic Park for the first time on Saturday, 6 March 1971, Raith Rovers the visitors in the quarter-final of the Scottish Cup. For once, Harry was not amongst the scorers in a 7-1 home win, albeit he was central to Celtic's attacking threat before making way for George Connelly late on. Bobby Lennox notched his latest hat-trick for the club, a Tommy Gemmell penalty and further strikes from Tommy Callaghan, Willie Wallace and Vic Davidson ended the Fifers dream. Aberdeen's hopes of a first-ever League and Cup Double would also be ended by their 1-0 defeat at Ibrox the same afternoon. Monday's semi-final ballot paired Celtic with Airdrieonians, whilst Hibernian would face Rangers, with both games to be played at Hampden.

It was Celtic's turn to be disappointed in midweek, as a collapse in the last half-hour saw Ajax build up a 3-0 lead in the first leg of their European Cup quarter-final in Amsterdam's Olympic stadium. Harry missed out as Jock Stein unusually went for a cautious defensive formation, Jim Craig restored at full-back allowing Davie Hay to carry out a man-marking role on Johan Cruyff. With an hour played, that plan was working perfectly before the Dutch maestro broke clear at the edge of the box to beat Evan Williams with a low drive. The Celtic keeper looked at fault for the second Ajax goal eight minutes later, Barry Hulshoff's curling free-kick eluding the wall to creep in at his far post. A difficult task was then pushed out of reach seconds before the final whistle, as some great work by Cruyff freed Piet Keizer on the right of Celtic's defence, the winger blasting the ball home to all but secure the tie.

Harry did start in the return a fortnight later, played at Hampden as work began on the refurbishment of the main stand at Celtic Park. Almost 84,000 turned out on a wild night to see the following teams.

CELTIC:

Evan Williams; Davie Hay & Tommy Gemmell; Tommy Callaghan, Billy McNeill & Jim Brogan; Jimmy Johnstone, Harry Hood, Willie Wallace, Bertie Auld & John Hughes. Substitutes; Tom Lally, Jim Craig, George Connelly, Bobby Lennox & Vic Davidson.

AJAX:

Heinz Stuy; Velibor Vasovic & Wim Suurbier; Barry Hulshoff, Ruud Krol & Nico Rijnders; Johan Neeskens, Horst Blankenberg, Gerrie Muhren, Johann Cruyff & Piet Keizer. Substitutes; Seis Wever, Dick Van Dijk, Arie Hann, Sjaak Swart & Ruud Suurendonk.

Jimmy Johnstone briefly restored hope with a goal on the half-hour, following a Tommy Callaghan free-kick, and a John Hughes strike was ruled out for offside late on, whilst Ajax keeper Heinz Stuy made a superb stop to prevent Billy McNeill's header setting up a tight finish. But there would be no further scoring as Celtic's European aspirations were dashed by a Dutch club for the second successive year. Ajax would meet and beat Atletico Madrid with identical 3-0 and 0-1 scorelines in the semi-final before defeating a Panathinaikos side managed by the great Ferenc Puskas in the Wembley final in June 1971.

As an aside, the Ajax skipper, who played in both legs against Celtic and would go on to lift the trophy at Wembley that season was 31-year-old Yugoslav defender Velibor Vasovic. The previous May, he had netted from the penalty spot against AC Milan in Madrid to become the ninth player to score in two separate European Cup finals. Three years earlier, the Belgrade-born stopper had opened the scoring for Partizan against Real Madrid in Brussels, before two late strikes sent the original trophy permanently to Spain. Having spent his youth career at Partizan, Vasovic bravely - or perhaps foolishly - crossed the great city divide in 1963, joining Red Star. That move prompted fan protests and even death threats, the strangest one of those coming from an officer in the Yugoslav People's army, who threatened to kill him during a game with a sniper's rifle in a letter which also included his full name, address and telephone number! That might explain why he was back at Partizan within six months.

The first player to score in two European Cup finals was Alfredo Di Stefano, whose record of netting in all five of Real Madrid's initial successes will probably never be equalled. Other Real stars to score in two finals were Hector Rial, Francisco Gento and Ferenc Puskas, who managed an incredible seven goals in his two appearances. Three Benfica legends also achieved the feat, Jose Aguas, Mario Coluna and Eusebio, as did Sandro Mazzola when he opened the scoring for Inter Milan against Celtic in Lisbon in May 1967. The man who equalized that day, Tommy Gemmell, would become the 10th, when he gave the Bhoys the lead against Feyenoord on that ultimately devastating night in Milan in 1970.

Between the Ajax matches, progress had continued on the domestic front for Celtic, with away wins over bottom-dogs Cowdenbeath then Kilmarnock. Harry scored a second-half double in a 5-1 win at Central Park on Saturday, 13 March 1971, as the restored John Hughes came in from the cold to star having withdrawn his recent transfer request. Yogi equalised an early Davie Hay own goal, with Billy McNeill and Bobby Lennox also on the scoresheet. Celtic's 'H Bombs' were at it again, seven days later in Ayrshire, as the Hoops fought back from an early Eddie Morrison goal down at the interval to win 4-1, despite Tommy Gemmell blasting a spot kick wide of the post. Ally Hunter was between the sticks for Killie, but he was helpless as Harry scored twice, either side of a Hughes strike, to give Celts a 3-1 lead, before making way for Bertie Auld. Vic Davidson completed the scoring seven minutes from time.

Despite the European hangover, Harry would then grab a third successive domestic brace as a highly productive March for him personally ended with a 4-0 victory over Falkirk at Parkhead. The "two goals in a minute blitz from HMS Hood" arrived early in the second half, after Willie Wallace and John Hughes had given Celts a two-goal lead at the interval. Perhaps the biggest roar of the afternoon, though, was reserved for the introduction of Bobby Murdoch for Jim Brogan with 20 minutes remaining, the Celtic powerhouse making a first top-team appearance since dislocating his shoulder in January. Over at Tynecastle, a Davie Robb hat-trick kept Aberdeen three points clear at the top of the table, albeit Celtic still had two games in hand. Third-placed St Johnstone, in turn, trailed a remote nine points behind the Hoops. The two-horse title race would now enter its final furlong in April.

Before that, there would be Scottish Cup business to attend to, Harry, quite remarkably, scoring a fourth consecutive domestic double as Celts twice blew a two-goal lead to share six goals with Airdrieonians in the semi-final at Hampden, on Saturday, 3 April 1971. Harry opened the scoring midway through the first half, following great work from man-of-the-match Jimmy Johnstone, with Jinky himself giving Celts one foot in the final with a header just before the break. Skipper Derek Whiteford started the Airdrie comeback three minutes after the restart before Johnstone once again set Harry up for 3-1. Billy Wilson immediately pulled one back for the underdogs before their 45-goal strikeforce of Drew Jarvie and Drew Busby combined for the latter to equalise with 20 minutes to play.

Harry would have to be content with just the one goal in the midweek replay, rounding Airdrie's Irish goalkeeper Roddie McKenzie for the clincher with seven minutes to play, after Jimmy Johnstone had continued his own excellent form with the opener early in the second half. With Harry now the top scorer in the country - having scored 18 of his 28 goals since the turn of the year – why both he and the on fire Jinky were ignored when Scotland boss Bobby Brown announced his 18-man squad the following morning for the Nations Cup match against Portugal in Lisbon will forever remain a mystery. Celtic's opponents in the May final would be Rangers, who had edged past Hibernian after a replay at Hampden two nights earlier, the Hoops win setting up a repeat of the 1969 season's showpiece finale.

Whilst Celtic had been involved in the clashes with Airdrieonians, Aberdeen had dropped a surprise point in a goalless draw at home to Motherwell. With young Kenny Dalglish rewarded for his excellent performance in the replay with a starting slot in midfield, the Bhoys then followed suit, drawing 1-1 with Dundee United at Parkhead on Saturday, 10 April 1971, as the Dons won 2-1 at Cowdenbeath. Indeed, only a late Willie Wallace equaliser prevented even more damage to Celtic's title hopes.

Jock Stein's men were now a daunting five points behind Eddie Turnbull's side, albeit with three extra games to play, leaving absolutely no margin for error as they faced Motherwell at Celtic Park in the first of those rearranged fixtures two nights later, Monday, 12 April 1971. Harry had been an injury doubt after taking a knock against

Dundee United but responded to treatment to take his usual place as the Hoops boss rang the changes and got the desired outcome. Jimmy Johnstone was once again in unstoppable form, setting up the opening goal for Willie Wallace 10 minutes before the break before adding a second with the last effort of the half. With 20 minutes remaining, Johnstone was again the architect as Harry fired past keeper Keith MacRae to secure a 3-0 victory over the Lanarkshire side with his 30th strike of the campaign, before being replaced late on by Bobby Murdoch. Harry's goal against Motherwell – his 27th in the three domestic competitions that campaign, also saw him finally overtake Aberdeen's Joe Harper at the top of the Scottish scoring charts, with the Airdrieonians duo of Drew Jarvie and Drew Busby tucked in just behind the Dons man. Remarkably, Harry had been 13 goals behind Harper at the end of January, before embarking on his incredible scoring spree.

The scene was now set perfectly for the match of the season, five days later, as Aberdeen hosted Celtic at Pittodrie. The Dons were three points clear, with Celtic having just three games to play beyond the trip north, a home victory on Saturday, 17 April 1971 thus leaving Aberdeen requiring only to win their final game at Brockville to secure a first title for the Granite City since 1955 and end Jock Stein's hopes of matching Willie Maley's six-in-a-row Scottish record, which had stood since 1910. On the other hand, a draw or Celtic win would see the advantage remain with the defending champions, albeit they would still require points from their final matches.

The full house 36,000 crowd included a 10-year-old Matt Corr, an overnight stay with the supporters' bus in Aberdeen the stuff of childhood dreams. For just £1, the dads on the Cairn CSC could bring one of their kids to see a virtual title decider. Happy days. We would be on the road by 8am, in those days before motorways and bypasses, stopping for lunch at Forfar before arriving at Pittodrie in good time for kick-off. I will always remember, as we approached the Granite City, one of those dads, Harry Docherty, bursting into a spontaneous version of *"The Northern Lights of Old Aberdeen,"* and the rest joining in. Wonderful times.

The big news surrounded the team selections, Joe Harper starting on the bench for Aberdeen whilst Jock Stein left out the vastly-experienced trio of Tommy Gemmell, Bobby Murdoch and John Hughes. The sides lined up as follows for this vital clash of Scotland's top two.

ABERDEEN:

Bobby Clark; Henning Boel & Jim Hermiston; Steve Murray, Tommy McMillan & Martin Buchan; Jim Forrest, Alex Willoughby, Davie Robb, Arthur Graham & George Buchan. Substitute; Joe Harper.

CELTIC:

Evan Williams; Jim Craig & Jim Brogan; George Connelly, Billy McNeill & Davie Hay; Jimmy Johnstone, Bobby Lennox, Willie Wallace, Tommy Callaghan & Harry Hood. Substitute; Jimmy Quinn.

Our seats were in the back row of what remained of the fire-damaged main stand, looking along the six-yard box at the Merkland Street end, and so we had a perfect view as Harry opened the scoring directly in front of us within three minutes, following a Jimmy Johnstone corner on the far side, goal number 31 of the season for Scotland's top marksman. Aberdeen had won the opening League fixture between the teams in Glasgow back in December, as they had done the previous May and then again in the 1970 Scottish Cup final a few weeks later. They were going for a fourth successive victory over Stein's men, quite unheard of in those days, and they would not be giving up their tilt at the title without a fight. There was pandemonium all around us seven minutes before the break when the Dons equalised, Springburn-born Alex Willoughby - the former Rangers striker now partnering his cousin Jim Forrest, himself a Garngad man and scourge of Celtic so often in the early 60s whilst at Ibrox - taking advantage of an error from Evan Williams to blast home at the Beach End for 1-1.

Celtic's title hopes would now hang in the balance over the final 45 minutes of football in the cauldron of Pittodrie. There is a defining moment in every season, and this one came 10 minutes into the second period. Castlemilk teenager Arthur Graham was enjoying his tussle with his hero, Celtic captain Billy McNeill, and history beckoned as he rounded Williams and prepared to give his side a precious lead. With the goal gaping and 15,000 Celtic supporters holding their breath, Cesar made a miraculous recovery to block the ball on the line. Celtic would not look back. Harry limped off near the end, to be replaced by Jimmy Quinn, and Joe Harper was introduced for George Buchan as Eddie Turnbull's last throw of the title dice, but Jock Stein's men dug deep, bringing all the experience of those previous big games to hold out for the point required, with McNeill magnificent. Now it was advantage Celtic.

The Glasgow Herald match report on the Monday morning highlighted Harry's key contribution.

"Individual skills were often subdued but there were men who tamed the pitch, the wind and the lively ball. Harry Hood and Alex Willoughby, the two scorers, were in a class by themselves. Hood certainly surpassed all in the Celtic side, even Jimmy Johnstone, from whom was expected the filigree artistry that can bewilder opponents. It was Hood who took the strain off Celtic immediately with a goal from a Johnstone corner kick after three minutes. This imposed extra stress on Aberdeen who had to open out more and thus become more vulnerable."

As an aside, the match programme for that day states that Aberdeen had tried to buy Harry from Clyde in November 1967 but had failed in a bid for his services. You may recall that Shawfield boss Archie Wright had dismissed such reports at that time. Both Aberdeen and Celtic were credited with a current interest in Rutherglen Glencairn's teenage sweeper Bob Houston. He would eventually make his name in the senior game as a talented winger, most notably with Partick Thistle, Kilmarnock and Morton.

The final fatal blow to Aberdeen's championship hopes occurred the following Saturday. With Celtic's 'home' match against Ayr United postponed due to a waterlogged Hampden pitch, the Dons lost their final League game 1-0 to Falkirk at Brockville, the hosts attack led by their experienced centre-forward, a certain Alex Ferguson! This meant that the Hoops required just three points from their final three matches, at home to Ayr United and Clyde and away to St Mirren, the title all but wrapped up now. There was some small consolation for Aberdeen as Martin Buchan was awarded the Scottish Football Writers' Association Player of the Year, the young Dons captain finishing ahead of Celtic's Jim Brogan. Another player who must have been a leading contender for the award - Harry Hood - was an interested spectator at Brockville. He was approached afterwards by *Evening Times* reporter Jim Blair.

"Wasn't much of a game," prompted Blair.

"No but I was quite pleased with the result!" replied Harry.

The three games which would confirm the destination of the 1970/71 Scottish League Championship would all take place in the coming week. On Tuesday, 27 April 1971, Harry returned to Love St, Paisley, the scene of his Celtic debut two years earlier, beating his old Holyrood keeper Denis Connaghan to equalise after 20 minutes with his 32nd goal of the season. St Mirren's teenage striker Ally McLeod had opened the scoring within eight minutes, and he gave them the lead again on the hour, in a game Saints had to win to avoid relegation and send Dunfermline Athletic down with Fife neighbours Cowdenbeath instead. However, within 60 seconds Bobby Lennox made it 2-2 with the final goal of the night, the Saltcoats hitman denied a winner late on by highly-rated defender Gordon McQueen. The Buddies thus took the dreaded drop, ending their three-year tenure in the top-flight, whilst Jock Stein's men moved to within one victory of history.

A groin strain sustained at Paisley would rule Harry out of the rescheduled match with Ayr United, played at Hampden two nights later, Thursday, 29 April 1971, Lou Macari skipping in. I have to confess that I never really understood why this game was moved there, as the 25,000 crowd could easily have been accommodated in the three open sides of Celtic Park, as they would be in the final fixture against Clyde two days later. History will record that Celtic won six consecutive League titles for the second time in their history that night, as goals from Bobby Lennox and Willie Wallace either side of the interval gave them the two points required to match Aberdeen's final tally of 54 points. And the Celtic supporters would no doubt enjoy the moment - including Ayr United's second-half substitute, a teenage Johnny Doyle - albeit I recall being inside Hampden that night and feeling a slight sense of anti-climax, the match at Aberdeen regarded by pretty much everyone around me as the day it would be won or lost. However, I have a slightly different take on this. If a catastrophic defeat in the final League game of the season had to be avoided at Motherwell in May 1966 and Dunfermline two years later, days recognised as title-clinchers, then exactly the same scenario existed in May 1971, where a 12-goal defeat at home to Clyde would have seen the flag flying at Pittodrie rather than Parkhead. Improbable? Absolutely, however, mathematically possible, just like the others. Thus, I believe the historic record-equalling 1970/71 League Championship was clinched on Saturday, 1 May 1971 by the immortal Lisbon Lions making their final appearance together. Now that's truly 'fairytale club' stuff.

Jock Stein's decision to field the Lions one last time was a PR masterstroke, drawing 35,000 supporters to pay homage for the last time and affording those youngsters like myself to say, *"I was there,"* 50 years after the event. The retired Ronnie Simpson, wearing that iconic green keeper's kit, led Celtic's greatest-ever team down a makeshift ramp through the old enclosure onto the pitch, 'Faither' warming up then passing the gloves to Evan Williams before kick-off as the crowd roared its approval. The game had been postponed from New Year's Day, fate now decreeing that we would witness a final 90 minutes from this magical team as they destroyed a Clyde side featuring a young Dom Sullivan and many of Harry's old teammates 6-1. The Lions were on fire. Bobby Lennox scored a hat-trick, Willie Wallace added a double and the last word went to Stevie Chalmers, just as it had done in Lisbon. There wasn't a dry eye in the house as the Immortals – the men who put the star above our crest - waved a final goodbye to their adoring support. It was Celtic theatre at its unparalleled and unbeatable best.

The League season ended with Celtic two points ahead of Aberdeen, Willie Ormond's St Johnstone a further 10 behind in a highly-creditable third place. An *Evening Times* review of Celtic's title-winning campaign highlighted Harry's immense contribution.

"Although, as always, Celtic's success was a team effort, special mention must be made of Harry Hood. He scored the goal which probably won the Stein Machine the Championship, when he beat Scotland's Bobby Clark in the third minute of the match with the Dons at Pittodrie on April 17. Aberdeen could manage only a draw, and the strain was taken off Celtic. Hood's marksmanship at other times also had a big say in the Celtic story. He scored 22 League goals which along with those he netted in other competitions made him Scotland's No.1 in the First Division with a total of 29. But the point is this. Hood got off to an indifferent start this season. He did not score his first goal in the League until match No.8, against Airdrie on October 17. He missed six of the remaining 26 matches, yet still managed that 22, which gave him an average of more than one an outing."

Seven days later, Jock Stein's men attempted to secure a third League and Cup Double in five seasons by beating Rangers in the Scottish Cup final at Hampden, at the same time looking to avenge their defeat by the Ibrox side in the League Cup final the previous October. The following teams took to the field just before 3pm on Saturday, 8 May 1971.

CELTIC:

Evan Williams; Jim Craig & Jim Brogan; George Connelly, Billy McNeill & Davie Hay; Jimmy Johnstone, Bobby Lennox, Willie Wallace Tommy Callaghan & Harry Hood. Substitute; Lou Macari.

RANGERS:

Peter McCloy; Alex Miller & Willie Mathieson; John Greig, Ron McKinnon & Colin Jackson; Willie Henderson, Andy Penman, Colin Stein, Alex MacDonald & Willie Johnston. Substitute; Derek Johnstone.

The first meeting of the clubs since the Ibrox tragedy four months earlier drew more than 120,000 spectators to Hampden. They would see Rangers start well before Celts gained the advantage just before the interval, Harry's clever reverse pass sending Bobby Lennox in for another cup final goal. With three minutes remaining, that looked like being enough, before substitute Derek Johnstone's header forced a replay, Celts appealing in vain to referee Tom 'Tiny' Wharton that the teenage striker had been offside. Whilst the form book had pointed to Celtic at the outset, history now favoured the Ibrox club, who had won all six of their Scottish Cup final replays since 1930. In contrast, Celts had not won a replay since 1931, losing each of their last four, dating back to Jock Stein's playing days in 1955.

Four nights later, the two sides went head-to-head again, a mere 103,332 supporters present this time on a beautiful May evening in the old stadium. Jock Stein made one change, Harry wearing the number nine shorts with Lou Macari replacing Willie Wallace, a senior cup debut for the Ayrshire teenager. That would be made unforgettable as he put Celtic ahead midway through the first half, tapping home at the near post from a Bobby Lennox corner. Jimmy Johnstone was in one of his unstoppable moods, and he would force Rangers centre-half Ron McKinnon into a rugby tackle to prevent him from scoring two minutes later, after an exquisite through ball from Tommy Callaghan had left him through on goal. Up stepped Harry in front of the massed ranks of the expectant Celtic support at the King's Park end of Hampden. But it could have been a training exercise, as he placed the ball on the spot, before coolly and expertly sending Peter McCloy the wrong way to give the Hoops one hand on the cup.

There would be one blip in the second half, a comedy cut goal we sadly all too often associate with our club arriving on the hour mark, as Evan Williams' parry struck one Celtic defender before Jim Craig sliced the ball into his own net to give the Ibrox side some hope of saving the match. Harry made way for Willie Wallace with 15 minutes remaining, as Rangers sought an equaliser. However, just as at Pittodrie a few weeks earlier, the experience and expertise of the Hoops would prevail, and it was once again Billy McNeill who lifted the famous old trophy above his head to the roars of the Celtic faithful, just as he had done in 1965, 1967 and 1969 and he would do again many times in the future.

For all the positive performances we had witnessed over the previous nine months, there was no doubt that Harry was the man of the season. His 33 goals in 49 starts included the effective title-clincher at Pittodrie, the Scottish Cup-winner at Hampden, a hat-trick in Europe and another in the Fir Park mud, plus no fewer than seven doubles, four of those in successive domestic matches in that crucial run-in to glory. Now proudly in possession of the full suite of domestic medals, it was time for Harry and Celtic to make another assault on the European Cup.

Chapter 20

Harry, Charlie, the Pope and the King

Season 1971/72 opened with Harry enjoying a new kid on the block as his striking partner. Kenny Dalglish had shown a glimmer of his world-class future by going on a scoring spree as the end of the previous season saw the transition from Lisbon Lions to Quality Street Gang accelerate, the 20-year-old hitting six of Celtic's seven goals against Kilmarnock at Rugby Park in a testimonial match for the Ayrshire side's championship-winning captain Frank Beattie, two nights after the Double had been secured at Hampden. He was then included in the party which enjoyed a short break in Israel at the end of the month, Harry, of course, scoring the only goal of the match against Hapoel in Tel Aviv. John Clark, Bertie Auld and Stevie Chalmers had all left Celtic to prolong their careers elsewhere, '10.30' to Hibernian and the others to wear the blue-and-white hoops of Morton. Other Lions would soon follow.

Dalglish then followed his six goals against Kilmarnock with another four as Celts beat Limerick 6-1 as part of a short pre-season tour of Ireland on Monday, 26 July 1971, two of those from the spot on a night when Tommy Gemmell missed another penalty and the hosts - captained by Al Finucane, who had made his international debut for Ireland beside Charlie Gallagher in Ankara back in February 1967 – also converted theirs to grab a consolation goal. There was real sadness a few hours later, when it was revealed that another of Celtic's Irish international players, Charlie Tully, had suddenly passed away at his home in Belfast. He had celebrated his 47th birthday just two weeks earlier.

Charles Patrick Tully is a true Celtic legend. My dad was one of those behind the goal when he scored twice from a corner kick in a Scottish Cup-tie at Brockville in February 1953, a feat he had also achieved for Ireland against England in his native Belfast, four months earlier, albeit just the once in that instance! There are perhaps more stories involving Charlie than any other Celt in history, and whilst most of these are funny - allegedly handing out comp tickets to defenders he was getting the better of during matches, for example - there is no doubting his talent. Tully was part of the squads who won the Coronation Cup in 1953, Celtic's first League and Scottish Cup Double in 40 years the following season, our first League Cup-winning side in 1956 and the Hampden in the Sun destruction of Rangers in October 1957. He is Celtic folklore, piling on the agony for those who played against him and putting on the style for the thousands who hung on his every move or touch. It was tragic that he should depart so young. He will no doubt be regaling the angels in heaven about the time no-one recognised the guy wearing all-white on the balcony next to him in St Peter's Square. Rest in peace, Charlie.

The new season opened with another tremendous Irish footballing Charlie returning to Parkhead. This time it was the aforementioned Gallagher, the man who had made way for the debut of Kenny Dalglish at Hamilton back in September 1968 now using his talent and experience to help the young players at Dumbarton. The Sons were Celtic's first-ever opponents in the new brewery-sponsored knockout competition, the Drybrough Cup, introduced as a pre-season taster for established events. It was open to the four highest-scoring League clubs in each of the two divisions at that time, which as it happened included Scotland's top three teams from 1970/71, Celtic, Aberdeen and St Johnstone, together with the clubs finishing in the first four positions in the Second Division - newly-promoted Partick Thistle and East Fife, plus Arbroath and Dumbarton. With one match remaining of the previous League season, the eighth Drybrough Cup place had looked a stick-on for Rangers, who had pipped Dundee to secure fourth spot in Division One. Mid-table Airdrieonians would then go goal crazy in their final League match, defeating Falkirk by, of all scores, 7-1, to pass the Ibrox club's tally by two and qualify.

It was a strange feeling walking up to Celtic Park on Saturday, 31 July 1971, the old stadium looking totally different as the steel skeleton of the new stand roof stretched imposingly into the sky. And there was much change on the pitch too, with only Jim Craig and John Hughes from the Lisbon squad included in the team named by Jock Stein, back from pall-bearing duties with Billy McNeill at Charlie Tully's funeral in Belfast, two days earlier. Jim Brogan would captain the side in Cesar's absence.

Celtic lined up as follows, in front of 22,000 curious spectators:

Evan Williams; Jim Craig & Jim Brogan; Tommy Callaghan, George Connelly & Davie Hay; Kenny Dalglish, Vic Davidson, Lou Macari, Harry Hood, & John Hughes. Substitute; Jimmy Quinn.

It was another of that immortal pool of players who struck first, Charlie Gallagher rolling back the years to strike a free-kick past Evan Williams after just eight minutes to give the Sons of the Rock a shock lead. Celtic's star man from the previous season, Harry, then started where he had left off in Tel Aviv, hammering the ball past Dumbarton keeper Laurie Williams with the aid of a deflection off defender Ian Bolton to square things at 1-1 after 20 minutes. By the half-hour mark it was 2-2, Kenny Dalglish scoring the first of so many marvellous goals in the Hoops at Celtic Park as he beat Williams to a left-wing cross from John Hughes to nod home, with former Rangers and Dundee United winger Davie Wilson then equalising within two minutes. As we approached the final quarter of the match, those who had bothered to attend on the day got their just reward. The Bhoy King Dalglish announced his arrival in spectacular fashion, with an eight-minute hat-trick to add to his earlier strike, taking his tally to 14 in three games, as Celts won 5-2 to move into the semi-final.

The other three first-round ties went with form, Aberdeen beating East Fife 3-0 at Bayview, Airdrieonians edging a three-goal battle at home to Arbroath and St Johnstone doing the same to Partick Thistle. The Perth side would now face Jock Stein's champions in midweek at Firhill, the game presumably moved from Celtic Park as the stadium refurbishment work continued.

There were few grounds I enjoyed visiting more than a packed Firhill, and packed it was on Wednesday, 4 August 1971 as we made the short trip from Springburn to cram into the Panmure Street end with around 30,000 others. It was some sight under the lights, Celts with an unusual combination of Hoops and dark green socks and Jock giving a debut to keeper Gordon Marshall, who had been freed by Hibernian in the close-season, having previously been a title-winner across the city at Tynecastle. The other change in personnel from the weekend saw Harry drop to the bench, Billy McNeill returning in a reshuffled half-back line with Tommy Callaghan moving further forward. Willie Ormond's Saints had enjoyed their best-ever season in 1970/71 and looked like they would record a second successive win over Celtic, two goals ahead before the hour mark with Marshall culpable for at least the first of those. The naivety or confidence of youth meant that I always believed we would pull those goals back, as that was what we did back then, and so it proved. In a 10-minute spell, Kenny Dalglish scored a double before Lou Macari put Celts in front, then, just for good measure, Dalglish added a hat-trick to his weekend quadruple with seven minutes to play. Incredibly, the 20-year-old who had never previously played up front for Celtic's first team had now scored 17 goals in 3 games.

The Bhoy King Dalglish would be in the line-up for the final against Aberdeen, played three days later at Pittodrie, the only time Hampden would not be used for a Drybrough Cup finale. The Dons had beaten Airdrieonians 4-1 at Broomfield in the other midweek semi-final and would now seek revenge for the heart-breaking end to the title race just three months earlier. Jock Stein brought back Evan Williams and Harry, in place of Gordon Marshall and the injured Jim Brogan, with Tommy Callaghan and Davie Hay stepping back. In the home dugout, new Dons boss Jimmy Bonthrone would have a baptism of fire, having stepped up from his role as assistant manager just 24 hours earlier, following the sudden departure of manager Eddie Turnbull to his beloved Hibernian.

Aberdeen took the lead after 20 minutes, in front of 28,000 spectators, a lead they held until the hour before John Hughes leapt to head home an equaliser for Celtic. The winning goal would come from the spot, just five minutes later, Callaghan somewhat harshly penalised for his challenge on Joe Harper. The former Morton striker only just beat Williams with his shot, however, only just is enough. The Dons would hold on for a 2-1 victory to claim the first Drybrough Cup, thus extending their run over Celts to four wins and a draw in the previous five clashes, albeit that draw had secured the 1971 title for the Hoops. Over the wall at the Beach End came the Red Hordes in triumph, Aberdeen sending an early signal that they would once again be the team to beat to secure the honours in Scotland.

The defeat at the hands of Aberdeen had to be put quickly to one side as Celtic sought to continue the most incredible domestic cup run of the modern era. Not since August 1963 and home and away 0-3 reverses against Rangers in the sectional fixtures had the Hoops been eliminated from the League Cup prior to the final itself, with five trophy wins following their loss to the Ibrox side at Hampden in October 1964. The goals that afternoon had been scored by Jim Forrest and Jimmy Johnstone, who had faced each other in that title decider at Pittodrie in April 1971, the Garngad man by now wearing the red of Aberdeen.

Harry's Clyde had come as close as anyone to ending that record, succumbing only to a late strike from substitute George Connelly at Hampden in the semi-final of October 1968, Jock Stein's men going on to complete a second treble in three seasons with a 6-2 thrashing of Hibernian the following April, the final deferred after a fire in the South Stand of the national stadium. Harry would be wearing Hoops by the time the next season's campaign got underway a few months later, and he had experienced the glory of a win and the pain of defeat since then, Bertie Auld's goal beating St Johnstone in October 1969 before a Derek Johnstone header ended the run of success at five-in-a-row, 12 months later.

Celts would find themselves drawn in a section with Rangers for the fourth time in five years, an added issue introduced this time around as the Celtic Park stand was still undergoing major refurbishment. Desmond White had taken over as Celtic chairman in April, as Bob Kelly's health deteriorated and he was made club President, and White made the offer to play both fixtures at Ibrox, a decision eventually agreed on after some initial pushback from Rangers. So, it was then that Celtic 'hosted' Willie Waddell's side at Ibrox on Saturday, 14 August 1971, with young Kenny Dalglish famously stopping to calmly tie his bootlaces in front of 73,000 spectators before sending Peter McCloy the wrong way from the spot, opening his competitive account for the club with Celtic's second goal of the afternoon, just three minutes after Jimmy Johnstone had added yet another strike against Rangers to his tally.

Harry had missed the visit to Ibrox through injury and he would remain on the sidelines as Celts won at Greenock and Ayr before losing to Morton at Celtic Park on the night the newly completed stand was opened for the first time, the final match that John Hughes, another hero of that great Stein team, would start for Celtic. Harry would then take a seat on the bench for the second visit to Govan, on Saturday, 28 August 1971, replacing Bobby Murdoch shortly after Kenny Dalglish had struck his second successive goal in the shadow of the high-rise flats in which he had been brought up in. Tommy Callaghan and Bobby Lennox then added superb goals as the Hoops emerged from the very real threat of elimination to put themselves in pole position to qualify from the section with an excellent 3-0 victory. They would duly do so two nights later against Ayr United at Celtic Park, Celts two goals up before visiting winger Johnny Doyle scored the best goal of the game just before the interval, beating man after man before slipping the ball past Evan Williams for 2-1. Dalglish secured the points early in the second half before making way for Harry, Davie Hay then ending the scoring at 4-1 on 85 minutes.

The embarrassment of attacking riches available to Jock Stein was highlighted by the fact that Celtic beat South American champions, Nacional, then opened their defence of their Scottish title by scoring nine against Clyde with Harry, last season's leading goalscorer, unable to command even a seat on the bench following his recovery from injury. He would make do with a goal in the reserves' 7-1 win at Shawfield. Harry would finally get an outing and a first competitive strike of the season in midweek, against Second Division Clydebank at New Kilbowie, as the Hoops won their League Cup quarter-final first-leg 5-0, then miss out again as Celts made it three wins at Ibrox in 28 days with a 3-2 victory in the League clash, thanks to a last-minute header from – yes, you've guessed it – Jimmy Johnstone. As that drama was playing out in Govan, Harry, John Hughes and Willie Wallace were lining up for Celtic's second-string in a resounding 4-1 win over Rangers, Yogi with the opening goal for the Mini Hoops.

Harry returned to League action for the home clash with Morton, a surreal experience to see John Clark and Stevie Chalmers in the blue-and-white version of the Hoops, whilst Celts wore a strange combo consisting of green shirts, white shorts and yellow socks. It was not a happy homecoming for either Lion. Poor Stevie was injured within five minutes whilst John had the misfortune to score Celtic's second goal, his cruel deflection from a Lou Macari shot beating Evan Williams, the keeper restored after Gordon Marshall had played his second and final game for the Bhoys in the shock midweek European Cup defeat by Boldklubben 1903 in Copenhagen. By contrast, Harry was having a field day, missing the target by inches before having a goal disallowed after Lou Macari strayed into an offside position. Harry then added a sensational late third goal for Celtic, a flick and volley past Erik Sorensen described as *"the best goal you will see all season"* by Allan Herron in *The Sunday Mail*, within a minute of Morton pulling one back through Borge Thorup, as the match ended in a 3-1 win.

Celtic Park was in mourning three days later, Tuesday, 21 September 1971, when Bob Kelly lost his battle with illness at the age of 68. The son of James, Celtic's first captain and superstar, he had served on the Board since the death of his father in 1932 and had been club chairman between 1947 and the spring of 1971. Kelly was a divisive character in many ways – a hero to supporters during the 1952 Tricolour 'flag crisis' and the man credited with the introduction of the youth policy dubbed 'The Kelly Kids,' which would come to such fabulous fruition in Lisbon but frequently accused of interfering with team selections to the detriment of results. He was, nevertheless, in my opinion, a man with Celtic in his blood. I'll leave the final word on Bob Kelly to the man he brought back in March 1965, Jock Stein.

"No man has done more for the club in every way than Sir Robert Kelly."

Jock introduced the latest from his conveyor belt of young prodigies 24 hours later, for the return leg with Clydebank in the last eight of the League Cup. I remember being excited at the prospect of seeing 16-year-old Brian McLaughlin making his debut, and he certainly did not let himself down, however, Harry was the star of the night, his latest hat-trick consisting of a goal within three minutes then one at the end of each half, his second another thing of real beauty. A Lou Macari double and Denis Ruddy own goal completed the scoring as Celts added to their 5-0 first-leg lead with a 6-2 win on the night, to march through to the semi-final for an eighth consecutive season.

Curiously, Harry's reward for that performance was to be omitted from the squad which travelled to Broomfield three days later, my first visit there made memorable by Lou Macari's first Celtic hat-trick in a 5-0 win over Airdrieonians. And whilst he would no doubt be concerned about his lack of first-team action, that scenario was about to get much worse for two of the remaining Lions. Willie Wallace would score twice against Danish amateurs Boldklubben 1903, as 53,000 supporters turned out to watch Celts overturn a 2-1 deficit from the Copenhagen first leg, his brace coming either side of a Tommy Callaghan header, the normally placid big Fifer a shade lucky to still be on the field after a retaliatory kick out at a defender in the first half. Wallace's late third had been set up by second-half substitute John Hughes, in pretty much his last act as a Celtic player. Yogi had earlier missed a penalty and would not be seen again in the Hoops, whilst Wispy would shortly join him at Crystal Palace, having just scored his final goals for the club.

Harry did get a recall after Celts suffered a second home defeat of the season, on Saturday, 2 October 1971, this time to St Johnstone, having scored twice that afternoon in a 5-0 victory for the reserves at Muirton Park. He and Tommy Gemmell returned in midweek as Jock Stein's men attempted to reach an eighth successive League Cup final against Second Division St Mirren at Hampden. Harry grabbed Celtic's second goal in the middle of an incredible three-minute spell around the hour mark, with Davie Hay and Bobby Lennox also on target as they eased through 3-0. The Saints defence included keeper Denis Connaghan, Harry's old Holyrood teammate who had been on Celtic's books as a youngster, and centre-half Gordon McQueen. Neither would be playing their football in Paisley the next season, Connaghan soon to become Jock's latest attempt at finding a permanent replacement for Ronnie Simpson, whilst McQueen would become the eventual successor to Jack Charlton at Leeds United.

Harry would come up against and his old Celtic colleague Bertie Auld in the green of Hibernian for the first time, on Saturday, 9 October 1971. This was another 'rite of passage' moment for 10-year-old me, as I attended a match at Easter Road for the first time, perched on the front boundary wall of that massive terrace opposite the main stand to watch Lou Macari score the only goal of the game late on in front of 41,000 spectators.

Seven days later, Saturday, 16 October 1971, it was Dundee's turn to take on the champions, a front four of Jimmy Johnstone, Harry, Kenny Dalglish and Lou Macari – how good does that sound? – proving far too powerful as the Hoops won 3-1 at Celtic Park. Star of the show was the young Dalglish, netting a hat-trick in a 15-minute spell either side of the interval and being brought down for a penalty, albeit Tommy Gemmell saw his effort saved by Mike Hewitt.

Celtic's preparations for the midweek European Cup-tie at home to Maltese champions Sliema Wanderers were dominated by the sale of Lisbon Lions John Hughes and Willie Wallace to Crystal Palace. Wispy would later recall that he was summoned to a breakfast meeting with Jock Stein at Seamill, to be told that the English club's representatives were already en route to meet him at Parkhead. This was the first he had heard about any transfer! Tommy Gemmell opened the scoring within three minutes with what would transpire to be his 67th and final goal for Celtic. Harry added a double before the break, Jim Brogan then Lou Macari rendering the trip to Malta a formality at 5-0.

Three days later, Saturday, 23 October 1971, I made my way excitedly to Hampden in the rain to see Celtic win the League Cup for the first time. Well, that was the plan, anyway. There was a certain symmetry in that the club's first victory in the final of this tournament had been against the Jags some 15 years earlier. I would finally be able to write that 3-1 defeat by Aberdeen in my only previous cup final from the memory bank, thus avoiding a trip to the adoption agency on the Monday morning. It was written in the stars. I waved goodbye to my mum at the door with a confident "*6-2*" prediction. I was very nearly right, albeit not quite in the way I had intended.

Bobby Murdoch led Celtic out in the absence of injured skipper Billy McNeill, as the following teams lined up before 63,000 spectators.

CELTIC:

Evan Williams; Davie Hay & Tommy Gemmell, Bobby Murdoch, George Connelly & Jim Brogan; Jimmy Johnstone, Kenny Dalglish, Harry Hood, Tommy Callaghan & Lou Macari. Substitute; Jim Craig.

PARTICK THISTLE:

Alan Rough; John Hansen & Alex Forsyth, Ronnie Glavin, Jackie Campbell & Hugh Strachan; Denis McQuade, Frank Coulston, Jimmy Bone, Alex Rae & Bobby Lawrie. Substitute; Johnny Gibson.

I guess we'll never really understand what happened in that first 45 minutes. From my perch high up on a barrier in the Celtic End, I can clearly recall the shock of seeing Alex Rae's dipping shot nestling in the back of those huge Hampden nets, then feeling that pretty much everything else Thistle hit in that first half seemed to end up in the same place. I don't recall that Ronnie Glavin's tackle ended Jimmy Johnstone's final at 2-0, or why Celtic, with such an embarrassment of attacking riches, had defender Jim Craig as the only available substitute. Of course, my piece de resistance at half-time was advising my dad that *"It was ok, we just needed five in the second half to win the cup."* If looks could kill.

As it transpired, like a certain night against Artmedia Bratislava in future years, Celtic actually had enough chances in the second period to score five and then some. Sadly, they would only get one, with 20 minutes remaining, Kenny Dalglish scoring the first of his cup final goals for Celtic which all ended with the same outcome, a Hoops defeat. I still find that an incredible statistic.

The victory by Partick Thistle at Hampden in October 1971 over Jock Stein's all-conquering Celtic - and the margin of it - remains one of the most sensational stories of all time in Scottish football.

So, two cup finals in the first three months of season 1971/72 had both ended in defeat. Things could only get better.

"Is that right, Dad?"

"Dad?"

Jock Stein reacted to the League Cup final defeat by Partick Thistle by going into the market for a new goalkeeper and striker. In came Denis Connaghan from St Mirren, having starred in the recent semi-final against the Hoops at Hampden, and John 'Dixie' Deans from Motherwell, despite the fact he was currently serving a six-week suspension for his most recent ordering off. Connaghan made his debut at East End Park in midweek, picking the ball out of his net after eight minutes from Jim Gillespie's header. Second-half goals from the returning Billy McNeill and Bobby Lennox kept the title campaign on track, albeit Celtic would now be without fellow Lion Bobby Murdoch for some time, after the influential midfielder sustained knee ligament damage.

Harry was delighted that his old Holyrood classmate Connaghan had joined Celtic.

"We were always great buddies and I think he'll do a job with us."

Denis would enjoy his first clean sheet as a CeltIc goalkeeper three days later, a late Kenny Dalglish goal enough to beat an Ayr United side including future Celts Joe Fillippi and Johnny Doyle at Somerset Park. Deans was then added to the first-team squad, but before he could pull on a jersey, there was European Cup business to conclude, Harry becoming the first Celt to score on the George Cross island of Malta when he equalised just before the interval in the return leg with Sliema Wanderers, on a surface which must have brought back memories of childhood games on the red ash of the old Broomfield Pitches in Balornock. Celts had been shocked after just 30 seconds in Gzira's Ta'Quali Stadium, Ronnie Cocks blasting the ball past Evan Williams to send the 12,000 home supporters into a frenzy. Harry then set up Bobby Lennox for the headed winner early second-half, on an afternoon which saw former Newtongrange Star forward Steve Hancock make his only appearance in the Hoops, the youngster replacing Vic Davidson as the Bhoys cruised through on a 7-1 aggregate.

The victory in Malta would also be the final match for another Lisbon hero, Tommy Gemmell. He was dropped as Celtic and Aberdeen once again met in a top-of-the-table clash, this time at Parkhead on Saturday, 6 November 1971. Each side had so far only dropped points in their matches with St Johnstone, played on successive Saturdays the previous month, the Dons draw at Muirton giving them the edge over Celtic, who had lost to the Perth outfit at home the week before. Aberdeen had also hammered new League Cup holders Partick Thistle 7-2 at Pittodrie, their visit attracting a huge crowd of 64,000 to Celtic Park, around 1,000 more than had watched their victory on the same ground 11 months earlier. Jock Stein handed a home debut to Denis Connaghan, as the sides lined up as follows.

CELTIC:

Denis Connaghan; Jim Craig & Jim Brogan, Davie Hay, Billy McNeill & George Connelly; Jimmy Johnstone, Harry Hood, Kenny Dalglish, Lou Macari & Tommy Callaghan. Substitute; Bobby Lennox.

ABERDEEN:

Bobby Clark; George Murray & Jim Hermiston; Steve Murray, Willie Young & Martin Buchan; Jim Forrest, Davie Robb, Joe Harper, Alex Willoughby & Arthur Graham. Substitute; Bertie Miller.

This is another one of those 'rite of passage' matches I remember so well from my childhood. I had been deemed too young to go to that corresponding match, when Joe Harper's header had continued Aberdeen's excellent record against Celtic at that time, however, this would now be the largest attendance I had ever witnessed at Celtic Park. The Bhoys were shooting into the 'wrong end' in the first half and despite dominating the play, it would take until the hour mark before Harry squeezed a low shot past Bobby Clark at the far end to give the Hoops the lead, and the top of the table beckoned. With 13 minutes remaining, however, that script was re-written, as Billy McNeill headed Harper's cross ball past Connaghan to nestle in those green nets before hiding his face in his hands, an image I can still recall clearly 50 years later. Aberdeen would hold out for the point which kept them clear at the top, thus extending their unbeaten record against Celtic to six games, stretching back to October 1969.

Three Celts did finally enjoy a victory at Pittodrie in midweek, albeit they were wearing the navy blue of Scotland, as an early goal from John O'Hare – Harry's old striking partner at Sunderland – was enough to beat Belgium in a qualifier for the European Championship finals to be held in the same country the following summer. Both Davie Hay and Jimmy Johnstone started the match, whilst it was a landmark evening for Kenny Dalglish, his rapid rise to fame continuing as interim Scotland manager Tommy Docherty awarded him the first of what would become a record number of international caps, the young Celtic striker replacing Hibernian's Alex Cropley early in the second half.

All three Scotland men were in an unchanged Celtic team which trailed at half-time to an Alan Gordon goal at Tannadice, three days later, before Jock Stein's revamped attacking formation for the second half changed the match completely. Harry was pulled down for a penalty within three minutes of the restart, confidently converting his spot kick before firing Celts in front 60 seconds later with his 14th goal of the season. Further counters from Lou Macari, Kenny Dalglish and his replacement Bobby Lennox - with his first touch of the ball - sealed an eventually emphatic 5-1 win over Dundee United.

The first snows of winter dropped on to the Parkhead pitch for the visit of Falkirk, on Saturday, 20 November 1971. With transfer-listed striker Jimmy Quinn brought in at left-back, Celts would keep up the pressure on Aberdeen with a. 2-0 win. Jim Craig set Kenny Dalglish up for an angled finish in five minutes, Billy McNeill heading home Tommy Callaghan's corner just after the restart to end the scoring.

The following Saturday was a pivotal one for the title race, and a big day for a couple of the Celts who lined up at Firhill with revenge very much on their minds. The re-run of the previous month's League Cup final was a 33,000 sell-out, meaning I was confined to barracks. It's a tough gig being a 10-year-old Celtic supporter sometimes. Dixie Deans was finally free of suspension and made his Hoops debut, whilst Jimmy Quinn retained the left-back slot he had filled so well during the previous week's home win over Falkirk. That would probably send out the clearest of signals to a fully fit Tommy Gemmell.

Within 15 minutes, Harry had successfully achieved that most unique feat – well, unique unless you're Charles Patrick Tully – by scoring directly from a corner kick to give Celtic the lead. And by the half-hour it was 3-0, another Hood corner headed home by Jimmy Johnstone, Kenny Dalglish piling on the agony with a third goal in 10 minutes. Jimmy Bone grabbed a consolation for the Jags before the interval, however, a Hugh Strachan own goal and a debut header from Deans in the final eight minutes served the revenge dish up cold at 5-1. Knowing me, I probably claimed that as an aggregate victory. And the good news kept on coming at full-time, as word filtered through that third placed Hearts had beaten leaders Aberdeen 3-2 at Pittodrie, all five goals coming after the interval with Donald Ford scoring a hat-trick. The loss of their unbeaten record would also cost the Dons top spot, as the five-star Celts now leap-frogged them by a point.

Jock Stein's December began in Berlin, on a night which would later have great significance to his Celtic side's continental aspirations. He was attending the replayed first leg of the European Cup second-round match between Borussia Munchengladbach and Inter Milan. The original game, played in Munchengladbach in October as Celts were hitting Sliema Wanderers for five goals at Parkhead, had ended in an incredible 7-1 victory for the West Germans, the Italians then successfully appealing to UEFA for the result to be annulled, claiming that their goalscorer - Roberto Boninsegna - had been struck by a can of Coca-Cola thrown from the crowd. A 4-2 win for Inter in the San Siro two weeks later had, in effect, become the first leg, and Stein and the 85,000 supporters would then witness a goalless draw in the Olympiastadion return which saw Borussia eliminated. The sour taste felt by most football supporters on hearing this result would be particular bitter in Glasgow's east end in the spring.

In the meantime, the new League leaders in Scotland would keep on winning. Kilmarnock were on the receiving end of a second consecutive 5-1 Celtic win on Saturday, 4 December 1971, thanks to doubles from Jimmy Johnstone and Kenny Dalglish plus a home debut goal for Dixie Deans. The new striker scored both goals the following Saturday in the 2-1 home win over East Fife, nodding home Harry's free-kick after 12 minutes, before doing the same to a Paul Wilson corner 15 minutes from time. The young winger was making his first start of the season in place of the injured Lou Macari.

A quirk of the fixture calendar then sent Dixie Deans back to Motherwell, as Celts faced the Steelmen at Fir Park on Saturday, 18 December 1971. He would show his old mates no mercy by opening the scoring within 10 minutes, a header from another Harry cross, thus continuing his goal-a-game start to his Celtic career. Kenny Dalglish added a double before Jackie McInally pulled one back for the hosts. With the new Bhoys having done their bit for the cause in the first half, it was the turn of the old brigade after the break, Bobby Lennox and Jimmy Johnstone both on target as Celts won 5-1 for the fourth Saturday in six weeks.

The day before that victory, another of the Lisbon Lions had finally left the colony, Dixie Deans' £20,000 fee recouped immediately with an additional 50% thrown in for good measure as the out-of-favour Tommy Gemmell headed south to join Nottingham Forest. The legend who scored in two European Cup finals for the club would follow Bertie Auld, John Clark, Stevie Chalmers, Willie Wallace and John Hughes in leaving Parkhead in the last six months, a massive transition by any standards.

The final game of 1971 was also the last time the Bhoys were in action on Christmas Day, my dad and I unusually travelling by car and heading for the east terracing, where we met up with my mum's two Celtic-mad brothers, the only time that happened in all my years following the club. Hearts were the team with the unwanted gift of facing Jock Stein's men in such formidable form, 34,000 supporters somehow escaping festive duties to pile into Parkhead. Harry was the first to unwrap the Tynecastle defence, heading home the opening goal within 60 seconds to get the party started, after Jim Cruickshank had parried an effort from Dixie Deans, then missing a great opportunity to double the lead the following minute. A masterclass in wing-play from Jimmy Johnstone was rewarded with a second, 10 minutes before the interval, just after the Gorgie men had equalised through Derek Renton, somewhat against the run of play. Harry was again heavily involved after the break, his fierce drive beating Cruickshank all ends up but crashing off the angle of crossbar and post. With 20 minutes remaining, he set up Deans for his by-now customary goal. Hearts defender Jim Brown would scramble a shot past Denis Connaghan to make the last 12 minutes or so more anxious than should have been the case, however, Celts would end the afternoon and the year one point clear of Aberdeen at the top of the table, after a five-goal Christmas cracker. The pursuit of an unprecedented seventh successive League Championship for Jock Stein's side was very much on.

Whilst the irrepressible Jinky earned star billing, Harry's contribution didn't go unnoticed by Jim Blair in his match report for Monday's *Evening Times*.

"For 90 minutes, the 34,000 crowd were given plenty of Christmas cheer, especially from Celtic right or left winger Jimmy Johnstone. The wee man was magic. As well as a good goal – Celtic's second – he treated us to a wonderful exhibition of close dribbling that teased and tormented Hearts' right flank."

"Back to form in a big way too came Harry Hood, the man the fans love to sing about. He had a great game in his pick-up role on the right. He headed the opening goal in 41 seconds, hit the crossbar twice, and gave Deans the pass that resulted in Dixie keeping that impressive goal-a-game record. Add to that first-class distribution and you'll see [why] Hood wasn't far behind Johnstone when the honours were being dished out."

Chapter 21

A record-breaking yet heartbreaking season's end for Celtic

Celtic's wonderful form in the closing weeks of 1971 carried over into the new year, the 'first-footers' at Shawfield ripping Clyde apart with a 7-0 victory. Harry began the slaughter of his old side by hooking home the opening goal in 15 minutes, the first of his double. His second was also a cracker, Kenny Dalglish's defence-splitting pass hammered passed keeper Phil Cairney on 74 minutes. Dixie Deans also grabbed a brace to continue his perfect scoring record, before making way for Danny McGrain seven minutes into the second half, the Celt joining his cousin – Danny McGrain of Clyde - on the pitch. Vic Davidson, Dalglish and an Eddie Mulheron own goal made it a magnificent seven on the day and an incredible 16 in two League games against the struggling Bully Wee that season. There was a lovely touch as the players left the field at the interval, captured by reporter William Hunter in the following Monday's *Glasgow Herald*, which perhaps summed up the type of man Harry was.

"Clyde did well. Five down at half-time, they came off in a condition of utter dejection. Their despair was so obviously total it was embarrassing. Entering the pavilion, Hood was moved to nudge Mulheron in the ribs in a gesture of unobtrusive sportsmanship that was part encouragement, part apology and most moving."

The mood on our car journey home was lifted further as word came through that Aberdeen had only drawn at Dens Park, Stein's Celts now two points clear at the top. It was a perfect start to the year.

Two days later, Monday, 3 January 1972, Willie Waddell's Rangers crossed the city looking to avenge those three defeats on their own turf back in August. Not since New Year's Day 1913 had Celtic managed to win both League fixtures against their traditional rivals in the same season, a quite incredible statistic for those of us brought up in the decades of success. A goal early in the second half by Jimmy Quinn had been enough to win at Ibrox back then, the Bould Bhoy from Croy having scored the winner in a five-goal Celtic Park thriller the previous October. These were the days of Alec 'The Icicle' McNair, 'Sunny Jim' Young, Andy McAtee, Jimmy 'Napoleon' McMenemy and, of course, the incomparable 'Mighty Atom'

Patsy Gallacher, early heroes whose names still roll off Celtic tongues with such love and respect over a century later.

The Mighty Quinn's grandson and namesake had recovered from an injury sustained in a friendly against Raith Rovers in Kirkcaldy the previous week, however, fatefully as it transpired, Jim Brogan would be selected by Jock Stein to wear the number three shorts, as the following teams lined up.

CELTIC:

Denis Connaghan; Davie Hay & Jim Brogan, Kenny Dalglish, Billy McNeill & George Connelly; Jimmy Johnstone, Bobby Lennox, Dixie Deans, Tommy Callaghan & Harry Hood. Substitute; Danny McGrain.

RANGERS:

Peter McCloy; Sandy Jardine & Willie Mathieson; John Greig Colin Jackson & Dave Smith; Tommy McLean, Derek Johnstone, Colin Stein, Alex MacDonald & Willie Johnston. Substitute; Alfie Conn.

The afternoon commenced on a sombre note, the players from both teams wearing black armbands and flags above the Jungle flying at half-mast in tribute to those who had lost their lives in the terrible crush which followed the corresponding fixture 12 months earlier. Rest in peace.

Having scored twice against Clyde, Harry would turn provider in this latest derby clash, played before almost 78,000 spectators. Ten minutes before the interval, he slung over a cross from his left wing beat beside the Jungle, picking out Jimmy Johnstone, lurking on the far side of the box. Jinky had been a major doubt for the match beforehand, however, there was no doubt in his mind as he powered yet another header past Peter McCloy to give the Hoops the lead. With 10 minutes remaining, Colin Stein forced his way through to score a late equaliser, negating Johnstone's goal, just as he had done in the match last January, however, on this occasion the last word would go to the most unlikely of heroes.

Jim Brogan was a tremendous Celtic player, powerful, consistent and capable of playing in a number of roles equally well. A fantastic man to have in your team. Like another great Celt to whom those attributes were often labelled - Danny McGrain - if there was ever a criticism of Brogan it could only be around the number of goals he scored for the club, just six in over 200 League games. But on this day, Jim would score his most famous goal for Celtic. Two days earlier, Rangers had snatched victory over Partick Thistle at Ibrox with a Derek Johnstone strike in stoppage time. Today, they would be on the receiving end of a late winner, and a fourth defeat of the campaign at the hands of Celtic, Harry's cute chipped pass finding the left-back running clear at the far post to steer a header past McCloy and win the match. To this day, the image of Jim Brogan against the backdrop of the illuminated main stand roof as he scores a late, winning goal against Rangers is right up there with the best of them.

Football being the unpredictable game it is, the champions would then drop a point against Morton at Cappielow five days later, Celts unable to build on Harry's equaliser on the half-hour after the Greenock club's player/coach Stevie Chalmers had set up an opening goal for Don Gillies 10 minutes earlier. The two-point gap would then be restored on Saturday, 15 January 1972, Aberdeen held to a goalless draw by Rangers at Pittodrie, whilst goals from Kenny Dalglish and Bobby Lennox saw off bottom-dogs Airdrieonians at Parkhead. Celtic's lead would duly become four points, seven days later, the Dons losing 1-0 for the second successive season at East End Park, Dunfermline, whilst Celts took revenge for their only League defeat of the campaign to date by beating St Johnstone 3-0 at Muirton, a match which had been in doubt all week. Dixie Deans ended his mini goal-drought with a late double after Dalglish had opened the scoring in the fifth minute. Harry linked up with Davie Hay in midfield, before making way for Tommy Callaghan in the closing stages.

The month ended on a highly satisfactory note as the prolific Deans began his one-man war against Hibernian with a late winner at Celtic Park. Harry had equalised early in the second half from a Davie Hay cross, his curling shot deflected past Jim Herriot by the player he later cited as his most difficult opponent – John Blackley - after Pat Stanton had given the visitors an interval lead in front of 38,000. There was a slightly unusual transfer thrown into the mix, Jock Stein allowing Gordon Marshall to join title challengers Aberdeen. The former Hearts, Hibernian and England Under-23 keeper had played just twice for Celtic since signing the previous summer, a 4-2 Drybrough Cup win over St Johnstone at Firhill in August then the 2-1 defeat by Boldklubben 1903 in Copenhagen the following month.

The highlight of a weather-ravaged February was Celtic's progression into the quarter-final of the Scottish Cup, following emphatic home wins over Albion Rovers and Dundee. Jock Stein used the game against his first senior club to bring back Bobby Murdoch and Lou Macari after their injury absences, Harry one of several Celts to enjoy a day off as both returning players scored in a 5-0 win over the Coatbridge outfit. The Hoops boss took his players through to Easter Road following Saturday, to see Aberdeen drop a point in a 2-2 draw with Hibernian, Celtic's match at Dens Park a victim of the weather. With the gap now three points but Celts having that game in hand, both challengers would squeeze out 1-0 home wins on Saturday, 19 February 1972, Macari Celtic's matchwinner on the hour against a Dunfermline Athletic side now propping up the table under new manager George Miller.

By far the most impressive February performance was reserved for the final Saturday of the month, as Dundee visited Celtic Park on Scottish Cup duty. The Dark Blues were also under new management, Davie White having succeeded John Prentice at Dens Park, just as he had at Shawfield in 1966. One goal up through an early Bobby Lennox header, the *"I was there"* moment arrived just before the hour, Kenny

Dalglish waltzing around Dundee keeper Mike Hewitt to score a wonderful solo goal, displaying the composure of a star. Further goals from Dixie Deans and Lennox sealed a 4-0 victory lapped up by the majority of the 47,000 spectators inside Celtic Park, as the holders cruised into the quarter-final. The month ended with both title contenders involved in transfer business. Aberdeen's hopes would surely be dented with the sale of skipper and current Scottish Player of the Year Martin Buchan to Manchester United, albeit they would take some comfort from their record cheque for £125,000. And over at Celtic, there would be sadness as another of the Lisbon Lions squad headed out of Paradise, long-serving goalkeeper John Fallon leaving for Motherwell on a free transfer after 14 years of service.

March opened with a visit from an Ayr United side again featuring future Jock Stein signings Johnny Doyle and Joe Filippi, the Celtic manager's most recent capture the transfer market - Dixie Deans - scoring both goals that day in a 2-0 victory. This was to prove another pivotal afternoon in the flag race, as Aberdeen lost 2-0 at Firhill, having beaten the Jags 7-2 in the home fixture back in November. The Dons were now five points behind the defending champions, having played one game more. The title finishing line was now in sight if Stein's Bhoys could now hold their nerve over the coming weeks.

There was another level of challenge completely for Celtic in midweek. Having beaten the champions of Denmark then Malta, next up for the Hoops was the dangerous Ujpest Dosza of Hungary, in the quarter-final of the European Cup. The last eight of the continent's elite competition was a mouth-watering prospect, featuring five previous winners. Ajax and Feyenoord were in there, the champions from the last two seasons, plus two clubs who had won it twice in the early 1960's, Inter Milan and Benfica. And, of course, Stein's Celtic, now shorn of many of its immortal Lions from that night in Lisbon in May 1967 but with his mixture of prudent signings and Quality Street Kids placing them once again amongst the favourites. Arsenal, having become the first English club to win their League and Cup double in a decade – and just the second to do so that century - joined the elite group, with Ujpest and Belgian champions Standard Liege completing the line-up. This was the European Champions Cup just as it should be, for me.

Celts travelled to Budapest for the first leg on Wednesday, 8 March 1972, Ujpest deciding to play the home tie at their compact Megyeri uti Stadion, rather than the larger Nepstadion. Perhaps this would prove a good omen, Celtic's previous visit to the national arena having ended in a 4-0 semi-final defeat by MTK in the Cup Winners' Cup which shattered dreams of a first European trophy back in April 1964. On the seventh anniversary of his arrival into the Parkhead manager's office, Jock Stein was forced to leave out Dixie Deans after his newest striker injured a shoulder in training in Budapest, whilst Jimmy Johnstone was left behind in Glasgow to continue his recovery from chickenpox. The following men were duly selected to lay the foundations of another last-four appearance for Scotland's champions.

CELTIC:

Evan Williams; Danny McGrain & Jim Brogan, Bobby Murdoch, Billy McNeill & George Connelly; Harry Hood, Davie Hay, Kenny Dalglish, Lou Macari & Bobby Lennox. Substitutes; Denis Connaghan, Jimmy Quinn, Tommy Callaghan, Vic Davidson & Paul Wilson.

The Celtic boss opted to partner Lou Macari and Bobby Lennox up front, and this would prove to be another master stroke, the youngster enjoying one of the highlights of his Hoops career. Unusually for those times, the game was shown live on television, the 4.30pm kick-off meaning a mad dash home from school in Sighthill for yours truly. It would prove to be well worth the effort.

With 20 minutes played in the midst of a thunderstorm, giant Ujpest defender Jozsef 'Joe' Horvath scored the first of his bizarre goal double of the afternoon…this one for Celtic. As own goals go, this was an award-winning effort, a spectacular diving header by the big man with the flowing long locks which flew high into the net, leaving his own goalkeeper helpless. He would atone for that - sort of - by unleashing an incredible 35-yard shot just after the hour which left Evan Williams stranded in the mud to tie things up at 1-1. With the match drifting towards an excellent away scoring draw, suddenly Macari got the goal his non-stop effort had deserved, the little striker turning sharply to lob goalkeeper Antal Szentmihályi and give Celts a vital advantage to take back to Glasgow.

Harry played and scored in major cup finals and against some of the best teams in Europe for Celtic. He represented his country at several levels, scoring against England at Hampden, and netted winners for Sunderland against Manchester United and for Clyde as a youngster at Ibrox. Yet when Harry was asked towards the end of his career to name his most memorable match, he chose that 2-1 victory over Ujpest in Budapest, his personal memento of the visit still on display at his home to this day.

Jock Stein's post-match comment would perhaps lend weight to Harry's choice.

"At this level, and when you consider the age of this team of ours, it is probably Celtic's best European Cup display since Lisbon."

As an aside, Joe Horvath, the man who scored at both ends that evening, also enjoyed a wonderful football career. Having won the Hungarian title in each of his seven seasons at Ujpest - adding the national cup for a double on three of those occasions - and being voted Hungarian Player of the Year as his club went all the way to the semi-final of the European Cup in 1974, the big defender would try his luck in Europe, appearing in Switzerland, Spain and West Germany. He then finished his playing days in the NASL in the United States, where his teammates included Johann Cruyff and future Celtic manager Wim Jansen at Washington Diplomats and George Best at San Jose Earthquakes.

Whilst the players would be making their way home to Glasgow immediately after the game, there would then be one of those stories which could only happen to Celtic fans. Welsh actor Richard Burton was also in Budapest that week, on location for his latest movie *'Bluebeard'* at the Wenckheim Palace in the centre of the city. He had been joined by his wife Elizabeth Taylor, the Hollywood 'A' list couple perhaps the most famous in the world at that time. It had to be, of course, that they were staying in the same hotel as a planeload of Celtic supporters, one thing leading to another as an impromptu party was held, the actress' recent 40th birthday all the excuse anyone needed to do so with Burton and Taylor taking centre stage. Burton put a four-figure sum behind the bar as this unusual mix of folk from California to the Calton drank and danced the night away to celebrate a famous Celtic away win.

If Carlsberg did European trips...

The big games kept on coming for Celtic, Jock Stein's men following up their superb victory in Budapest with a trip to face nearest title challengers Aberdeen at Pittodrie three days later, Saturday, 11 March 1972. The Hoops boss, unsurprisingly, went with the men who had played so well in midweek. Harry once again excelled in his midfield role, as did George Connelly in central defence, as Celts went for the victory which would effectively seal a seventh consecutive League title. It was Connelly who would be instrumental in the Bhoys taking the lead, 17 minutes from time, a clever overlap allowing him to take Bobby Murdoch's quick free-kick in his stride before passing across the goal for Bobby Lennox to stride in and beat Gordon Marshall, the keeper who until recently had been his teammate at Parkhead.

It was almost 2-0 five minutes later, Harry showing wonderful control to set up Kenny Dalglish, only for Dons centre-half Willie Young to pluck the ball from the foot of the young Scotland striker in the nick of time. Celts would regret that missed opportunity within moments, as Joe Harper flashed a shot past Evan Williams to equalise. There would be no further scoring as a third successive League match between the country's top two sides ended 1-1, a result which undoubtedly suited Celtic much more than the hosts on this occasion.

The following Saturday was Scottish Cup quarter-final day, with Hearts the visitors to Celtic Park, a crowd approaching 48,000 rolling up to see if the Hoops could take another giant step towards a possible Double. Fit-again Dixie Deans returned at the expense of the fatigued Kenny Dalglish, the youngster dropping to the bench with Tommy Callaghan coming in for George Connelly, who had sustained an injury on international duty in midweek. Hearts featured future Celt Andy Lynch on the left-wing, ahead of 21-year-old full-back Jim Jeffries.

Things looked good at the interval, Celtic ahead through a Deans strike on the half-hour, however, as the match progressed, they seemed to be pushed further and further back, perhaps the efforts of the previous fortnight taking their toll. I recall a sense of dread and disappointment as the equaliser which had been coming finally arrived, from Derek Renton in the last minute up at the far end of the ground. Now

Celts would have to win at Tynecastle, another difficult away match. At least Stein's men were still in the running, Aberdeen's 2-0 defeat at the hands of Hibernian and their former manager Eddie Turnbull at Easter Road meant their own hopes of a domestic double had effectively been killed off in just eight days. Kilmarnock plus either Motherwell or Rangers would complete the semi-final line-up.

Four days later, Wednesday, 22 March 1972, a special gift was discovered in my 11th birthday card, a stand ticket for that night's European Cup quarter-final second-leg match against Ujpest Dosza. Those of you of a certain vintage will remember those old stand briefs, a huge yellow paper ticket which unfolded like an Evening Citizen. There was no better sight to behold as a kid. This would be a real treat. My first big European match. Somehow, I managed to get through the school day and took my seat to witness the magical spectacle of a packed Celtic Park under the floodlights. I will never, ever forget that moment. Jock Stein started with the line-up which had won the first leg in Hungary a fortnight earlier. Back into the side came George Connelly and Kenny Dalglish, with Tommy Callaghan and Dixie Deans moving onto the bench beside Jimmy Johnstone, the talismanic winger having been on the sidelines since the defeat of Hibernian at the end of January. This would be vital.

The significance of that fantastic result in Budapest was emphasised for the 75,000 supporters as Ujpest star man Ferenc Bene gave the Celtic defence a torrid time, the vastly experienced Hungarian international striker setting up a tie-equalising goal for his partner Antal Dunai in the fifth minute. My young heart sank into the Upper Stand seat, as a purple tide threatened to sweep the Hoops out of the tournament. But then there was Jinky, hero of so many European nights in the east end arena. Parkhead erupted as he came off the bench to replace the injured Jim Brogan on the hour mark, as yet again Jock flexed his tactical muscles, moving Davie Hay to full-back to accommodate the little maestro. Within minutes, Lou Macari had scored against Ujpest once again, gloriously lobbing the goalkeeper at the packed Celtic End to kick off wild celebrations which would continue until full-time. Celts would duly march through to a fifth European semi-final in nine years, four of them under Jock.

The line-up for the last four of the European Cup was mouth-watering, previous winners one and all. Holders Ajax had beaten Arsenal home and away, and word on the street was that they would prefer to meet Celtic next. The second quarter final had paired their bitter rivals Feyenoord with Benfica, two sides from Celtic's ultimately disappointing Road to Milan in 1970. The Dutch took a 1-0 lead to Lisbon but were then swept away by the Eagles, 5-1 on the night, to exit the competition with a whimper. The Celtic connection continued with the fourth side in the draw, Inter Milan. Having controversially qualified for the last eight despite that 7-1 mauling in Monchengladbach, the Italians rode their luck once again at that stage. A late Jair goal gave them a 1-0 home lead from their first leg against Belgian champions Standard Liege, with Sandro Mazzola, the man who opened the scoring in the 1967 final in Lisbon, repeating that in Liege to see the Nerazzurri squeeze through on away goals after losing 2-1. Friday's draw paired Ajax and Benfica, whilst Celts would face old foes Inter Milan in a repeat of that 1967 finale. No doubt all associated with the club would happily settle for a repeat of that outcome.

Inter manager Gianni Invernizzi was an interested spectator three days later as Celts got back to the business of setting a new domestic landmark, a seventh successive Scottish League title, a visit to Brockville being the latest challenge. The hosts included David Cattenach, their recent signing from Celtic, in defence, whilst Jock Stein rested a number of top stars ahead of the vital Scottish Cup quarter-final replay with Hearts 48 hours later. Bobby Murdoch, Jimmy Johnstone, Harry and Bobby Lennox all joined the injured Jim Brogan in sitting this one out, whilst European Cup hero Lou Macari dropped to the bench. Macari would be introduced after the interval, albeit in the most distressing of circumstances, Danny McGrain sustaining a fractured skull in a collision with Falkirk striker Doug Somner, just six minutes in, yet bravely playing on until half-time. They broke the mould of courage when they made the legend that is Daniel Fergus McGrain.

Somner and partner Alex Ferguson would enjoy then miss the best of the chances in this game before Celts hit them with a sucker punch in the final five minutes, a goal made in Quality Street. The move was started by George Connelly, with Macari then Paul Wilson involved before Vic Davidson secured another two crucial points with a low angular shot past Ally Donaldson. Meanwhile back in Glasgow, Stevie Chalmers chalked up yet another goal against Rangers, the equaliser in Morton's 2-1 win which saw the Ibrox club fall a massive 10 points behind League leaders Celtic in the table.

The Celtic army quickly mobilised again, travelling in huge numbers through to Edinburgh on Monday, 27 March 1972, swelling the Tynecastle attendance to over 40,000 for the replayed Scottish Cup-tie. It was another 'backs to the wall' performance from Stein's men, the only goal of the tie coming 10 minutes before the break as Lou Macari, the smallest man on the pitch, somehow got on the end of Harry's perfect corner delivery to head home. Harry was back in the team, but he spent most of the second half as a virtual passenger on the wing after taking a heavy challenge on his ankle, Celts having already used substitute Jimmy Quinn as the full-back curse struck again. This time, Davie Hay was the man hobbling off, joining Jim Brogan on the treatment table with Danny McGrain still hospitalised. Early thoughts were that all three plus Harry would struggle to recover in time for the trip to Milan, leaving Jock Stein with a massive problem to solve. The match at Tynecastle would end amidst ugly scenes, play stopped for several minutes as trouble erupted in the covered enclosure opposite the stand. Police would eventually restore order and clear the field, allowing the closing stages to play out, however, the spectre of segregation inside football grounds would once again rear its ugly head.

Harry would still be nursing that ankle as the first day of April involved a home League fixture with Partick Thistle. Jock Stein rested Lou Macari and moved Kenny Dalglish to the bench, bringing back Jimmy Johnstone, Vic Davidson and Dixie Deans up front. Jim Craig and Jimmy Quinn became the latest to be named in the dreaded full-back slots for what was Celtic's final game before the visit to the San Siro. The match was finished as a contest within 12 minutes, by which time Davidson had scored his second of the afternoon, 11 minutes and 44 seconds after his first! Johnstone would add another headed goal to his collection when he beat Alan Rough before the half-hour, the Jags managing one in response through Frank Coulston as the interval beckoned. That would be it in terms of scoring, as Celtic ran out comfortable 3-1 winners on a miserable wet afternoon for the 30,000 spectators, albeit the majority would be further cheered as news of Aberdeen's 1-0 defeat to Hearts at Tynecastle saw Celtic's lead at the top of the table restored to five points but the Bhoys now with two games in hand.

The feelgood factor would be somewhat diluted as fate dealt another blow to another Celtic full-back. This time it was young stand-in defender, Jimmy Quinn, hurt early in the game against Partick Thistle and joining Harry, Davie Hay and Jim Brogan in intensive treatment ahead of the midweek Italian Job. The Celtic party flew out to Lake Como on Monday, 3 April 1972 for the first leg of their European Cup semi-final with Inter Milan in the San Siro. The 20-man squad included walking wounded Harry, Jimmy Johnstone and the full-back trio of Hay, Brogan and Quinn, all five men clearly struggling to be fit for the vital midweek clash. The fourth defensive casualty - Danny McGrain - would now continue his recovery from the fractured skull suffered at Brockville at home.

The years immediately following their defeat by Celtic in Lisbon had been challenging for former world club champions, Internazionale, the Nerazzurri failing to qualify for European football in either of the next two seasons. A fourth-place finish in the 1968/69 Serie A, won by Fiorentina, would give them entry into the Inter-Cities Fairs Cup the following season, however, as Celtic were beating Leeds United at Hampden, having already disposed of Italian champions Fiorentina in the quarter-final, Inter Milan were blowing an excellent 1-0 semi-final first-leg victory in Brussels by losing 2-0 to Anderlecht in that same San Siro where the Hoops would come up short against Feyenoord just three weeks later. Inter would then lose in the first round of the following year's competition to Newcastle United.

The goals of Roberto Boninsegna had then taken Inter to the Italian title in 1971, and he would be a key figure in this season's European Cup campaign. The international striker was on target in both legs of the first-round clash with AEK Athens, as Inter won 6-4 on aggregate, however, as mentioned previously, the major controversy took place in Monchengladbach on Wednesday, 20 October 1971. The Italian club claimed that he had been struck by a can of Coca-Cola thrown from the crowd shortly after his equaliser against Borussia, a game the West Germans would go on to win 7-1. UEFA would then render that incredible result invalid and order the game to be replayed at a neutral venue, hence Jock Stein's visit to Berlin in December. Boninsegna would score for the fourth successive game as Inter won 4-2 in the San Siro in the scheduled second leg, before that run - and Borussia's European involvement - ended in a goalless draw in the Olympiastadion. Like most football supporters, as I recall, I felt that Monchengladbach had been very harshly treated at the time, and I still do. The quarter-final then saw the Italians progress on away goals following a 2-2 tie with Belgian champions Standard Liege, thus setting up the last-four reunion with Jock Stein's Celtic. Surely, their good fortune could not continue much longer.

Boninsegna would not score against Celtic. Neither Harry nor Jimmy Quinn was deemed fit enough even for the bench in the San Siro, Davie Hay named as a substitute whilst old warriors Jim Brogan and Jimmy Johnstone were patched up and included in the starting line-up, albeit obviously not in the greatest condition. Indeed, Brogan would last only an hour, Hay's lack of fitness clearly forcing Jock Stein to choose teenager Pat McCluskey as the replacement. This would be a real baptism of fire, the Kilsyth-born defender having enjoyed only 55 minutes of competitive first-team football, spread over a home Scottish Cup-tie with Albion Rovers then a trip to Somerset Park earlier in the year. A Hoops supporter who lived the dream, Pat would come through with flying colours as Stein's young Lions matched the performance of his 1969 vintage by emerging from the cauldron of the Giuseppe Meazza and its 85,000 fanatical Inter supporters with a hard-fought goalless draw. Italian Job – half-done.

Pat McCluskey would get his first Celtic start as the double-header with Kilmarnock commenced at Rugby Park three days later, partnering Jim Craig at full-back as goals from Dixie Deans, Vic Davidson and Paul Wilson saw a makeshift Hoops team close to within two points of the League title with a 3-1 win. Harry made his comeback 48 hours later, on target at Parkhead as Celtic's second-string beat East Fife's reserves 6-0, but he missed out again as that 3-1 victory over Killie was replicated in the Scottish Cup semi-final at Hampden on Wednesday, 12 April 1972. A Dixie double and a late Lou Macari strike enabled Celts to march through to an incredible seventh Scottish Cup final in eight years. Their final opponents would be Rangers or Hibernian, who were due to meet at the same venue that weekend.

Before that there was history to be made.

Harry, Kenny Dalglish and Jimmy Quinn would all return to the team for the visit to Methil on Saturday, 15 April 1972, as Jock Stein's men sought to break Celtic's own Scottish record for consecutive Scottish League Championship wins, which had been held by Willie Maley's wonderful side since 1910. The current Parkhead boss chose the following line-up to secure the two points required against East Fife.

Evan Williams; Jim Craig & Jimmy Quinn; Bobby Murdoch, Billy McNeill & George Connelly; Harry Hood, Kenny Dalglish, Dixie Deans, Tommy Callaghan & Lou Macari. Substitute; Pat McCluskey.

Having witnessed title-clinchers five and six, I was excited and proud to take my place behind the goal on a beautiful afternoon in Fife as the Hoops Class of '72 sought to extend the sequence to seven. The result was never in doubt, Dixie Deans grabbing another brace in the comfortable 3-0 win at Bayview. Harry was instrumental in the victory which sealed his fourth title as a Celt, heading home the second goal just before the break then setting Deans up perfectly for a late third, to get the party underway.

With the title secured and one cup final place already booked, it was time for the toughest test of all against Inter Milan four nights later. It would be the biggest night of my life, albeit it very nearly wasn't, my dad sensibly deciding that the terracing would be too busy for me and only forced to relent after I had locked myself in the bathroom to break my heart, something I feel guilty about to this day! Thus, an hour or so later, dry-eyed and perched on my stanchion in the Celtic End to take in the spectacular scene, I would watch as the Bhoys attempted to reach a third European Cup final in six years.

They would have to do so without Harry, who was carrying a knock after the win at Methil, his place going to Jimmy Johnstone. Two other changes from the weekend saw Jimmy Quinn and Dixie Deans drop to the bench, whilst Pat McCluskey and Bobby Lennox came into the team. For Inter, star striker Roberto Boninsegna remained in Milan nursing a leg injury. As 75,000 voices roared Celtic on, Inter's game plan was evident from the kick-off, delay, spoil and defend with your life, then hit on the break or take your chances in a shootout. The Italians were and are past masters at it. Three years earlier, another goalless draw in the San Siro had been negated by a single slip in the home leg, as AC Milan and not Celtic went through to the last four. And it would, agonisingly, come down once again to one misjudgement. Deans had replaced Kenny Dalglish on the hour to receive his first taste of the European big-time as a Celt, however, he would probably rather have stayed on the bench. With 90 minutes in Milan then 120 in Glasgow failing to produce a goal, and Sandro Mazzola repeating his Lisbon trick by scoring the first goal of the night from the penalty spot, Deans stepped up to level things off with the first shootout kick for the Hoops at the far end. He would no doubt be full of confidence, having been knocking them in for fun during the week as Stein's men practised them at Seamill...just in case. There are career-defining moments, and this was one, Dixie and the huge Celtic support looking on in anguish as his shot sailed over the crossbar. One by one the remaining penalty-takers walked from the halfway line, jeered or cheered as appropriate, and one by one they found the net. Jim Craig, Jimmy Johnstone and Pat McCluskey keeping home hopes alive until the Brazilian veteran Jair, an absentee in Lisbon, pierced a dagger through Celtic hearts with a fifth successful strike for Inter, rendering Bobby Murdoch's subsequent conversion irrelevant. For the four Italians who did play in Lisbon five years earlier - Tarcisio Burgnich, Giacinto Facchetti, Gianfranco Bedin and Mazzola, they would now have the opportunity to win a third European Cup for Inter. To do so they would have to beat holders Ajax - 1-0 aggregate winners over Benfica - at the home of Feyenoord in Rotterdam.

Jock Stein was philosophical afterwards.

"There's no question about blaming Dixie. We had been cracking penalty kicks home all week in practice. When the crunch comes, that's another matter. Naturally, we are disappointed. But with so many young players and with so many injuries, we have done better than we thought we would. We didn't lose on football. We lost on a circus act. We certainly don't approve of playing to this penalty kick business, but it is in the rules and we must always abide by the rules. We knew beforehand that we would have to settle the issue by penalties if we were still level. We have no complaints."

The Football Gods can be an unforgiving bunch and so, of course, Celtic's next game, three days later, would see Dixie Deans at the heart of the action with penalties to the fore, as his old Motherwell pals made the short trip along the old London Road, possibly bringing the match ball back from midweek, if the cruel and tactless newspaper cartoons of the time were to be believed. The 20,000 crowd gave the Hoops striker a huge ovation as he ran out at Celtic Park, as they did for visiting keeper John Fallon, one of our own whatever colours he was wearing that afternoon. Deans had replaced Lou Macari, whilst Harry and Jim Brogan continued their recovery in the reserves, as they lost 2-0 at Fir Park.

With Celts a Jumbo Muir goal down just after the half-hour mark, they were awarded a penalty when Jackie McInally punched a Bobby Murdoch header off the line. Sections of the crowd immediately chanted for Dixie Deans to take the kick but instead it would be Murdoch himself who stepped up to rifle the ball past his old colleague Fallon in the Well goal. Deans did get his goal within minutes, before Bobby Lennox made it 3-1 on the stroke of half-time. McInally pulled one back for the Steelmen on the hour, before referee R K Wilson awarded a second spot kick of the afternoon to Celtic, Bobby Watson penalised for a challenge on Murdoch. Again, the cries went up for Deans, again Bobby obliged and again Dixie immediately followed up with a goal from open play, as the match ended at 5-2.

Harry enjoyed another outing with the second-string 48 hours later, in a 2-0 win over Dundee United at Celtic Park in the second leg of the Scottish Reserve League Cup semi-final. With the teams tied at 2-2 on aggregate after extra-time, they met again the following night as a prelude to the final first team League match, Harry again playing the 90 minutes in a 3-1 win, as did Davie Hay. The League side duly followed that up with a 3-0 win over the Tannadice outfit, thanks to second-half goals from Jimmy Johnstone, Bobby Lennox and Dixie Deans. Celts finally welcomed Harry and Davie back to the first team for the visit to Tynecastle, the following Saturday, on what would turn out to be a bizarre afternoon in Scotland's capital. Tired and weary of their treatment in Gorgie, the chaos at the recent Scottish Cup replay being the final straw, thousands of Celtic supporters took part in a boycott of the match, the attendance dropping by a remarkable 30,000 from that night to just over the five-figure mark. Even Jock Stein gave it a miss, preferring to take in England's 3-1 defeat by West Germany at Wembley. The new Scottish champions took the pre-match ovation from their hosts then the lead with another Bobby Murdoch penalty within 10 minutes, however, that was as good as it got. By full-time, Hearts had scored four, missed a penalty and had another goal ruled out for offside. The 4-1 defeat would be the only domestic loss on their travels all season, and was the biggest League hammering I could ever recall as a Celtic supporter, dating back to Jock Stein's arrival in 1965.

There would be one last awayday before the Scottish Cup final, a trip to Dens Park to face Dundee on Monday, 1 May 1972 in the final League match of the season. Harry dropped to the bench as a Lou Macari equaliser on the hour stretched Celtic's final advantage at the top of the table to a round 10 points over Aberdeen, following a low-key 1-1 draw. Now it was all about Hampden, five days later.

The following morning, Harry was included in the 14-man squad announced by Jock Stein for the Scottish Cup final, as Celts headed to Troon to complete their preparations. Having scored the goal which clinched the Double in the win over Rangers 12 months earlier, it would no doubt be a sickening blow to Harry to learn on the Friday that he would miss out on the opportunity to win another trophy, as would Davie Hay, injuries bringing a sad end to the season for two of Celtic's most influential players. Together with the crowd of 106,102, they would watch history being made on what turned out to be the best afternoon of my Celtic-supporting life pre-adulthood.

Having finally beaten Willie Maley's record for successive League title wins, Jock Stein now sought to emulate the great man by recording back-to-back League and Cup doubles, a feat first achieved by the Bould Bhoys in 1908. For Hibernian manager Eddie Turnbull, the challenge was equally historic, win the personal duel with Stein - as he had in the 1970 final but lost three years earlier - to deliver a first Scottish Cup for Leith in seven decades. The legends chose these teams to deliver on their dreams.

CELTIC:

Evan Williams; Jim Craig & Jim Brogan; Bobby Murdoch, Billy McNeill & George Connelly; Jimmy Johnstone, Dixie Deans, Lou Macari, Kenny Dalglish & Tommy Callaghan. Substitute; Bobby Lennox.

HIBERNIAN:

Jim Herriot; John Brownlie & Eric Schaedler; Pat Stanton, Jim Black & John Blackley; Alex Edwards, John Hazel, Alan Gordon, Jim O'Rourke & Arthur Duncan. Substitute; Bertie Auld.

Hibernian had destroyed Rangers in the semi-final and were favourites with many to defeat a Celtic side still struggling with the aftermath of that European Cup exit. But they were never in with a chance. Billy McNeill opened the scoring within 90 seconds with his THIRD goal in the showpiece event in eight years, quite a record for a centre-half. And records would be the watchword of this magical day, Dixie Deans becoming the first player to score a Scottish Cup final hat-trick since the Bhoy from Croy,

Jimmy Quinn, had overturned a 0-2 deficit against Rangers in the first such final to take place at the third and present Hampden, back in April 1904. As Dixie forward-rolled his way into folklore with his treble – the second goal a quite incredible solo effort which defies logic to this day – he could reflect on an incredible personal turnaround and finale to his first season as a Celt, following the abject misery of the penalty miss against Inter just 17 days earlier. Two late strikes from Lou Macari - both following assists from Jim Craig - took the tally to 6-1, thus equalling the record Scottish Cup final winning margin achieved by Renton over Cambuslang in the final of February 1888, three months before their captain James Kelly and double-goalscorer Neil McCallum appeared in the first-ever Celtic line-up. It was a fairytale afternoon for this wonderful football club to bring the curtain down on a tremendous season.

As Jim Craig became the latest Lisbon Lion to announce his departure from Parkhead - the big full-back announcing that he would be emigrating with his family for a new life in South Africa - there would be mixed emotions for those with Celtic in their hearts. A near-perfect domestic campaign had been soured only by that inexplicable defeat to Partick Thistle in the previous October's League Cup final, whilst the pain of that penalty shootout elimination at the hands of Inter Milan - who many believe should have been knocked out of the European Cup long before the semi-final, following their 7-1 humiliation by Borussia in Monchengladbach - would live long in the memory.

For Harry personally, it had been a mixed bag, his 21 goals in 40 appearances a decent return, if not quite matching that of the previous campaign. There had been the highs of Budapest and seven-in-a-row then the crushing heartbreak of missing out against Inter and the cup final win over Hibernian. Both he and Celtic would now go again with renewed hopes and expectations after the summer break.

Chapter 22

Unhappy sequels in Hungary and at Hampden

Following his injury disappointments at the tail end of the previous campaign, Harry's 1972/73 season commenced in much the same vein. He would miss out on the home Drybrough Cup victories over promoted Dumbarton then holders Aberdeen, which set up a rematch of May's Scottish Cup final with Hibernian at Hampden on Saturday, 5 Aug 1972. Harry was one of a number of first team players involved in a friendly with Queen's Park at Lesser Hampden on the eve of the Dons game, opening his account for the season with Celtic's sixth in a 7-1 win, a match which saw the return of Danny McGrain from his horrific skull fracture. Whilst Danny was immediately brought back to the first-team fold, both Harry and Vic Davidson were given the opportunity to play their way into the cup final squad with a run out against Alloa Athletic at Recreation Park on the night before the clash with Hibernian. Both scored in the 4-0 win, but neither would make the cut for Hampden, as Celtic thrillingly fought back from three goals down to take the match to extra-time, before succumbing to two further goals as the sponsors' trophy headed to Leith.

Harry would continue playing his way back to full match sharpness with another 90 minutes against Hamilton Academical at Douglas Park on Tuesday, 8 August 1972, 24 hours after the first team had defeated UEFA Cup-holders Tottenham Hotspur 1-0 at Celtic Park thanks to a second-half Tommy Callaghan strike. Jim Brogan and Dixie Deans were also on duty in South Lanarkshire as an otherwise youthful squad fought back from three goals down to lose 3-2, Harry adding the late second for Celtic.

Dixie and Harry were joined by out-of-favour goalkeeper Evan Williams for the start of the competitive season, on Saturday, 12 August 1972. All three men had been key to Celtic's Double-winning campaign in the spring but now found themselves at a deserted Celtic Park for the Reserve League Cup section match with Airdrieonians. Harry continued his scoring run with a delicate lob from a Jackie McNamara pass on the half-hour, Celtic's equaliser in a 1-1 draw. The duo then played their way into Jock Stein's thoughts with fine displays in a 4-1 win over Ayr United's reserves at the same venue 48 hours later.

Both men returned to the first-team picture at Gayfield Park, Arbroath on Saturday,

19 August 1972, as Celts continued to make progress through a rather uninteresting League Cup section, which also included Stirling Albion and East Fife. The newly promoted Red Lichties would be no match for Jock Stein's Double Winners, sporting their new hooped shirts with the white v-insert collar, as the group reached the halfway point with a 5-0 victory for Celtic. Kenny Dalglish and Dixie Deans showed early signs of what would become a prolific striking partnership that season with doubles apiece after Bobby Murdoch had opened the scoring from 12 yards, use of the 'P word' still a bit raw to the ears of Celtic fans after the events of April and Inter Milan.

Kenny grabbed another brace in midweek as Celts returned to Bayview Park, Methil, the venue of their historic seventh successive title victory four months earlier. The Hoops would again take a 3-0 lead - Bobby Lennox having opened the scoring - as they had that day, before two late Kevin Hegarty goals made the scoreline look tighter than should have been the case. And qualification was secured on Matchday 5, Saturday, 26 August 1972, as once again a Bobby Murdoch dead ball from 12 yards was followed by goals by the Terrible Twins, Dalglish and Deans, albeit only one apiece this time in another 3-0 win, this time over Stirling Albion at Parkhead.

I remember the final match well, albeit not for the happiest of reasons. The home game with Arbroath had already been moved to Hampden to facilitate work on the press box, which was suspended from the new stand roof at Celtic Park, however, 24 hours earlier a fire had damaged the stand itself, presumably adding to the complications and subsequent delay in playing matches again at our spiritual home. The Hampden experience that Monday evening in August 1972 was entirely surreal, just 5,000 spectators in the vast arena once measured to hold 150,000 plus. A young Arbroath forward would have better memories of this match though, enjoying the night of his football life by scoring a hat-trick against the side who had been a PK away from the European Cup final a few months earlier. Derek Rylance opened the scoring with his first-ever goal for the Angus club, then added two more late on as Arbroath fought back from 3-1 down to share the points. Harry had opened his own Celtic account for the season to put the Hoops 2-1 ahead just before the interval, after the unfortunate Cargill had beaten his own keeper Gordon Marshall to level things off on the half-hour. Kenny Dalglish then appeared to secure the win on 57 minutes before Rylance completed his own piece of football history. Photos of this match show that the Celtic team wore the old crew neck kit that evening, which to the best of my knowledge, was the final time that the Lisbon strip was on show. The end of an era.

Celts started their quest for an incredible eighth successive Scottish League title with another strange experience five days later, Saturday, 2 September 1972. The opening match of the campaign would again be at their temporary Hampden home, a combination of that and a 7pm kick-off on a Saturday night reducing the attendance to under 12,000. Not that this seemed to bother the players so much, Harry netting a first Hampden hat-trick and Dixie Deans a double as only Ally Hunter in the Kilmarnock goals kept the score at six. The Ayrshire club did manage a couple of their own with Bobby Murdoch's late…er…shot from 12 yards out allowing the champions to declare at 6-2. David Stirling was in no doubt of the key Celt in his match report for Monday's *Evening Times*.

"Of the original Celts who started the great monopoly back in 1965, Bobby Murdoch and Billy McNeill looked as good as ever. It was a slimmer-looking Murdoch who faced Killie, and he's coming back to the form that made him the best midfield player in Scotland. But for me, the man who gets the excitement going is Harry Hood. He's the most graceful of players. He's also one of the most intelligent, the man who can make Celtic tick. Hood started the rot with a shot that Jackie McGrory deflected into the net. Dixie Deans, who's coming back to scoring form, got the second, and Hood the third after Alistair Hunter had failed to hold a raging shot from Murdoch. After the restart, Hood got the fifth, heading between Hunter's legs after Deans had headed on a throw-in by Dalglish."

There was an additional 3,000 on the gate as Celtic visited Cappielow the following Saturday, a Bobby Murdoch double beating a Morton side which included his old friends John Clark and Stevie Chalmers, and then it was back to a sparsely populated Hampden in midweek as the Bhoys faced Norwegian Double-winners Rosenborg and their 30-year-old coach Nils Arne Eggen for the first time. Less than 20,000 were on the vast slopes to see first-half goals from Lou Macari - from Harry's corner kick - then Dixie Deans appear to have the tie pretty much sewn up before a Bjorn Wirkola effort after the break made the trip to the Artic Circle that bit more daunting. That goal was a story in itself, as Wirkola was actually a world champion ski-jumper who played football as a sideline! The Rosenberg keeper that night, Geir Karlsen, suffered a broken ankle in a collision with Macari and was stretchered off. Karlsen would later follow in the footsteps of Aarhus keeper Bent Martin in the mid 1960s, by trialling for Celtic after playing against them in a European tie before making his name at Dunfermline Athletic.

Like the 'Hampden season' which would follow two decades later, highlights of this temporary decant were like supporters who enjoyed the experience, thin on the ground, however, one would certainly be the early afternoon of Saturday, 16 September 1972, when the Hoops beat Rangers 3-1 in the most one-sided of derbies before 50,460 spectators. The match kicked off at noon and the contest was over before most folk had thought about lunch, Kenny Dalglish within two minutes, Jimmy Johnstone with his obligatory strike 15 minutes later then Lou Macari five minutes after the break all beating Peter McCloy, with the missed opportunities bordering on the farcical. Harry replaced Jinky with 12 minutes remaining and would witness first-hand the extraordinary sight of John Greig scoring a consolation goal in the dying seconds which drew huge cheers from the Celtic support in the ground, the Rangers captain acknowledging the applause with a raised fist. These were strange times.

Two nights later, an unchanged Celtic team faced Manchester United in a testimonial game for Bobby Charlton, over 60,000 cramming into Old Trafford to watch the first two European champions from outwith the continental landmass lock horns before settling for a goalless draw. Harry replaced Jimmy Johnstone for the entire second half, thus making his first-ever appearance at the Theatre of Dreams, having missed out on the only match between the clubs in Manchester during his spell at Sunderland. The United side did feature three of the men who had faced Sunderland at Roker Park on Wednesday, 24 February 1965 - the great Charlton himself, Denis Law and full-back Tony Dunne - when Harry had scored the goal which beat the English champions-elect in front of over 50,000 cheering Wearsiders.

The change of setting could hardly be more pronounced, as Celts travelled north from Manchester to pay a first-ever visit to Stair Park, Stranraer, two nights later. Harry returned to the starting line-up and set up Celtic's 75th minute winner as goals from Vic Davidson and Bobby Lennox gave the Hoops a 2-1 advantage in the first leg of their League Cup quarter-final tie in front of 5,000 spectators. At the weekend, though, Harry would again be turning out for the reserves, scoring the second goal in a 3-2 win over Dundee's second string at Parkhead, whilst the first team went down 2-0 at Dens Park.

That combination of circumstance perhaps brought Harry back into contention for the midweek trip to Trondheim, as Jock Stein's men looked to complete the task of qualifying for the second round of the European Cup in Celtic's maiden competitive match in Norway. Stein was unusually blunt in his briefing to the media before the match, clearly throwing the gauntlet down to Harry whilst dropping an incredible compliment his way.

"I'll probably call in Harry Hood. He's another who could do a lot for us. He's got a load of talent, probably more than Johnstone even, but he hasn't been getting involved. Harry has seemed content to flit about on the outskirts. I want authority from him tonight. He knows the game. He's got talent and physique. We want more from him than we've been getting."

There were shades of the defeat in Copenhagen 12 months earlier, as Rosenborg took the lead before the interval in the Stadion Lerkendal, however, a close-range strike from last season's European hero Lou Macari had tied things on the night by the hour, and late goals from Harry and Kenny Dalglish saw Celts through on a comfortable if not entirely convincing 5-2 aggregate.

Harry retained his starting slot as the last day of September saw Celtic finally make their return to Paradise after a month on the road, the home match with Ayr United preceded by the unfurling of the 1971/72 League flag. The eight flagpoles above the Jungle proudly displayed the presentation banners from each of the seven glorious seasons in the run, with the one nearest the Celtic End of the ground flying a special 'seven-in-a-row' commemorative flag. As often happens on such occasions, the game itself was fairly low key, an early Dixie Deans header separating the teams at the end of 90 minutes, Celts remaining top of the table on goal difference from Aberdeen and Dundee United.

They would lose that lead seven days later, as Airdrieonians left Parkhead with a point following a frustrating 1-1 draw. Evan Williams, Jimmy Johnstone and Dixie Deans were the latest Celts to drop out of the team as Jock Stein sought an end to his side's indifferent and inconsistent form. Both goals were scored in the first half, John Fury cleverly chipping Denis Connaghan in 15 minutes with Bobby Lennox equalising seven minutes from the break. Harry made way for Vic Davidson with 12 minutes remaining as the Diamonds held on for a well-earned point.

Harry was back on reserve team duty in midweek, scoring twice in a 6-5 loss to Partick Thistle at Celtic Park. On the same night, Dundee followed up their recent 2-0 League victory over the champions at Dens Park with another home win in the first leg of the League Cup quarter-final, this time a single goal from Gordon Wallace setting things up nicely for the return.

Harry found himself on the bench the following Saturday as Celts made the short trip to Firhill. He would join the fray with the Bhoys 2-0 up and 25 minutes remaining, Jim Brogan finally succumbing to an injury sustained in the opening stages. Goals from Bobby Lennox and Kenny Dalglish would then add to earlier strikes from Davie Hay and Dixie Deans as Celts ran out 4-0 winners. He would play a key role in Celtic's next game, a home League fixture with East Fife seven days later, coming on for Bobby Murdoch with just half an hour played. Seconds before the interval, Harry fired home from close range as defiant Methil goalkeeper Dave Gorman was finally beaten. Late goals from Dixie Deans and Bobby Lennox then put a bit more gloss on the scoreline at 3-0, and saw the Celts return to the top of the table following a defeat for previous leaders' Dundee United to Falkirk at Brockville.

Midweek saw the return of the European Cup. Jock Stein had asked for a tough second-round draw, and he received exactly that, an early re-match with Ujpest Dosza just six months after the Bhoys had defeated the Hungarian champions to set up the ultimately heartbreaking semi-final with Inter Milan. This time the first leg would be at home and the outcome of the tie would sadly be very different. In the absence of the injured Bobby Murdoch and Jim Brogan, the Celtic manager went with the following team on Wednesday, 25 October 1972, in front of 52,000 expectant supporters at Parkhead.

Evan Williams; Davie Hay & Danny McGrain; George Connelly, Billy McNeill & Tommy Callaghan; Jimmy Johnstone, Kenny Dalglish, Dixie Deans, Lou Macari & Harry Hood. Substitutes; Denis Connaghan, Bobby Lennox, Pat McCluskey, Vic Davidson & Brian McLaughlin.

Ferenc Bene had been a thorn in Celtic's side back in March, and he would be so again, the Ujpest veteran striking to give the Hungarians the lead on 20 minutes. The closing stages of the first half saw Harry inches away from equalising, before he became the first victim of Jock Stein's tactical reshuffle, making way for Pat McCluskey at the interval with George Connelly pushed into midfield. Within five minutes of the restart, the decision of the Hoops boss would be vindicated, Connelly crossing for the immaculate Kenny Dalglish to sidefoot the ball home. With 15 minutes remaining and the game locked at 1-1, Stein made his second move, Jimmy Johnstone withdrawn, and his great friend Bobby Lennox introduced, much to the displeasure of large sections of the crowd. His impact would be immediate, though, Lennox's far post cross picking out Dalglish to nod home for 2-1. Despite incessant pressure, there would be no further scoring, the tie now beautifully balanced ahead of the second leg.

By a quirk of fate there would also be a Hungarian influence in Celtic's next match, the trip north to face closest challengers Aberdeen at Pittodrie, three days later. The Dons fielded their new Magyar signing Zoltan Varga, christened *"Salt'n'Vinegar"* by the home fans in those days when any player not from Scotland or Scandanavia was still very much a novelty. Varga had enjoyed an interesting career, to say the least. A gold medalist with Hungary at the Tokyo Olympics of 1964, he had played in that great Ferencvaros team which beat Juventus in their own Stadio Comunale to win the Inter-Cities Fairs Cup the following spring, partnering the wonderful Florian Albert. Albert would, of course, pip Bobby Charlton and Jimmy Johnstone to the European Footballer of the Year award in 1967. He and Varga would lead Ferencvaros all the way to the final of the Fairs Cup again the next season, this time losing a two-leg tie with Leeds United by a single goal. In the summer of 1968, Varga travelled with the Hungarian national team to defend their Olympic title in Mexico City, following which he chose to defect to the west as the Prague Spring saw huge conflict and unrest in many of the Warsaw Pact countries. He would land in Berlin via Standard Liege, playing for three seasons with Hertha before being cited in the Bundesliga bribes scandal in 1971 and subsequently banned from playing in Germany for two years. Hertha then sold him to Aberdeen, allegedly against the player's wishes. If that were true, it did not appear to impact his form, as I recall him being a real star player in Scotland at the time. He certainly played his part against Celtic on Saturday, 28 October 1972, scoring both home goals as the Bhoys edged a five-goal thriller at a packed Pittodrie, thanks to strikes from Dixie Deans, Lou Macari and Kenny Dalglish. Harry was in the pool of 13 players who travelled to Aberdeen before finding himself the man left out on the day. Incredibly, outwith an extra-time 3-2 Drybrough Cup win at Parkhead back in August, this was Celtic's first victory over Aberdeen since October 1969.

Harry would be back on the bench in midweek as Jock Stein's men recorded a second successive 3-2 win, to square off the League Cup quarter-final tie with Dundee, following the first-leg defeat at Dens Park. It was a terrific game, despite the best efforts of controversial referee R H Davidson of Airdrie, who somehow managed to upset both teams, a 40,000 crowd and Jock Stein, who marched across the Parkhead pitch to remonstrate with him as the teams summoned up the energy for extra-time. Harry replaced Kenny Dalglish for the additional 30 minutes but there would be no further scoring, a play-off now required to decide who would join Aberdeen, Hibernian and Rangers in the last four.

It was the turn of Dundee's Tannadice Street neighbours to visit Celtic Park three days later, Saturday, 4 November 1972. Harry was again the 12th man, getting the nod to replace Dixie Deans after an hour with the Hoops 2-1 ahead against Jim McLean's Dundee United. He would be heavily involved in Celtic's third and clinching goal, his exquisite lob beating Hamish McAlpine but crashing back off the crossbar, Lou Macari applying the finishing touch for 3-1.

The recent domestic recovery would be quickly forgotten after a dreadful night in Budapest in midweek. Wednesday, 8 November 1972 would be one of the low points of the wonderful Jock Stein tenure, as his former European champions were put to the sword by a lightning quick Ujpest Dosza attack, spearheaded by Ferenc Bene and Antal Dunai. In three previous meetings between the clubs, they had threatened to convert that pace and skill into goals and tonight they would make good on that threat. I suppose the writing was on the wall when after rushing home from school Groundhog Day-style, just as I had done exactly eight months previously, I tuned in to the sad face of Arthur Montford advising that the satellite link had failed. That would not be the only failing as Celts found themselves three goals down within 20 minutes, news of each goal relayed by the bold Arthur with an expression which would have done the Reverend I M Jolly proud. Perhaps the only surprise was that the Hungarians did not add to their tally, however, their job was done long before Jock Stein finally introduced Harry and Dixie Deans for Bobby Lennox and Danny McGrain for the closing stages.

The Hungarian champions would progress to face Juventus in the quarter-final, recording an excellent goalless draw in Turin's Stadio Comunale then producing the same lightning start to the return leg that had destroyed Celtic, Ujpest 2-0 up after 13 minutes and with one foot in the last four. On this occasion though, the Old Lady would use her vast experience to claw her way back into the tie before going through on away goals. Ujpest would make the European Cup semi-final the following season, holding eventual winners Bayern Munich to a 1-1 draw in Budapest before finally succumbing to two late German goals in the Olympiastadion. Further evidence, as if any were needed, that the Hungarian champions were a more than useful side over that three-year period.

Back in Glasgow, Jock Stein would have much to reflect on, as for only the second time since his appointment as Celtic manager, his side had failed to reach the last eight of a European competition. The contrast in those two matches in Budapest in the spring and autumn of 1972 could hardly have been greater, the euphoria of what he had called the *"best performance since Lisbon"* replaced by headlines such as *"Celts outclassed"* and *"14 minutes of disaster."* There would be no heroic last-gasp winners or after-match parties with Hollywood royalty this time around, and his focus could now turn on the quest to secure a third domestic Treble.

The hangover from Budapest was blown away with the Motherwell players as Celts unleashed their frustration to hit the Steelmen with everything on the muddy Fir Park pitch on Saturday, 11 November 1972. Harry and Dixie Deans were recalled to the starting line-up, the former vindicating his selection with a first-half double. Harry opened the scoring after seven minutes, having had a shot cleared off the line within 90 seconds of the kick-off. His second goal arrived just before the interval, Motherwell keeper Keith MacRae doing well to stop a Deans thunderbolt only to look on in despair as the ever-alert Hood knocked the loose ball home. Kenny Dalglish was also in sparkling form, on an afternoon when Celtic did not have a failure, the King striking twice either side of the break from 20 yards. A fifth goal duly arrived with 20 minutes remaining, Harry's shot deflected over MacRae by the outstretched leg of Willie McCallum, the defender discredited with an own goal to deny Harry his second hat-trick of the season. Celts ran out convincing 5-0 winners as the Euro recovery started with a bang, with the contribution made by Harry highlighted by Malcolm Munro is his *Evening Times* report on the Monday.

"Harry got himself involved against Motherwell and had Celtic ticking over like a Rolls-Royce. He's a big strong boy is Harry, yet he fades out of a game. But his strong dribbling and accurate crossing at the weekend was worth watching. He was taking on opponents and giving others space to move. Because of the attention that was being paid to him, Kenny Dalglish had a cracker of a game. They shared four goals."

Celtic had won that match minus three injured stars in captain Billy McNeill, Bobby Murdoch and Lou Macari, the trio still missing as was George Connelly as Hearts arrived at Celtic Park seven days later for what would prove another classic encounter. Exploiting his squad resources to the full, Jock Stein selected the following team.

Evan Williams; Danny McGrain & Jimmy Quinn; Pat McCluskey, Davie Hay & Jim Brogan; Jimmy Johnstone, Dixie Deans, Kenny Dalglish, Harry Hood & Tommy Callaghan. Substitute; Bobby Lennox.

The Tynecastle men started well in their new Ajax-style kit, regular nuisance Donald Ford scoring in the opening quarter after both Jimmy Johnstone and Harry had tested the woodwork. The immaculate Kenny Dalglish would then beat Kenny Garland in the Hearts goal with another superb strike to level things at 1-1 just before the break. Ford again gave the Gorgie side the lead within minutes of the restart with the Hoops defence claiming offside, and there was controversy too as Dixie Deans scored a second equaliser with 25 minutes remaining, the visitors protesting furiously that Dalglish had been ahead of the last defender in the build-up to the goal. Celtic's star men on the afternoon then won the match. Harry laid on a third goal for Johnstone on 73 minutes, the winger repaying the compliment with seven minutes remaining, allowing Harry to beat the tracksuit-bottomed Garland and complete the scoring at 4-2, sending the majority of the 28,000 supporters home happy. They would be happier still as news came through of Hibernian's surprise 2-1 defeat at home to Rangers, Celtic's lead at the top now extended to four points over their Edinburgh rivals and the runners-up from the previous two seasons, Aberdeen.

The play-off to decide the fourth semi-final slot in the League Cup took place at Hampden, two nights later, Monday, 20 November 1972. I was amongst the 36,500 crowd inside the national stadium to watch Celts face Dundee for the fourth time in two months, unusually standing in that schoolboy enclosure in front of the main South Stand. That would allow me a close-up view of the action, and there was plenty of it, particularly in an incredible first half. The Dark Blues started brightly against a Celtic side which welcomed back George Connelly, driven on by their fine attacking trio of Gordon Wallace, John Duncan and Jocky Scott. Within 15 minutes, each had threatened the Celtic goal, Wallace hitting the bar before Scott conjured up his second goal of the tie to give Dundee the lead. Celtic's response when it arrived was simply devastating, the Hoops scoring with four headers before the interval, three of those in a six-minute spell which finished the match at 4-1. Harry was again on target to level things before the half-hour, nodding home at the far post following a corner. Dixie Deans and Kenny Dalglish then took turns at crossing for each other to head home, before a superb move the length of the pitch culminated in Deans arriving perfectly to dispatch Harry's sublime cross past Thomson Allan. Perhaps not surprisingly, the second period struggled to match the first, the key moment seeing Harry denied his second goal of the night by the crossbar. It was a performance that even to my 11-year-old eyes was clearly something special to behold.

The last Saturday of the month saw Celts travel to Brockville, Denis Connaghan replacing Evan Williams between the sticks and Bobby Lennox stepping in for Jimmy Johnstone, with Harry moving wide right. The Terrible Twins Dalglish and Deans would share three goals, Kenny striking twice before the break after Tom McLeod had given Falkirk the lead midway through the first half, Harry then teeing up Dixie for a header five minutes into the second period. Eight months earlier, Danny McGrain had suffered a fractured skull at Brockville, and sadly this afternoon would see another full-back badly injured, Jim Shirra stretchered off on 70 minutes with a fractured leg after a collision involving Deans. With former Celt Davie Cattenach on as his replacement, McLeod gave the Bairns some hope of a comeback by completing his own double late on, but Celts held out for the two points as the match ended 3-2.

Two nights later, Celtic ended November as they had ended October, with another 3-2 victory over Aberdeen, their third such success this season after three years without a win over the Dons. Just under 40,000 supporters braved the elements at Hampden on the horrendous evening of Monday, 27 November 1972, for the League Cup semi-final between Scotland's top sides of the decade to date. Joe Harper scored his customary goal against the Hoops, as the recent Celtic trend of going behind then fighting back continued unabated. Harry equalised from the spot within three minutes, after Kenny Dalglish had been brought down in the box, however, with 17 minutes remaining, a Davie Robb header threatened to end Celtic's run of League Cup final appearances, which stretched back eight years to 1964. Yet again, the champions found an immediate response, Jimmy Johnstone equalising before Tommy Callaghan scored the goal of the night, the big Fifer rifling the ball past Bobby Clark in the 80th minute to send the Hoops through to yet another Hampden final.

Saturday, 2 December 1972 was a red-letter day for the good folk of Dumbarton, as Celtic paid a first competitive visit to Boghead for half a century. The Sons of the Rock included former Celts John Cushley and Willie Wallace plus future Parkhead signing Tom McAdam in their line-up, but it was a current Hoops star who would get the party started, Harry's blistering free-kick screaming past Laurie Williams in the home goal after four minutes. It would also be a special afternoon for Pat McCluskey, Harry setting up the young wing-half for a first Celtic goal on 15 minutes, Jimmy Johnstone adding a third midway through the first half as the match threatened to become a rout. Pat obviously enjoyed the feeling, scoring again 10 minutes before the break then competing an unlikely hat-trick with Celtic's sixth goal 12 minutes from time. The unfortunate Cushley had deflected a Hood shot past Williams a few minutes earlier to make it 5-0, however, the last word would go to a Lisbon Lion, Wallace getting Dumbarton on the scoresheet with six minutes remaining as the Hoops won 6-1.

Next up for Celts was the League Cup final at Hampden, a rematch of the memorable Scottish Cup final with Eddie Turnbull's Hibernian seven months earlier. The Bhoys had been in incredible form that afternoon, however, like the clash with Ujpest Dosza the previous month, the contrast between the two cup final meetings with Hibernian in 1972 could hardly have been starker. Hampden in December was a dark, cold, gloomy alternative to that magical May afternoon, and the attendance of 72,000, whilst decent, was still 30,000 less than that which watched the Double clinched in such spectacular style. However, the main difference was in the Celtic teams. Of the three cup-winning goalscorers, Dixie Deans would miss out whilst Billy McNeill returned from injury and Lou Macari from flu, neither appearing fully fit. Midfield dynamo Bobby Murdoch was also injured, whilst his partner Tommy Callaghan was fit enough only for a seat on the bench. And to literally add insult to injury, George Connelly had been badly hurt, deliberately as he later admitted, by Southampton defender Jim Steele, a guest player in a Jersey select team whom Celts had faced in a rather ill-timed friendly in the Channel Islands five days earlier, Harry scoring Celtic's first two goals in an 11-1 rout. Connelly would play at Hampden, but like McNeill and Macari, he would be in far from peak condition for such a vital match.

And then there was the kit. It may just have been me, but I could never take to the v-insert collar, certainly not at that time anyway. This had been the first change in the hooped jersey of my conscious lifetime. The crew-neck top had been worn since 1962. It had witnessed the arrival of Jock Stein's wonderful team. It was the strip of Lisbon. It was THE Celtic jersey, just as Jock was the manager, Cesar was the captain and Celtic were the champions. These were all givens. Somehow, in my 11-year-old mind, the change of strip marked changing times. The fact that it was last worn in earnest in that 1972 Scottish Cup final, the highlight of my Celtic childhood, if anything made that line in the sand even clearer. Jock Stein and Eddie Turnbull named the following teams, the Celtic boss seeking to end a run of two losing League Cup finals.

CELTIC:

Evan Williams; Danny McGrain & Jim Brogan; Pat McCluskey, Billy McNeill & Davie Hay; Jimmy Johnstone, George Connelly, Kenny Dalglish, Harry Hood & Lou Macari. Substitute; Tommy Callaghan.

HIBERNIAN:

Jim Herriot; John Brownlie & Eric Schaedler; Pat Stanton, Jim Black & John Blackley; Alex Edwards, Jim O'Rourke, Alan Gordon, Alex Cropley & Arthur Duncan. Substitute; Johnny Hamilton.

Turnbull had inherited then developed a tremendous side at Easter Road since moving from Aberdeen in the summer of 1971, and Hibernian would succeed the Dons as Celtic's main challengers for a few seasons. In any other era, they would most likely have been champions, and on that dark afternoon at Hampden, they would enjoy their finest hour, as they matched Jock Stein's Celts blow for blow before taking the ascendancy in the second half. I didn't have many favourite players who earned their living somewhere other than Parkhead, however, Pat Stanton was one of that select band. As the clock ticked towards the 60-minute mark, the Hibs skipper grabbed the final by the scruff of the neck and within six minutes, the trophy was heading to Leith for the first time. First, he displayed wonderful control to evade several lunges in the Celtic penalty area before rifling the ball high past Evan Williams for the opener, then he glided down the right flank before picking out striker Jim O'Rourke with a perfect cross, his header beating Williams at his near post to put Hibernian 2-0 up. It could have been worse, Williams flapping at a cross ball to allow Alan Gordon the chance to score his second cup final goal against Celtic, the alert Billy McNeill managing to get back onto the goal-line and block the shot. With 13 minutes remaining, Kenny Dalglish, Celtic's best player on the day, carved out his own piece of magic to bear down towards the Celtic End before hammering the ball past Jim Herriot for 2-1. Sadly, just like the previous season's League Cup final – and any other cup final in which Kenny scored for Celtic for that matter – it would prove to be no more than a consolation goal, as the Hoops, having won the trophy five times in succession, now suffered a third consecutive final defeat.

Chapter 23

Celts overcome setbacks and spots of bother to deliver eight-in-a-row

There were two very different matches for the League Cup finalists on Saturday, 16 December 1972, seven days after their Hampden efforts had seen the trophy head to Leith for the first time. Strangely, only 12,000 supporters turned up at Easter Road to welcome home their heroes, with those who didn't missing a goalfest which started after only 12 seconds. Ayr United were put to the sword as Hibernian won 8-1, their cup-winning goalscorers Pat Stanton and Jim O'Rourke contributing four of those, the latter with a hat-trick. Beaten finalists Celtic had a much trickier afternoon in the mud of Gayfield, losing a goal to Arbroath's Eric Sellars within 30 seconds. Indeed, it took two late strikes from Harry to avoid a shock defeat and maintain their four-point advantage over Hibernian at the top of the table, ahead of the vital League clash between the teams the following Saturday.

More than 45,000 supporters headed to Celtic Park on Saturday, 23 December 1972 for the third successive pre-Christmas clash there between Scotland's top two sides. Aberdeen had won then drawn in the previous two seasons, albeit Celts had recovered to claim the title on both occasions, Eddie Turnbull now returned with his League Cup-winners Hibernian as the main challengers, the following teams taking the field for this latest summit meeting.

CELTIC:

Evan Williams; Davie Hay & Jim Brogan; Pat McCluskey, Billy McNeill & George Connelly; Jimmy Johnstone, Dixie Deans, Kenny Dalglish, Harry Hood & Tommy Callaghan. Substitute; Bobby Lennox.

HIBERNIAN:

Jim Herriot; John Brownlie & Eric Schaedler; Pat Stanton, Jim Black & John Blackley; Alex Edwards, Jim O'Rourke, Alan Gordon, Alex Cropley & Arthur Duncan. Substitute; Johnny Hamilton.

The three main talking points of the first half all went against Celtic, who were wearing an unusual all-yellow kit. Firstly, a linesman's flag robbed Harry of a critical goal, after a Dixie Deans header had come back off the crossbar. Then Jimmy Johnstone, in dazzling form, found himself the meat in a Pat Stanton and Jim O'Rourke sandwich – yes, those two again – the winger forced to limp off the Parkhead pitch just before the half-hour, with Bobby Lennox his replacement. Then eight minutes from the break, the tall figure of Alan Gordon stole in, to head home yet another goal against Celtic.

The second half consisted of a siege towards Jim Herriot's goal. Within eight minutes he was beaten, as Harry's spectacular long-range shot hit his post then rolled along the line behind the Hibernian keeper before rolling to safety on the other side of the goals. Just as we were marking this one up as 'one of those days,' the Bhoys struck. With 12 minutes remaining, George Connelly's exquisite pass released Davie Hay down the Jungle right, his pinpoint cross finding the head of Kenny Dalglish, for the young King to glance past Herriot for 1-1. In the dying minutes, the woodwork saved the Edinburgh men once more, this time substitute Lennox producing some magic which deserved to win the match, his shot from outside the box beating Herriot but this time crashing off his crossbar, as the game ended with the teams sharing a point apiece.

As 1972 gave way to 1973, there were a number of setbacks at Celtic Park which had the potential to derail any thoughts of an eighth successive championship win. Firstly, Jock Stein was taken to hospital after complaining of heart pains, where he would remain for a further fortnight, thus missing the three crucial matches planned for the holiday period. Then a flu epidemic which had commenced with Harry and skipper Billy McNeill spread to include a further six first-team players, causing the cancellation of Celtic's visit to Rugby Park on Saturday, 30 December 1972 then the home game with Morton on New Year's Day. In the meantime, Hibernian would beat Aberdeen 3-2 at Easter Road before enjoying an incredible 7-0 win at Tynecastle to join Celts at the top of the table, albeit having played two games more. Even third-placed Rangers were now in the title mix, one point behind the leaders having played an additional three games but due to host the Bhoys the following Saturday.

In those days Rangers claimed 1873 as their starting point, and they would open their Centenary Stand – basically the old covered enclosure fitted with benches – on Saturday, 6 January of this year with a win over the team who had been their fiercest rivals for the majority of that first century. The only goal of the first half came, controversially, via the spot, Pat McCluskey harshly penalised by Bothwell referee John Paterson midway through the half for a challenge on Alex MacDonald. Derek Parlane saw his kick saved by Evan Williams but reacted first to squeeze the ball home at the second attempt. Six minutes after the break, Celts found an equaliser, Dixie Deans' instinctive shot deflected past Peter McCloy by Dave Smith. Bizarrely for such a prolific striker, this was the only goal Dixie would score in Celtic's colours against Rangers. With Celts now in the ascendancy and Interim Manager Sean Fallon introducing Harry for McCluskey, they were caught by a sucker punch, Alfie Conn glancing a header past Williams in those final, agonising seconds to allow the Ibrox men to leapfrog their visitors into second place behind Hibernian. Eddie Turnbull's side had narrowly beaten East Fife 1-0 that afternoon, albeit that win had come at a horrific cost, as their outstanding full-back John Brownlie broke his leg.

The weekend then went from bad to worse for Celtic, as Lou Macari handed in a transfer request, his comments providing some insight to the reasons behind his desire to move.

"I just think it's a better, more decent life in England. Certainly, the money matters, but there's more to it than that. The whole atmosphere is different down there. It's not easy being a Celtic player. I don't go out much socially because you can run into stupid people who resent you for what you do for a living. It's too small up here. I want to go somewhere where I can leave my football behind me when I leave the club. Last night, after the Rangers match, well, it was difficult… I've had supporters ringing me to ask why I want away from Celtic. But I have nothing against them, they are a great club. I feel you have to make a move sometime and it's best to do it when you're on top. Take John Brownlie. He was worth £250,000 on Friday, but what happens to him if his leg doesn't mend properly? I hope it does, but…"

This was the first time I could recall any 'first-pick' Celtic player asking to leave the club. Many of the Lions had, of course, moved on since the summer of 1971, however, for most of those it was to prolong a career after they had dropped out of the first-team picture, whilst for others they had been sold after decisions made in the boardroom rather than being driven by the player. Sadly, there would be many more taking this path over the coming years, with traditional 'one-club men' becoming very much the exception to the rule.

Macari would be missing from the team for the next League match, against Dundee at Celtic Park on Saturday, 13 January 1973 He was replaced by Harry, whilst Danny McGrain came in for the injured Davie Hay at right-back and Bobby Murdoch for Pat McCluskey. Jock Stein made a welcome return to Paradise, the Boss given a huge ovation from the crowd as he took his seat in the stand before kick-off. The four previous meetings between the clubs that season had been highly dramatic, and this would be no exception, the returning Hood the best player on the pitch as he set up chance after chance for his teammates. It was Harry's cross which allowed Jimmy Johnstone to give Celtic the lead on 15 minutes, and he would do the same for Kenny Dalglish as the match entered its closing 10 minutes level at 1-1, Doug Houston's deflected effort on the half-hour having earlier restored parity for the Dens Park men. That winning goal would prove crucial as news filtered through that Hibernian had lost at Tannadice, enabling Celts to catch up with them on points. Rangers were now the leaders by one point, having played three games more.

The worst-kept secret in Scottish football was revealed five days later, Thursday, 18 January 1973, when Lou Macari became the first of the Quality Street Gang to leave Celtic for a big-money move south of the border. Despite travelling down to Anfield with Sean Fallon to have a look around the set-up at League leaders Liverpool, it was no real surprise when new Manchester United manager Tommy Docherty signed a £200,000 cheque to take the man he had capped whilst Scotland boss the previous year to Old Trafford. Whilst Macari had managed 58 goals in 110 appearances in the Hoops since making his debut at Somerset Park in August 1967, he had only really emerged as a regular fixture in the first team three years later, with around half of those goals and games achieved in the Double-winning season of 1971/72. Now, just eight months later, it appeared he was leaving the scene as quickly as he had arrived. What now for the *"Harry, Harry, Lou Macari,"* chant?

Life after Macari began ironically in his native Ayrshire, with a hard-fought 3-1 win at Somerset Park 48 hours later, Kenny Dalglish with a late double after Dixie Deans had cancelled out an early Johnny Graham opener. Jock Stein then used some of the transfer money to finally buy an international goalkeeper, Ally Hunter signed from Kilmarnock on Wednesday, 24 January 1973, for a fee thought to be in the region of £40,000. Hunter would make his debut three days later at Broomfield, a last-minute goal from Airdrieonians winger Kevin McCann ruining the occasion and putting another dent in Celtic's hopes of eight-in-a-row. Harry came closest to breaking the deadlock in the first half, his beautiful dipping volley beating Roddy McKenzie all ends up but crashing back off the crossbar. Dixie Deans then gave the Hoops the lead early in the second half, only for the hosts to equalise on the hour through debutant Billy Hulston, who you may recall was the striker signed by Clyde to replace Harry four years earlier. Within seconds, Deans had earned a penalty kick, but for once, Bobby Murdoch's aim was just a fraction out, his shot crashing off McKenzie's post to safety, as once again the woodwork came to his rescue. Celts would pay the price for that miss in the dying seconds, McCann's follow-up after a goalmouth scramble allowing the bottom-dog Diamonds to put one over on the champions. The final whistle triggered a series of unsavoury personal feuds as the teams left the field, as a second January League defeat for Celtic saw Rangers lead at the top now stretch to three points.

February brought the welcome return of Jock Stein to the dugout, following his recent health scare, together with another signing from the Macari war chest. The month opened with a comfortable 4-1 win over East Fife at Celtic Park as the quest for a third successive Scottish Cup triumph got underway. Harry moved onto the bench and would get the call on the hour to replace Tommy Callaghan, by which time Dixie Deans and Kenny Dalglish had helped themselves to a double apiece. Another £35,000 cheque saw left-winger Andy Lynch fulfil a Bhoyhood dream by joining from Hearts on Wednesday, 7 February 1973. He watched on from the Rugby Park stand that very evening as Celtic managed to play one of their three games in hand on Rangers. This is another one of those nights which I can remember so well despite the near five decades which have passed since. The main reason for that is that I was one of thousands of Celtic supporters who travelled to Ayrshire on a horrific night in the hope that we would witness Celtic's 6,000th League goal. It was by no means guaranteed, given that Stein's men required to score five against a team battling for survival, however, they would get within touching distance before the woodwork, yet again, played a part in denying a Hoops goal.

From my vantage point on the back wall of the old covered enclosure opposite the stand, I had a birds-eye view as Ally Hunter marked his early return to Kilmarnock by producing a series of tremendous saves. He would provide the platform for a rather flattering victory on the night, as goals from Kenny Dalglish and Jimmy Johnstone saw the Bhoys head down that narrow Rugby Park tunnel two goals to the good at the interval. The hosts had seen a valid-looking claim for offside dismissed as Celts took the lead, and they would be up in arms again within five minutes of the restart as Tommy Callaghan stroked home a third goal with the Killie defence having stopped on seeing a linesman's flag raised. Referee John Paterson again ignored the assistant's advice to award the goal, Kilmarnock's night going from bad to worse as Harry, a second-half replacement for Dixie Deans, set up Dalglish for his second of the match with seven minutes remaining. With only one goal now required to hit the 6,000 mark, the atmosphere inside the enclosure where the majority of the spectators were seeking refuge from the rain was lifted by several decibels. With two minutes to play, history was there for the taking, Celts awarded a late penalty kick after Johnstone was impeded in the box. Up stepped King Kenny to face Hunter's replacement, Jim Stewart, a hat-trick and a place in the record books then denied as his shot clattered off the crossbar and into the night air.

Andy Lynch replaced Harry on the bench as the circus rolled back to Celtic Park that weekend for the visit of Partick Thistle, the prospect of seeing the historic goal swelling the attendance to 32,000. The Jags fielded Lisbon Lion Stevie Chalmers plus three men who would later wear the Hoops, Alan Rough, Ronnie Glavin and Joe Craig. They took the lead through Bobby Lawrie 10 minutes before the break, on an afternoon where referee Ian Foote appeared to be making his own attempt at creating history by denying Celtic no fewer than five penalties, albeit given our recent record from the spot those were no guarantee of goals. Lynch replaced Bobby Lennox on the hour for his Celtic debut and was in pole position to witness the 6,000th goal, 11 minutes later, Bobby Murdoch firing home after Rough had blocked a Kenny Dalglish header. With the record now secured, the anxiety of the supporters then switched to winning the game and the vital two points. In the dying seconds, Tommy Callaghan looked to have done that as his shot beat the Thistle goalkeeper, 30,000 groans filling the Parkhead air as yet again the crossbar rather than the net stopped his effort, and another point slipped agonisingly away.

In midweek, there was another historic occasion which did not quite go to plan. A Scotland team featuring Kenny Dalglish and the recently departed Lou Macari took on England at Hampden in a match to celebrate the centenary of the SFA. It was a first match in charge of the national team for new Scotland manager, Willie Ormond, and my first live taste of a fixture I had followed for years on television and print. It was also the night English skipper Bobby Moore made it a century of caps, and he can rarely have enjoyed such an easy 90 minutes in the 99 which preceded this St Valentine's Massacre. A few months earlier, I had stood in the schoolboy enclosure in front of the main stand at Hampden and watched Celtic tear a terrific Dundee team apart in a League Cup quarter-final play-off. Tonight, ankle-deep in snow, the coldest I have ever felt at a football match, I had a worms-eye view from the same spot as the English attack of Mick Channon, Martin Chivers and Allan Clarke - all three appearing about 7' tall - helped themselves to goals in a 5-0 rout, something I thought I would never witness at Hampden. It was 3-0 within 15 minutes as the nightmare unfolded before my eyes. Scotland goalkeeper Bobby Clark had looked less than clever at several of the goals and would never play for his country again, leaving the door open for the new Celtic stopper, Ally Hunter, to receive his chance.

Three days later, Saturday, 17 February 1973, it was back to Celtic business as we headed for Methil and a League fixture with East Fife. We took up position immediately behind the goal, just as we had done 10 months earlier as Jock Stein's Class of '72 created a new Scottish record of seven successive titles. That would be the only comparison on an afternoon when the quest for an eighth flag could have been seriously derailed. The romp in the April sunshine would be replaced by a dark slog on a muddy Bayview for a match that will live long in the memory. Harry returned to the starting line-up as Jock Stein went with the following team.

Ally Hunter; Danny McGrain & Jimmy Quinn; Bobby Murdoch, Billy McNeill & George Connelly; Jimmy Johnstone, Dixie Deans, Kenny Dalglish, Harry Hood & Tommy Callaghan. Substitute; Bobby Lennox.

The frozen weather during the week had taken its toll on many of the other fixtures scheduled for that afternoon, amongst those Rangers home clash with struggling Arbroath. This meant that a Celtic victory would see them replace the Ibrox club at the top of the table, whilst still having a game in hand. All was going according to script at the interval, Celts ahead through a Dixie Deans strike midway through the first half, however, the second period would produce incredible drama from the kick-off. Within six minutes, the Fifers had turned the game around, a rather soft penalty award converted by Billy McPhee before Walter Borthwick gave the hosts the lead. Cue the fightback, as the champions battled back from the ropes. With 13 minutes remaining, their efforts looked to have paid off, as referee George Smith pointed to the spot for the second time. One of the pleasures I really miss from those days is being so close to the action behind the goals at such grounds as Bayview. We could almost see the whites of Bobby Murdoch's eyes as he placed the ball in the mud, his shot beating Ernie McGarr but yet again striking woodwork, just as he had done against Airdrieonians and Kenny Dalglish at Kilmarnock with Celtic's two previous penalties. There was an instant reprieve and sharp intake of breath as Smith indicated a retake for intrusion by one or two East Fife defenders. With Murdoch having recorded two successive misses, up stepped Harry to equalise for Celts…only for the bold McGarr to stick out a foot and keep it at 1-2. Another 10 minutes of desperate attacking play from the Hoops led to a third spot kick of the afternoon, four if you include that retake. This time Kenny Dalglish was the man entrusted to get the job done, his low shot heading for the corner before McGarr produced a tremendous save at his post. With three penalty attempts failing to produce an equaliser, we could be forgiven for filing this in the 'not our day' folder, however Stein's men were nothing if not resilient. As the clock headed for 90 minutes and excitement at fever pitch, a Tommy Callaghan corner was headed home by Deans to a sigh of joy and relief which would have been heard back in Glasgow.

The seven League games played so far in 1973 had produced just three Celtic wins, whilst two matches had been drawn and two lost. Hardly, the form of champions, enabling rivals Hibernian and Rangers to smell blood and create a genuine title race. Further to that record, Celtic had now missed with five successive attempts from the penalty spot, with three different players involved. There would be much work to be done if the holy grail of eight-in-a-row was to be realised.

Jock Stein made two changes from that remarkable draw at Methil for the tricky Scottish Cup-tie at Fir Park, Motherwell on Saturday, 24 February 1973. Davie Hay and Bobby Lennox came back in with Harry moving on to the bench and the injured Tommy Callaghan dropping out of the squad. Quite remarkably, this was the first time Celts had been drawn away from home in the competition since the quarter-final clash at Tynecastle all of seven years earlier.

On a beautiful but cold afternoon, Celtic would be up for the task from the off, Kenny Dalglish curling an opener past Keith MacRae within six minutes. There was a certain inevitably after the four spot kicks at Methil the previous weekend that we would be talking about these again today, and so it proved, Billy McNeill penalised for handball after 15 minutes. For once, though, this would result in a positive for Celts, Ally Hunter diving to his left to save in spectacular fashion from Peter Millar. This would prove the crucial moment in the tie. Dalglish and Dixie Deans had shared four goals in the defeat of East Fife at Celtic Park in the previous round, and they would combine brilliantly again, Kenny linking up with Danny McGrain to set his strike partner up for a five-minute double midway through the first half. And having saved a penalty so early in his Parkhead career, keeper Hunter now turned goal provider as his long clearance found Bobby Lennox running into the opposite box to lash the ball past MacRae for 4-0. Harry would join the fray with 15 minutes remaining to give man-of-the-match Davie Hay a rest on his return from injury. All round it had been a great day for the Celtic.

Brian McLaughlin replaced Harry on the bench for the midweek visit of a St Johnstone side now under new management, as Dumbarton boss Jackie Stewart succeeded Willie Ormond. The youngster came on for Jimmy Johnstone just after the hour with Celtic a Bobby Lennox goal ahead, and he would earn praise for his contribution as Davie Hay, Kenny Dalglish then Lennox again took the final score to 4-0 and brought

Jock Stein's men to within one point of the summit with a game in hand.

The weekend would bring a recall for Harry as Davie Hay found himself on the injured list once again following the win over St Johnstone. The visitors to Glasgow's east end on Saturday, 3 March 1973 were Aberdeen, a dress rehearsal for the Scottish Cup quarter-final tie due at the same venue later that month. Harry came closest to breaking the deadlock in a one-sided first half, his shot beating Scotland keeper Bobby Clark all ends up before crashing off his post. The match remained goalless for an hour until Dons centre-half Willie Young handled Jimmy Johnstone's netbound effort on the line. On the back of five successive failed attempts from the spot for Celtic, it would fall to Bobby Lennox to take his first-ever penalty in senior football and give the Bhoys the lead. With seven minutes remaining, Danny McGrain and Kenny Dalglish produced another example of the world-class talents they would become, the Quality Street graduates combining brilliantly for Dalglish to seal a 2-0 win.

The fickle nature of football was demonstrated again three nights later, as a Paul Wilson goal just before the interval gave Celts a 1-0 home victory over Morton, the two points secured by winning their game in hand over Rangers taking the Hoops back to the top of the League but insufficient to avoid the chorus of booing at the final whistle. And there was further frustration after the weekend clash at Tannadice ended 2-2, Bobby Lennox with a double as the dropped point meant that only goal difference now separated Celtic and the Ibrox men at the summit with just seven games remaining.

There was a break from League business on Saturday, 17 March 1973, quarter-final day in the Scottish Cup attracting 40,000 spectators to see a rematch of the 1970 final between Celtic and Aberdeen at Parkhead. The main character on the day would be referee R H Davidson of Airdrie, just as he had been on that dreadful day at Hampden. He would rule out a Jimmy Johnstone goal within the first minute, having initially awarded it, then add insult to injury by sending the winger off on the hour, having consulted with his linesman in front of the Jungle, a decision with sparked a hail of missiles to be launched in his direction. The St Patrick's Day stalemate would see the circus travel north for a midweek replay at a packed Pittodrie, with Celtic's hopes of back-to-back Doubles now seriously under threat on two fronts. However, yet again, when the chips were down, Jock Stein's men found a way to win. Having missed out on Saturday, Harry came in for Kenny Dalglish and he was involved in most of the game's key moments, hitting the post early on before going close with a spectacular, flying header. Then with just four minutes remaining, his corner kick found the flashing head of Billy McNeill to bring back memories of that wonderful winning goal in the final against Dunfermline Athletic in April 1965, the imperious Cesar rising above two Dons defenders to beat Bobby Clark and send Celtic through to the last four.

The stakes were high again as Jock Stein's men travelled to Tynecastle on Saturday,

24 March 1973, a venue where they had failed to win a League match since October 1968. As Celts had faced off with Aberdeen in the midweek cup replay, Rangers had taken advantage by beating Airdrieonians 6-2 at Broomfield, meaning that the Bhoys were once again playing catch-up at the top of the table. A superb early strike from Dixie Deans set Celtic up for another valuable two points, Bobby Lennox sealing the win on the hour following good work by Vic Davidson. Harry suffered a back injury and was replaced by Paul Wilson early in the second half.

Controversial referee Bobby Davidson was back at Celtic Park on the last day of March, as the Hoops entertained Falkirk, however, even the Airdrie official was powerless to stop a Celtic side from romping to a 4-0 victory, with Harry very much to the fore after the interval. Dixie Deans again opened the scoring, just before the half-hour, with Bobby Lennox successfully converting his second penalty kick of the month a few minutes later after Tom Young had pulled him down in the box. Just before the hour, the lightning-fast Lisbon Lion took advantage of an exquisite Harry defence-splitting pass to make it 3-0, and within five minutes it was four, Harry combining beautifully with Davie Hay before shooting past Ally Donaldson in the Bairns goal for his first strike in more than three months. With the points in the bag, he then made way for young Brian McLaughlin having picked up another knock.

April opened with a Tuesday evening rescheduled match at home to Motherwell, second-half goals from the deadly duo of Kenny Dalglish and Dixie Deans securing the two points which brought Celtic level at the summit with Rangers but now 11 goals better off than the Ibrox side, both teams now with four games remaining. Harry had enjoyed another fine match against the Steelmen, but he would then be struck by illness on the Saturday morning which ruled him out of the Scottish Cup semi-final with Dundee at Hampden later that day. Jimmy Johnstone was drafted into the squad and would play for the final 10 minutes but the match ended in a frustrating goalless draw in front of 53,000 spectators.

That set up an incredible seventh meeting of the sides that season the following midweek, the third of those to be played at Hampden. The 90 minutes in the replay would again fail to produce a goal, Celts requiring extra-time before a Jimmy Johnstone double either side of a Kenny Dalglish strike sent the Hoops into an eighth Scottish Cup final in nine seasons, a fourth against Rangers. Having recovered from illness, Harry made a late cameo appearance from the bench to replace the injured Dixie Deans.

Rangers had again taken advantage of Celtic's Scottish Cup commitments to play and win a League match, a solitary John Greig goal enough to take the points against his boyhood team at Tynecastle. Thus, as Celtic travelled to face St Johnstone at Muirton Park on Saturday, 14 April 1973, the Hoops were back in second place in the table, two points behind with a game in hand. With Dixie Deans failing to recover from injury, Jock Stein named the following men to maintain the push for the title.

Ally Hunter; Danny McGrain & Jim Brogan; Bobby Murdoch, Billy McNeill & George Connelly; Jimmy Johnstone, Harry Hood, Kenny Dalglish, Davie Hay & Tommy Callaghan. Substitute; Bobby Lennox.

On a ground where Celts had often struggled and would do so again many times in the future, this was one of those afternoons when Stein's machine clicked into place, Kenny Dalglish on hand to tap home Billy McNeill's header midway through the first half to ease the pressure on the travelling Hoops. The lead was doubled 10 minutes after the break, Jimmy Johnstone stealing in at the far post to convert a Tommy Callaghan cross and Dalglish sealed the points in the 66th minute, taking a Bobby Murdoch pass to beat Jim Donaldson at his near post. The only negative on the day was the late strike by Jim Pearson which finished the scoring at 3-1, the first goal Ally Hunter and his defence had conceded since the 2-2 draw at Tannadice in early March, a most un-Celtic-like sequence of seven clean sheets in a row. Hopefully, that failure to complete the eighth was not an omen. Back at Ibrox, Rangers beat Dundee United 2-1 on the same afternoon, Greig with a double as he maintained his one-man battle to steal Celtic's crown.

Wednesday, 18 April 1973 became the latest critical date in the titanic struggle for the 1972/73 Scottish League Championship. Jock Stein made one change to his Perth starting line-up for the visit of Dumbarton, Dixie Deans returning with Harry moving to the bench and Bobby Lennox dropping out. His selection would be totally vindicated as Deans netted a hat-trick, Tommy Callaghan and Kenny Dalglish making it a nap hand as the champions returned to the top of the table on goal difference. Jimmy Johnstone had again been at his mercurial best, withdrawn by Stein after 70 minutes at 4-0 having suffered an ankle injury, allowing Harry a late piece of the action. Now enjoying a 16-goal advantage over their Ibrox rivals, Celts now required only to match Rangers results in the final two fixtures to retain their title and extend their winning sequence to an unprecedented eight-in-a-row.

The title odds then finally tilted in Celtic's favour three days later, as Arbroath travelled to Parkhead whilst Rangers faced the tricky trip to Pittodrie. Harry retained his place at the expense of the injured Jimmy Johnstone, with Bobby Lennox returning to the bench. It would have been difficult to predict the outcome at the interval as Celts struggled against an Arbroath side who had come back from 3-1 down to snatch a point at Hampden earlier in the season then taken the Hoops all the way before succumbing to a late defeat at Gayfield just before Christmas. The sigh of relief from inside Celtic Park when Harry headed the vital breakthrough goal past Gordon Marshall from a Bobby Murdoch cross eight minutes into the second half would have been heard at Pittodrie, and we then had one of those incredible moments when the stadium erupts with nothing to justify that on the pitch, a thousand transistor radios advising that the Dons were now leading against Rangers. There was still much work to be done here, Harry and Tommy Callaghan switching flanks to great effect as goals from Davie Hay, Dixie Deans and Kenny Dalglish in the final 20 minutes had the champagne on ice. As things stood, only a Celtic defeat at Easter Road and a 20-goal swing in favour of Rangers on the final day would prevent eight-in-a-row. But with the celebrations in full flow, there was yet another twist in this extraordinary season. Back in January, Alfie Conn had turned one point into two with his last-minute headed winner against Celtic at Ibrox. He would now turn a defeat into a draw at Pittodrie in the final seconds, the point secured enough to halt the party at Parkhead. Crucially, Celtic would still have to avoid defeat in Leith to ensure that the flag would be flying above the Jungle in the summer. Easter Road was a notoriously difficult place to secure a result. This title race would go right to the wire.

Harry and Jimmy Johnstone would be the only players to report to Parkhead for treatment 48 hours later, with Malcolm Munro from *The Evening Times* providing some insight on Harry's recent struggles.

"One player who played an important part in the defeat of the Red Lichties, Harry Hood, will be trying harder than most to get into trim for the big one. Jock Stein tells me Harry lost 7lb in weight after a severe bout of flu recently. That's a lot of weight for any athlete to lose at one time, though I must say Hood's Saturday form didn't suggest any weakness at all, and he is a potent factor for his club when he goes all out."

What is it they say about football history repeating itself?

On Saturday, 17 April 1954, a Celtic team including that immortal half-back line of Evans, Stein and Peacock and a forward line which featured legends Willie Fernie, Sean Fallon, Charlie Tully and Neil Mochan, had travelled to Easter Road requiring a point to claim a first title win in 16 years. They had done so, following a 3-0 victory, thanks to a Mochan brace then a late strike from John Higgins. Fallon would then score the winning goal in a 2-1 win over Aberdeen in the Scottish Cup final seven days later, giving Jimmy McGrory's Celtic a first League and Cup double in 40 years, the only one achieved by the great man as either a player or manager in a wonderful career.

Seven days before the 1973 Scottish Cup final against Rangers, on Saturday, 28 April, Jock Stein, Sean Fallon and Neil Mochan would swap the Easter Road pitch for the dugout. Harry dropped to the bench beside them to accommodate Jimmy Johnstone as the following men sought to write another chapter into Celtic's illustrious history.

Ally Hunter; Danny McGrain & Jim Brogan; Bobby Murdoch, Billy McNeill & George Connelly; Jimmy Johnstone, Dixie Deans, Kenny Dalglish, Davie Hay & Tommy Callaghan. Substitute; Harry Hood.

Just as back in April 1954, there was a crowd of over 45,000 packed into the old Leith terraces, the vast majority hoping to see their Bhoys secure the title. Having witnessed five, six then seven-in-a-row being clinched, I was heartbroken to be told by my dad that the potential crushing at Easter Road meant that I would be listening to the match at home, rather than being part of one of the biggest Celtic travelling supports ever to attend a game. Sometimes it's rubbish being 12. That would not be a concern for Stein's men as they attacked down the famous slope, Billy McNeill almost adding to his collection of vital goals as his shot crashed back off Jim McArthur's crossbar within seven minutes of kick-off. The opening goal was merely delayed a further 15 minutes, Tommy Callaghan's angled drive blocked on the line by Derek Spalding only for Dixie Deans to gleefully hammer home the loose ball. Nerves inevitably would creep in, both on and off the park, as the two sides fought for that vital next goal. Ironically, perhaps, the mistake which made sure of Celtic's victory was down to two Hibernian defenders, McArthur and Des Bremner getting into a horrible tangle, allowing Kenny Dalglish an open goal for 2-0 with 20 minutes remaining.

Now the party could really get underway, both in Leith and Springburn, Deans putting the icing on the championship cake when he rose at the far post to head home Davie Hay's superb cross. The little striker was, perhaps appropriately, wearing the number eight shorts on the day, his double securing the title just as Neil Mochan's had done on the same ground back in 1954. At full-time, both men would embrace on the pitch as the players and management celebrated yet another unique achievement, in front of the massed ranks of the delirious Celtic support. The soundtrack for the party would be provided by the 40,000-plus Hoops fans who had witnessed history. The chants began to ring out from the vast terracing opposite the main stand, firstly an acknowledgement of the manager who had recovered from a health scare in January to maintain his record of winning the title in every season he had kicked off as Celtic manager.

"Jock Stein! Jock Stein!"

Then the chant of *"Eight in a row!"* resounded from all four sides of the stadium, as the green-and-white scarves and banners were raised in triumph.

As the celebrations continued, the man who had planned and delivered the Eight slipped quietly down the Easter Road tunnel, Jock Stein's focus already on the next challenge. Seven days from now, his men would face a wounded Rangers at Hampden as Celts attempted to secure the Scottish Cup for a third successive year for the first time in the club's history, whilst becoming the first side ever to win three consecutive League and Cup doubles.

Chapter 24

Harry's game

If Harry had been disappointed to remain on the bench as Celtic clinched an eighth successive League Championship at Easter Road, then no doubt he would have been heartbroken to miss out completely on the Scottish Cup final against Rangers, seven days later, Jock Stein going with the same line-up but selecting Bobby Lennox as his substitute on this occasion.

With a Treble Double up for grabs, Saturday, 5 May 1973 would sadly not be Celtic's day, a miskick from the late Tom Forsyth on the hour trundling barely over the line for Rangers' winner, his first-ever goal for the club. Earlier, the match had swung one way then the other. Kenny Dalglish had scored a terrific opener for the Bhoys midway through the first half, his third cup final goal, following great work from Dixie Deans. Goals either side of the interval from Derek Parlane and Alfie Conn then saw the Ibrox club lead briefly before John Greig dived full-length to deny Deans the cup final goal he deserved, the Ibrox skipper punching the ball clear on the line. The bizarre rules in place at that time meant that the only punishment for such a blatant act of cheating by Greig was the award of a penalty kick to Celtic, a penalty kick which could quite easily be missed! Thankfully, Scotland's new Player of the Year, George Connelly, stepped up to take the most exquisite spot kick, sending Peter McCloy for chips as the ball nestled sweetly in the net for his second Scottish Cup final goal in four seasons against the same opposition. Within 10 minutes, however, Forsyth would have his moment in the sun as the scoring ended at 3-2 before 122,714 spectators, the last six-figure crowd to attend a game in Scotland.

The two Glasgow rivals were paired once again as the 1973/74 season kicked off with the League Cup sections, Arbroath and Falkirk the unfortunate makeweights in the group. Harry would be in midfield with new £50,000 signing Steve Murray from Aberdeen as an unfamiliar looking Celtic attack with Brian McLaughlin and Andy Lynch on the flanks beat the Red Lichties 2-1 on Saturday, 11 August 1973, thanks to first half goals from Lynch and Bobby Lennox. Harry was replaced by Dixie Deans for the second half after injuring his finger, although an X-ray would show nothing to be broken. This was the day on which new rules were introduced allowing clubs to make two substitutions during a match. The roles would be reversed in midweek as Harry came off the bench following a sickening first-half clash at Brockville involving John Young and Dixie Deans which left the Celt with a fractured jaw. Danny McGrain had suffered a fractured skull at the same venue just the previous year. Second-half strikes from Davie Hay and Bobby Lennox, the latter from the spot, secured a comfortable 2-0 win for Celtic.

Saturday, 18 August 1973 saw the first meeting of Celtic and Rangers since the cup final three months earlier. The Ibrox club were going for an unprecedented third consecutive victory over a Jock Stein Celtic team as they welcomed them to Govan for the first of two clashes which would decide the winner of their league Cup section. The teams lined up as follows before 63,000 spectators.

RANGERS:

Peter McCloy; Sandy Jardine & Willie Mathieson; John Greig, Derek Johnstone & Alex MacDonald; Tommy McLean, Tom Forsyth, Derek Parlane, Alfie Conn & Quinton Young. Substitutes; Ally Scott & Dave Smith.

CELTIC:

Ally Hunter; Danny McGrain & Jim Brogan; Steve Murray, Billy McNeill & George Connelly; Jimmy Johnstone, Brian McLaughlin, Kenny Dalglish, Davie Hay & Bobby Lennox. Substitutes; Tommy Callaghan & Harry Hood.

Rangers created the better chances in a goalless first half, but the game changed with the introduction of Harry and Tommy Callaghan for Kenny Dalglish and Brian McLaughlin either side of the hour mark. Harry's number 13 shorts proved unlucky for the hosts, as two of his interventions won the game. With eight minutes remaining, he turned Willie Mathieson and Dave Smith inside out before setting Bobby Lennox up for his customary goal against Rangers, then, within five minutes, it was 2-0, Lennox this time returning the favour to leave Harry with a clear shot at goal for his first strike of the season, after a lightning counterattack. A last-minute own goal from Billy McNeill then ended the scoring at 2-1 as Celts took the initiative in the group, albeit unlike previous seasons, the two top clubs from each section would qualify in a dreadfully unexciting format. This would be significant for both Harry and Celtic later in the year.

Harry reverted to the traditional number 9 shorts in midweek as an early Bobby Lennox double in the home tie with Falkirk secured qualification with two matches remaining. The return match with Rangers, though, on Saturday, 25 August 1973 would be a different matter. Harry dropped to the bench as Kenny Dalglish regained his starting slot, Celts totally dominating the first half but heading down the Parkhead tunnel with only a Lennox goal to show for that. The Ayrshire Lion had another goal disallowed in controversial circumstances, whilst Dalglish struck the post. With a Celtic victory looking inevitable, the game turned on its head in a five-minute spell early in the second half, a volley from Alex MacDonald and a dubious

Derek Parlane strike, which brought Jock Stein to the touchline to calm his players down, giving the visitors an unlikely lead. Moments later, Jimmy Johnstone reacted to MacDonald's crude challenge, the winger immediately dismissed by Fife referee J R P Gordon as Celts were left to play the remaining 30 minutes with 10 men. Jock Stein introduced Harry for young Brian McLaughlin in a final attempt to save the match, however, a late solo effort from Alfie Conn sealed the visitors first win at Celtic Park since September 1968.

The section was rounded off with a 3-1 victory over Arbroath at Gayfield on Wednesday, 29 August 1973, Harry returning and young Highlander Roddie MacDonald making his Celtic debut as goals from Kenny Dalglish, Bobby Lennox and Paul Wilson secured the points. As one new Celt joined the ranks, those present would be witnessing another stage in the break-up of the Lisbon Lions. We would not know it that day, however, this would turn out to be the last appearance in his beloved Hoops for the incomparable Bobby Murdoch, put forward by many observers as the finest player in Celtic's greatest-ever team. Praise really does not come any higher than that. Steve Murray had been the preferred right-half since arriving from Aberdeen in May, and that would continue. Bobby had played as The Eight was secured at Easter Road in April then in the Scottish Cup final the following Saturday, and earlier in the year, he had scored Celtic's 6,000th League goal against Partick Thistle at Parkhead. That would now prove to be his 110th and final strike for the club. After 507 appearances for his Bhoyhood team, stretching back 11 years to his debut against Hearts in August 1962, two days before he turned 18, the much-revered Murdoch would sadly find himself surplus to requirements at Celtic Park.

The campaign to win an unprecedented ninth successive League title kicked off in Dunfermline three days later, on Saturday, 1 September 1973, Jock Stein selecting the following team against the newly-promoted Pars.

Ally Hunter; Danny McGrain & Jim Brogan; Steve Murray, Billy McNeill & George Connelly; Brian McLaughlin, Harry Hood, Kenny Dalglish, Davie Hay & Bobby Lennox. Substitutes; Tommy Callaghan & Paul Wilson.

The main talking point was the inclusion of dynamic midfielder Davie Hay, who had just been placed on the transfer list at his own request, Tommy Docherty amongst his alleged list of suitors, eight short months after he had lured Lou Macari to Manchester United.

I'm not sure why we were not in Fife that day, a venue I had yet to attend despite ticking off most of the others in the top Division, however, I do clearly recall watching the highlights that night on our new colour television. Harry opened the scoring for Celts after 20 minutes, the game heading towards that narrow Hoops victory before an unexpected 'goalfest' in the final 10 minutes. Alex Kinninmonth briefly brought the hosts level, only for substitute Paul Wilson, barely 60 seconds after replacing Brian McLaughlin, to restore the lead with his first kick of the ball, getting on the end of Harry's cross to beat John Arrol. In the final moments, there was further drama. Under pressure from Steve Murray, future Dunfermline Athletic manager Jim Leishman conceded an own goal to make it 3-1, before Jackie Sinclair beat Ally Hunter to pull another one back for the hosts with literally the last kick of the ball.

The following Saturday is another I remember well, albeit for the saddest of reasons. The other promoted side, Clyde, unbeaten under the new management of Stan Anderson - Harry's old teammate - were the visitors to Celtic Park as the champions unfurled their eighth successive League flag. The Jungle flagpoles all displayed those distinctive white-and-green flags - a quite wonderful sight to behold - and all of the players wore the number eight on their shorts to mark the occasion. Jock Stein again went with the team who had started at Dunfermline, the only change being Jimmy Johnstone for Tommy Callaghan on the bench beside Paul Wilson. Eight was indeed the magic number, as by the eighth minute Celts were already two goals ahead through a Bobby Lennox penalty and a superb Kenny Dalglish header. Tragically, the party atmosphere was crushed along with the ligaments in poor Brian McLaughlin's knee, as a quite disgraceful challenge from Clyde defender Willie McVie ended his afternoon and effectively his career on the half hour. Jimmy Johnstone entered the fray in time to see his old pal Lennox complete a hat-trick, whilst Danny McGrain would score the first of his impressive (Sorry, Danny!) catalogue of goals on the day he lined up against his namesake and cousin.

Jinky would replace Brian McLaughlin in the only change to the Celtic team for the midweek trip to Motherwell in the first leg of the League Cup second round. He would set up Harry for the opening goal with a beautiful back-heeled pass midway through the first half, Steve Murray opening his Celtic account with a second just before the interval. John Goldthorpe would be involved in the main talking points after the break, the Motherwell striker fortunate to remain on the pitch after a late challenge on Hoops keeper Ally Hunter within seconds of the restart, the irony not lost on those present as he then kept the Steelmen in the tie with a goal a few minutes later. Still, it would be advantage Celtic for the second leg.

Bobby Lennox had limped off Fir Park in the first half and he would miss out as Celtic made a second visit of the season to Ibrox on Saturday, 15 September 1973, this time on League duty. Paul Wilson replaced the Celtic talisman in the only change to the starting line-up, with Pat McCluskey coming in from the cold to take a seat on the bench. Jimmy Johnstone had been cast as the villain in some quarters following his ordering off in the previous clash of the clubs three weeks earlier, however, once again he would prove the matchwinner, his header from Davie Hay's cross with 15 minutes remaining being the only goal of the game. Incredibly, it was the fifth goal the little winger had scored at Ibrox, the third with his head. On a day when regular forwards Brian McLaughlin, Bobby Lennox and fractured jaw victim Dixie Deans were sitting in the stand, forcing a clearly unfit Kenny Dalglish to play his part on the pitch, it would no doubt be a happy Jock Stein who contemplated that 1-0 victory later that evening. This was the day that Bobby Murdoch was handed a free transfer by Celtic, presumably to accept the offer made by Jack Charlton, manager at English Second Division side Middlesbrough. Bobby would then go on to make himself a hero to a whole new generation of football fans in the industrial north-east of England, future Scotland captain Graeme Souness one of the youngsters to learn his trade under the great man. This meant that from the team who lined up in the Hoops in the heat of Lisbon six years earlier, only Billy McNeill, Jimmy Johnstone and Bobby Lennox now remained.

Jock Stein's Class of '73 would commence their quest to emulate the Lions in Turku, in south-western Finland, four nights later, Wednesday, 19 September. Three years earlier, Harry had bagged a hat-trick as the current Finnish champions KPV Kokkola were beaten 14-0 on aggregate at the same stage, still a record European victory for Celtic. Harry would be on target again in the 6-1 first-leg win over Turun Palloseura, putting Celts 2-1 up midway through the first half before making way for returning fractured jaw victim Dixie Deans on the hour. Tommy Callaghan had opened the scoring in the first minute and completed his double just before the end. Jimmy Johnstone, with a superb curving shot, substitute Deans with a trademark diving header and George Connelly from a twice-taken penalty were the other yellow-clad Celts on the scoresheet, whilst the hosts would enjoy five minutes of parity after their own spot kick was converted by Teuvo Andalmin, following a Danny McGrain handball.

With five Celts in the Scotland team due to play Czechoslovakia in a vital World Cup qualifying match the following midweek, the scheduled League fixture with Morton that Saturday was postponed. I was fortunate enough to be taken to Hampden by my brother to join 96,000 fans on what would be an era-defining evening. The quintet of Bhoys all started and played their part in a memorable 2-1 victory, which secured a first place in the finals for 16 years, the first of my 12-year-old lifetime. Only negative note was the loss of the Czech goal by Ally Hunter, something I felt he never truly recovered from, having been our best shotstopper since Ronnie Simpson. Ivo Viktor was the man beaten by the late Jim Holton then Joe Jordan, who had earlier replaced Kenny Dalglish. The great Czech keeper had been at the opposite end of the pitch to 'Faither' during Celtic's epic clashes with Dukla Prague in 1967.

All five Scottish heroes came back to earth with a bump three days later, Saturday, 29 September 1973, as the Hoops lost 2-1 at Muirton, so often a problematic venue for Celtic. Dixie Deans had given Celts the perfect start, scoring within two minutes after Steve Murray had cleverly headed Harry's cross back from the byeline, only for a lack of communication between Ally Hunter and Jim Brogan to allow John Muir to equalise for St Johnstone three minutes later. Harry suffered a back injury and was replaced at the interval by Tommy Callaghan. The final goal action was reserved for the closing 10 minutes, following a lethargic second-half display by the champions, Jim Pearson heading past Hunter from John Lambie's cross before Deans had a second goal ruled out by the referee. Meanwhile, 60 miles south of Perth, Rab Prentice had continued his excellent start to the season after his release from Celtic by scoring as Hearts went top of the table following a 3-0 victory over Rangers at Ibrox.

Harry would not be risked for the midweek dead rubber against Finnish champions TPS at Parkhead. With Celtic leading 2-0 at the interval through goals from Dixie Deans and Jimmy Johnstone, Jock Stein took the opportunity to hand Jackie McNamara a first-team debut, the youngster replacing Kenny Dalglish. Jinky would add a superb solo third early in the second half as the Bhoys cruised through to the next round of the European Cup 9-1 on aggregate. Harry's disappointing run of illness and injury continued as he and Davie Hay developed flu symptoms, Harry fit enough only for the reserve fixture at Fir Park on the Friday night, scoring in the second-string's 2-0 win. He would then sit out the first part of the home double-header with Ian St John's Motherwell the next afternoon, late goals from Deans against his old team and Paul Wilson securing a 2-0 League win. Harry would replace Wilson from the bench in midweek, as John Goldthorpe's first-half goal levelled the League Cup second round aggregate score at 2-2. With 20 minutes to play, Harry was brought down for a penalty, Motherwell keeper Keith MacRae brilliantly saving George Connelly's spot kick to take the tie to a third match, as Dundee had done at the quarter-final stage the previous season.

Saturday, 13 October 1973 would be a strange day in the career of Harry at Celtic Park. As rumours abounded of his inclusion in a transfer package proposed to Dundee to secure the signing of striker John Duncan, he replaced the suspended Jimmy Johnstone and turned in a man-of-the-match display at Dens Park against his suggested new employers, setting up the only goal of the game for Tommy Callaghan in the third minute. In the Dundee ranks, Harry's old Celtic teammate Tommy Gemmell rolled back the years with an excellent performance in central defence, the Lisbon Lion now skipper at Dens Park following his move from Nottingham Forest via Miami Toros three months earlier. I recall that game well, for the strangest of reasons. Standing at the Provost Road end of the ground, we had to endure the constant rants of a fellow supporter for the 85 minutes which he managed to witness. Problem was, he had arrived after TC's goal had been scored at the far end and, having had one or two drinks, he only discovered that Celtic had actually won the match rather than drawn after letting rip with his final volley of insults at the full-time whistle! I suspect my memory of that afternoon will be better than his.

Shearer Borthwick was singing the praises of Harry in his Monday column for *The Evening Times*.

"One of the highlights was the display of Harry Hood of Celtic, especially in the first half, and if there is any question of a player-exchange deal in the offing then surely Harry is not to be one of the men involved. He showed that he is still one of the most attractive, useful and intelligent forwards in the game and he was the mainspring of

the Celtic attack. He threw over a perfect ball right into the path of Tommy Callaghan for the big chap to leather the ball into the net after only three minutes."

It was back to Celtic Park the following weekend for one of my favourite fixtures of that era, the Battle of the Greens with Hibernian. Jock Stein brought back top scorer Bobby Lennox after a seven-game absence as he sought to keep the pressure on League-leaders Hearts, ahead of the imminent visit to Tynecastle. Celtic lined up as follows.

Ally Hunter; Danny McGrain & Jim Brogan; Steve Murray, Billy McNeill & George Connelly; Harry Hood, Kenny Dalglish, Bobby Lennox, Davie Hay & Tommy Callaghan. Substitutes; Dixie Deans & Pat McCluskey.

The two teams served up a feast of football for the 34,000 hardy supporters who braved a constant downpour. Celts suffered a blow just before the interval as skipper Billy McNeill was helped from the pitch following an accidental collision with goalkeeper Ally Hunter. Stein brought Pat McCluskey on to play in midfield, with Davie Hay going back to partner his good friend George Connelly in central defence. When the breakthrough came on the hour it went the way of the visitors, and in controversial fashion. Arthur Duncan looked to all the world offside as he received the ball on the main stand side, however, as the home players stopped in anticipation of a flag which would not come, the lightning-fast winger made ground before picking out Alan Gordon with a perfect pass, the blond striker adding yet another to his collection of goals scored against Celtic to put Hibernian one up. With 20 minutes remaining, the Hoops finally fashioned an equaliser, Kenny Dalglish's sublime chipped pass finding Pat McCluskey charging into the Hibs penalty box. The substitute's finish was unerring, the net bulging behind Jim McArthur as another crucial point was added to the Celtic tally.

McCluskey would remain in the team in the skipper's continued absence for the midweek European tie at home to Danish champions Vejle. On his return from suspension, Jimmy Johnstone was given a rare opportunity to lead out the side after a decade in the Hoops, Billy McNeill failing to recover from his chest injury. The Danes had caused the major sensation of the first round by holding French champions Nantes 2-2 at home before following in the footsteps of giants by winning in the Stade Marcel Saupin, thanks to a second-half strike from Knud Norregaard. On one of the most frustrating European nights that I can ever recall, they very nearly added a win in Glasgow to that record, only Ally Hunter's legs preventing Jorgen Markussen from giving Vejle an early lead. As Celtic toiled to break down the amateurs' defence, Jock Stein changed his formation several times then eventually his personnel, Paul Wilson replacing Harry on the hour, however, a combination of bad luck, poor finishing and great goalkeeping from Niels Wodskou would see the players leave the field to a chorus of derision after a disappointing goalless draw, all to play for now in the Jutland return in a fortnight's time.

The performance against Vejle had hardly been the ideal preparation for the top of the table clash with Hearts at Tynecastle three days later, with the critics piling the pressure on with the usual nonsense regarding burst bubbles etc. This is another of those matches which I can recall, albeit unlike midweek, for all the right reasons. Teenage Highlander Roddie MacDonald was given a League debut, thrown in at the proverbial deep end by Jock Stein as Billy McNeill again missed out following that accidental clash against Hibernian, as did both Harry and Bobby Lennox. MacDonald had been a promising striker at Brora Rangers under former Celt, Sammy Wilson, the 'Hampden in the Sun' goal hero then converting him to a central defender, before recommending the player to his old Parkhead skipper Stein. After one League Cup tie at Arbroath, Roddie would now face a different test entirely against a free-scoring Hearts attack which included former Airdrieonians striker Drew Busby, Scotland's top marksman Donald Ford and the in-form ex-Celtic winger, Rab Prentice.

When the going gets tough, well, you know the rest. Written off in so many quarters, and minus their inspirational skipper, Celtic came out of the blocks like the champions they are against the would-be contenders. George Connelly beat Hearts keeper Kenny Garland with a long-range rocket within seven minutes to open the scoring, Kenny Dalglish adding a double to finish the match as a contest before the interval. Ford would get his goal in the second half, but the destination of the points was never in doubt, Celtic reclaiming leadership of the League table by a solitary goal, whilst still having that postponed Morton game in hand. It was a huge result in the context of the season.

There was no time to reflect on that win as Celtic faced the possibility of two League Cup ties in three days in midweek. Monday, 29 October 1973 saw Motherwell return to Celtic Park for the third time that month, Billy McNeill having guessed the coin toss correctly as he had in Lisbon four years earlier, albeit this time only home advantage was at stake. The Hoops legend would once again be missing through injury for the second-round play-off, MacDonald again given the nod, if you pardon the pun. Another exciting clash went right to the wire, Jimmy Johnstone grabbing the fifth and winning goal with just 15 seconds remaining, Motherwell's defenders protesting furiously that he was offside. The visitors had twice recovered from a goal down following strikes either side of the interval by Steve Murray and Dixie Deans, before Jinky's last-gasp finish set up a quarter-final clash with Aberdeen.

The first leg took place at Celtic Park just 48 hours after the victory over Motherwell. Back into the side came Billy McNeill, Harry and Davie Hay, with Roddie MacDonald, Jimmy Johnstone and Tommy Callaghan dropping out. Celts were rocked when Drew Jarvie gave the Dons the lead in the third minute, before a quickfire double from Kenny Dalglish had the Hoops back in front within the opening quarter, a lead they held until the break. Jarvie completed his double 10 minutes into the second half, but within seconds, Pat McCluskey again came to Celtic's rescue, as he had against

Hibernian, this time cracking home a wonderful drive from outside the box which flew past Bobby Clark for 3-2.

The series of six games in 14 days continued with a 4-2 win over East Fife at Celtic Park on Saturday, 3 November 1973. The scoreline is slightly misleading, Celts four goals clear and coasting before easing off in the final 10 minutes and paying the price as the Methil outfit grabbed two consolation strikes. The match was finished as a contest in the opening quarter, by which time Dixie Deans and Kenny Dalglish had continued their deadly partnership by putting Celtic 2-0 up. Deans then headed his second with 20 minutes remaining, allowing Jock Stein to replace Dalglish and Jim Brogan with Tommy Callaghan and Andy Lynch. The former Hearts winger's first contribution was to set up Harry for Celtic's fourth, before a late rally from the Fifers put a slightly different complexion on the final score.

On the Monday, the Celtic party travelled to eastern Jutland for the return European tie with Vejle the following night. There was a huge scare within 14 seconds of the kick-off when a George Connelly error allowed Jorgen Markussen in to score for the hosts, only for the Swedish referee to rule it out for offside. Jock Stein shuffled his team again, bringing back Bobby Lennox and Davie Hay whilst Jimmy Johnstone and Harry dropped to the bench. Yet again his selection would be vindicated, midfield powerhouse Hay having a goal harshly disallowed for offside before the veteran hitman Lennox pounced on a mistake in the Danish defence to score what would prove to be the only goal of the tie. Whilst Celtic had been anything but convincing over the two legs, in knockout football only one thing matters, qualification, and a place in the quarter final of European competition had been secured for the seventh time in nine seasons under Stein. Other contemporary giants had not been so fortunate. Last season's beaten finalists, Juventus, had been eliminated by East German champions Dynamo Dresden in the opening round, and they would now be joined on the sidelines by holders and three-time winners Ajax, beaten in extra-time by CSKA in Sofia. Ujpest Dosza, Celtic's conquerors from 12 months earlier, knocked out the great Eusebio and Benfica in Budapest, whilst Liverpool suffered home and away defeats to Red Star Belgrade.

Next up domestically was a tricky trip down to Somerset Park four days later, Saturday, 10 November 1973, to face an Ayr United side minus the injured Johnny Doyle but featuring future Celt Joe Filippi in defence and former Ibrox strikers Alex Ferguson and George McLean up front. Both had been made scapegoats for cup defeats at Rangers, McLean following the shock Scottish Cup exit at Berwick in 1967 and Ferguson for his part in the 4-0 humiliation by Celtic in the final two years later. Celtic's first three scorers at Hampden that day - Billy McNeill, Bobby Lennox and George Connelly – all lined up in the Hoops, whilst Tommy Callaghan came into midfield in place of leg strain victim Davie Hay as Harry remained on the bench and Jimmy Johnstone on the sidelines. The match was settled by a disputed Kenny Dalglish goal four minutes before the interval, the home defenders claiming in vain for offside as the Scotland striker skilfully controlled a Dixie Deans head flick to beat Ally McLean in the Ayr goal.

The next week would prove to be one of the more bizarre periods of this or any other season. Harry was one of several Celts not involved in midweek international duty who played against Highland League outfit Inverness Thistle on the Monday, Hood impressing enough to return to the first team for Saturday's visit of Partick Thistle. Davie Hay would have been involved in the SFA Centenary match against West Germany at Hampden, a game I attended, however, the transfer speculation surrounding one of Celtic's prized assets had reached fever pitch, Tommy Docherty at Manchester United, Don Revie across the Pennines at Leeds and Bill Nicholson at Tottenham Hotspur all vying for his signature. George Connelly did play at Hampden, however, he then failed to appear for training at Celtic Park on the Friday, sadly not for the first or last time. And finally, Jimmy Johnstone would again be missing, rumours of problems behind the scenes refusing to go away, despite his absence being attributed to a mystery illness. As with the build-up to the vital fixture at Tynecastle the previous month, and combined with a couple of poor displays, it did little to inspire confidence within the Celtic support.

So, of course, on Saturday, 17 November 1973, this cobbled-together team wearing the Hoops would go out and destroy a strong Partick Thistle line-up by 7-0. Dixie Deans was the star of the show with a Scottish post-war scoring record of six goals, the last four of those set up by Harry, who hadn't featured for a fortnight but now turned in a display described by *Evening Times* reporter Jim Blair as "one of his best-ever games in a Celtic jersey." Deans, in turn, laid on a goal for Bobby Lennox, as the great McGrory looked on from the stand. In that same Parkhead arena some 45 years earlier, Jimmy had achieved the all-time record, netting eight of Celtic's nine goals against Dunfermline Athletic. He would admit later to believing that record would go, as Deans actually contrived to pass up several other opportunities. A number of players had scored five in one game, Lennox himself and Stevie Chalmers incredibly doing it in the same match - a 10-0 victory over Hamilton Academical – whilst Neil Mochan and Bertie Auld had both managed it in different games at the same ground, Broomfield against Airdrieonians, however, Deans would add the post-war scoring record to his Scottish Cup final hat-trick of the previous year. As an aside, that Partick Thistle team included no fewer than four players who would later play for Celtic, Alan Rough, Ronnie Glavin, Johnny Gibson and Joe Craig, whilst on their left-wing was Bobby Houston, a huge Hoops supporter and a lovely man I would have the pleasure of getting to know well many years later, being the brother of my friend and neighbour.

Whilst Dixie was setting Parkhead alight, Hearts were going down to a 3-1 defeat at Pittodrie, which meant that both they and Aberdeen were now three points behind Celtic at the top of the table. The Dons were next up for Celtic, Davie Hay and George Connelly still missing for the midweek trip to the Granite City, as Celts defended their 3-2 lead in the League Cup quarter-final, Jimmy Johnstone listed as a substitute. The worsening situation in the country had led to the declaration of a state of emergency, with 1.45pm kick-offs in midweek to avoid the use of floodlighting during the ongoing fuel shortages. Six-shooter Dixie Deans experienced the fluctuating fortunes of football as he hobbled from the pitch injured after just 20 minutes, Jinky returning to the fold, as a disciplined performance saw Celts achieve a 0-0 draw and a place in the last four of the competition for the 10th successive year.

League duty continued on the road three days later, Saturday, 24 November 1973, with a visit to Boghead to face Dumbarton, their ex-Celts John Cushley and Willie Wallace in the usual places, whilst a young Colin McAdam was on the bench. On a muddy surface, the power of Pat McCluskey and the finesse of Kenny Dalglish would prove the difference. Dalglish opened the scoring in the 10th minute after good work from Tommy Callaghan, and a similar period had elapsed in the second half when the King was barged in the box by Sons defender Denis Ruddy, Bobby Lennox making his usual expert job of the conversion to end the scoring at 2-0.

December brought heavy snowfall to most parts of Scotland, Celtic's match at Arbroath the only top-flight fixture to survive on the first day of the month. Kenny Dalglish was again the main man, beating his former teammate Gordon Marshall with some style to set the Hoops on their way within the opening five minutes. The Bhoys enjoyed the vast majority of possession, however, with 15 minutes to play, they were made to pay for their failure to add a second goal, Eric Sellars running in to meet Andy Penman's free-kick and beat Ally Hunter. In danger of dropping a vital point, or worse, the champions were rescued in the closing minutes as Paul Wilson combined well with Jimmy Johnstone before firing past Marshall for 2-1, sending the Hoops five points clear of Hearts at the top of the table.

Hampden was the venue in midweek, for the first major semi-final meeting of Celtic and Rangers in my lifetime, a place in the League Cup final against Davie White's Dundee at stake. Jock Stein had played his cards close to his chest and when the line-up was announced there was a return for Davie Hay for the first time in a month, with another two Celts who had been out of favour - George Connelly and Jimmy Johnstone - making up the substitutes' bench. Dixie Deans was again missing with a back injury, Paul Wilson retaining his place and leading the line as the following teams lined up.

RANGERS:

Peter McCloy; Sandy Jardine & Willie Mathieson; John Greig, Colin Jackson & Doug Houston; Tommy McLean, Tom Forsyth, Derek Parlane, Alfie Conn & Alex MacDonald. Substitutes; Derek Johnstone & Dave Smith.

CELTIC:

Ally Hunter; Danny McGrain & Jim Brogan; Steve Murray, Billy McNeill & Pat McCluskey; Harry Hood, Davie Hay, Paul Wilson, Tommy Callaghan & Kenny Dalglish. Substitutes; Jimmy Johnstone & George Connelly.

The match would prove to be a personal triumph and a landmark in Harry's wonderful career. The man who ironically had been linked with a move to Dundee just weeks earlier would add another goal against Rangers to his collection as he gave Celts the lead 10 minutes before the break, Harry perfectly positioned to head past Peter McCloy after Kenny Dalglish had seen his first attempt blocked by Willie Mathieson on the line. That scourge of Celtic, Alex MacDonald, then levelled things before the break when his cross-shot deceived Ally Hunter, like the Czech goal at the same venue perhaps not one that the Celtic keeper would enjoy watching again. The Harry Hood Show would then come to life in the second half, as the Hoops battled against the elements to destroy Rangers and win through to a 10th consecutive League Cup final, before 55,000 spectators. Ten minutes after the restart, Harry's striker's instinct again put him in the right position to beat McCloy following Billy McNeill's back post header, and with 17 minutes remaining, he strode on to a sublime Dalglish pass to complete his hat-trick. Seconds later, Harry hit another marvellous effort past the Rangers keeper, only for referee Alistair McKenzie to incredibly rule it out for offside, a ridiculous call which angers me to this day. Thus, Harry was cruelly deprived of the honour of being the only Celt ever to score four goals in this fixture.

He would still join a select band.

The Mighty Jimmy Quinn was the first to score a hat-trick against Rangers in a competitive fixture. He managed it in two cup finals, the British League Cup final of April 1902 at Cathkin then the first Scottish Cup final at the current Hampden, two years later. The great man then achieved a third treble with all three goals in the New Year's Day fixture of 1912 at Celtic Park. Malcolm MacDonald was next, with three in Celtic's 6-2 home League victory in September 1938. Post-war, the McPhail brothers would both do it in Hampden finals in the same decade, John in front of Danny Kaye in the Glasgow Charity Cup final of 1950 and Billy as Seven Passed Niven in the October sunshine, seven years later. And two of Harry's contemporaries had also got in on the act, Stevie Chalmers bringing in the New Year with a Treble in the foggy dew of Paradise in 1966, whilst his partner-in-crime Bobby Lennox would match that feat at Ibrox in the Glasgow Cup that summer, as the quest for the Quintuple got underway.

But if one record was stolen from Harry with the disallowed fourth, then happily one will remain with him forever. In the four decades which followed before the liquidation of the Ibrox club in 2012, no Celtic player would manage to repeat Harry's hat-trick.

Not Dixie or Kenny in the remainder of the seventies. Not Nicholas, McGarvey, McClair or McAvennie, those marvellous Celtic strikers of a decade later. Nor any of the Three Amigos who briefly graced Paradise as the 20th century drew to a close.

Not even the Terrible Trio who made Celts the dominant force in the new Millennium under Martin O'Neill, The King of Kings Henrik, the Evil Genius Sutton or Big Bad John.

No, that record is one for the Hood family to treasure for all time.

Last word to the man himself, as quoted in *The Celtic View* after the game. Modesty personified.

"It's not every day you score three goals – especially against Rangers in a cup-tie. It was fantastic. It was an even bigger thrill to be in the team at all. With George Connelly, David Hay, Dixie Deans and Bobby Lennox back in the reckoning I wasn't too sure about keeping my place. That's how tough it is at Parkhead. The competition for first-team spots is really fierce. The hat-trick wasn't too important – beating Rangers and qualifying for the League Cup final was the thing that mattered."

Chapter 25

Celts storm back after the League Cup final from Hell

Hat-trick hero Harry Hood started where he had left off in midweek, as an unchanged Celtic team faced Dundee United three days later, Saturday, 8 December 1973, on the winter wonderland which was Celtic Park. This is a game which most supporters of my vintage will recall, played with a ball which was as, er, tangerine as the visitors' shirts, to allow the game to take place on a snow-covered pitch. It would never have been played in the modern era. Harry followed up his three strikes which counted against Rangers and the one which didn't by hitting the opener in the seventh minute, following up a Billy McNeill header to score, just as he had done at Hampden. With Harry and the other Celts defying the atrocious underfoot conditions to turn on the style, the game appeared to be in the bag before the interval, despite a horrendous decision by Edinburgh referee Eddie Pringle which handed Jim McLean's United an equaliser on 17 minutes. Hoops keeper Ally Hunter was the meat in an Archie Knox/George Fleming sandwich as he leapt to collect a high ball in his box, the tangerine sphere squirming from his grasp to present Andy Gray with a belated 18th birthday gift for 1-1, Celtic captain McNeill chasing the Edinburgh official to the halfway line to protest the injustice, to no avail.

Two goals in the final 15 minutes of the half allowed that anger to be somewhat dispelled, Tommy Callaghan scoring after Kenny Dalglish's effort had crashed off the crossbar then the King himself beating Hamish McAlpine after a wonderful interchange with Harry. At 3-1, it seemed that Jock Stein also believed it was job done, man-of-the-moment Harry withdrawn to let Bobby Lennox loose on the United defence and finish them off, although it would later transpire that Harry was still struggling with a back injury. Fleming reduced the deficit within 10 minutes of the restart before Pringle's second dreadful call of the afternoon saw the visitors leave Glasgow with an unlikely point. There were only seconds remaining when Knox tapped the ball home from a clearly offside position. As we all looked for a linesman's flag, none was forthcoming, the match ending 3-3 much to the disappointment of the majority of the frostbitten 19,000 spectators inside Parkhead.

That state of frozen disappointment would manifest itself again seven days later against the other club from Tannadice Street, in the most surreal cup final atmosphere I ever witnessed. A generator ban introduced 24 hours earlier meant that the 1973/74 Scottish League Cup competition would be brought to a conclusion at lunchtime on Saturday, 15 December 1973, a combination of the early kick-off, appalling weather conditions and the national state of emergency - perhaps even the opposition - reducing the attendance to an all-time low, at that time, for a national cup final of just under 28,000. We were shivering high up in the North Stand, but at least we were under cover, a luxury many of those dotted around the frozen slopes of the vast stadium would not enjoy. The old Hampden packed with 100,000 spectators or more was a truly awesome sight, however, as we had witnessed against Arbroath and Rosenborg over the past year, as an empty bowl it often produced a performance from the players to match the flat atmosphere. Sadly, that was about to unfold in front of us once more.

As Harry was putting Rangers to the sword 10 days earlier, Dundee were already reflecting on a job well done, having beaten Kilmarnock 1-0 at the national stadium in front of less than 5,000 spectators on the Monday evening, thanks to a goal from captain Tommy Gemmell. The match had been postponed from the previous midweek due to, yes, you've guessed it, snow. The Dark Blues were managed by Davie White, who had played alongside Harry at Clyde in his first spell there, then brought him back to Shawfield from Sunderland as manager in 1966 as the club finished third that season, equalling their highest-ever League position, whilst taking the Lisbon Lions to a replay in the Scottish Cup semi-final, the first game of which Harry had played in before injury saw him miss out in midweek. White's performance would see him move to Ibrox as assistant manager to Scot Symon that summer before replacing him a few months later. After two years without a trophy as Rangers manager, in the autumn of 1969 he would become the first man to be sacked from that post, despite his side leading the League. Jock Stein's shadow was a very cold place for anyone connected with Ibrox to live.

White then took over from his and Harry's old Clyde manager, John Prentice, at Dens Park in 1972, and had forged an excellent side which you may recall had taken Celtic to three games in the quarter-final of the previous season's League Cup, before succumbing to a four-goal first-half aerial blitz in the Hampden play-off. He had beaten Stein's Celtic in both League and Cup home matches on Tayside that campaign. They were a decent side with excellent players. In this current League Cup competition, Dundee had topped a group including Hearts, Partick Thistle and St Johnstone, before eliminating both Dunfermline Athletic and Clyde in the two-legged knockout stages then securing that 1-0 victory over Kilmarnock in the semi-final.

This would be the club's fourth appearance in the League Cup final. They had become the first club to successfully defend the new trophy when they followed up their 3-2 win over Rangers in October 1951 with a 2-0 victory over Kilmarnock 12 months later. That great team had also reached the Scottish Cup final in April of that year, losing heavily to Motherwell, and included Doug Cowie at left-half. Doug was capped

20 times for his country in the mid-1950's and at the time of writing is believed to be the oldest surviving Scottish international player, having celebrated his 95th birthday in May 2021.

As an aside, the beaten Kilmarnock side in October 1952 featured my uncle, Willie Jack, at inside-left. Willie had scored a last-minute winner against Rangers in the semi-final, which prevented a re-run of the previous season's finale. His goal involved an attempted clearance from an Ibrox defender taking a ricochet off his stomach to win the match, an event subsequently caricatured in the national media. It was often wheeled out at family parties and remains in the possession of my cousins to this day, its place in our family history reinforced by its inclusion in his Order of Service when he passed away a few years ago. Willie had won the Scottish Junior Cup with Shawfield before signing for St Mirren then joining Albion Rovers, where he was a teammate of Jock Stein. As Stein headed to Llanelli in 1951, Jack was signed by former Celt Malcolm MacDonald for Kilmarnock. Jock and Willie would later face off when the Big Man returned to Scotland with Celtic - one of those matches in the Scottish Cup memorably captured in classic Pathe footage in 1955 - and they would remain friends in later years.

Dundee's third League Cup final had been against Stein's Celtic in October 1967, played immediately before the current European champions headed out to South America for the ill-fated World Club Championship clashes with Racing Club. Celts had gone there in fine fettle after a 5-3 win over the Dark Blues had extended their sequence of successes to three, thanks to a Steve Chalmers double and further goals from John Hughes, Bobby Lennox and Willie Wallace.

Dundee's goals at Hampden that afternoon had been shared between the two McLeans, George and Jim. Both had featured against this current Celtic team in recent weeks, 'Dandy' as a player for Ayr United and 'Wee Jum' as the Dundee United manager in the 3-3 snow fight the previous Saturday.

Some of their 1967 vintage would again feature in the final six years later, Bobby Wilson at full-back and George Stewart in central defence, whilst Steve Murray would now be wearing the colours of Celtic, having arrived in Glasgow in May 1973 via a four-year spell at Aberdeen. Murray would make his only international appearance on home Pittodrie soil in December 1971 beside Scotland debutant Kenny Dalglish, who was now his club teammate.

The Celtic team from that previous final meeting would also include survivors in December 1973. Tommy Gemmell, of course, would now lead Dundee out at Hampden, alongside his friend Billy McNeill, whilst Jock Stein would again be in the Hoops dugout. The incredible turnaround of players at Parkhead was illustrated further as only Bobby Lennox from the other 10 players who took part that afternoon for Celtic remained at the club. Bobby would not be in the cup final squad, he and Dixie Deans left out as Stein went with the same men who had clinched the last-four victory over Rangers.

The full line-ups were as follows.

CELTIC:

Ally Hunter; Danny McGrain & Jim Brogan; Pat McCluskey, Billy McNeill & Steve Murray; Harry Hood, Davie Hay, Paul Wilson, Tommy Callaghan & Kenny Dalglish. Substitutes; Jimmy Johnstone & George Connelly.

DUNDEE:

Thomson Allan; Bobby Wilson & Tommy Gemmell; Bobby Ford, George Stewart & Iain Phillip; John Duncan, Bobby Robinson, Gordon Wallace, Jocky Scott & Duncan Lambie. Substitutes; Davie Johnston & Ian Scott.

Apart from Gemmell and Murray, there were some other interesting side stories associated with the match. Dundee keeper Thomson Allan had shipped six goals to Celtic in his previous appearance in a League Cup final, for Hibernian in April 1969, whilst Jock Stein had allegedly tried and failed recently to bring Iain Phillip back to Scotland from Crystal Palace, the player choosing instead to return to Dens Park. And, of course, there was a suggestion that a deal involving Harry plus cash had been proposed to Dundee a few weeks before the final to bring John Duncan to Parkhead. As it transpired, there would be no such reunion of Harry and Davie White at Dundee, whilst Duncan would eventually join Tottenham Hotspur for big money.

Celtic's route to a 10th successive League Cup final had been tortuous, six section games in August, which included two Glasgow derbies with Rangers, followed by home and away second round games with Motherwell which produced a tie, the European 'away goals' rule which would have seen Celts qualify disregarded in favour of a play-off. The third Motherwell game and the first leg of the quarter-final with Aberdeen were both squeezed into a 72-hour midweek period in the middle of the European Cup schedule, with a three-week gap before the second-leg at Pittodrie. And after all that, Celtic were paired again with section rivals Rangers in a midweek semi-final played in early December, 10 days before the final itself, our 13th game in the competition. You genuinely could not make this stuff up.

To add insult to injury, the Hampden surface was in dreadful condition on the day of the final, the snow having been cleared only to form pools of water all over a muddy surface above a rock-hard base. Unsurprisingly, both managers wanted the game postponed on safety grounds, adding to the momentum in the wider media to defer the final until spring to provide half a chance of making it the showpiece it once was, even despite the tedious competition it had become. However, common sense once again took a holiday. The Ghost of Hampden Past – Bobby Davidson of Airdrie – was the referee, as he had been in the 1967 final, and he decided or was told it was going ahead. And that was that.

The League Cup had been a bizarre competition for Celtic. We had managed to qualify from the initial sections only twice in the first decade following its introduction to the domestic calendar at the start of season 1946/47, succeeding the old wartime

Southern and North East Regional League Cups. Then, like corporation buses, when one trophy arrived, another followed shortly, Celts beating Partick Thistle in October 1956 then Rangers 12 months later, Hampden in the Sun. The Hoops then failed to reach another final until a defeat by Rangers in 1964 - the first of the current sequence of 10 - taking revenge by beating the Ibrox men in the finals of 1965 and 1966. That became three-in-a-row with the aforementioned defeat of Dundee in October 1967, then five as both Hibernian and St Johnstone were beaten in the calendar year 1969, the first final deferred after a fire at Hampden in the autumn of 1968. No other club has ever dominated the competition over such an extended period, so it was a real disappointment when the shock defeat to Ross County in November 2020 removed the possibility of Celtic matching that achievement last season, Scott Brown having lifted the previous four trophies.

The rollercoaster continued. Having won five in a row between 1965 and 1969, Jock Stein's Hoops had then failed to win any of the next three League Cup finals, Rangers, Partick Thistle then Hibernian all enjoying an unexpected Hampden success at Celtic's expense. I had been at the two previous defeats and still awaited a first win. Surely, even on this dismal afternoon, Jock Stein's men would prevail.

Leaving aside the conditions and atmosphere, which applied equally to both teams, there is no doubt that Dundee deserved to win on the day. Harry had showed up well in flashes but early in the second half he was limping out on the flanks, eventually making way for Jimmy Johnstone on 68 minutes. The solitary goal arrived eight minutes later, and probably reflected the only real combination of play worthy of the final. A free-kick on the halfway line was launched into the Celtic box by Bobby Wilson, a veteran of the League Cup final six years earlier, the ball clearing the first jumping Celtic defender. Dundee striker Gordon Wallace then showed superb control to take it on his chest before swivelling to beat Ally Hunter low at his post. There would be a late Hoops flurry but no reprieve, as for the first time, Tommy Gemmell lifted a trophy at Hampden which was not welcomed by the Celtic support.

A fourth consecutive League Cup final defeat was hardly the ending envisaged 10 days earlier, as Harry made Celtic history with his Hampden hat-trick. Still, there was the slight matter of nine successive League titles to be won, by way of compensation, as well as the European and Scottish Cups.

The Hampden hangover was clearly in evidence as only 11,000 hardy souls turned up for the first of a Parkhead double-header either side of Christmas, which would conclude a mixed calendar year of 1973. Those who didn't attend would be the losers, as Celts chalked up scores more associated with Wimbledon in south-west London than the east end of Glasgow, the Hoops hammering both Falkirk then Dunfermline Athletic in straight sets by the same margin, 6-0 6-0.

My dad recorded the Golden Goal time for the club competition at that time, seated at the back of the stand next to his Celtic Supporters' Association colleague Jim

Divers, who did the Hospital Broadcast. I would often head over early to sit with him there, rather than travel with the supporters' bus to our normal Celtic End spot. As a 12-year-old boy, it was exciting to park in the old London Road school where the players left their cars then met up with their families afterwards. VIP stuff. Dad had an official pass to get in there, albeit that didn't stop 'George the Janny' from peering in our car window suspiciously as we approached every week. It became part of our routine, keeping a straight face before bursting into laughter as he finally and reluctantly let us through. These two matches were cases in point and remain firm and fond memories of watching Celtic with dad almost five decades on.

Jock Stein recalled Dixie Deans and Bobby Lennox for the first of those two games, against Falkirk on Saturday, 22 December 1973, with Paul Wilson and Tommy Callaghan dropping to the bench, whilst Hampden substitutes Jimmy Johnstone and George Connelly travelled to Brockville with the reserves. The visitors were struggling at the foot of the table, still without a win after a dreadful run of results and they would feel the full power of Celtic's wrath on another horrible, wet Glasgow afternoon. Their game plan did work for 35 minutes, in fairness, before the roof caved in, Kenny Dalglish heading the League leaders in front following a wonderful exchange with Danny McGrain, comeback man Lennox then adding a second after Harry had created the opportunity. The teams turned around at 2-0 before Deans, making his first start since scoring a post-war record six goals against Partick Thistle in October, decided to put his back-injury problems behind him, literally, by joining the goal trail again. Cometh the hour, cometh the prolific Celtic striker, Dixie burying two shots behind Ally Donaldson within eight minutes before saving his best for the final 10 minutes. In memory's view, I can still see him diving McGrory-esque to meet Lennox's cross for 5-0, before repeating the feat from Dalglish's assist in the dying moments to make it a personal tally of 10 goals in two games. Up on Tayside, the fickleness of football fortunes was highlighted yet again as League Cup-winning captain Tommy Gemmell was sent off in the 1-0 home defeat by Motherwell for disputing the award of a throw-in!

Dixie Deans would make that 12 goals in three matches seven days later, denied a hat-trick against Dunfermline Athletic only by a linesman's flag. His double arrived in a seven-minute spell either side of a Kenny Dalglish strike on the half-hour, all three headed goals flying past Pars keeper Geir Karlsen, who had faced the Hoops the previous season in the European Cup with Rosenborg, before arriving in Fife via a trial period at Parkhead. With Celts enjoying a 3-0 interval lead, there was more perfect symmetry in the second half, this time Dalglish's second goal splitting a pair of superb Harry efforts, with only a desperate goal-line clearance from Jim Leishman preventing a second December hat-trick for Hood. Celtic's sixth and final goal – Harry's second - was a devastating piece of play involving Deans, Dalglish and 17-year-old substitute Andy Ritchie, who had replaced Billy McNeill with 20 minutes remaining to make his senior debut. Former Kirkintilloch Rob Roy star Ritchie had it all, and there were huge hopes for his future at Celtic Park, as the calendar year 1973 ended on a high, defeats for closest challengers Hearts, Hibernian and Ayr United allowing fifth-placed Rangers to climb to second spot, six points behind the champions. The year had been a real mixed bag, with three Hampden cup final defeats following the securing of an unprecedented eighth consecutive League title at Easter Road.

Tuesday, 1 January 1974 saw the now traditional biennial trek to Shawfield for Celtic to first-foot east end neighbours Clyde, for once Dixie Deans not on the scoresheet as goals from Bobby Lennox and Kenny Dalglish without reply allowed Harry to enjoy a return to his first senior ground. Across the city, Rangers were fortunate to escape with a point from a 1-1 draw with Partick Thistle at Ibrox, the gap at the top of the table now seven points. Five days later, it was the turn of the Ibrox outfit to travel to the east end of Glasgow, looking to avoid a third successive defeat at the hands of Celtic, whilst seeking the win which would be required to keep any remote hope of stopping the march of Stein's machine to nine-in-a-row. The Celtic boss stuck with the same team for a fourth successive game as he sought to pull nine points clear of Rangers, the players wearing black armbands as a gesture of respect for former captain and manager, Jimmy McStay, who had sadly passed away on Hogmanay.

The teams lined up as follows in front of 55,000 spectators.

CELTIC:

Ally Hunter; Danny McGrain & Jim Brogan; Pat McCluskey, Billy McNeill & Davie Hay; Harry Hood, Steve Murray, Dixie Deans, Kenny Dalglish & Bobby Lennox Substitutes; Jimmy Johnstone & George Connelly.

RANGERS:

Peter McCloy; Sandy Jardine & Willie Mathieson; John Greig, Derek Johnstone & Doug Houston; Quinton Young, Tom Forsyth, Derek Parlane, Alex MacDonald & Ally Scott. Substitutes; Johnny Hamilton & Dave Smith.

The talk in the media beforehand had all been about the monopoly Celtic currently enjoyed in the League and the remote prospect of that ending anytime soon, such dominance being blamed as the major factor in dwindling attendances, which would see the introduction of a new 10-team Premier League from summer 1975. The 90 minutes which followed would do nothing to dispel that argument, despite the misleading 1-0 scoreline in favour of Celtic. Jock Stein's men would once again enjoy the majority of possession, skilled players on view and clear goalscoring chances. The goal which did count once again came from the boot of derby specialist Bobby Lennox, however, it owed much to Harry in terms of creation. Just before the half-hour, he picked up the ball 40 yards from his own goal before slipping it to Steve Murray on his right. The former Dundee and Aberdeen midfielder then showed great courage to release the ball up the touchline to Kenny Dalglish, a split second before he was 'rollerballed' by Tom Forsyth in front of the dugouts. The King would continue the move by passing the ball around the Rangers defence to pick out Harry, who had sprinted another 40 yards to the edge of the Rangers box. As Peter McCloy approached to narrow the angle, Harry clipped the ball perfectly to his left where Lennox was sprinting clear of his marker. There was nothing faster on two legs than the Buzz Bomb in full flight, all those sessions on Saltcoats beach giving him pace others could only dream about. Often that would cost he and Celtic goals, linesmen raising flags assuming he must have started ahead of the defender he had just outstripped, and yet again there were calls for offside as he slid in to win the match, but the goal would stand as Celts took a massive step towards nine-in-a-row.

Weather caused the cancellation of Celtic's next fixture, against Morton at Cappielow seven days later, Hibernian's 3-1 win over Dundee United enabling them to reduce the gap at the summit to five points. And in midweek thoughts turned back to the chase for continental glory, Celtic paired once again with Swiss champions FC Basel, as the draw for the last eight of the European Cup was made in Paris. This would be a third pairing of the two clubs in 12 years, with Celts unbeaten in the four matches played to date. The domestic action resumed with a comfortable 3-0 home victory over St Johnstone on Saturday, 19 January 1974, Vic Davidson coming in for the injured Dixie Deans as Celts once again extended the lead to six points, Hibernian only managing a 1-1 draw with Ayr United at Somerset Park. St Johnstone defender Jim Argue got the ball rolling on the half-hour, deflecting a Bobby Lennox drive past his own goalkeeper after an expertly worked free-kick taken by Harry. A late scoring burst sealed the points, Danny McGrain setting Steve Murray up to notch Celtic's 100th goal of the season before Lennox converted a spot kick awarded after Davie Hay had been upended in the box.

Having missed out on the win over St Johnstone with his third injury of the season, a foot problem suffered at Shawfield on New Year's Day and aggravated against Rangers, Dixie Deans recommenced his reign of terror on opposition defences as Sunday football received an introduction eight days later. Almost 30,000 spectators rolled up to Celtic Park for the Scottish Cup third-round tie with Clydebank, a combination of the novelty and the drought of football during a weather-ravaged month perhaps the main factors in such a higher-than-average attendance. Deans would mark the occasion and his return with a first-half hat-trick, as Celts scored six goals at home for the third time in six weeks. The Hoops striker was actually unlucky not to better the double treble he had scored personally against Partick Thistle two months earlier, being denied by the woodwork no fewer than four times, missing another chance by inches then being blinded by the sun late on as he shaped to head home in an incredible performance. Bobby Lennox added a brace either side of the break before substitute Vic Davidson made it 6-0 with 25 minutes still remaining. As Deans tried and failed to increase his tally, the only remaining goal arrived at the other end in stoppage time, Bankies defender Jim Fallon scoring against his boyhood heroes to trigger a storm of booing, after Bishopbriggs referee Kyle had awarded a ludicrous penalty for a shot driven against the arm of Jim Brogan at point-blank range.

There was another contentious and this time costly refereeing error as February opened with a League visit to Fir Park. Celts had been coasting at 2-0 an hour into the game, thanks to goals from Steve Murray and Bobby Lennox either side of the break, before Alex Martin pulled one back for the hosts. With 20 minutes to play, Dixie Deans appeared to have sealed the points against his old club when his perfect header sailed past Stuart Rennie in the Motherwell goal. With no flag raised from the linesman, why Kilmarnock referee McCririck decided to rule the goal out for offside will be between him and his God, Kenny Dalglish booked in the follow-up. Within two minutes, Bobby Graham beat Ally Hunter with a header to equalise before a late rally saw John Goldthorpe score his third goal of the season against Celtic to win the game. Hibernian celebrated the signing of Joe Harper from Everton for a Scottish record transfer fee by beating his old side Aberdeen 3-1, to move within four points of Celtic.

The first Sunday League game at Celtic Park followed eight days later and would end in defeat for the Bhoys for the second successive week, this time League Cup winners Dundee shocking a 40,000 crowd by beating the Champions 2-1. The continuing problems behind the scenes with George Connelly had seen the wonderfully talented Fifer placed on the transfer list, however, he was preferred to Pat McCluskey beside Billy McNeill in central defence to make a first-team appearance for the first time since November. Celts found themselves 2-0 down to early strikes by Duncan Lambie and Hoops target John Duncan before Davie Hay reduced the deficit 10 minutes from half-time. Harry was replaced by Tommy Callaghan in the second half, but Celts could not find a way past Thomson Allan in the visitors' goal. The keeper's old club, Hibernian, had stumbled at basement-dwellers Falkirk, 24 hours earlier, leaving Brockville with a disappointing draw which would now see the gap at the top of the table reduced to just three points, Scotland's top two teams scheduled to meet at Easter Road in a fortnight.

It was Groundhog Day the following Sunday as Celtic repeated their 6-1 Scottish Cup thrashing of Clydebank by doing the same to Stirling Albion at Parkhead, albeit this time only 23,000 bore witness to the win. The tie was over by half-time, by which time Celtic were 4-1 ahead, goals from Kenny Dalglish and Paul Wilson followed by a Harry double, taking his season's tally to 13 after Mickey Lawson had pulled one back for the Second Division side. Steve Murray added his own brace in the second half, having recovered from the toe problem which would later effectively end his career, but the biggest cheer of the afternoon was reserved for full-time, word coming through that Dundee had followed up their victory at Celtic Park the previous week by hammering cup-holders Rangers 3-0 at Ibrox, effectively ending their season. That would no doubt have been a real source of satisfaction to Dundee manager Davie White, sacked from his Ibrox post four years earlier, and indeed his captain Tommy Gemmell, a Lisbon Lion in the lion's den. There were no real lions in there, obviously.

Saturday, 23 February 1974 was another red-letter day in my young Celtic-supporting life, as we travelled through to Edinburgh for the much-anticipated 'title decider' with Hibernian at Easter Road, having missed the clincher 10 months earlier at the same venue. Against a tide of dwindling attendances, the desire to watch this one play out live drew almost 50,000 to the Leith ground, by some distance the largest crowd I have ever seen there. We were seated in the covered enclosure behind one of the goals, the scene of much unrest as a terracing when I had first visited Easter Road in October 1971. It was an incredible atmosphere and a truly awesome sight, to see that vast bank of bodies to our left and behind the other goal. Jock Stein had, perhaps surprisingly, moved into the transfer market in midweek to sign twice-capped Scotland striker Jimmy Bone from Sheffield United for £25,000. With Bobby Lennox failing to recover from an injury against Stirling Albion, former Partick Thistle star Bone would be given an immediate taste of life as a Celt on the bench at Easter Road. Billy McNeill had also been a fitness doubt with the back injury which saw him forced off in the same match, however, Cesar would be in his normal place for the vital clash as the following teams lined up.

HIBERNIAN:

Jim McArthur; Derek Spalding & Eric Schaedler; Pat Stanton, Jim Black & John Blackley; Alex Edwards, Jim O'Rourke, Alan Gordon, Alex Cropley & Arthur Duncan. Substitutes; Joe Harper & Des Bremner.

CELTIC:

Ally Hunter; Danny McGrain & Jim Brogan; George Connelly, Billy McNeill & Davie Hay; Harry Hood, Steve Murray, Dixie Deans, Kenny Dalglish & Paul Wilson. Substitutes; Pat McCluskey & Jimmy Bone.

The titanic game got off to a sensational start when Dixie Deans hammered the ball past Jim McArthur in the opening minute to draw first blood for the Hoops, Harry going close to doubling the lead on 20 minutes as his shot crashed back off Jim McArthur's post. In a thrilling match with twists throughout, Hibernian winger Arthur Duncan equalised midway through the first half, only for Kenny Dalglish to score a second goal for Celtic eight minutes before the break, the King showing all the poise, balance and control which would become his trademark throughout a world-class career to sidefoot home. There was nothing quite like King Kenny.

Eight minutes into the second half, Jim O'Rourke levelled things for the second time, a third Hibernian goal looking likely and having the potential to totally derail the quest for nine-in-a-row. However, once again the Champions dug deep. Just after the hour, Paul Wilson squeezed a third home off McArthur's post, Harry then going close twice, as first John Blackley – the man Harry acknowledged as his most difficult opponent – cleared his effort off the line before his drive arrowed inches wide minutes later. The coup de grace arrived in stoppage time, a spectacular effort as Dixie Deans stretched those neck muscles to beat the Hibs keeper for a second time from an impossible angle, just a few yards in front of us, striking the most decisive blow yet to the hopes of the title contenders. The celebrations at the full-time whistle, which blew seconds later, suggested that the hard work had largely now been done, the defending champions now holding a five-point gap over Hibernian with a dozen games remaining.

It was a happy Celtic party which gathered at Glasgow Airport on Monday, 25 February 1974, just 48 hours after the tremendous victory at Easter Road which made them odds-on to retain their Scottish title for an incredible ninth successive year. Their destination was Switzerland, for the first leg of the European Cup quarter-final tie against FC Basel. The Swiss had been scoring goals for fun in this season's competition, notching up 11 over the two legs in their first-round victory over Icelandic champions, Fram Reykjavik. Peruvian star Teofilo Cubillas had been on the scoresheet in both matches. He first came to my attention during that magical World Cup finals tournament in Mexico in the summer of 1970. I would be less enamoured with him eight years later, as he hammered two screamers past Alan Rough in Argentina, ruining my night and Scotland's tournament before either had really started. Cubillas would still be in Switzerland as Basel overturned a 2-1 deficit from Brugge by beating the Belgian champions 6-4 at their St Jakob Stadium in the second round, with German striker Ottmar Hitzfeld netting a hat-trick to set up the last-eight clash with Celtic in the spring. In the interim, the Peruvian legend would sign for FC Porto for a not insignificant transfer fee of £200,000.

This would be the third meeting of the clubs in just over a decade of continental competition. They had first been paired back in the autumn of 1963, in the opening round of the Cup Winners' Cup, Celtic's second European tie after the inaugural clash with Valencia 12 months earlier. The Hoops were doing their best to live up to their 'consistently inconsistently' tag at that time, having built up a 4-0 lead at home to Third Lanark on the Saturday only to see that vanish before the hour as the game ended 4-4. Three nights later, Tuesday, 17 September 1963, they would manage to rack up five goals without reply against Swiss Cup-holders Basel in the St Jakob, before a late goal from Heinz Blumer reduced the damage to 5-1. John Hughes would become the first Celtic player to score a European hat-trick that night, whilst John Divers and Bobby Lennox also notched their maiden continental strikes, club legends Billy McNeill and Karl Odermatt in opposition for the first of their many tussles.

Celts would suffer League defeats at Falkirk and Paisley, then share the points at home to Jock Stein's unbeaten table-topping Dunfermline Athletic, after again conceding a two-goal lead, before the return match with Basel took place on Wednesday, 9 October 1963. A combination of poor results, a 5-1 lead and the most atrocious weather reduced the attendance to just 8,000, which remains Celtic's lowest European home crowd to this day. In fairness, the players did their job professionally, with a comprehensive 5-0 victory, John Divers netting a double to join Yogi at the top of the club's European scoring charts, whilst future Lions, Jimmy Johnstone, Bobby Murdoch and Steve Chalmers all broke their European scoring ducks. That initial tie with Basel reflected Celtic's first wins at home, away and on aggregate in continental competition. The games are part of our long and proud European history.

The previously struggling Celts would then go on the rampage with five consecutive League wins, over which they amassed no fewer than 25 goals. Airdrieonians were on the end of the heaviest defeat, losing 9-0, Hoops goalkeeper Frank Haffey missing a penalty which would have meant double-figures. On the same afternoon, the 19-year-old Harry had scored the winner as Clyde edged a five-goal thriller with Cowdenbeath at Central Park in the old Second Division, however, he was on the Celtic bench for his first continental tie the next time they faced FC Basel, in the first round of the 1969/70 European Cup in the St Jakob on Wednesday, 19 September 1969. As in 1963, Celts had again come into the tie on the back of poor domestic form, having lost to Dunfermline Athletic and Hibernian either side of a goalless draw at Pittodrie. They would secure another 0-0 draw in Switzerland, Harry replacing Stevie Chalmers at half-time, which set things up nicely for the return leg in Glasgow a fortnight later.

Harry would return to the team and grab the winner as Celts got back to winning ways at Ibrox, three days later, followed up by victories over Aberdeen and his old pals at Clyde. He would then celebrate his first European start for Celtic by scoring in the opening minute against Basel, in front of 50,000 spectators at Parkhead, Tommy Gemmell sealing a 2-0 win and the tie with a fabulous shot just after the hour, as the first step in the Road to Milan was safely negotiated.

The aftermath of that match would see Ronnie Simpson suffer a recurrence of the dislocated shoulder which forced his retiral, Jock Stein going into the transfer market to sign former Third Lanark keeper Evan Williams from Wolverhampton Wanderers. Williams would see off competition from John Fallon to retain the gloves, playing in the European Cup final in Milan in 1970, then Denis Connaghan, signed from St Mirren the following year after the 4-1 League Cup final defeat by Partick Thistle, before the arrival of Scottish international keeper Ally Hunter from Kilmarnock in January 1973 brought his run of over 150 appearances to an end. A back injury sustained by Hunter in the 4-2 victory at Easter Road in February 1974 forced him out of the trip to Basel in the first leg of the European Cup quarter-final the following midweek, Williams finding himself back in the spotlight again more than a year since his last first-team match. He would probably wish that he hadn't bothered, 90 minutes later, as his Celtic career ended in a series of blunders in Switzerland.

Jock Stein named the following men for Celtic's third visit to the St Jakob Stadium, on Wednesday, 27 February 1974, the match having been brought forward by a week at the request of the Swiss to avoid a clash with a local carnival, despite that date coming before the end of their scheduled winter break.

Evan Williams; Danny McGrain & Jim Brogan; George Connelly, Billy McNeill & Davie Hay; Harry Hood, Steve Murray, Dixie Deans, Kenny Dalglish & Paul Wilson. Substitutes; Ally Hunter, Roddie MacDonald, Pat McCluskey, Tommy Callaghan & Vic Davidson.

Despite an eye injury suffered by Billy McNeill in the opening exchanges, Celtic started on the front foot and took the lead on 20 minutes. Harry began the move by finding Jim Brogan wide on the left, the full-back making great progress down the flank before pitching over a cross which took out the Swiss central defence, Paul Wilson connecting perfectly to send a stunning volley straight over Frenchman Jean-Paul Laufenberger in the Basel goal. The tie then turned on its head in a three-minute spell around the half-hour, with Evan Williams badly at fault on both occasions, first allowing a low shot from Ottmar Hitzfeld to squirm out of his grasp and over the line for the equaliser, then left looking on as Karl Odermatt's 25-yard free-kick flew past him at the post he was covering for 2-1.

Celts would regroup and storm back after the interval, Kenny Dalglish and Danny McGrain combining brilliantly to allow The King to float in the most exquisite equaliser, 10 minutes into the second half, the club's 100th goal in European football. With two vital away goals secured and the home crowd deflated, sadly it would be Williams who allowed Basel back into the game again. This time his fluffed clearance landed at the feet of Otto Demarmels. A slick one-two saw the Basel midfielder chopped down in the box by George Connelly, Hitzfeld blasting the spot kick high past Williams to give the Swiss a 3-2 advantage from the home leg. Otto Hitzfeld, of course, would go on to win the trophy as manager of Borussia Dortmund and Bayern Munich. Evan Williams would not play for Celtic's first team again.

Ally Hunter would return between the sticks for the visit of Hearts, three days later, on Saturday, 2 March 1974, albeit he suffered another injury early on which appeared to hamper his movement and would cost him his place in the following game. Still, he kept a clean sheet, as a Celtic side minus birthday Bhoy Billy McNeill won 1-0, thanks to a strike from Dixie Deans on the half-hour. Jimmy Bone appeared in place of the matchwinner at the start of the second half to make his Hoops debut.

Eight days later, an excellent crowd of 46,000 rolled up to Parkhead for the Scottish Cup fifth-round tie with Motherwell, a sixth meeting of the season between the two clubs. Ally Hunter's latest injury gave Denis Connaghan the opportunity to wear the first-team gloves again, the big keeper yet to taste defeat in his 18 games at the club since joining from St Mirren in October 1971, whilst Billy McNeill, twisted knee victim Danny McGrain and long-term absentee Jimmy Johnstone were all still missing from action. The star of the show for Celtic was Harry, who twice equalised to keep the Bhoys in the Cup after first Bobby Graham then Ian Kennedy had given the visitors the lead in the first half. Just before the half-hour, Harry fastened on to a Dixie Deans flick to restore parity, then, within two minutes of the restart, he made it 2-2, beating Motherwell keeper Stuart Rennie all ends up *"with as magnificent a shot as I've seen all season,"* according to *The Daily Record's* Hugh Taylor.

The circus would now move on to a seventh performance in midweek, Jimmy Bone received his first Hoops start at a jam-packed Fir Park on Wednesday, 13 March 1974 in place of Paul Wilson, but it was his strike partner Dixie Deans who would be the difference on the night. As the clock ticked towards the hour mark, Harry sent substitute Tommy Callaghan down the left with a deft pass, the big Fifer making ground before slinging the ball into the centre. That was the trigger for Dixie to launch himself full-length amongst the bodies to make a perfect connection with his forehead, the ball arrowing past Rennie to knock his old team out of the Scottish Cup, as they had in the League Cup in October. Jock Stein's men now awaited the winners of the replay between Dundee and Hibernian in the last four.

There were two novel sights as League business recommenced with a home clash with Ayr United three days later. The obvious one was the first appearance of Celtic's new change kit, black and green vertical stripes with black shorts and socks. From memory, it had been made popular by Coventry City and it would later be recycled in the Gordon Strachan era, a Champions League game at Old Trafford and a title-clincher at Kilmarnock immediately springing to mind.

The second sight was a welcome one, Jimmy Johnstone making his return to first-team action after a three-month absence, with various reasons put forward as to why he had not featured in the interim. Harry dropped to the bench, replacing Kenny Dalglish late on as Jinky promptly turned in a man-of-the-match performance, showing all the old moves and scoring twice from the penalty spot, as did the prolific Dixie Deans from open play in a 4-0 victory. With Hibernian's home game with Motherwell postponed that day, Celts duly stretched their advantage at the top of the table to seven points.

Both Johnstone and Hood would be in the starting line-up in midweek, as Celts set out to overturn a 3-2 deficit from the first leg of their European Cup quarter-final clash with Basel, on Wednesday, 20 March 1974. The ineligible Jimmy Bone was the player to miss out from the weekend, as Jock Stein went with the following selection.

Denis Connaghan; Davie Hay & Jim Brogan; Steve Murray, Billy McNeill & George Connelly; Jimmy Johnstone, Kenny Dalglish, Dixie Deans, Tommy Callaghan & Harry Hood. Substitutes; Ally Hunter, Pat McCluskey, Bobby Lennox & Paul Wilson.

This was one of the classic European games from my childhood, perhaps the last great European victory of the Stein era. My recollection is that it was pay-at-the-gate, and just two days short of my teens, I recall being overwhelmed at the size of the crowd and the crushing in the old Celtic End prior to kick-off. The attendance was given officially as 71,000. It felt like much more at that time.

What an emotional roller-coaster of a night. There was a crushing disappointment early on as first star defender George Connelly was stretchered off with what would prove to be a broken ankle, ending his season within five minutes of the kick-off, then Dixie Deans had TWO goals disallowed by the French referee within 60 seconds, shortly afterwards. Celtic then showed the spirit of true champions by storming into a two-goal lead by the 20th minute, to take the initiative back in the tie. Tommy Callaghan's inswinging corner from the left was met perfectly by the head of Kenny

Dalglish to open the scoring, then Harry slipped Steve Murray in to deliver a low cross from the right, Deans making it third time lucky by sweeping the ball past Jean-Paul Laufenburger for 2-0. Just after the half-hour, the aggregate score was level again, skipper Karl Odermatt's curling free-kick from the left bulleted past Denis Connaghan by defender Walter Mundschin. Laufenburger then became the second casualty of the evening, limping off to be replaced by Marcel Kunz, a veteran of the 1969 clashes between the sides. An incredible first 45 minutes still had one final twist, in stoppage time, Swiss international striker Walter Balmer on hand to tap the ball home after Connaghan had parried Odermatt's shot, yet another goalkeeping error giving Basel the aggregate lead back once again at 5-4.

There would only be one goal in the second half, as the tie continued to swing one way then another, but what a goal it was. The ball was played to Jimmy Johnstone from a short corner on the right, before Harry swung over a cross which reached Callaghan at the far post, the tall midfielder controlling it on his chest before unleashing a fierce left-foot volley past Kunz. Now the aggregate scores were level on away goals, and extra-time loomed. The winner, when it arrived, was a real seminal moment in the career of Steve Murray. With five minutes of the first period of extra-time remaining, Harry again showed wonderful poise and footwork in the box to hit the byeline, before pitching a cross to the far post, where Jimmy Johnstone was always second favourite to beat his Swiss marker in the air. However, pressure from the little winger forced the defender to miscue his clearance, the ball dropping towards Murray in the six-yard box. One stretch of his neck muscles sent the ball past Kunz, Celts into the last four and Steve Murray into Celtic folklore. There was pandemonium in the old stadium and this time there would no way back for Basel, as the Hoops marched into the semi-final.

So, who would lie in wait for Celtic? There was the possibility of a third successive meeting with Ujpest Dosza, the Hungarians having eliminated Czechoslovakian champions Spartak Trnava following a penalty shootout, after two 1-1 draws. They would be dangerous but familiar opposition. Also in the draw were the powerful West Germans of Bayern Munich, who had overcome Bulgarian champions CSKA - conquerors of holders Ajax - despite a second-leg defeat in Sofia. Bayern had ridden their luck earlier in the competition, requiring penalties to beat Swedish champions Atvidaberg then a late Gerd Muller strike to defeat East Germans Dynamo Dresden by the odd goal in 13. They would now progress to their first-ever European Cup semi-final, but it would be another 24 hours before the third potential opponent was known, albeit Atletico Madrid would start their second leg as favourites, having beaten Red Star 2-0 in Belgrade.

Chapter 26

It's football but not as we know it, as Argentina Madrid come to town

After the highs of the midweek victory over FC Basel, the start of my teenage years would bring me crashing back down to earth just three days later, Saturday, 23 March 1974, as two Ronnie Glavin strikes in the final quarter – both set up by Stevie Chalmers - gave Partick Thistle a 2-0 victory over European Cup semi-finalists Celtic at Firhill. The match was watched by Juan Carlos Lorenzo, manager of Atletico Madrid, who had been drawn to face Celtic in the last four of Europe's elite competition 24 hours earlier in Zurich. Jimmy Bone returned to face his former side, allowing Harry a chance to recover from his exertions against the Swiss on the bench before replacing him at the interval. It was a performance which saw the struggling Jags take some measure of revenge for their 7-0 defeat at Parkhead five months earlier and nudge Thistle skipper Glavin closer to a transfer to Celtic, which would be sealed later that year. Remarkably, it was also a first taste of defeat between the posts for Denis Connaghan, signed in October 1971. The gap at the top remained seven points, following the cancellation of Hibernian's match at Dens Park, albeit the Edinburgh club now had two games in hand.

Harry returned to the starting line-up seven days later, as did Ally Hunter and Danny McGrain, Jock Stein ringing the changes as his Celts hosted Dumbarton, Scotland stars Davie Hay and Kenny Dalglish dropped to the bench following their midweek trip to West Germany, whilst Jimmy Bone dropped out of the squad completely. King Kenny would be required at half-time, replacing Tommy Callaghan, after goals from the two McAdam brothers Tom and Colin had given the Sons an unlikely interval lead, and he added to Paul Wilson's early strike to level things by the hour. The post-Euro hangover would continue, though, and it took a late Dixie Deans goal to salvage a point after Peter Coleman had put Dumbarton 3-2 up in the 76th minute. Hibernian also shared six goals that day, with St Johnstone at Easter Road, allowing Rangers to move into second place in the table, six points behind Celtic.

April opened with a midweek Scottish Cup semi-final with Dundee at Hampden. The rematch of the League Cup final attracted almost 60,000 supporters to the national stadium, more than twice as many who had suffered those atrocious conditions at the same venue four months earlier. Celts ensured there would be no repeat of that result by taking the game to the Dark Blues from the kick-off. The only surprise was perhaps that it took a solitary Jimmy Johnstone goal to send Celtic through to a ninth Scottish Cup final in 10 years, a quite incredible record. Two minutes before the interval, the legendary winger thrashed the ball past Thomson Allan, after Billy McNeill had headed on Harry's corner kick. The Hoops would now meet either Hearts or Dundee United in the final.

It would take another single goal victory to defeat Dundee's Angus neighbours Arbroath at Celtic Park, three days later, this time it was Kenny Dalglish with a header on the hour beating former teammate Gordon Marshall to inch the Hoops two points closer to a ninth successive League title. Harry would sustain a head injury late on which forced his substitution by Paul Wilson, but thankfully he would recover in time for the midweek visit of Atletico Madrid. Having remained on the bench for the epic victories over Leeds United then the gut-wrenching disappointment of Milan in 1970, then missed out through injury as Celts and Inter fought out two goalless stalemates two years later, Harry would now have the opportunity to play in the final stages of the European Cup. It would be quite an experience.

The events which took place at Parkhead on the night of Wednesday, 10 April 1974 will live long in the memory of anyone who witnessed them. That number would include myself. It was another Celtic date with destiny, a second European Cup semi-final in three seasons and, unlike the Inter Milan game of two years earlier, I had not had to fight to get taken to see this one. At 13, it was more of an accepted rite of passage and so I made my way with the other adults and the 'greetin'-faced weans' as Spanish champions Atletico Madrid stood between Celtic and a third European Cup final.

It had started off so well, sat perched on a stanchion in the old Celtic End with another 73,000 with hope in their hearts on a lovely spring evening, giving me a glorious panorama of the most spectacular version of "You'll never walk alone" I had ever seen. The old stadium was packed to the rafters with a sea of green and white scarves, the fanatical passion in those legions and generations of voices filling the night air. There was and is nothing quite like it. Anywhere. It is a cry from the very soul which still tingles my spine as I complete my sixth decade.

Unlike quarter-final opponents FC Basel, this would be a first meeting between the two clubs, although only the most remarkable of comebacks had prevented that clash taking place on the Road to Lisbon. Having pipped European champions and bitter city rivals Real Madrid to the 1965/66 La Liga title by a single point, Atletico had enjoyed home and away wins over Sweden's Malmo FF in the first round of the 1966/67 European Cup, before drawing the powerful Yugoslavs, Vojvodina. A 3-1 defeat in Novi Sad would leave them with much to do at their as-yet-unfinished new home, the Estadio Manzanares, opened the previous month on the banks of the

Madrid river which bears its name, however, goals from club legends Luis Aragones and Adelardo had levelled the aggregate by half-time. With no further scoring and no 'away goals rule' in place as yet in the major continental competition, unlike the two others, which would of course have seen the Spaniards qualify, a play-off would now be required.

Atletico would presumably win the coin toss for home advantage, although, strangely, when this prospect reappeared at the quarter-final stage of the competition for Celtic, it had already been agreed that any play-off would take place in neutral Rotterdam. In any case, in the interim, the draw for the last eight of the European Cup had paired the winner of this tie with Jock Stein's Celtic, who had just beaten French champions Nantes home and away. The Parkhead boss would be in Madrid on Wednesday, 21 December 1966 to witness the second-round play-off in person, and he would probably have felt safe to leave after just six minutes, happy in the knowledge that his side would be returning there in the spring. By that time, goals from Adelardo and Enrique Collar had the hosts 2-0 ahead, whilst Irish referee Willie O'Neill would later send off two Vojvodina players. Game over? Not a bit of it. The Yugoslavs levelled the tie just after the hour, thanks to goals from Silvester Takac and Dimitrije Radovic, and when Takac scored his second on the night towards the end of the first period of extra-time, it would be the nine men from Serbia who would progress to provide the opposition for Celtic, for what would turn out to be the most memorable night in Glasgow's east end in March 1967.

Ironically, Atletico would again have to overcome Yugoslav opposition to qualify for the semi-final meeting with Celtic in April 1974, this time Red Star Belgrade their opponents in the last eight, following aggregate wins over Galatasaray and Dinamo Bucharest. This time the hard work was done by Atletico in the Serbian capital, with a 2-0 victory in the first leg, their third successive away win in the competition. Unusually, the Spaniards had drawn all three of their home games.

Time can sometimes play tricks with the memory, in the sense that I don't specifically recall whether or not the background of Atletico's coach and compilation of their playing squad was made much of an issue before the match. Argentinian Juan Carlos Lorenzo had followed the path of his illustrious countryman and predecessor Helenio Herrera to Italy and Spain, in his case as a player at Boca Juniors, Sampdoria then Atletico Madrid. His management CV included spells at both Rome clubs, sandwiched between leading the Argentinian national side at the World Cups of 1962 and 1966. It was his Argentina team to whom England manager Alf Ramsey had directed his infamous 'animals' reference, after the Wembley quarter-final had witnessed ridiculous scenes involving his captain, Antonio Rattin. Celtic would sadly experience this somewhat different approach to football the following year themselves, in three games against Racing Club de Avellaneda, incidentally another club who would later be managed by Lorenzo.

There would be four Argentinians in Atletico's starting line-up in Glasgow, the most notorious of whom being left-back Ruben Diaz, who had kicked Jimmy Johnstone up and down the Hampden pitch in the colours of Racing Club back in October 1967. He was nicknamed 'The Baker,' presumably as 'The Butcher' had already been claimed when he signed up, although, surprisingly, Diaz did not feature in rounds two and three of the battle in Buenos Aires and Montevideo.

Of Atletico's Spanish contingent, Adelardo was in his usual place, however, there was no sign of the talisman Luis Aragones, whilst international goalkeeper Miguel Reina was between the sticks. Reina's son Jose, better known as Pepe, would play against Celtic in the UEFA Cup for Villarreal, 30 years later, before moving to Liverpool then Napoli.

The teams lined up as follows, as Jock Stein sought a first-leg advantage to take to Madrid.

CELTIC:

Denis Connaghan; Davie Hay & Jim Brogan; Steve Murray, Billy McNeill & Pat McCluskey; Jimmy Johnstone, Harry Hood, Dixie Deans, Tommy Callaghan & Kenny Dalglish. Substitutes; Ally Hunter, Danny McGrain, Bobby Lennox & Paul Wilson.

ATLETICO MADRID:

Miguel Reina; Francisco Melo & Ruben Diaz; Domingo Benegas, Iselin Overjero & Eusebio Bejerano; Ruben Ayala, Adelardo Rodriguez, Jose Garate, Javier Irureta & Ramon Heredia. Substitutes; Quique Vicente & Alberto Fernandez.

There is a critical moment early in the match which tends to be overshadowed by subsequent events. Tommy Callaghan's pass found Harry and Kenny Dalglish springing Atletico's offside trap, Hood doing superbly well to round Reina and clip the ball back for Dalglish to tap home. Incredibly, the Turkish officials ruled the goal out, presumably on the basis that the ball had crossed the line before Harry cut it back. Photographic evidence should later show this to be a travesty of justice. Had the Spanish game plan been blown away so early and had Celts had that vital lead to build on in front of that massive home support, who knows how history may have changed.

Instead, the match became a battle of attrition, Atletico allowed to commit foul after horrible foul for 90 minutes, more than 50 in total, with Celtic's attacking play broken up constantly. The yellow card count soon began to rack up, before the reds started to appear from referee Babacan's pocket. The waist-high assault on Jimmy Johnstone by Paraguayan defender Domingo Benegas early in the second half - after 'The Baker' Diaz had tried unsuccessfully to slice him in half - was worthy of an ordering off in itself, however, incredibly, he survived with a caution.

Argentinian international striker Ruben Ayala would be the first to walk. In his first season in Madrid, following a transfer from Argentinian 'Invincibles' San Lorenzo and looking forward to representing his country in the summer World Cup finals, this would not be his finest hour. Ayala had already been booked early on for a pointless challenge on Denis Connaghan when he brought Davie Hay crashing to the ground with a two-footed lunge from behind right in front of the dugouts, a quick check of his number from referee Babacan enough to send him packing.

Next up was another Ruben, this time Diaz. He had gone through the full repertoire of tricks on Jimmy Johnstone, including a first-half rugby tackle which went unpunished, when the winger skipped past him for the umpteenth time. Having failed to stop Jinky legally, up went the boot to catch the winger's trailing leg before the look of innocence and hands clasped behind his back would surely convince the Turkish referee that no wrongdoing had occurred. I suspect that by this time, even Babacan had had enough. Out came the red card and into the early Argentinian bath trudged the shocked and shocking Diaz. And then there were nine.

The shameful tactics adopted by the visitors continued, goalkeeper Miguel Reina actually elbowing Dixie Deans in the ribs as he cleared from his penalty area, only to then writhe about the ground in agony, despite the Celt making no contact whatsoever. Amongst all this, there would be the occasional outbreak of football, Harry glancing his header inches wide of the post from a Tommy Callaghan cross before the keeper dived to hold a Kenny Dalglish effort.

Normal service was soon resumed, substitute Quique deciding to seek his own form of retribution, 15 seconds after his introduction, by following through on a clearance to kick out at Jimmy Johnstone. He limped back to his feet before being shown the third red card of the night by referee Babacan. With only eight players remaining on the pitch, one further misdemeanour would see the match abandoned, however, Atletico were too streetwise to allow that to happen. Callaghan would again deliver a perfect cross to pick out the head of Johnstone, and how fitting it would have been had the bruised and battered winger found the net to give Celts one foot in the Brussels final. Sadly, the ball would drift wide, and with it would go the last hope of a home lead on a night when football and whatever reputation Atletico had was shamed in Glasgow. The final whistle triggered yet further disgraceful scenes, with both sets of players, officials and even police officers involved in an unseemly rumble as they headed down the tunnel. No beautiful game tonight.

Harry recalled the events of that infamous evening in April 2011.

"We just thought it would be a nice Spanish football side who play nice, clever football and it would be a nice game of football because we were an attacking side, and we were hoping that this being a normal Spanish side it would be something similar. We had a goal disallowed in the first couple of minutes and why it was disallowed I don't know. The ball most certainly was not over the line. What happened after that was just incredible. Football was not allowed to be played. If I remember rightly, we still got our match bonus because of the way we conducted ourselves."

Celtic boss Jock Stein had sought out Atletico counterpart Juan Carlos Lorenzo after the full-time whistle, unsuccessfully as Harry remembers.

"I think Mr Stein lost the plot a little because he wasn't happy with their manager and I think he tried to get a hold of him, but he couldn't because their manager had run all the way to the dressing room and barricaded himself in there. I think Billy and I ran after Mr Stein and we tried to get hold of him. So, it was all happening behind us, but I think there was a fair Donnybrook going on."

Three days later, Saturday, 13 April 1974, Celts travelled to Tayside for a League match with Dundee United at Tannadice. This would now be a dress-rehearsal for the following month's Scottish Cup final, Jim McLean's men having overcome Hearts 4-2 in a midweek replay at Hampden to reach the club's first-ever national cup final, 24 hours before Celtic's bout with Atletico Madrid. The attendance at the national stadium for the Tuesday night fixture had failed to reach 13,000, for a match which would have doubled that crowd and produced an atmosphere worthy of the occasion if played at Dens Park or Easter Road, whilst also helping those out who don't seem to feature prominently in such decisions, the paying customer. What wonderful governance we enjoy in the best little country in the world.

Jimmy Johnstone's legs were presumably still in ice as he missed the game, with Tommy Callaghan and Dixie Deans dropping to the bench. Into the starting line-up came Danny McGrain, Paul Wilson and Jimmy Bone. Celts applauded the cup-finalists onto the pitch then promptly blew them off it, Steve Murray hammering in the opener within two minutes. The match was over as a contest 10 minutes before the break, this time Davie Hay beating Sandy Davie in the United goal with a fierce shot. Harry would make way for Callaghan on the hour as Jock Stein attempted to balance game time with rest in this hectic schedule, as Celtic chased glory on three fronts. The quest for a ninth successive League title was helped by surprise defeats to both of Celtic's closest challengers, Rangers at home to Dundee and Hibernian away to Arbroath.

That squad rotation continued in midweek in Methil, Jimmy Quinn, Dixie Deans and Bobby Lennox all returning, the Lisbon Lion after a 10-week injury absence, whilst Jim Brogan, Paul Wilson and Jimmy Bone dropped out. There was none of the three missed spot-kicks and last-minute equaliser drama experienced in the previous trip to Bayview, 14 months earlier, albeit Bertie Miller gave East Fife a shock lead midway through the first half. Lennox levelled the match with 10 minutes of the first half remaining, his 250th goal of a wonderful Celtic career, Kenny Dalglish then wrapping up the points before the interval with a superb quickfire double. A similar scoring burst midway through the second period saw the Hoops run out emphatic 6-1 winners on the night, Harry grabbing his own brace either side of a Deans strike, to take his personal tally to 17 and Celtic within three points of nine-in-a-row.

Harry in the red shirt of Clyde at Shawfield in 1962: *Photo courtesy of John Taylor*

Clyde F.C. — 1962-63

Back row (left to right): Davy White, Jim Moffatt, John Finnigan, Harry Haddock, Tommy McCulloch, Andy Donnelly, Dan Currie, Newman. Middle row: Danny Malloy, Willie Finlay, John McHugh, Tommy Burke, Dick Grant, Jim McLean, Willie McCulloch, Dave Thomson. Front row: George McFarlane, John McLaughlin, John Divers, Bobby Steel, Danny Blair and John Colrain

Harry threatens the Celtic goal at Shawfield in a League match on 12 September 1964

Harry in his first season at Roker Park (1964/65)

Harry challenges with Celtic's Tommy Gemmell in the Scottish Cup semi-final at Hampden on 1 April 1967

Clyde's 1967/68 squad: *Photo courtesy of Dick Staite*

Harry with Bobby Brown's Scotland Under 23 team which faced England at Hampden in February 1968

Above: Harry makes his Celtic debut at Love Street, Paisley on 29 March 1969

Left: Harry signs for Celtic watched by managers Archie Robertson and Jock Stein on 16 March 1969

Harry opens the scoring against Rangers in the Glasgow Cup at Celtic Park on 11 April 1969

Harry in action against Raith Rovers in a League match at Celtic Park on 16 August 1969

Harry runs out to face Rangers at Celtic Park in the League Cup on 20 August 1969

Harry leaves the field after the European Cup win over FC Basel at Celtic Park on 1 October 1969

Harry and his Celtic teammates celebrate his first cup final win at Hampden on 25 October 1969

Harry's header makes it 3-0 against Benfica in the European Cup at Celtic Park on 12 November 1969

Jimmy Johnstone secures a Scottish Cup victory over Rangers at Celtic Park on 21 February 1970

Harry sets up Willie Wallace's last-minute goal against Fiorentina at Celtic Park on 4 March 1970.

Pre-season photoshoot at Celtic Park for 1970/71

Harry scores against Kilmarnock at Rugby Park on 20 March 1971

Harry scores that vital League goal against Aberdeen at Pittodrie on 17 April 1971

Harry in action at Pittodrie on 17 April 1971

Harry in action against Rangers at Hampden in the Scottish Cup final on 8 May 1971

Black-eyed Bhoy. Harry receiving treatment in the Scottish Cup final replay on 12 May 1971

Harry puts Celtic 2-0 up from the spot in the Scottish Cup final replay at Hampden on 12 May 1971

Harry and Kenny Dalglish in Drybrough Cup action against Dumbarton at Celtic Park on 31 July 1971

Jim Craig, Billy McNeill, Tommy Gemmell and Harry take a stroll at Seamill on 19 October 1971

Above: Harry equalises for Celtic in the European Cup tie with Sliema Wanderers in Malta on 3 November 1971

Harry scores directly from a corner kick against Partick Thistle at Firhill on 27 November 1971

Titanic battle between Celtic and Ujpest Dosza in the European Cup quarter-final on 22 March 1972

Davie Hay looks on as Harry scores against Falkirk at Celtic Park on 31 March 1973

Harry's historic Hampden hat-trick is underway on 5 December 1973

Celtic and Atletico Madrid clash in the infamous European Cup semi-final tie on 10 April 1974

Harry leads the Celts out after Kenny's goal secures a ninth successive title at Brockville on 27 April 1974

Top left: Harry opens the scoring in the Scottish Cup final against Dundee United on 4 May 1974
Top right: Celtic goalscorers Steve Murray, Harry and Dixie Deans pose with the Scottish Cup on 4 May 1974
Above: A smiling Harry holds the Scottish Cup aloft at Hampden on 4 May 1974

A fitting finale for Cesar as Celts win the Scottish Cup, beating Airdrieonians 3-1 at Hampden on 3 May 1975

Left: Harry scores his final goal for Celtic, against Hearts on 4 October 1975.
Right: Harry warms up at Hampden ahead of the Scottish League Cup final on 25 October 1975

Harry in the colours of San Antonio Thunder (left) and Motherwell (right) in 1976

Bobby Moore and the Thunder squad prior to Harry and Tommy Callaghan joining up

Looks like Harry is on his own for Thunder against Seattle Sounders at Alamo Stadium on 12 July 1976

That would become one point three days later, following a 2-0 home victory over Aberdeen on Saturday, 20 April 1974, Celtic's last match before the trip to Madrid. The Hoops were pretty much at full strength with the return of David Hay, Jim Brogan and Jimmy Johnstone, Dixie Deans getting things underway in the fifth minute when he lashed Johnstone's cutback past Bobby Clark. With the midweek Atletico clash in mind, Jock Stein withdrew both Deans and Johnstone on the hour, introducing Bobby Lennox and Tommy Callaghan, however, despite total superiority, it took until five minutes from time before Celts clinched the points, albeit what a goal it was. A clever free-kick ploy involving Lennox, Dalglish and Hood saw the Dons defence follow Kenny the decoy, as Harry slipped the Buzz Bomb through to finish, Bobby expertly racking up goal number 251 in his beloved Hoops.

Celts landed in Madrid 48 hours later amidst unprecedented security protocols in the Spanish capital, for a football match at any rate, the now renamed Estadio Vicente Calderon resembling a war zone with its high military presence and water cannons. Both Jock Stein and Jimmy Johnstone had received death threats, with the team confined to their heavily guarded hotel. UEFA had performed its usual pointless governance role by fining the Spaniards a mere £15,000, around a tenth of the income they could expect from the full house on the night of the game. There would be no proper warm-up or pitchside bench for the Celtic officials, who could only look at the backs of their Spanish counterparts from a ground-level dugout. It was beyond parody. *"It's football, but not as we know it, Jim,"* as the *Star Trek* philosopher Mr Spock would perhaps have said.

Six of the Atletico team booked or ordered off in Glasgow would be missing, the Spaniards fielding a team more geared to playing football than stopping it as it turned out. Nevertheless, the Hoops would be on the front foot before a baying mob of 70,000, to a man or woman convinced by the local media that their team had been the victims and not the aggressors at Celtic Park.

ATLETICO MADRID:

Miguel Reina; Domingo Benegas & Ramon Heredia; Eusebio Bejerano, Jose Capon & Adelardo; Jose Ufarte, Luis Aragones, Jose Garate, Javier Irureta & Heraldo Bezerra.

CELTIC:

Denis Connaghan; Danny McGrain & Jim Brogan; Davie Hay, Billy McNeill & Pat McCluskey; Jimmy Johnstone, Steve Murray, Kenny Dalglish, Harry Hood & Bobby Lennox. Substitutes; Ally Hunter, Tommy Callaghan, Dixie Deans & Paul Wilson.

Jock Stein's main selection dilemma had been up front, the Parkhead boss eventually going for the pace of the recently invigorated Bobby Lennox over the aerial power of Dixie Deans. Midway through the first half, the explosive turn of speed possessed by Lennox would see him through on goal, only to pull his effort wide. Kenny Dalglish forced Miguel Reina into a decent save before the interval then missed the chance of the match shortly after the break, the Hoops striker caught in two minds and his effort cleared. As in the first leg, what price a goal to put the pressure on the Spaniards?

The hosts would eventually impose themselves on the game, Celtic defending deeper and deeper before conceding late on, as extra-time loomed. Fully in line with the way this tie had gone, there was huge controversy over Atletico's opener 13 minutes from time. Striker Jose Garate had been born in Argentina to Spanish parents, and was now a naturalised Spaniard, an international player in his adopted country since 1967. He had been a prolific goalscorer for Atletico since the year before that, finishing as the country's leading marksman for three successive La Liga seasons as that decade came to an end, before twice scoring the winning goals in the final of the Copa del Rey. Garate had been anonymous in Glasgow, before being replaced by the subsequently dismissed Quique, but he would strike now to turn the tie in Atletico's favour, albeit looking for all the world offside as he poked the ball past the previously unbeatable Denis Connaghan. With noise levels in the Vicente Calderon reaching a crescendo, Celts threw everything into snatching the late away goal which would send them into a third European Cup final in eight years. Then, as so often happens, they were caught with a sucker punch, Madrid skipper Adelardo seizing on a loose ball to blast it high past Connaghan with four minutes to play.

As a footnote to this tie, having disgraced the game of football in Glasgow, Juan Carlos Lorenzo and his Atletico Madrid side came within seconds of winning the European Cup in Brussels the following month. Bayern Munich had defeated Ujpest Dosza in the other semi-final and would enjoy the bulk of the play in the Heysel Stadium, however, a goalless 90 minutes saw the teams play out an edgy extra half-hour. With just six minutes of that period remaining, Luis Aragones whipped a delightful free-kick past Sepp Maier in the Bayern goal, and it looked like the trophy was heading back to Madrid after an eight-year absence, a first-ever triumph for *The Mattressmakers*. Then with the referee looking at his watch, Bayern defender Hans-Georg Schwarzenbeck launched a speculative shot from fully 30 yards, Miguel Reina beaten low at his post to give the Germans a second bite. They would gleefully take that two nights later, doubles from Uli Hoeness and Gerd Muller taking the Big Cup to Bavaria.

History would repeat itself for Atletico 40 years later, in Lisbon of all places and against Real Madrid of all teams. Diego Godin's first-half goal would see them again have one hand on the elusive trophy as the match entered the third minute of stoppage time, before the head of Sergio Ramos gave the nine-time winners a lifeline. As in Brussels four decades earlier, that would be it for Atletico's hopes, extra-time strikes from Gareth Bale, Marcelo and a Cristiano Ronaldo penalty giving Real Madrid their cherished Decima.

And just to complete the set, the same two sides clashed again in the Milan final two years later, all four Real Madrid scorers from Lisbon converting shoot-out spot-kicks as they secured their 11th European Cup at their neighbours' expense, Sergio Ramos and Yannick Carrasco strikes in normal time having been followed by a goalless additional period in the San Siro.

At the time of writing, Atletico Madrid have yet to place that gold star above their crest.

Karma may not always be instant, but it can still be a bitch.

Chapter 27

World records and domestic Doubles

There was no time for Jock Stein or his Celtic players to mull over the events in Madrid, or for that matter in Glasgow, two weeks earlier. Three days after that late defeat in the Vicente Calderon, the Hoops were on their travels again, this time the much shorter journey to Falkirk.

The final scheduled League programme of the season had thrown up a classic Top v Bottom clash at Brockville, on Saturday, 27 April 1974. For the home side it was win or bust, only the two points on offer for an unlikely victory over the champions-elect giving them any hope of avoiding relegation, in what was their 34th and final match of a difficult campaign. Falkirk also needed results involving East Fife, Clyde and Dunfermline Athletic to go their way. Having won only four of their 33 League games to date, it was a long shot at best for The Bairns.

In contrast, due to their Scottish Cup commitments, Celtic would still have three games to play after Falkirk and had the luxury of knowing that they required only a single point from these four matches to secure a ninth title in succession, and even that assumed that second-placed Hibernian would pick up wins in each of their final three fixtures. It had long since been a matter of when and not if the holy grail of nine-in-a-row would be clinched by Stein's side.

Celtic, of course, had been setting and breaking domestic records since the days of The Bould Bhoys, following on from inaugural champions Dumbarton - who had shared then won the first two Scottish League titles - by claiming the next two, then becoming the first side to win three, and then four of the first eight competitions by 1898. No new club has ever had such an impact in Scottish football. They would create a new benchmark under Willie Maley by winning five-in-a-row in 1909, then extend that to six the following season, a record which stood for six decades until this current Hoops regime eclipsed it at Bayview in 1972. One point would now see that latest run stretched to a magical nine.

Achieving 'The Nine' would allow Celtic to match a world record for successive League Championship wins, something only two other clubs in history could claim. Old European foes MTK Budapest had lifted the Hungarian title between 1916/17 and

1924/25, before bitter rivals Ferencvaros stopped the 10. Strictly speaking, the first two of those were wartime titles, which unlike many other countries were recognised by the Hungarian FA. In the interests of balance, MTK had also won the last national championship before war broke out in 1914. As an aside, Willie Maley's Celtic had faced FA Cup-winners Burnley in Budapest in May 1914, the English side wearing the blue-and-white jerseys of MTK at the request of the organisers to contrast with Celtic's green-and-white, the colours of Ferencvaros, thus adding a bit of spice to the contest. It clearly worked, as no prisoners were taken in a match which ended with players swapping punches on the pitch. This was the infamous Budapest Cup game.

The other team to have claimed nine successive titles before 1974 was CSKA Sofia. The Bulgarian Army club had won the national championship between 1954 and 1962, albeit, ever the pedant, I should point out that this included a transitional 'half-season' in the early part of 1958, to facilitate a move to the more traditional autumn-spring calendar favoured by most European nations. To win that particular competition, CSKA played just 11 games, as opposed to the normal 'home and away' 22, with no promotion or relegation taking place. By the time the Plovdiv duo of Spartak and Botev had finished ahead of them in the spring of 1963 to end CSKA's run, the top division had been extended to 16 teams. CSKA Sofia would have to wait until May 1966 to reclaim their crown, just as Celtic's latest reign was commencing in Scotland. So, it is a fact that no club from any of the western European Leagues had ever achieved the level of dominance enjoyed by Jock Stein's wonderful sides in Scotland from the mid-sixties onwards, and there would be no intention of stopping anytime soon. The Celtic manager sent out the following team to ensure the world record was matched at Brockville.

Denis Connaghan; Davie Hay & Jim Brogan; Steve Murray, Billy McNeill & Pat McCluskey; Harry Hood, Kenny Dalglish, Dixie Deans, Tommy Callaghan & Bobby Lennox. Substitutes; Danny McGrain & Jimmy Johnstone.

I had been attending Celtic games since the autumn of 1965, so had not known anything other than Celts being champions in my young lifetime. It was a given, just as Jock was the manager, Billy was captain and Dad went to the match on a Saturday afternoon. I had been too young to go to Motherwell or Ibrox to see the first two flags being secured, or the school night games at Dunfermline and Kilmarnock which saw the run stretch to four. However, I had been very fortunate to witness three of the last four clinched, at Tynecastle, Hampden and Bayview, as Willie Maley's record finally ceded into the history books. April 1973 at Easter Road was the exception, Dad, probably wisely, feeling that was a risk not worth taking with 50,000 supporters expected.

We were both in Falkirk today though, stood in the higher of the two ends behind the goal. Up behind us on a gantry was a TV camera crew, this being perhaps the only match I can recall being recorded from behind the goal for the BBC Sportsreel highlights programme later that night. We would see Celts get off to a dreadful start, as home striker Kirky Lawson took advantage of some hesitancy in the Hoops defence to put the Bairns 1-0 up within three minutes. The hopes of the home support would not last long, dashed by a goal which will live long in the memory of Celtic fans of a certain vintage. As we approached the 20-minute mark, there seemed little danger as Kenny Dalglish picked up the ball in midfield, however, The King was now displaying the full range of powers which would mark him out as world-class long before he ever wore the red shirt of Liverpool. As the Falkirk defenders backed off, he advanced menacingly towards the home goal, before unleashing a shot which left keeper Ally Donaldson helpless as it nestled in those old curved stanchions just a few yards in front of us.

It was a goal fit to clinch a world record, albeit out of keeping with much of the other play on offer. There was little else on the pitch to entertain the bulk of the crowd, the remainder of the afternoon consisting of a celebratory singsong, the old stuff, the good stuff, the impromptu concert only ended by the whistle which made Celtic champions and consigned Falkirk to Second Division football the following season. Over the wall went the youngsters and a few of those who might have known better, much to the displeasure of Dad and most of the 'old team' in our company, a view I am certain would have been shared by Jock Stein. Rather reluctantly, it seemed to me, the Celtic team reappeared from the tunnel to take their well-earned lap of honour around Brockville, their facial expressions not those normally associated with such an occasion, perhaps as a result of their uninvited escort.

This would mark a low point in the career of Falkirk manager, John Prentice. He had captained the Brockville club to a Scottish Cup victory over Kilmarnock back in 1957, completing his own domestic set of honours after a spell at Ibrox had seen him claim League and League Cup medals there. He moved into management with Arbroath in 1960 and was the man who replaced Johnny Haddow to develop the teenage Harry for Clyde two years later, then sold him to Sunderland in 1964. John had succeeded Jock Stein as Scotland manager by the time his old skipper Davie White brought Harry back to Shawfield in 1966. Ongoing tensions between him and the SFA brought the international role to an end, with Prentice resurfacing at Falkirk in October 1966, then moving to Dundee two years later. In the small, incestuous world that is Scottish football, Prentice had given up his role as Dundee manager in 1971 to commence a second spell in charge at Brockville, his replacement at Dens Park being...Davie White! They would enjoy mixed fortunes this season, White leading the Dark Blues to a League Cup final victory over Stein's Celtic, whilst his old boss would now be relegated against Harry's new team.

Bizarrely, two of Celtic's remaining three League games would be squeezed into a 24-hour period in the midweek before the Scottish Cup final. On Monday, 29 April 1974, a much-changed side travelled to Aberdeen, teenage centre-half Frank Welsh awarded a first-team debut. Harry came off the bench to replace Dixie Deans for the final 20 minutes of a drab goalless draw at Pittodrie. And the following evening, Morton were the visitors to Parkhead as Harry unusually donned the number four shorts in the never-to-be-repeated half-back line of Hood, McNeill and Welsh. With the scoreline blank at the interval, there was a welcome return for Brian McLaughlin, missing from first-team action since the brutal assault by Clyde's Willie McVie almost eight months earlier, Andy Lynch making way. The opening goal was scored on the hour by young Greenock winger Alex McGhee, however, within seven minutes, McLaughlin would light up Celtic Park, beating future teammate Roy Baines in the Morton goal with a delightful lob to end the scoring at 1-1. As an aside, this match features in a trivia question, as apparently it marked the only League starts for two Celtic players during the Jock Stein nine-in-a-row sequence, those being Lynch and Jackie McNamara.

Three successive League draws in four days marked the beginning of the build-up to that Saturday's Scottish Cup final against Dundee United. This would be a first-ever appearance in a national showpiece for the Tayside club, Jim McLean becoming the first manager to lead a team into its maiden Scottish Cup final since a certain Jock Stein at Dunfermline in April 1961. Stein had an incredible record in the competition, following up that success with the Pars by leading Hibernian into the last-four in March 1965, then taking over at Celtic to guide The Bhoys past Motherwell in the semi-final then his old Dunfermline players in the final the next month. He would then reach the Scottish Cup final with Celtic in all but one of the next nine seasons, the only exception being 1968, when the Hoops were beaten in the third round at home by... Dunfermline Athletic, who went on to beat Hearts in that year's final. Of those nine Hampden appearances with his two clubs, Jock had won six, losing out in 1966, 1970 and 1973, whilst the recent record in the League Cup finals, where Celts had contrived to lose four-in-a-row, had dented a record and reputation previously thought to be invincible. Indeed, between Drybrough, League Cup and Scottish Cup finals, Celtic had actually lost the previous five, the 6-1 win over Hibernian in May 1972 being the last success. It was time to get back on track, the game with Dundee United also offering the opportunity for Stein and his men to add to their tally of four League and Cup doubles since 1967.

Harry had experienced mixed fortunes in Scottish Cup finals since joining Celtic in March 1969. Having played against the Hoops for Clyde in the fourth-round ties the previous month, he would be ineligible for that April's 4-0 hammering of Rangers, and despite making 46 appearances in his first full season at Parkhead, Harry would lose his place at the critical run-in stage to miss out on the Scottish and European Cup final defeats 12 months later. He would bounce back from that disappointment to score the winning goal in the 2-1 win over Rangers in May 1971, the last of the 33 he had netted in that top-scoring, Double-winning season. An injury sustained at Tynecastle in late March effectively ended Harry's chances of featuring in that 6-1 destruction of Hibernian in the 1972 Scottish Cup final, whilst an illness suffered in the build-up to the 1973 semi-final with

Dundee would ultimately see him drop out of the team which lost 3-2 to Rangers in the centenary cup final. But today would be a good day.

The teams lined up as follows on a damp afternoon at Hampden on Saturday, 4 May 1974, in front of 76,000 spectators.

CELTIC:

Denis Connaghan; Danny McGrain & Jim Brogan; Steve Murray, Billy McNeill & Pat McCluskey; Jimmy Johnstone, Harry Hood, Dixie Deans, Davie Hay & Kenny Dalglish. Substitutes; Tommy Callaghan & Bobby Lennox.

DUNDEE UNITED:

Sandy Davie; Pat Gardner & Frank Kopel; Jackie Copland, Doug Smith & Walter Smith; Graeme Payne, Archie Knox, Andy Gray, George Fleming & Doug Houston. Substitutes; Tommy Traynor & Andy Rolland.

Whilst this was United's first Scottish Cup final, full-back Pat Gardner was looking for his second winner's medal in the competition. Playing alongside Tommy Callaghan, he had scored the second and decisive goal at Celtic Park in January 1968 which saw the Pars eliminate the European champions and cup-holders before going all the way to the final, where Gardner would score twice as Dunfermline Athletic beat Hearts 3-1 to claim a second - and to date last - success. Gardner had helped to knock his old side out in a quarter-final replay in this season's Road to Hampden, after a 1-1 draw at East End Park, the Tangerine Terrors having earlier beaten both Airdrieonians and Morton at Tannadice before defeating Hearts in the last four.

Doug Houston had spent a decade along the road at Dens Park from the early 1960s, much of that in the company of Steve Murray. The pair had lined up for the Dark Blues against Celtic at Hampden in the League Cup final of October 1967, as the Hoops won 5-3, but, like Gardner and Callaghan, they would now be in opposite camps for Scottish football's 1974 showpiece.

On the back of three Hampden cup final defeats in the past 12 months, there was a certain anxiety as we took our spots on the Kings Park terrace before the match. Two years earlier, I sat on a stanchion high up in that same section to watch Dixie and co beat Hibernian to record my only cup final victory to date, defeats either side of that against Aberdeen, Partick Thistle, Hibernian and Dundee giving me a record which placed me at serious risk of adoption. But today would be a good day.

The destination of the 1974 Scottish Cup was effectively decided in a five-minute spell midway through the first half, with Harry and Dixie Deans to the fore. Both men had enjoyed that special feeling of scoring for Celtic in a winning Scottish Cup final, indeed Deans had followed up his 1972 masterclass by doing everything other than find the net 12 months later against Rangers, setting up Kenny Dalglish for the Hoops opener before being cruelly robbed of the goal his performance had deserved when John Greig dived to punch his netbound shot off the line, the Rangers skipper conceding the penalty kick from which George Connelly equalised. As the clock moved on to 20 minutes, Dixie would again be the provider, his lobbed pass leaving Harry and United keeper Sandy Davie in a race for the ball at the edge of the box. We had a fantastic view as Harry timed his leap perfectly to meet the bouncing ball and nod it over Davie for 1-0, his 18th goal of the campaign and his second in a major cup final.

Five minutes later, the pair combined brilliantly again to seal the game, this time Harry playing a one-two with Deans on the left side of the box before slicing the ball towards Jimmy Johnstone on the penalty spot. The little winger, in turn, nudged it right to the feet of Steve Murray, whose low drive beat Davie at his near post to give the Bhoys a two-goal lead.

United worked hard to claw their way back into the final, their best spell coming immediately after the interval, the efforts of Andy Gray and Archie Knox up front foiled by Denis Connaghan, as gradually Celts regained the initiative. With the ribbons being laid out for the imminent presentation, there was one final, wonderful twist of the afternoon. Kenny Dalglish had never – and would never – score in a cup final which Celtic won, so perhaps the fates or the King's conscience persuaded him to pass to Deans when clean through in the dying moments of the match. Dixie drew Sandy Davie before clipping the ball over him towards goal, the back-peddling Walter Smith looking back in anguish as he raced to cover the other post, the ball passing him on its way into the opposite corner of the net for 3-0. That was a 33rd goal of the season for Scotland's top marksman, all but five scored since November, sadly not enough to book his place in the Scotland squad for the summer World Cup finals in West Germany.

At full-time, we had that fabulous and familiar sight of Jock Stein rushing on to the Hampden turf to embrace his captain, Billy McNeill, the man who had walked up those stairs so often to receive the silverware earned in this current, unsurpassed era of success. Before he did so, Billy would lead his players on a lap of honour to thank the supporters. Such traditions had been suspended following an invasion of the pitch by Rangers supporters after the Celts had defeated their favourites in the League Cup final of 1965, the players now getting around that ban by doing so without the cup, much to the displeasure of SFA supremo Willie Allan. Then it was time to make their way up the famous steps to provide the images for the Sunday newspapers and lifetime memories for the tens of thousands of us who had filled Hampden praying for this very moment.

'Our Cup' was back in Paradise, after a 12-month hiatus, for the sixth time in a decade under Jock Stein. The League and Cup double had been secured for the fifth time in that period, Stein's incredible impact on the club illustrated by the fact that this feat had only been achieved four times in the 80 years which preceded his arrival as Celtic manager, the last of which had been achieved when Jock had been the captain of the club, back in April 1954.

For Harry, who had played a key part in securing three of those Doubles, it was a second Scottish Cup winner's medal in two final appearances, the skilful Celt having scored crucial goals in both games.

And for me…well, those adoption papers could perhaps go on hold meantime.

Chapter 28

A glorious era ends in Athens

Double-winners Celtic ended the 1973/74 season by beating English FA Cup-winners Liverpool 4-1 on their own Anfield turf, the testimonial match for the Reds' former Dundee United centre-half, Ron Yeats, memorable for the sight of Bobby Charlton in the Hoops, who thrilled the 10,000 travelling supporters by opening the scoring early in the match. Harry followed up his Hampden strike with the last of Celtic's goals, eight minutes after the break, Vic Davidson and Bobby Lennox having scored in the interim. Liverpool's guest substitute Bob Tynan netted a late consolation goal just before the end.

That summer saw the departure of two players who had won a host of medals over the past five years at Parkhead. Goalkeeper Evan Williams had managed just one first-team appearance in 18 months, and sadly he was at fault for all three goals that night, as Celtic slumped to defeat in Basel. He was released and would later join Clyde, against whom, co-incidentally, I had seen him make his debut in a Glasgow Cup-tie back in October 1969. A week or so after that game, an ordering off for Tommy Gemmell whilst on Scotland duty in Hamburg provided a major opportunity for young full-back David Hay, chosen by Jock Stein to replace the Lisbon Lion for the League Cup final victory over St Johnstone. By the summer of 1974, Hay was one of the finest midfield players on this island, tipped by many as the natural successor to Billy McNeill as captain at Celtic. There had been ongoing contractual issues between Hay and the club for some time now, triggering rumours of a 'big-money' move to England, which refused to go away. He had excelled in the World Cup finals for Scotland and on his return from Germany, a cheque for £225,000 saw him start a new career at Chelsea. Celtic would effectively lose two players in that deal, as his close friend George Connelly would never really be the same again once David had left Glasgow. More on George to follow.

The new season got underway with yet more silverware for Celtic…albeit only just. After three failed final attempts in the first three competitions, and a semi-final scare at Dens Park when it took a last-minute Dixie Deans goal to take the tie to extra-time, the Drybrough Cup was won following a penalty shootout victory over

Rangers at Hampden on Saturday, 3 August 1974. Celts seemed to have secured victory, when Paul Wilson's header early in extra-time gave them a 2-1 lead, but a late Pat McCluskey own goal ensured that the trophy would be decided on that most nerve-wracking of finales. Harry had been replaced earlier by Jackie McNamara, robbing the Hoops of an expert penalty-taker, and when Bobby Lennox saw his first effort saved by new Ibrox keeper Stewart Kennedy before Sandy Jardine converted his, things looked ominous for the Hoops. Denis Connaghan had contrived to throw the ball into his own net against Airdrieonians at Broomfield in the opening tie of this season, with Jock Stein presumably looking for Evan Williams' phone number at that point, however, the big keeper would now be the hero, saving from Derek Parlane then Tommy McLean. One by one, the remaining Celts stepped up to beat Kennedy, McCluskey, then Steve Murray, then Tommy Callaghan. All of a sudden, it was all down to Jimmy Johnstone. Score and Celtic win. Jinky had made a habit of netting against Rangers throughout his career, and he would do so again, thrashing the ball past Kennedy into the net as Harry added a Drybrough Cup medal to his list of honours achieved at Celtic.

As an aside, Tommy Callaghan expressed his regret to me at having never scored a cup final goal. Well, I think netting in a penalty-shootout against Rangers that day ticks that box nicely for you, Tommy.

The path to an 11th successive League Cup final began with a section which included Dundee United, Motherwell and Ayr United, Harry featuring in five of the six games as Celts qualified from the group with a game to spare, despite an early defeat at Somerset Park. Jock Stein fielded his Drybrough Cup-winning side for the opening fixture against Motherwell at Celtic Park on Saturday, 10 August 1974, first-half strikes from Kenny Dalglish and Paul Wilson securing the points in a 2-1 win. Two nights later, Harry dropped to the bench as Billy McNeill's testimonial season kicked off with a glamour match against Liverpool at Celtic Park, 60,000 supporters paying tribute to the club's greatest-ever skipper as the Hoops drew 1-1 with the FA Cup-holders, playing under their legendary manager Bill Shankly for the final time. Harry and Paul Wilson replaced Bobby Lennox and Kenny Dalglish after the restart, and it was Wilson who grabbed the equaliser to cancel out John Toshack's first-half header.

Within 48 hours, Celtic would suffer a first defeat at the hands of Ayr United since November 1959, coincidentally by the same 3-2 scoreline as that afternoon at Parkhead almost 15 years earlier. Goals from Steve Murray and George Connelly had twice brought Celtic level at Somerset Park, before a blunder by restored keeper Ally Hunter handed Alex Ingram the chance to win the match for the hosts.

Harry dropped back on to the bench for the visit of section leaders Dundee United on Saturday, 17 August 1974. He would replace Jackie McNamara, but only after the midfielder had scored the only goal of the game from a knockdown by Dixie Deans, just after the half-hour. The pivotal night in the group was the return against Ayr United in midweek, Celts again trailing twice before emerging 5-2 winners on the night. Johnny Doyle gave the visitors an early lead they held until 10 minutes before the break, Jimmy Johnstone diving full-length to head an equaliser from a Kenny Dalglish corner kick. Ayr scored again at the start of the second half through centre-half Rikki Fleming but found themselves 3-2 down within five minutes, Bobby Lennox then Paul Wilson doing the damage. Both man-of-the-match Johnstone and Wilson would complete personal doubles to secure the points at 5-2, Jinky then receiving a tremendous ovation as he made way for Harry with five minutes remaining.

As an early Paul Wilson strike gave Celts the victory required for qualification up at Tannadice on Saturday, 24 August 1974, Harry joined Jim Brogan and Dixie Deans in the reserve side beaten 2-1 by Dundee United at Celtic Park. He returned in midweek as the Hoops completed the section by sharing four goals with Motherwell at Fir Park, Kenny Dalglish with a double either side of the interval. The strongest group saw Hibernian emerge ahead of cup-holders Dundee and Rangers. They would face Kilmarnock in the two-legged quarter-final whilst Celtic would meet Hamilton Academical.

The last day in August saw the League campaign open with a 5-0 home victory over Willie Fernie's newly-promoted Kilmarnock. Scottish Cup-final heroes Harry and Dixie Deans received a painful reminder that there is often little sentimentality in football, both on reserve team duty at Rugby Park as Jock Stein opted for Paul Wilson and Vic Davidson alongside Kenny Dalglish and Jimmy Johnstone up front, with Bobby Lennox on the bench. Their case wouldn't be helped much that day as all four forwards scored before Steve Murray converted a last-minute penalty.

Harry was again missing seven days later, as Celts made the short trip to his old Shawfield stomping ground, to face a Clyde team with Evan Williams between the posts, the keeper having swapped clubs in the summer. Jock Stein was still struggling to choose an established number one, Denis Connaghan having literally 'thrown one in' at Broomfield whilst Ally Hunter's gaffe in the Somerset defeat had seen him quickly hand the gloves back to the former St Mirren man. Wouldn't you just know that the bold Evan would play a blinder in the first half, by which time his Clyde team were two goals to the good, thanks mainly to future Celtic midfielder, Dom Sullivan, who set up both for Gerry Marshall and Bobby Ferris. Jock's alterations, with George Connelly and Pat McCluskey swapping roles, would quickly pay dividends, the latter scoring Celtic's third from his new midfield beat, after Kenny Dalglish and Vic Davidson had levelled the match. Substitute Bobby Lennox made it 4-2 late on.

Harry returned to the starting line-up and got off the scoring mark for the season with a double over Hamilton Academical in the first leg of the League Cup quarter-final at Celtic Park on Wednesday, 11 September 1974, his first a quite exquisite lob over keeper Rikki Ferguson on the half-hour. If that was down to accuracy and touch then his second just after the restart was all about power, Harry blasting home on the volley after Jimmy Johnstone had worked his usual magic down the right wing.

The midweek double saw Harry return to the League squad for the visit of Rangers three days later, a rite of passage day for yours truly, as I attended this fixture for the first time. Dad still wasn't too comfortable about me going to these matches, so it was left to my older brother, now in his late teens, to do the needful. I can recall clearly walking along Janefield Street and, for the first time ever, hearing chants ringing out from our ground which were not the ones I had grown up to love. Once inside, tingling with excitement, we took our place much further back in the traditional Celtic End than normal. My recollection is that most of the singing started back there in those days. Harry was listed as one of the substitutes as the following teams lined up on Saturday, 14 September 1974.

CELTIC:

Denis Connaghan; Danny McGrain & Jim Brogan; Pat McCluskey, Billy McNeill & Tommy Callaghan; Jimmy Johnstone, Steve Murray, Kenny Dalglish, Vic Davidson & Paul Wilson. Substitutes; Harry Hood & Bobby Lennox.

RANGERS:

Stewart Kennedy; Sandy Jardine & John Greig; Ian McDougall, Colin Jackson & Tom Forsyth; Quinton Young, Derek Johnstone, Derek Parlane, Alex MacDonald & Graham Fyfe. Substitutes; Ally Scott & Tommy McLean.

There was plenty of singing going on around us just after the half-hour, as King Kenny blasted a shot over Stewart Kennedy which flew into the net off the crossbar to give the Hoops the lead. At that point, my brother leaned over to say something along the lines of, *"That's the first of many,"* however, sadly, those adoption papers would soon be getting wheeled out again, as the second half proceeded to go downhill rapidly. A young and largely unknown Ian McDougall equalised out of the blue before a clash between Jim Brogan and Derek Parlane saw the Celt sent off but the Ibrox striker, remarkably, remain on the pitch. The goalkeeping problems then once again came back to haunt the 10-man Celts, as Denis Connaghan misjudged a cross, allowing Colin Jackson a free header for 2-1 with 15 minutes remaining. As the niggles continued all over the pitch, Jimmy Johnstone's 82nd-minute booking saw him immediately replaced by Harry, and by the time Parlane had finally been given his marching orders, in the dying seconds, the loss of an unbeaten home run against Rangers, which had stretched back six years to the autumn of 1968, would sadly be the legacy of my first major Glasgow derby. Celtic now slipped to third place in the table, behind new leaders Hibernian and Rangers.

The mystery of George Connelly's non-appearance in that game would be cleared up in the immediate aftermath, reports indicating that the brilliant but troubled Celt had not turned up at the scheduled time and place and, at 25, had basically had enough of the limelight he attracted by playing football at that level. Between that news and Saturday's defeat, it would be fair to say that preparations could have gone better for the midweek European Cup first-round tie with Olympiakos Piraeus, the reigning Greek champions. This would be Celtic's ninth consecutive assault on European football's blue riband competition under Jock Stein, whilst on only two of those occasions, in 1967 and 1973, had his team failed to reach at least the quarter-final, Dynamo Kiev and Ujpest Dosza, respectively, the two clubs to breach that proud record. That would be seriously under threat after a frustrating and ultimately disappointing night at Celtic Park, on Wednesday, 18 September 1974. I remember the headlines after a heavy defeat endured by Scotland in Portugal under Andy Roxburgh, "the night a team died," or something similar. I always equate the Olympiakos tie with a similar feeling about the great Celtic sides under Jock. Just over two years previously, I had witnessed perhaps the last truly wonderful performance by a Hoops side in a major match, the 1972 Scottish Cup final, a 6-1 demolition over the finest Hibernian team of my lifetime, a side who would have been champions in any other era. Perhaps symbolically, it was the last time Celtic would wear that Lisbon crew-neck jersey on a big occasion, a decade after it had replaced the old rugby-collared Hoops.

From that fabulous afternoon, whilst two further League titles had been secured plus, indeed, a recent Double, it was hard to escape the possibility that we were watching a side in decline, and it was not difficult to fathom why. The genius of Bobby Murdoch had peaked, then left the following season, with the three remaining Lions, Billy McNeill, Jimmy Johnstone and Bobby Lennox, all now the wrong side of 30. Of those three, only Cesar was an automatic pick, Jinky disappearing from the team for long periods, often unexplained, leading to unhelpful speculation. Stein had planned and, in many cases, proactively created the space for their successors to follow, however, the changing world of football had seen Lou Macari then Davie Hay move to England, whilst George Connelly was now also lost to the Celtic manager. These were top-class players, whose individual and collective loss would have been felt by any team. The career of the next young hope, Brian McLaughlin, was effectively ended after a horrific Willie McVie challenge in September 1973, whilst the goalkeeping position had never been adequately filled since Ronnie Simpson's injury, some five years ago now. Ally Hunter could and should have been the answer, however, ironically, the first Celtic keeper since 'Faither' to play at international level lost his confidence after losing a goal for Scotland. Ally was never the same for me.

Then there was the curious case of Dixie Deans, hat-trick hero at Hampden in 1972, following that up with 33 goals in each of the two following campaigns. He had been a peripheral figure since his excellent performance in the most recent Scottish Cup final - where he had scored one and made the other two as Celts beat Dundee United 3-0 - starting just twice this season. Despite being linked with moves to Fulham and Partick Thistle, a hat-trick in the 6-1 weekend reserve victory over Rangers would see him return to the bench for the visit of Olympiakos, as Jock Stein went with the following team.

Denis Connaghan; Danny McGrain & Jim Brogan; Steve Murray, Billy McNeill & Pat McCluskey; Jimmy Johnstone, Harry Hood, Kenny Dalglish, Tommy Callaghan & Paul Wilson. Substitutes; Ally Hunter, Jackie McNamara, Roddie MacDonald, Dixie Deans & Bobby Lennox.

Celtic's first-ever meeting with Greek opposition followed on perfectly from their previous tie in the competition, against Atletico Madrid, as a South American was booked within a minute for a foul on Jimmy Johnstone. In fairness, the chap concerned, Uruguayan midfielder Milton Viera, was a player. Barely out of his teens, he had featured in all three of his country's group games in London at the 1966 World Cup finals, as unbeaten Uruguay progressed with England to the quarter-final, before missing out on the 4-0 defeat by West Germany at Hillsborough. At that time, he played his club football at Nacional, and he could very well have faced Celtic the following year. In August 1967, after goalless draws in both legs of the final of the Copa Libertadores, Viera's Nacional would lose 2-1 to Racing Club of Buenos Aires in the Santiago play-off. It would thus be the Argentinians who would progress for their infamous clashes with Celtic.

After a brief spell with Boca Juniors, Viera returned to Uruguay to sign for new champions Penarol in 1968, suffering defeat once again in the final of the Copa Libertadores in May 1970 with his new club, this time to another Argentinian side, Estudiantes. After a trophy-laden decade in his native Uruguay, he headed for Europe to sign for Olympiakos in 1972, as did Penarol teammate Julio Losada, the duo having added two Greek championships and a Greek Cup medal to their tally before lining up in Glasgow in September 1974. That would be an eventful night for Viera, following up his early booking by putting Olympiakos ahead 10 minutes before the interval, having played a delicious one-two with Losada, then becoming the fourth player to see red against Celtic in successive European matches at Parkhead by tugging Harry's shirt as the Celt sought an equaliser. He would merely delay that goal by 60 seconds, Paul Wilson volleying a Bobby Lennox cut-back past keeper Panagiotis Kelesidis. There would be much for Celts to do in Athens in a fortnight to avoid the old *"Greek Tragedy"* headlines.

As a footnote to this match, a section of the Celtic support had grown restless as the second half progressed with no sign of a breakthrough, eventually breaking into the inevitable chants for Dixie Deans. This was a common occurrence at that time, with Jimmy Johnstone often the player involved. My dad would just as inevitably turn to me and say, "Well, we won't be getting him then," in reference to Jock's alleged stubbornness in bowing to the demands of the crowd if it didn't suit him. As always, Dad was correct, Dixie stayed on the bench, Stein introducing Bobby Lennox for Jim Brogan instead.

There was still no sign of the prolific Dixie Deans at his old Fir Park stomping ground, three days later, two Bobby Lennox penalties either side of the break enabling the Hoops to bounce back from that European disappointment with a 2-1 win, on both occasions the veteran hitman brought down by Motherwell keeper Graham Lloyd. The hosts were currently between managers, Ian St John having accepted an offer from Portsmouth with Harry's old Clyde teammate Willie McLean due to arrive from Queen of the South to take over. Harry sustained an ankle injury at Fir Park and was replaced by Deans in the shadow Hoops team which qualified for the League Cup semi-final at nearby Douglas Park the following midweek, the striker drawing Celtic level late in the first half after an early Billy McNeill own goal reduced the aggregate deficit to 2-1. Second-half goals from Tommy Callaghan, Jackie McNamara and Bobby Lennox sealed a 4-2 win, with Accies' young striking prospect Paul Hegarty also on target.

Harry returned for the home game against bottom-dogs Ayr United on the last Saturday of September, his seventh-minute goal controversially ruled offside by the linesman. Dixie Deans did open the scoring in the 20th minute then set Paul Wilson up to head the Bhoys into a 2-0 lead by the half-hour. Doug Somner replied for the visitors from a Johnny Doyle assist before Kenny Dalglish sent Celts in at the break 3-1 ahead. Two sensational second-half strikes by Wilson then Harry ended the contest at 5-1 with 40 minutes still remaining. No doubt Jock Stein would have been annoyed at the loss of further goals to John Dickson and future Celt Joe Filippi, which ended the scoring at 5-3. Such slackness at the back could be fatal in Athens in midweek. A shock home defeat for Hibernian at the hands of St Johnstone that afternoon saw Rangers go top with Celtic one point behind in second place.

The squad which left for Greece 48 hours later would not include the long-serving duo of Jimmy Quinn and Vic Davidson, or the much more recent signings Andy Lynch and Jimmy Bone, all of whom found themselves on the transfer list, as Jock Stein looked to revamp his team. Despite Olympiakos missing their suspended talisman Milton Viera, the Celtic manager must have feared the worst when he saw the state of the Karaiskakis pitch, described in one newspaper report as a "patchwork quilt" and by Stein himself as the poorest he had ever encountered in Europe. With Celts needing to score at least once to qualify after the disappointing home draw, he fielded an attack-minded formation with Jimmy Johnstone and Paul Wilson either side of Dixie Deans, the trio supported by Steve Murray, Kenny Dalglish and Tommy Callaghan. Harry watched on from the bench as the Hoops got off to the worst possible start, Michalis Kritikopoulos wandering unchallenged into the Celtic box to head a free-kick under Denis Connaghan within two minutes. Midway through the first half the tie had gone, a cruel deflection sending another dead-ball effort from Haralambos Stavropoulos into the opposite corner, with the Hoops keeper stranded, both goals sparking a pitch invasion by the local photography corps. Quite bizarre scenes.

On the hour, Stein's last throw of the dice was to introduce Harry and Bobby Lennox for Kenny Dalglish and Jimmy Johnstone, however, the hopelessness of the night was perhaps summed up perfectly as the mild-mannered Lisbon Lion was sent off by East German referee Rudi Gloeckner in the most ridiculous circumstances. He received a yellow card for pointing out to the bungling official that the Greeks were trying to make a substitution, then saw his match ended following a 'nothing' challenge late on. The 40,000 Greek supporters would have no interest in any of that, as they claimed the biggest scalp in their history. More than 40 years later, I would visit the stadium whilst in Athens for the Champions League qualifier with AEK, to be greeted with various celebratory images of that night. As an aside, that was also the case in Atletico Madrid's new stadium, in which I also took a tour a couple of years back. It's perhaps difficult to imagine nowadays just how huge Celtic were back then in European terms, however, sadly that night in the port of Piraeus would be a watershed for the club. We would not know it then, but we had just seen Billy McNeill's last European match as a player.

As a final word on this tie, Milton Viera returned to score from the penalty spot as Olympiakos' next European Cup game ended in a 5-1 defeat by Anderlecht in Brussels. UEFA responded to the use of firecrackers in the stadium for the victory over Celtic by forcing Olympiakos to play their next European match at a neutral venue, thus the second leg of that second-round tie with Anderlecht was played in Patras, 150 miles from Athens. A hat-trick from Maik Galakos, who did not feature in either of the matches against Celtic, secured a 3-0 win on the night, taking the Greek champions to within one goal of a stunning comeback against the Belgians. But they would now join Celtic on the European sidelines.

Chapter 29

The five-year wait for League Cup glory ends with another Dixie hat-trick

From the Athens Riviera, the Celtic party moved on to the Clyde estuary for the match at Dumbarton. Harry returned to the starting line-up two days after his 30th birthday and there was a reminder of another era, as sixties Celts John Cushley, Donald Watt and Willie Wallace all performed admirably for the Sons, Wispy pulling a goal back from the spot on 70 minutes after Jimmy Johnstone and Dixie Deans had given the Hoops a 2-0 interval lead. The restored Ally Hunter then produced a crucial save from future Bhoy Tom McAdam to prevent an equaliser, before the man Tom would in effect be signed to replace, Kenny Dalglish, put his disappointing display in Piraeus behind him with a stunning 82nd minute strike to make it 3-1.

Four nights later, Wednesday, 9 October 1974, Hampden was the venue as Celtic faced Airdrieonians in the League Cup semi-final. The competition had faced increasing criticism over recent years, turning spectators off, with the 'Snow Final' of the previous December a real low point. Less than 20,000 supporters bothered to turn up to see this tie involving the country's top club, another real cause for concern for the organisers. Those who stayed away would not have too many regrets, a Steve Murray goal on the hour the only real highlight as the Bhoys booked their place in an incredible 11th successive League Cup final. Forty miles or so to the east, Hibernian were edging out Falkirk by the same margin at Tynecastle, to set up a repeat of the April 1969 final between the sides, which Celts had won 6-2.

Steve Murray was again the matchwinner in that Saturday's home victory over Arbroath, just 16,000 spectators inside Celtic Park, perhaps reflecting some disappointment and disillusionment at the level of performances witnessed in the season so far. As always, Jock Stein would take action to address the problem, the Celtic manager deciding to bring his players in for double-training sessions over the course of the following week. It would have a dramatic effect.

Hibernian had been level with Celtic, a single point behind League leaders Rangers, when they arrived in Glasgow for a vital clash on Saturday, 19 October 1974, a dress rehearsal for the League Cup final due seven days later. The fact that supporters will turn up when they fancy the product on offer was once again demonstrated as almost 40,000 packed into Celtic Park for Part 1 of The Battle of the Greens, as the media loved to describe it back then. I remember the day so well, as out of nowhere, my Celtic were back, the Hoops rolling back the years with a vintage display of attacking football.

The tone of the match was set from the kick-off, Harry racing fully 40 yards to contest a throw-in. For the third successive match, Steve Murray opened the scoring, this time from the penalty spot in 15 minutes, after Hibernian keeper Jim McArthur had hauled Dixie Deans down in the box. Deans and Jimmy Johnstone then began to run riot, Jinky scoring a glorious second five minutes later, nutmegging Derek Spalding before poking a low shot just inside McArthur's post for 2-0. Within five minutes, the game was over, this time Dixie somehow squeezing the ball in at the far post from an acute angle, with Jinky following up to make sure. The only negative in a scintillating first half was the accidental clash of heads between Jim Brogan and Billy McNeill which saw the former stretchered off, Roddie MacDonald introduced to partner the dazed Cesar in central defence. With the huge crowd lapping it up, Celts went for the jugular after the interval, Deans making it 4-0 within 90 seconds as he hammered the ball past McArthur before rounding things off with a header 15 minutes from time, completing his second hat-trick against Hibernian. It had been a wonderful display, which few if any had seen coming, making it all the more special. Football has this incredible knack of changing your mood over the course of an afternoon.

It also has a rare habit of throwing up some incredible co-incidences, and there would be a classic case in hand, as Jock Stein listed the same 13 men as the previous week in front of a disappointing crowd of under 54,000 at a damp Hampden for the Scottish League Cup final on Saturday, 26 October 1974.

Ally Hunter; Danny McGrain & Jim Brogan; Steve Murray, Billy McNeill & Pat McCluskey; Jimmy Johnstone, Kenny Dalglish, Dixie Deans, Harry Hood & Paul Wilson. Substitutes; Roddie MacDonald & Bobby Lennox.

Hibernian had followed up that 5-0 defeat at Celtic Park by losing 4-2 to Juventus at Easter Road in their midweek UEFA Cup-tie. Eddie Turnbull chose the following men to deliver a second League Cup final victory over Celtic in three years.

Jim McArthur; John Brownlie & Des Bremner; Pat Stanton, Derek Spalding & John Blackley; Alex Edwards, Alex Cropley, Joe Harper, Iain Munro & Arthur Duncan. Substitutes; Bobby Smith & Willie Murray.

Folk tend to remember this game mainly for two reasons, Dixie's hat-trick and his bizarre third goal in particular, perhaps three in fairness, as most recall that Joe

Harper also scored a treble whilst his team were losing the match. I have an additional observation, the sheer quality of the six Celtic goals, which brought the League Cup home for the first time since Bertie Auld's early strike had beaten St Johnstone back in October 1969, in Harry's first major cup final. This would be a rare masterclass of attacking play from Jock Stein's men to consign the experimental offside rule to the dustbin of football history.

The Hoops started where they had left off at Celtic Park seven days earlier, taking the lead within six minutes with a superb team goal. Pat McCluskey's raking pass down the left picked out Dixie Deans with a marker tight on him, the striker producing a sublime flick which Kenny Dalglish took in his stride to drive past another Hibernian defender towards the byeline. The King then showed great composure to look up before sliding the ball across goal for Jimmy Johnstone to net his second League Cup final goal, almost a decade to the day he had scored his first in the 2-1 defeat by Rangers which had kicked off the present run of 11 appearances.

I always felt that McCluskey was an underrated player, often subjected to jibes about his weight which bordered on offensive for a man who wore the sacred Hoops in two European Cup semi-finals. Pat had started the move for the first goal, and he would be even more directly involved for Celtic's second, 10 minutes before the break, taking a pass from Harry before pitching the most perfect 40-yard ball into the path of Deans at the edge of the Hibernian box. Dixie did not need to break stride as he slipped his shot past Jim McArthur.

There was a brief attempt to spoil the Celtic party just before the interval, a spot of head tennis following a Hibernian corner allowing Harper to hook a shot over Ally Hunter from point-blank range to see the Hoops lead reduced to 2-1. However, within two minutes of the restart, Stein's men would produce another wonderful team goal. Danny McGrain fed Johnstone on the right, the little winger totally wrong-footing Hibs sweeper John Blackley before slipping a lovely pass into the path of Paul Wilson, whose unerring finish across McArthur found the inside of the far post for 3-1. Fabulous stuff.

On the hour, the untidiest goal of the afternoon arrived, Pat Stanton sending Alex Edwards down the right and the playmaker's cross deflecting off the outstretched boot of Billy McNeill to beat Hunter with Harper in close attendance. I'm fairly certain that this was given as an own goal at the time, and looking at footage now, it still appears to me that the Hibernian striker did not get a touch on the ball, but history has since recorded this as Harper's second of the day, as the score moved to 3-2. Within five minutes, that wouldn't matter anyway, as Deans added a second Hampden hat-trick against Hibernian to his CV, a third against them overall after his exploits the previous Saturday. The first was another wonderful piece of football from a Celtic side now in full flow. Harry did brilliantly to avoid a couple of challenges on the left before finding midfield partner Steve Murray on the opposite flank. Murray's clipped pass into the feet of Deans left the striker with much to do, however, his superb swivel and second touch left his defender for dead and him one-on-one with McArthur. There would be only one outcome as Dixie fired his shot through the keeper's legs to find the far corner and restore the Hoops' two-goal lead.

The next goal was either football genius or pantomime, depending on your mood or outlook. Harry's deep corner from the left cleared everyone except the lurking Johnstone, wide of the far post. His instinctive volley was heading back towards Harry or Govanhill, whichever it struck first, before Deans launched himself McGrory-esque to connect and bullet a header past a bewildered McArthur in the Hibernian goal. Jinky's reaction said it all, as he looked to the heavens, rolled his eyes and laughed. It was an *"I was there"* moment for all involved.

Hard to believe, perhaps, but there was still another sublime team goal to grace the final. With 15 minutes remaining, Murray began and ended the move which put Celts out of sight at 6-2, a classic example of pass and move. His interchange with Dalglish via a slick one-two with Wilson found the midfielder running at the left angle of the penalty area. As McArthur approached, Steve slipped a low left-foot shot back across the keeper into the bottom corner of the net for his fourth goal in as many games. Another wonderful strike, stunning in its build and execution, all of Celtic's goalscorers from the previous week's League win having now repeated the dose at Hampden against the same team.

It almost felt like bad manners that the ninth and final goal of the afternoon fell to Hibernian. There were only seven minutes between Celtic and a first success in this competition of the decade when Iain Munro beat McGrain to reach the left byeline. His low cross should have been food and drink to Hunter, however, once again there was disappointment as the keeper spilled the ball onto the arm, shoulder or back of Harper and over the line for 6-3.

That would be a minor irritation on the day, as we watched Billy McNeill lift the League Cup high above his head to the delight of the Celtic support, a sixth such success for Cesar, a long-awaited second for Harry, and a first for seven of his colleagues and myself. For the time being at least, all four trophies available for top-flight teams in Scotland would sit proudly side-by-side in the Parkhead trophy room.

October's purple patch for Dixie Deans and Jimmy Johnstone was recognised and rewarded with the inclusion of both Celts for Scotland's friendly with East Germany at Hampden four days later, Dixie receiving his international debut at the age of 28 beside Parkhead colleagues Jinky and Kenny Dalglish, whilst young Graeme Souness, now receiving expert tutelage from Bobby Murdoch at Middlesbrough, wore his country's colours for the first time in midfield. Dalglish would score Scotland's third with 15 minutes to play, in a comfortable 3-0 victory on the night.

November opened with a couple of narrow and fortunate wins for Celtic, as the race for 10-in-a-row resumed in earnest. Aberdeen winger Ian Purdie saw two shots come back off the woodwork, the second from a late penalty, as a Paul Wilson strike late in the first half saw Celts claim two points at home against the Dons on the opening Saturday. And it took a last-minute winner from Kenny Dalglish at Firhill in midweek to take Celts level with Rangers at the top of the table, both clubs now sharing an identical goal difference as well as points, the Ibrox club's win at Parkhead in September since offset by draws at Somerset and Tynecastle. Partick Thistle manager Bertie Auld faced his old club for the first time as a manager, and he saw his team fall behind early in the second half to a Dixie Deans header. On-loan English striker Eddie Prudham squared the match with 20 minutes remaining but Bobby Houston' second yellow card left the Jags with 10 men for the closing 12 minutes. Then with only seconds remaining, Dalglish beat Alan Rough with a low shot to secure the two vital points.

Rangers would edge back in front three days later, narrowly beating Dundee at Ibrox as Celts were held to a goalless draw at Tannadice. Dundee United keeper Hamish McAlpine crowned a fine personal performance by saving a Steve Murray penalty on the hour, after Vic Davidson had been fouled by Frank Kopel. The following week saw a number of positives at Parkhead, George Connelly restarting training after a two-month absence whilst Jock Stein broke the club's transfer record to bring in Ronnie Glavin from Partick Thistle, the fee believed to be in the order of £80,000. Harry would drop out as Ronnie made his debut in the number eight shirt for the home game against Airdrieonians 24 hours later, an afternoon which saw Jimmy Johnstone return from the hip injury suffered against Aberdeen at the start of the month to take a seat on the bench. He would be introduced for Kenny Dalglish for the closing 25 minutes, just moments after a long-range shot from Glavin had allowed the new Celt to celebrate a debut goal, the green-clad Bhoys' third of the day. Earlier, Ronnie had set Steve Murray up for the opener before Billy McNeill headed what would prove to be his final goal of a fabulous career to give Celtic a 2-0 interval lead. With the Diamonds down and out, further strikes from Murray, Paul Wilson and a Bobby Lennox spot kick would cap an excellent afternoon's work at 6-0.

Both Dixie Deans and Jimmy Johnstone started Scotland's crucial European Championship qualifier with Spain at Hampden in midweek, with on-form Kenny Dalglish bizarrely left on the bench. The 94,000 spectators saw an early Billy Bremner strike cancelled out by a Quini double, Deans making way for Dalglish after the Spaniard's second goal on the hour, having just played for his country for the second and final time. The full-time whistle would also bring the international career of the one and only Jimmy Johnstone to an end after a decade which saw him amass just 23 Scotland caps.

Celtic's roller-coaster season continued three days later with a dropped point against struggling Hearts at Tynecastle, albeit it could be argued later it was a point gained as news came through of Rangers defeat by Hibernian at Ibrox. The key moment of the match occurred seven minutes before the break, with Celts leading by an early Paul Wilson goal. Bobby Lennox was brought crashing to the ground and dusted himself down to take the resultant penalty. Hearts veteran keeper Jim Cruickshank had saved a Tommy Gemmell spot kick to save a point for his team on my first visit there, the title-clincher four years earlier, and he would deny another Lion by diving to his left to parry then smother Lennox's shot. Within three minutes, Tynecastle striker Drew Busby beat Ally Hunter to end the scoring at 1-1.

Harry remained on the first-team periphery as the month ended with another tricky away fixture, this time against Morton at Cappielow. Steve Murray's goal on the stroke of half-time, following good work from the newlywed Kenny Dalglish, was the only counter as Celtic and Rangers continued to vie for supremacy at the top of the table, the Ibrox club now ahead only on the basis of goals scored after a 4-2 win over Dundee United at Ibrox.

Both sides would record 2-1 victories seven days later, on Saturday, 7 December 1974, Rangers at Pittodrie and Celts at home to Dunfermline Athletic. Harry had not featured in the first-team since the arrival of Ronnie Glavin the previous month, but he returned to the bench before having the final say of the afternoon. With Jimmy Johnstone and Dixie Deans still recovering from injury, Jock Stein could have done without losing Pat McCluskey to a chest knock within 15 minutes, the powerful defender's final contribution being to inadvertently set up an opening goal for Graham Shaw. With youngster Frank Welsh now in central defence, transfer-listed Jimmy Bone – only in the team due to the absence of Deans - immediately equalised with his one and goal for Celtic. Billy McNeill and Harry had managed a few between them, and they would combine in the dying seconds to secure a precious point for the Hoops, Harry having replaced Bone just after the hour. Kenny Dalglish had created the first goal for Bone, and he would now claim a second assist, his curling corner-kick met by the head of Cesar, who knocked it into the danger area, Harry spinning to slam the ball past Dunfermline keeper Geir Karlsen and win the match for Celtic, his first goal since netting against Ayr United in late September.

I mentioned earlier about football throwing up co-incidences and there was yet another example of that in midweek, Wednesday, 11 December 1974, as Benfica arrived at Celtic Park for a charity match in aid of UNICEF. The former European champion clubs had clashed once before, in the second round of the European Cup in November 1969. On that occasion, both sides had won their respective home legs by 3-0, with Billy McNeill twice guessing correctly in the coin toss lottery which sent Celts through to a quarter-final match with Fiorentina, and, eventually, to a second European Cup final in May 1970. Sadly, the great Eusebio would miss out on a second appearance at Celtic Park through injury, as would Johann Cruyff, the Barcelona star having previously agreed to play as a guest.

Portuguese keeper Jose Henrique had lost three goals at Parkhead that night in 1969 and he would do so once more, whilst McNeill would again decide the issue, albeit not in the way he would have liked. Benfica had started on the front foot to open up a two-goal lead within 10 minutes, thanks to striker Vitor Moia's double, before Celtic, who included George Connelly for the first time since his walkout in September, fought back superbly. Paul Wilson won a penalty, Pat McCluskey beating Henrique, then the returning Connelly picked out Jimmy Johnstone expertly for the winger to level things at 2-2. When Ronnie Glavin and Harry weaved magic through the Benfica defence to allow the former Partick Thistle midfielder to edge the Hoops in front, it looked like that fightback had produced the desired outcome, but within minutes it was 3-3, thanks to a goal from legendary Portuguese striker Nene. Celts went close to winning the match with 10 minutes remaining, Harry crashing a shot off the crossbar with Henrique beaten, before a penalty shootout was required to decide the outcome. Celts successfully converted all first four kicks, Pat McCluskey followed by Paul Wilson, Tommy Callaghan and Jimmy Johnstone, Benfica doing likewise, to create a sudden-death situation. Despite the presence of dead-ball experts George Connelly, Ronnie Glavin, Harry and Kenny Dalglish on the pitch, perhaps it was fate who chose Billy McNeill to take the final kick, the Celtic skipper playing his part in the drama as he stroked the ball past the post, allowing Toni to seal the victory. The real winners would be the children's charity though, a 30,000 attendance on the night producing a £20,000 windfall for UNICEF.

Three days later, I witnessed perhaps the last great Celtic performance of the Jock Stein era as the Bhoys travelled to Dens Park on the winter's afternoon of Saturday, 14 December 1974. Those of us privileged to be there that day will never forget it, including Rod Stewart, sitting nearby in the main stand, the first time I can recall him being at a Celtic match. His love for the Scottish national team had presumably triggered a friendship with Jimmy Johnstone and Kenny Dalglish, and if that were the case then he chose his fixture well. The pair were simply sublime that day, although the game got off to a difficult beginning as Harry laid claim to be the earliest-ever Celtic substitution when he replaced the injured Ronnie Glavin in the first minute. Within five minutes, Jinky had taken advantage of a Thomson Allan error to give the Bhoys the lead, the keeper making another faux pas on the half-hour to let Johnstone in for his second. Between those strikes, King Kenny had served notice of what was to follow from him, finishing off a great team move to beat the Dundee keeper for 2-0. The Scotland star then turned provider, robbing former Parkhead target Iain Phillip to set up Paul Wilson for a lethal strike which saw the Hoops head down the tunnel at the interval with a four-goal cushion. The highlight of the day arrived in front of us in - appropriately enough - the 67th minute, Dalglish beating Dundee defender George Stewart with a sublime dummy before clipping the ball over Allan for the most wonderful goal. As the old Dens Park stand shook to the sound of a delirious Hoops support, Kenny then delivered the coup de grace, taking Steve Murray's pass to waltz around the shellshocked Dundee keeper to make it 6-0, sending the Bhoys three goals clear of Rangers at the top of the table. A few weeks earlier, Scottish pop band Pilot had created a huge chart hit with their single *"Magic,"* the song quickly adapted and adopted by the Hoops support, declaring our belief that the mythical 10-in-a-row was on its way. That performance raised supporter hopes of The Ten to new levels, whilst sending out a chilling message to the challengers that Jock Stein's champions were now back in the groove.

I have written previously that I believe this is the day Rod Stewart fell in love with Celtic.

We had been there for a while before him, and days like this were part of the reason why. It was indeed magical.

Chapter 30

No magic ten for Jock Stein's Celts

Seven days after the stunning 6-0 victory at Dens Park in December 1974, which sent the Hoops to the top of the League on goal difference, there was a further sign that things were beginning to swing in Celtic's favour, Rangers losing 4-3 at Broomfield to an Airdrieonians side upon whom the Bhoys had inflicted another six-goal defeat just five weeks earlier.

A dozen or so miles to the west, Jock Stein's team recovered from the loss of an early goal by former Hibernian striker Jim O'Rourke to beat St Johnstone 3-1 at Parkhead. The key moment in this match was the dismissal of Perth striker Bobby Thomson, who would later make his name partnering Andy Ritchie at Morton. He took umbrage to a challenge from Pat McCluskey to adopt a Marquis of Queensberry response, 10 minutes into the second half. At that point, the sides were level at 1-1, McCluskey continuing his good record from the penalty spot midway through the first half after Danny McGrain had been brought down. The 10 men conceded a goal within three minutes of that red card, Kenny Dalglish curling a delightful free-kick high beyond Derek Robertson in the Saints goal. Celtic's third, with five minutes to play, was less pleasing on the eye, Steve Murray's header from Harry's cross creeping between goalkeeper and defenders to give Celts some welcome daylight at the summit.

The last game of the calendar year saw the Hoops travel down the A77 to face Kilmarnock at Rugby Park on Saturday, 28 December 1974. Ronnie Glavin and Jim Brogan returned in place of Jimmy Johnstone and Pat McCluskey, whilst Dixie Deans was deemed fit enough to take a seat on the bench, following a five-week injury absence. Former Celtic legend Willie Fernie's attractive Killie side included two young wingers making their name in the game, Davie Provan on the right and Gordon Smith on the left, whilst his strike partnership of Ian Fleming and Eddie Morrison had amassed 27 goals between them at the halfway stage of the season. Celtic's defence would cope well with those threats, whilst at the other end, one moment of magic from Kenny Dalglish saw the points head back up to Glasgow. Seven minutes from the interval, Harry's left-wing cross was headed into the danger area by Glavin. King Kenny, as always, was a split-second ahead of his marker in both thought and movement, and that was enough to give him the yard he required to blast the ball beyond Jim Stewart.

The two-point lead at the top of the table was maintained after a comfortable 5-1 victory over Clyde at Celtic Park on New Year's Day. Jimmy Johnstone and Dixie Deans returned with Harry dropping to the bench and Steve Murray missing out, and it was Deans who started the year in some style, opening the scoring within seven minutes. Tommy Callaghan added a double either side of the break and Kenny Dalglish chipped in with his regular goal as the Hoops went four goals clear with more than half-an-hour remaining. Perhaps with the weekend match at Ibrox in mind, the Celtic feet came off the gas, Ronnie Glavin's late strike ending the scoring after Peter Boyle had pulled one back for Clyde.

The game which turned the title tide against Celtic and their dreams of a tenth successive League championship took place at Ibrox on Saturday, 4 January 1975. With George Connelly recovering from a badly cut leg sustained during the Clyde match, Pat McCluskey returned to partner Billy McNeill at the heart of the Hoops defence, whilst further forward, Steve Murray and Harry were restored to the exclusion of Jimmy Johnstone and Dixie Deans, the latter not even on the bench. The teams lined up as follows in front of 72,000 spectators.

RANGERS:

Stewart Kennedy; Sandy Jardine & John Greig; Tom Forsyth, Colin Jackson & Derek Johnstone; Tommy McLean, Ian McDougall, Derek Parlane, Alex MacDonald & Ally Scott. Substitutes; Alex Miller & Quinton Young.

CELTIC:

Ally Hunter; Danny McGrain & Jim Brogan; Steve Murray, Billy McNeill & Pat McCluskey; Harry Hood, Ronnie Glavin, Kenny Dalglish, Tommy Callaghan & Paul Wilson. Substitutes; Roddie MacDonald & Jimmy Johnstone.

This was the strangest of games, in the sense that Celtic could quite easily have won had they taken some gilt-edged opportunities in the first half yet ended up facing their biggest derby defeat in 12 years. The hosts got off to a great start, when Tommy McLean's lofted cross to the far post was headed home by Derek Johnstone, however, Paul Wilson was thriving on Celtic's left flank, beating defenders for fun before setting up Harry then Kenny Dalglish for chances they would normally have buried. Five minutes into the second half, those misses would come back to haunt the Hoops, McLean sent clear through the middle to squeeze the ball past Ally Hunter for 2-0. With Jimmy Johnstone on for Harry but struggling to make any impact on the game, the crucial third goal also occurred at the traditional Celtic End, sadly a carbon copy of the first. McLean was allowed the time and space to deliver another aerial bomb, this time Derek Parlane first to connect and send a header looping back over Ally Hunter for 3-0. That would be significant, completing the six-goal swing which saw the Ibrox side go top. Now Celtic had a problem, as the two title contenders would not meet again in the League that season.

The two-goal deficit became two points, seven days later, as a late Willie Pettigrew strike gave Motherwell a 3-2 win at Celtic Park. Pettigrew and partner Bobby Graham were an excellent striking duo, who seemed to save their best performances for matches against Celtic at that time, this being a case in point. Each had scored within the first 20 minutes, leaving an already under-pressure home team facing a long afternoon, referee JRP Gordon not helping matters by ruling out a Harry goal for offside then denying the Hoops a clear penalty when Paul Wilson was chopped down, seconds before Graham made it 2-0. Harry did his best to correct the situation, pulling one back on the half-hour before levelling the match 10 minutes into the second half, after Kenny Dalglish had created the opening. As the Bhoys piled forward in search of that vital winner, there was always the fear of being caught on the break. That script was written, Pettigrew's pace seeing him outstrip the Celtic defence to win the match with 15 minutes to go, plunging a dagger through our hearts and dreams of The Ten.

There was an opportunity to make up some lost ground the following Saturday, as Rangers home game with Kilmarnock was one of the casualties of the unrelenting January weather, Celtic's visit to Somerset Park in Ayr one of three fixtures to survive. Jock Stein reacted to the two recent defeats by recalling Jim Brogan, George Connelly and Tommy Callaghan, with Pat McCluskey dropped and Ronnie Glavin and Roddie MacDonald on the bench. Three successive League losses for the first time under Jock looked a possibility as the other Dixie, Ayr's Ingram, put the hosts ahead on the half-hour, before goals one minute either side of the break from Steve Murray and Harry calmed a frustrated away support. Our Dixie – the Deans variety – then netted a superb double to secure the two points, a late Danny McDonald own goal wrapping up a much-needed 5-1 victory for the defending champions.

Saturday, 24 January 1975 was Scottish Cup third-round day, and I suspect the last thing Celtic wanted was an away draw to title challengers and League Cup finalists Hibernian. Jock Stein named the same team, and his faith would be rewarded as goals at either end of a 90 minutes dominated by the visitors sent the Hoops safely through. Harry was the creator-in-chief as Celts took the lead in 12 minutes, his cross mishandled by debutant keeper Hugh Whyte to allow Dixie Deans the chance to nod the ball home, his seventh goal in three games against the Leith men that season. With 10 minutes remaining, Steve Murray slid in at the back post to make it 2-0, after more great work from man-of-the-match Harry Hood. The main losers at this stage were Rangers, beaten 2-1 by Aberdeen in an Ibrox replay after a 1-1 draw at Pittodrie. Whilst this would be a major boost to Celtic's chances of retaining the cup, it would also leave their rivals with only the title race upon which to focus all of their efforts.

Harry's recent return to form had not gone unnoticed, Scotland manager Willie Ormond criticised for omitting him from his latest squad, for the European Championship match against Spain in Valencia by Jim Blair of *The Evening Times*, Ormond opting for Chelsea's Charlie Cooke in a pool dominated by men plying their trade in England.

"I question Ormond's choice and his obvious lack of faith in home players. Harry Hood, two years younger than Cooke, showed great form against Hibs on Saturday at Easter Road. Ormond was there, and if he is to pick players on a one-game basis what was wrong with Hood, for instance? Or George Connelly? Harry Hood had a great game. He was all over the place, and his close control was tremendous – as was seen when he wriggled along the by-line to set up Murray's goal. He took on the role that is normally Kenny Dalglish's."

Saturday, 1 February 1975 saw the fixture balance restored as Celtic's home game with Dumbarton was called off before Rangers drew 1-1 at Cappielow, the Ibrox club nosing back in front by a point after grabbing a late equaliser. It would soon be two points. Seven days later, the Hoops travelled north to Gayfield to face bottom-dogs Arbroath, who fielded new signing Jimmy Bone at centre-forward. He had left Parkhead just three weeks earlier in a £15,000 deal, half the price Jock Stein had paid Sheffield United less than a year earlier, a move that sadly for both parties had not worked out. Of course, you would not have got a bet on Bone equalling his Celtic goal tally in one match, and this he duly achieved within 10 minutes of the kick-off to give the hosts the lead. Harry's right foot brought Celts level on 17 minutes, before Kenny Dalglish fired them in front just before the break, and the second half was a procession towards teenager Alan Campbell in the Arbroath goal, that third goal just refusing to come along. As we have seen this season, just as winning becomes a habit so does failing to see games through. Back in August 1972, Arbroath's Derek Rylance had scored a hat-trick against Celtic in a League Cup sectional match played at Hampden, his first-ever goals for the club securing an unlikely 3-3 draw, after strikes from Harry and Kenny had seen the Hoops coasting at 3-1. He would now come back to haunt the ailing champions again, as would Bone. With 15 minutes remaining, the former Parkhead striker's cross found Rylance with all the time in the world to blast the ball past Ally Hunter and place another nail in the 10-in-a-row coffin, as the match ended 2-2.

That would also be the score three nights later, on Tuesday, 11 February 1975, as Celts failed to beat another side struggling at the bottom of the table, having established a winning position, this time Dumbarton at home in the rescheduled fixture. Harry was again first on target for Celtic, cutting in from the left to curl the ball beyond Sons keeper Ian McGregor just after the half hour, his ninth goal of the season. And within five minutes the points should have been safe when new Scotland cap Paul Wilson headed home Kenny Dalglish's cross for 2-0. Then the old failings returned. Ally Hunter and Danny McGrain engaged in a spot of *"after you, Claude"* to allow John Bourke to pull one back 10 minutes into the second half, before Tom McAdam atoned for a series of earlier misses by nodding a rebound past Hunter for 2-2 with 20 minutes remaining. Yet again, Jock Stein's men had failed to capitalise on a night when their opponents were idle, those two damaging draws leaving the Hoops one point behind Rangers having played a game more.

Not surprisingly, Stein rang the changes as Scottish Cup business recommenced with a home tie against a fast-improving Clydebank outfit five days later, Saturday, 15 February 1975. Out went skipper Billy McNeill, Jim Brogan and big-money signing Ronnie Glavin, Steve Murray handed the captain's armband on the day. However, the biggest surprise was between the sticks, with Bothwell teenager Graham Barclay wearing the gloves for what would prove to be his only first team appearance. Perhaps the most unusual Celtic team selection of the 1974/75 season lined up as follows.

Graham Barclay; Danny McGrain & Pat McCluskey; Steve Murray, Roddie MacDonald & George Connelly; Harry Hood, Jackie McNamara, Dixie Deans, Kenny Dalglish & Paul Wilson.
Substitutes; Tommy Callaghan & Jimmy Johnstone.

The Bankies fielded the nucleus of the side which would win successive promotions in the new three-tier League set-up being introduced the following season, regular defensive stalwarts Jim Gallacher and Jim Fallon supporting an attacking duo of Davie Cooper and Mike Larnach. They had knocked out top-flight Dunfermline Athletic in the previous round and boosted their chances of a much bigger upset when Joe McCallan's opportunist strike gave them the lead midway through the first half. Three devastating Celtic shots from outside the box ruined that dream as the interval approached, Jackie McNamara levelling things from a Dixie Deans pass before Kenny Dalglish produced two sublime efforts within 60 seconds which flew past Gallacher to send the teams inside at 3-1. The final goal did not arrive until the 83rd minute, Roddie MacDonald opening his Celtic account with a far-post effort to conclude the scoring at 4-1 and keep Celtic's bid to retain the famous old trophy on track. On the same afternoon, Rangers required yet another late equaliser to salvage a 3-3 draw with Kilmarnock at Ibrox, to move two points clear at the top of the table. Celts would be left to rue once again their inability to pile the pressure on to the Govan side by failing to beat Arbroath and Dumbarton recently.

The next week saw the arrival of a new goalkeeper at Parkhead. Peter Latchford was one of three Birmingham-born brothers to make a career in professional football. Whilst striker Bob and keeper Dave were learning their trade with City at St Andrews, Peter was working his way up the ranks at nearby West Bromwich Albion. His breakthrough season of 1972/73 would be bittersweet, Peter's 26 appearances in England's top division ending with a first relegation for the Baggies since the Second World War. He would then be a stand-out as Albion battled for instant promotion, Latchford an ever-present between the sticks, his form attracting the notice of the England selectors. In October 1973, just 24 hours before that famous match at Wembley which saw Poland eliminate Alf Ramsay's men from the World Cup, Peter would make his international bow in the under-23 clash between the two sides at Home Park, Plymouth, the match ending goalless. He then faced the third team in England's section, Wales, at Bristol City's Ashton Gate in February 1974, this time alongside his brother Bob on a proud evening for the Latchford family, the game again finishing 0-0. The following season would not go so well, West Brom making a disappointing start to the League campaign which would see Peter lose both his club and international place. By January 1975, he was a peripheral player at The Hawthorns, Jock Stein receiving a recommendation from Don Revie before agreeing a loan deal with his Baggies counterpart Don Howe which saw Latchford move to Glasgow until the summer.

The big Englishman would make an immediate debut, as Celtic returned to Easter Road just four weeks after their Scottish Cup victory at the same venue, the keeper surprisingly the only change from the win over Clydebank. It would not be the most auspicious of starts, Peter picking the ball out of his net twice in the opening 15 minutes as an Arthur Duncan double piled on the agony for Celtic's support and their fading title hopes, Latchford and young centre-half Roddie MacDonald both at fault for the first goal. A late Paul Wilson strike was scant consolation on the day, as even the most fervent optimist now struggled to make the case for 10-in-a-row, Rangers now four points clear with just nine games remaining after their narrow win at Shawfield.

The opening day of March involved a home clash for Celts with Bertie Auld's Partick Thistle, Billy McNeill and Ronnie Glavin returning to the team at the expense of Roddie MacDonald and Jackie McNamara. It would again be an afternoon Peter Latchford would want to forget, the Englishman inexplicably allowing a Danny Kellachan free-kick from the halfway-line to float over his head and put Thistle 2-1 up midway through the first half, after future Celtic striker Joe Craig's early goal had been cancelled out by a Pat McCluskey penalty. The rescue act would commence with 20 minutes to play, Kenny Dalglish equalising before he and Harry lined up to take a free-kick in the final minute. The King had broken Bertie's heart at Firhill in the earlier League clash back in November, scoring the winner in the dying seconds, and no doubt a Jags defence which included Alan Rough and both Hansen brothers would be aware of that as they prepared for the attack. This time, though, Dalglish would shape to shoot then run over the ball, Harry expertly clipping it over the wall and into the opposite corner for a sensational winner, a rare ray of hope and light amidst some dark times. Across at Ibrox, yes, you've guessed it, a last-minute winner against Hearts saw Rangers maintain their four-point lead at the top.

The quarter-final draw of the Scottish Cup sent Celts along the coast to Dumbarton seven days later, Saturday, 8 March 1975, the big news being the exclusion of Dixie Deans and George Connelly, which saw Andy Lynch and Roddie MacDonald start at Boghead, whilst Tommy Callaghan replaced flu victim Steve Murray. The free-kick ruse which beat Partick Thistle worked again within five minutes, this time Harry playing the decoy and Ronnie Glavin the ball, to beat Laurie Williams in the home goal. Three minutes later, the Ghosts of Parkhead Past and Future combined to level the tie, Lisbon Lion Willie Wallace setting up Tom McAdam for another goal against the Hoops. Harry was again involved in the move which decided the contest on the hour, playing in Paul Wilson from another set-piece for 2-1. In the tie of the round, Aberdeen were beaten at home by Motherwell, Celts later drawn to face either Hearts or Dundee in the semi-final, whilst the Steelmen would have a local derby with Airdrieonians in the last four, if the Broomfield outfit could overcome Arbroath in the other replayed match.

The Scottish Cup would sadly be the only focus for Celtic by the end of March, as three defeats in four League games finally crushed dreams of La Decima. Four days after the cup victory over Dumbarton, the Hoops headed to Pittodrie to play their game in hand, the defending champions now six points behind Rangers. With George Connelly restored for young Roddie MacDonald, this would be a night when the headlines would be made by players not normally in the spotlight. Dumfries-born Billy Williamson had spent the majority of his five years at Aberdeen as a full-back, whilst left-winger Andy Lynch had struggled to secure a regular place at Celtic since his transfer from Hearts in 1973. Transfer-listed Williamson had only recently been used as a midfield player by Dons boss Jimmy Bonthrone, and he would now enjoy the greatest 90 minutes of his career by scoring the hat-trick which defeated the Hoops. Twice Lynch would reply for Celtic to bring the visitors level by the hour, his first League goals for the club, before Connelly hauled Aberdeen substitute Duncan Davidson down in the box with 13 minutes to play. Up strode Williamson to beat Peter Latchford via an upright to complete a most unlikely treble and put another huge dent in Celtic's championship aspirations.

George Connelly and the previously ever-present Paul Wilson were the men dropped for the home match with Dundee United three days later, the big Fifer missing completely, whilst the striker would at least have the opportunity to maintain his record from the bench beside Dixie Deans. Roddie MacDonald and Jimmy Johnstone were the incomers as Jock Stein hoped for the miracle which would salvage their title record, a championship having been delivered in each of his nine full seasons in charge at Parkhead. Even that sliver of hope disappeared as Celtic slumped to another defeat against a team they had destroyed in the Scottish Cup final 10 months earlier. The only goal of this Glasgow clash was scored by Andy Gray, a Drumchapel teenager with a preference for the blue half of the city, his header from a corner on the half-hour bouncing over a posse of defenders on the line. Deans would replace Tommy Callaghan at the interval before Wilson was introduced for Pat McCluskey as Stein went for broke, however, the best chance of the second half fell to Gray, this time Peter Latchford producing an excellent save. Meanwhile, 90 miles to the north, Rangers recovered from a goal and a man down – the returning Colin Stein ordered off - to beat Dundee 2-1 at Dens Park, thanks to another last-minute winner, to move eight points clear at the top of the table with just six games remaining.

There was some respite in midweek as the Glasgow Cup made a return to the schedule after a four-year absence, Jock Stein fielding a strong team as he tried to get performances back on track for the bigger matter of Celtic's defence of the

Scottish Cup. Partick Thistle's second visit of the month to Parkhead would again end in defeat by a single goal, however, there was no cute, last-minute free-kick from Harry involved this time around. Danny McGrain is one of the most incredible footballers I have ever seen play the game. He had everything, strength, pace, touch, plus the capacity to fight back from the most dreadful of setbacks, the fractured skull at Brockville three years earlier and more recently, his diagnosis as a diabetic on his return from the World Cup in West Germany the previous summer. Well, he had almost everything. He rarely scored a goal. In fact, most of Danny's goals are items of note, due to how few he managed. JFK moments. McGrain would create another on this night by scoring the best goal of his career. As we approached the half-hour, he picked the ball up on the halfway line, charging into the box to beat several Thistle defenders before placing his shot past former Scotland keeper Jim Herriot, sending Celts into a final meeting with Rangers.

As birthdays go, my 14th on Saturday, 22 March 1975 was bittersweet. Celtic's collapse since the New Year had coincided with the first spell in my life in which I had not been attending games, following my decision to resume playing instead, a huge call. Together with friends, I had started training with St Roch's Boys Guild in the Garngad, and unfortunately their games were played at 3pm on a Saturday afternoon. We tended to do really well at home, urged on by the men pouring out of the old Hibs Club on Royston Road at 2.30, but less so on the road. On that particular afternoon, we would break our away duck by hammering Our Lady & St George 4-1, somewhere in the Penilee or Cardonald area. Behind enemy lines, if you like. Sadly, that news was tempered as we heard that Celtic had lost at Broomfield and were now a massive 10 points behind Rangers following their win over Motherwell at nearby Ibrox. The Ibrox outfit was now just a point away from winning the League for the first time in my Celtic-supporting lifetime. If Carlsberg did birthdays, it would certainly not have been that one.

Jock Stein had again shuffled his pack for the trip to Airdrie, making five changes from the side who lost to Dundee United as he sought to avoid a third successive League loss for the first time in his tenure. A revamped defence saw the loss of the injured Billy McNeill and Danny McGrain covered by George Connelly and Jim Brogan, whilst young Frank Welsh had done enough in the midweek Glasgow Cup-tie to see him preferred to Roddie MacDonald. Further forward, Dixie Deans and Bobby Lennox came in for Harry and Andy Lynch. The changes would not have the desired effect, Willie McCulloch's angled shot beating Peter Latchford to bounce home off the post seven minutes from the interval, for the only goal of the game, allowing Hibernian to leapfrog Celtic into second spot in the table.

There was a certain irony that having toiled for most of the year to throw away the chance of 10-in-a-row, Celts then produced an excellent performance at home to Hearts seven days later, on the day Rangers secured the point they required at Easter Road. The Hoops had welcomed back Billy McNeill, Danny McGrain, Harry and

Paul Wilson, with Jim Brogan, Frank Welsh, Dixie Deans and Bobby Lennox making way, and they were four goals clear and coasting before Drew Busby headed a late consolation goal for the visitors. The main damage was done in a 15-minute spell just after the break, Kenny Dalglish looking more like his old self as he blasted a double past Jim Cruickshank before laying on a third for Paul Wilson then a fourth for Ronnie Glavin. The King then left the field to a standing ovation, on this strangest of days, Stein choosing to rest him ahead of the midweek Scottish Cup semi-final.

Cup favourites Celtic and Motherwell had been kept apart in the semi-final draw, the Hoops instead facing Dundee at that stage for the third successive season, a fourth time in six years. The Dark Blues had been seconds from elimination in the quarter-final at Tynecastle, before a Gordon Wallace equaliser set up a replay at Dens which they would edge by the odd goal in five. The latest chapter in the by now annual series took place at Hampden on Wednesday, 2 April 1975, Celts protecting an unbeaten record over these fixtures and choosing to make just one change from Saturday's winning line-up, Bobby Lennox replacing Jimmy Johnstone. Tommy Gemmell had been a teammate of Jinky and the Buzz Bomb for that first meeting in March 1970, Lennox netting the winner after the prolific Wallace had equalised for Dundee, and fate would deal the big full-back a cruel blow on this night. With the match still goalless after an hour's play, Dens skipper Gemmell suffered a fatal lack of concentration as he dallied with the ball at the edge of the box. The lurking Ronnie Glavin had struggled to justify the club record fee paid by Celtic five months earlier, however, he would now start to repay that in some style, dispossessing Gemmell to slot the ball past Thomson Allan for the only goal of the game. Thus, Celts would end the 1974/75 season with no League title for the first time in a decade but with a place in a seventh consecutive Scottish Cup final, a ninth in 10 years under the legend that is Jock Stein, a quite incredible record.

The Celtic manager was blunt in his assessment of his team's performance in the latter half of a season which had promised so much, even as recently as December, as quoted in The Celtic View.

"To be honest, we have slipped more than I had thought possible. Changes will have to be made but these will not be effected before next season. The new players will be brought in as a unit. It will be a fresh start with fresh faces."

Chapter 31

It's three cups for Celtic and a fitting finale for Cesar

Following the Hampden win over Dundee, the remainder of April 1975 saw that inconsistency of performance which had plagued Celtic all season continue to affect the final League fixtures. It began with a 1-1 home draw with Morton, three days later, which saw Kenny Dalglish captain the team for the first time, Danny McGrain score an own goal to level things after an early Paul Wilson strike and Brian McLaughlin come off the bench for his first appearance of the season. We then had the bizarre sight of George Connelly simply giving up on a chase with a Morton forward late on, an indication that all was clearly not well with him. That would be confirmed on the Saturday by his non-appearance at East End Park for Celtic's 3-1 victory over Dunfermline Athletic, after his latest walkout. Harry dropped to the bench as winger-cum-striker Andy Lynch was deployed for the first time in the left-back role which he would later make his own, whilst Paul Wilson - with a double - and Bobby Lennox shared the goals and the honours up front.

As Connelly's once-brightly shining star appeared to be on the wane, we had a first glimpse of another future Hoops legend as Dundee rolled back into Glasgow on League business on Saturday, 19 April 1975. Jock Stein named an unchanged starting line-up from Dunfermline but gave youngsters Andy Ritchie and Tommy Burns a seat on the bench, perhaps with a view to next season, whilst Harry was on target as he joined Tommy Callaghan, Jimmy Johnstone, Dixie Deans, Ally Hunter and Jim Brogan in the vastly experienced reserve team which drew 1-1 at Dens Park. Back at Celtic Park, 18-year-old Burns came on for Paul Wilson to receive his Celtic debut on 65 minutes, just after makeshift striker Ronnie Glavin had headed the Hoops level at 1-1. The performance of the two goalkeepers would determine the destination of the points, Thomson Allan foiling Celts time and time again before Peter Latchford was caught stranded off his line by Wilson Hoggan in the dying moments, the ball sailing over the Englishman's head from fully 35 yards to consign Celtic to a defeat which allowed Hibernian to leapfrog them into second place, as this special League season went from bad to worse.

That third-place finish was confirmed as Celtic went down to a second consecutive 2-1 loss in the final League match of the two-Division era, at Muirton Park on Saturday 26 April 1975. St Johnstone were one of three clubs scrambling for the last two places in the new Top Ten Premier Division due to commence in August, and they urgently required the points from the clash with Celtic which would seal that for them. For Jock Stein's part, he had a Scottish Cup final the following Saturday to consider, with selection dilemmas throughout the team and the added problem of Paul Wilson sadly unavailable due to family illness. Stein's choice was to recall the experience of Johnstone, Hood, Deans and Callaghan from the reserves but exclude Hunter and Brogan, as he went with the following 13 men.

Peter Latchford; Danny McGrain & Andy Lynch; Steve Murray, Billy McNeill & Roddie MacDonald; Jimmy Johnstone, Ronnie Glavin, Dixie Deans, Tommy Callaghan & Kenny Dalglish. Substitutes; Harry Hood & Bobby Lennox.

Saints striker Jim O'Rourke had been a thorn in Celtic's side as a Hibernian player and he would again play that role today, winning his team a penalty within three minutes as Roddie MacDonald blocked his run into the box. There was a reprieve for Celts as Duncan Lambie shot wide. Having struggled badly earlier in the year, Ronnie Glavin was finally enjoying a decent spell of form and he provided Celtic's biggest threat in the first half, crashing a shot off the crossbar before giving the Hoops the lead on the half-hour after a neat interchange with Dixie Deans. The hosts then enjoyed the benefit of a controversial decision three minutes from the interval, which changed the tide of the match, O'Rourke breaking from an offside position to beat Peter Latchford for 1-1. There was a significant moment on the hour, as both Jimmy Johnstone and Deans were withdrawn by Stein, both having struggled on an afternoon where cup final places were at stake. For Jinky, it would have even sadder implications, the man voted Celtic's greatest-ever player in 2002 would never start a match in his beloved Hoops again. Substitutes Harry Hood and Bobby Lennox would fare better, only Perth keeper Derek Robertson preventing further goals for the visitors, however, just as against Dundee, it would be a problem at the other end which would seal the fate of the points. Just seven minutes after the Celtic changes, O'Rourke broke clear after Billy McNeill and Danny McGrain had got in each other's way, Latchford bringing him down to concede a second penalty. Saints would now change their taker and receive the desired outcome, Gordon Smith sending Latchford one way and the ball the other to end Celtic's poorest League campaign in a decade on another low note. St Johnstone and Motherwell would claim the final two places in the inaugural Top Ten for 1975/76, edging out Willie Fernie's Kilmarnock and Scottish Cup finalists Airdrieonians, whose last-day victory at Ibrox saw them complete a double over Rangers, as they finished the campaign in 11th place.

Whilst the Lanarkshire club would be on a high following their win, the build-up to Celtic's seventh successive Scottish Cup final saw several off-field scenarios playing out. A number of the senior players were clearly still in contention for a place in the

Hampden line-up, Harry, Dixie Deans and Tommy Callaghan again on reserve duty in midweek whilst Jimmy Johnstone was battling against a leg strain picked up at Perth. The saddest news involved Paul Wilson, the winger suffering the tragic loss of his mother, with the funeral taking place that week. He would ask Jock Stein to consider him available for selection if required, such bravery bearing testament to the man he was, God rest him.

As the day of the match arrived, Saturday, 3 May 1975, the most momentous news of all had been kept quiet, the decision of Billy McNeill to announce his retirement after a wonderful 17-year career in the Hoops, commencing effectively after the game. I have mentioned previously how Cesar, like Jock and the League flag flying high above the Jungle every summer, were constants in my Celtic life. Now two of those constants would be gone. Things would never quite be the same again.

When Jock Stein made his selection, it would be good news for Harry, Bobby Lennox, Pat McCluskey and the grieving Paul Wilson, all included in the starting line-up, whilst there would be disappointment for Jimmy Johnstone and Dixie Deans, the two men who had lit up Hampden in the League Cup final victory over Hibernian just six months earlier. Tommy Callaghan and the young apprentice Roddie MacDonald would have the possibility of taking part at some stage from the bench, as the Celtic manager listed the following team.

Peter Latchford; Danny McGrain & Andy Lynch; Steve Murray, Billy McNeill & Pat McCluskey; Harry Hood, Ronnie Glavin, Kenny Dalglish, Bobby Lennox & Paul Wilson. Substitutes; Tommy Callaghan & Roddie MacDonald.

Airdrieonians manager Ian McMillan selected the following men to bring the Scottish Cup back to Broomfield for the first time since 1924.

Dave McWilliams; Paul Jonquin & Mark Cowan; Derek Whiteford, Jim Black & John Menzies; Kevin McCann, Tommy Walker, Willie McCulloch, John Lapsley & Billy Wilson. Substitutes; Jim March & Tommy Reynolds.

Hampden was blessed with perfect Scottish Cup final weather, most within the 75,457 crowd unaware they would be saying goodbye to a Celtic icon, seeking a seventh winner's medal in this particular competition, perhaps even another goal to add to his strikes in 1965, 1969 and 1972, a wonderful record for anyone far less a defender. The goalscoring hero today though would be the grief-stricken Paul Wilson, with a double. Paul had scored in both finals in which the Hoops had featured that season, the Drybrough Cup shootout win over Rangers in August then the 6-3 destruction of Hibernian in the League Cup two months later. He would soon have the distinction of making it three when he headed past Dave McWilliams in the 15th minute, after a delightful combination between Danny McGrain and Kenny Dalglish down the right allowed the King to pick him out with a perfect cross.

With half-time imminent, the game exploded into life, young Airdrieonians winger Kevin McCann writing his own name into the history books as he lashed a shot high past Peter Latchford to square the match, after some heroic defending by the Celtic defence had blocked two previous efforts. Within seconds, the Hoops were ahead again, Bobby Lennox curling his corner-kick from the left into the danger zone, where Wilson timed his run to perfection to connect with the ball a split-second before McWilliams, sending Celts in 2-1 up at the interval. Lennox would also be involved in the third and clinching goal, eight minutes into the second half. A quick throw-in from Dalglish sent the veteran Lion scampering down the left flank with a posse of Diamond defenders on his tail, a sudden burst of acceleration then taking him clear into the box before a desperate lunge sent him sprawling. As referee Ian Foote pointed to the spot, all eyes turned to Paul Wilson, now on a rare cup final hat-trick. But the striker was happy to leave it to the nominated penalty-taker, and up stepped Pat McCluskey to stroke the ball into the net and ensure that Cesar's Last Stand would end the way of so many others since April 1965, with green-and-white ribbons bedecking a major trophy.

There was many an irritant eye being scratched as, for the last time, the great man led his cup-winners up and down the Hampden pitch he had graced with club and country for the best part of two decades, scarf outstretched. Celtic to the core. And then it was that familiar climb up the steps, a brief handshake then the silverware is held aloft for his adoring support to raise the metaphorical roof. This is how it felt to be Celtic under Jock Stein and Billy McNeill. There was nothing quite like it.

Life after Cesar began with another Hampden cup final, just seven days later, the conclusion of the recently resurrected Glasgow Cup against Rangers. The absence of the Celtic legend wasn't the only obvious difference from the previous week, the match played in a constant downpour as opposed to glorious sunshine. Despite the atrocious conditions, both teams served up a fast, entertaining first-half for the 70,000 spectators. As expected, Roddie MacDonald came in for Billy McNeill, whilst Jock Stein's other enforced change was to recall Jim Brogan for Ronnie Glavin - the midfielder cup-tied with Partick Thistle just weeks before his transfer and thus ineligible - following a seven-week absence. The award of the captain's armband to the long-serving defender was perhaps a sign that Jim would be playing his last game for Celtic. Jimmy Johnstone came in for his farewell appearance on the bench, as a fabulous era truly ended with the following Celtic line-up.

Peter Latchford; Danny McGrain & Andy Lynch; Pat McCluskey, Roddie MacDonald & Jim Brogan; Harry Hood, Steve Murray, Kenny Dalglish, Bobby Lennox & Paul Wilson. Substitutes; Tommy Callaghan & Jimmy Johnstone.

Rangers fielded the following players.

Stewart Kennedy; Sandy Jardine & John Greig; Bobby McKean, Colin Jackson & Tom Forsyth; Tommy McLean, Colin Stein, Derek Parlane, Alex MacDonald & Derek Johnstone. Substitutes; Alex Miller & Quinton Young.

With many supporters still shuffling into position, Celts took the lead, Rangers full-back Sandy Jardine celebrating his Player of the Year award by passing the ball back beyond his own goalkeeper, Stewart Kennedy, the ever-alert Paul Wilson running in to gleefully knock the ball into the empty net. By doing so, he created a record which will surely never be beaten, Paul scoring in his fourth Hampden cup final that season. By the seventh minute, it was 1-1, Colin Stein the last link in the head tennis chain as he beat Peter Latchford from Tommy McLean's corner kick. However, the best goal of the game arrived 10 minutes later. Kenny Dalglish advanced to the edge of the Rangers box before slipping a pass to Wilson on his right, the talented Celt leaving Colin Jackson sprawling on the sodden turf with a shake of his hips, before rounding Kennedy and slamming the ball between John Greig and Tom Forsyth into the Hampden net for a quite stunning goal. A strike fit to grace any occasion, completing Wilson's second cup final double in seven days and taking his tally at the national stadium to six in four games in this, the best season of his career.

The fourth goal, by comparison, was a scrambled effort, partly down to the conditions, McLean's shot skidding off Pat McCluskey to wrongfoot Latchford just before the break. The first half would prove a tough act to follow, the second period memorable only for the wrong reasons. Jim Brogan's 12-year Celtic career ended on the saddest of notes, the skipper-for-the-day stretchered off, his replacement Tommy Callaghan later making way for Jimmy Johnstone, as the genius from Viewpark brought the curtain down on his own magical spell at Parkhead. With the teams still level at 2-2 after 90 minutes, somewhat bizarrely, there would be no extra-time or penalties to decide the outcome, the powers-that-be no doubt aware of the potential for another huge payday early in the new season. If this all sounds uncannily like the scenario at the 1909 Scottish Cup final between the clubs at the same venue, then thankfully, we did not witness the ensuing riots and burning of goalposts. It was probably too wet to be honest. And that replay never did take place.

As a final footnote to the bittersweet campaign of 1974/75, the wonderful *Celtic Wiki* throws up a piece of trivia which I had never been made aware of and which may be of interest.

Four nights after the Glasgow Cup final, on Wednesday, 14 May 1975, Celtic sent a team comprising free transfers, senior players and a trialist to face East Kilbride Thistle in a benefit match for one of the Lanarkshire club's players, Dougie Thomson. The Hoops forward line makes interesting reading, as follows.

Andy Ritchie, Harry Hood, Mark McGhee, Dixie Deans & Bobby Lennox.

After Bobby Lennox had opened the scoring, Celtic's 17-year-old trialist Mark McGhee added a second, the Hoops going on to win 6-2. Sadly, McGhee would not be offered a professional contract at Celtic, moving to Morton during the close-season.

Chapter 32

More heroes depart but the Boss survives and the King remains

Celtic Park would have been a strange place to be over the summer of 1975 as life began without some of the huge personalities who had graced the old ground over the previous decade. Cesar, of course, had bowed out after the Scottish Cup final victory over Airdrieonians in May, whilst two men who had starred beside him so often through those wonderful years, Jimmy Johnstone and Jim Brogan had been given free transfers. Jinky recalls being *"in bits"* after Jock Stein told him it was all over, whilst the versatile Brogan states that he was told of his release by Billy McNeill! Nothing with Jimmy was ever straightforward it seemed, and so it continued, with San Antonio Thunder and Rochester Lancers both claiming they had verbal agreements for him to sign before he opted for a spell with San Jose Earthquakes, where he would come up against Harry's hero Pele, playing with New York Cosmos. Jim Brogan moved to the English top-flight with Coventry City, causing a stir as he arrived for his first day at training in July driving a Rolls-Royce! He would soon demonstrate that same high quality on the pitch, as the Sky Blues made their best-ever start in the First Division, with Jim a fixture in the team.

Jimmy Johnstone and Jim Brogan would be joined in the departure lounge by the hugely talented Vic Davidson, the former Quality Street Gang forward having not featured in the first-team scene since November 1974. Vic was quickly snapped up by Motherwell. It would later transpire that his old strike partner Kenny Dalglish had submitted a transfer request, which had been rejected by the Board.

There was very nearly another Celtic legend leaving us in tragically different circumstances. On the morning of Saturday, 5 July 1975, we awoke to the horrible news that Jock Stein had been seriously injured in a collision whilst driving home from Manchester Airport on the notorious A74, following a holiday with friends in Minorca. The Celtic boss would, thankfully, recover in time, by far the most important concern, however, that would be not be for some considerable period, the first-team reins being passed to his friend and right-hand, Sean Fallon, in the interim. It would be the Iron Man from Sligo who would lead Celtic into the brand-new Scottish Premier League era the following month.

One early piece of business for Sean to conclude was to make Peter Latchford's loan deal permanent, the Englishman signed from West Bromwich Albion for £30,000 on 14 July. The next Hoops transfer target had a slightly more exotic background than the West Midlands. Most Celtic supporters of a certain vintage will immediately think of one player when Iceland is mentioned, Johannes Edvaldsson, better known whilst he was in Scotland as 'Big Shuggy!'

The son of a former Estonian international goalkeeper, Evald Mikson, who was accused of war crimes and fled his homeland after the Second World War to settle in Reykjavik, the current Icelandic national team captain Edvaldsson was plying his trade as an amateur with Danish outfit Holbaek when he was invited to join Celtic on trial for a short tour of Ireland. Johannes was wearing the number six shorts as he lined up with Harry and Ronnie Glavin in midfield against Dundalk at Oriel Park on Thursday, 24 July 1975 for the opening game of the season, the new Bhoy capping a fine debut by heading home Celtic's fifth goal with 15 minutes remaining. Earlier, the 5,000 spectators had witnessed two classic strikes from Harry and Kenny Dalglish which would have blessed any occasion, with Glavin and tour skipper Bobby Lennox adding to those to create a 4-0 lead early in the second half. A late Paul Wilson strike completed a 6-0 win. Harry had been replaced by Jackie McNamara after an hour having sustained an injury to his right arm, triggering his first-ever visit to hospital for a football-related problem. An X-ray showed only severe bruising, Harry duly coming up with a novel recovery plan.

"I've been told to keep it moving as much as possible, so I am going to the golf course to do just that. If it stands up to a round of golf, I should be ok."

Despite Sean Fallon's earlier assertion that Harry would not be risked, he did make an appearance in the second half three days later in the goalless draw with Finn Harps in Ballybofey. Edvaldsson again impressed before flying back to Reykjavik to captain his country in the 2-0 defeat by the USSR. Harry returned to the starting line-up for the third and final game of the tour, Sean Fallon returning to his native Sligo as Celtic manager to see his team enjoy a 6-1 victory over the local Rovers. Bobby Lennox was in dazzling form with four goals, adding to Ronnie Glavin's opener and Pat McCluskey's penalty kick. Five years earlier, the teenage McCluskey had enjoyed a year-long loan spell with the 'Bit o'Red,' as Sligo Rovers went all the way to the FAI Cup final in Dublin in April 1970, before losing to Bohemians.

As Jock Stein commenced the first stage of his long road to recovery, leaving hospital in Dumfries on Friday, 1 August 1975, 24 hours later there was a first opportunity for Scottish-based Celtic supporters to take a look at Johannes Edvaldsson, a combination of that prospect and the glorious sunny weather drawing over 44,000 to Parkhead for the pre-season challenge match with English champions Derby County. The Rams were managed by former Hearts and Tottenham Hotspur legend Dave McKay, who had led them to promotion in 1969 under Brian Clough, before succeeding him as a title-winner with the East Midlands club in 1975. They were a side packed full of internationalists, with Bruce Rioch and Archie Gemmill perhaps the names most familiar to Scottish football supporters.

There was a welcome first sighting of the summer of George Connelly, but suspended Dixie Deans and the injured Steve Murray were still missing, as Sean Fallon selected the following team.

Peter Latchford; Danny McGrain & Andy Lynch; Pat McCluskey, Roddie MacDonald & Johannes Edvaldsson; Harry Hood, Ronnie Glavin, Paul Wilson, Kenny Dalglish & Bobby Lennox. Substitutes; Jackie McNamara & George Connelly.

I recall it being a thoroughly enjoyable afternoon in the summer sunshine, with Celtic very much on the front foot. The headline-writers would have a field day as the only goal of the game was scored on the hour by Edvaldsson, the big Icelander swivelling to rifle the ball past Graham Moseley in the visitors' goal after good work by Danny McGrain and Paul Wilson.

Edvaldsson's transfer from Halbaek was duly completed before Aberdeen's visit to Celtic Park to open the League Cup campaign, seven days later. Another large crowd of 32,000 basking in the sunshine saw the feelgood factor continue with the first two League Cup points secured, an early Kenny Dalglish strike proving to be the winner, with the Dons defenders protesting bitterly that two other Celts had been in offside positions. Harry made way for Jackie McNamara with 12 minutes remaining.

That positive feeling would come to a halt in midweek at Tynecastle, as Sean Fallon tasted his first defeat as Celtic manager. The game would be a tale of two goalkeepers and two penalties, Peter Latchford badly at fault as former Hoops midfielder Steve Hancock, making his Hearts debut, pounced on his mistake to score the opening goal on 15 minutes. The Englishman's opposite number, Jim Cruickshank, then continued his series of spot kick saves from Celtic players as he turned away Pat McCluskey's effort on the half-hour, after Danny McGrain's shot had been blocked by Allan Anderson's arm. Cruickshank was in inspirational form, defying Celtic time and again, and when he was beaten by a Johannes Edvaldsson header from Harry's free-kick, the upright came to his rescue. The match was settled by another regular scourge of Parkhead, striker Donald Ford, who earned then converted a penalty kick for the hosts with 17 minutes remaining to seal a 2-0 win, throwing the section wide open.

Harry dropped to the bench as Dumbarton travelled to Glasgow to complete the first round of League Cup fixtures three days later, Sean Fallon handing Jackie McNamara a starting berth. Kenny Dalglish was once again the star of the show albeit he would be missing from the scoresheet in a 3-1 win. Just after the half-hour mark, the King left three defenders for dead to create an opening tap-in for Paul Wilson at the back post. Wilson himself would turn provider within three minutes, Bobby Lennox the happy recipient as his volley sent Celtic in 2-0 up at the break. In a lacklustre start to the second half, Tom McAdam added another goal to his growing collection against the Bhoys before McNamara's ankle injury saw him stretchered off 10 minutes later. With Harry introduced, the mood was lifted around the ground with six minutes remaining, Johannes Edvaldsson scoring his first competitive goal for Celtic. Once again, Dalglish was the architect, rounding Sons keeper Laurie Williams before laying the ball back for Parkhead's new cult hero 'Big Shuggy' to blast it home and secure the points.

Revenge was in the air as Hearts rolled into Glasgow for the return match seven days after their victory at Tynecastle. There was a pre-match boost for Celtic as Kenny Dalglish ended the speculation around his future by penning a new two-year deal, the Hoops talisman promptly named as the new club captain. The man who had been fulfilling those duties, Bobby Lennox, missed out through illness, Harry promoted from the bench to replace him. Two long range strikes at the beginning and end of the first half ensured there would be no repeat of the earlier result, Ronnie Glavin lashing the ball home within two minutes with Andy Lynch accepting the challenge to send a rocket past former teammate Jim Cruickshank from even further out just before the interval from Harry's corner kick. Five minutes after the break, Johannes Edvaldsson made it two goals in as many games with a fine header following another teasing corner delivery from Hood. The only negative on the night occurred with 15 minutes remaining, Drew Busby ruining Peter Latchford's clean sheet hopes by pulling a goal back for Hearts.

Qualification from the League Cup section was virtually assured three days later, Saturday, 23 August 1975, as Celts ran riot at Boghead against Dumbarton. There was a sideshow to the main event as Ally Hunter refused the offer of a switch between the clubs as part of a package designed to have Tom McAdam score goals for Celtic rather than against them. The in-demand Sons striker was in his usual place at kick-off, but he was a mere onlooker as the Hoops attacking players filled their collective boots, Harry opened his scoring account for the season with a double, as did both Kenny Dalglish then Paul Wilson in the second half. Danny McGrain added a rare strike and substitute Tommy Callaghan was also on target as Celts cruised to an 8-0 victory with a stunning display of attacking strength.

Harry sustained a bad cut on his foot in an accident which caused him to miss Celtic's midweek trip to Pittodrie, Ronnie Glavin also out with a leg strain. The final game of the League Cup group stage was, to all intents and purposes, a dead rubber, such was the Hoops massively superior goal difference. Nevertheless, Sean Fallon's men took the game to Aberdeen from the kick-off, Kenny Dalglish slipping Bobby Lennox in to open the scoring within five minutes. The only other goal of the night came right at the end, and it was a special moment for young substitute Andy Ritchie, who had barely warmed up after replacing Paul Wilson when a defensive error left him with a clear run in on goal. The former Kirkintilloch Rob Roy teenager showed great touch, confidence and composure to beat Bobby Clark.

The rationale of the decision-makers in Scottish football governance was once again called into question as the first fixture of the new Premier League era saw Celtic travel to Ibrox to witness Rangers unveil their first championship flag in 11 years, strangely something which had never happened in the previous decade of Celtic dominance. Not surprisingly, protests would follow from Hoops supporters, local authorities and law enforcement agencies alike at this senseless, needlessly provocative and insensitive call. Perhaps less surprisingly, those protests were ignored, with the subsequent numbers of arrests and injured both hovering around the century mark. The more things change…

With Harry and Ronnie Glavin still unavailable, Sean Fallon named the following Celts for the inaugural Top 10 match on Saturday, 30 August 1975.

Peter Latchford; Danny McGrain & Andy Lynch; Pat McCluskey, Roddie MacDonald & Johannes Edvaldsson; Jackie McNamara, Paul Wilson, Kenny Dalglish, Tommy Callaghan & Bobby Lennox. Substitutes; Andy Ritchie & George Connelly.

Rangers manager Jock Wallace went with this line-up.

Peter McCloy; Sandy Jardine & John Greig; Tom Forsyth, Colin Jackson & Alex MacDonald; Tommy McLean, Bobby McKean, Colin Stein, Derek Johnstone & Quinton Young. Substitutes; Alex Miller & Alex O'Hara.

Just under 70,000 spectators watched Celtic dominate but contrive to lose the match following Kenny Dalglish's sublime opening goal just before the break. The move started from an unlikely source, young Roddie MacDonald showing lovely control to work the ball clear at his own corner flag under pressure from Sandy Jardine, before playing a one-two with Jackie McNamara. The big Highlander then played a long pass down the right touchline, where a beautiful head-flick from Danny McGrain picked out the run of Dalglish driving at the Rangers defence. With Paul Wilson clear on the left, the King shot just as Jardine's recovery sprint saw him slide in to make a block, the ball skidding over Peter McCloy to nestle in the far corner of the net, giving Celts an interval lead.

The match would then turn unexpectedly in the opening 20 minutes of the second half, as Celtic's collection of missed opportunities came back to haunt them, Derek Johnstone's shot beating Peter Latchford before the hosts were reduced to 10 men as Alex MacDonald made one crude challenge too many for the liking of referee Ian Foote. With the game there for the taking, Ibrox winger Quinton Young was fortunate to get away with a clear shove on Pat McCluskey before cutting in to net what would prove to be the winner with 20 minutes to go. Bobby Lennox then scorned another great chance before being replaced by Andy Ritchie, with McNamara making way for

George Connelly. Ritchie came closest to writing his name into the history books in the dying minutes, his close-range header stopped by the legs of McCloy with the keeper eventually falling onto the ball. It would be a sore result to take, as the brave new dawn of Scottish football served up the same old issues, on and off the pitch.

There was a better afternoon for the 25,000 Celtic supporters inside Parkhead to enjoy seven days later, Saturday, 6 September 1975, with the visit of Dundee for the club's first home game in the Premier League. Ahead of kick-off, the return of Jock Stein to Paradise was a sight for sore eyes, the Celtic manager gingerly taking his seat in the Directors' Box to huge applause. Ronnie Glavin returned to the side as Sean Fallon shuffled his pack to accommodate the loss of the injured Roddie MacDonald. Sadly, the news on Harry's injury would provide the one negative, the skilful playmaker now requiring specialist advice to resolve his painful foot problem.

Stein's one remaining Lisbon Lion was the star of the show, Bobby Lennox scoring the first hat-trick of the new era, just reward for a typically energetic performance, whilst Jackie McNamara was also on target in an emphatic 4-0 win over the Dark Blues. After the gloom of losing the cherished Ten, followed by the summer departures of our legends, then the serious threat to the life of our greatest-ever manager, it was a huge relief to witness a team in Hoops once again playing football the Glasgow Celtic way. The fightback to reclaim our crown as Scottish football's dominant force was underway.

There would be further arrivals and departures at Celtic Park as the month progressed. Wednesday, 10 September would be the saddest of days a decade later, as Jock tragically lost his life in Cardiff, but in this particular year it marked the club's first visit to Stenhousemuir's Ochilview Park since January 1937, the previous Hoops goalscorer at that venue being his predecessor as Celtic manager, James Edward McGrory. In the interests of pure, unashamed Celtic nostalgia, this was the Hoops side that day, which began the path to a Hampden Scottish Cup final with Aberdeen in April 1937 which would attract the largest football crowd ever to watch a club match outside Brazil, some 147,365 officially.

Joe Kennaway; Bobby Hogg & Jock Morrison; Chic Geatons, Willie Lyon & George Paterson; Joe Carruth, Willie Buchan, Jimmy McGrory, Johnny Crum & Frank Murphy.

The 1975 Hoops vintage had some way to go to match the achievements of that wonderful team, however, the 4,700 diehards who attended the first leg of the League Cup quarter-final at Ochilview would witness the first sighting of Celtic's latest young hope, 16-year-old Ayrshire schoolboy Robert Syme Aitken handed a spot on the bench next to a fit-again Harry. Known as Roy, he would become a legend in his own right wearing the number four shorts, his rampaging runs often accompanied by chants of *"Feed the Bear"* in a throwback to the support given to winger John 'Yogi' Hughes, a decade earlier. Co-incidentally, Billy Murdoch, the younger brother of Yogi's teammate, Bobby Murdoch - perhaps our greatest-ever right-half - lined up against the Hoops that night in that same position. In the absence of injured Roddie MacDonald, George Connelly returned to partner Johannes Edvaldsson in central defence, with Jackie McNamara, Ronnie Glavin and Tommy Callaghan supporting a strike force of Paul Wilson, Kenny Dalglish and Bobby Lennox.

After a goalless first half, where Edvaldsson, McNamara and Lennox all struck woodwork, the Lisbon Lion continued where he left off against Dundee, nodding Callaghan's corner past Ray Dunlop in the home goal 10 minutes after the break, before the big Fifer made way for Harry. The highlight of the evening arrived in the 80th minute, the majestic Dalglish, in the form of his life, producing another magnificent shot from the edge of the box to tie things up at 2-0. That was the cue for the young cub, Roy Aitken, to replace Edvaldsson and commence his own wonderful career in the famous Hoops.

Three days later, the League match at Fir Park, would mark the end of the road for another fabulous Celtic player, George Connelly playing what would prove to be his final 90 minutes for the club. It was a strange old day all round, as Vic Davidson, just four months after leaving Parkhead on a free transfer to join Motherwell, beat Peter Latchford to put his new club ahead in the 10th minute, with his old sparring partner Kenny Dalglish equalising for Celts just before the interval. The crucial moment in the match came on the hour, Stewart MacLaren punching a Bobby Lennox shot off the line to concede a penalty. With Pat McCluskey dropped to the reserves following the infamous nightclub incident in Copenhagen whilst on Scotland duty, and Lennox himself having seen his previous attempt saved at Tynecastle, it fell to Tommy Callaghan to win the match for Celtic. In fairness, his kick was struck well, low and hard, but home keeper Stuart Rennie produced a fabulous save to keep his side level, Celts, with Harry replacing Paul Wilson, were unable to find a winner as another vital point was shipped.

The following midweek saw Johannes Edvaldsson back on home soil within a month of joining Celtic, the Hoops drawn against his old club Valur in the first round of the 1975/76 European Cup Winners' Cup, a first match in that competition since the controversial defeat at Anfield a decade earlier. Sean Fallon's first European match as Celtic manager, played on Tuesday, 16 September 1975 at Reykjavik's national stadium, Laugardalsvoller, would be an emotional occasion for the Edvaldsson family, the Icelandic Cup-winners featuring younger brother Atli whilst Johannes was wearing the captain's armband for the Bhoys. There was also a nice reunion for Harry with his former Clyde teammate, Joe Gilroy, the striker who also enjoyed spells at Fulham and Dundee now in the final weeks of a stint coaching Valur. Bobby Lennox was suspended, following his ridiculous ordering off against Olympiakos in Greece 12 months earlier, the first Celtic team to play on Icelandic soil duly lining up as follows.

Peter Latchford; Danny McGrain & Andy Lynch; Pat McCluskey, Roddie MacDonald & Johannes Edvaldsson; Harry Hood, Jackie McNamara, Kenny Dalglish, Tommy Callaghan & Paul Wilson. Substitutes; Ally Hunter, George Connelly, Jim Casey, Ronnie Glavin & Andy Ritchie.

It would be an ultimately successful evening as Celts won 2-0, an early goal from Paul Wilson following good work by Kenny Dalglish settling any nerves then Roddie MacDonald heading a fine second from Harry's corner just after the hour. The only sour note on the night was a twice-taken, twice-missed penalty with 20 minutes remaining, after Wilson had been fouled in the box. The script was set up perfectly for Edvaldsson's happy homecoming, only for the Celtic skipper to blast the ball over the crossbar then watch his retaken effort saved brilliantly by Valur keeper Sigi Dagsson, a third successive miss from the spot for Celtic.

Domestic duties resumed four days later, with a trip to Perth to face St Johnstone, always a tricky fixture for Celtic. Dixie Deans would finally be free of the lengthy suspension carried forward from the previous season, a hat-trick in the reserves convincing Sean Fallon that he was ready for a return to first-team action after a five-month absence. Bobby Lennox was also restored from the naughty corner with Harry moving to the bench and the injured Jackie McNamara dropping out. It was a memorable afternoon for another Celt recently in the doghouse. With Celtic having missed their three previous penalty kicks, Sod's Law determined that they would be awarded two at Muirton Park, both times the driving runs of Paul Wilson forcing a mistake from the Saints defence and both times Pat McCluskey showing how it should be done by calmly placing the ball beyond home keeper Derek Robertson. McCluskey would then lay claim to a rather unique hat-trick by adding St Johnstone's goal in a 2-1 win for Celtic, 60 seconds after completing his double at the right end, the big defender unable to prevent an attempted clearance from Andy Lynch from bouncing back off him past Peter Latchford.

There was a huge double-blow in the lead-up to the midweek League Cup return with Stenhousemuir at Celtic Park. Firstly, Steve Murray's severe toe injuries forced the midfielder to announce his early retirement from football, just before his 31st birthday. Murray would reconsider and would briefly return to action early in the new year, but he would not be a first-team regular again. George Connelly was five years younger, and his challenges were perhaps more emotional than physical in nature. Whatever troubled him, it was enough for George to yet again walk away from Celtic and professional football, this time for good. Rated by many as one of the greatest players of his generation - on the planet never mind Scotland - to this day I still regret that Connelly was lost to Celtic and to football so young and with so much still to give and to enjoy. He was a wonderful player, and he could have been anything, but he was George. He had decided that he had had enough, and it was his life after all.

With all that going on, at least there was good news for two other young Celts. Danny McGrain had been replaced by Harry at Muirton with a badly cut shin and he would not be fit to face Stenhousemuir, Roy Aitken receiving his first Celtic start at right-back in his absence. And midfielder Jim Casey would come off the bench in the closing stages to sample first-team action for the first time, replacing Johannes Edvaldsson, with Bobby Lennox later making way for Harry, who promptly saw a shot come back off the post. Celtic's dreadful record from the penalty spot had continued earlier, Pat McCluskey, fresh from his Perth double, managing to blast the ball wide of the post after Kenny Dalglish had been brought down midway through the first half. The only goal of a low-key encounter played in driving rain before just 6,000 spectators came 10 minutes after the break, Andy Lynch playing a one-two with Dalglish before beating Warriors' keeper Ray Dunlop with a tidy finish to seal a spot in the last-four draw for the cup-holders. That would take place the following morning and pair Celtic with Bertie Auld's Partick Thistle, who had won a section including Dundee United, Kilmarnock and St Johnstone with a perfect 12 points from six games before beating Clydebank over two legs in the quarter-final.

Celtic's last fixture of the month was a home League game with Dundee United, which took place on Saturday, 27 September 1975. The previous night, both Harry and Dixie Deans had turned out for the reserves at Tannadice, Harry on the target as the hosts edged the match by the odd goal in 11. Both men would be named as substitutes for the main event at Celtic Park. This time it was the visitors who would be saying goodbye to a key player, star striker Andy Gray sold to Aston Villa for a six-figure fee on the morning of the match, replaced at Parkhead by another teenager, Paul Hegarty. On the sort of damp, dark, dreich day Dundee media man Dick Donald would have dreamed of, Celts secured the points thanks to second-half headers from Kenny Dalglish and Roddie MacDonald, both from deadly deliveries from Bobby Lennox, sadly not Dixie Deans! Of course, there would have to be more penalty drama, although fortunately the award would go to the visitors rather than ruining someone else's day in the Hoops, Graeme Payne doing the needful in the 73rd minute to complete the scoring at 2-1. Harry would get a brief taste of first-team action when he replaced Ronnie Glavin late on.

October opened with the return leg of the European Cup Winners' Cup tie with Valur, Sean Fallon showing the appropriate respect for his part-time opponents by fielding a strong side, with starting slots for Harry and Dixie Deans. Johannes Edvaldsson had passed up the chance to score on native soil two weeks earlier, but he did find the net in Glasgow, the powerful Icelandic star opening the scoring from a Deans centre within seven minutes. Other goals would quickly follow as the Bhoys romped to a 7-0 win, Harry setting up Kenny Dalglish to double the early lead on 12 minutes before Pat McCluskey broke both the penalty bogey and his European duck by making it 3-0 from the spot on the half-hour, after keeper Sigi Dagsson had brought down Deans. The former Motherwell striker was involved in most of the good things on the night, providing a third assist for Harry to fire home a spectacular fourth for Celts 10 minutes from the break, before making it 5-0 himself soon afterwards. Fallon took the opportunity to blood another youngster for the second half, 18-year-old striker George McCluskey introduced for Paul Wilson. Tommy Callaghan took Celtic's tally to six shortly after the break, before making way for Jim Casey, and the latest substitute would raise his profile with 10 minutes remaining when his strong running set up a second goal of the evening for Harry. As well as qualification, the tie with Valur saw Celtic receive one of its most unusual gifts, the Polar Bear Trophy, a stone image presented to the club by their Icelandic opponents, which I prefer to think of as a bear getting friendly with a seal, rather than the official description of the artwork, which has him eating it.

For once, perhaps the chant was amended to *"Don't feed the bear!"*

This chapter is dedicated to the memory of Johannes Edvaldsson, another wonderful Celt, who sadly passed away during the writing of this book.

Rest in peace, Johannes.

Chapter 33

A last Celtic goal and cup final for Harry

Saturday, 4 October 1975 would be a significant day in the wonderful Celtic career of Harry Hood, albeit neither he nor anyone else present at Parkhead would have been aware of that at the time. Sean Fallon stuck with the team who had scored seven goals without reply in the midweek European tie for the visit of Hearts, Harry's double and link-up with Dixie Deans against Valur seeing both fan favourites maintain their places in the following attack-minded line-up.

Peter Latchford; Danny McGrain & Andy Lynch; Pat McCluskey, Roddie MacDonald & Johannes Edvaldsson; Harry Hood, Kenny Dalglish, Dixie Deans, Tommy Callaghan & Paul Wilson. Substitutes; Jim Casey & Bobby Lennox.

The 21,000 faithful supporters who braved wet, blustery weather conditions witnessed an explosive start from Celtic, which finished the match as a contest within 20 minutes. In the 12th minute, the now world-class combination of Danny McGrain and Kenny Dalglish sent Paul Wilson down the right flank, his cross met at the far post by the reinvigorated Deans to put the Hoops 1-0 up. Five minutes later, Dixie and Johannes Edvaldsson set up an opportunity for Harry in front of goal which he gleefully accepted, slamming the ball past Jim Cruickshank for the 125th strike of his Celtic career. The third goal would arrive just as quickly, McGrain's magnificent full-back play again taking him to the by-line, a pinpoint cross picking out Wilson who showed superb skill to beat the Hearts keeper for 3-0. With a League Cup semi-final against Partick Thistle looming 48 hours later, understandably Celts played out the remainder of the match very much within themselves, a slight dampener, as if any were needed, coming in the shape of Drew Busby's late consolation for the visitors. Those of us who trudged home in a happy mood despite the constant drizzling rain would be unaware that we had just witnessed Harry's last goal in the colours of his beloved Celtic, the day after he had celebrated his 31st birthday.

Bertie Auld's Jags now stood between Celtic and a 12th successive League Cup final. The Maryhill outfit had enjoyed a wonderful tournament, the bottom seeds in a tough section comprising Dundee United, St Johnstone and Kilmarnock proceeding to defy the odds by winning all six matches to secure the only perfect qualifying record in the competition. They then finished the quarter-final in the first leg by beating Clydebank 4-0 at Firhill. Bertie arrived at Hampden with high hopes of his team inflicting another painful League Cup defeat on Celtic at the national stadium, whilst his old Parkhead teammate Sean Fallon named an unchanged side. Over 31,000 spectators witnessed a tense match settled by a single strike from Johannes Edvaldsson just before the half-hour, the big Icelander reacting first to a defensive clearance to launch the ball spectacularly past Thistle keeper Alan Rough. Celts would now await the winners of the other semi-final tie between Rangers and First Division Montrose, who had caused a sensation by knocking out Hibernian, beaten finalists the previous season, after extra-time in their last-eight clash. The Ibrox club had also required an additional 30 minutes to overcome Queen of the South the same night.

Next up for Celts was a tricky League fixture against Aberdeen at Pittodrie, five days later, on Saturday, 11 October 1975. Sean Fallon again went with the same starting 11 but that would be reduced by one within 12 minutes, as Paul Wilson reacted angrily to a challenge by Dons defender Eddie Thomson. The Celtic winger threw the ball in Thomson's face, a rare flash of temper which had referee George Smith reaching for his red card. Two minutes later, the Bhoys would have better luck as Drew Jarvie's hesitation was punished by the lightning reflexes of Kenny Dalglish, the Celtic striker coolly chipping Bobby Clark to give the 10-men an unexpected early lead. And it was another defensive disaster by the hosts just before the break which saw the points heading back to Glasgow, this time Harry robbing Jim Henry to fire a shot at goal, Clark's parry falling nicely for Dixie Deans to roll the ball into the empty net. Jocky Scott had caused Celtic many problems in the past whilst wearing the colours of Dundee, and he raised hopes of a fightback when he slammed the ball past Peter Latchford on the hour, however, a Celtic side who had played for almost 80 minutes one man short would hold out for a deserved 2-1 win. That would see the Hoops move to the top of the table for the first time in the Premier League era, following Rangers 3-0 defeat by Ayr United at Somerset Park. Aberdeen's fourth League defeat of the season would trigger a parting of the ways between the club and manager Jimmy Bonthrone over the weekend, early favourite for the Pittodrie role being Ayr's manager Ally MacLeod.

The man Bonthrone had replaced at Aberdeen, Eddie Turnbull, would be in the news seven days later, following one of the more controversial Scottish matches of that decade. On Saturday, 18 October 1975, he brought his Hibernian side to a Celtic Park enveloped in the thick mist which had plagued the city for days. Sean Fallon once again named an unchanged side – in those days a player sent off did not automatically miss the next match – as 33,000 spectators turned out for one of the glamour fixtures of the 1970's. Sadly, it would be ruined by the weather, which as it turned out was a huge stroke of luck for Celtic, but not their opponents, whose name I believe translates as *"Men of Ireland."*

Hibernian enjoyed the best of the early exchanges, scoring the only goal midway through the first half thanks to a header from midfielder Des Bremner. In those days, it was possible for supporters to switch ends at half-time, and on that particular afternoon, this 14-year-old left his Dad in the Celtic End to walk around the ground to view the second half from the east terracing, presumably as the Hoops would be shooting towards that goal after the break. Whatever the reason, I can recall clearly standing up there alone for the second half, albeit that will be the last time I mention the word 'clearly' in this paragraph. Newspaper reports advise that first Dixie Deans then Kenny Dalglish had to leave the field due to injury, but I have no recollection of that or indeed a second goal for Hibernian scored by Joe Harper with 15 minutes remaining. In over 50 years of watching football, I have, quite literally, never seen anything like this, a cloud of thick fog descending which rendered anything happening beyond that invisible. I genuinely still thought the score was 1-0, when word eventually spread around our area that the game had been abandoned. The referee that day was a certain RH Davidson of Airdrie. Suffice to say he was no friend of Celtic, so for him to do that with Hibernian 2-0 up at Celtic Park, where I believe they had not won for six years, and with only five minutes of play remaining, perhaps gives you a sense of just how farcical things had become. Presumably, those in the Jungle had some idea of what was going on, as some supporters spilled on to the pitch, which I guess was the final straw. Despite the outrage of Eddie Turnbull at the decision, the match would have to be replayed. And despite their excellent performance, the original Irish football club would not get their foggy due.

Celts swapped the misty gloom of Glasgow for the sunshine of northern Portugal in midweek as they travelled to face Boavista in the first leg of their second-round tie in the European Cup Winners' Cup. The club from the western Oporto suburb of the same name, who wore those unique black-and-white chequered shirts, had just enjoyed their best-ever season, finishing fourth in the Primeira Divisao behind the Portuguese holy trinity - Lisbon giants Benfica and Sporting Club and Boavista's own city rivals, FC Porto - whilst beating the mighty Eagles to win their first major trophy, the Taca de Portugal, on Saturday, 14 June 1975. The winning goal that day had been scored against his old Benfica teammates by Boavista's star midfielder, Joao Alves, the first player I can ever recall who wore gloves on the pitch as a matter of course.

That Portuguese Cup win would see the Panthers compete in European football for the first time, their Cup Winners' Cup first-round opponents being Czechoslovak Cup-holders Spartak Trnava. A goalless draw in the first leg in what is now western Slovakia would be followed by an emphatic 3-0 triumph in the return match at the Estadio do Bessa, as Celts were dumping Valur 7-0 in Glasgow. The sides were then drawn together in the second round, with Boavista the current Portuguese League leaders.

Neither Celtic captain Kenny Dalglish nor striker Dixie Deans would recover from injuries sustained in the abandoned match with Hibernian in time to line up in Portugal. With his European suspension over, Bobby Lennox returned to lead the side with Jackie McNamara given a marking role on the dangerman Alves, but the hero of that afternoon was goalkeeper Peter Latchford, who capped his best performance for Celtic to date by saving a late Alves' penalty, after Tommy Callaghan had handled in the box. That would enable the Bhoys to leave Portugal with a very respectable goalless draw.

As an aside, Boavista would go on to make that 1975/76 season their finest ever, this time finishing just two points behind champions Benfica in second place whilst retaining their Taca de Portugal by beating Vitoria Guimaraes 2-1 in the final, that victory perhaps tasting even sweeter as it took place at the Estadio das Antas, the home of local rivals Porto.

The last match of the month took place three days later, Saturday, 25 October 1975, and it was no ordinary game. Two nights after Celtic's defeat of Partick Thistle at Hampden, Rangers had beaten Montrose to set up a first League Cup final meeting between the clubs for five years. On that afternoon in 1970, a Derek Johnstone header had ended the Hoops five-year dominance in the competition before over 106,000 spectators, the last time a League Cup match had drawn a six-figure attendance. A controversial decision to bring forward the kick-off time to 1pm for this latest clash would be one of the reasons why the 1975 final would attract less than half that crowd to the national stadium, less than 58,000 making the effort. Lunchtime kick-offs for Celtic matches remain one of the bugbears of my football life. I detest them. Nevertheless, I was excited at the prospect of attending my first-ever cup final against Rangers, something I had grown up hearing all about from my dad and my brother. It was a first final also for Sean Fallon as Celtic manager, and it would turn out to be the last for the Sligo man and a number of his players that day, including Harry Hood.

Kenny Dalglish would be fit enough to return and captain Celtic in a cup final for the first time, Jackie McNamara moving to the bench in the only change to the midweek line-up in Portugal as the ongoing injury problem for Dixie Deans ruled him out of the squad completely. The full teams were as follows.

CELTIC:

Peter Latchford; Danny McGrain & Andy Lynch; Pat McCluskey, Roddie MacDonald & Johannes Edvaldsson; Harry Hood, Kenny Dalglish, Paul Wilson, Tommy Callaghan & Bobby Lennox. Substitutes; Jackie McNamara & Ronnie Glavin.

RANGERS:

Stewart Kennedy; Sandy Jardine & John Greig; Tom Forsyth, Colin Jackson & Alex MacDonald; Tommy McLean, Colin Stein, Derek Parlane, Derek Johnstone & Quinton Young. Substitutes; Alex Miller & Bobby McKean.

My recollections of this game are of huge anti-climax and disappointment, a half-empty national stadium rather than the Hampden Roar, and a struggling Celtic side who rarely looked like winning the match. From my spot high up in the old North

Enclosure, I had a bird's-eye view of the only goal, which arrived, of all times, in the 67th minute. There seemed little danger as Quinton Young's lofted cross looked to be heading out for a goal-kick, Rangers striker Derek Parlane and the ball being shepherded out by Roddie MacDonald. Perhaps a little inexperience crept in, Parlane somehow allowed to retrieve the ball and cross into the danger area, where Johannes Edvaldsson's defensive header appeared to have ended the threat. Sadly, it was nodded straight back in towards the penalty spot, where Alex MacDonald completed the session of head tennis by diving to beat Peter Latchford low at his right-hand post. Harry would mark his last cup final appearance by picking up a booking, before he and Paul Wilson made way for Jackie McNamara and Ronnie Glavin. Sadly, it would be John Greig rather than Kenny Dalglish who would climb the stairs to receive the trophy, as the green half of Glasgow trudged home to lick their wounds after a fifth League Cup final defeat in six seasons.

Seven days after the damp squib at Hampden, Celtic faced an unchanged Rangers side again, this time in a League fixture at Parkhead. Despite their League Cup victory, the Ibrox side had followed up their loss at Ayr with another League defeat, this time at Motherwell, as the fog was descending on Celtic Park. A Hoops win today would see them open up a three-point gap with a game in hand. Sean Fallon made two changes in his attack, Dixie Deans finally fit enough to return and joined by a 17-year-old George McCluskey making his first competitive start. Harry moved to the bench with Bobby Lennox and Ronnie Glavin dropping out the squad, Celts lining up as follows on Saturday, 1 November 1975.

Peter Latchford; Danny McGrain & Andy Lynch; Pat McCluskey, Roddie MacDonald & Johannes Edvaldsson; George McCluskey, Kenny Dalglish, Dixie Deans, Tommy Callaghan & Paul Wilson. Substitutes; Harry Hood & Jackie McNamara.

The first Premier League fixture to be impacted by the decision to kick off these matches at lunchtime attracted an attendance of just 55,000, some 15,000 below the set limit. We also witnessed the introduction of another unwelcome guest, one consequence of the mini pitch invasion against Hibernian a fortnight earlier, the installation of a perimeter fence, which now ran the length of the Jungle. The times they certainly were a-changing, and sadly not for the better.

Not surprisingly, the match would be a huge improvement on the Hampden non-event of the previous Saturday, with Celts playing the better football but Rangers missing the better chances. It would finish with honours even at 1-1, after a four-minute spell late in the game which provided the only goal action. That commenced with a Keystone Cops opener from the visitors with 15 minutes remaining. As Andy Lynch and Tommy Callaghan discussed options over a Celtic free-kick on the halfway line beside the newly-caged Jungle. I suspect none of those included a pass straight to Tommy McLean, who instantly sent Derek Parlane clean through on Peter Latchford. There was a certain inevitability about the outcome as the Ibrox striker raced in on goal unchallenged to round the keeper and put his side 1-0 up. Thankfully, there would be an instant and positive response from the Bhoys, with young George McCluskey the catalyst. He showed great skill in finding the yard of space required to deliver his cross from the right flank, the onrushing Dixie Deans failing to connect properly but Paul Wilson arriving at the far post to bundle the ball home for an inelegant but timely equaliser. The youngster would then make way for Harry after an excellent debut. The draw kept Celts one point ahead of a chasing pack of Hibernian, Motherwell, Rangers and Hearts, the Hoops still enjoying games in hand.

Four nights later, the return leg of the European Cup Winners' Cup tie with Boavista saw another break with tradition, a UEFA directive forcing the club to wear huge black numbers on the back of the sacred Hoops for the first time, Celts looking more like Sporting Lisbon than themselves. Sean Fallon made one change from the weekend, Jackie McNamara reinstated with goal hero Paul Wilson listed with Harry as one of his substitutes. Some 37,000 supporters avoided Bonfire Night distractions to attend and many of those would still be outside as Kenny Dalglish fired Celtic ahead within 35 seconds. There seemed little danger as the King played a speculative ball towards the far post, with Boavista keeper Antonio Botelho stepping off his line to claim under no pressure whatsoever. From my view in the front stand, it was unclear what happened next, however, the highlights footage would suggest he was already thinking of his next move, as the ball escaped his grasp and dropped into the empty net.

Celts received another lucky break on 20 minutes. Portuguese midfielder Manuel Barbosa is a Boavista club legend, his 14-year career tally of 345 League appearances unmatched by any other player. This would not be a moment for him to remember fondly, though, Barbosa's attempted clearance from Andy Lynch's free-kick travelling straight to the feet of Johannes Edvaldsson, who promptly rifled it straight back under Botelho for 2-0. The crucial next goal would then go the way of the visitors, 10 minutes from the interval, Boavista star Alves playing a sublime reverse pass which gave Mane a glimpse of goal, the Brazilian striker conjuring up an equally brilliant finish which ripped past Peter Latchford into the roof of the Celtic net. A nervous second half would produce just one more goal, and the roar of relief would have been heard in Oporto. Just four minutes were left on the clock when Dalglish's pass saw Dixie Deans scampering down the right flank unchallenged, Portuguese defenders with raised arms waiting for a flag which would not be forthcoming. The deadly Deans would bore down on the Boavista goal, before clipping the ball over Botelho to seal the tie, as the roof came off the old stadium. One of the great European moments for those of us of a certain vintage.

The European Cup Winners' Cup had long been regarded by many as the easiest of the three major UEFA tournaments to win, given the number of second-tier teams who would gain access, on occasion as runner's-up to teams who had completed a League and Cup double. Thus, you would occasionally see clubs win the trophy who could only dream of success at the real summit of continental football. This year's competition would be no exception, with Welsh Cup-winners Wrexham progressing to the quarter-final, whilst England was represented by FA Cup-winners, West Ham United, who had won it at Wembley back in 1965. Of the other top nations, old foes Atletico Madrid were beaten by Eintracht Frankfurt whilst the shock of the round was the exit of Coppa Italia holders Fiorentina's at the hands of East Germany's Sachsenring Zwickau, thanks to a shoot-out penalty converted by their long-serving goalkeeper, Jurgen Croy. More on them to follow later. The last eight was completed by Anderlecht, Austrians Sturm Graz and Dutch Cup-winners ADO Den Haag. Celtic had knocked on the door of the European Cup final in recent seasons, just short of the quality in depth possessed by Ajax and Bayern Munich, however, there was no doubt in my mind that this competition had just opened up.

The often mentioned but dreaded 'Euro Hangover' would be in evidence three days later, as League leaders Celtic travelled to Dens Park, some 11 months after Kenny Dalglish and Jimmy Johnstone had run riot against the Dark Blues there in a 6-0 win. Jinky had, of course, since departed Parkhead and was at that point still considering his next move after a brief stint in the USA. King Kenny had not left the building, but he would be outshone on the day by a young red-haired midfielder called Gordon Strachan, as a Celtic side with Harry and Bobby Lennox in for George McCluskey and Tommy Callaghan struggled to make any impact. Hoops keeper Peter Latchford limped through the vast majority of the 90 minutes, following an early ankle injury, and Sean Fallon would probably have accepted the point that was still within our grasp as the clock ticked down towards full-time. However, with three minutes remaining, Dundee's Scottish international midfielder Bobby Robinson suddenly found himself in the clear with only the toiling Latchford to beat, his unerring finish securing a 1-0 victory which enabled both Motherwell and Hearts to leapfrog Celtic at the top of the table.

Perversely, Celtic would then make the journey down to Somerset Park in midweek and produce their best performance since that December 1974 victory at Dens Park. Paul Wilson and Tommy Callaghan returned to the team, replacing Harry and Bobby Lennox, as Sean Fallon sought a winning formula against an Ayr United side unbeaten at home but now minus their manager Ally MacLeod, who had taken over at Aberdeen, coach Sam McMillan in charge. Once again, as on that memorable afternoon at Dundee, Kenny Dalglish was the destroyer-in-chief, the King elevating his performance that night to a higher plain, although the main headlines quite justifiably would reflect the fact that Johannes Edvaldsson had scored his first hat-trick in Scottish football. The Iceland captain benefitted from two Wilson deliveries to power the Hoops 2-0 up within 20 minutes, Dixie Deans, Dalglish himself with a glorious goal then Roddie MacDonald piling on the agony as Celts went nap just after the half-hour mark. The hosts' fightback was led by winger Johnny Doyle, the future Celtic hero felled by a current one in Danny McGrain to allow Johnny Graham to pull one back from the spot, just before the interval. Doyle himself would make it 5-2 by scoring against his Bhoyhood team 10 minutes into the second half, before a late burst saw two further Celtic goals take their tally to a magnificent seven. With 15 minutes remaining, we had the spectacular sight of Big Shuggy and Wee Dixie both diving to meet the same cross, Edvaldsson's head making contact to bullet the ball past Hugh Sproat for 6-2. Deans would duly get his own second in the closing stages, as a fabulous 7-2 victory saw Celts go top once again.

The yo-yo season continued at the weekend, with a summit meeting between Celtic and Motherwell at Parkhead. Harry found himself on reserve team duty on the Friday night, scoring Celtic's third goal in a 3-1 win at Fir Park. The following afternoon, an unchanged team from Wednesday's seven-goal mauling of Ayr United took the game to the visitors from the outset, the crossbar twice coming to keeper Stewart Rennie's rescue, as first a wonderful free-kick from Andy Lynch then a header from Dixie Deans against his old club rattled the goalframe. Celts were then sucker-punched in the seconds immediately before the break, Willie Pettigrew finishing off a classic counter-attack by nodding the ball past the previously untroubled Peter Latchford. The classy Motherwell striker was being watched by European champions Bayern Munich and he would do his chances of a dream move to the Bundesliga no harm by putting his team 2-0 up within six minutes of the restart, this time the predator forcing the ball past Latchford at the far post after good play by Bobby Graham. There would be no way back for Celtic as Motherwell defended that lead resolutely to the final whistle, the game ending in defeat much to the disappointment of the vast majority of the 33,000 spectators.

Seven days later, Saturday, 22 November 1975, it was the turn of bottom-dogs St Johnstone to visit Celtic Park on League duty. With Paul Wilson commencing a suspension following his October red card at Pittodrie, there was a return for George McCluskey, whilst Bobby Lennox replaced the injured Jackie McNamara and both Harry and Ronnie Glavin were restored to the bench. Neither would see action, the veteran Lennox striking either side of the break to cancel out opportunist goals from Jim O'Rourke and Charlie Smith, which had threatened to further derail Celtic's title hopes. The Lisbon Lion also struck the woodwork twice in the first half in a typically energetic performance, on the day a flag commemorating Celtic's world record of nine consecutive League titles was unfurled. However, it was the cool head of Kenny Dalglish which conjured up the winning goal for Celtic, just seven minutes into the second half, the Parkhead skipper's turn and shot beating Saints reserve keeper Dave Nicoll, as the Hoops eventually edged a five-goal thriller to maintain their push for a first Premier League title.

There was a trip home to the English Midlands for Peter Latchford in midweek, as Celts travelled to St Andrew's to face Birmingham City in a match to celebrate the centenary of the club formed as Small Heath Alliance back in 1875. Sadly, his brother Dave would not be between the sticks for the English top-flight outfit, and there would be no place for defender and future Celtic assistant manager Gary Pendrey or star forward Trevor Francis. Familiar names in the Blues line-up included Howard Kendall and the Scottish duo of Kenny Burns and Jimmy Calderwood. This was a golden opportunity for young Irish forward Hilary Carlyle, who had impressed against Celtic in a pre-season game for Finn Harps and would now play in a live trial in front of 15,000 spectators. He struggled to get a positive verdict on the night, replaced by Harry as the Hoops went down to a strike in first-half stoppage time by Peter With, whose goal would later win the 1982 European Cup for Aston Villa. Celtic passed up a great chance to level the match with 15 minutes remaining, a goalbound shot from Kenny Dalglish punched off the line by City full-back Ray Martin with his keeper Steve Smith well beaten. The ongoing saga of penalty misses continued, Pat McCluskey's effort saved as the hosts enjoyed a 1-0 win.

The final match of a roller-coaster November saw the introduction of segregation, another concept which would have been alien to the spirit of the game a decade earlier. Prior to that day, my only experience of fans being separated inside the ground had been for games where Celtic faced Rangers, however, at Tannadice on Saturday, 29 November 1975 it was Dundee United fans who exclusively occupied that spot in the steep terracing opposite the main stand where I had stood to watch my first game at that venue just a few years earlier, a no-man's land and police cordons now in place between the home and visiting supporters. Suspension-free Paul Wilson replaced George McCluskey with Harry listed as one of the substitutes as Celts entered this not-so-brave new world with the following team.

Peter Latchford; Danny McGrain & Andy Lynch; Pat McCluskey, Roddie MacDonald & Johannes Edvaldsson; Paul Wilson, Kenny Dalglish, Dixie Deans, Tommy Callaghan & Bobby Lennox. Substitutes; Harry Hood & Ronnie Glavin.

On a bitterly cold afternoon, Dixie Deans warmed the cockles of visiting hearts by putting the Hoops ahead within three minutes, the striker following up after United keeper Hamish McAlpine had parried an effort from Kenny Dalglish. The points were then settled with two superb goals in a five-minute spell midway through the second half. First Bobby Lennox took advantage of a defensive error to make it 2-0 with a glorious angled drive, then a short free-kick taken by Dalglish was lashed past the helpless McAlpine by Andy Lynch to make the game safe. Both Harry and Ronnie Glavin remained on the bench as a Paul Hegarty header with seven minutes remaining gave the home fans something to enjoy before the match ended 3-1. Celts ended the month ahead of Hibernian and Motherwell on goal difference, defending champions Rangers tucked in one point behind the leading pack.

Two days after the victory at Tannadice, Harry was back on Tayside for a match 200 yards along the street at Dens Park. Dundee's long-serving full-back Bobby Wilson had been granted a well-deserved testimonial and, as was often the case, it would be Jock Stein's Celts who were invited to provide the opposition. Technically, it was a Celtic select, with current stars Harry and Paul Wilson lining up alongside Hoops legends Tommy Gemmell, Billy McNeill, Davie Hay and Bertie Auld, together with a couple of guest players who would later represent the club with very different results, Pat Stanton and Frank Munro. This game, played on Monday, 1 December 1975, is also worthy of note as it would be the only occasion where future Parkhead manager Gordon Strachan would ever wear the Hoops.

The performances of the talented, diminutive redhead Strachan on the right flank for Dundee were drawing inevitable comparisons with the recently departed Jimmy Johnstone, who had made his debut for former Celt Jimmy Sirrel's Sheffield United just 10 days earlier, after a brief spell in the USA with San Jose Earthquakes. As an aside, Jinky's first match for the Blades was against a Stoke City side featuring England internationalists Peter Shilton and Mike Pejic, whom he had tormented for Scotland at Hampden just 18 months earlier, whilst still at the peak of his powers. How quickly things change in football. There were strong rumours that 18-year-old Strachan was on the radar of Sean Fallon, managing the Parkhead first team whilst Jock Stein recovered from his injuries, as well as talk of a potential return for David Hay. Sadly, neither signing would come to pass, albeit both wore the green-and-white Hoops as the following men represented Celtic at Dens Park on that first day of December.

Thomson Allan (Dundee); Tommy Gemmell (Dundee) & Jim Hermiston (ex-Aberdeen); Pat Stanton (Hibernian), Billy McNeill & Frank Munro (Wolverhampton Wanderers); Harry Hood, Davie Hay (Chelsea), Paul Wilson, Bertie Auld & Rab Prentice (Hearts). Substitutes; Gordon Strachan & Bobby Ford (both Dundee).

The game, of course, was much more about fun and honouring Bobby Wilson than the result, however, in the interests of completeness, Pat Stanton gave Celtic the lead midway through the first half before the hosts recovered to win 5-1.

Looking back now, November 1975 really marked a watershed in Harry's Celtic career, a month where his only competitive first-team action was a few minutes against Rangers as a substitute and a single start, against Dundee at Dens Park the following weekend. That would now become the norm for the remainder of his time at Parkhead, Harry, Dixie Deans and Tommy Callaghan finding themselves increasingly on the periphery as the next batch of promising youngsters were phased into the team.

Having scored for the reserves in a 4-2 win over Hearts in midweek, Harry would line up with the Class of '75 for the first time in a month, five days later, as Celts won a tricky fixture at Tynecastle to remain at the top of the table on goal difference, thanks to a late strike from Dixie Deans. That would set them up well for the visit of Hibernian in midweek, the replay of the October match controversially cancelled due to fog with the visitors leading 2-0 in the dying minutes. Things looked promising for the majority of the 33,000 spectators in the old ground as Deans yet again plundered a goal against the Leith men on the hour, taking a pass from Harry to bury a low shot past Jim McArthur. However, Joe Harper enjoyed scoring against Celtic every bit as much, and he levelled things off with 18 minutes remaining, claiming the final touch after peter Latchford had misjudged an Erich Schaedler free-kick. In normal circumstances, a draw at Parkhead would be considered a point dropped by Celtic, but like most folk, I suspect, given the situation with the original game, I was more than happy to accept that particular result, which enabled the Bhoys to move one point clear of Motherwell at the top of the table, with Hibernian one further back, all of the top sides now having completed 15 League fixtures.

That would all change on Saturday, 13 December 1975, as new Aberdeen manager Ally MacLeod brought his team to Glasgow. Paul Wilson came in for Harry in the only change from the midweek line-up, with young Roy Aitken also on the bench. Two goals in the opening half-hour from Drew Jarvie and Arthur Graham gave Celts a mountain to climb, and despite pushing the influential Johannes Edvaldsson into midfield from his sweeper role then introducing Harry for Wilson, the Hoops would draw a rare blank at Parkhead. Hibernian's home win over Motherwell the same afternoon would see them leapfrog the Steelmen to join Celtic on points at the top, ahead of their meeting seven days later.

The latest Battle of the Greens, which took place at Easter Road on Saturday, 20 December 1975, drew only 21,000 to Leith, perhaps a combination of changing times and the dreaded 'Saturday before Christmas' to blame for an attendance less than half what those great teams of just a few years earlier would have attracted. Nevertheless, it would prove to be another occasion when the Hoops rose to the challenge, with an excellent 3-1 win in perhaps their finest display of the season. With Jock Stein looking on from the stand, Sean Fallon opted for the more defensive Jackie McNamara to either Paul Wilson or Harry, his only change, and the midfielder would seal victory with a delightful lob in the final minute, after Dixie Deans had created the opening. Dixie had, of course, opened the scoring early on with one of his trademark headers, before two goals in a minute midway through the first half saw Celts emerge with that lead intact. Arthur Duncan's equaliser for Hibernian was cancelled out by Johannes Edvaldsson seconds later, the big Icelander following up to knock the ball home, after yet another Deans header had been touched onto the crossbar by keeper Jim McArthur. Some 50 miles to the west, Motherwell's 3-2 defeat at Ibrox would create some daylight between the trio of previous leaders, albeit Rangers were now making their own charge in the background.

Harry had been an unused substitute at Easter Road, and the following Saturday he travelled with the reserve squad for a match at Somerset Park against Ayr United. The team would include Steve Murray, now attempting a comeback having earlier announced his retiral from football, plus future Celtic stalwarts Roy Aitken, Tommy Burns and George McCluskey. Murray and McCluskey grabbed the goals in a 2-1 win. Back in Glasgow, an unchanged starting line-up secured two vital points by beating the Honest Men 3-1. Fresh from his Christmas trip home to Iceland, Johannes

Edvaldsson was the key man, his headed double either side of the interval putting Celts 2-1 up. The visitors were then reduced to 10 men, as Johnny Doyle, who had excelled in the recent clash between the clubs at Somerset, despite the 7-2 scoreline, finally had enough of the Andy Lynch treatment to give some of it back. Edvaldsson then rounded off a man-of-the-match performance by setting up Kenny Dalglish for Celtic's third and clinching goal with six minutes remaining. Results elsewhere would see the year end on a happy note, both Hibernian and Rangers drawing and only Motherwell of the leading pack matching the Hoops with a victory over Dundee.

There would be some final football action of 1975 for Harry, turning out again for the reserves on Tuesday, 30 December, as Rangers' second string made the short journey across the city. A strong attacking Hoops line-up, which included George McCluskey, Ronnie Glavin, Tommy Burns and Paul Wilson, would prevail, Harry adding to Alex O'Hara's own goal to give Celts a morale-boosting 2-1 win, ahead of the first-team clash at Ibrox two days later.

Chapter 34

It's anyone's title in a four-way race

Thursday, 1 January 1976 would be a double rite of passage day for yours truly, a first Ne'erday derby and my first visit to Ibrox. Harry and Paul Wilson had both done enough in the reserve fixture 48 hours earlier to merit inclusion on the Celtic bench, as the following teams kicked off the year.

RANGERS:

Stewart Kennedy; Alex Miller & John Greig; Tom Forsyth, Colin Jackson & Alex MacDonald; Bobby McKean, Johnny Hamilton, Martin Henderson, Tommy McLean & Derek Johnstone. Substitutes; Ally Scott & Alex O'Hara.

CELTIC:

Peter Latchford; Danny McGrain & Andy Lynch; Johannes Edvaldsson, Roddie MacDonald & Pat McCluskey; Jackie McNamara, Kenny Dalglish, Dixie Deans, Tommy Callaghan & Bobby Lennox. Substitutes; Harry Hood & Paul Wilson.

With the hosts three points behind the League leaders at the 2pm kick-off, it was pretty much a must-win game for them, whilst any sort of positive result would see Celtic remain in pole position for the second half of the season. What was not in the Hoops favour was a second consecutive New Year visit to Ibrox - a fixture they had not won since a Joe Cassidy double secured the points on the opening day of 1921 - an unhappy consequence of the move to four fixtures per season between the clubs.

Jock Stein's hopes of a cherished 10-in-a-row had been dashed on the Ibrox rocks 12 months earlier, with a painful 3-0 defeat, and sadly today would be another significant day in the inaugural Premier League title race. The only goal of the game came on the half-hour via that familiar Rangers tactic, a lofted Tommy McLean free-kick towards the head of Derek Johnstone. Once again, the burly striker won the aerial battle to beat Peter Latchford from close range, and despite a second-half bombardment of the Rangers goal following the introduction of Paul Wilson and Harry for Dixie Deans and Bobby Lennox, the hosts would stretch their unbeaten run against Celtic to seven games. That would be Harry's final first-team action for Celtic against Rangers. Both Motherwell and Hibernian opened 1976 with home wins, all three main challengers now lurking just a single point behind the table-topping Hoops with 17 of the 36 games remaining. Game on.

That defeat would be compounded two days later as Gordon Strachan swapped his December Hoops for the navy jersey of Dundee to make his first senior appearance at Celtic Park. Like many of those to follow, the skilful midfielder would cause Celtic no end of damage as a 3-1 lead early in the second half disappeared before the final whistle. With Paul Wilson in for Bobby Lennox and Steve Murray making his comeback from retiral on the bench at Harry's expense, the Bhoys recovered from the setback of an early Andy Lynch own goal to take a winning lead, Dixie Deans' quick equaliser followed by a Kenny Dalglish double, the Celtic captain looking more like himself after, by his own exceptional standards, a disappointing spell of form. The alarm bells which sounded upon Wilson Hoggan's goal for Dundee on the hour were set aside as the stadium rose to welcome Murray's introduction for Roddie MacDonald with 15 minutes remaining, Johannes Edvaldsson stepping back into central defence. We were into the final minutes when Gordon Strachan's corner was met by the head of visiting full-back David McIntosh, Peter Latchford helpless as the ball floated over him to steal away a precious point. With Motherwell drawing at Pittodrie and Hibernian's visit to Tannadice falling victim to the weather, a narrow win for Rangers at Tynecastle enabled the Ibrox club to join Celtic at the top of the table, only a superior goal difference now keeping Parkhead noses in front.

With the pressure now truly on, Sean Fallon's men produced two fighting performances to take maximum points from the difficult visits to Motherwell and Perth. The reserve fixture with Motherwell was brought forward to midweek, Harry one of a number of international players involved and on target in a 3-0 win at Celtic Park. The match at Fir Park three days later, on Saturday, 10 January 1976, brings back memories for me, as I was approached outside the main stand and invited to be the featured 'Celtic Boy' in the following edition of *The Celtic View*. Those of a certain vintage will recall that you are photographed and asked to name your favourite player, who you then meet at a future home game as a guest of the club. Before I could explain how much grief I would receive at school for this, my dad was right in there, and Celtic Boy I was, like it or not. That's my version anyway!

My choice of player had been Dixie Deans, and as it happened, he would be the key man on a day when Celtic again looked like champions. After a goalless first half, the striker scored twice against his old club in the opening 15 minutes of the second period to put the Hoops in the driving seat. There was a brief Groundhog Day feeling as that lead was halved just two minutes later, former Celt Vic Davidson knocking the ball over the line for 2-1 to save Johannes Edvaldsson the embarrassment of an own goal after the big sweeper had sliced a clearance. But Celtic fought back, the restored midfield duo of Steve Murray and Ronnie Glavin adding a freshness and dynamism to the team which had been missing in recent weeks and allowing captain Kenny Dalglish to operate slightly further forward. The King would have the final say, with eight minutes remaining, Deans yet again involved as Dalglish beat Stuart Rennie, the Hoops roaring back to form with an exhilarating 3-1 victory over one of their main rivals for the Scottish crown. Celtic now led Rangers at the top of the table only on goals scored.

Although named in the travelling squad, Harry had missed out on that Motherwell match and he would again be on reserve duty as the first team travelled to face bottom-dogs St Johnstone at Muirton Park, on Saturday, 17 January 1976. This is without doubt my favourite visit to the old Perth stadium, which so often witnessed a negative result for Celtic. There was an early shock for the unchanged visitors as Duncan Lambie gave Saints the lead after 15 minutes, Celts replying within six minutes after Dixie Deans and Kenny Dalglish combined again for the skipper to equalise. Just after the half-hour, Bobby Thomson beat Peter Latchford all ends up with a long-range effort, the Saints looking good value for their interval lead before Deans headed his fourth goal in three games just seconds from the whistle.

The feelgood half-time factor disappeared in the opening minute of the second period, this time Andy Lynch harshly penalised for a challenge in the box and Thomson stepping up for his double. Latchford denied the Perth striker with an excellent save, only to look on helplessly as Gordon Crammond was first to react and put Saints ahead for a third time. With Celts now piling forward towards the goal a few yards in front of us, there was a huge sense of relief when Roddie MacDonald soared to power his header home for 3-3 with 20 minutes remaining. Derek Robertson and his defensive line then led a charmed life, as all attempts to secure a winner were defied, word soon coming through on a thousand transistor radios that Rangers were beating Hibernian at Ibrox and were poised to go top, that news only adding to the feeling of impending gloom.

Then cometh the hour, cometh The Iceman.

With seconds remaining, Celts were working the ball up the far side in a desperate bid to win the match, that world-class combination of Danny McGrain and Kenny Dalglish weaving closer to the danger area. All of a sudden, the King has delivered a cross, which clears everyone in the middle to drift towards us, watching beyond the far post, before the powerful figure of Johannes Edvaldsson launches himself at the ball, his connection perfect as the net bulges behind the despairing Robertson to create bedlam all around us. It was an incredible end to an incredible afternoon, the Hoops showing the mark of champions to stay level with their closest rivals.

After two thrilling away victories in the League, the mood of the Celtic supporters was upbeat as they made their way to Motherwell in their thousands on Saturday, 24 January 1976. The defence of their Scottish Cup would commence at one of the most difficult venues in the country at that time, Fir Park. However, just two weeks earlier, Celtic had dismantled the Steelmen on their own turf, emerging as 3-1 winners to maintain their narrow lead at the top of the table.

Whilst some of the Celtic constants of my childhood had now gone - Billy McNeill, the League title and the annual European Cup entry - the Scottish Cup had been retained. Jock Stein had a quite incredible record in the competition, having lifted it as Hoops captain in April 1954 then as Dunfermline Athletic manager against Celtic seven years later. His last act as Hibernian boss had been to eliminate Rangers and take the Edinburgh side into the last four in March 1965, and by the time those ties came around, Stein was in charge at Parkhead and leading his new charges to their first major trophy since Hampden in the Sun, more than seven years earlier. In 11 years at the helm, Jock had taken Celtic to 10 Scottish Cup finals, winning seven of those. The only blight on that cup final record had been 1968, the Bhoys losing out, rather ironically, to Stein's old Dunfermline Athletic team in a 2-0 defeat at Celtic Park in the third-round tie played on Saturday, 27 January. The referee that day, Bobby Davidson of Airdrie, had controversially ruled out a Jim Brogan strike with the game goalless and would play a huge part in Aberdeen's defeat of Celtic in the final two years later. He and Jock would be at loggerheads for many years after that. Davidson was no friend of Celtic. I'll just leave it at that.

Whilst Stein was missing from the Celtic dugout at Fir Park, as he recovered from the severe injuries sustained in a road accident the previous summer, Davidson would again be the man in the middle. Celts were attempting to achieve a third successive Scottish Cup triumph, a feat never before managed by a team in the famous Hoops. Perhaps this would be the year. Caretaker boss Sean Fallon was forced into making one change, Steve Murray's attempted comeback from the toe injury which had forced his retiral the previous year sadly over, following a recurrence in training ahead of the match. He would not play for Celtic again. Jackie McNamara moved off the bench to replace Murray in midfield whilst Harry came back into the first-team squad after a spell in the reserves, Celtic lining up as follows.

Peter Latchford; Danny McGrain & Andy Lynch; Pat McCluskey, Roddie MacDonald & Johannes Edvaldsson; Jackie McNamara, Kenny Dalglish, Dixie Deans, Ronnie Glavin & Bobby Lennox. Substitutes; Harry Hood & Tommy Callaghan.

The high terracing at Fir Park was one of my favourite spots for watching football, offering a great view of the action. I had stood there on my first visit to Motherwell, back in November 1969, when an early Harry strike was cancelled out before the interval by none other than Dixie Deans, before John Hughes, 'Big Yogi,' beat Peter McCloy to win the game late on. In years to come, I would watch Charlie and another Bear, Roy Aitken, destroy Jock Wallace's Motherwell by scoring seven without reply, then a St Patrick's Day Scottish Cup victory which ended 6-0. Even after ground reconstruction, I liked the fact that Motherwell had erected a two-tier visitors' stand which still pretty much did the same job. I had enjoyed some great times in there too, most memorable being the night Henrik scored four and Lubo curled another wonderful free-kick past - would you believe - Stevie Woods. Great times.

By the interval, it would appear for all the world that this game would be added to that list. This was the first time I ever recall the Rod Stewart anthem *"Sailing"* being belted out by the Celtic support accompanied by a sea of green-and-white scarves, *"Walk On"* style, particularly in that covered enclosure to our right. The majority of the 25,000 spectators appeared to be favouring the Hoops and the match was going to script. On the half-hour, Kenny Dalglish exploded a free-kick past Stuart Rennie to get the party started, and when Andy Lynch popped up to head home a loose ball 10 minutes later it looked done and dusted.

The proverbial game of two halves would see that turnaround completely. Almost exactly 12 months earlier, a Motherwell side inspired by Bobby Graham and Willie Pettigrew had won 3-2 at Celtic Park to hammer another nail in the 10-in-a-row coffin, despite a Harry double. Whilst the headlines usually centred around Pettigrew, and which big-name club would be signing him, I thought Graham was a tremendous player, and he had pedigree. Born in Motherwell, he would follow another local lad Ian St John by heading to Bill Shankly's Liverpool in 1961. He scored a hat-trick against Aston Villa on his League debut and, despite the presence of St John and partner Roger Hunt, made over 100 League appearances for that first great Anfield side. Bobby would then rejoin Ian St John at both Coventry City and Tranmere Rovers before his old friend brought him home to Motherwell in 1973. Graham would complete a rare treble by making over a century of appearances at Fir Park then again as he ended his career at nearby Hamilton Academical.

In January 1976, the 31-year-old Graham would inspire the comeback of comebacks. Within seven minutes of the restart, he was first to reach Bobby Watson's curling cross to nod the ball down past Peter Latchford for 2-1. Ten minutes later, Celtic's English keeper had another moment to forget. Ian Taylor's long-range shot from a free-kick should have been food and drink for Latchford, however, agonisingly he allowed it to squirm from his grasp over the line. At that point, the graffiti was on the wall. With 20 minutes remaining, a long ball left Willie Pettigrew in a chase with Roddie MacDonald and Pat McCluskey in the Celtic half. There would only be one winner. Pettigrew's pace saw him reach the pass first, a sublime first touch taking both defenders out. And although he still had much to do, his angled shot was perfectly placed, fate drawing it onto the inside of Latchford's far post then the net for the winner. A wonderful run had come to an end from a seemingly unassailable position, and the good ship Celtic was sailing out of the Scottish Cup at this stage for the first time since 1968.

As an aside, I will always maintain that Motherwell were robbed of their best chance of winning the famous trophy since their defeat of Dundee back in April 1952. Having knocked out another top side in Hibernian over three games in an epic quarter-final, I recall clearly watching the highlights of their last-four tie with Rangers at Hampden. Motherwell were 2-0 up and coasting with around an hour played, when the Ibrox club were awarded the most ridiculous penalty kick to get them back into the match. Two late goals then turned the game around and sent the Steelmen out of the competition. The more things change…

Harry had remained on the bench at Motherwell, and he would have moved to Fir Park by the time Celtic made their next appearance in the competition 12 months later. Hence, his last Scottish Cup action as a Celt would be back in the Hampden final of May 1975 against Airdrieonians, where he had played a key role as the Bhoys made sure the great Cesar's last stand would end in victory, as so many had in the decade before that. Not a bad way to bow out, Harry.

He would again be listed as a substitute seven days after the cup exit, caretaker manager Sean Fallon reacting to the Motherwell defeat by ringing the changes for the visit of Dundee United on the last day of the month. Out went Peter Latchford, Roddie MacDonald and record-signing Ronnie Glavin altogether, with Bobby Lennox joining Harry on the bench. In came Ally Hunter between the posts for the first time since he carried the can for the loss of a two-goal lead to Dumbarton the previous February, as dreams of The Ten crashed and burned. There was a first competitive start for young Andy Ritchie, Tommy Callaghan coming in to bring his experience to bear alongside him and Jackie McNamara in midfield, whilst Paul Wilson returned up front after several weeks out in the cold.

Hunter's long-awaited comeback would be a personal nightmare for the former Scotland keeper. Within the first minute, he had failed to deal with a passback from Johannes Edvaldsson, Henry Hall seizing on the error to put United ahead. This was an afternoon where Celtic would ride their luck with the benefit of a strange refereeing performance from Tommy Muirhead. Tom McAdam had scored Dumbarton's equaliser in Ally's previous appearance for Celtic, and now wearing the tangerine of the Tayside outfit, he beat the keeper twice in the first half, albeit on both occasions Muirhead would rule them out for offside with no flag raised by his lineman. To compound United's fury, the Stenhousemuir official had allowed a Kenny Dalglish equaliser to stand with the Celt, at best, playing on the very margins of the defensive line. There was even a hint of good fortune for Celtic's winner, scored by Paul Wilson just before the break, the winger's shot deflected past a wrong-footed Hamish McAlpine for 2-1. One can only imagine Jim McLean's press conference afterwards. There would be no further scoring in the second half, Harry replacing Tommy Callaghan for the final 25 minutes to get his first taste of the action since the 2-0 defeat by Aberdeen at Celtic Park in mid-December.

With Rangers drawing 1-1 draw with Dundee at Dens Park, Celts edged one point clear again at the top of the table with 13 matches of the inaugural Premier League campaign now remaining, including a clash between the top two at Celtic Park scheduled for March. It was thus still very much in the hands of the Parkhead club to claim a 10th title in 11 seasons. Those hands would not belong to Ally Hunter, though, the loss of that first-minute goal to Dundee United the last he would concede in the colours of Celtic. Like Steve Murray, Ally played his final first-team match for the Hoops in January 1976, as the major transition period at Celtic Park continued.

Jim Casey was next up for a starting debut, drafted into central defence for the visit of Hearts on Saturday, 7 February 1976. Pat McCluskey pushed forward into midfield beside Andy Ritchie and the restored Ronnie Glavin, with Tommy Callaghan dropping out of the squad. Peter Latchford replaced Ally Hunter between the sticks whilst Harry was joined on the bench by another youngster, Roy Aitken, albeit neither would get the call. This was another memorable day for a third young Celt, yours truly, invited to meet and have my photo taken with Dixie Deans in the Parkhead tunnel before the game as the latest 'Celtic Boy.' Dixie must have wondered what on earth was going on, as rather than the usual cute kid, he was confronted with this skinny teenager with a moustache to rival his own and a giant feather cut, wearing flares which could have quite comfortably smuggled two friends into Celtic Park, suspended above platform shoes which Elton John would have rejected as being too outrageous. It was probably all Dixie could do to keep a straight face.

Deans would definitely be smiling an hour or so later, his head flick setting up Kenny Dalglish for a stunning lob over Jim Cruickshank which broke the deadlock. With 10 minutes to go, the Celtic skipper then nodded home a second, after Andy Ritchie's cross had taken out the Hearts keeper. All three challengers - Hibernian, Motherwell and Rangers - also enjoyed victories, as the destination of the flag remained unclear, Celts still a single point in front.

With a redundant Saturday looming due to the Scottish Cup and the European tie with East Germans Sachsenring Zwickau fast approaching, Celts took the opportunity to set up a friendly on Wednesday, 11 February 1976. Initial plans to play against Iron Curtain opposition in the shape of Dinamo Kiev fell through and instead it was Leeds United who rolled up at Parkhead. The Yorkshire club had finally reached a European Cup final the previous May, five years after their home and away defeats by Jock Stein's men in the historic last-four clashes, before losing to Bayern Munich somewhat controversially in Paris. Hoops-mad captain Billy Bremner had scored Leeds' only goal of that 1970 tie, but he would be missing on this occasion, albeit several others who declared their allegiances to Celtic were in the line-up, such as Peter Lorimer, Joe Jordan and the Gray brothers. Castlemilk Bhoy Eddie Gray caused yet another nightmare for a Hoops goalkeeper, his corner-kick punched into the net by Peter Latchford just before the break to equalise for the visitors after a piece of genius from Andy Ritchie had given Celts the lead on the half-hour. Picking the ball up on the halfway line, the big midfielder proceeded to waltz past several Leeds defenders before sending a screamer over David Harvey to send the 27,000 spectators into raptures. Harry replaced Dixie Deans at the interval as Celtic, with Kenny Dalglish in wonderful form, continued to look the part moving forward, but a late sucker-punch saw the honours head south. With Jim Casey and George McCluskey on to reduce the average age of Sean Fallon's team still further, defensive hesitancy again proved fatal. Neither Latchford nor his defenders attacked another cross from Eddie Gray, Leeds ace hitman Allan Clarke gleefully accepting the free gift with 10 minutes remaining, before former Scottish schoolboy star Dave McNiven twisted the knife, his shot deceiving Latchford to end the scoring at 3-1.

Harry was back on reserve team duty the following Saturday, as the title race resumed for Celtic with a tricky fixture to Pittodrie, the Dons at that time involved in a struggle to remain in the top-flight with the Tayside trio of St Johnstone, Dundee and Dundee United. The centre-half berth was taken by Roy Aitken, a League debut for the Saltcoats teenager. He would never look back from there, whilst at the other end of the field a young Willie Garner was beginning his senior career at Aberdeen. The pair would briefly become teammates at Parkhead in the early 1980's. On an afternoon of missed chances, the match turned in a five-minute spell late in the second half. With the game goalless, the hosts went close to breaking the deadlock as a Davie Robb shot crashed back off the crossbar with Peter Latchford beaten. The Englishman's opposite number, Bobby Clark - back after a three-month absence - would then have his own moment of horror, completely misjudging a cross from Kenny Dalglish which drifted over his head to the far post. Whether it was going in or not, substitute Bobby Lennox was taking no chances, the Lisbon Lion applying the finishing touch to secure another vital two points. As supporters pressed radios to ears, news came through that both Rangers and Hibernian had won away from home, the Ibrox club at Ayr and the Hi-bees effectively knocking Motherwell out of the title race.

Hibernian would travel to Celtic Park for the final game of the month, on Saturday, 28 February 1976. The flu virus which had swept across Scotland that week claimed its first Parkhead victims, youngsters Andy Ritchie and Jim Casey missing out. That allowed Bobby Lennox to reclaim a starting slot, and Harry and Roddie MacDonald a seat on the bench. Sean Fallon sent the following men out to keep the Hoops ahead at the top of the table.

Peter Latchford; Danny McGrain & Andy Lynch; Pat McCluskey, Roy Aitken & Johannes Edvaldsson; Paul Wilson, Kenny Dalglish, Dixie Deans, Ronnie Glavin & Bobby Lennox. Substitutes; Harry Hood & Roddie MacDonald.

Despite the blustery conditions, this would be another day when the real Celtic would turn up, the visitors literally blown away in the first half. Bobby Lennox and Dixie Deans would be front and centre as Celts built a three-goal lead, the veteran Lennox felled for a penalty which Deans converted for his 20th, and as it turned out, his final goal against the club he just loved scoring against. Five minutes before the break, Bobby himself, another Celt with a Hampden cup final hat-trick against Hibernian on his CV, got in on the act, this time Dixie with the assist as the Saltcoats Lion made it 2-0. And as the pie queues gathered momentum, only the woodwork prevented a second goal for Deans, strike partner Paul Wilson not hanging around to quickly dispatch the rebound past Mike McDonald for 3-0. With the points in the bag, there would be just one more goal for the 33,000 spectators to enjoy, but what a goal it was. In memory's view, a trademark Kenny Dalglish goal would involve the Hoops superstar looking up before curling a shot over defender and goalkeeper into the top corner. Just after the hour mark, he would do just that, a goal perfect in both its design and execution to complete a wonderful afternoon for those with Celtic flowing through their veins. Hibernian's defeat combined with Motherwell's single goal loss at home to Rangers meant the title race would now be between the two Glasgow rivals, Celtic one point ahead with 10 games remaining.

Chapter 35

A magnificent seven seasons at Celtic ends for Harry

March 1976 would commence with Celtic's first-ever European tie against German opposition. Having faced Portugal's Boavista in November, there was a sense of disappointment as the Hoops were paired with unknowns Sachsenring Zwickau in the quarter-final of the Cup Winners' Cup, rather than one of the bigger continental names, such as Eintracht Frankfurt or Anderlecht, or easy travel options - the Welsh Cup-holders Wrexham or Brother Walfrid's other favourite Eastenders, West Ham United.

The club from the motor city of Zwickau had enjoyed occasional success in the post-war world of East German football in its various guises, with names often changed and clubs rebranded or merged to suit the needs of individuals or organisations as they were used, quite literally, in the very definition of political footballs. Originally formed as the Planitzer Sportclub in April 1912, they won the first championship of the Eastern Zone (essentially East Germany) in 1948, before permission to travel to Stuttgart to face Western Zone winners 1FC Nurnberg for the German Championship was withdrawn for - once again - political reasons. Two years later, now known as ZSG Horch Zwickau, the club won the inaugural DDR Oberliga, the second and last time it would be East German champions.

There would be three successes in the national cup competition, the FDGB-Pokal, the first of those in May 1963, when the club now known as BSG Motor Zwickau beat Chemie Zeitz 3-0 in Altenberg. This allowed entry to the European Cup-Winners' Cup that autumn, where a first-round bye preceded their first-ever competitive continental tie, a meeting with MTK Budapest. A 1-0 home win in the Georgi-Dimitroff Stadion in Zwickau on Wednesday, 20 November 1963 was overturned by two second-half goals in the Hungarian capital 10 days later. MTK, of course, would overcome a 3-0 first-leg deficit in Glasgow to knock Celtic out at the penultimate stage the following spring, before losing the replayed final to another club wearing the green-and-white Hoops, Sporting Club of Portugal.

As Jock Stein's Bhoys were becoming European champions in Sporting's home city three years later, Motor Zwickau were defeating Hansa Rostock 3-0 to win a second FDGB-Pokal. Like the Celts, the East Germans' European dreams the next season would be dashed in the first round by a Russian side, in Zwickau's case an excellent goalless draw in Moscow wasted following a 1-0 home defeat to Torpedo.

On May Day 1968, exactly five years after that first East German Cup success, Motor Zwickau was renamed as BSG Sachsenring Zwickau, in line with the major club sponsor, who in turn had adopted the name from the Saxony racing track (literally the ring or circuit of Saxony). It was as Sachsenring Zwickau that they would win their third FDGB-Pokal in East Berlin on 14 May 1975, against favourites and fierce rivals Dynamo Dresden. This was the first national cup final to be decided by a penalty shootout, with goalkeeper Jurgen Croy the name on the lips of the 55,000 spectators at the end. Twice Sachsenring had denied Dresden the trophy by fighting back to equalise, Peter Nestler's goal in the last minute of extra-time tying things up at 2-2. Croy saved two Dynamo shootout attempts before switching roles to take the final kick himself, the big keeper converting to win the cup for the Swans.

Born in Zwickau on 19 October 1946, Jurgen Croy joined his local club as a teenager in 1963 before making his senior debut two years later. In May 1967, Croy celebrated a personal double as Motor Zwickau won the FDGB-Pokal and he earned a first international cap against Sweden, in Henrik's home city of Helsingborg. In 1972, he was named East Germany's Player of the Year - a feat he would repeat in 1976 and 1978 – and by summer 1974, Croy was the automatic first-choice goalkeeper for East Germany and well on his way to completing a total of 86 caps between the sticks for his country. Those would include an appearance against Scotland at Hampden on Wednesday, 30 October 1974, the international debut of Dixie Deans. Neither Deans nor his pal Jimmy Johnstone, both in unstoppable form domestically at that time, would manage to score that night, although the 40,000 spectators would witness Kenny Dalglish beating Jurgen Croy to score Scotland's third in a 3-0 victory.

That 1974/75 season saw Sachsenring Zwickau finish in their normal mid-table position in the DDR-Oberliga, however, their shootout victory over Dynamo Dresden in the FDGB-Pokal allowed the Swans a third entry into the European Cup Winners' Cup. Their first-round opponents were Panathanaikos, European Cup-finalists just four years earlier, a goalless draw in Athens followed by a 2-0 victory in Zwickau, the club thus winning its first competitive tie in Europe. The next round produced another tough task, Coppa Italia holders Fiorentina, the first leg ending in a 1-0 defeat for Sachsenring in Florence. With that result matched in Zwickau, there was a real sense of deja-vu as the tie went to a shootout, this time Jurgen Croy saving from legendary Italian midfielder Giancarlo Antognoni, before once again successfully scoring with the final kick to take the East Germans into the last-eight. Next up would be former European champions Celtic, Sachsenring looking to emulate current East German title-holders FC Magdeburg, who had defeated AC Milan to win the competition two years earlier.

The flu bug which had spread through Parkhead at the end of February now added Ronnie Glavin to its list of casualties ahead of the first leg in Glasgow on Wednesday,

3 March 1976. The big pre-match news was that Harry would come in to replace him for his first start in three months, as Alan Davidson of *The Evening Times* recorded.

"Harry Hood, the man who has come in from the cold of reserve football to the white-hot atmosphere of European competition, will have a vital role to play at Parkhead tonight as Celtic attempt to build up a decisive lead against Sachsenring Zwickau. Hood has been unhappy playing second team football recently and hasn't been slow to say so. But with flu victim Ronnie Glavin ruled out of caretaker manager Sean Fallon's match plans, the experienced, subtle Hood returns to the top team. He could hardly wish for a bigger occasion on which to display his undoubted skills. Celtic are going for a place in the semi-finals of the Cup Winners' Cup, with all the prestige which that entails."

"The ball is at Harry's feet now," Fallon said from Celtic's training headquarters at Seamill today. "He's back in the top side and it's a great game for him in which to return."

"Hood will slot into the midfield tonight and will be asked to help supply the ammunition with which Celtic hope to cut down the East Germans."

Celtic lined up as follows before 46,000 spectators.

Peter Latchford; Danny McGrain & Andy Lynch; Pat McCluskey, Roy Aitken & Johannes Edvaldsson; Paul Wilson, Kenny Dalglish, Dixie Deans, Harry Hood & Bobby Lennox. Substitutes; Ally Hunter, Roddie MacDonald, Jackie McNamara & Tommy Callaghan.

That crowd would not include an extremely unhappy yours truly, who at that point would be midway through an 'outward bound' school break with another 40 or so victims from the Garngad at Faskally House on the shores of Loch Tummel, near Pitlochry in Perthshire. Orienteering rather than football was the order of the day that week, so I would miss out as Celts laid siege to Jurgen Croy's goal on what would prove an ultimately disappointing night for the Hoops.

Not that they didn't have chances, none better than midway through the first half when a foul on Kenny Dalglish gave Bobby Lennox an opportunity from the spot. With Celtic's record from 12 yards combined with the heroics of Croy, any 1976 analyst worth his salt would probably have predicted the outcome, the big keeper leaping high to stop the Lion's shot and keep his side level. He was finally beaten, just before the break, and just as at Hampden some 18 months earlier it would be the King who would do the damage, Danny McGrain finding Dalglish who slammed the ball home for 1-0.

Kenny was one of several Celts guilty of passing up chances in the second half, and with seconds remaining it looked like they would travel to East Germany with the slimmest of leads. Then disaster struck. Sachsenring had drawn a blank all night in terms of being an attacking threat, until they…er…drew a Blank, Ludwig Blank. The

Zwickau striker found himself in a race for the ball with Euro debutant Roy Aitken, his pace proving too much for the teenage defender before he beat Peter Latchford for the unlikeliest of equalisers, to turn the tie on its head.

That would not be the only problem facing Fallon and Celtic over the days ahead, as the flu epidemic spread to affect Paul Wilson, Peter Latchford, Dixie Deans and Kenny Dalglish, causing the cancellation of the scheduled League fixture with struggling Ayr United at Somerset Park three days later, on an afternoon when Rangers were on Scottish Cup duty and the potential for a three-point lead was there for the taking. By midweek, Danny McGrain, Andy Lynch and Tommy Callaghan were also ill, and plans to play the Ayr match in midweek were abandoned. The flu virus then struck at Ibrox, meaning a postponement of Celtic's vital home clash with Rangers the following Saturday, 13 March 1976. As we have seen many times since then, timing is often everything in football, where a match which could have significant implications is deferred to a date when it is no longer relevant. Celts were on a run of six successive League victories when these postponements kicked in and wins over Ayr United and the Ibrox club would have extended their lead at the top of the table and piled all the pressure across the city. Sadly, we will never know what may have transpired that season. It was a cruel break indeed.

As Celtic headed to their St Patrick's Day of destiny in East Germany, they had not played a single minute of competitive football since Blank's last-gasp equaliser in Glasgow, a fortnight earlier. There were three other very different background stories playing out ahead of the vital match. The first involved the deadline-day signing of Ayr United winger, Johnny Doyle - a player red-carded in his previous visit to Celtic Park - in a club record £90,000 deal. On the morning of Monday, 15 March 1976, in the unusual surroundings of Glasgow Airport, the Viewpark Bhoy's childhood dream came true as he signed for his beloved Celtic. Some big footsteps to follow there, Johnny.

The second story concerned Roy Aitken, only recently introduced to the first-team defence. Having turned 17 years old the previous November, Roy was not yet considered an adult by the East German authorities, and as discussions ensued it became clear the only way that he would be allowed to enter the country would be as an adoptee of the club. Thus, legend will relate that manager Sean Fallon would quite literally adopt the role as father figure to the teenage Roy for the purposes of the trip.

Whilst there was general mirth at that one, the final part of the Parkhead puzzle would definitely be no joke. Several members of the first-team squad had come through the worst of the illness and would now be required to play in Zwickau, including skipper Kenny Dalglish, Celtic's other world-class talent Danny McGrain, striker Paul Wilson and goalkeeper Peter Latchford. Others would not be so lucky, Dixie Deans, Bobby Lennox and Andy Lynch amongst the regular 'first-picks' who would miss out. Fallon would be forced to play centre-half Roddie MacDonald as an emergency striker and Tommy Callaghan at left-back, as this Celtic side fought to keep the club in Europe.

Peter Latchford; Danny McGrain & Tommy Callaghan; Roy Aitken, Johannes Edvaldsson & Pat McCluskey; Paul Wilson, Ronnie Glavin, Roddie MacDonald, Kenny Dalglish & Harry Hood. Substitutes; Ally Hunter, Jackie McNamara, Jim Casey & Bobby Hannah.

Like the European Cup-tie with Ujpest Dosza in Budapest four years earlier, the match at the Georgi Dimitroff Stadion was a rare opportunity for Celtic supporters to watch the game live on television, albeit the 2pm kick-off would present a few difficulties for some in that regard. Nevertheless, I recall watching that game at home in Springburn, and it would again be a tale of missed opportunities after Sachsenring had opened the scoring in the third minute with a sensational strike from Ludwig Blank, which caught Peter Latchford and the viewers at home unawares.

The communist politician Georgi Dimitroff was regarded as a hero far and beyond his native Bulgaria, and he had famously defended himself against the charge of setting fire to Berlin's Reichstag back in 1933. In the Zwickau stadium which now bore his name, it would be Jurgen Croy and his Sachsenring colleagues who would perform the defensive heroics to time and time again deny the yellow-clad Celts a precious away goal. Add to that some horrific misses, with the unfortunate Roddie MacDonald, reverting to his Highland League days as a striker, the main culprit, and then a coup de grace applied by the Spanish referee Franco Martinez with five minutes remaining, which finally sealed Celtic's fate. From Harry's corner-kick, MacDonald rose cleanly to power the ball past Croy for a perfectly legitimate equaliser, only to reel in horror as Martinez chopped the goal off for a non-existent foul on the Sachsenring keeper. There had been no contact whatsoever, and with that scandalous decision went Celtic's last hope of a European semi-final place.

It would be an angry, frustrated and disappointed Celtic party who headed home to Scotland with only the Premier League left to fight for, after a decade of pretty much unparalleled success. They had been beaten by a team which would not have lived with a fully fit Celtic line-up that season, far less the wonderful Parkhead sides which had gradually broken up over the previous few years. We would not know it then, but this would be the last appearance of a Celtic team in the final stages of a European competition under Jock Stein. The Big Man would be back in charge of the club, in time, but those heady days were gone now. It was a sad end to a very special era.

The fallout from those changing times would also impact Harry, by now a fringe player at his beloved Celtic after seven seasons of glorious service. That assist for Roddie MacDonald for the goal that never was would be his European Swan song, as Harry bade auf wiedersehen to continental competition.

Still boiling with a sense of injustice following the midweek events in East Germany, the Celtic party took the road and the miles to Dundee on Saturday, 20 March 1976 for a vital League match at Dens Park. Included in the squad was new club record signing Johnny Doyle, whilst there was no sign of midfielder Jimmy Smith, a seemingly somewhat reluctant loanee from Newcastle United who had finally arrived that week. Both men had featured in the reserve team which beat their Dundee counterparts 4-0 at Celtic Park 24 hours after the defeat in Zwickau. The unfortunate Smith would quickly return to Newcastle with a recurrence of the knee injury which had dogged his career and without playing a first-team match for Celtic, leaving Sean Fallon still short of creative options. On the flip side, no doubt lifelong supporter Doyle would have loved the fact that he had scored in his first match wearing those sacred Hoops.

Two days later, Johnny would make his senior Celtic debut against a Dundee side captained by Lisbon Lion Tommy Gemmell and with future Parkhead boss Gordon Strachan on the bench. Fallon's side was again decimated by a combination of flu and injuries, Ronnie Glavin having recovered from the former then struck by the latter against Sachsenring in midweek. That meant defender Roddie MacDonald would again adopt a central striking role at Dens Park, as Celts went with the following line-up.

Peter Latchford; Danny McGrain & Andy Lynch; Pat McCluskey, Roy Aitken & Johannes Edvaldsson; Johnny Doyle, Kenny Dalglish, Roddie MacDonald, Jackie McNamara & Harry Hood. Substitutes; Paul Wilson & Tommy Callaghan.

I recall being one of the 15,000 inside the ground, standing with my dad and some of the older guys and their sons, in the covered enclosure opposite the main stand as the teams ran out that afternoon, Johnny proudly wearing those number seven shorts. Irishman Frank Dolan, a friend of my dad's, proclaimed to one and all that *"we had signed the new Jinky,"* before being roundly scorned for such sacrilege. Johnny was a great talent, with the heart of a lion and is rightly still revered by Celtic supporters to this day. But there was only one Jinky.

Sadly, Doyle's Bhoyhood dream lasted only half-an-hour, the winger carried off after one crunching Dundee tackle too many just before the interval, having gamely tried to carry on. The crude challenge by home defender Dave Johnston had cost him a booking from referee Davidson of Airdrie but it would rule Johnny out of action for the next month, the latest in a series of blows for Sean Fallon. The one shining light at the end of the tunnel was the form of captain Kenny Dalglish. Yet again, he would step up to secure the points for Celtic, this time with the aid of a subtle assist from emergency striker Roddie MacDonald. As we approached the hour still goalless, a swivel of the King's hips took him clear of Thomson Allan in the home goal, opening up the target for an unerring finish. Thus, another difficult fixture had been ticked off with Celts still clear at the top of the table. Now just nine games remained.

Those matches commenced with the visit of Motherwell to Celtic Park on Saturday, 27 March 1976. There was revenge in the air, the visitors chasing a third successive victory at Celtic Park for surely the first time ever, Willie Pettigrew having grabbed doubles in each of the last two games in Glasgow's east end, followed by the winner as the Steelmen knocked the holders out of the Scottish Cup just two months earlier. Sean Fallon made two changes from the team which won narrowly at Dundee, Bobby Lennox replacing the injured Johnny Doyle whilst Harry made way for the return of Dixie Deans.

Celtic had inexplicably blown a two-goal interval lead at Motherwell in that January cup-tie, however, there was never any danger of history repeating itself on an afternoon where the match was won in a blistering first-half display, the Bhoys scoring four without reply, despite playing against a strong wind. Tormentor-in-chief once again was Kenny Dalglish, the skipper opening the scoring after 15 minutes with a low shot then making it 3-0 on the half-hour with a sublime goal, the King weaving his way along the byeline to leave two defenders for dead before curling the ball past Motherwell keeper Stuart Rennie from an impossible angle. In between those strikes, Dixie Deans helped himself to his usual goal against his old team by rifling a Pat McCluskey pass past Rennie, albeit with some suggestion of handball in the build-up. The wonderful Danny McGrain then capped his first-half masterclass of full-back play by setting up Bobby Lennox for a fourth five minutes from the break. Perhaps the only surprise was that the second half did not provide the same excitement for the 30,000 spectators, Paul Wilson replacing makeshift forward Roddie MacDonald for the closing 15 minutes as Celts coasted to a 4-0 victory which few would have envisaged at kick-off. That result would see the Hoops maintain their single-point advantage at the top of the table, with Rangers winning 3-0 against relegation-haunted St Johnstone up in Perth. Eight games to go.

The Saints' cause was hardly helped by a fixture schedule which sent them to Celtic Park, the following Saturday. Once again, Celtic's plans to play the outstanding fixture with Ayr United in midweek had had to be shelved, with the Somerset Park pitch waterlogged, another valuable opportunity to get points on the board wasted. For the weekend visit of St Johnstone, Sean Fallon named an unchanged line-up, the Celtic boss introducing young Robert Hannah to the bench in place of Tommy Callaghan. A disappointing crowd of just 16,000 watched the Hoops maintain the push for the title by beating the Perth side by the odd goal for the fourth time that season. At Muirton Park back in January, it had required a last-gasp header from Johannes Edvaldsson to edge a seven-goal thriller. This time the key moment came midway through the first half, and once again it would be Kenny Dalglish who would make the difference. The Celtic captain sent Dixie Deans down the left flank before racing into the box in expectation of a return pass. Deans would duly do the honours to allow Dalglish to beat Davie Nicol at the far post for the only goal of the game. The news from Easter Road would reinforce just how vital Kenny's solitary strike had been, Rangers winning one of their most difficult away fixtures by 3-0 in Leith to remain hard on Celtic's heels with seven games to play.

The title would start to tilt away from Celtic following a damaging defeat at

Tannadice seven days later, Saturday, 10 April 1976. This was also a significant day in the wonderful career of Harry Hood, recalled after a three-week absence to make his 325th and final appearance in his beloved Hoops. Just over seven years earlier, on Saturday, 29 March 1969, the 24-year-old Harry had made a scoring debut against St Mirren at Love Street, two weeks after signing from Clyde, as part of this team chosen by Jock Stein ahead of a month where he would win a second Treble.

John Fallon; Jim Craig & Tommy Gemmell; Bobby Murdoch, Billy McNeill & Jim Brogan; Jimmy Johnstone, Harry Hood, Willie Wallace, Bobby Lennox & John Hughes. Substitute; Tommy Callaghan

Only Bobby Lennox of that starting line-up would be beside Harry on Tayside, as he drew a line under that part of his life, with the evolution then dissolution of that team making for interesting reading. The group would remain intact for Harry's first two seasons before the departure of Willie Wallace and John Hughes to Crystal Palace in October 1971, the duo quickly followed by Tommy Gemmell as he headed to Nottingham Forest just before Christmas. John Fallon signed for Motherwell in March 1972 and Celtic's 6-1 victory over Hibernian in the Scottish Cup final two months later was the final hurrah for Jim Craig before he left to start a new life with his family in South Africa. Bobby Murdoch joined Jack Charlton at Middlesbrough in September 1973, but the close-season of 1975 was perhaps the most significant of all, as Billy McNeill, Celtic's greatest-ever captain, Jimmy Johnstone, the genius voted our best-ever player, and that wonderful servant Jim Brogan all left the club.

The class of '76 selected by Sean Fallon to keep the title dream going against a Dundee United side fighting for their Premier League lives at Tannadice was as follows.

Peter Latchford; Danny McGrain & Andy Lynch; Pat McCluskey, Roy Aitken & Johannes Edvaldsson; Harry Hood, Kenny Dalglish, Dixie Deans, Ronnie Glavin & Bobby Lennox. Substitutes; Paul Wilson & Roddie MacDonald.

Harry saw an early effort ruled out for offside in a tense match, played in difficult, blustery conditions. The game appeared to be heading towards a goalless first half before that scourge of Celtic, Tom McAdam, threw the flag race wide open by hooking the ball over Peter Latchford to put United 1-0 up seconds from the interval. With Harry making way for Paul Wilson 10 minutes after the restart - his last act as a first-team Celt - a below-par Hoops side found the strength to fight back, and once again it was the skipper to the rescue, Kenny Dalglish taking aim from 25 yards to beat Hamish McAlpine with a low shot on the hour. Within two minutes, the hosts had regained their advantage, George Fleming on the end of a slick passing move to head past Latchford. Dalglish saw another excellent effort crash off McAlpine's crossbar before Jim McLean's men sealed the two vital points with five minutes to play, McAdam again on target with a diving header at the far post to push a dagger through the hearts of the huge travelling support. Kenny would have the last word with a close-range finish to give Celts a flicker of hope at 3-2, however, the news of Rangers 3-0 victory over United's city and relegation rivals Dundee at Ibrox would complete a great afternoon's entertainment for the home fans, whilst we poured out onto Sandeman Street with heavy hearts. A lead at the top of the table, which Celtic had held since November, had gone in a flash, the Hoops now one point behind with six matches to play. It felt like we had seen this particular movie before, about 12 months earlier, in fact.

The fixture calendar would once again conspire to hurt Celtic in midweek, as Hearts Scottish Cup replay with second-tier Dumbarton meant the Hoops would be idle as all other Top 10 clubs played League matches. Rangers dropped a point in a goalless draw at Pittodrie and then found themselves further out in front, rather than see their hard-fought lead disappear immediately. As I mentioned earlier, sometimes in football timing is everything.

Celtic would then compound the situation at the weekend with a little help from our old friend JRP Gordon, as Aberdeen faced a second title challenger in four days. Like Dundee United the previous Saturday, the Dons were fighting for survival in this first Premier League season. With St Johnstone already all but down, the second team to face the trapdoor would come from Aberdeen and the two Dundee clubs. There was another selection headache for Sean Fallon following the demoralising defeat at Tannadice. Andy Lynch and Pat McCluskey had accumulated a level of bookings which saw both suspended for the visit of Aberdeen, Tommy Callaghan recalled from a spell on the sidelines to cover at left-back, whilst young Tommy Burns came in for his starting debut in midfield. Better news for the Celtic boss was the return of Johnny Doyle, now recovered from the injury sustained at Dundee to make his first home appearance in the Hoops, albeit that would come to the exclusion of Harry. I had never appreciated before that those two great friends and Celts, Tommy and Johnny, had made their first Parkhead starts together. Somehow, that just feels right.

As he had done so often this season, Kenny Dalglish opened the scoring for Celtic, the Hoops skipper following up to beat Bobby Clark after the Dons keeper had parried his close-range header midway through the first half. Seconds before the interval, there was dreadful misfortune for Celtic defender Johannes Edvaldsson, a man enjoying a wonderful first season in Scottish football. His attempted clearance from an Aberdeen free-kick sliced horribly past Peter Latchford to bring the visitors level. The drama continued immediately after the restart, with a first coming together of those two warriors Roy Aitken and Willie Miller. The young Celt found himself running in on goal before Miller illegally brought that to an end, a challenge which produced a red card from referee Gordon. Celts then laid siege on the 10-man Dons and, with seconds remaining, it appeared they had secured the vital two points which would have kept the advantage with them. Clark inadvertently played the ball yards too far in front of him as he prepared to clear upfield, the ever-alert Dalglish pouncing to win the race and force the ball home. As Parkhead erupted and the linesman sprinted to the halfway line to signal the goal, Gordon, from his position 40 yards up the pitch, incredibly charged back into the box to award a free-kick to Aberdeen. It was a scandalous decision, a sliding doors moment which would have huge consequences at both ends of the Premier League. The Dons eventually pipped relegated Dundee only on goal difference, whilst the dropped point meant Celtic's fate was once again out of their own hands. Such are the fine margins in football. It was a monumental call in the context of season 1975/76.

The feeling that the title odds had now swung towards Ibrox was confirmed by two dreadful results in the following seven days. In midweek, Celtic travelled to Easter Road to face Hibernian in the latest 'must win' encounter. The suspended duo of Andy Lynch and Pat McCluskey returned to the starting line-up with Tommy Callaghan dropping out and young Tommy Burns moving on to the bench where he would be joined by George McCluskey. Johnny Doyle's unfortunate start to his Parkhead career continued as illness forced him to miss out, Paul Wilson stepping in. It was a night of abject misery for Celtic supporters in the 20,000 crowd, a Hibernian goal in each half leaving hopes of reclaiming our League crown hanging by a thread. Bobby Smith opened the scoring directly from a free-kick midway through the first half, following a challenge by Johannes Edvaldsson which may have merited the award of a penalty kick. The hosts did get a spot kick just after the hour, the big Icelander again involved, this time Ally McLeod converting for 2-0, Celts never really threatening to pull that lead back at any time. A late Rangers winner at home to Motherwell would now leave them tantalisingly close to a second consecutive title, five points clear with just four matches remaining.

That fate would be sealed three days later, Saturday, 24 April 1976. Harry lined up for the reserves at Somerset Park, as an Andy Ritchie brace and Paul Wilson secured a 3-1 win. Thirty miles away, the first team would not fare so well at Parkhead, Malcolm Robertson's double giving Ayr United a shock 2-0 lead, with the only home counter coming on the hour from a Dixie Deans penalty, a final Celtic goal for the wonderful striker as it turned out. The Bhoys' defeat, combined with a 1-0 Rangers victory at Tannadice, ensured there would be no major trophy in the Celtic Park boardroom for the first time in 12 years. Just three weeks earlier, the title advantage had still remained with Celtic, despite a series of really bad breaks. One point in four games had put paid to that, with horrific consequences.

So, it was with a sense of trepidation combined with youthful defiance that we made our way along the Gallowgate again 48 hours later, the evening of Monday, 26 April 1976. The Football Gods had decided to inflict an additional insult to our injury, as the March fixture with Rangers deferred due to the flu outbreak would now take place with the Ibrox club crowned Scottish champions. Talk about rubbing it in. The goalless match is best remembered for an excellent performance from Tommy Burns, which gave us at least some hope for the future, following a season where the Hoops had failed to register a win over the Ibrox club in five attempts.

Three nights later, Thursday, 29 April 1976, there would inevitably be a degree of sadness in many Celtic hearts as Harry's magnificent seven-year career in the Hoops formally came to an end with news of his release on a free transfer. He had packed more into that period than most players can even dream about, with a glittering array of silverware the tangible reward for some fabulous personal and team achievements. Since signing in March 1969, Harry played his part in Celtic winning the League Championship in each of his first six seasons at the club, a brief cameo role in the spring of that year followed by star performances in the first five titles of the 1970's, including the early goal at Pittodrie in April 1971 which pretty much ensured that a record-equalling sixth Scottish Championship would be heading for Paradise. He would then be a key man as that six became a world record nine-in-a-row.

Cup-tied with Clyde, and thus ineligible for the Scottish and League Cup finals of April 1969, Harry would go on to enjoy a 100% winning record in Scottish Cup finals, featuring in the major showpiece occasions of 1971, 1974 and 1975, and scoring in two of those Hampden finals to secure League and Cup Doubles. As for all Celts of that period, the League Cup would prove more elusive, Harry enduring the pain of defeat five times in the final as the club struggled to repeat the dominance of the 1960's. Nevertheless, he played in the two winning finals Celts managed for which he was eligible, the victories over St Johnstone and Hibernian in the autumns of 1969 and 1974.

And whilst the 1973 League Cup would end in farce, Harry's hat-trick against Rangers in the Hampden semi-final would be the first in that particular derby fixture by a Celtic player in more than seven years, and the last ever achieved by a Parkhead player before the liquidation of the Ibrox club in 2012, almost 40 years later. And he was cruelly robbed of a fourth goal that night, which would have made his achievement even more unique.

There would be major highlights in European football to sit alongside his domestic success, a goal within a minute of his home continental debut against FC Basel in October 1969, followed by the vital third against Benfica the next month, which ultimately allowed Celtic to progress towards a second European Cup final, after a 3-0 second-leg defeat in Lisbon. Injury prevented an appearance in the final stages that season, the matches with Leeds United and Feyenoord, and the semi-final with Inter Milan two years later, however, he would be in the last Celtic teams to play in the last four of the European Cup, Harry featuring in both of the infamous matches against Atletico Madrid in April 1974.

Harry would end his spell at his boyhood club having scored 125 goals in 325 appearances, his finest season statistically being that 1970/71 campaign, where his

33 goals included the highest League tally in the country – 22 – a virtual title decider at Aberdeen, plus the winner in the Scottish Cup final replay against Rangers, which secured another double for Celtic.

By any standards, his was a remarkable Celtic career, bringing pleasure to many thousands of us who hold the club so dear to our hearts.

Thank you for those magical memories, Harry.

Now altogether…

"Oh Harry, Harry,

Harry, Harry,

Harry, Harry,

Harry Hood."

Chapter 36

Loan stars shine deep in the heart of Texas

Life after Celtic would certainly be different for Harry. His next port of call would see him follow in the footsteps of his sister Irene, by moving to Texas. Back in 1961, she had married Bob Bacon at the family ranch in Brownsville, where the Lone Star state borders Mexico. Fifteen years later, Harry took up an offer to play that summer with NASL outfit San Antonio Thunder, some 300 miles north of Brownsville, on the edge of the triangle which links the major Texan cities of Austin, Dallas and Houston.

San Antonio Thunder were due to begin their second season in the North American Soccer League, having finished bottom of the Central Division in 1975, St Louis Stars progressing to the play-offs by winning a group which also included teams from Chicago, Denver and Dallas. Thunder were owned by Herman Warden Lay junior, known as Ward, son of the founder of Frito-Lay, the biggest snack food company in the USA. They had played that first season at the 10,000 capacity North East Stadium but Lay had secured the Alamo Stadium for the 1976 campaign, with seats for over 22,000 spectators, as he sought to raise the profile and performance levels of his franchise in the American game.

Ward Lay had also secured the services of coach Don Batie from California State University in Chico - known as Chico State - in June 1975. Batie could not believe the situation at the club, on and off the pitch, with primitive facilities and an attitude which explained a record of one win from their opening nine games. That would be too much to turn around in the present campaign, but together with assistant coach Jim Forrest, the former Rangers and Aberdeen striker, Lay and Batie worked tirelessly to put things into place for the 1976 season. It would be Batie who would create the iconic shirt design.

Key to the success would be the recruitment of players, and Lay was aiming high. Having failed to sign Jimmy Johnstone the previous spring - Jinky choosing San Jose Earthquakes instead - he would also be rejected by George Best, who dropped out of several arranged meetings before admitting that he was going to LA Aztecs following a request from Elton John, a part-owner of that club. As part of their strategy, Batie retained legendary Aberdeen scout Bobby Calder to help him sign Scottish players of a calibre required to move the club forward. The two men watched the Anglo Scottish Cup semi-final between Motherwell and Fulham at Fir Park on Tuesday, 4 November 1975, where Batie identified the visiting central defender as the player he wanted. The coach later recalled the conversation.

"The game started, and I was immediately drawn to one player, Fulham's number six. I had never seen a player play the game so easily, who was so much in control, and so much ahead of the game. I said to Bobby Calder, "That's the player we need. That's the player we can build a team around."

"Calder just laughed and said, "Don't you know who that is? That's Bobby Moore. You will never sign Bobby Moore."

But sign him Batie did, after a series of discussions. The former England captain would be joined by a number of Scottish professionals, most nearing the end of their top-flight careers, some like Moore taking the opportunity of going to the USA on loan over the summer and others now freed from their contracts. Harry was in that latter category, whilst his old Queen's Park teammate Bobby Clark would spend summer in Texas before returning to Aberdeen. Another two men with Pittodrie connections would join them, midfielder Jim Henry and defender Eddie Thomson, whilst Neil Martin - Ian McColl's unwanted 21st birthday present for Harry at Sunderland - was also on San Antonio Thunder's 1976 roster. Bobby Moore would have another ex-England cap to keep him company in Texas, with the arrival of Bob McNab, a full-back who had won the English League and Cup Double with Arsenal in 1971, just as Harry was making a huge contribution to Celtic's own Double success north of the border.

The North American Soccer League (NASL) of 1976 involved 20 teams from the USA and Canada, split into two Conferences - Atlantic and Pacific – then four Divisions of five teams (Northern & Eastern Divisions within the Atlantic Conference, Western & Southern Divisions within the Pacific Conference). There would be 24 games played by each team in the 'regular season' before a series of knockout play-offs produced an overall winner. Matches would be played between April and August 1976.

San Antonio Thunder were placed in the Southern Division and would play the other nine teams in the Pacific Conference home and away for a total of 18 games. They would also face three teams from each of the two Atlantic Divisions on a one-off basis – either home or away - those six games taking the total for the regular season to 24. If you are still following me, then you will have worked out that there would be seven of the other 19 sides who would not feature for each club in its schedule. Sadly, for Harry, New York Cosmos with their star attraction Pele would be one of those seven teams for San Antonio Thunder. To add insult to injury, whilst Harry was on the periphery for his final days as a Celtic player, Pele's Cosmos had actually opened the Alamo Stadium as one of six matches played by them to generate interest in the NASL. Thunder beat the great Brazilian et al 1-0 in front of 20,000 spectators on Wednesday, 31 March 1976, thanks to a goal from Canadian international Victor

Kodelja. So, having missed out numerous times as plans for Celtic to face Santos had been cancelled during his stint at Parkhead, once more fate would come between Harry and the chance to play against his Brazilian idol.

By the time of his arrival in Texas in early May, Harry had also missed the first four games of the NASL regular season. Thunder had kicked off with a 2-1 win over St Louis Stars on Wednesday, 14 April 1976 before just 5,300 supporters in the Alamo Stadium. Derek Currie - a winger from Glasgow who was one of a number of recruits who had played in Hong Kong - scored both Thunder goals, those being the inaugural strikes of what was known as the Bicentennial League campaign.

Next up was an away fixture – or road game – three days later with the new franchise San Diego Jaws – think 1975 movies and "We're gonna need a bigger boat!" Another crowd of 5,000 witnessed a 1-0 win after extra-time for the hosts in the Aztec Bowl, described by Derek Currie as the worst field he had ever seen. As an aside, the star man for Jaws that season was none other than Hilary Carlyle, the Irish triallist whom Harry had replaced against Birmingham City at St Andrews five months earlier.

Matchday three for Thunder involved a short trip north for a Texan derby against Dallas Tornado on Saturday, 24 April 1976, which resulted in another 1-0 defeat. Best known Tornado player was former West Bromwich Albion midfielder Bobby Hope, who had played with Harry for Scotland on the global tour of summer 1967. The only goal was scored by Scottish winger Jimmy Ryan, who spent seven seasons with Manchester United in the 1960s and later returned there to work as a coach and assistant under Alex Ferguson.

The final game missed by Harry was the home fixture with Minnesota Kicks seven days later. Goals from Victor Kodelja and Eddie Thomson secured a 2-1 win for Thunder and saw them continue with the 50% win/loss record which would pretty much become the story of the season. Harry made his US debut against LA Aztecs at the Alamo Stadium on Saturday, 8 May 1976. The Californian side included Scottish international midfielder Charlie Cooke and Welsh striker Ron Davies, but the star of the show was undoubtedly Irishman George Best. Nevertheless, the points would stay in Texas following Harry's first experience of league football, American style. Both Neil Martin and Bobby McAlinden – George Best's flatmate, business partner and 'Best man' – scored doubles, leaving the sides tied at 2-2 after 90 minutes followed by extra-time. With no draws permitted in the NASL, a penalty shootout was required to decide the outcome. Thankfully, Thunder would prevail by 3-2 to claim the victory.

In true Davie Crockett style, it was back to defend the Alamo the following Saturday for the clash with Washington Diplomats, Thunder's first opponents that season from outwith the Pacific Conference. The Eastern Division side were managed at that time by former Manchester United striker Dennis Viollet, a survivor of the Munich Airport crash in February 1958. The Diplomats would later boast Dutchmen Johan Cruyff, Wim Jansen and Guus Hiddink in their playing rosters, and they took the spoils back to the capital that day, winning by 3-2, despite goals from Eddie Thomson and Bobby Moore.

The fixtures continued for Thunder with a long trail north-west to Oregon to take on Portland Timbers on Wednesday, 19 May 1976. There would be a familiar face in the hosts line-up in the shape of Pat McMahon, who had started the 1968/69 season wearing the number eight shorts at Parkhead, a position which would belong to Harry by the end of that campaign. Croy Bhoy Pat would have the last laugh on this occasion though, as the Timbers won with the only goal of the game, scored by English striker Tony Betts in Portland's historic Civic Stadium in front of an impressive 19,000 crowd.

As the NASL commenced a two-week break for the USA Bicentennial Cup – a tournament involving Team America, Brazil, England and Italy, held to celebrate the 200th anniversary of the Declaration of Independence - there would be more familiar faces for Harry. He had gone out to Texas ahead of his family, but now they would join him for his Stateside adventure. Harry's younger daughter Siobhan was approaching her 18th birthday then, but she clearly recalled that reunion recently with a smile.

"We arrived at the airport and it was red hot, and then I saw dad coming towards us, wearing a cowboy hat. He said he was embracing the culture! He always did have a presence."

Team America was a side drawn from the NASL rosters and saw old rivals Bobby Moore and Pele play together against their respective countries, as did Cosmos' Giorgio Chinaglia, who had played against Harry for Fiorentina back in March 1970. The Americans would lose all three games, beaten 4-0 by Italy in Washington DC, 2-0 by tournament winners Brazil in Seattle and 3-1 by England in Philadelphia, where ironically their goal was scored by Tampa Bay Rowdies' Stewart Scullion, a winger from Bo'ness!

The NASL season recommenced for San Antonio Thunder with the visit of another superstar whom Harry and Celtic had faced on the Road to Milan in 1969/70. Portuguese striker Eusebio was the jewel in Benfica's crown for much of that decade, and at 34 he now worked his magic with Toronto Metros-Croatia in the Northern Division of the NASL. The man from Mozambique was again to the fore at the Alamo Stadium on Friday, 4 June 1976, winning the match 2-1 for Toronto with a late free-kick, after Harry had opened his NASL account in front of 7,000 spectators. Thunder coach Don Batie had another reason to recall Eusebio's performance that night, as related by the Texas Soccer Journal.

"Batie remembered that Eusebio made an ugly tackle from behind in front of the Thunder bench. He then told him in a low voice, "Eusebio, I'm disappointed in you." Eusebio looked at Batie and walked away with his head down, but after a few minutes Batie said he forgot about the incident. Then 30 minutes or so after the game, Eusebio ran up to Batie at full speed, causing him to wonder if he was about

to get decked. Eusebio stopped in front of him and said, "Coach, forgive me. Forgive me, I am sorry. This is not how I am as a player." Batie said he told him to forget it and they parted ways on friendly terms, noting, "He surprised me that he played that very humble role."

Harry would come up against one of Eusebio's old Benfica teammates in Thunder's next match, two days later, as they travelled to northern California to face San Jose Earthquakes in front of 17,000 spectators at the Spartan Stadium. Legendary Portuguese winger Antonio Simoes had quite literally won everything in a glorious 14-year career with the Eagles, a European and World champion with 46 caps for his country. He had faced Harry three times previously, in both legs of that epic European Cup clash in November 1969 when Celts had scraped through on the toss of a coin then the UNICEF match in Glasgow five years later, which Benfica won on a shootout. The honours would be with Harry in San Jose that Sunday, as Thunder turned in perhaps their best performance of the season to win 3-0. Harry and Neil Martin were both on the scoresheet, as was American international forward Dan Counce.

There was a second successive Thunder road win as they made the trip to Florida to face Miami Toros on Thursday, 10 June 1976. Former Manchester United and Scotland defender Jim Holton was in direct opposition to Harry but a solitary goal from full-back Bob McNab took the points back to Texas. The San Antonio club's record now stood at five wins and five losses after their first 10 fixtures. Thunder remained in Florida to complete the double-header with East Division opponents two days later with a match against reigning Soccer Bowl champions Tampa Bay Rowdies at Tampa Stadium before 11,000 spectators. The Rowdies included English internationalists Rodney Marsh, Tommy Smith plus Bobby Moore's old West Ham United teammate Clyde Best in their ranks. Neither side managed a goal in regular or overtime, forcing another penalty shootout and Thunder's only televised match ever had a controversial ending, the referee disallowing a successful Jim Henry conversion during the shootout, as he hadn't blown his whistle. Tampa Bay eventually won the shootout by 5-4, leading to a formal protest by Thunder coach Batie to the NASL, which was ultimately unsuccessful.

Thunder bounced back from that disappointment to record their biggest win of the season, a 6-1 rout of Vancouver Whitecaps at Alamo Stadium on Saturday, 19 June 1976 watched by a 'crowd' of 4,418. Dan Counce scored a hat-trick with Harry, Eddie Thomson and Brazilian Jose Berico also on target. They would follow that up with a 4-3 shootout win over Northern Division's Chicago Sting at the same venue, seven days later, after Harry's goal had secured a 1-1 draw in regular time. Sting were coached by another survivor of the Munich Airport tragedy, former Manchester United defender Bill Foulkes.

The last day of June required a trip north to Connecticut to face the Hartford Bicentennials, less than 1,700 spectators inside Dillon Stadium to see goals from

Victor Kodelja and former Newcastle United and Middlesbrough striker Alan Foggon tie the match at 1-1. There was then another bizarre episode in the world of American 'soccer.' Play was suspended late in the second half due to violent electrical storms, but rather than replay the match, the NASL decided that the result would be settled by a penalty shootout the next morning, which took place in front of just 40 spectators a few hours before the Thunder squad were due to fly home to San Antonio! At least Thunder won the shootout by 3-2.

July would see Harry reacquainted with his old friend, Tommy Callaghan, who joined Thunder on loan from Celtic, following a request from his old teammate. More from Tommy on that story to follow. As it transpired, the first game would involve a trip to Los Angeles to face the Aztecs at Murdock Stadium on Saturday, 3 July 1976. George Best would be put in the shade as Harry's double secured a 2-1 win for the Thunder before 8,000 spectators, leaving the Texas side in a strong Play-off position.

That objective would be seriously derailed following five straight defeats, the first of those away to Minnesota Kicks in midweek, Neil Martin's goal insufficient to prevent Thunder going down 3-1 at the Metropolitan Stadium in Bloomington, in the southern suburbs of Minneapolis. The Kicks were on a run which would see them go all the way to the Soccer Bowl, the NASL Championship decider, their goals that day coming from a Ron Futcher double and Alan Willey.

Harry was on target for Thunder again on Monday, 12 July 1976, as they lost 2-1 at Alamo Stadium to Seattle Sounders in extra-time. One of Sounders' goals was scored by former St Mirren and Tottenham Hotspur winger Jimmy Robertson, who had played against Harry all the way from schoolboy football in Glasgow in the early 1960's. The Seattle outfit also featured another Spurs player from that era, the multi-capped Welsh defender Mike England, together with two former colleagues of Bobby Moore from Upton Park, Geoff Hurst and Harry Redknapp.

Back home in the relative normality of Scottish football, plans were afoot to recruit Harry for the new domestic season. Alan Davidson published this piece in *The Evening Times* earlier that day, suggesting two and possibly three former Celts would potentially be hooking back up in Maryhill.

"Partick Thistle manager Bertie Auld hopes to add the experience of ex-Celt Harry Hood to his player squad for next season's campaign in the Premier Division. Hood, released by Celtic at the end of last season, is currently playing in the United States, but he discussed his future with Auld before flying out and will give the Firhill boss his decision on his return."

"I'm very interested in Harry. I feel he has the qualities I require for next season. He's experienced, but more important he's got ability and that's really what it's all about. I spoke to Harry before he left, and the only snag could be that he's already had an offer from another Scottish club. However, I feel that a move to Thistle would be good for both Harry – who has business interests in the West of Scotland – and for ourselves."

"Auld is also interested in Celtic's experienced Tommy Callaghan, although his position is rather different to Hood's. Callaghan has been retained by Celtic for next season, but Thistle could move in with a bid for him."

Thunder's NASL campaign continued with a third consecutive loss, this time 3-0 on Thursday, 15 July 1976 at Vancouver's Empire Stadium to a Whitecaps side they had beaten 6-1 the previous month. English strikers Tommy Ord - with a double - and Billy Woof scored for the hosts. World Cup-winning striker Geoff Hurst then scored the only goal of the game as Seattle Sounders inflicted another defeat on Thunder 48 hours later, in front of 26,000 spectators at the Kingdome. Off the pitch, the strange goings-on continued in this fixture, when 10 minutes allegedly 'disappeared' from the stadium clock! Coach Batie would once again protest but like the Tampa appeal, it would be rejected, and the result allowed to stand. Perhaps the only surprise was that prolific hitman Gordon Wallace - a former Scottish Writers' Player of the Year whilst with Raith Rovers and scorer of the winning goal for Dundee in that dreadful League Cup final three years earlier - was not on target for either of Seattle's victories over Thunder over that five-day period.

The five-match losing sequence for Thunder continued with a 1-0 defeat to Portland Timbers at home on Friday, 23 July 1976, another former Middlesbrough striker Malcolm Smith with the only goal. The following day, Thunder would be in action in Missouri, beating St Louis Stars 3-0 at Francis Field, the stadium built as the main venue for the 1904 Olympic Games. A Victor Kadelja double and another from Dan Counce ended the run of defeats and restored hope of qualification for the play-offs.

Those hopes would suffer a crushing blow seven days later, as Thunder lost 3-2 at Alamo to bottom club San Diego Jaws, despite goals from Harry and Dan Counce. The final two regular season matches would both take place in San Antonio in August, the first of those on the seventh of the month ending 3-2 to Thunder against Dallas Tornado, Harry adding to Jose Berico's double for the hosts whilst Bobby Hope was on target for the visitors. That would provide some silverware from Harry's stint in the USA in the shape of the Texas Challenge Cup, a trophy played for between Thunder and Tornado and currently held by Dallas. With the head-to-head record for the 1976 meetings between the two Texas sides level at 3-3, the trophy went to San Antonio on the basis that Thunder had been in the opposition penalty area more often, thus perhaps reflecting Harry's most unusual ever success.

What would turn out to be San Antonio Thunder's last-ever game took place at Alamo Stadium on Friday, 13 August 1976, a 2-0 win over San Jose Earthquakes in front of just 4,147 spectators. Thunder beat the Southern section winners thanks to first-half goals from Harry and his former Sunderland teammate Neil Martin. Harry's 10th goal of the season confirmed him as Thunder's all-time top scorer, with his seven assists making him their Most Valuable Player for 1976. Former Dundee keeper Mike Hewitt was in goals for the Quakes, preventing the third Thunder goal which would have ensured an automatic play-off spot, whilst Harry also saw his effort hit the post.

Thunder were now eight points ahead of LA Aztecs in the play-off position but needed a favour from Dallas Tornados in their match with the Aztecs 24 hours later, with nine points potentially up for grabs. Harry remained optimistic.

"Now all we have to do is cross our fingers for Dallas."

Sadly, the Aztecs would score four goals without reply in the final half-hour of the regular season, thus securing the maximum nine points required to pip the Thunder by 108-107. The LA outfit would then meet Tornado in the first round of the play-offs four days later and be eliminated after a 2-0 defeat!

The Soccer Bowl of 1976 would eventually be won by Eusebio's Toronto Metros-Croatia, who beat Minnesota Kicks 3-0 in the final at Seattle's Kingdome on Saturday, 28 August 1976.

Don Batie's plans to bring back Bobby Moore – an ever-present in the 1976 campaign – as Thunder's player/coach the following season were dashed as Ward Lay, disillusioned by the lack of local support from both the business community and the 'soccer public' decided to relocate his franchise to Hawaii.

It would be left to the Scots to sum up that summer of 1976, Seattle sounders' Gordon Wallace with this observation.

"They know how to promote football in the States. It's simply fantastic the way they go about promoting the game. We know nothing about it here. The advertising on radio and television, sponsorship and the flow of information to the crowds before, during and after the game is really fantastic."

Tommy Callaghan would not forget the Stateside experience, as he reflected recently.

"I was hugely disappointed to miss out on the opportunity to play in Bobby Moore's testimonial game at Upton Park in November 1970. I had been stretchered off against St Johnstone at Parkhead with a badly cut leg a few weeks before that game. A horrific injury that was. Anyway, I was still out when the boys left for London. Bobby had been my idol as a kid so gutted wasn't the word. I would get to live the dream, right enough, by playing in the same team as the great man. You'll enjoy this, Matt."

"In the summer of 1976, towards the end of my time at Celtic, Jock Stein took a call from Harry, asking about the possibility of me being made available to play some games for San Antonio Thunder in Texas. Harry had been over there with his family for a while and said I would like it. I was really keen but Jock less so, for whatever reason. Anyway, long story short, the Boss agreed, so we headed to San Antonio."

"Apart from Harry, there were a few players I knew who were already at the club. Jim Henry, who played with Dundee United, Eddie Thomson who you might recall from his time at Hearts and Aberdeen, and Billy Semple, who spent some time at Ibrox. Bob McNab, the former Arsenal full-back from their Double-winning team was also there, although he was injured at the time but the captain was Bobby Moore! It was all a bit surreal, especially the time we played in Los Angeles and met up with

George Best. He was an absolute God over there. Film star. They loved him. After the game, we're all in George's pub. I'm coming back from the bar with a jug of beer in each hand and Bobby Moore is telling me to fill George's tumbler up! Totally surreal. George was a lovely guy. Great company."

"I managed nine games with Thunder then we got knocked out before the play-offs, so that was that. I came back and signed for Clydebank!"

Within a few days of Thunder's final game, speculation around Harry's future was making the news back in Scotland, with Alan Davidson commenting in *The Evening Times* of Tuesday, 17 August 1976.

"Partick Thistle will face fierce competition for the signature of Harry Hood, because today the former Celt revealed that he has had signing offers from three Premier League clubs. Hood returned only last night from a three-month spell in United States' football, playing for San Antonio Thunder, and he's not going to rush into an immediate decision on his future."

"I'm still very tired from the long flight, so I'm going to think things over very carefully before deciding which offer to accept," Harry told me. "Including Thistle, I've been contacted by three Premier Division clubs, and I hope to make my mind up within the next couple of days. I've to meet the managers of two of the clubs tonight, and I'll be in touch with the other by telephone."

"However, before Hood can play for whichever club he decides on, he will have to get clearance from the United States. That should come through within the next day or two. Certainly, it's no surprise that the talented, experienced Hood is in big demand in Scotland. As well as Thistle, his name has been linked with Motherwell and Kilmarnock – both, of course, from the Premier Division. Thistle manager Bertie Auld expects to get an answer to his offer before the Firhill board meet tomorrow night, 24 hours later than scheduled."

Last word on the Stateside adventure goes to the man in the airport wearing the stetson, Harry Hood.

"It's terrific how the Americans go about things. It was a real eye-opener to me."

Chapter 37

Harry joins the Steelmen

Harry's immediate future was settled quickly on his return from Texas, as he opted to sign for his old Clyde teammate Willie McLean at Motherwell. Alan Davidson confirmed that a return to Shawfield for a third spell with the Bully Wee was one of the options on the table in his report for *The Evening Times* on Wednesday, 18 August 1976.

"Motherwell have won the race for Harry Hood. Fir Park manager Willie McLean signed the ex-Celt today, beating off opposition from Partick Thistle, Kilmarnock and Clyde, who had also made offers to the experienced, talented Hood. McLean completed the deal late today and Hood, who only returned to Scotland on Monday after a three-month spell in United States football, will start training at Fir Park immediately.

"I'm delighted to have signed for Motherwell," he told me. "They're a progressive and an ambitious club. They did well last season and I'm sure they're going to be even better this time. Also, I'll stay a full-timer at Fir Park, and that was an important factor in my decision to join Motherwell."

"The signing of Hood gives further depth to an already impressive top-team squad built up by McLean. He shared Hood's enthusiasm at the signing."

"I'm very pleased to have fixed up Harry," he said. "He has signed a one-year contract with a one-year option clause."

"Hood has still to get his clearance from the States, where he was playing with San Antonio Thunder, but is expected to do so within the next day or so. He's match fit and could be included in McLean's team plans for Saturday's match with Hearts at Tynecastle."

Signing for Motherwell that morning would be the first part of a double celebration for Harry, as he left Fir Park to stand as best man at his brother George's wedding to Mary Sullivan later that day!

Having failed in his bid to bring Harry to Firhill, Partick Thistle manager Bertie Auld immediately turned his attention to signing Jackie McNamara from Celtic, in a player plus cash deal, with Joe Craig, Bobby Houston or Alan Hansen potentially moving to Parkhead, depending on which report you believed. As it transpired, McNamara knocked the offer back as he wanted to remain full-time, and he would head to Easter Road at the end of the month in a deal which brought Hibernian captain Pat Stanton to Celtic, whilst Craig joined Celtic in a £60,000 deal two weeks after that.

Motherwell had started the season poorly, knocked out of the Anglo Scottish Cup by Willie Fernie's newly promoted Kilmarnock on a 5-1 aggregate, following a 4-0 defeat at Rugby Park. They then took just one point from their opening two League Cup sectional games, a 1-1 draw with Partick Thistle at Fir Park on Saturday, 14 August 1976 then a 2-1 defeat to Dundee at Dens Park four nights later, on the day Harry signed for the club. Harry was duly named in the 16-man pool for the third match, a clash with leaders Hearts at Tynecastle on Saturday, 21 August 1976, albeit his international clearance had not yet come through from the USA. The player himself remained optimistic.

"I've had verbal assurance that it will come through on time, but I'll have to wait for official word."

Manager Willie McLean was also keeping his fingers crossed, Harry very much in his thoughts.

"Harry certainly has a chance of playing."

As it transpired, his clearance did not arrive in time, Harry having to make do with being a spectator at Tynecastle, as Motherwell lost 2-1 to remain bottom of the section. It finally came through on the Tuesday, clearing Harry to play against Dundee at Fir Park the next night, making his Motherwell debut beside a couple of former Celtic teammates, Ally Hunter and Vic Davidson, in the following line-up.

Ally Hunter; Peter Millar & Joe Wark; Stewart MacLaren, Willie McVie & Gregor Stevens; Harry Hood, Willie Pettigrew, Bobby Graham, Vic Davidson & Peter Marinello. Substitutes; Willie Watson & Jim O'Rourke.

It was the most positive start, Vic Davidson heading Motherwell ahead from Harry's cross after just seven minutes, before the game swung one way then the other. Billy Pirie scored twice for Dundee either side of the break then a second from Davidson and a Bobby Graham strike put Well 3-2 up. Pirie completed his hat-trick from the spot with six minutes remaining to end the scoring at 3-3, as the Steelmen remained bottom of the section with two points from four games, five behind Hearts. The feedback on Harry's debut was complimentary, this from *The Glasgow Herald* the next morning.

"The inclusion of Harry Hood brought some composure to the attack and his intelligent running and positional play should have been exploited by his colleagues."

Three days later, Saturday, 28 August 1976, Harry scored his first – and as it would transpire, only goal for Motherwell to give them a 16th minute lead against Hearts at Fir Park with a shot which *"scorched into the net."* Drew Busby equalised two minutes later, and Hearts were 3-1 ahead by the half-hour through Ralph Callachan and Donald Park, Motherwell winger Peter Marinello seeing his penalty kick saved by visiting keeper Brian Wilson at 2-1. Busby grabbed his second early in the second half from the spot as Hearts won 4-1 to clinch the section with a game to spare, Harry replaced by Jim O'Rourke late on, *"to the disgust of the Motherwell fans."*

Amidst reports of Motherwell interest in signing Peter Cormack from Liverpool, Harry found himself on the bench for the visit to Firhill on Wednesday, 1 September 1976. His new side were beaten 2-0 by Partick Thistle, ironically one of the clubs who tried to sign him a few weeks earlier, the Steelmen finishing bottom of the section without a victory. Harry came on with the Jags leading 1-0 thanks to an early Doug Somner strike, Thistle substitute Joe Craig completing the scoring 10 minutes from time.

Harry was restored to the starting line-up to make his Premier League debut for Motherwell at Rugby Park on Saturday, 4 September 1976. Kilmarnock were managed by former Celt Willie Fernie, a player renowned for his talent on the ball, and his side boasted two of Scotland's most prized young wingers in Davie Provan and Gordon Smith. Harry's corner kick set up transfer-seeking defender Willie McVie to equalise on 17 minutes, after Paul Clarke had headed the hosts in front early on. That would be that in terms of scoring as the sides settled for a point apiece. As an aside, George Best and Rodney Marsh made their Fulham debuts the same day, following their summer in the NASL, the Irish genius scoring the winner in a 1-0 victory over Bristol Rovers at Craven Cottage in the English Second Division.

Harry retained his place in the team for the visit of Hibernian, seven days later, Motherwell behind within 30 seconds as Ally Scott knocked the ball home after Stuart Rennie had parried a John Brownlie drive. Harry – *"who gives Motherwell a nice touch of composure"* - was again involved in Motherwell's reply, 15 minutes later, his "craftiest of free-kicks" picking out the run of Bobby Graham to beat keeper Mike McDonald for 1-1. Midway through the second half, Jackie McNamara set up Willie Murray to put the visitors in front once more, and there were only two minutes remaining when substitute Peter Marinello equalised against his old club to end the scoring at 2-2.

Bob Cuthill was full of praise for Harry in his match report for the following Monday's *Evening Times*.

"Though his name did not appear on the scoresheet, the man who took most credit for 'Well's creditable performance was Harry Hood. The ex-Celt was behind both the goals. He lofted a free-kick to Bobby Graham for No.1 in 16 minutes and also started the move which allowed Peter Marinello to equalise two minutes from time after keeper Mike McDonald palmed away a Willie Pettigrew shot. Harry's class provided the poise Motherwell have been lacking this season, and his play evoked just the right response from strikers Graham and Pettigrew."

Motherwell's winless start to the season continued on Saturday, 18 September 1976, with a quick return to Firhill, an unchanged team losing 2-0 to Partick Thistle thanks to goals from Maryhill strike duo Doug Somner and Jim Melrose. Bertie Auld had sold

Joe Craig to his old manager Jock Stein 24 hours earlier. Harry was then missing from the side which gained that elusive first victory seven days later, with a 4-1 win over Ayr United at Fir Park, the old double-act of Willie Pettigrew and Bobby Graham sharing the goals. He would again be absent as October opened with a daunting test, a trip to Tannadice to face a Dundee United side boasting a perfect record of four wins from their opening four games. Second-half strikes from Paul Hegarty and Paul Sturrock extended that sequence to five.

Harry celebrated his 32nd birthday on Sunday, 3 October 1976. The League programme was cancelled the following Saturday, due to Scotland's World Cup qualifier against Czechoslovakia in Prague the following midweek. There was a first-ever match for Harry against his old club Sunderland to look forward to, played at Fir Park on Monday, 11 October 1976, albeit he would remain on the bench as Motherwell won 3-1, thanks to a Bobby Graham double either side of Jimmy O'Rourke's strike. Alan Foggon had earlier equalised for Sunderland. He was one of two visiting players whom Harry had faced in his spell in the NASL, former Manchester United and Scotland defender Jim Holton being the other.

Harry would remain on the periphery of the action as the campaign progressed, Willie Pettigrew's demotion to the bench for the home clash with Hearts on Saturday, 16 October triggering a transfer request from the Scotland striker. With Jim O'Rourke struggling with a throat infection, Pettigrew was restored to the starting line-up as Motherwell hosted Rangers seven days later, Harry listed as one of the substitutes. He would look on as Pettigrew destroyed Rangers, his scintillating performance rewarded with a double in Motherwell's 3-1 win. Legendary defender Joe Wark scored the other goal.

Things would not go so well for Harry or the Lanarkshire side the following Saturday, Jim O'Rourke's return to the bench meaning Harry missed out on the opportunity to play against Celtic at Parkhead. It's not clear if Harry watched Kenny Dalglish score both goals in a 2-0 home victory or if he played in the reserve side which suffered the same fate at Fir Park, thanks to goals from Bobby Lennox and Brian McLaughlin. If it was the latter, then he would have his old friend Tommy Callaghan for company, the big Fifer at left-back for the second-string in his final match in the Hoops. He signed for First Division Clydebank the following Thursday for a fee of £6,000.

Harry was again missing for Motherwell's trip to face League Cup finalists Aberdeen at Pittodrie on Tuesday, 2 November 1976, the Dons winning 3-1, then the home match with bottom-of-the-table Kilmarnock the following Saturday, a Jim O'Rourke hat-trick enabling the Steelmen to twice come from behind to edge a nine-goal thriller, but he returned to the bench after the international break as Anglo-Scottish Cup semi-finalists Partick Thistle arrived at Fir Park on Saturday, 20 November 1976. Harry replaced Peter Marinello with Motherwell 2-0 up early in the second half, thanks to another Willie Pettigrew double, Vic Davidson securing the two points with a third goal on 65 minutes.

Motherwell consolidated their position in the top half of the table in midweek, recording their third successive win in the Premier League by beating Hibernian 2-0 at Easter Road. Willie Pettigrew scored his 10th goal of the season early on then limped off to be replaced by Bobby Graham, Harry coming on for Vic Davidson before Graham sealed the victory with 20 minutes remaining. That sequence would come to an abrupt halt at Somerset Park on Saturday, 27 November 1976. Harry was again on the bench as Joe Fillipi and Gordon Cramond gave second-bottom Ayr United an early 2-0 lead, Peter Marinello's header reducing the deficit for the Steelmen before the break. Former Aberdeen striker Walker McCall restored the two-goal cushion for the hosts 10 minutes after the restart, Willie McLean sending Harry on for Stewart MacLaren in a bid to rescue a point. But McCall would have the last word, a second excellent solo goal from the tall hitman consigning Motherwell to a disappointing 4-1 defeat.

The icy weather then put paid to next two weekend's fixtures, Motherwell not back in action until a second visit of the season to Tynecastle on Saturday, 18 December 1976. Harry was again on the bench with Colin McAdam, introduced by Willie McLean to replace Willie Pettigrew with 20 minutes to play and the sides level at 1-1, Gregor Stevens having equalised Graham Shaw's 30-yard opener for Hearts. With Motherwell chasing a winner, there was a cruel twist in the 83rd minute, Stevens completing an unwanted double by knocking the ball past his own keeper Stuart Rennie to gift the hosts a 2-1 win.

The build-up to the Boxing Day clash with Rangers at Ibrox was dominated by leaked reports linking Motherwell's controversial defender with a move to Govan, with Iain Munro going in the opposite direction. Larkhall-based McVie - suspended six times previously with one case pending - had been in dispute with the club for most of the current season and made no secret of his wish to make that happen. The stories would fizzle out ahead of the clash which Rangers won 1-0 thanks to a late goal from Alex O'Hara. The New Year's Day fixture with Celtic at Fir Park was another victim of the Scottish winter but Harry was back in the starting line-up for the visit to Rugby Park on Monday, 3 January 1977. Motherwell came out of the blocks flying, a Willie Pettigrew double within the first 10 minutes giving the visitors the perfect start to the year. But Kilmarnock fought back bravely, in front of 7,000 spectators, Ian Fallis making it 2-1 before the break, then a second-half onslaught by the home side rewarded by a late equaliser from George Maxwell. There is a sad footnote to this paragraph as Ian Fallis was killed in a car accident near his home in North Lanarkshire later that year, aged just 23.

Harry was wearing the number 11 jersey as Motherwell entertained Hibernian five days later, the kick-off deferred by 15 minutes as one of a series of initiatives by the Steelmen to increase attendances. There were almost 9,000 supporters inside Fir Park to see Harry set up Willie Pettigrew for a header which shaved the crossbar, before the visitors went ahead through a long-range John Brownlie effort. Hibernian held that lead until the opening minutes of the second half, and it was one of their favourite sons who inflicted the damage with Motherwell's equaliser, Jim O'Rourke following up his own header to beat Mike McDonald from close-range. The hosts would then hit the Leith men with everything but the proverbial kitchen sink, but Eddie Turnbull's men held out for a share of the spoils.

Plans to play the home match with Celtic - postponed on New Year's Day - on Wednesday, 18 January 1977 were again dashed by the severe weather. This would now be pushed back until the end of the season and would prove to be significant for one of Harry's former teammates. More on that later.

Saturday, 22 January 1977 would be another landmark day in the career of Harry Hood, as he started a League match in top-flight football for the final time, albeit he would not know that as Motherwell and Ayr United lined up at Fir Park as follows.

MOTHERWELL:

Stuart Rennie; Peter Millar & Joe Wark; Colin McAdam, Willie Watson & Gregor Stevens; Harry Hood, Willie Pettigrew, Jim O'Rourke, Vic Davidson & Ian Kennedy. Substitutes; Bobby Graham & Peter Marinello.

AYR UNITED:

Andy Geoghegan; Davie Wells & John Murphy; Rikki Fleming, Alex McAnespie & Joe Filippi; Jim McSherry, Walker McCall, Danny Masterton, Gordon Cramond & Davie McCulloch. Substitutes; Malcolm Robertson & Alex Ingram.

Motherwell had convincingly won the opening meeting of the clubs in September by 4-1 with Ayr reversing that result two months later. The key man this afternoon would again be visiting striker Walker McCall, who repeated his Somerset Park double to secure another victory for the Honest Men. Honours were even at the break, Jim McSherry giving United the lead against the run of play on 18 minutes before Willie Pettigrew headed an equaliser on the half-hour. Danny Masterton then headed Ayr's second immediately after the restart, but Jim O'Rourke fired home from Harry's corner on the hour mark to leave the sides still deadlocked at 2-2. McCall immediately restored the visitors' lead and then capped another fine display with a superb solo effort three minutes from time, beating three Motherwell defenders before shooting past Stuart Rennie for 4-2.

Saturday, 29 January 1977 was Scottish Cup third-round day, Willie Fernie's Kilmarnock getting a break from their relegation dogfight as they travelled through to Fir Park. Harry dropped to the bench beside Gregor Stevens as Bobby Graham and Peter Marinello received a recall, as did Willie McVie. The tie was over by half-time, by which time Motherwell were 3-0 to the good. Willie Pettigrew scored within 30 seconds of kick-off, Vic Davidson doubling the lead 15 minutes later with a fierce strike. Pettigrew then brought the house down with a 30-yard free-kick which flew past Jim Stewart three minutes from the break. There would be no further scoring as the Steelmen progressed comfortably to the fourth round, on a day where the major surprise was First Division St Mirren's 4-1 hammering of Premier League high-flyers Dundee United at Love Street before 16,000 spectators.

Motherwell's losing battle with the winter weather continued as matches on successive Saturdays at Tannadice then Pittodrie were called off. The Dundee United fixture was rescheduled for Wednesday, 16 February 1977, Harry watching from the bench as the game exploded into life in the final 20 minutes. Paul Sturrock appeared to be well offside when he opened the scoring for United, but the goal stood, and it took another piece of Willie Pettigrew magic to save a point for the visitors. With 12 minutes remaining, he bent a free-kick around the wall and past Hamish McAlpine to make it 1-1. The talismanic striker continued where he left off three days later, as Hearts arrived at Fir Park, his first-minute header giving Motherwell the lead. The Gorgie side equalised just before the break when Willie Gibson capitalised on an error by 'Well keeper Stuart Rennie to force the ball home. Harry was introduced on the hour mark and Motherwell immediately regained the lead, Jim O'Rourke picking up a pass from Gregor Stevens to hammer it past Jim Cruickshank for what would prove to be the winner. Gibson and Pettigrew moved on to the 17-goal mark for the season, tied with Celtic's Joe Craig in third place in the Scottish top-flight scoring stakes. Long-time leader Joe Harper of Aberdeen still topped the chart with 25, although Parkhead skipper Kenny Dalglish had closed the gap behind him to four.

There was huge excitement the following Saturday as St Mirren boss Alex Ferguson brought his combination of fearless youngsters and experienced pros to Fir Park for the most hyped-up tie of the Scottish Cup fourth round. More than 26,000 spectators packed into Fir Park to see the following sides.

MOTHERWELL:

Stuart Rennie; Willie Watson & Joe Wark; Colin McAdam, Stewart MacLaren & Gregor Stevens; Peter Millar, Willie Pettigrew, Jim O'Rourke, Vic Davidson & Peter Marinello. Substitutes; Harry Hood & Bobby Graham.

ST MIRREN:

Donald Hunter; Alex Beckett & Billy Johnston; Tony Fitzpatrick, Bobby Reid & Jackie Copland; Frank McGarvey, Billy Stark, Bobby Torrance, Lex Richardson & Derek Hyslop. Substitutes; Donny McDowell & John Young.

The game was 10 minutes late in kicking off due to the huge crowds at the turnstiles, Stewart MacLaren's timing similarly tardy as he tackled Bobby Torrance five seconds into the action. Alex Beckett's name then went into referee Ian Foote's notebook for his challenge on Vic Davidson, the St Mirren full-back fortunate to stay on the park after committing another bad foul minutes later. The goal action commenced early in the second half, Davidson following up to give Motherwell the lead after Willie Pettigrew's shot had come back off a post. Within two minutes, the Buddies were level, Frank McGarvey's unerring finish beating Stuart Rennie. On the hour,

Pettigrew would yet again win a cup-tie for Motherwell, Davidson fouled in the box and the Scotland striker making no mistake from 12 yards to take his tally for the season to 18. St Mirren would lodge a protest at how Foote allowed the early challenges on their players to go without cautions, setting the tone for the rest of the match, but Motherwell would progress to the last eight, where they would face cup-holders Rangers at Ibrox. Aberdeen and Hibernian would not be joining them in the quarter-final, the two Premier teams losing home replays to lower League teams sides Dundee and Arbroath respectively.

There was a dress rehearsal of the Scottish Cup clash on Saturday, 5 March 1977, albeit Motherwell enjoyed home advantage for this one. Willie McLean's only change was to bring Ian Kennedy on to the bench beside Harry to the exclusion of Bobby Graham, the former Liverpool striker a Hearts target, having asked way due to lack of current first-team action. Harry got a taste of the action, replacing the injured Vic Davidson, before being hurt himself as Rangers won 2-0 with goals from Alex MacDonald and Kenny Watson to take a psychological advantage back to the Glasgow ahead of the cup clash.

There was a certain symmetry in the events which took place seven days later, Saturday, 12 March 1977. Having made his senior debut for Clyde as an 18-year-old at Ibrox back in November 1962, Harry was named in Motherwell's line-up at the same venue for the Scottish Cup clash with Rangers the best part of 15 years later, wearing number seven but playing wide left in a midfield four for what would be his final start as a top-flight footballer. The sides lined up as follows in front of 35,000 spectators.

RANGERS:

Stewart Kennedy; Sandy Jardine & John Greig; Tom Forsyth, Colin Jackson & Kenny Watson; Tommy McLean, Bobby McKean, Derek Parlane, Alex MacDonald & Derek Johnstone. Substitutes; Chris Robertson & Alex Miller.

MOTHERWELL:

Stuart Rennie; Willie Watson & Joe Wark; Colin McAdam, Stewart MacLaren & Gregor Stevens; Harry Hood, Willie Pettigrew, Bobby Graham, Vic Davidson & Ian Kennedy. Substitutes; Jim O'Rourke & Peter Marinello.

Harry set up an early chance for Ian Kennedy before the hosts took the lead five minutes in, Bobby McKean glancing a header past Stuart Rennie from John Greig's cross. Harry then tested Stewart Kennedy in the Ibrox goal before sending Willie Pettigrew to do likewise, as the sides turned at 1-0. Rangers would enjoy the bulk of the second-half possession and chances, but it took a last-minute free-kick from Kenny Watson to confirm their passage to the semi-final.

Whether Harry was injured at Ibrox or paid the price for Willie McLean's displeasure at Motherwell's performance is unclear, in any case both he and Ian Kennedy were missing from the 13 names listed for the midweek visit to Celtic Park. Jimmy Miller made a second appearance there in just four days, having been part of the Queen of the South team beaten 5-1 in the Scottish Cup quarter-final before signing for Motherwell for £!2,000 on the eve of the match. He started on the bench with Tommy O'Neill as Ronnie Glavin continued his tremendous scoring run by netting from the penalty spot within 60 seconds, after Joe Craig had been barged in the box by Gregor Stevens, his 21st goal of the season for the League leaders. Goals either side of the break from Bobby Graham and Johannes Edvaldsson had Celts 2-1 ahead as we entered the final 10 minutes, but substitute Miller – on for Willie Pettigrew - then set up Vic Davidson to equalise against his old club and end the scoring at 2-2.

Jimmy Miller's introduction would see Harry drop out of the first-team picture for the rest of that month, as Motherwell caught up their backlog of fixtures with a series of mixed results. Miller started against Kilmarnock three days later in a 2-0 home win, Bobby Graham netting a double, then again in midweek at Pittodrie as the Steelmen lost their 1-0 lead late on to strikes from Duncan Davidson and Arthur Graham. He retained his place at Easter Road on Saturday, 26 March 1977, as Motherwell came from behind to win 2-1 with a Willie Pettigrew double and in the goalless draw with Partick Thistle at Firhill the following midweek, a match where Stuart Rennie's broken finger provided an opportunity for Harry's old Parkhead teammate Ally Hunter to regain a first-team spot. Harry was restored to the bench on Saturday, 2 April 1977, as Motherwell fought out another draw with Bertie Auld's men, this time 1-1 at Fir Park, Dixie Deans featuring for Thistle against his old club. Alan Rough saved a Willie Pettigrew penalty before Harry came on for Gregor Stevens, five minutes into the second half, Chick Young deeming him "the man most likely to succeed" in terms of breaking the deadlock in his *Evening Times* match report. It would be yet another former Celt who would do so with 15 minutes remaining, Vic Davidson on target, but Thistle equalised immediately through Ian Gibson as the game ended 1-1.

Harry was again on the bench for the visit of Aberdeen, on Tuesday, 5 April 1977. Vic Davidson would become the second Motherwell striker in successive games to see a penalty saved as Dons keeper Ally McLean blocked his effort in first-half stoppage time. The Steelmen then took the lead midway through the second period when Willie Pettigrew smashed a tremendous shot home from outside the box, but with seconds remaining, Scotland's top marksman Joe Harper rescued a point for Aberdeen. Harry was then missing from the squad which lost 3-2 to Ayr United at Somerset Park the following Saturday, Willie Pettigrew with yet another double for Motherwell but Ayr's Gordon Cramond going one better with a hat-trick. Midweek saw Jock Stein's Celtic head to Fir Park looking for the victory which would give them the Premier League title if Dundee United slipped up the same evening against Aberdeen. The Taysiders duly lost 3-2 at Tannadice but an incredible game in North Lanarkshire saw Motherwell win 3-0, despite being under the cosh for much of the match. Ian Kennedy opened the scoring against the run of play just before the interval, with Celtic full-back Andy Lynch beating his own keeper Roy Baines twice in the closing three minutes to keep the Parkhead champagne on ice.

Harry had missed out on the opportunity to face Celtic in midweek and he was absent as Motherwell made it seven goals without reply in five days against the top two sides in the country by beating Dundee United 4-0 at Fir Park on Sunday, 17 April 1977. Willie Pettigrew's early opener was followed by a Bobby Graham double and an Andy Rolland own goal as the two points won by Motherwell consigned Hearts to their first-ever relegation from the top-flight of Scottish football. Pettigrew was on target again in midweek, putting Motherwell ahead at Ibrox then crashing another shot against the bar before Rangers turned the game around with four of their own to end the Steelmen's good run.

The next match followed a similar pattern, Ian Kennedy giving Motherwell the lead on the half-hour at home to Aberdeen on Saturday, 23 April 1977 before the roof caved in with 12 minutes remaining, a Duncan Davidson double and Arthur Graham strike sealing a 3-1 win for the Dons. Harry was still an absentee as Motherwell travelled to Tynecastle, seven days later, to face a Hearts side under new management, Willie Ormond resigning as Scotland boss to replace John Hagart. Prolific duo Willie Pettigrew and Willie Gibson traded goals to send the teams in level at the break. Ally Hunter had toiled with an injured ankle for much of the first half and it was his error which allowed Gordon Smith a free header for 2-1 shortly after the restart, Hearts' new signing Malcolm Robertson returning the favour by putting through his own net with 20 minutes remaining before Eamon Bannon scored the winner.

Harry was released by the club as Motherwell duly completed a disappointing campaign with two home fixtures, the first a 1-1 draw with Dundee United on Wednesday, 4 May 1977. Bobby Graham lobbed Hamish McAlpine to give the hosts the lead seconds before the half-time whistle, Billy Williamson equalising on the hour mark. The second would be more significant, albeit from a visitors' perspective. Jock Stein named an unchanged Celtic team from that which had had clinched the Double at the weekend with a 1-0 Scottish Cup final victory over Rangers, for the final League match of the season at Fir Park on Tuesday, 10 May 1977. The man who had scored two own goals on his visit to Motherwell, left-back Andy Lynch, had clinched the trophy at Hampden by converting his first-ever penalty kick in the Hoops. The new champions were rocked when Motherwell scored twice in as many minutes just before the interval, Gregor Stevens and Peter Marinello beating Peter Latchford to put the hosts in control. Stein introduced Tommy Burns for Johannes Edvaldsson at the interval, and the youngster vindicated that decision by grabbing his first Celtic goal on the hour, following good work from Alfie Conn and Kenny Dalglish. And it was the skipper who completed the scoring eight minutes later, Dalglish slipping the ball past third choice 'Well keeper Jim Muir for 2-2. Whilst Kenny would feature in a Glasgow Cup-tie at Shawfield that weekend - Celtic beating a Clyde side now managed by Billy McNeill 4-2, with Cesar's good friend Harry watching two of his old clubs do battle from the stand - and some pre-season friendlies later that summer, this would prove to be his last goal and final competitive outing in the Hoops before signing for Liverpool for £440,000 in August.

There was an interesting postscript to that scenario involving Cesar and Clyde, which gave a strong indication as to where Harry saw his future, reported by Shearer Borthwick in *The Evening Times*.

"Harry Hood might have been the Clyde manager had Billy McNeill not appeared on the scene just at the right time to pip his former colleague. Harry was very much in the running but of course was still playing with Motherwell when Clyde directors made their appointment. So, it's that fact that has brought Harry to the notice of the Dundee directors who will get down to the job of naming a successor to David White next week. Harry's name has been mentioned in the top circles, but the ex-Motherwell man, who is now a free agent, says he hasn't thought about the Dens post."

"I would be interested in either a manager's job – ultimately, I want to be a manager – or as a player-coach or a coach. I'm now available for a full or part-time post, for I've just got my brother George into the family hotel business, and so I would be free to concentrate on football. I've been 15 years in the game now and it's hard to think of giving it up. I'd like to remain in football."

"Harry will be attending the SFA coaching course at Largs this summer."

That situation took another twist as Aberdeen manager Ally MacLeod was appointed to replace Willie Ormond as Scotland boss, the Pittodrie club turning to Clyde's Billy McNeill as MacLeod's successor in the Granite City in early June, with Harry again tipped to take over at Shawfield. Clyde then offered the post to Craig Brown, who had been Willie McLean's assistant manager at Motherwell. Harry would later reflect that missing out on the Shawfield job was one of his biggest disappointments in his career.

Chapter 38

King of the South

First Division Queen of the South caused the first major upset of the 1977/78 Scottish football season, Mike Jackson's men following up their 2-1 win at Easter Road on Wednesday, 17 August 1977 with a goalless draw at Palmerston seven nights later, to knock Premier League Hibernian out of the League Cup at the first stage. Their reward was a second-round tie with Second Division Brechin City, Queens doing the damage at home this time with a 2-0 win before sharing four goals at Glebe Park. Next up for the Dumfries outfit would be a clash with Dundee, now under a new management duo of Tommy Gemmell and Willie Wallace, with a third Lisbon Lion on the playing staff, a certain Jimmy Johnstone.

By the time that tie came around in early October, Queens would have a new player in their ranks, as Harry signed for his sixth senior club, the news covered by the local *Dumfries & Galloway Standard.*

"Harry Hood, the former Celtic star, became a Queens' player on Friday after much speculation. Harry had been training with the Queens' squad in Glasgow for the past few weeks and had turned out for the reserves a couple of times. Said chairman, Mr William Harkness: "We in no way pressurised Harry into signing. When we first approached him, he wanted time to decide whether or not he still had the appetite for the game but now he has made up his mind. I'm confident he can do a job for us."

"Harry started his senior career with Clyde, then moved to Sunderland. After two years at Roker Park, he returned to Clyde before signing for Celtic, and during his seven years at Parkhead was a great favourite with the Celtic fans and won a cap for the Scottish League. After leaving Parkhead he was in America for a short period and on his return joined Motherwell with whom he ended last season. Harry, who is 32, now owns a hotel in Uddingston."

Signing up at Palmerston would see Harry link up again with Mike Jackson, who had briefly been a teammate at Shawfield in that memorable 1966/67 campaign, before moving to Dumfries. He made his Queen of the South debut in the First Division clash with Arbroath at Gayfield on Saturday, 24 September 1977. Former Celtic colleague Jimmy Bone led the attack for the hosts, as Jackson selected the following side.

Allan Ball; Iain McChesney & Tommy O'Hara; Billy McLaren, Nobby Clark & Crawford Boyd; Jocky Dempster, Peter Dickson, Ian Reid, Harry Hood & George Dickson. Substitutes; Alan Munro & Les O'Neill.

It would be a losing debut without a goal for once for Harry, who made way for Allan Munro in the second half, both Bone and future Hoops hero Albert Kidd on target as Queens went down 3-1. Harry would then start on the bench in midweek before replacing Les O'Neill to make his home debut against Dundee, but old pals Tommy Gemmell and Willie Wallace held the bragging rights that night following a 2-0 win at Palmerston, which gave them a boost ahead of the imminent League Cup tie between the sides. Harry did score his first goal for Queens three days later, pulling one back after Stirling Albion had established a two-goal by the break, but Alex Smith's men eventually edged a five-goal thriller.

The first leg of the League Cup third round tie at Dens Park in midweek ended goalless, leaving it finely balanced for the return in Dumfries three weeks later. In the interim, Harry retained his starting slot for three of the four League games played, a 1-0 defeat by East Fife in Methil and single-goal victories over Montrose at Palmerston and League leaders Morton at Cappielow, ending an unbeaten run of 27 games for the Greenock side. Harry missed the 2-2 draw at home with St Johnstone on Saturday, 15 October 1977. In stark contrast to his previous season at Motherwell, that would be the only match in which he would not feature after joining the club.

The highlight of the campaign would be the second leg match with Dundee at Palmerston, played on Wednesday, 26 October 1977. Aberdeen manager Billy McNeill had made the long journey south to take a look at Dundee's highly rated young midfielder Gordon Strachan, but he picked the wrong night. Jocky Dempster scored within seven minutes before Cesar's old pal Harry set up George Dickson for a second, and by half-time the tie was over at 4-0, Ian Reid, and Peter Dickson piling on the agony. Five minutes after the break, Harry's free-kick allowed George Dickson to head a fifth for Queens before Reid completed his own brace in the closing minutes. The Dumfries side would now meet Forfar Athletic for a place in the League Cup semi-final, the Angus outfit having eliminated Premier League Ayr United the same evening.

There was another familiar face in opposition three days later, as Queens headed up the M74 to face Hamilton Academical at Douglas Park. Harry and Bobby Graham had been teammates at Motherwell a few months earlier, but the new Hamilton assistant manager and striker was on fire that afternoon, hitting a hat-trick as Accies won by the odd goal in seven. And the Parkhead connection was in full force on Saturday, 5 November 1977, as a Dumbarton side in third spot and featuring new signing Pat McCluskey and future Hoops star Murdo MacLeod visited Palmerston. Having beaten both leaders Morton and second-placed Dundee, the Sons were next to bite the dust, and it was Harry who scored the only goal of the match. That came in the third minute of the second half and was set up by Queens left-back Tommy O'Hara, who had spent time at Celtic as a youngster and would later follow Harry to the NASL, where he would play beside Johan Cruyff and Wim Jansen for Washington Diplomats.

The first leg of the League Cup quarter-final with Forfar Athletic was played at Palmerston on Tuesday, 8 November 1977. With an hour gone, Queens were odds-on favourites to progress, holding a 3-1 lead over their Second Division opponents, but veteran midfielder Alex Rae turned the tie on its head, adding to his earlier penalty conversion to complete a late hat-trick to end the scoring at 3-3. Four days later, Mike Jackson's men made the trip up the A76 to Kilmarnock, Harry experiencing deja vu at kick-off as he looked across the line to see Colin Stein facing him, the Rangers striker on loan at Rugby Park. But it was a Celtic star of the future who opened the scoring, Davie Provan smashing a 25-yard shot past Allan Ball on the stroke of half-time. Harry set up the equaliser with a cross on to the head of Jocky Dempster on the hour mark, the winger beating Jim Stewart to end the scoring at 1-1.

Queens' Hampden dream would come to an end at Station Park in midweek, a Billy Gavine goal 10 minutes from the break enough to send Forfar Athletic into their first-ever League Cup semi-final, the visitors paying a huge price for that late collapse at Palmerston. Harry was a constant threat, Ian Reid hitting the woodwork from one of his crosses, but the Angus side would now meet Rangers in the last four. Harry had featured in seven successive League Cup finals with Celtic, and Jock Stein's men would also progress that night to reach the penultimate stage for an incredible 14th consecutive year, with a 5-1 aggregate win over Alex Ferguson's St Mirren. This was Harry's final League Cup match.

Bottom dogs Alloa Athletic were the visitors to Palmerston on Saturday, 19 November 1977, Harry again creating chance after chance for the hosts. The only goal, though, came from the penalty spot, right-back Iain McChesney converting seconds from half-time after a Peter Dickson cross was handled. Arbroath were also struggling near the foot of the table, but the Red Lichties returned north with both points seven days later, following their 2-1 win.

There would be a two-week gap before Queens' next match, as the winter weather impacted the Scottish fixture calendar, albeit it was worth the wait, as they shared six goals with East Fife at Palmerston on Saturday, 10 December 1977. Harry set up Tommy Bryce to make it 1-1 on 20 minutes, before scoring the third goal for the hosts himself. The following Saturday saw the Doonhamers fight back for an excellent 2-1 win against St Johnstone at Muirton. Trailing at the break to a Derek O'Connor strike, two goals in two minutes from Peter Dickson and Benny Ferrie midway through the second half saw Mike Jackson's team claim the points.

Tommy Bryce made the Christmas Eve headlines against Airdrieonians at Palmerston, the Queens striker levelling Sandy Clark's opener before being sent off in a crazy spell just before the break. Peter Dickson put the 10-man hosts ahead early in the second half, but the Broomfield outfit fought back to make it 2-2. The Hogmanay show at

Boghead was much quieter, Dumbarton's Donald McNeill beating his own keeper to give Queens the lead 10 minutes after the restart before Jimbo Muir equalised on the hour, as the calendar year ended with a share of the spoils against the promotion-chasing Sons.

Queens were the 'first-footers' at Rugby Park on Monday, 2 January 1978 but headed home on the back of a 2-0 defeat to Kilmarnock, a George Maxwell penalty and Colin Stein making it a disappointing start to the year in front of the biggest crowd of the season to date, over 5,000 spectators. The first home game of the year produced a point from a 1-1 draw with Hamilton Academical, five days later.

A visit to Tynecastle to face Willie Ormond's title-chasing Hearts was the next challenge for Harry and his Dumfries teammates, more than 12,000 spectators inside the old Gorgie ground on Saturday, 14 January 1978 to see the teams set up as follows.

HEARTS:

Ray Dunlop; Walter Kidd & Cammy Fraser; Dave McNicoll, Jim Jefferies & Lawrie Tierney; Rab Prentice, Eamon Bannon, Willie Gibson, Drew Busby & Malcolm Robertson. Substitutes; Graham Shaw & Jim Brown.

QUEEN OF THE SOUTH:

Allan Ball; Peter Dickson & Tommy O'Hara; Billy McLaren, Nobby Clark & Crawford Boyd; Benny Ferrie, Chris Balderstone, Tommy Bryce, Harry Hood & Jimmy Coughlin. Substitutes; Iain McChesney & Jocky Dempster.

The two best chances of a goalless first half saw Jimmy Coughlin hit the Hearts crossbar from Harry's corner before Allan Ball's superb save thwarted Cammy Fraser. The only goal of the match came from Hearts midfielder Lawrie Tierney, the two points keeping Hearts tucked in third spot just behind joint leaders Dundee and Morton.

The weather claimed the next weekend's home fixture with Arbroath as a casualty, the Scottish Cup third round tie with Montrose beating the freezing conditions to take place on Saturday, 28 January 1978. Jimmy Coughlin got Harry's first Scottish Cup-tie for the club off to a perfect start with a goal inside two minutes, Bobby Livingston equalising for the visitors just after the half-hour. The sides would manage a goal apiece after the break to set up a replay at Links Park, the winners facing a difficult but lucrative trip to Tannadice in the next round. Harry would be instrumental as Queens won the replay 3-1, taking advantage of Les Barr's error to put his side one up early on then setting up George Dickson for a second-half tap-in as the sides clashed again on Monday, 6 February 1978. Tommy Bryce secured the tie with six minutes remaining, Montrose scoring a consolation penalty in the dying seconds through defender Dennis D'Arcy. That strike at Links Park would prove to be Harry's last-ever goal in the Scottish Cup, having twice scored in winning finals for Celtic earlier in the decade.

The freezing temperatures decimated the fixture card through February, with only two further games taking place, both played in the final days of the month. There was a brave fightback from Queens on the last Saturday at Palmerston, after St Johnstone had taken a two-goal lead through John Brogan and John Pelosi. Harry set up Benny Ferrie to give the hosts a foothold in the game just before half-time then Jocky Dempster salvaged a point with an equaliser after the break. The Scottish Cup fourth-round tie with Dundee United took place at Tannadice two nights later, Monday, 27 February 1978, having been postponed nine days earlier. The teams lined up as follows, in front of 8,000 spectators.

DUNDEE UNITED:

Hamish McAlpine; Alex Rennie & Frank Kopel; George Fleming, Paul Hegarty & David Narey; Paul Sturrock, John Holt, John Bourke, Billy Kirkwood & Graeme Payne.

Substitutes; Davie Dodds & Andy Rolland.

QUEEN OF THE SOUTH:

Allan Ball; Peter Dickson & Iain McChesney; Crawford Boyd, Nobby Clark & Chris Balderstone; Jocky Dempster, George Dickson, Harry Hood, Tommy Bryce & Jimmy Coughlin. Substitutes; Robert Thorburn & Benny Ferrie.

Another superb performance from Queens keeper Allan Ball – whom Harry had scored against in the same competition back in January 1971 whilst with Celtic – kept the match goalless for the first hour, but once George Fleming had put the hosts ahead from a Billy Kirkwood cross the result was never in doubt. Within two minutes, Paul Hegarty made it 2-0 from the spot after Nobby Clark felled Fleming in the box and John Bourke, a recent signing from Dumbarton, ended the scoring in the 80th minute. That would provide another two landmarks in Harry's playing career, his final Scottish Cup-tie and last match against top-flight opposition. His two previous clubs did not fare any better, going out of the competition at the same stage to lower-league opposition. Motherwell were humbled 3-1 by Second Division Queen's Park at home, whilst a late Derrick McDicken strike in the Rugby Park replay saw Jock Stein succumb to his first Scottish Cup defeat outwith a final in a decade, and only his second ever as Celtic manager. Sean Fallon had been in charge of the Hoops for the 3-2 exit at Fir Park two years earlier. Like Harry, Jock would not be involved in the prestigious old tournament again.

Revenge would be on the home menu as Mike Jackson took his men back up to Montrose on the opening Saturday in March, Harry scoring perhaps the quickest goal of his career after just 20 seconds at Links Park after an error from Dennis D'Arcy. The visitors would then concede four goals before the break and eventually lose the match by 5-2, despite that fantastic start. That would be the first of six straight defeats in the League as Queens struggled for the remainder of the campaign. The home match with Stirling Albion in midweek followed much the same pattern as

Montrose, Tommy Bryce putting the Dumfries side ahead before the roof caved in, Matt McPhee and Ian Browning grabbing doubles in a 4-1 win for the visitors, which would have been more but for the heroics of Allan Ball.

Veteran Queen of the South goalkeeper Ball was at the centre of attention the following weekend, as he played two games in 24 hours to reach 700 appearances between the sticks for the club he had served with such distinction for 15 years. The Sunderland-born stopper had been signed in December 1963 by goalkeeper George Farm, whose first act was to promptly drop himself to give Ball his debut. The first match was a daunting trip to face League leaders Dundee, no doubt smarting from their 6-0 defeat in Dumfries back in October. A second-half double from Billie Pirie and an Ian Redford counter saw Tommy Gemmell's men retain a two-point lead over Hearts. Queens would then cross the Tay for a rescheduled game the following afternoon at Bayview, East Fife captain Colin Methven presenting Ball with some whiskey to acknowledge his landmark before goals from Ken Mackie and John Huskey gave the side propping up the table a rare win in their first-ever Sunday fixture and made it a fruitless weekend in terms of points if not spirits for the visitors, as the losing run stretched to four. Former Ayr United, Coventry City and Rangers winger Quinton Young broke his leg early in the second half.

Two back-to-back home games in the next week failed to provide any respite. A Billy McMillan own goal allowed Arbroath to take the points home on an evening where less than 700 supporters bothered to turn up at Palmerston. Harry would meet up with some familiar faces again on Saturday, 18 March 1978, Benny Rooney's championship-chasing Morton side featuring his former Holyrood and Celtic teammate Denis Connaghan plus Andy Ritchie, who had moved from Parkhead to Greenock in a deal which saw goalkeeper Roy Baines make the reverse journey. Billy McLaren opened the scoring early on for the Doonhamers before another of Harry's old colleagues – former Motherwell striker John Goldthorp – headed Morton level midway through the half. The visitors would eventually prevail by the odd goal in five as Queens' recent run saw them drop to fourth-bottom in the 14-team Division.

Mike Jackson's men would finally end the run of defeats with two draws on the road within the next seven days. Allan Ball was beaten by a 40-yard strike from Stirling Albion's Ian Browning at Annfield in midweek, but he had a brilliant match as Tommy Bryce's equaliser in first-half stoppage time ended the scoring at 1-1. It could have been even better for Queens, had Ball's opposite number George Young not denied Harry with an excellent save seven minutes from time. The match at Cappielow on Saturday, 25 March 1978 also ended 1-1, Morton taking the lead through another Goldthorp header before Tommy Bryce put a huge dent in Greenock title hopes by equalising just before the interval.

Peter Dickson was the man who gave Queen of the South a first League victory since mid-December by scoring the only goal of the game against lowly Alloa Athletic five minutes into the second half at Palmerston on Saturday, 1 April 1978. Sadly, that would prove to the final victory of the campaign. Airdrieonians were the side above Queens in the table and the clubs met at Broomfield the following Saturday, Mark Cowan missing a penalty for the hosts in a goalless first half. Harry beat Airdrie keeper Marshall Poulton after the break for what would be his final goal as a professional player, but Sandy Clark enhanced his growing reputation with a double as the Diamonds won by the odd goal in three.

Queens hosted League leaders Hearts on Saturday, 15 April 1978, Harry almost ending his goalscoring career by repeating the feat he achieved with Celtic at Firhill back in November 1971. His corner-kick put visiting keeper John Brough in all kinds of trouble, the Hearts stopper just about keeping the ball from crossing the line. Brough then denied Harry an equaliser by saving his penalty after Donald Park had given the title favourites the lead. Willie Ormond's men were all set to take a massive step to reclaiming their top-flight status after one season when Peter Dickson scored a last-minute leveller.

With Dundee now trailing second-placed Morton by a point, Tommy Gemmell's men could afford no slip-ups as he welcomed his close friend Harry to Dens Park on Saturday, 22 April 1978. Harry did go close to opening the scoring, but the Dark Blues would get the victory required to keep them in the title race, running out 3-0 winners with goals from Eric Sinclair, Dave McKinnon and Billy Williamson.

Saturday, 29 April 1978 was a landmark date in Harry's life, as a journey that started in the red shirt of Clyde at Ibrox in November 1962 ended in the blue of Queen of the South not far from his Lanarkshire home some 16 years later. A second visit to Broomfield Park, Airdrie in three weeks would be Harry's final game as a professional footballer, the teams lining up for the occasion as follows.

AIRDRIEONIANS:

Marshall Poulton; Paul Jonquin & Mark Cowan; Jim Black, Jim March & Tommy Walker; Willie McGuire, Norrie Anderson, Sandy Clark, Joe Cairney & Billy Wilson. Substitutes; John Lapsley & Kevin McCann.

QUEEN OF THE SOUTH:

Allan Ball; Iain McChesney & Robert Thorburn; Crawford Boyd, Nobby Clark & George Dickson; Jocky Dempster, Peter Dickson, Harry Hood, Tommy Bryce & Jimmy Coughlin. Substitutes; Ian White & Benny Ferrie.

The hosts enjoyed the best of the game, going ahead through an early Sandy Clark penalty. Jocky Dempster looked to have equalised just before the break only to see his effort ruled offside by referee Bob Valentine. The only goal of the second half came from home striker Joe Cairney as Queens ended the 39-game campaign in 12th spot, one place but five points clear of relegated Alloa Athletic and 10 points ahead of bottom-dogs East Fife. Morton and Hearts finished one point ahead of Dundee to gain promotion, and Queens would be joined by Harry's old club Clyde in the First

Division of 1978/79, Craig Brown's men winning the title on goal difference from Raith Rovers.

The defeat at Airdrie was also the last match in charge of Queen of the South for Mike Jackson, who left the post the following month to take up the assistant manager role at newly promoted Morton. Jackson would be succeeded at Palmerston by former Motherwell and Scotland forward Willie Hunter, who had been assisting his old Fir Park colleague Ian St John as his number two at Portsmouth.

For Harry, after the disappointing end to his spell at that same Fir Park the previous spring, his final season in professional football had seen him once again a first-team regular, missing only one of the 40 games played by Queen of the South since he signed, contributing five goals and countless assists.

Epilogue

A wonderful legacy and a poignant last farewell

Harry would remain involved at Palmerston the following season, as a coach for the Glasgow-based Queen of the South players. That would allow him to focus on what had effectively been his second career, as founder and owner of the pub and management company Lisini, the name of the family business - very appropriately - derived from the first two letters from the Christian names of the three Hood children, Lisa, Siobhan and Nicholas. A lovely touch.

His involvement in the licensed trade had commenced back in 1970 with the purchase of a hotel on the Old Edinburgh Road in Uddingston, which Harry and Kathleen took over and renamed Sherwood Manor, although in truth both had been working in that business for many years before that. You may recall that Kathleen's parents, Tony and Mary McGinley, had owned Tony's Bar in Bridgeton from the 1950's. Kathleen would spend many hours working there between her school and university studies, particularly after the sudden death of her father, whilst Harry also helped out in the pub and had worked as a sales representative with the Dunn family's drinks business whilst with Clyde.

The Hoods bought a second Uddingston establishment in 1979, the Plough Inn, which would become Angels, perhaps the venue now most associated with Harry and the Lisini Pub Co portfolio. Over the years, through a combination of astute leadership, quality service and a desire to put customer needs at the forefront of everything they do, that portfolio developed into an award-winning family business.

DRAM is an industry magazine, which over the decades to follow would recognise that devotion and the success it brought Lisini in the form of awards. More on that later. Susan Young, DRAM's editor, recalled the early days of the Hood family's Lisini adventure.

"Harry knew that he had to have something in place to support his young family when he finally hung up his boots. Having devoted his early years to football, he didn't have an education to fall back on. Chatting to some of the Celtic players on the team bus returning from a game in Edinburgh in 1970, they passed a pub in Viewpark called The Mirn, and Harry overheard Jimmy Johnstone – who came from

Viewpark - saying to Billy McNeill that it had potential. The following Monday, he put an offer in and once the sale went through, they changed the name to the Sherwood Manor Hotel."

"Speaking to a local newspaper at that time, Harry said, "It's been my ambition for some time to own a pub or a hotel. I was a rep at one time, so I know something about the licensed trade, and my wife's mother had a pub, so between us we know something about the business."

"After enjoying success with the Sherwood Manor, Harry continued to keep his eye on the trade. He spotted a pub in Bellshill called the Iron Maiden, which was said to be the 'in' place to go."

"He added: "I thought to myself, if Bellshill can have an 'in' place, Uddingston can too, and that's how Angels came about."

"In 1979, an offer was placed and accepted for The Plough Bar in Uddingston, which began a journey of unbridled success and established a legacy which was to see it become the number one venue in Lanarkshire. The building itself dates back to 1906, so Harry and Kathleen had their work cut out making the changes they wanted. The Plough was a short-lived name, having been The McKinnon Arms for a number of years. The Hoods decided to change the name to Angels, after seeing a building in Los Angeles with the name and thinking it would work well for a hotel."

His move into the licensed trade would also be the trigger for personal friendships which would last for the remainder of Harry's life, Malcolm McNeill being a case in point. Both Harry and Malcolm lived in Bothwell and had links with Motherwell, one as a player and the other a director, so of course they would meet for the first time in...Argentina! Malcolm picks up the story.

"I first met Harry whilst on a trip to the World Cup in Argentina 1978. He was a guest of the brewers, Tennents from memory, and me and three friends had travelled with the Scottish Football League. We were walking through Córdoba and, as usual, fancied a pint. We found a little bar just off the main square and spied some other guys within and heard from their accents that they were Scottish, so we joined them and introduced ourselves. They did likewise and we had a couple of drinks with them. The trip to Argentina was a real long haul, 27 hours from memory. I knew Harry stayed in Bothwell and I mentioned that I had just moved into the village. The next time we met was back in the local pub, the Camphill Vaults, and from there our friendship grew."

"Harry was a member of the Jock Stein Suite at Celtic Park and the Vice Presidents Club at Fir Park. His first love, of course was Celtic, although we had many happy days at Motherwell. Over the years, I found him to be a very good businessman. He never rushed into any big decisions, rather he was very focused and kept his own council. Along with, first of all, Kathy, then the other members of the family, they built up a very strong portfolio of licensed premises, including Dalziel Park

Golf Club. Harry was a very active member of the famous Glasgow Vintners Golf Society. They played each Thursday at different courses across the West of Scotland, and Kilmarnock Barassie in the winter. They had a very enthusiastic membership, including Billy McNeill, Davie Reilly, Joe Gillan, Tony Capaldi, Ricky Monaghan, Brendan McLaughlin, some publicans and many more. Harry was also a member of Cathkin Braes and Aloha Golf Club in Marbella. He enjoyed a handicap of around 12 but that was much less on his day. His biggest problem with his game was when he developed the dreaded yips, which for the uninitiated is when "Yer bottle goes whilst addressing the ball when ready to putt."

"He had a wicked sense of humour. Whilst playing a fourball in a Vintners tournament at Dalmahoy, Harry teed off, followed by his partner, Tony Capaldi. Their balls went straight down the middle, but they were hitting over a large mound and did not see them land. Harry and Tony volunteered to go over and watch where their opponents' balls came to rest. Davie and Brendan hit much the same shots, down the middle. When they descended, Davie could see Harry standing over a ball which was lodged against a big rock, just off the fairway. Harry shouted, "Davie, can I have a ruling here?" Davie shouted in reply, "No relief. You must play the ball from where it sites." Harry paused briefly, looked again at the ball and then declared, "Good. It's yours!"

"The Vintners was also where Harry met another man who would become a friend and confidant for the best part of four decades, Davie Reilly. He had another batch of 'Harry stories' to relay, including that one above from Dalmahoy, which Davie reckoned Harry must have told "at least 990 times!"

"I first met Harry when I joined The Glasgow Vintners Golf Society in 1983 at Old Prestwick Golf Club in Ayrshire. Having watched Harry play for Celtic and witnessed his fantastic hat trick against Rangers, I was surprised to see him approach me to welcome me to the Vintners. Little did I know then that this was the start of a lasting friendship, spanning over 36 years."

"Over the years we had great times, especially playing golf in Scotland and Spain. Our families came together, and we had many nights with Harry's other great friends, Ricky and Ina Monaghan. Harry had a great and generous personality, although on occasion, if needed, he could be quite outspoken. He was the king of the one-liner, especially on the golf course."

"Having first met Harry at Old Prestwick, the following week I was drawn out to play with him at Lenzie Golf Club. On the fourth hole, I had already played six shots, when Harry offered some advice, "You're swinging too fast!" The next hole was a par three, and that's when I heard one of Harry's favourite sayings. He hit the ball through the green, to which his comment was, "I hit that too good." It was amazing how often he hit the ball "too good!" After a few bad drives, he would hit a good shot and we would hear, "Right, I know what I am doing wrong!"

"On one of the Belhaven golf trips, we landed in the Prince William Bar. As anyone

who drank with Harry knows, a BOTTLE of coke is a must with a Bacardi. The barman, however, committed the cardinal sin of pouring DRAUGHT coke, to which, Harry, in his inimitable fashion, suggested that he should take them back. The barman did indeed take them back but ordered us out of the pub!"

"On another of our trips to Spain, we were in a restaurant near San Pedro. At the end of the night, I noticed there was a keyboard, so I sat down and started to play. Fifteen minutes later, the waiter came and handed me the bill. Only then did I notice Harry and the boys had all left (sneaked out more like). I told the waiter, "You better go and stop the minibus. I've no money."

"The licensed trade used to have a national golf tournament covering the whole of the UK, called the White Horse Trophy, the finals for which the Glasgow Vintners had never qualified. Harry was captain on the occasion we first made it to the finals at the Rosemount in Blairgowrie. The final was held over two rounds and we were leading by two points with one game to come. Not able to contain himself, Harry and I walked down to the 18th tee. We were in with a shout and our last man was Lawrence Garvie, a fellow Vintner."

"Harry asked him, "How are you playing and how many points do you have?"

"Lawrence replied, "How many do you need?"

"Harry: "We need 32 points!"

"Lawrence, "That's ok. I already have 35 points."

"Queue celebrations."

"As it was our first time qualifying, Harry was a very proud captain. Always a winner."

That same sense of fun came shining through in all of my dealings with Harry's family, as I researched and wrote his biography. I asked Kathy to describe each of their children as youngsters in a few words.

"Lisa loved her sports. We thought she would be a gymnast when she grew up, instead she ended up as a PE teacher, playing hockey for Scotland. Siobhan was always drawing and had a very imaginative mind. Perhaps that's why she went for a marketing degree. And she was a bit accident prone. She had numerous accidents including the near-fatal car crash with young Jonathan Stein, which ultimately led to her suffering a brain haemorrhage when she was in the army. Nicky was a boisterous torag, always kicking a ball, although sending him to St Aloysius meant he played rugby. Then he discovered a wee white ball and got hooked on golf. He's a superb player. Please use your talent and make them sound more interesting than this, Matt!"

I had no need to do that. I found each one to be talented, funny, interesting and instantly likeable.

And self-deprecating, Nicky claiming that when he was born the doctor slapped the midwife.

I also thoroughly enjoyed reading Lisa's description of her family and of the time the Hoods auditioned for the television show Family Fortunes.

"As a family, we actually auditioned for Family Fortunes a few years ago. My father had always said, "We'd be great in Family Fortunes…let's audition!" So, we did. In the introduction, we all stated our names and what we did for a living. "We work in a pub," echoed my sister Siobhan, Nicky, Uncle George (dad's brother) and my mum. My dad said, "Well, I own the pub!" Actually, Siobhan was so shell-shocked, that she forgot her name! Mum kept calling Les Dennis, "Des," and my dad - the TV expert - couldn't quite get his brain into gear and he couldn't answer anything. Needless to say, we didn't succeed. I think that sums our family up!"

"As an immediate family, we have very different but complimentary skills. Siobhan is a natural publican, and in so many ways emulates my late father's passion for the customer and service. She is also a genuinely creative person and a tough negotiator. My cousin, Grant Hood, is Operations Director. He runs the company on a day-to-day basis, has the most incredible personable nature and is regarded highly by all who meet him. He has a gift of getting the absolute best out of his teams. Nicky - although ageing rapidly - is still a cool cat and has an incredible knack of knowing what is current and what will work. People love him. He's witty like my father. As a senior team, it is often hard to differentiate between family life and work life, and inevitably business conversations extend beyond 'traditional working hours'… if there is such a thing anymore. I think our longevity derives from several things. A lifelong passion for service but with a mutual respect for each other's strengths and weaknesses. We fiercely debate many issues that we face but have a healthy respect for each other's opinions and position. I often say to members of my family, "I would agree with you, but then we would both be wrong!"

Siobhan also recalls her dad's wit and his ultra-competitiveness, themes which were constantly played back to me as I spoke to those close to Harry over the years.

"Dad was 'the man.' He had a presence. The only time I ever saw him in any way reticent was when Jock Stein was around. Papa Jock. The shift in presence was palpable when Mr Stein was in the room. And dad was always kidding. I would be around 13 and someone told him that I had a new boyfriend. He comes back immediately with, "What? Is he blind?"

"I joined the Officer Training Corps – a sort of TA for students - and passed out at Sandhurst in 1988. Mum and dad came down and brought Auntie May O'Gara with them. Later, I was living in Germany and the whole family came over for the Officers' Mess Ball. Dad won the rifle-shooting competition, up against regular army personnel! He was asked to present the trophy for an army football game, soldiers stationed on the Rhine split up as Celtic v Rangers, then he was invited to be a guest

at the Sergeants' Mess. I told him that was a great privilege then we found out that he was to do the after-dinner speech. No warning whatsoever but he just winged it. That was dad."

Harry was clearly a rare breed who enjoyed not one but two highly successful careers. Whilst speaking with his family, I formed the opinion that he was every bit as proud - if not more so – of what he and his family achieved with Lisini than anything he ever did as a footballer. Nevertheless, Harry would dip his toes back into the waters of Scottish football again, twice in fact, on both occasions as a manager.

In February 1981, he accepted an offer from Albion Rovers chairman Tom Fagan to succeed Sam Goodwin as manager at Cliftonhill. Goodwin had been in the role for almost five years and would now become a director of the Second Division club. Harry's first match in charge was a 3-2 home win over East Fife on Saturday, 14 February 1981. For his second, three days later, his old friend Billy McNeill brought his Premier League-leading Celtic to Coatbridge for a game which saw Murdo MacLeod continue his comeback from injury by scoring the Hoops opener in a 2-0 victory, George McCluskey with the other goal for Celts. Harry would face another two of his former clubs in the shape of Queen of the South and Clyde in Second Division fixtures, albeit with mixed results. Queens were defeated 1-0 at Cliftonhill on Saturday, 14 March 1981 but his Rovers team lost 4-0 at Shawfield, seven days later. It would be a brief spell in charge for Harry, winning six and losing six of his 12 League matches before calling it a day following a 2-0 defeat to Stenhousemuir at Cliftonhill on Saturday, 18 April 1981.

Harry's second and final post in football management followed a very similar pattern, 12 months later, as he returned to Palmerston Park as the manager of Queen of the South in February 1982. Dumfries club historian Iain McCartney provides the context, with Queens newly promoted to the First Division.

"Chairman Willie Harkness, and his fellow directors could for once stand acclaimed instead of being pilloried for their head-in-the-sand decisions. They had taken the decision following George Herd's departure to take over the reins and it was to their credit that they had guided the team to promotion."

"I am very emotional" said the Queens chairman. "It is the greatest thing to have happened to Queens for years. It took me back to the 1930's."

"Flushed with their success of the previous season, the directors decided to continue to run the show, at least as far as season 1981-82 was concerned, but they were soon to find that everything in the garden was certainly not rosy. Having finished the previous season as Division Two Player of the Year, Jimmy Robertson, who was also Queens top scorer with 20 goals, was suddenly at loggerheads with the club in a contract dispute and was subsequently left out of the team as the League programme got under way."

"Asking for the moon," was how Willie Harkness described the player's demands."

"We possibly pay the best part-time wages in the First Division and there is no way the club will alter its whole structure to suit Jimmy Robertson. I don't think the public would want us to do that."

"So, the big winger found himself out in the cold, as Queens began to find that if getting into the First Division was difficult, then it was going to be much more of an effort to remain there, with their first victory not materialising until the eighth game of the campaign, in late September, when they beat Hamilton Academical 3-2. Two months later, a 4-2 defeat by that same Hamilton team, this time at home, saw Queens hit the bottom of the First Division, a position they would still find themselves in come January, with severe weather rather than severe thumpings keeping them there. Robertson had by then returned to the fold but made little difference, with the Standard correspondent writing that "Queen's only consolation was that they could not play any worse," following an appalling display against Falkirk at home. The situation was now becoming rather desperate, as it had been 11 games since they had last won, and it would be a further nine before they did so again."

"Deciding that they had had enough of organising training and whatever, the directors appointed Harry Hood in a coaching capacity towards the end of February, but it was too late for Hood, or anyone else for that matter, to be able to salvage anything from the serious situation that the club found itself in. Having been with the club as a player towards the end of his career, Hood would have known how the club was run and he was prepared to do what he considered best, as he tried to secure enough points to avoid a swift return [to Division Two] from whence they had come 12 months previously. He had barely got accustomed to what was kept in which drawer of his office desk, before resigning from his post after only eight weeks."

"Although the results had continued to be disappointing, he resigned on a matter of principle, as he had wanted to suspend two players - Jimmy Robertson and Peter Dickson - for missing training but failed to obtain the backing of the board on the matter. This issue was raised at a showdown meeting prior to the 3-1 defeat by Dumbarton on 17 April 1982, a game which ensured that Queens would indeed play Second Division football again the following season. It was believed that Harry Hood had given the directors the ultimatum – complete player control, or I resign. Failing to get the required backing, he stood by his words and quit, telephoning his decision to the Queens board."

"He was later to say: "I left on a matter of principle. I was not prepared to have these two players miss three weeks' training and allow them to come back without anything being done about it. I would have had no standing with the rest of the players. I played for 18 years and trained whether or not I was in the first team. In fact, if I wasn't in the first team, I didn't take the huff, I tried all the harder to get back into it again."

"Following the Harry Hood scenario, chairman Willie Harkness found himself

strongly attacked by supporters, with the protests leaving the board in no doubt as to who they felt was in the right, with the Standard editorial agreeing. It read: "As president of the SFA, Willie Harkness has been away from Dumfries for long spells during the past four miserable years. It is rumoured that during that time, he has offered to stand down as chairman of Queen of the South, to make way for someone with more time to devote to the running of the club. It seems a pity that did not happen. Having continued as chairman, Mr Harkness cannot now abdicate responsibility, but his fellow directors should stand up and take the blame with him. The most honourable – but also the most impractical – course for them would be to resign and make way for new faces. Failing this they should appoint a manager, if any is still willing to risk his neck in Dumfries and give him full support in any decision he proposes, to get them quickly out of the Second Division."

"The season drew to an inglorious end, a meagre crowd of 300 at the penultimate home fixture against Queen's Park making themselves and their opinions heard, as they protested about the recent events."

Harry's spell in the Palmerston dugout involved just seven weeks and nine games, commencing with a 3-3 draw against St Johnstone at Muirton on Saturday, 27 February 1982 and ending with that aforementioned 3-1 loss to Dumbarton at Boghead on Saturday, 17 April 1982. He left with a record of two wins, two draws and five defeats as Queens were relegated back to the Second Division. They would be replaced for the new campaign by his old club Clyde, who had won the third-tier title under Craig Brown, whilst the Premier and First Divisions were clinched by his other two former Scottish teams, Celtic and Motherwell, now managed by his old friends from his Parkhead days, Billy McNeill and Davie Hay respectively. As the late Jimmy Greaves used to say, *"It's a funny old game."*

Leaving football for the final time would allow Harry time to enjoy the new apartment by the beach in Puerto Banus, just west of Marbella, which they had bought in 1981 and which the family retain to this day, described by Nicky as his dad's *"pride and joy."*

He recalled an event which must have been a bit surreal for a 12-year-old football-mad boy.

"It must have been summer '83. Ron Atkinson was renting the apartment next door. Lo and behold I've come in one afternoon and he, my dad and George Best are sitting having a beer, talking about football. They disappeared to a local beach bar called Tramps and many hours later, around 3am, my dad told George to crash out at our apartment. I awoke the following morning and with a mixture of shock and awe realise there's George Best, out to the world and snoring like a baby in the spare bed!"

Puerto Banus was also the setting for one of Harry's nephew John Wagner's fondest recollections.

"I met my Uncle Harry on four or five occasions. He came over to Montana to visit

my mum - his sister Pat – and we visited Yellowstone National Park amongst other things. I graduated in New York City and we flew to Glasgow. That would have been around 1996. I stayed for two weeks and he showed me around, took me golfing and drinking at Angels. He was extremely friendly, a second father figure to me. Instantly warm and I felt like we bonded. It was a unique experience with this long-lost family who look like you and act like you, with the same mannerisms. He said he could see my mum in my face. He, Jack and George were very similar. I don't think Peter kept the best of health at that time."

"Uncle Harry was a pretty funny jokester. We met up in Marbella on our honeymoon. One night, we're out with him and Nicky and there's a police car with a couple of officers standing there. Harry says to me, "Right, John, take our picture." Over he goes with Nicky and the two of them put their hands together, faking arrest like they're being 'cuffed, just so that I can get a photo! He really liked his kids."

That devotion to, and love for, his family would be extended over the years as the next generation arrived, Harry's grandchildren. First to be born was Peter Henry Edwards in December 1998, a son to Siobhan and her husband Pete Edwards, named after both of his grandfathers and known as Harry. He would welcome a 'wee brother' in April 2001, Andrew Callum Edwards, then baby sister Mackenzie, born in Canada in December 2003 and named after the country's longest river. That same year, Lisa and her husband Keith Wishart were blessed by a son, Jamie, and in August 2004 little Helena Hood arrived, Nicky's daughter, to complete a fabulous quintet of grandchildren for Harry and Kathleen.

In the vicious circle that is life, sadly that period would also see Harry lose some of his older siblings, first of those being brother Peter in 2003, aged 77. Harry's oldest sister Maggie had died in infancy, back in October 1941, almost three years to the day before he was born. His surviving sisters Irene and Pat had spent much of Harry's life living in the USA, and they would both pass away there within a few years of each other, Pat in Missoula, Montana in September 2013 during her 81st year and Irene in South Carolina in March 2017, aged 86. God bless and rest them all.

Harry continued to work hard and live his own life to the full, with no shortage of humorous stories from his various trips and events. Malcolm McNeill recalled another from a holiday closer to home.

"Harry and Kathy, my wife Angela and I formed a very strong friendship, and it was a coincidence that we both had properties on the Costa del Sol and the East Neuk of Fife, so we had many good times together. Once we went out for dinner to an excellent restaurant in the East Neuk called The Peat Inn, where we had a lovely meal. Jimmy Tarbuck was sitting at the next table and we started chatting. He was telling us that he was up working in Kirkcaldy and had played The Old Course that afternoon. When we were ready to leave, Harry asked for the bill and then asked Kathy for the money. You should have seen the look on her face. "Harry, I've come

away without it." I said, "No problem. I'll get it." "No," said Harry. "It's my turn. I've just remembered, I've got money in the car." He left the restaurant and swiftly returned with two sacks of coins - £1 and 50p pieces - and he explained that he'd emptied the puggy machines in the pub that day. The bags were taken to the kitchen and the manageress counted out the amount due. I bet it's the first time the staff have been tipped in £1 and 50p coins. Jimmy Tarbuck looked over and said, "I've heard about you Scots being tight, but this beats the lot!"

Kathleen recalls the night a meeting with another celebrity at Hampden caused a few chuckles.

"Harry and Malcolm played golf at the Aloha course in Marbella, which was also the club used by Sean Connery, who lived close by our house. Talking about Sir Sean, Harry and I were with Tommy and Mary Gemmell for the Champions League final in May 2002. Sean and King Juan Carlos of Spain were behind us. Sean was obviously intrigued with talking to the lads, but I was gobsmacked at seeing royalty and so at half-time I called my mother to let her know I had just met King Juan Carlos. Mum was hard of hearing and there was a lot of background noise, so I had to repeat myself several times. "King Juan Carlos! King Juan Carlos!" Mum then muttered that she didn't know any Kings from Cardross! Those were the days."

There was also recognition for Harry from two of the football clubs whose colours he graced with such elegance and honour in his playing career. In 2012, Harry was inducted into Clyde's Hall of Fame in his own right and two years later, he was honoured again, as part of that wonderful squad of 1966/67.

Between those two inductions, Harry was invited to Celtic Park in December 2013, to mark the 40th anniversary of his hat-trick in the League Cup semi-final at Hampden against Rangers in 1973. He and his family were guests of the club for the match against Hibernian at Celtic Park on Saturday, 14 December 2013, Harry making the *Paradise Windfall* draw on the pitch at half-time before raising his right arm one more time to acknowledge the support to whom he had given so much over the years.

That hat-trick back in the 1970's would be the precursor for another lovely occasion which took place at the end of May 2017. Angels had undergone a transformational overhaul in the seven months or so leading up to its reopening, Harry receiving a wonderful surprise from his family as the revamped premises included Harry's Bar. And who better to formally open the bar named after a legendary Celtic striker than the man currently starring in that position, Moussa Dembele. He had become the next name marked in the record books as having scored a hat-trick for Celts against Rangers, following his performance for Brendan Rodgers' Invincibles in the 5-1 rout of the Ibrox club in September 2016. There were some lovely scenes and photos taken as Harry made an emotional response to the gesture, clearly and momentarily taken aback, having whispered in Moussa's ear, *"I never knew about this!"*

But only after a tongue-in-cheek opening remark, of course.

"I'll just say one thing. It was a long arduous thing and I never once lost my temper! I'd like to apologise to all the people that I did shout at. You know that's what I'm like. But pressure gets to you eventually. As a football player there was no pressure. (Harry turns to Moussa) Wasn't there not? I'd love to be just playing football like this young man just now and if I miss anything, I miss my fitness. I miss the training and I miss all that. And I wish Moussa all the best. We've got a big Treble coming up etcetera and he's had a great season, and I wish you all future success."

Moussa would later recall the words Harry left him with.

"What you achieved will last in history forever."

That meeting was witnessed by Harry's friend, Malcolm McNeill.

"It was great to see him and Moussa Dembele, who came along to the opening of Harry's Bar in Angels. I looked across to see the two of them having a discussion, I would imagine the perfect hat-trick might have got a mention. Harry claims he scored another that night which was knocked off for offside."

Malcolm wasn't wrong. Back to Harry.

"Moussa was such a nice lad. I didn't have the heart to tell him I actually scored four goals in that game against Rangers. The linesman decided to call one offside. It was never offside."

Despite his outward humour, Harry had been battling against cancer for some time by then, although typical of his generosity of spirit, he and the family had used that major personal setback as a trigger to raise tens of thousands of pounds for charity, most notably for the Beatson and latterly Marie Curie. He did not let that prevent him from continuing to enjoy his breaks in the sun, leading to a classic encounter with another pair of celebrities in the Cote d'Azur in 2018. Malcolm takes up the story.

*"We also holidayed in the South of France each year and on one occasion we're going out for dinner and decided to have a drink before going on to the restaurant, which was La Colombe d'Or, in Saint-Paul-de-Vence, just behind Nice. We entered the cocktail bar, and the ladies took a seat at the window. Harry and I went to the bar to order a drink. Who walks in then but none other than Rod Stewart, his wife Penny, and her mother. They walked over to where the ladies were sitting and Rod asked, "Do you mind if we join you?" Kathy replied, "Of course not." Rod said, "I like that accent, ladies." Angela replied, "Well if you like our accent, you'll love those guys at the bar. One of them is Harry Hood." Rod turned around swiftly and exclaimed, "Harry ****** Hood! You are about the only Celtic player whom I've not had my photograph taken with!" He rushed over and embraced Harry and for the next 45 minutes quizzed him about Jimmy Johnstone, Jock Stein, Billy McNeill etc. Incidentally, it's said that Rod is quite tight with his money, but not that night. He would not let us pay for a drink. Harry asked to have his photograph taken with*

Penny and she stood up and came over, next to Harry. He said, "Penny, I wish you'd have worn your flatties tonight." She replied, "Harry, I'm wearing them!" She must be about 6'2"! Penny then went back and joined the ladies, who were discussing tv programmes, children and grandchildren."

Lisini's success would be formally recognised by a series of industry awards, three events in particular which struck me as being highly appropriate, all occurring in the final years of Harry's life. In 2016, Lisini was chosen as Family Business of the Year at the Scottish Bar and Pub Award ceremony, whilst Kathleen was inducted into the Scottish Licensed Trade Hall of Fame the same evening. In April 2018, Harry was presented with Scottish Entertainment & Hospitality's Lifetime Achievement Award by his friend James Mortimer and four months later, he and Kathleen became the first joint recipients of the Scottish Bar and Pub Lifetime Achievement Award at the Glasgow Hilton. That last award, recognising five decades of achievement, was perhaps particularly poignant. As well as recognising the couple as a team, the ceremony also took place in the skyscraper hotel which overlooked the beautiful, old church of St Patrick's, Anderston, where all the way back on Friday, 24 October 1924, Harry's parents – Henry Hood and Mary Scott – had pledged their marriage vows and a lifetime of love and devotion. Lisini would now provide a fitting legacy and platform for the next generation of family to build on.

On Saturday, 25 May 2019, Celtic faced Hearts at Hampden in the Scottish Cup final, seeking the win which would give the club - formed back in November 1887 in Glasgow's east end to support an impoverished community - an unprecedented Treble Treble, a clean sweep of the domestic trophies in Scotland for a third consecutive season. History in the making but with the saddest of backdrops.

Watching on television at home in Bothwell was a man who had scored in two such occasions in the past. He would see the tributes paid to two of his dear friends and colleagues from those wonderful days at Celtic Park under Jock Stein. The march of time had claimed two of our own in recent weeks, Cesar and Stevie, McNeill and Chalmers. Two of those we think of as immortal, but whom God still chooses to take. Poignantly, they would be honoured on this day of all days. May 25. Lisbon Day. One scored the goal which won the Big Cup and the other fought through crowds and his tears to lift it. Billy famously described the club has having a fairytale element to it. No-one could write this script.

But today this was a dad and his son watching their last Celtic match together, as Nicky Hood recalls.

"In my dad's final weeks, when he was bedridden, the illness had taken his body but certainly not his mind. He was as sharp as a tack until the end. It was so sad to watch but he was stoic till his last breath. He was very much aware of the Treble Treble under Brendan Rodgers and I firmly believe that he held on to watch that part of Celtic's history being made. It was an incredibly emotional day in more ways than

one. Dad let go early the next morning, surrounded by his family, just the way he would have wanted it. A good, humble man who truly lived the dream."

Siobhan spoke of her dad's battle with illness, and in true Hood tradition, found time to thank those who had helped make that dreadful burden just a little bit lighter.

"Dad was first diagnosed with bowel cancer five years ago, then it was his liver and then it was his lung. He was successful in beating all those cancers. In January this year, the cancer returned, and we all hoped in our hearts he was going to beat it, as he was such a fighter. But after his first round of chemotherapy, this time he became too weak and wasn't able to beat it. We were able to spend time with dad as a family and make so many memories with him."

"The Marie Curie nurses are absolute angels. The strength these people have and the support they offer families going through this is incredible, and this is something we will be forever grateful for. As a family, we have been touched by the outpouring of messages we have had from people and just how much dad touched people's lives. We've had messages from all over the world, from the punters he used to talk to in his pubs. It's been hard to take in."

And after all those anecdotes earlier, a final heartfelt tribute to his great friend from Malcolm McNeill.

"During his illness, I can honestly say I never heard Harry complain about anything. It was a long, slow battle. However, he made the best of it and I'll never forget the courage he showed."

"I miss him very much."

Davie Reilly expressed similar thoughts.

"I have so many memories from my long friendship with Harry. He was a kind, generous and charitable man. I am just glad that I had the good fortune to count Harry as a friend all those years and he will always be in my memory."

The eulogy at Harry's service was delivered by another of his long-term friends. Stuart Ross and he had met in the earliest days of Lisini, one the new landlord of the Sherwood Manor and the other a rep with Belhaven, at that point a small company employing 30 staff. The two men quickly hit it off and Harry gave Stuart and Belhaven the business, an arrangement which would continue throughout their respective careers. However, the relationship would grow from a working basis to that which saw Stuart asked by the family to write and present Harry's eulogy, which I replicate below.

"Kathleen and the family have asked me to say a few words about Harry's life and times in the Scottish hospitality industry. It is not for a frustrated and forlorn follower of the Jags like myself to comment on Harry's ability as a footballer but no one could dispute the fact that Harry had quick feet. And he was to prove equally nimble-footed in his foray into the Scottish licensed trade. And when I say Harry,

I really do mean Harry and Kathleen. They built the business together. Bacon and eggs, bread and butter, Harry and Kathleen. You cannot separate them. Their special togetherness was honoured only last year when they jointly received the prestigious Scottish licensed trade Life Achievement Award, the first and only time the award has not been made to a single individual."

"Kathleen's mum was in the trade at Tony's Bar, where they both helped out in their younger days and Harry, when playing for Clyde, got a good feel for the pub game when working part time as a salesman for Dunn and Moore, the well-known Glasgow drinks wholesaler. That grounding helped them evolve Lisini from a one-shop 'boozer' into a broad-based multi-unit leisure company now employing more than 300 people, which has become a bellwether of West of Scotland hospitality."

"Their first pub in 1970 was the Sherwood Manor in Viewpark, Jimmy Johnstone's local, but it was the purchase of the Plough Inn in Uddingston in 1979, after Harry had finished with football, which was to prove the cornerstone of their future success. They transformed the Plough and renamed it Angels, presumably after Kathleen, and from there they never looked back. After Angels, they expanded Lisini through further purchases and reshaping of the Croft Bar near Hampden, the Castle Rooms, Uddingston, the Parkville in Blantyre and the Dalziel Park in Motherwell. Harry didn't do 'posh,' but he did do top quality, always offering great grub at affordable prices, attractive and comfortable bars and superb facilities for weddings, conferences and other functions. He even managed to get into golf course management at the nine-hole course within the Dalziel complex."

"Along the 50-year path of progress, the children got involved in the business. The Lisini name is derived from the abbreviated forms of Lisa, Siobhan and Nicky. Lisa now heads it up for the close family, but the wider family is also involved, with nephew Grant in charge of operations and brother George still doing regular shifts in the Parkville at the age of 82."

"Harry was always ambitious and visionary, with a great eye for the next opportunity. He never put a foot wrong. He led Lisini with total pride and passion and he had an innate intuition to deliver exactly what his customers wanted. As we all know, he was a big personality, his charisma could fill a room. He could be fiery, at times intimidating especially if his short temper fused, but he had tenacity, energy and determination in spades. A great competitor. He was always very modest about his business and sporting successes. A very intelligent and grounded person. Henry Hood did not come up the Clyde on a water biscuit. Always generous of spirit and hugely supportive of so many different causes, including most recently the Beatson."

"After his family and his business, Harry enjoyed the golf, the third passion in his life. He was a prominent member of the Glasgow Vintners or, as they prefer to be known, the famous Glasgow Vintners. He enjoyed the banter in the clubhouse, washed down with the occasional Bacardi, with his cronies such as David Reilly, Tony Capaldi and

Ricky Monaghan, to name but three. And the Vintners gave him the ideal platform to display his mischievous sense of humour. When I asked his lifelong friend David Reilly to sum Harry up in three words, he texted me back "ONE, LINE, ER." He was a master of the quick quip, the cheeky chappie remark. But he could take it as well as give it. I remember at one of our charity golf days at Cardross, where Andy Cameron auctioned the teams and the banter flowed relentlessly, Harry pushed his heckling a bit too far and Andy snapped, "Oh shut up Harry. I had to watch you when you were crap!"

"My abiding memory of Harry is the way he chatted to everyone no matter rich or poor, no matter colour or creed. He had a word for and with everyone. Like Scotland's Ploughman's poet, Rabbie Burns, Harry treated princes and paupers in exactly the same way. Burns articulated that respect for people so well in 'A man's a man for a' that,' and I can think of no more appropriate way of saying goodbye to Harry than by reading the final verse of that wonderful poem."

Then let us pray that come it may, As come it will for a' that,
That Sense and Worth, o'er a' the earth, Shall bear the gree an' a' that.
For a' that an' a' that, It's comin yet for a' that,
That Man to Man the warld o'er, Shall brithers be for a' that

"Farewell Harry."

"You leave us as one of Scotland's most beloved brothers of both Scottish football and hospitality."

"We will all miss you so very much."

Sentiments echoed my many.

Harry Hood.

Twice as good.